The Mammals of Canada

A.W.F. BANFIELD

Illustrations by

Allan Brooks, Claude Johnson, John Crosby,

Charles Douglas, Robert Thompson, John Tottenham

Cartography by

Geoffrey Matthews and Jennifer Wilcox

Published for the

National Museum of Natural Sciences

National Museums of Canada

by University of Toronto Press

© University of Toronto Press 1974

Toronto and Buffalo

Reprinted 1977 (with corrections), 1981

Printed in Canada

ISBN 0-8020-2137-9

LC 73-92298

Preface

The publication of *The Mammals of Canada* has long been planned by the National Museums of Canada.

The coloured illustrations by the Canadian artist Allan Brooks, which are here published for the first time, were commissioned for this work about 1923. The late Dr R.M. Anderson, formerly Chief of the Biology Division, worked on the project for a number of years during the 1930s and early 1940s. He accumulated a mass of distributional data on Canadian mammals which forms part of the Anderson library, housed at the National Museums. His main effort in this project was the publication of his *Catalogue of Canadian Recent Mammals* in 1946, the year of his retirement. Dr Austin L. Rand, who succeeded Dr Anderson, continued work on the project during 1947 and 1948 and prepared manuscript keys to the identification of Canadian mammals and diagnostic descriptions of the species. Later, Dr Austin W. Cameron, as Curator of Mammals, during the period 1958 to 1960 abstracted the literature on the life history of a good number of species. On completion of my caribou monograph in late 1961, the year of Dr Cameron's resignation, I commenced writing this book, species by species, as a companion volume to Godfrey's *Birds of Canada*. However, the change of duties from Chief Zoologist to Director of Natural History delayed completion until the end of 1968. The whole manuscript was revised during the winter of 1973–74 prior to publication. Much of the information is based on my own observations while studying mammals in every province and territory of Canada.

The purpose of the book is to provide a popular account of the mammals of Canada for students, lay readers, and professional biologists. Less emphasis has been placed on the descriptions and distributions of the subspecies, which are considered to be the special interest of systematic mammalogists. Besides, there are several excellent texts available on these aspects, such as E.R. Hall and K.R. Kelson's *The Mammals of North America* (1959) and R.L. Peterson's *The Mammals of Eastern Canada* (1966). Neither is this book to be considered as an authoritative text on the classification or physiology of the class Mammalia. For such information the reader is referred to *The Principles of Classification and a Classification of Mammals* by G.G. Simpson (1945), *Mammals of the World* by E.P. Walker (1964), *Recent Mammals of the World* by S. Anderson and J. Knox Jones (1967), and *Principles in Mammalogy* by D.E. Davis and F.B. Golley (1963). An excellent text on the methods of collecting and preserving mammal specimens has already been published by the National Museum (R.M. Anderson, *Methods of Collecting and Preserving Vertebrate Animals*, 4th rev. ed., 1965).

In this book are listed 196 species of recent mammals known to have occurred since historic times in Canada or in her coastal waters.

ACKNOWLEDGMENTS

Free use has been made of the manuscript notes prepared by Rand and Cameron, a privilege I gratefully acknowledge. In the earlier stages of preparation, the Hall and Kelson text referred to above was constantly in use for checking names and distributions. At the final stage, Peterson's *The Mammals of Eastern Canada* was similarly useful. Many items of life history were taken from scientific papers of authors too numerous to mention. To all these anonymous authors I owe a debt of gratitude. I have singled out the most important references at the end of each species section. Consultation of these papers will lead the reader to the pertinent literature.

The illustrations were prepared by several artists formerly on the staff of the Museum (the contribution of Allan Brooks has been previously mentioned). Other coloured plates are the work of Claude Johnson, long-time artist of the old Biology Division, and of John Crosby, Robert Thompson, and Charles Douglas in more recent times. The pen drawings are the work of Claude Johnson, Robert Thompson, John Crosby, and Charles Douglas. A number of line drawings of skulls and dentitions, and of the whales, were prepared under my direction by John Tottenham in 1962. Much of the appeal of this book is due to their efforts, and I am pleased to express my gratitude to them.

I would also like to thank Miss Lorraine Ourom and other members of the University of Toronto Press staff, for their assistance beyond the call of duty during the production of this book.

The French names were taken from 'Noms français des mammifères du Canada,' by R. Bernard, R. Cayouette, C. Delisle, P. DesMeules, L. Lemieux, and G. Moisan, published in *Les Carnets de Zoologie* 27(2): 25–30 (Quebec, 1967).

A.W.F.B.

PREFACE TO SECOND PRINTING

The reprinting of *The Mammals of Canada* has provided a welcome opportunity to review the text and to make some corrections and amendments. I am grateful to the authors of several detailed reviews for pointing out errors, and particularly to William Fuller and Robert Wrigley for their assistance in substituting more recent literature references for various species. A number of distribution maps have been amended on the advice of correspondents.* Marginal dots for museum specimens have not, however, been added because I believe that such dots represent the distribution of mammalogists rather than of the mammals themselves. Scales have been included for the drawings of skulls and other parts of mammals.

One point which might be clarified here is the use of the generic name *Lontra* for the North American river otter. This choice was made on the basis of C.G. Van Zyll de Jong's *A Systematic Review of the Nearctic and Neotropical River Otters (Genus* Lutra, *Mustelidae, Carnivora)*, published in 1972 as Life Sciences Contribution No. 80 of the Royal Ontario Museum. I might mention as well that the reproductions of various watercolour paintings by C.E. Johnson and Allan Brooks were of necessity printed in black and white because the originals were unavailable at the time of publication.

Finally, I would mention two excellent handbooks of North American mammals that are useful for identifying small mammals: William H. Burt and Richard P. Grossenheider, *A Field Guide to the Mammals* (Houghton Mifflin Co., Boston, 1964); and Ralph S. Palmer, *The Mammal Guide: Mammals of North America North of Mexico* (Doubleday & Co., Garden City, N.Y., 1954).

A.W.F.B.

*NOTE ADDED IN PROOF A number of other corrections to both maps and text should have been made in the light of P.M. Youngman's *Mammals of the Yukon Territory* (Publications in Zoology No. 10, National Museum of Natural Sciences, Ottawa, 1975) but unfortunately the volume reached me too late.

Contents

Colour Plates

The artist is given in italics, and the facing page at the end.

Figures

Introduction

WHAT IS A MAMMAL?

To begin a book with a definition is an awkward practice, but because of the confusion between animals and mammals among lay readers, it is unfortunately necessary for this book. Often the general term 'animal' is applied to a mammal, as if fishes, birds, and insects belonged to some other category of living things.

How then can one characterize mammals? Their very name is derived from their fundamental characteristic: the possession of mammary glands. All young mammals are nurtured on milk. The second general characteristic is the possession of a body-covering of hair, though this is much reduced in certain mammals such as man, armadillos, and whales. Also a number of anatomical features, in combination, separate them from other classes of animals. These features include a four-chambered heart, with the left aortic arch forming the main artery leading from the heart, and a diaphragm. The bony skeleton has a characteristic lower jaw consisting of a single pair of dentary bones; a skull, which articulates with the vertebral column by means of paired occipital condyles; vertebrae, which show regional differentiation; and a pelvic girdle, which comprises a pair of innominate bones. The mammalian dentition is unique. It consists of two sets of teeth: first the deciduous or milk teeth, and then the permanent set, which replaces them. The dentition is also separated into different kinds of teeth: incisors, canines, premolars, and molars. However, between different kinds of mammals there is generally much variation in tooth form and number, and this variation constitutes an important criterion for their classification.

Mammals have been the dominant form of life for the past 65 million years of the earth's history, an era known as the Cenozoic, just as dinosaurs dominated the previous 140 million years of the Mesozoic. Even during the last part of the latter era, insignificant small ancestral mammals existed along with the giant dinosaurs. Mammals are believed to have evolved from the reptilian order Therapsida some time during the Triassic period, about 175 to 200 million years ago. The fossil skeletal remains of those reptiles are remarkably mammal-like with a differentiation in teeth, in the formation of a bony palate, in the enlarge-

ment of the dentary bone in the mandible, and in the remarkably mammal-like limbs. Unfortunately there is no key to the nature of the soft parts of these animals to determine whether they were mammalian in character. It is not known whether they had hair or scales, or what the method of reproduction was, or the form of the heart, or the body temperature. The implication is that these early reptiles may have been mammal-like in some of these traits, although their brains were small (the present-day crocodiles also possess four-chambered hearts).

CLASSIFICATION OF MAMMALS

Living mammals exhibit a diverse array of forms, from the undoubtedly primitive egg-laying duck-billed platypus of Australia to such highly adaptive groups as the oceanic whales, bats, horses, dogs, and even man himself. The scientific classification of all forms of life dates from the revolutionary work of the Swedish botanist Carl von Linné (1707–78), who used a hierarchical system as a basis, grouping similar forms at different levels of relationship. For example, the wolf found in Ontario and Quebec would be classified as follows:

TAXON		RELATIONSHIPS
Kingdom	*Animalia*	All animals
Phylum	*Chordata*	Animals with notochords
Subphylum	*Vertebrata*	Animals with skeletons of bone or cartilage
Class	*Mammalia*	Mammals as described
Order	*Carnivora*	Carnivores
Family	*Canidae*	Dogs, foxes, etc.
Genus	*Canis*	Dogs
Species	*lupus*	Wolves
Subspecies	*lycaon*	Northeastern American wolves

The genus, species, and subspecies names form the trinomial scientific name of the mammal. These names are composed of Latin or latinized Greek words, or, rarely, words from other languages, and are conventionally written in italics. So the scientific name of the wolf found in Ontario and most of Quebec is *Canis lupus lycaon* (the generic name being capitalized, by convention, but not the specific and subspecific names). The great advantage in the use of scientific names is that for each species and subspecies there is only one valid name that is recognized throughout the world, irrespective of language.

Today the emphasis is placed on the species as a biological unit. This is by definition an interbreeding population sharing a common gene pool and relatively isolated in time and space. Well-marked geographical variants are described as subspecies. This is not to say that it is always easy to distinguish whether one is dealing with a species or subspecies; it is sometimes difficult because of interrupted distributions. Species hybrids and even generic hybrids add confusion, but these cases are generally rare in nature and for the most part indicate close relationships. Usually such hybrids are sterile or possess a much-reduced fertility rate.

In this book, the treatment is on a species level, but lists of the currently recognized subspecies are provided. There is still considerable interest and activity in describing new subspecies and shifting boundaries, but it is unlikely that many new species of mammals will be found in Canada and its coastal waters.

The most widely accepted classification of the class Mammalia is that of Simpson (1945) for the higher categories – orders, families, tribes, and genera. This classification is followed in general outline here, except in a few cases where more recent individual studies have indicated minor realignments.

DISTRIBUTION OF MAMMALS IN CANADA

From coast to coast in this vast land, mammals are found everywhere – except possibly on remote small islets. Our shores are frequented by members of the seal clan, Pinnipedia, and our coasts are visited by the less-known pelagic whales. Canada's land area is 3,846,000 square miles, or 6.9 per cent of the world's total land area of 55,786,000 square miles. Out of an estimated 3,200 species of land mammals, 163 species or 5 per cent of the total mammalian land fauna are known to inhabit Canada. In addition, 33 of a total of 85 species of whales have been known to visit our coasts. This can be considered a fairly high proportion, if one bears in mind that the tropics have a richer fauna than the temperate regions and that our post-glacial history is short.

Embracing half a continent, Canada contains many climatic, physiographic, and vegetative zones. The most widely accepted description of the forest regions of Canada is that of Rowe (1959). Each species of mammal has special environmental requirements for the necessities of shelter, food, and reproductive facilities. Each species is said to occupy its own ecological niche. For large cursorial carnivores, such as the wolf, this may permit a broad geographical distribution, but most small sedentary mammals, with distributions generally conforming well to the vegetative zones, are restricted to smaller ecologically uniform areas. Because of the restrictive ecological requirements, few mammals occur right across Canada. More usually, each physiographic, climatic, and vegetative zone has its own particular fauna.

Competition for food and shelter between closely related species also limits the distribution of many species. For that reason, when one finds a large variety of related mammals, such as various species of mice, in one area, it can safely be assumed that their food habits and life styles differ greatly.

The patterns of mammal distribution in North America were studied by Hagmeier and Stults in 1964, and Hagmeier brought his findings up to date in 1966. He concluded that there were twelve 'mammal provinces' in Canada, and a total of thirty-five for the United States and Canada. The Canadian 'provinces' may be united to form parts of five super-provinces or, further, parts of three subregions: Tundran, Coniferan, and Deciduan. These are subdivisions of the classical biogeographic Nearctic region, including North America and Greenland.

The present array of native mammal species in Canada suggests considerable antiquity for the fauna, but this is not the case. At the height of the last glaciation, the Wisconsin, a mere 18,000 years ago, most of Canada and the northern part of the United States were covered by a thick sheet of ice, and therefore were devoid of mammals. A few unglaciated areas did provide a refuge for them, the following being the most important: south of the continental glacier in the central United States; northwestern Yukon Territory and Alaska; the northern tip of Greenland (Pearyland); parts of the northwestern arctic islands; possibly a few isolated mountain-tops (nunataks) in the Queen Charlotte Islands, British Columbia; a drained portion of the continental shelf surrounding Sable Island, Nova Scotia; and the Grand Banks of Newfoundland. The rest of Canada has therefore been populated by immigration of mammals from these refuges since the Wisconsin glaciation. The two most important components of the recent mammal fauna are the holarctic group, which crossed the Bering landbridge from Asia and passed through the Yukon Territory, and the temperate American group, which migrated northward from the United States. There are indications of the immigration of a few mammals from Pearyland, such as the Peary caribou, and at least two species, the porcupine and the opossum, are immigrants from the Neotropical region.

HISTORY OF CANADIAN MAMMALOGY

Fur-bearing mammals were the first Canadian natural resource exploited by Europeans. The pursuit of the valuable beaver and the search for new trapping areas spurred on the exploration of this country in the eighteenth and early nineteenth centuries. (Even in 1972 the value of raw furs produced in Canada was 33 million dollars – a figure of some consequence.) About a century later, a second mammalian resource – whale oil – encouraged the exploration of the arctic seas around our northern shores.

Samuel Hearne (1795) gave an accurate account of his observations of mammals during northern explorations. This is surprising because the writings of other authors of his period, such as Pennant (1784), still contained many fanciful accounts of mysterious beasts such as 'sea apes.'

The scientific study of Canada's mammalian fauna began with John Richardson's *Fauna boreali-americana*, *volume 1: Mammals*, published in 1829. During the nineteenth century the accounts of fur traders, big-game hunters, geologists, explorers, and missionaries added to our knowledge of Canadian mammals, but it was not until 1888 that another summary was attempted, a brief list by J.B. Tyrrell.

Canada has been fortunate in having a number of naturalists who have made valuable contributions to knowledge of the biology of mammals through their writings. The best known was Ernest Thompson Seton, whose *Life Histories of Northern Animals* (1909) was originally an account of the mammals of Manitoba. This led to the enlarged *Lives of Game Animals* (1929), which has been accepted as a classic among reference books in this field. Other naturalists – such as the Criddle brothers, Stuart and Norman, of Aweme, Manitoba; James Munro, of Okanagan Landing, British Columbia; Kenneth Racey, of Vancouver; and W.E. Saunders, of London, Ontario – have all made significant contributions to Canadian mammalian literature.

The National Museums of Canada have supported continued research on the mammals of Canada through a distinguished line of professional staff mammalogists: R.M. Anderson, J.D. Soper, A.L. Rand, A.W. Cameron, P.M. Youngman, and C.G. van Zyll de Jong. During this period, research has been conducted throughout Canada from Newfoundland to the Queen Charlotte Islands and from Ellesmere Island to Pelee Island in Lake Erie. Museum officials have also been active in the preparation of provincial and other local annotated lists of mammals.

PUBLICATIONS IN CANADIAN MAMMALOGY

National and Provincial Lists of Mammals

CANADA
Anderson, R.M. 1946. Catalogue of Canadian recent mammals. National Museum of Canada Bulletin 102. King's Printer, Ottawa.
Peterson, Randolph L. 1966. The mammals of Eastern Canada. Oxford University Press, Toronto.

ALBERTA
Soper, J. Dewey. 1965. The mammals of Alberta. Hamly Press, Edmonton.

BRITISH COLUMBIA
Cowan, Ian McT., and C.J. Guiguet. 1956. The mammals of British Columbia. British Columbia Provincial Museum Handbook 11.

MANITOBA
Soper, J. Dewey. 1961. The mammals of Manitoba. Canadian Field-Naturalist 75(4): 171–219.

NEW BRUNSWICK
Morris, R.F. 1948. The land mammals of New Brunswick. Journal of Mammalogy 29(2): 165–76.

NEWFOUNDLAND
Cameron, Austin W. 1958. The mammals of Newfoundland. *In* Mammals of the islands in the Gulf of St. Lawrence. National Museum of Canada Bulletin 154: 71–106. Queen's Printer, Ottawa.

NORTHWEST TERRITORIES
Preble, E.A. 1902. A biological investigation of the Hudson Bay region. North American Fauna 22. Washington.
– 1908. A biological investigation of the Athabasca–Mackenzie region. North American Fauna 27. Washington.

NOVA SCOTIA
Smith, R.W. 1940. The land mammals of Nova Scotia. American Midland Naturalist 24(1): 213–41.

ONTARIO
Cross, E.C., and L.L. Snyder. 1929. The mammals of Ontario. Royal Ontario Museum Handbook 1.
Dagg, Anne Innis. 1974. Mammals of Ontario. Otter Press, Waterloo.

PRINCE EDWARD ISLAND
Cameron, Austin W. 1958. The mammals of Prince Edward Island. *In* Mammals of the islands in the Gulf of St. Lawrence. National Museum of Canada Bulletin 154: 40–53. Queen's Printer, Ottawa.

QUEBEC
Anderson, R.M. 1938. Mammals of the Province of Quebec. Annual Report Provancher Society 1938: 50–114.
Dionne, C.E. 1902. Les mammifères de la province de Québec. Dussault et Proulx, Quebec.

SASKATCHEWAN
Beck, W.H. 1958. A guide to Saskatchewan mammals. Saskatchewan Natural History Society, Special Publication 1. Regina.

YUKON TERRITORY
Rand, A.L. 1945. Mammals of Yukon. National Museum of Canada Bulletin 100. King's Printer, Ottawa.

The following scientific periodicals regularly publish papers on the distribution, taxonomy, biology, and ecology of Canadian mammals.

Canadian Periodicals
The Canadian Field Naturalist (Ottawa Field-Naturalists' Club, Ottawa).
The Canadian Journal of Zoology (National Research Council of Canada, Ottawa).
Les Carnets de zoologie (la Société zoologique de Québec, Inc., Quebec).
Le Naturaliste canadien (l'Université Laval, Quebec).

International Periodicals
Acta theriologica (Polish Academy of Sciences, Bialowieza, Poland)
Journal of Mammalogy (American Society of Mammalogists, Lawrence, Kansas, U.S.A.).
Mammalia (Musée national d'histoire naturelle, Paris).
Zeitschrift für Säugetierkunde (Deutschen Gesellschaft für Säugetierkunde, Hamburg and Berlin).

EFFECTS OF CIVILIZATION

The first European explorers to our country were impressed by the abundance of mammal life, which formed the cornerstone in the hunting culture of most of Canada's aboriginal inhabitants, the Eskimos and the Indians. With their scattered populations, their nomadic culture, and their primitive hunting weapons, it seems that they had not exterminated any species during the previous several thousand years.

The introduction of European culture and weapons, however, has had a disastrous effect on the populations of many mammals. Hunting and trapping reduced the populations of fur-bearers and deer. Agricultural developments on the prairies displaced bison, pronghorn, and wapiti herds. Deforestation and forest fires deprived many mammals such as caribou, marten, and fisher of the required climax forest habitat. Finally, since the natural feeding habits of many mammals such as rodents and carnivores were found to be deleterious to man's agricultural interests, control programs by poison and trap were put into practice, and these greatly reduced their populations.

So far as we are aware, only one species, the sea mink (*Mustela macrodon*), and two subspecies, the Queen Charlotte Island caribou (*Rangifer tarandus dawsoni*) and the eastern wapiti (*Cervus elaphus canadensis*), have been exterminated. But several species such as the black-footed ferret (*Mustela nigripes*), the swift fox (*Vulpes velox*), and the sea otter (*Enhydra lutris*) have been extirpated from the Canadian portions of their distribution (Alaskan sea otters have been recently reintroduced to an undisclosed portion of their former distribution on the British Columbia coast), and their numbers have been greatly reduced elsewhere. One subspecies, the wood bison (*Bison bison athabascae*), has been reduced to the point of extermination on its natural range, and the plains bison (*Bison bison bison*) continues mainly as an inhabitant of enclosed ranges in parks.

A few other species such as the mountain beaver (*Aplodontia rufa*), the black-tailed prairie dog (*Cynomys ludovicianus*), and the northern elephant seal (*Mirounga angustirostris*), although of restricted distribution in Canada, occur elsewhere in some numbers. Many whales and the harp seal, which are regular visitors to our shores, have also been seriously reduced in numbers as a result of international exploitation.

One must admit that with the exploding world population of human beings, the outlook for the maintenance of adequate habitat for other species of mammals is not very bright. The outlook is not, however, completely black. In recent decades, populations of game and fur-bearing mammals such as moose (*Alces alces*), deer (*Odocoileus* sp.), and beaver (*Castor canadensis*) have increased as a result of wise hunting and trapping laws. In addition, some varied habitats are being maintained in national and provincial parks, which support small populations of many species.

SPECIES ACCOUNTS

An attempt has been made to maintain uniform species accounts so that comparative life history details are presented for each species. Often it has been possible to point out gaps in our knowledge of the life histories of some species.

The accounts begin with the English and French name followed by the currently recognized scientific name and the authority for that name. For a starting point I have followed Jones, Carter, and Genoways' (1973) check list of names of North American mammals, but I have deviated in a few cases where there are more familiar Canadian vernacular names (for example, I have used the 'bighorn' sheep in place of 'mountain' sheep, which is the name applied to several species of wild sheep elsewhere). In the same vein I have occasionally added the adjective 'American' to a species (such as the badger) when the name is applied to other species on other continents. The check list may also be considered as a starting point for the scientific names, although I have deviated in a few cases where I have followed the conclusion reached by different authors of systematic studies. *Plecotus townsendii* was placed closer to *Myotis* on the basis of Handley's (1959) study. *Nycticeius* was similarly listed after *Eptesicus* to show closer affinities. *Ochotona collaris* is considered conspecific with *Ochotona princeps* on the basis of Broadbooks's (1965) report. I also consider *Spermophilus saturatus* as only subspecifically distinct from *Spermophilus lateralis*.

All the rats and mice are placed in the broad family Muridae after Ellerman (1940–45) and most European authors. If one raises the cricetines to family rank, surely the microtines deserve the same treatment. The cricetines are now considered only primitive murine mice, and the raising of the group to family rank (Cricetidae) is considered only a matter of convenience in view of the large number of species involved. *Peromyscus oreas* Bangs has been recognized as a full species as a result of Sheppe's (1961) work. The arrangement of the genera of microtine rodents was suggested by the analysis of Hooper and Hart (1962), although it is realized that it is impossible to indicate reticulate evolutionary relationships in a linear arrangement. *Clethrionomys* is generally accepted as the most generalized genus, and the lemmings *Lemmus* and *Dicrostonyx* are not closely related. *Microtus* is listed last. I have followed Rausch (1953) and many other recent authors in using the holarctic names *Lemmus sibiricus* and *Dicrostonyx torquatus* for the North American lemmings. The arrangement of the species of *Zapus* follows Krutzsch (1954). I included the jumping mice with the jerboas in the family Dipodidae after Klingener (1964) and many European authors.

Whale classification is a controversial subject, and two opposing viewpoints have been proposed. Hershkovitz (1966) holds that the toothed whales (Odontoceti) are the more primitive suborder and begins his classification with the toothy river dolphins; but Fraser and Purves (1960) believe that the whalebone whales (Mysticeti) are more primitive, based upon the structure of their accessory air sacs. Not being a specialist in the group, I have chosen to follow the traditional order commencing with the beaked whales (Ziphiidae). The list closely follows that of Rice and Scheffer (1968).

I have placed the weasel *Mustela nivalis* next to the black-footed ferret *Mustela nigripes*, because of the similarity in their reproductive physiology as distinct from the other weasels, *M. erminea* and *M. frenata*.

The arrangement of the seals follows that proposed by King (1964).

I have followed my own inclination in the order of the deer, commencing with *Rangifer* of the Neocervinae.

The sections called Description include information on historical background, body form, limbs, diagnostic features, skull and skeletal features, dentition, coat texture, colour and moults, sexual variation, measurements, and weights (usually provided in the metric system for smaller mammals, because it is the universally recognized scientific system). A conversion table from English to metric measurements is provided in Appendix 2. Length refers to total length, from snout to tip of tail. Tail is tail length from base to tip. Hind foot refers to length of foot from claws to heel. Ear length is measured from base of lobe to tip. Tables of dental formulae and numbers of digits and mammae for each species may be found in Appendix 1. A glossary of unfamiliar scientific terms and a drawing of a skull in which the bones are labelled are also provided at the back of the book.

Under Habits, information is given on sociability, migrations, senses, voice, diurnal activity, hibernation, winter nests, burrows, dens, population densities and fluctuations, home ranges, longevity, seasonal diet, and predators.

The natural environmental preferences are described under Habitat.

The section on Reproduction provides information on male and female annual sexual cycles, mating habits, gestation period, number and position of mammae, litter size, and period during which young are born. The appearance of the young at birth and their early development are described, including the opening of the eyes, juvenile coats, weights, weaning, and age of independence.

Under Economic Status are described the importance of the species to the aboriginal Canadian populations, modern hunting techniques, the importance of the species as a fur-bearer, its injurious habits and their control, and its importance as a vector of human diseases.

The current populations of certain species may be given with some certainty under Status. Others may be described as extinct in Canada after a certain date.

The world distribution of the species is provided under Distribution, and under Canadian Distribution the currently recognized subspecies found in Canada are listed by their scientific name, author, date of publication, and bibliographic reference. A brief description of their Canadian distribution is included, as are also general comments on

their appearance if the subspecies are easily recognizable. The Canadian distributions are also given in distribution maps for each species. The small inset maps give the original distribution, before human interference.

The most important recent publications for each species are listed under References. In this section preference has been given to Canadian authors.

REFERENCES

Anderson, R.M. 1946. Catalogue of Canadian recent mammals. Nat. Mus. Canada Bull. 102.

– 1965. Methods of collecting and preserving vertebrate animals. Nat. Mus. Canada Bull. 69, 4th rev. ed.

Anderson, S., and J. Knox Jones. 1967. Recent mammals of the world – A synopsis of families. Ronald Press, New York.

Broadbooks, H.E. 1965. Ecology and distribution of the pikas of Washington and Alaska. American Midl. Nat. 73(2): 299–335.

Davis, David E., and Frank B. Golley. 1963. Principles in mammalogy. Reinhold Press, New York.

Ellerman, J.R. 1940–45. The families and genera of living rodents. 3 vols. British Mus. (Nat. Hist.), London.

Fraser, F.C., and P.E. Purves. 1960. Hearing in cetaceans: Evolution of the accessory air sacs and the structure and function of the outer and middle ear in recent cetaceans. Bull. British Mus. (Nat. Hist.), 7(1).

Hagmeier, Edwin M. 1966. A numerical analysis of the distributional patterns of North American mammals. II. Re-evaluation of the provinces. Syst. Zool. 15(4): 279–99.

Hagmeier, Edwin M., and C.D. Stults. 1964. A numerical analysis of the distributional patterns of North American mammals. Syst. Zool. 13(3): 125–55.

Hall, E. Raymond, and Keith R. Kelson. 1959. The mammals of North America. 2 vols. Ronald Press, New York.

Handley, Charles O. Jr. 1959. A revision of the American bats of the genera *Euderma* and *Plecotus*. Proc. United States Nat. Mus. 110: 95–246.

Hearne, S. 1795. A journey from Prince of Wales Fort in Hudson Bay to the Northern Ocean ... in the years 1769, 1770, 1771 and 1772. A. Serahan and T. Cadell, London.

Hershkovitz, Philip. 1966. Catalog of living whales. Smiths. Inst. United States Nat. Mus. Bull. 246.

Hooper, Emmet T., and Barbara S. Hart. 1962. A synopsis of recent North American microtine rodents. Misc. Pub. 120, Mus. of Zool. Univ. Michigan, Ann Arbor.

Jones, J. Knox Jr., Dilford C. Carter, and Hugh H. Genoways. 1973. Checklist of North American mammals, north of Mexico. The Museum, Texas Tech. Univ. Occas. Papers 12.

King, Judith E. 1964. Seals of the world. The British Museum (Natural History), London.

Klingener, D. 1964. The comparative myology of four dipodoid rodents (genera *Zapus*, *Napaeozapus*, *Si-*

cista, and *Jaculus*). Misc. Pub. Mus. Zool. Univ. Michigan 124.

Krutzsch, Philip H. 1954. North American jumping mice (genus *Zapus*). Univ. Kansas Pub. Mus. Nat. Hist. 7(4): 349–472.

Pennant, Thomas. 1784. Arctic zoology, vol. 1: Mammals. Henry Hughs, London.

Peterson, Randolph L. 1966. The mammals of eastern Canada. Oxford University Press, Toronto.

Rausch, Robert. 1953. On the status of some arctic mammals. Arctic 6(2): 91–148.

Rice, D.W., and V.B. Scheffer. 1968. A list of the marine mammals of the world. United States Fish and Wildlife Serv. Spec. Sci. Rept. – Fisheries, 579.

Richardson, John. 1829. Fauna boreali-americana: Pt. 1, containing the quadrupeds. John Murray, London.

Rowe, J.S. 1959. Forest regions of Canada. Dept. Northern Affairs and National Resources, Forestry Branch Bull. 123. Ottawa.

Seton, E. Thompson. 1909. Life histories of northern animals: An account of the mammals of Manitoba. 2 vols. Chas. Scribner's Sons, New York.

– 1929. Lives of game animals. 4 vols. Doubleday Page, New York.

Sheppe, Walter. 1961. Systematic and ecological relations of *Peromyscus oreas* and *P. maniculatus*. Proc. American Phil. Soc. 105(4): 421–46.

Simpson, George G. 1945. The principles of classification and a classification of mammals. Bull. American Mus. Nat. Hist. 85.

Tyrrell, J.B. 1888. The mammalia of Canada. Copp, Clark Co., Toronto.

Walker, Ernest P. *et al.* 1964. Mammals of the world. 3 vols. Johns Hopkins Press, Baltimore.

ARTIFICIAL KEY TO THE ORDERS OF CANADIAN MAMMALS

Choose from alternatives 1 and 1′, then proceed to alternatives 2 and 2′, or 3 and 3′, etc., as indicated at the right.

1	Forelimbs modified as flippers	2
2	Hind limbs modified as flippers, tail short	PINNIPEDIA
2′	Hind limbs absent, tail modified as horizontal flukes	CETACEA
1′	Forelimbs not modified as flippers	3
3	Forelimbs modified as wings	CHIROPTERA
3′	Forelimbs and hind limbs similar	4
4	Feet terminating in cloven hooves	ARTIODACTYLA
4′	Feet terminating in four or five toes	5
5	First digits (thumb or toe) opposable	6
6	Thumb opposable	PRIMATES
6′	Big toe opposable, females with pouch	MARSUPIALIA
5′	First digits not opposable	7
7	Two pairs of large incisor teeth visible in front of mouth with space between incisors and cheek teeth	8
8	Two pairs large incisors, only	RODENTIA
8′	A second pair of small upper incisors immediately behind the first, ears moderate to large, tail powder-puff-like	LAGOMORPHA
7′	Three or more pairs of incisiform teeth, teeth in continuous row	9
9	Snout pointed, eyes small, ears small, teeth numerous, canines not developed	INSECTIVORA
9′	Incisors three pairs of similar teeth, canines long, shearing carnassial teeth, eyes large, ears moderate to large	CARNIVORA

Check List of Canadian Mammals

CLASS MAMMALIA

SUBCLASS THERIA

Infraclass Metatheria

ORDER MARSUPIALIA / MARSUPIALS / 3

Family Didelphidae / New World opossums / 3
Didelphis virginiana Kerr / Virginia opossum / 3
  virginiana Kerr

Infraclass Eutheria

ORDER INSECTIVORA / INSECTIVORES / 8

Family Soricidae / Shrews / 8
Sorex cinereus Kerr / Masked shrew / 8
  acadicus Gilpin
  cinereus Kerr
  haydeni Baird
  miscix Bangs
  streatori Merriam
  ugyunak Anderson and Rand
Sorex vagrans Baird / Vagrant shrew / 10
  vagrans Baird
  vancouverensis Merriam
Sorex obscurus Merriam / Dusky shrew / 11
  alascensis Merriam
  calvertensis Cowan
  elassodon Osgood
  insularis Cowan
  isolatus Jackson
  longicauda Merriam
  mixtus Hall
  obscurus Merriam
  prevostensis Osgood
  setosus Elliot
  soperi Anderson and Rand
Sorex palustris Richardson / American water shrew / 13
  albibarbis (Cope)
  brooksi Anderson
  gloveralleni Jackson
  hydrobadistes Jackson
  labradorensis Burt
  navigator (Baird)
  palustris Richardson
  turneri Johnson
Sorex bendirii (Merriam) / Bendire's shrew / 15
  bendirii (Merriam)
Sorex fumeus Miller / Smoky shrew / 16
  fumeus Miller

  umbrosus Jackson
Sorex arcticus Kerr / Arctic shrew / 17
  arcticus Kerr
  laricorum Jackson
  maritimensis R.W. Smith
  tundrensis Merriam
Sorex gaspensis Anthony and Goodwin / Gaspé shrew / 19
Sorex trowbridgii Baird / Trowbridge's shrew / 19
  trowbridgii Baird
Microsorex hoyi (Baird) / Pigmy shrew / 20
  alnorum (Preble)
  eximius (Osgood)
  hoyi (Baird)
  washingtoni Jackson
Microsorex thompsoni (Baird) / Thompson's pigmy shrew / 21
  thompsoni (Baird)
Blarina brevicauda (Say) / Short-tailed shrew / 22
  angusta Anderson
  brevicauda (Say)
  hooperi Bole and Moulthrop
  manitobensis Anderson
  pallida R.W. Smith
  talpoides (Gapper)
Cryptotis parva (Say) / Least shrew / 25
  parva (Say)

Family Talpidae / Moles / 26
Neürotrichus gibbsii (Baird) / American shrew-mole / 26
  gibbsii (Baird)
  minor Dalquest and Burgner
Scapanus townsendii (Bachman) / Townsend's mole / 28
  townsendii (Bachman)
Scapanus orarius True / Pacific coast mole / 30
  schefferi Jackson
Parascalops breweri (Bachman) / Hairy-tailed mole / 31
Scalopus aquaticus (Linnaeus) / Eastern mole / 33
  machrinus (Rafinesque)
Condylura cristata (Linnaeus) / Star-nosed mole / 35
  cristata (Linnaeus)
  nigra Smith

ORDER CHIROPTERA / BATS / 40

Family Vespertilionidae / Smooth-faced bats / 40
Myotis lucifugus (LeConte) / Little brown bat / 40
  alascensis Miller
  carissima Thomas
  lucifugus (LeConte)
  pernox Hollister
Myotis yumanensis (H. Allen) / Yuma bat / 45
  saturatus Miller

The Mammals of Canada

Order **Marsupialia** / Marsupials

The marsupials are the most primitive group of the viviparous mammals (i.e. those which bear their young alive). They are separated from the other groups by the absence of a true placenta and the possession of a fur-lined pouch (marsupium) covering the female's mammae. A diagnosis of the group reveals, however, that, as so often occurs in nature, there are exceptions to the rule. The long-nosed bandicoot of Australia (*Peramales*) has a true chorionic placenta, and several species possess only rudimentary pouches.

There are a number of other primitive skeletal features that unite the group. The number of teeth may be much higher than regularly found in the placental mammals. Yet fewer of the milk teeth are replaced by permanent teeth than in placentals, the fourth premolar being the only one having a milk predecessor. The skull is characterized by a very small brain-case; the tympanic (ear) bones are circular or tubular; and the angle of the mandible is inflected. The pelvis includes two primitive epipubic bones.

Although living marsupials are found only in Australia, New Guinea, the Celebes, and the Americas, the palaeontological record indicates a much wider distribution in earlier times.

Figure 1 Virginia opossum

Family **Didelphidae** / New World Opossums

The New World opossums are in many ways a generalized group, possessing many primitive features, on the whole not highly adapted to any particular mode of life. This generalized condition explains why our opossum is so successful. It has fifty teeth, a generally long, scaly prehensile tail, five digits on each foot, a big toe (hallux) that lacks a nail and is opposable to the other four, and generally it possesses only a rudimentary pouch.

VIRGINIA OPOSSUM
Opossum d'Amérique. *Didelphis virginiana* Kerr

Description. A full-grown opossum is cat-sized. It has a pointed muzzle, large naked paper-thin ears, a long scaly prehensile tail, white toes, and a fleshy clawless hallux opposed to the other four digits, as found in the monkey. The female possesses a fur-lined abdominal pouch (Figures 1 and 2).

The long, loose pelage (coat) is composed of a thick, short grey undercoat and long, coarse, white or black-tipped guard hairs. There is no set season of moult, a few hairs being replaced continuously all year. Black, reddish, and albino colour phases are known. The naked nose pad is large, pink, and porcine; the hair on the face is short and white; the large black eyes are surrounded by a black patch; the ears are black with white rims; the legs are

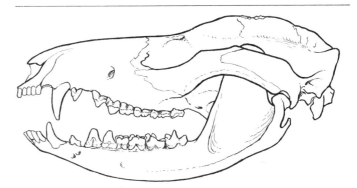

Figure 2 Opossum skull (× 2/3)

3

black; the toes are white; and the tail is white with a black-furred base. The male has a gland on the throat, which stains the fur with its yellowish discharge.

In winter, towards the northern limit of their distribution, opossums suffer from frozen extremities. Rarely is a full-grown opossum found without its ears frozen (back) to about half normal size, and its tail ending in a stub, lacking two inches or more.

Average measurements: total length 767 (686–835), tail 321 (290–348), hind foot 68.5 (60–74) mm. Average weight: of males 2.79 (1.36–5.04), of females 1.89 (1.36–3.23) kg.

Habits. The opossum is a solitary nocturnal hunter. Its deliberate ambling gait makes it easy for an active boy to overtake one. It climbs and swims well. Opossums remain active all winter in spite of cold spells. They do not burrow, but take over abandoned skunk or ground-hog burrows for their dens; or they build dens in brush piles or occupy hollow trees or logs and fill them with dry leaves. They generally utilize a home range of about fifty acres but may wander as far distant as seven miles.

One of the opossum's best-known habits is its ability to feign death when first captured. At the moment of crisis it may topple over, and lay immobilized on its side, mouth gaping and eyes glazed. If there is no further activity, it gradually comes around and totters off. This act of 'playing possum' has for a long time been considered a voluntary performance, but recent research has suggested that it is an involuntary state of tonic immobility brought on by shock. Opossums handled repeatedly seldom resort to this action but defend themselves with their teeth.

Opossums have catholic food tastes. Practically all animal and many plant forms within reach are considered grist for the metabolic mill. Insects form a large portion of their food: adult crickets, grasshoppers, beetles, and butterflies, or the larvae and grubs from the forest floor. They eat small mammals such as mice and moles as well as the young of larger species such as rabbits and squirrels. They also relish toads, frogs, salamanders, and snakes. Birds' eggs and nestlings, too, form part of their diet during the spring and summer. They also consume a wide range of berries, nuts, seeds, grasses, and clover. The opossum is an opportunist and will not disdain carrion found on its forays.

The opossum itself has such a disagreeable odour that most of the larger predators give it a wide berth. Great horned owls are known to kill opossums regularly, but, judging by roadside kills, one would conclude that the automobile is its worst enemy.

Opossums become sexually mature as yearlings and often live to an age of seven years.

Habitat. These mammals prefer to live in moist woods not far from streams. Though they may forage in higher and drier situations such as cultivated fields, they generally den in the bottomlands.

Reproduction. The reproduction of the opossum was considered one of the greatest animal mysteries of the eighteenth century. Many legends are expounded, and the fact is as fabulous as the fiction. The females are polyoestrous, with generally two peaks in breeding activity: late

January to March and late May to early July. If the female does not become pregnant, the oestrous cycle recurs in about twenty-eight days. The gestation period is thirteen days (perhaps the shortest known for any mammal). The young are born in an embryonic state, about 14 mm long and weighing approximately 0.6 g, or one ten-thousandth of the mother's weight. The whole litter can easily be accommodated in a teaspoon. At birth they have no external ears, eyes, or jaws; the tail and hind legs are rudimentary, and only the forelimbs are well developed, with digits fitted with claws; a circular orifice, which serves as a mouth, possesses a well-developed tongue.

The marsupium contains an average of thirteen teats arranged in the shape of a horseshoe, twelve around the perimeter and one in the centre. It has a strong sphincter muscle, which can draw tightly closed so that the young may be kept secure and dry even when the mother is swimming.

As the time for birth arrives, the female carefully cleans the pouch and licks down a pathway in the fur between the cloaca and the pouch entrance. She then props herself up in a sitting position. As the tiny foetuses appear, they are carefully licked dry, one by one. They then squirm blindly hand-over-hand, with a head-waving motion, up the moistened pathway to topple into the pouch. Inside, the first thirteen seek out the minute teats and fasten on. The litter may consist of up to twenty-five foetuses, but some do not find the pathway and fall to the ground, and others, the late arrivals, finding the teats all taken, are also doomed.

The pouched young remain attached to the teats for nine to ten weeks before they appear at the pouch entrance to take their first glimpse of the outside world. They do not grow onto the teat, nor is the milk pumped into them by the mother, as was originally thought. Rather, they suck quite ordinarily but continuously. By the time they are ready to leave their mother, the average litter size has been reduced to 8.6 by intramarsupium mortality. They remain with their mother until they are about three months old, clinging tightly to her back with their claws.

Economic Status. The opossum is probably of no consequence as far as man's economy is concerned, but it does destroy a great number of noxious insects. A few do, however, become hen-house marauders. The opossum has been found to be highly resistant to rabies infection.

Our friends in the southern United States consider roasted 'possum and taters' a delicacy. Opossums are classified as small game and hunted at night with hounds and flashlights. They usually quickly 'tree' in small bushes, from which they are easily shaken. It is doubtful if they will ever become a popular game animal in Canada.

Distribution. The opossum is found from Brazil and Peru northward to the eastern United States and southern Canada.

Canadian Distribution. According to Peterson and Downing (1956), opossums appear to have reached southern Ontario in waves of immigrants. The first wave was between 1892 and 1906, the second was in 1934, and the third began after 1947. Although most records refer to southwestern Ontario, one was taken in 1952 at Morris-

4

Map 1 Distribution of the Virginia opossum, *Didelphis virginiana*

burg on the St Lawrence River and others from near Lansdowne and Kemptville in 1961. This race reached the lower Fraser valley of British Columbia in 1949, where they are now common as far as Hope (see Map 1).

The subspecies found in Canada is the nominate race:

Didelphis virginiana virginiana Kerr, 1792, The animal kingdom ..., p. 193. Northeastern North America.

REFERENCES

Hartman, Carl G. 1952. Possums. University of Texas Press, Austin.
Peterson, R.L., and S.D. Downing. 1956. Distributional records of the opossum in Ontario. Jour. Mamm. 37(3): 431–5.

COLOUR PLATE

1

Comparison of Canadian shrews and bats: (a) American water shrew, *Sorex palustris*; (b) masked shrew, *Sorex cinereus*; (c) pigmy shrew, *Microsorex hoyi*; (d) arctic shrew, *Sorex arcticus*; (e) hoary bat, *Lasiurus cinereus*; (f) red bat, *Lasiurus borealis*; (g) small-footed bat, *Myotis leibii*; (h) silver-haired bat, *Lasionycteris noctivagans*; (i) little brown bat, *Myotis lucifugus*; (j) big brown bat, *Eptesicus fuscus*; (k) long-eared bat, *Myotis evotis*

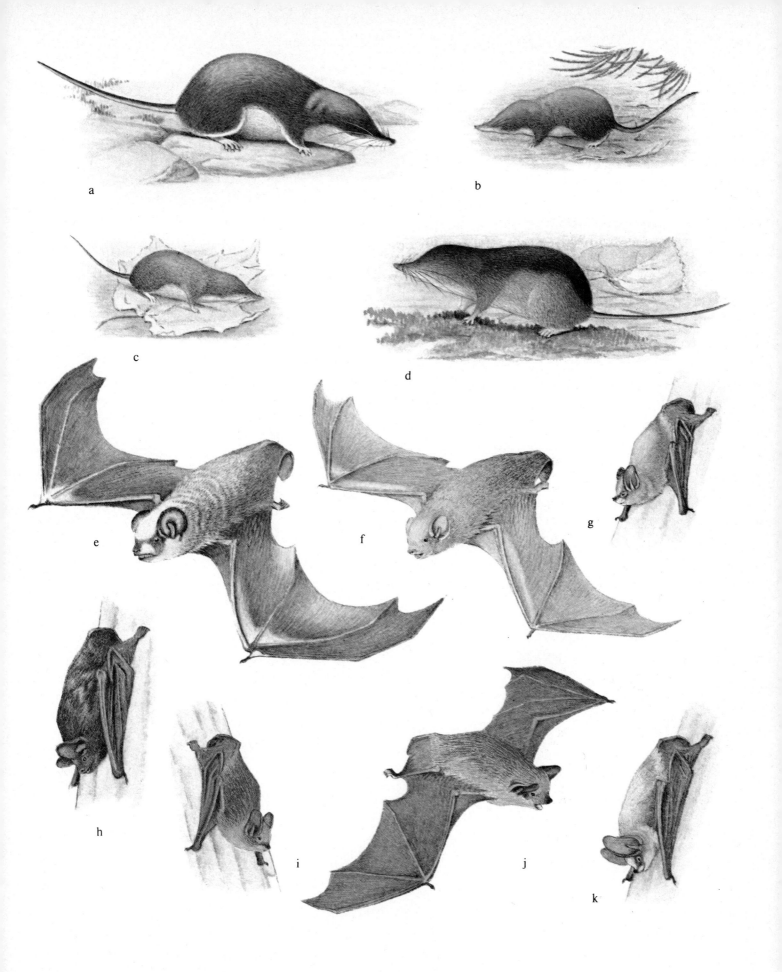

a

b

c

d

e

f

g

h

i

j

k

2

3

COLOUR PLATE

2

Short-tailed (*Blarina brevicauda*) and masked (*Sorex cinereus*)
shrew, masked shrew in background

3

Ord's kangaroo rat, *Dipodomys ordii*

Order **Insectivora** / Insectivores

It has been suggested that this order constitutes a waste-basket into which small primitive mammals of uncertain affinities have been dumped. The insectivores are the most primitive of the placental mammals and possess many fundamental characteristics found scattered through the higher groups. They are generally small mammals with long pointed snouts and short legs, each possessing five clawed digits. They generally walk with the heel on the ground (plantigrade). The typical Eutherian tooth formula (3 pairs of incisors, 1 pair of canines, 4 pairs of premolars, and 3 pairs of molars, both top and bottom jaw, totalling 44 teeth) first appears in this group. The replacement of the milk dentition by incisors, canines, and premolars is rapid and is completed in infancy. The tooth structure is relatively simple. The skull is triangular; the brain is small; the tympanic bones are annular. Insectivores are found throughout most of the world, except in Australia, Antarctica, Greenland, and most of South America.

ARTIFICIAL KEY TO FAMILIES OF CANADIAN INSECTIVORA

1 Forefeet broader than hind feet, no ear pinnae.   TALPIDAE

1' Forefeet the same width as hind feet, with ear pinnae.
                                                SORICIDAE

Family **Soricidae** / Shrews

The shrews are among the smallest living mammals. They have long pointed snouts, short velvety fur, minute black bead-like eyes, fairly prominent ears, and short but regular legs. Internally, the skull is narrow and lacks the zygomatic arch (cheek-bones); the tips of the teeth are red-stained (in Canadian species); the mandible articulates with the skull by two facets. The milk teeth are shed *in utero* and are never functional. Scent glands on the flank give a characteristic musky odour to several species.

MASKED SHREW
Musaraigne cendrée. *Sorex cinereus* Kerr

Description. The masked shrew is commonly and widely distributed in Canada. It is a diminutive beast, approxi-

mately 4 inches long, with a long flexible snout, minute eyes, readily discernible ears, small delicate feet, and a fairly long tail about the diameter of the lead in a pencil (Plates 1b and 2). The five maxillary unicuspid teeth are arranged in a graduated series from the largest in front to the smallest behind (Figures 3 and 4h).

The upper parts are a dull sepia brown in summer, shading into pale grey underparts. The winter pelage is longer, glossier, and greyer than in summer. The tail is bi-coloured, darker above. There are two moulting periods in spring and autumn, and the moults progress quite rapidly.

Average measurements: total length 100 (92–110), tail 40 (37–46), hind foot 11.5 (10–13) mm; weight 4.1 (2.9–6.6) g.

Habits. These voracious little hunters appear to be atoms of nervous energy and savagery. They are more or less active throughout the twenty-four-hour period, with peaks of activity after dusk and during the early morning hours. Within this framework there are also short-term periods of activity and rest, each of about an hour's duration. They are active all year, hunting in burrows under the snow. Occasionally their minute tracks may be seen on the snow leading from one snow collar about a shrub stem to another.

Shrews are not very congenial among even their own kind. Strangers avoid encounters, but when cornered they

Figure 3 Masked shrew head and skull (× 2)

8

fight. In confinement, shrews show cannibalistic tendencies; even litter mates destroy each other if confined after they leave the nest. Only when mating or rearing their young will the females tolerate the company of their mates. Shrews vigorously defend their nests and territories and drive intruders away.

Little information is available on population densities of masked shrews. The home range has been calculated to be about one-tenth of an acre, and populations that varied from less than one to as many as nine per acre in favourable habitats have been studied. Populations of these shrews show marked fluctuations from year to year.

The masked shrew forages for its food primarily among the leaves and debris of the forest floor, although it sometimes preys upon bird nestlings in trees. Its feet are probably too weak to dig its own burrows unless the soil is light or mossy; it therefore frequently utilizes the tunnels of larger species. Its food consists of about 65 per cent insects (adults, larvae, pupae, and eggs), 7 per cent vertebrates (salamanders and young mice), and 7 per cent centipedes; worms, molluscs, sowbugs, and vegetable matter account for the remainder of its diet. In order to maintain a high metabolic rate, it eats its own weight in food each day. Pregnant females have been known to consume over three times their body weight in a day. The shrew's voracious appetite accounts for its continual activity and quick death when deprived of food. The apparent high metabolic rate of shrews may be artificial, however, since their animal food has a higher moisture content than the plant seeds consumed by small rodents of equal size.

Unexpectedly, shrews are quite vocal, uttering as they

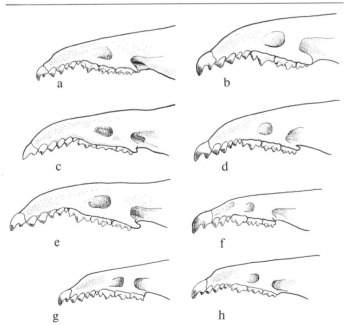

Figure 4 Comparison of dentitions of species of *Sorex* and *Microsorex*: (a) Trowbridge's shrew, *Sorex trowbridgii*; (b) American water shrew, *Sorex palustris*; (c) smoky shrew, *Sorex fumeus*; (d) arctic shrew, *Sorex arcticus*; (e) Bendire's shrew, *Sorex bendirii*; (f) pigmy shrew, *Microsorex hoyi*; (g) vagrant shrew, *Sorex vagrans*; (h) masked shrew, *Sorex cinereus* (× 4)

forage a twittering sound, or when angry a rapid series of shrill staccato notes.

Shrews usually live only fourteen to sixteen months – two summers and the intervening winter (maximum, twenty-three months) – and so they may be considered to be 'annuals' among mammalian populations.

In spite of their malodorous glands, masked shrews are preyed upon by a wide variety of small predators – larger shrews, weasels, hawks, owls, and snakes.

Habitat. The masked shrew lives in a wide variety of habitats, from dense forests to arctic tundra and from the seashore to alpine meadows. Humidity seems to be an important restricting factor, for shrews inhabit runways and forest floors where the air is saturated. In humid periods they may colonize open fields, but they retreat to moist shrubby or forested areas when the grasslands dry out under the hot sun. Ground cover in the form of leaves, stumps, decayed logs, and herbaceous vegetation seems to be ideal for the species.

Reproduction. Although the masked shrew is one of the commonest and most widely distributed of small mammals in North America, many facets of its life history are unknown. Females born in the spring may occasionally reach sexual maturity at the age of four months, in the autumn, but most breed for the first time the following spring. At that time there is a great relative growth in the sex organs of both male and female. The females possess six inguinal teats, arranged roughly in a v. However, the mammary tissue extends from the ventral surface around the flanks to the back. The breeding season lasts from late April to late September or October. Regularly one litter, occasionally two, are born in a season. Ovulation is induced by copulation. The period of gestation is thought to be about eighteen days. The number of young in a litter is two to ten, with an average of 4.4. At birth the young weigh 0.1 g or one-thirty-eighth of the female's weight. The young are born in a nest of grass, built under a log, board, stone, or stump; one or two small tunnels in the punky wood or vegetation lead away from the nest. The period of lactation and the length of time the young remain in the nest are not known. Growth is relatively slow. The eyes of the European species *Sorex araneus* do not open until the eighteenth to twenty-first day. Adult-sized young shrews, awkward in movements, are sometimes found in the nest in the summer months.

Economic Status. Shrews are beneficial to man's endeavours because of the large numbers of insects they consume. They have been found to make significant inroads into the pupae of such injurious species as the larch and spruce sawflies, and were introduced to Newfoundland in 1958 to control the depredations of the former. Apparently the results have been successful, and the shrews have spread over much of the island during the past decade.

Distribution. The masked shrew is found in northern North America from the southern Appalachians and central Rocky Mountains in the United States to Ungava and Alaska. It has also been identified in eastern Siberia.

Canadian Distribution. Six geographical subspecies of

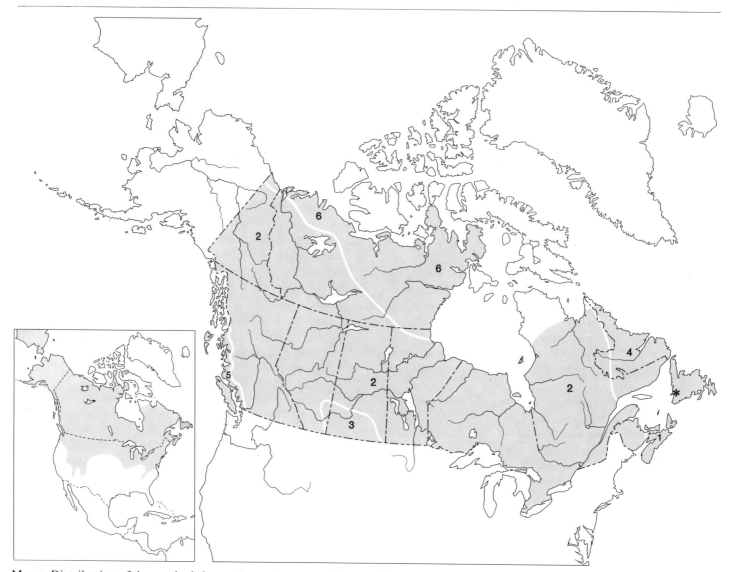

Map 2 Distribution of the masked shrew, *Sorex cinereus*: 1 *S. c. acadicus*, 2 *S. c. cinereus*, 3 *S. c. haydeni*, 4 *S. c. miscix*, 5 *S. c. streatori*, 6 *S. c. ugyunak*, * introduced

the masked shrew are currently recognized in Canada (see Map 2). They are distinguished primarily by colour differences and, secondarily, by size. For example, *ugyunak* has uniform pale flanks, which give it a tri-tone effect, while *haydeni* is smaller and dorsally paler.

Sorex cinereus acadicus Gilpin, 1867, Proc. and Trans. Nova Scotian Inst. Nat. Sci. 1(2): 2. Maritimes.
Sorex cinereus cinereus Kerr, 1792, The animal kingdom ..., p. 206. Boreal Canada.
Sorex cinereus haydeni Baird, 1858, Mammals: Rept. Expl. Surv. ... Rail. to Pacific 8(1): 29. Southern Prairie Provinces.
Sorex cinereus miscix Bangs, 1899, Proc. New England Zool. Club 1: 15. Labrador.
Sorex cinereus streatori Merriam, 1895, N. American Fauna 10: 62. Coastal British Columbia.
Sorex cinereus ugyunak Anderson and Rand, 1945, Canadian Field-Nat. 59: 62. Northwest Territories and Yukon Territory tundra.

REFERENCE

Moore, J.C. 1949. Notes on the shrew, *Sorex cinereus*, in the southern Appalachians. Ecol. 30(2): 234–7.

VAGRANT SHREW
Musaraigne errante. *Sorex vagrans* Baird

Description. It seems to be a natural rule that if two long-tailed shrews (genus *Sorex*) occupy the same habitat, one must be larger than the other. In eastern Canada the smoky shrew (*Sorex fumeus*) is frequently found with the masked shrew. However, in western Canada it is the vagrant shrew which appears as the big brother of the masked shrew (although their relations are far from brotherly). The vagrant shrew is about 4½ inches in length and is more heavily built than the masked shrew. Its tail is about 40 per cent of the total length. The colour ranges from reddish brown to greyish in summer, depending upon the subspecies. The silky winter pelage is longer than the summer one; it is sooty coloured with a mixture of white-tipped hairs in the Pacific coast populations, and more dusky in the interior races. The tail and feet are brownish. Fortunately the trenchant unicuspid dental pattern of the species provides a means of quick identification; in this species the third maxillary unicuspid tooth is noticeably smaller than the fourth (see Figure 4g).

The spring moult occurs in May and June, and the autumn moult in October. There is much individual variation in the time of moult. The new hair first appears on the rump and gradually spreads forward. A secondary focus of new hair develops on the nose and spreads over the face. A band between the ears is usually the last part of the body to change. A midsummer moult has been described for one or two individuals.

The usual shrew flank glands are evident in this species. They are insignificant in juvenile males but rapidly increase in size with the onset of the breeding season in February. They are also found in about 30 per cent of the mature females.

There is considerable variation in size between the various geographical subspecies. Average measurements for the species are: total length 117 (107–125), tail 50 (41–54), hind foot 13.5 (12–15) mm. The average weight for both sexes during the period of reproductive quiescence is 4.75 g. In March, with the onset of the breeding season, the mean weight of males rises to 7.2 g and remains at that level. The average weight of females during the same period rises to 7.82 g.

Habits. In summer the daily activity rhythm of the vagrant shrew is characterized by two nocturnal peaks, a lower morning peak, and an afternoon period of relative inactivity. Within this daily pattern is a short-term rhythm of nine to fifteen activity periods of forty-five minutes' to an hour's duration, alternating with rest periods of equal length. This shrew remains active all year. The average home range has been estimated to be approximately 4,000 square feet.

No information is available on the populations, predators, age, or mortality of this species, but it probably has similar characteristics to other long-tailed shrews.

This species has been found to feed primarily on insect larvae and adults as well as on earthworms. Other small invertebrates such as molluscs and spiders are taken, as well as a considerable amount of vegetable matter.

Habitat. Vagrant shrews are found from the Pacific shore to an elevation of approximately 7,500 feet in the Rocky Mountains. They are seldom found far from water in the form of marshes or streams, and may be found in moist coniferous forests or alpine meadows near mountain streams. Mossy forests, willow-clad brook banks, horsetail (*Equisetum*) stands along streams, and sphagnum bogs appear to be their favourite haunts.

Reproduction. Sexual activity commences in the males in February. Matings occur in March, and pregnant females have been found from April 1 to August 8. No data are available on gestation or lactation periods. The average litter size has been found to be 6.4, varying from two to nine. Post-partum mating has been described for several

species of shrews, and there is some evidence that two litters may be born rarely in this species as well. It is also possible that occasionally young females born early in the year may themselves bear young in late summer.

Young vagrant shrews are born in nests of dry grass about four inches in diameter, commonly placed in decayed logs. Although the grass ball usually has no central cavity, the young burrow through the centre. The eyes are still closed even when the young shrews are almost fully grown. Little is known of the growth of these shrews.

Economic Status. This species also feeds upon many forms of forest insects.

Distribution. The vagrant shrew occurs in western North America from northern Mexico to Alaska.

Canadian Distribution. This species seems to be divided into two family stocks: one is smaller and dark and inhabits the Pacific coastal forests (*vagrans*); the other is larger and paler and inhabits marshes in the Rockies and Great Plains areas (*obscurus*). Over much of the species range in the western United States the various geographic subspecies replace each other in orderly fashion, but in the coastal area, including southern British Columbia, these two family groups are found to occur together independently.

Such a situation of sympatric subspecies is thought to have occurred as a result of range extensions and contractions during the alternating glacial and interglacial stages of the Pleistocene epoch. It is postulated that during the penultimate glaciation the *vagrans* ancestors were distributed continuously across western North America south of the ice-sheet. During the last interglacial stage the range was extended northward to include northwest Canada and Alaska. However the high, dry plateau between the Rocky Mountains and the coast range was abandoned because of lack of suitable habitat. During the last glaciation the northern portion of the range was obliterated, leaving the coastal and Rocky Mountains separated. Increasing moisture again made the interior plateau habitable, and the Rocky Mountain part of the population reinvaded the coastal area occupied by the parent forest stock. In the intervening time, however, differentiation proceeded to such an extent that reproductive barriers were established, and the two forms behaved as independent species. Elsewhere to the south the two groups interbred because the separation had been less complete.

The number of slightly differentiated insular populations found in this region would lead one to suppose that a few of these shrews must have been transported accidentally to several islands off the British Columbia coast on natural rafts from landslides on precipitous coasts.

The dusky shrew, *Sorex obscurus* Merriam, has recently been given full specific rank by Hoffmann (1971) as distinct from its close relative the vagrant shrew, *Sorex vagrans*. The dusky shrew has the wider distribution in northwestern North America, as represented by eleven subspecies. The vagrant shrew only reaches extreme southern British Columbia (*Sorex vagrans vagrans*) and the southern tip of Vancouver Island (*Sorex vagrans vancouverensis*) (see Map 3).

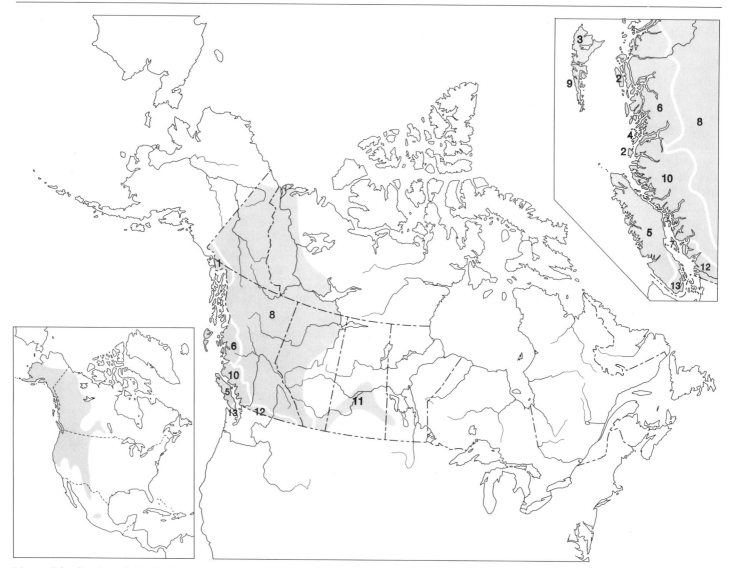

Map 3 Distribution of the dusky shrew, *Sorex obscurus*, and the vagrant shrew, *Sorex vagrans*: 1 *S. o. alascensis*, 2 *S. o. calvertensis*, 3 *S. o. elassodon*, 4 *S. o. insularis*, 5 *S. o. isolatus*, 6 *S. o. longicauda*, 7 *S. o. mixtus*, 8 *S. o. obscurus*, 9 *S. o. prevostensis*, 10 *S. o. setosus*, 11 *S. o. soperi*, 12 *S. v. vagrans*, 13 *S. v. vancouverensis*

Sorex obscurus alascensis Merriam, 1895, N. American Fauna 10: 76. Extreme northwest British Columbia.

Sorex obscurus calvertensis Cowan, 1941, Proc. Biol. Soc. Washington 54: 103. Banks and Calvert islands, British Columbia.

Sorex obscurus elassodon Osgood, 1901, N. American Fauna 21: 35. Graham, Hippa, and Moresby islands, Queen Charlotte Islands, British Columbia.

Sorex obscurus insularis Cowan, 1941, Proc. Biol. Soc. Washington 54: 103. Bardswell Island Group, British Columbia.

Sorex obscurus isolatus Jackson, 1922. Jour. Washington Acad. Sci. 12: 263. Vancouver Island, British Columbia.

Sorex obscurus longicauda Merriam, 1895, N. American Fauna 10: 74. North coast of British Columbia.

Sorex obscurus mixtus Hall, 1938, American Nat. 72: 462. Texada Island, British Columbia.

Sorex obscurus obscurus Merriam, 1895, N. American Fauna 10: 72. Alberta, British Columbia, Yukon Territory.

Sorex obscurus prevostensis Osgood, 1901, N. American Fauna 21: 35. Kunghit Island, Queen Charlotte Islands, British Columbia.

Sorex obscurus setosus Elliot, 1899, Field Columbian Mus. Pub. 32: 274. South coast of British Columbia.

Sorex obscurus soperi Anderson and Rand, 1945, Canadian Field-Nat. 59: 47. Central Manitoba and Saskatchewan.

Sorex vagrans vagrans Baird, 1858, Mammals: Rept. Expl. Surv. ... Rail. to Pacific 8(1): 15. Extreme southern British Columbia.

Sorex vagrans vancouverensis Merriam, 1895, N. American Fauna 10: 70. Southern Vancouver Island, British Columbia.

REFERENCES

Clothier, R.R. 1955. Contribution to the life history of *Sorex vagrans* in Montana. Jour. Mamm. 36(2): 214–21.

Hoffmann, Robert S. 1971. Relationships of certain holarctic shrews, genus *Sorex*. Zeits. f. Säugetierkunde 36(4): 193–200.

AMERICAN WATER SHREW
Musaraigne palustre. *Sorex palustris* Richardson

Description. Swift-flowing forest streams form a productive habitat that has been colonized by a variety of small carnivorous mammals throughout the world. In West Africa it is the giant water shrew *Potamogale*, and in Australia and New Guinea, the water rats of the genus *Hydromys*. The Eurasian water shrew belongs to a different genus (*Neomys*) from ours. The similarity in appearance of these diverse mammals, as a result of their adaptation to the particular environmental niche, is remarkable. All possess long-pointed snouts, long strong tails, large webbed or fringed hind feet, and a short dark velvety coat.

The American water shrew (Plate 1a) is a large shrew (about 6 inches long, including its relatively long tail). The large hind feet are fringed with a row of stiff hairs; the middle toes are partially webbed. The pelage is particularly soft and velvety, fuscous black above and silvery to brownish beneath. The tail is distinctly bi-coloured, silvery below (Figure 5). There is a spring moult from April to June, beginning anteriorly and working back. The autumn moult occurs in late July and August, when the animals renew their thicker winter pelage. Flank glands have been found only in the males. The skull is relatively large and is heavily constructed. The first two unicuspid teeth are noticeably larger than the next two (Figure 4b).

Average measurements: total length 153 (143–161), tail 73 (63–78), hind foot 20 (18–21) mm. Average weight: immature males 9.7 g, mature males 15.4 g, and mature females 12.3 g.

Habits. The water shrew is a secretive creature, spending most of its time hunting under the cover of overhanging banks. Even in its favourite habitat it is seldom observed in life. I have seen water shrews on only two occasions. The first time I caught a glimpse of one was when I was about to step across a swift mountain brook and a small black furry creature scuttled from under my foot and leaped into the clear water. Immediately it was transformed into a silver object by the film of air trapped in its fur. It swam quickly under water to the opposite bank, where it vanished. The second time I had a better glimpse of one as it scampered over lakeshore boulders high in the Alberta Rockies.

These shrews are active to some extent throughout the total twenty-four-hour period but have two activity peaks: one hour before sunrise and the three hours following sunset. They have an average rhythm of approximately thirty minutes of activity, followed by a sixty-minute rest period. Like all shrews they are active all winter, and it is easy to trap them under the shell of ice clinging to the banks of fast-flowing streams.

They are scrappy little beasts but do not show any social hierarchy or territoriality. They build many resting nests, they hoard food, and they rob the caches of others. Little is known of their home ranges or population densities. Although the species is usually uncommon, sizable populations have been noted occasionally in favourable locations.

The large webbed and fringed hind feet (Figure 6), the close pile of the fur, and the long tail give this shrew an amazing buoyancy in water. It has been observed scampering across the surface of a still pool, apparently 'walking on the water.' Air bubbles have been observed trapped under its feet. As with other species, its sense of sight seems to be poorly developed, and the sense of smell and the tactile sense in the long vibrissae on the mobile snout give most aid in finding food. In aquaria, water shrews appear to stay under water with difficulty, paddling furiously and probing the bottom with their snouts. After a swim, the water shrew dries its coat by combing it with the stiff hairs on its hind feet and by giving a quick shake.

Figure 5 American water shrew

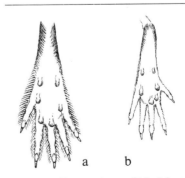

Figure 6 Comparison of hind feet of (a) American water shrew, *Sorex palustris*, and (b) arctic shrew, *Sorex arcticus* (× 2)

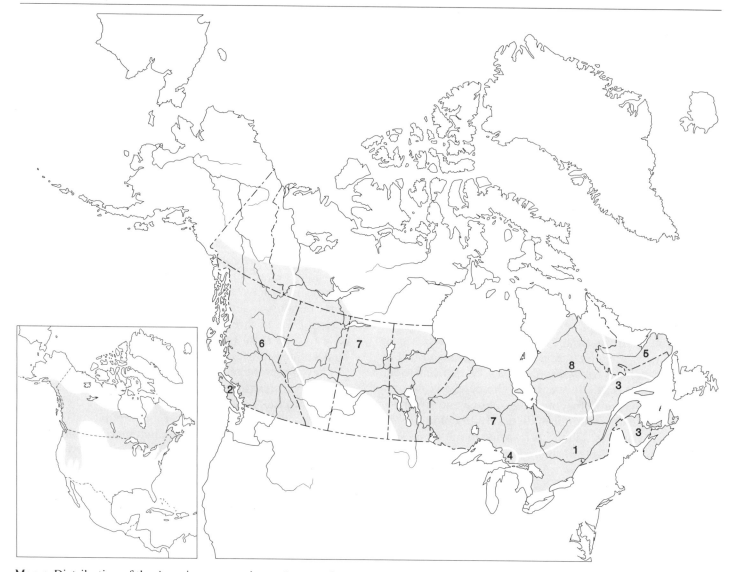

Map 4 Distribution of the American water shrew, *Sorex palustris*: 1 *S. p. albibarbis*, 2 *S. p. brooksi*, 3 *S. p. gloveralleni*, 4 *S. p. hydrobadistes*, 5 *S. p. labradorensis*, 6 *S. p. navigator*, 7 *S. p. palustris*, 8 *S. p. turneri*

This shrew's food consists primarily of insects, about 50 per cent of which are aquatic larvae of stoneflies, caddisflies, and mayflies. Other aquatic invertebrates such as planarians are eaten, and small fish are also captured. A water shrew has been seen diving in a shallow pool and seizing a 2½-inch salmon parr, which it brought back to a rock to eat. Shrews have also been known to eat fish eggs in hatchery pools.

Evidence points to the conclusion that water shrews are annuals, dying after their second summer.

Habitat. These shrews are physically adapted to an aquatic environment and are seldom found far from water. They inhabit stream banks, lakeshores, and marshes, in the coniferous forest region from sea level to 7,000 feet in the mountains. Their favourite haunts are mossy banks, rocks, and logs along the banks of swift-flowing streams in dense climax coniferous forests. Though seldom taken more than thirty feet from such locations, they are occasionally found in nearby wet meadows.

Reproduction. It seems that young males do not become sexually mature until December or January of their first year, but they remain sexually active until the following August. No old males have been recorded after this month. Reproductive activity in females commences in late January. Ovulation is induced by copulation. First matings probably occur in February, the earliest pregnancy being reported for February 24. The exact gestation and lactation periods are unknown. Since virtually all adult females taken between April and August are pregnant or lactating, it is suspected that two or three litters are produced by adult females in their second summer. The evidence points to a polyoestrous cycle and post-partum matings. Five to eight embryos have been recorded with the mode six for litter size (the same number as the teats). There is some evidence to suggest that a few young females born in the early spring may breed in their first summer.

A water shrew's nest containing young has been found

in a beaver lodge. The nest, about four inches in diameter, which was composed of sticks and leaves, had been placed just above the water line. It contained four half-grown young on May 11.

Economic Status. Water shrews are probably neutral in man's scheme of things. They live on the aquatic nymphs of certain obnoxious insects such as biting flies, but individual shrews can become quite destructive to eggs and in fish hatcheries.

Distribution. The American water shrew is found from the Appalachian Mountains, the southern Rocky Mountains, and the Sierra Nevada Range in California north to southern Alaska and Ungava.

Canadian Distribution. Eight geographical subspecies are recognized in Canada (see Map 4). The Cordilleran subspecies *navigator* is quite distinctive, with its silvery underparts contrasting strongly with the black back.

Sorex palustris albibarbis (Cope), 1862, Proc. Acad. Nat. Sci. Philadelphia 14: 188. Eastern Ontario, southern Quebec.

Sorex palustris brooksi Anderson, 1934, Canadian Field-Nat. 48: 134. Vancouver Island, British Columbia.

Sorex palustris gloveralleni Jackson, 1926, Jour. Mamm. 7: 57. The Maritimes.

Sorex palustris hydrobadistes Jackson, 1926, Jour. Mamm. 7: 57. Sault Ste Marie, Ontario.

Sorex palustris labradorensis Burt, 1938, Occas. Papers Mus. Zool. Univ. Michigan 383: 1. Southern Labrador.

Sorex palustris navigator (Baird), 1858, Mammals: Repts. Expl. Surv. ... Rail. to Pacific 8(1): 11. Western mountain region in Alberta, British Columbia, and Yukon.

Sorex palustris palustris Richardson, 1828, Zool. Jour. 3(12): 517. Central Canada.

Sorex palustris turneri Johnson, 1951, Proc. Biol. Soc. Washington 64: 110. Ungava.

REFERENCES

Conaway, C.H. 1952. Life history of the water shrew (*Sorex palustris navigator*). American Midl. Nat. 48(1): 219–48.

Sorenson, M.W. 1963. Some aspects of water shrew behavior. American Midl. Nat. 68(2): 445–62.

BENDIRE'S SHREW
Musaraigne de Bendire. *Sorex bendirii* (Merriam)

Description. This shrew, measuring about 6½ inches in total length, is the longest of the North American shrews. It, too, shows aquatic modifications but to a lesser degree than the water shrew. The hind feet are only faintly fringed with stiff hairs. The colour is dark chocolate brown, only slightly paler on the abdomen. The tail and feet are similarly coloured. The summer pelage is slightly paler than the winter coat. The spring moult occurs between mid-June and mid-July, and the autumn moult between late August and late October. Individuals moult fairly quickly,

Map 5 Distribution of Bendire's shrew, *Sorex bendirii*

but there is considerable variation in the date of moulting.

Bendire's shrew is easily distinguished from the water shrew in western Canada because of its chocolate-coloured underparts in contrast to the silvery underparts of the water shrew. However, in the Olympic Peninsula of Washington State, there is a white-bellied Bendire's shrew. To distinguish it, then, one must rely on the trenchant skull characteristics, which include a much longer, slightly hooked rostrum and a flattened cranium (Figure 4e).

Average measurements: total length 161 (155–167), tail 72 (65–81), hind foot 19 (18–21) mm.

Habits. Very little is known of the biology of this species.

Habitat. Bendire's shrew is found in dense, moist coniferous forests, on beaches, and in marshes. It is usually trapped near water and is known to swim readily.

Reproduction. No particulars are known for this species.

Economic Status. Unknown.

Distribution. This shrew is found on the Pacific coast from northern California to southern British Columbia.

Canadian Distribution. The species occurs only in the lower Fraser valley of British Columbia (see Map 5). The Canadian form is the typical one.

Sorex bendirii bendirii (Merriam), 1884, Trans. Linn. Soc. New York 2: 217.

Map 6 Distribution of the smoky shrew, *Sorex fumeus*: 1 *S. f. fumeus*, 2 *S. f. umbrosus*

SMOKY SHREW
Musaraigne fuligineuse. *Sorex fumeus* Miller

Description. The novice eastern mammalogist is early confronted with the problem of distinguishing between smoky and masked shrews in the hand. The smoky shrew is larger (about 4½ inches). In summer it is grizzled brown dorsally and only slightly paler below. The tail is longer and fuscous-coloured; it is relatively naked in adults, and lightly tufted with brownish hairs in juveniles. The ears are also fuscous and more prominent. The winter pelage is strikingly different. Then the smoky shrew wears its characteristic dense, velvety, slate-coloured coat, which has a silvery sheen on the belly. The winter coat is worn from late September to early May. An autumn juvenile coat of 'concolor buff' has also been described. The flank glands are well developed in both sexes (Figure 4c).

Average measurements: total length 116 (110–127), tail 44 (40–52), hind foot 13 (13–15) mm. Average weight: males 9 (6.4–11) g, females 7.5 (6.7–10) g.

Habits. Smoky shrews are active throughout the twenty-four-hour period, with the usual alternating periods of activity and rest. They are also active throughout the winter.

Since their feet are weak, they do not burrow but use the burrows of other species in the leaf mould of the forest floor. The baseball-sized nest of shredded leaves is placed in the tunnels, from four to nine inches below the soil surface, under a stump or log.

Smoky shrews twitter in characteristic shrew fashion when foraging, and pipe shrilly when cornered. Their long facial vibrissae appear to act as sensory organs. When hunting, the shrew frequently holds its snout in the air, vibrissae twitching, to sense danger. Eyesight and hearing seem to be well developed in this species, but the sense of smell seems less reliable.

About 80 per cent of the food items eaten in summer consists of insect forms; earthworms, vegetable matter, centipedes, and snails make up most of the remainder. Salamanders, sowbugs, spiders, and bird remains are occasionally eaten.

Smoky shrew populations appear to fluctuate from year

16

to year, but the causes remain unknown. Generally, the species is much less common than the masked shrew. Occasionally, in ideal habitat, fair numbers of smoky shrews may be secured. They have the same annual life-span as other shrews. Owls and small predators such as the short-tailed shrew prey upon this species.

Habitat. Smoky shrews prefer moist leaf mould in the mature deciduous forests of eastern North America. They also frequent mossy rocks, logs, and alders along stream banks. Their smaller neighbour, the masked shrew, is usually less demanding in choice of habitat. Although the masked shrew may occur with the smoky shrew, its keener senses may serve to preserve it from its larger competitor.

Reproduction. Young smoky shrews do not become sexually mature during the year of their birth. The males reach breeding condition in March, with a great development of the sex organs and flank glands, and continue to maintain their fecundity through August. Females become sexually mature in March as well. Matings probably commence in April since the first pregnant females were secured in late April. Although the gestation period is thought to be slightly less than three weeks, it has not been definitely determined. The females possess the usual three pairs of teats arranged in a v, and the mammary glands extend subdermally on the flank and around the hind legs onto the back. The litter size averages 5.5 (2–8) in number. Since the reproductive period extends until August and since the species is probably polyoestrous, there are indications of a second litter.

Economic Status. These shrews must be thought of as beneficial to man because they destroy large numbers of insect larvae and pupae, which are probably injurious to forest trees.

Distribution. The smoky shrew is found in eastern North America from the Great Smokies of the Carolinas north to the Maritimes and central Ontario.

Canadian Distribution. Two subspecies are recognized in Canada (see Map 6).

Sorex fumeus fumeus Miller, 1895, N. American Fauna 10: 50. Ontario and western Quebec.
Sorex fumeus umbrosus Jackson, 1917, Proc. Biol. Soc. Washington 30: 149. Maritimes and southern Quebec.

REFERENCE

Hamilton, W.J. Jr. 1940. The biology of the smoky shrew (*Sorex fumeus fumeus* Miller). Zoologica 25(4): 473–92.

ARCTIC SHREW
Musaraigne arctique. *Sorex arcticus* Kerr

Description. The arctic shrew is a relatively heavily built long-tailed shrew, about 4½ inches in length. Adults are easily recognized in the hand (in most areas of Canada) by their tri-toned coat. In winter the adult's back is glossy fuscous black; its flanks are cinnamon brown, and its belly is grey. Its summer coat, somewhat subdued in colour, is much shorter; it is chocolate brown on the back, which

still contrasts sharply with the grey-brown of the flanks and belly. The tail is cinnamon brown, paler beneath and rather scantily haired in summer adults (Plate 1d). The arctic shrew is closely related to the common shrew (*Sorex araneus*) of Europe and Asia.

It was necessary to qualify the arctic shrew's easy separation from other Canadian shrews because the northern subspecies of the masked shrew (*Sorex cinereus ugyunak*) is similarly tri-coloured. However, its larger size, robust build, and short tail usually serve to identify the arctic shrew, except when dealing with immature shrews, when it may be necessary to examine cranial characters for proper identification. The larger, more robust skull and the concurrence of a post-mandibular canal in *Sorex arcticus* then makes identification definite (Figures 7a and 4d).

The juvenile coat is dull chocolate brown above, paler below. The moult takes place in October, and the young assume the adult tri-coloured coat by November. The spring moult occurs in June, but the change is less noticeable.

Average measurements of adult males: length 114 (100–121), tail 42 (37–45), hind foot 14 (12–15) mm; weight 8 (6–12.3) g. Measurements of adult females: length 116 (105-124), tail 42 (36–45), hind foot 14 (13–15) mm; weight 8.3 (5.3–13.5) g.

Habits. These shrews are rather docile and are unafraid in captivity. They are continually on the run, digging and constructing grass nests. They spend much time grooming their faces with their forepaws. Arctic shrews are active throughout day and night.

This shrew is reported to construct its own trails, but it has been known to use those constructed by larger rodents as well. There are also indications of territoriality in the species. The average cruising range, determined to be 146 feet, suggests a home range of about one-tenth of an acre. Populations as high as five per acre have been measured in favourite habitat in Manitoba, though they are generally less than one per acre. This shrew is known to survive at least eighteen months. Nothing is known of its feeding habits or of its enemies.

Habitat. The arctic shrew has been most frequently taken on the edges of sphagnum bogs and marshes, often on the edge of the alder or willow shrub zone. It seems to

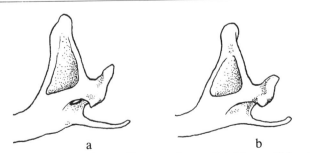

Figure 7 Comparison of inner surfaces of right mandibles of (a) arctic shrew, *Sorex arcticus*, and (b) masked shrew, *Sorex cinereus* (× 8)

Map 7 Distribution of the arctic shrew, *Sorex arcticus*: 1 *S. a. arcticus*, 2 *S. a. laricorum*, 3 *S. a. maritimensis*, 4 *S. a. tundrensis*

favour a slightly drier habitat than other species. It also occurs on the arctic tundra. Trapping records suggest that it may be a species typical of the subclimax or transitional vegetation stages.

Reproduction. Very little information is available on this aspect of the biology of the species. The fact that pregnant females have been taken from late April to September suggests that there are two litters each season. The number of embryos counted has varied from six to ten (average 6.3). The reproductive organs of the males enlarge in February and regress from July to August. Juvenile females rarely breed during their first summer.

Economic Status. Specific details are lacking for this species.

Distribution. The species is found primarily across Canada from the Maritimes to the Yukon and into Alaska. Its range includes a small section of the mid-western states, from Lake Michigan to North Dakota.

Canadian Distribution. Four subspecies are recognized in Canada (see Map 7). The form found on the tundra of Alaska, Yukon, and the Mackenzie delta (*S. a. tundrensis*) is quite distinctive. The winter pelage is extremely long and silky, and the back is rich chocolate brown without any slaty tone. This race is appreciably smaller than the typical forest subspecies and may constitute a distinct species.

Sorex arcticus arcticus Kerr, 1792, The animal kingdom ..., p. 206. Central Canada.

Sorex arcticus laricorum Jackson, 1925, Proc. Biol. Soc. Washington 38: 127. Southern Manitoba.

Sorex arcticus maritimensis R.W. Smith, 1939, Jour. Mamm. 20: 244. Maritimes.

Sorex arcticus tundrensis Merriam, 1900, Proc. Washington Acad. Sci. 2: 16. Yukon Territory and the Mackenzie delta, Northwest Territories.

REFERENCE

Clough, G.C. 1963. Biology of the arctic shrew, *Sorex arcticus*. American Midl. Nat. 69(1): 69–81.

GASPÉ SHREW
Musaraigne de Gaspé. *Sorex gaspensis* Anthony and Goodwin

Description. The Gaspé shrew is one of the rarest and least known of Canadian mammals. Its exact taxonomic status is not settled. It is considered closely related to *Sorex dispar* of the Appalachian Mountains, and may be only subspecifically distinct from that species.

It is a slender, long-tailed shrew. Although the total length is similar to that of the sympatric smoky shrew, the latter species is much heavier and has a shorter tail. The Gaspé shrew has larger ears and long vibrissae. In summer it is a uniform mouse-grey colour, only slightly paler beneath. The winter coat is unknown.

The skull is long (particularly the rostrum) and depressed. The unicuspid teeth are narrow, the third and fourth being approximately equal in size.

Average measurements: total length 95–115, tail 47–55, hind foot 12 mm; weight 5 g.

Habits. Virtually nothing is known of the life history of this species. The stomachs of three *Sorex dispar* examined from Pennsylvania contained centipedes. Although generally rare, these shrews may be fairly common in their chosen habitat.

Habitat. The closely related *Sorex dispar* seems to occupy a particularly specialized ecological niche. It inhabits cool, moist, dark mossy talus rocks. There it lives in a network of galleries in the moss and leaf mould under the surface rocks. Most specimens have been taken underground in talus slopes beneath rock outcroppings in dense forests. Although they seem to prefer coniferous forests, they also inhabit climax oak–beech forests.

The Gaspé shrew has been taken from beneath mossy boulders along swift-flowing stream banks in spruce forests, a habitat similar to that of the water shrew. However, the stream-bank habitat may also be equivalent to the rock talus slope of the long-tailed shrew farther south.

Reproduction. No data are available on the Gaspé shrew. Females of *Sorex dispar* taken in late April showed increased sexual activity. Two specimens taken in May were pregnant, each containing five embryos. Others taken from July to March indicated no sexual activity.

Ecomomic Status. The Gaspé shrew is of no known economic importance.

Distribution. The long-tailed shrew, *Sorex dispar*, is found in the Appalachian Mountains from North Carolina to Maine.

Canadian Distribution. The Canadian species is monotypic (see Map 8).

Sorex gaspensis Anthony and Goodwin, 1924, American Mus. Novit. 109: 1. Gaspé Peninsula and the Eastern Townships, Quebec; northern New Brunswick.

REFERENCE

Richmond, N.D., and W.C. Grimm. 1950. Ecology and distribution of the shrew *Sorex dispar* in Pennsylvania. Ecol. 31(2): 279–82.

Map 8 Distribution of: 1, the Gaspé shrew, *Sorex gaspensis*; and 2, Trowbridge's shrew, *Sorex trowbridgii*

TROWBRIDGE'S SHREW
Musaraigne de Trowbridge. *Sorex trowbridgii* Baird

Description. Trowbridge's shrew is of average size (about 4½ inches long). In winter its coat is slate black above, only slightly lighter beneath; its tail is strikingly bi-coloured, brown above, white below. Its hind feet are white, and its forefeet are strongly developed. Its ears are fairly large. Its summer coat is shorter and dark brown in colour. The spring moult commences in late April and may occur as late as the summer months in the high mountains. Few adults may survive to assume their second summer coat, and rare indeed is the one that lives to acquire a second winter coat. The young shrews get their slate grey winter coats any time from late August to early November.

This shrew's skull is of average size and is relatively flat. The third unicuspid is smaller than the fourth (Figure 4a).

Average measurements: total length 119 (109–125), tail 55 (48–58), hind foot 13.5 (13–15) mm; weight of non-breeding shrews of both sexes 4.0–5.5 g; weight of breeding adults 6.0–7.5 g.

Habits. Trowbridge's shrew probably displays the usual daily and annual activity pattern. It also has the same short life-span typical of other soricids. The population from

19

autumn until spring is composed of only one age class, each barely overlapping its successor. The individuals live only long enough to bring forth a new generation in spring. By summer the adults gradually drop out, until by the first of September only 2 per cent of the population is a year old. The maximum age for the species is eighteen months. The oldsters are recognized by their heavily worn teeth. Starvation is thought to be one of the main causes of death among these oldsters.

During most of the year this shrew lives primarily on insects. Remains of alderflies, beetles, flies, butterflies, ants, and bugs have been recognized in shrews' stomachs. Besides, insects, spiders, centipedes, and worms are eaten, particularly during the winter months. This species is unique in that it has been found to consume a larger portion of vegetable matter, especially in winter, than other soricids. In one study it was found to be particularly fond of Douglas fir seeds.

Habitat. This species inhabits coniferous forests from sea level to an elevation of 6,000 feet in the mountains. It prefers the moist litter of the forest floor for its domain, where it seeks shelter among logs, stumps, and decaying vegetation. If the area is logged, the shrew population is much reduced.

Reproduction. Both sexes mature rapidly in February with a coincident rapid development in the reproductive organs. The males mature perhaps two weeks earlier than the females. At this period, winter conditions of cold temperatures and deep snow still prevail in the mountains. Pregnancy occurs as early as February 25 but is most common in April and May. Reproduction generally ends in June; however, one late lactating female was taken on August 8. The average number of embryos carried is five, the range being three to six. The reproductive organs of the males rapidly regress after June. The occurrence of females that are both pregnant and lactating points to the conclusion that post-partum oestrus occurs regularly and that two litters are born during the spring without interruption.

Nothing is known of the development of the young.

Economic Status. It has been suggested that the consumption of Douglas fir seeds by Trowbridge's shrews limits the regeneration of the trees after logging and fire.

Distribution. Trowbridge's shrew occurs on the Pacific coast from California to southern British Columbia.

Canadian Distribution. This species occurs in Canada only in the lower Fraser valley of British Columbia, where the typical race is found (see Map 8).

Sorex trowbridgii trowbridgii Baird, 1858, Mammals: Repts. Expl. Surv. ... Rail. to Pacific 8(1): 13. Southern British Columbia.

REFERENCE

Jameson, E.W., Jr. 1955. Observations on the biology of *Sorex trowbridgii* in the Sierra Nevada, California. Jour. Mamm. 36(3): 339–45.

PIGMY SHREW
Musaraigne pygmée. *Microsorex hoyi* (Baird)

Description. The pigmy shrew, which is only 3½ inches long, is the smallest mammal in the New World and one of the smallest in the whole world. It has another claim to fame, because it is also one of the rarer of the American small mammals.

In the hand, the pigmy shrew closely resembles a small edition of the masked shrew, but it appears slimmer and greyer and has a decidedly shorter tail (Plate 1c). To make its identity certain, one must examine the upper unicuspid tooth row. In the pigmy shrew, the third and fifth unicuspids are so small that a magnifying lens is necessary to see them (Figure 4f). Upon lifting the upper lip, one has the impression of only three unicuspids behind the front incisors; in contrast, five appear in the other long-tailed shrews of the genus *Sorex*. There are other cranial differences in the museum specimen. The feet are extremely small and delicate; the flank glands, which are well developed, emit a characteristic musky odour when the animal is excited.

The summer pelage is sepia brown above, smoke grey beneath. The winter pelage is olive brown above, paler beneath. Moulting animals have been taken from late April to early May and from early October to early November.

Average measurements: total length 81 (73–88), tail 26 (22–29), hind feet 10 (9–12) mm; weight 2.5–6.3 g.

Habits. Very little is known of the life history of this little creature. It has been kept in captivity for short periods on only two occasions. Both observers were impressed by its agility and tempo of activity. In both instances the animals were active throughout the total twenty-four-hour period, taking only intermittent, short rest periods. At those times one lay curled up with its feet tucked under its body, much like a sleeping dog. When active it scampered over the ground with tail elevated. It also climbed and jumped distances up to four and a half inches, and even swam passably well. The other observer reported that his shrew dug in soft earth under moss. Its long snout twitched, and it piped shrilly as it hunted for its food. Undoubtedly insects form the bulk of its natural diet; however, one observer fed his pigmy shrew mostly the carcasses of other small mammals such as masked shrews, deer mice, and red-backed voles, and it seemed to relish the brains and viscera of these offerings. In a ten-day period this immature female, which weighed 3.4 g, ate 107.5 g of such meat, besides a variety of flies, grasshoppers, and craneflies, or approximately three times its weight each day.

Although pigmy shrews are rarely trapped, they have been taken in large numbers on several occasions by means of water buckets sunk in the ground in favourable habitats. This suggests that the shrews may not be as rare as is indicated by the scarcity of specimens.

Habitat. The pigmy shrew seems to be a denizen of the boreal forest zone, although it does not seem to occupy the

Map 9 Distribution of the pigmy shrews, *Microsorex hoyi* and *Microsorex thompsoni*: 1 *M. h. alnorum*, 2 *M. h. eximius*, 3 *M. h. hoyi*, 4 *M. h. washingtoni*, 5 *M. t. thompsoni*

forest itself but rather the grassy glades within. Sometimes the grassy meadows are quite dry. On other occasions the shrews are found in sphagnum bogs or shrubby borders of bogs and wet meadows.

Reproduction. This species is believed to bear only one litter each year.

Economic Status. This shrew is probably of little economic importance.

Distribution. The pigmy shrew is found in northern North America from the southern Appalachians and the Maritime Provinces northwest to Alaska.

Canadian Distribution. This genus has recently been revised by Long (1972). He recognizes four subspecies of the pigmy shrew in Canada and elevates the tiny shrew of the Maritimes and Appalachians to full specific status (see Map 9) as Thompson's pigmy shrew.

Microsorex hoyi alnorum (Preble), 1901, N. American Fauna 22: 72. Northern Quebec and Ontario and northeastern Manitoba.

Microsorex hoyi eximius (Osgood), 1901, N. American Fauna 21: 71. Yukon Territory and northwestern British Columbia.

Microsorex hoyi hoyi (Baird), 1858, Mammals: Repts. Expl. Surv. ... Rail. to Pacific 8(1): 32. Northwest Territories and central Canada including the Gaspé Peninsula.

Microsorex hoyi washingtoni Jackson, 1925, Proc. Biol. Soc. Washington 38: 125. The Rocky Mountains of eastern British Columbia.

Microsorex thompsoni thompsoni (Baird), 1858, Mammals: Repts. Expl. Surv. ... Rail. to Pacific 8(1): 34. The Maritimes and Eastern Townships of Quebec.

REFERENCES

Long, Charles A. 1972. Notes on habitat preference and reproduction in pigmy shrews, *Microsorex*. Canadian Field-Nat. 86: 155–60.

– 1972. Taxonomic revision of the mammalian genus *Microsorex* Coues. Trans. Kansas Acad. Sci. 74(2): 181–96.

Prince, L.A. 1940. Notes on the habits of the pigmy shrew (*Microsorex hoyi*) in captivity. Canadian Field-Nat. 54(7): 97–100.

– 1941. Water traps capture the pigmy shrew (*Microsorex hoyi*) in abundance. Canadian Field-Nat. 55(5): 72.

SHORT-TAILED SHREW
Grande musaraigne. *Blarina brevicauda* (Say)

Description. The short-tailed shrew is the largest American shrew from the standpoint of weight, although the larger long-tailed shrews (American water shrew and Bendire's shrew) exceed it in total length. It is also one of the commonest of the small mammals in eastern Canada. So common is it that students trapping small mammals in a favourable *Blarina* year sometimes despair of ever capturing any other creature. Fortunately, it has been the subject of considerable study, and its life history is pretty well delineated.

The short-tailed shrew is a medium-sized, mole-like animal, almost black in colour, with a robust body, a somewhat blunt nose, a bobbed tail, small pinkish feet, little beady eyes, and scarcely noticeable ears. It is approximately 5 inches long, including the short tail. The well-developed flank glands give off a characteristic pungy odour when the animal is held in the hand. The same odour may be detected about its burrows. There is also a glandular, hairless area on the mid-ventral region. The skin is remarkably thick and tough. The skull is large and heavy. The unicuspids are arranged in two pairs, the first and second being much larger than the third and fourth (Figure 8).

The pelage is short and has a velvety texture. It is slate black dorsally, fading to slate grey ventrally. There is little difference in colour between the summer and winter pelages; however, the latter is longer and denser (Plate 2).

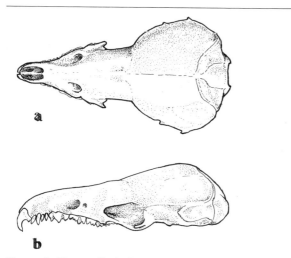

Figure 8 Short-tailed shrew skull: (a) dorsal view, (b) lateral view (× 3)

The young are born naked. The first juvenile pelage is rather woolly and more brownish than the adult's. Those born in the spring moult to the adult coat in summer, and those born in summer moult directly to the adult coat as soon as winter comes. The post-juvenile moult begins on the nose and spreads back to the tail. Often the ventral surface moults more quickly than the back. The adult spring moult, which commences in February, begins in the head region of females and progresses backwards in a normal way. The moult of males is more irregular, and some are still moulting in July. The autumn moult, starting on the rump and spreading forward to include, finally, the head (the opposite progression of the spring moult), occurs in October and November. This reverse pattern is typical of American shrews studied.

Average measurements: total length 124 (95–134), tail 25 (17–30), hind foot 15 (12–17) mm. Average weight of both sexes 19.3 (12–27) g.

Habits. This is the most fossorial of the American shrews, usually inhabiting tunnels in the friable forest loams and leaf litter. It constructs its own tunnels but does not hesitate to use the tunnels of other species such as moles or pine voles. Also, it frequently hunts on the surface in vole runways or among decaying leaves. It prefers the air in its tunnels to be saturated with water vapour. Its nest, which is about eight inches in diameter, is built of leaves and grass and sometimes lined with hair; it is placed in a partially buried log or stump about a foot underground, and usually has two entrances. Smaller nests for resting may be found elsewhere in the home range.

The short-tailed shrew seems more congenial than other species of shrews. Several individuals may sleep together, rolled into a ball. Although there is some individual variation, strange shrews become accustomed to each other's presence and may eventually live together. It seems likely that mated pairs live together for some time. Young shrews indulge in play, pushing one another around.

Although in this species the sense of sight seems to be poorly developed, the tactile sense and the sense of vibration appear to be well developed. Hearing is acute, and there is some evidence that these animals may be able to smell meat through the snow cover in winter. They utter a variety of sounds – twitters when feeding, shrill squeals when fighting, and a clicking sound made by the males when pursuing females.

Short-tailed shrews are active all winter, and their diurnal activity follows the general shrew pattern. They exhibit a short-term rhythm of alternating periods of activity and rest, the bursts of activity averaging about forty-nine minutes in duration and the rest periods about ninety-nine minutes. In captivity the shrews appear only slightly less active in daytime than at night. Light seems to have little effect upon their activity, and it is speculated that the rate of digestion is an important factor in the rhythm.

Studies have indicated that the short-tailed shrew may occupy a home range of 1 to 1 1/4 acres. Populations have been found to vary from less than one in unfavourable habitats to 11.6 per acre in good habitats. The population of this species fluctuates widely, and in some years the forests seem to be teeming with these shrews. Densities of up to forty-eight shrews per acre have been recorded in Ohio.

This species seems to have a potentially greater longevity than the long-tailed species. Six per cent of shrews trapped during winter in one study were shown to be in their second winter, as determined by their worn teeth. Only 2 out of 184 shrews trapped survived two winters until the third spring. In captivity three shrews lived to be twenty-nine to thirty-three months of age. When they reached two years of age they were practically toothless. However, this potential longevity is probably of little importance in nature because the few shrews that do survive more than eighteen months die of starvation.

As one might expect, insects form the bulk of the short-tailed shrew's diet. In a study of 244 stomachs in New York State, representative of all seasons, the following bulk percentages were determined: insects 47.8, plants 11.4, worms 7.2, sowbugs 6.7, snails 5.4, vertebrates 4.1, centipedes and millipedes 5.5, as well as various other items in smaller amounts. Even in winter, insects form over 50 per cent of the diet. There is evidence that these shrews undertake a certain amount of snail hoarding, groups of live terrestrial snails of the genus *Polygya* having been found in subterranean chambers of *Blarina* burrows. In one experiment some were marked, and the empty shells were later found discarded at the surface, and new snails had been added to the hoard. The small piles of snail shells often found on the forest floor are frequently the work of this species.

Although mice usually form only a small item in the normal shrew diet, short-tailed shrews may prey upon voles to a much greater extent during years when meadow voles (*Microtus pennsylvanicus*) are abundant. In one study, mouse remains were found in 56 per cent of the shrew stomachs examined. During the winter of 1942–43, vole populations near Ithaca, New York, reached eighty per acre; and by spring short-tailed shrews were thought to have accounted for fourteen to twenty-seven voles per acre.

The poisonous bite of the shrew is a bit of folklore shared by many European peasants. Naturally this item was dismissed by serious scientists as superstition until 1942. Dr O.P. Pearson then recalled the tale when he learned that the salivary glands of the short-tailed shrew contained unusual granular cells. He injected small amounts of extract from the submaxillary gland into mice, and noted uncontrolled twitching, slowed respiration, and a depressed condition. When the amount of extract was increased, convulsions were followed by death, due to respiratory failure. He concluded that the saliva contained a poison derived from the submaxillary gland.

There are two principal types of snake venom: that found in viperines (vipers, rattlesnakes, and copperheads), which is primarily haemorrhagic in action; and elapine (coral snake and cobra) venom, which is more neurotoxic in action. The evidence on hand suggests that the *Blarina* poison resembles the cobra venom in action. It would appear that the bite of the short-tailed shrew injects a neurotoxic poison into its prey, which helps to subdue it.

The pungent odour of the short-tailed shrew offers some protection against larger predators. However, it does not provide complete immunity, for remains of short-tailed shrews have often been found in hawk and owl pellets. Weasels are also known to prey upon shrews. Domestic cats and dogs frequently worry shrews to death but show a reluctance to partake of their offensive prey.

Habitat. The eastern hardwood forests are the favourite haunt of the short-tailed shrew. High humidity and loose humus are the prime physical requirements of its environment. Moist hardwood forests form the foci of its distribution. Under favourable conditions of moisture, the shrew population may expand into meadows, bogs, and fields, but when drought occurs, the population retracts to the favourable refugia. Frequently a high number of males have been trapped in unfavourable subclimax forest situations, a result of the tendency of males to invade new territory.

Reproduction. Although the females possess the usual six mammae common to shrews, they are farther apart than in other species. The anterior pair is more widely spaced than the posterior pair. The flank glands enlarge during the breeding season, but those of the females do not develop as much as those of the males. Mating of adults over six months of age usually commences in March, although the males may be ready to mate by late February. The first pregnancies are usually noted in April, and the young may be born in that month. The gestation period is twenty-one to twenty-two days after the first mating. However, since ovulation is induced by copulation, a better measure of gestation would probably be from ovulation and fertilization to birth; this period is thought to be eighteen or nineteen days.

The average litter is 4.5 young, although the average number of foetuses in pregnant females is 6.7. The young measure about 22 mm at birth and weigh approximately 0.8 g. They grow rapidly. Seventeen days after birth they weigh between 9 and 12 g and commence to move out of the nest. The spring litters mature early, and females become sexually receptive at about six weeks of age. The young males are probably not sexually mature until about twelve weeks old. In any event, young females born in the spring probably have autumn litters, whereas the yearling females probably have two or three litters per year. The breeding season normally closes in September, although some sexually active males have been taken as late as October 20. It does not appear as though post-partum oestrus occurs in the species. Females are not generally receptive after the birth of their young unless they lose them.

Economic Status. The larger populations of this shrew in eastern Canada may be of considerable economic benefit because they destroy forest insects in great quantities. There are indications that they may also act as a controlling agent in meadow vole population explosions.

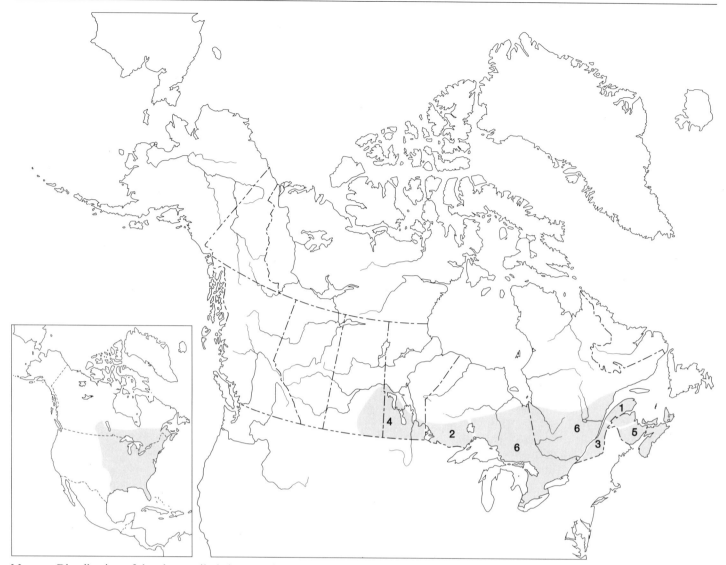

Map 10 Distribution of the short-tailed shrew, *Blarina brevicauda*: 1 *B. b. angusta*, 2 *B. b. brevicauda*, 3 *B. b. hooperi*, 4 *B. b. manitobensis*, 5 *B. b. pallida*, 6 *B. b. talpoides*

The short-tailed shrew is strong enough to break the skin in its bite. People who have been bitten have complained of local swelling and intense shooting pains caused by its poisonous saliva. Though painful, its bite is not dangerous to humans.

Distribution. The short-tailed shrew is found in eastern North America from the Gulf of Mexico north to eastern Saskatchewan, Lake Superior, and the Gaspé Peninsula of Quebec.

Canadian Distribution. Six geographic subspecies are recognized in Canada (see Map 10). These vary somewhat in size, paleness of colour, and skull conformation.

Blarina brevicauda angusta Anderson, 1943, Ann. Rept. Provancher Soc. Nat. Hist., Quebec, p. 52. Gaspé Peninsula and northern New Brunswick.

Blarina brevicauda brevicauda (Say), 1823, *in* Long, An account of an expedition ... to Rocky Mts. 1: 164. Northwestern Ontario.

Blarina brevicauda hooperi Bole and Moulthrop, 1942, Sci. Pub. Cleveland Mus. Nat. Hist. 5: 110. Lake Champlain area of Quebec.

Blarina brevicauda manitobensis Anderson, 1947, Nat. Mus. Canada Bull. 102: 23. Manitoba and Saskatchewan.

Blarina brevicauda pallida R.W. Smith, 1940, American Midl. Nat. 24: 223. Nova Scotia, Prince Edward Island; and southern New Brunswick.

Blarina brevicauda talpoides (Gapper), 1830, Zool. Jour. 5: 202. Central Ontario and Quebec.

REFERENCES

Mann, P.M., and R.H. Stinson. 1957. Activity of the short-tailed shrew. Canadian Jour. Zool. 35(2): 171–7.

Pearson, O.P. 1944. Reproduction in the shrew (*Blarina brevicauda* Say). American Jour. Anat. 75(1): 39–93.

LEAST SHREW
Petite musaraigne. *Cryptotis parva* (Say)

Description. The least shrew rivals the pigmy shrew for the title of the smallest mammal in America. Its claim is by reason of its stubby tail, which gives it an extremely short over-all length, although it has a longer and more heavily built body than the pigmy shrew. In many ways it looks like a small edition of the short-tailed shrew, but it is less robust, its nose is more pointed, and its short tail is slenderer. There are trenchant dental differences as well: the fourth unicuspid is much smaller than the third (Figure 9).

The colour of the least shrew is greyish brown above, becoming silvery greyish beneath. The winter pelage is darker, and the upper parts lack the sepia-tipped hairs of the summer coat. The spring moult occurs in March, and the autumn moult from late August to September. In the autumn moult, the new winter fur appears simultaneously on the face and rump and seems to spread over the body to meet behind the shoulders.

Average measurements: total length 81.9 (75–92), tail 17.5 (15–21.5), hind foot 11.2 (10–12.5) mm. Average weight of adults 4.9 (4.4–5.7) g.

Habits. This species is much less subterranean than *Blarina brevicauda*, its large competitor. It hunts on the surface of the ground and builds its small baseball-sized nests of leaves and grass at the base of a shrub or under a log, board, or piece of tin. It may construct shallow trenches in the neighbourhood of its nest. It appears to be active at all times but does not exhibit any rhythmic activity, periods of frenzied activity being interspersed with irregular rest periods. Least shrews seem to be more active by night than by day. When hunting, they scurry about with noses elevated and vibrissae twitching. Their tiny squeaks can scarcely be heard beyond a distance of ten feet. The senses of sight and hearing do not seem to be particularly well developed, but their olfactory sense is.

The least shrew seems to be the most sociable of the American shrews. Several adults often occupy the same nest and sleep together, rolled into a ball of fur. Both parents care for the young and live together for extended periods. One observer had a group living together in a cage and occupying a common nest. When a litter was born, the observer broke the nest and scattered the young as an experiment. All the adults assisted the mother in collecting the young and in rebuilding the nest. The hardy young survived this traumatic experience.

The food of the least shrew is similar to that of other shrews and includes insects, molluscs, amphibians, lizards, and mammals. It has been suggested by one observer that the least shrew favours frogs as food, and by another that it prefers bees. It also eats fruit such as apples. It appears that the metabolic rate of the least shrew is not as high as that of the long-tailed shrews (genus *Sorex*) because specimens under experimental conditions consumed only about three-quarters of their weight per day and rested for periods of up to six hours. However, its rate of digestion is extremely rapid. Food took from ninety-five minutes to three or four hours to pass through the alimentary canal.

Since, generally speaking, least shrews are seldom trapped by researchers, the impression has grown that the species is relatively rare. However, least shrew remains often turn up abundantly in owl pellets. In one study the species constituted 41 per cent of the small mammals preyed upon by barn owls. Its apparent rarity is a result of its reluctance to visit baited traps. The first Canadian specimens were taken from the stomach of a milk snake.

No information is available on population densities. Specimens held in captivity have survived twenty months, but the normal longevity in the wild is probably approximately eighteen months.

Habitat. The least shrew inhabits open grasslands, coastal salt marshes, and forest glades. It has been trapped at an elevation of 3,000 feet in the Smoky Mountains of Tennessee. The only Canadian locality is a grassy sand dune area.

Reproduction. The reproductive period lasts from March to November in the northern part of the species range and perhaps throughout the year in the south. The gestation period varies from twenty-one to twenty-three days from the last mating to birth. The number of young varies from four to six per litter. Post-partum oestrus is of regular occurrence, and the mother may conceive again immediately. If she is not mated immediately, she is probably not receptive again until after the litter is weaned, twenty-two days later. It is therefore likely that two or three litters are born during a summer.

The young shrews grow exceedingly rapidly. At birth they are naked, pink, and wrinkled, with disproportionately large heads and forefeet, measuring about 20 mm in total length and weighing about 0.32 g. By the end of the first week they are covered with silvery fur. By the end of the second week, their eyes are open, and they can wobble short distances from the nest. At the time of weaning, the combined weight of the litter is about three times the weight of the mother. A failing milk supply may stimulate the young to take off on their own at the age of approximately twenty-two days, which is soon after they reach adult weight. It is not known whether young least shrews breed in their first year of life.

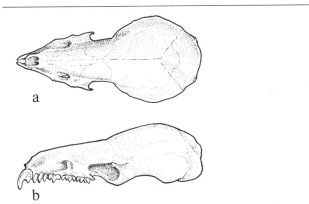

Figure 9 Least shrew skull: (a) dorsal view, (b) lateral view (× 3)

Map 11 Distribution of the least shrew, *Cryptotis parva*

Family **Talpidae** / Moles

Although several groups of mammals have taken to a subterranean existence, the moles are the ones that have become the most highly adapted to the fossorial way of life. Some variation which still persists in fossorial specialization among the group indicates a variation in dependence upon this way of life or a difference in the time that the various animals have been committed to live continually underground.

Moles have thick streamlined bodies: the nose is long and pointed, and the limbs are short. The shoulder girdle has moved forward so that the front limbs are opposite the base of the skull and has rotated so that the enlarged palm faces outwards. There is little external evidence of the neck. External ears (pinnae) are lacking, and the eyes are embedded in the skin. The hind legs are more normal in position but are relatively weak. There are five toes on each foot. The fur has a dark, short, dense pile, which may be brushed in either direction. The forefeet are armed with long, flattened claws for digging.

Some of the most striking characteristics of the group are found in the skeleton. The skull possesses weak zygomatic arches, which are absent in shrews, and double-rooted canines. The long sternum is keeled for the attachment of strong chest muscles. The scapula is similarly long and slender. The humerus, on the other hand, is almost as broad as it is long. The powerful hand is reinforced by a slender sesamoid bone in the wrist, which appears to act as a sixth finger. The terminal phalange of the forefeet is bifurcate.

Economic Status. The least shrew is too rare to be of any economic importance in Canada.

Distribution. This species is found in southeastern North America from the Gulf of Mexico to the Great Lakes.

Canadian Distribution. This species has been found only on Long Point, on the north shore of Lake Erie, Ontario (see Map 11). Extensive trapping elsewhere along the north shore of Lake Erie for many years has failed to disclose any other colonies. The evidence strongly suggests that the original colonizers must have been rafted across the lake on a floating log from the south shore, where the species occurs normally. The Canadian subspecies is the nominate race.

Cryptotis parva parva (Say), 1823, *in* Long, An account of an expedition ... to the Rocky Mts. 1: 163. Long Point, Ontario.

REFERENCES

Conaway, C.H. 1958. Maintenance, reproduction and growth of the least shrew in captivity. Jour. Mamm. 39(4): 507–12.
Hamilton, W.J., Jr. 1944. The biology of the little short-tailed shrew, *Cryptotis parva*. Jour. Mamm. 25(1): 1–7.

AMERICAN SHREW-MOLE
Taupe naine. *Neürotrichus gibbsii* (Baird)

Description. The shrew-mole is the smallest of the American moles and the least adapted to the subterranean life. It resembles the shrew in so many of its characters that one is tempted to call it a primitive mole, but this is not necessarily the case.

The shrew-mole is about 4½ inches long. About a third of its total length consists of a thick scaly tail, which is constricted at the base. The sparse, coarse hairs of the tail project between the annular scales except for the stiff brush at the blunt end. The body is thick, although it is not as cylindrical as in the larger moles. There is no neck, and the face terminates in a prolonged slender proboscis. This flexible snout, which is lightly furred at its base, terminates in a naked pink pad with lateral nostrils. The eyes are concealed under a small hairless patch of skin, and the ears are merely slits in the skin on the side of the head. The feet are small and have pink soles. The hind feet are not exceptional, but the forefeet are slightly enlarged, and they are rotated so that the palms face outwards. The digits have long, curved, flattened claws, which make the feet decidedly longer than broad. The females possess eight mammae.

The shrew-mole's sooty blue-black pelage is rather thin

and lacks the thick mole 'plush,' as shrews do. The spring moult occurs from late April to early June, and the autumn moult during October. The new summer coat first appears on top of the head, soon to be followed by new areas on the back and breast. These areas expand and grow back until they unite on the flanks. In spite of its many shrew-like external characters, the internal anatomy strongly indicates that the creature is a true mole. The skull and dentition are typically mole-like (Figure 10a), but the auditory bullae are incompletely ossified and the pelvic girdle is less modified for fossorial locomotion. The shrew-mole has a strong, pungent, musky odour.

Average measurements of both sexes of the nominate race: total length 119 (113–125), tail 40 (37–45), hind foot 16.5 (16–18.5) mm; weight about 11 g.

Habits. The unique morphology provides hints to the shrew-mole's strange mode of life. It is the least fossorial of the moles and spends much of its time scuttling about the leafy litter of the forest floor. When walking above ground, it curls its palms and claws under so that it walks on its knuckles. It swims with great rapidity and even climbs bushes with ease so that it is far more agile above ground than its subterranean relatives. Even stranger is its use of the proboscis. When it is hunting, it throws this flexible organ upwards, twists it sideways, or uses it to tap the ground in front of it. When it is moving among dry

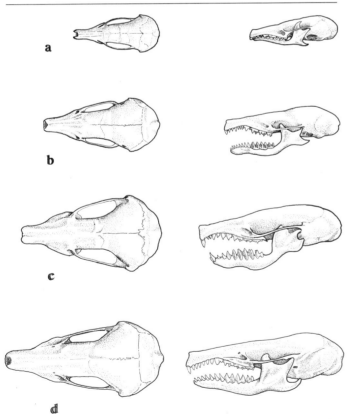

Figure 10 Skulls of Canadian moles: (a) American shrew-mole, *Neürotrichus gibbsii*; (b) hairy-tailed mole, *Parascalops breweri*; (c) eastern mole, *Scalopus aquaticus*; (d) Townsend's mole, *Scapanus townsendii* (× 1)

leaves a series of rapid taps of its snout on the ground may be heard.

This creature seems to be blind and to have little sense of smell. It shows little response to low-frequency sounds but does respond to those of high frequency. It utters a faint, high-pitched twittering sound. Apparently its hearing is adapted to high-frequency sounds that are perhaps beyond our ken. The senses of touch and vibration seem to be highly developed, particularly in the facial vibrissae. The long, prehensile snout serves as a blind man's cane to guide the animal through life.

Shrew-moles construct a maze of shallow runways, just under the forest litter, which are essentially troughs about an inch in diameter. They do not push up molehills but leave many characteristic small openings for ventilation in the roof of the runways. The true tunnels are deeper, about five inches below the surface, and less extensive. They differ from the other mole tunnels in having open entrances. The nesting chamber contains a minimum of dry grass or leaves. One nest of willow leaves was found above ground in an old rotten alder stump. Moles use their forefeet to construct tunnels by pushing the soft earth first to one side and then to the other.

This animal is active at all periods of the day and night. Periods of hunting are followed by rest periods, which vary from one to eight minutes in length, between periods of two to eighteen minutes of activity. There is no season of hibernation. They seem to be remarkably sociable for insectivores, and there is (some) evidence that they occur in bands.

The amount of food they consume is comparable to that eaten by shrews. One specimen ate 1.4 times its body weight in twelve hours. Their diet consists of about 42 per cent earthworms, 36 per cent sowbugs, 12 per cent insect larvae and pupae, and the remainder assorted invertebrates. The rate of digestion is also remarkably fast, tracer food items usually being found in the faeces thirty-five to forty minutes after being eaten.

The blind, blundering shrew-mole probably is an easy prey for a number of small predators such as snakes, raccoons, hawks, and owls. The last two avian predators are perhaps the most important since their limited olfactory senses would not carry to them the shrew-mole's strong odour.

Habitat. This animal inhabits loose friable humus, primarily under deciduous underbrush in ravines and river banks. The soils are usually saturated and are not covered by a thick sod. It also occurs at higher elevations in the Coast Range of British Columbia.

Reproduction. The breeding season of the shrew-mole is prolonged. Moles in breeding condition have been taken as early as February 23, and nursing females as late as September 26. Pregnant females have been taken from March 7 to late May. The gestation period is not known. The size of the litter varies from one to four. At birth the young shrew-mole measures about 26 mm long and weighs about 0.67 g. Its body is pink and naked, and its eyes appear as black dots.

Map 12 Distribution of the American shrew-mole, *Neürotrichus gibbsii*

Economic Status. The range of the shrew-mole in Canada is so restricted that it probably has no economic importance in any broad sense.

Distribution. The shrew-mole is found on the humid Pacific coast from northern California to southern British Columbia.

Canadian Distribution. The shrew-mole's distribution barely reaches southwestern British Columbia, where two geographical subspecies are recognized (see Map 12).

Neürotrichus gibbsii gibbsii (Baird), 1858, Mammals: Repts. Expl. Surv. ... Rail. to Pacific 8(1): 76. Coast Range, Hope-Princeton Highway, Lihumitson Mountains, and Vancouver, British Columbia.

Neürotrichus gibbsii minor Dalquest and Burgner, 1941, The Murrelet 22: 12. Puget Sound lowlands north to Fraser River delta, British Columbia.

REFERENCE

Dalquest, W.W., and D.R. Orcutt. 1942. The biology of the least shrew-mole, *Neürotrichus gibbsii minor*. American Midl. Nat. 27(2): 387–401.

TOWNSEND'S MOLE

Taupe de Townsend. *Scapanus townsendii* (Bachman)

Description. Townsend's mole, which measures about 8 inches in length, is the largest American mole. Its form is

streamlined from a relatively broad but pointed snout and a heavy, depressed cylindrical body to a short, stout tail. The short upper portions of the legs are enclosed in the body integument. The front feet are large and broad and are armed with long, flattened nails. The palms are rotated outwards. The hind feet are much smaller but relatively broad, with long, curved claws. The vestigial eyes are usually hidden in the fur of the face behind the fine vibrissae, but, when disturbed, Townsend's mole can flatten the surrounding hair, part the hairless minute eyelids, and protrude two tiny eyeballs (Figure 10d).

The flesh-coloured snout, feet, and tail are covered with sparse, short, fine white hairs. The naked tip of the muzzle carries the dorsal crescentic nostrils. The tail has scaly annulations, between which the fine hairs project. The females possess eight mammae. The pelage is composed of dense silky fur of constant length, and is not divided into the usual longer guard hairs and shorter underfur. The resultant 'plush'-like effect offers a minimum of resistance to the mole's progress through its subterranean tunnels.

The coat colour is slaty black with a marked copper sheen. It is darker in winter and paler in summer. The spring moult occurs in April, and the autumn moult in October. The sequence of moulting is rather irregular but appears to start on the abdomen, work around to the flanks, and terminate on the back.

Average measurements for adults: total length 210 (202–218), tail 40 (35–55), hind foot 25 (24–26) mm. There is little difference between the sexes. The weight is approximately 148 g.

Habits. The species exhibits the characteristic fossorial existence of the group. Rarely appearing above ground, it lives in a labyrinth of tunnels below the sod of fields and meadows. The tunnel system may be divided into two main kinds: the deeper permanent tunnels about two feet in depth, which serve as highways and living quarters, and the shallow foraging tunnels, which are usually situated only a few inches below the surface.

Although awkward above ground, the mole has specialized forelimbs which enable it to tunnel with ease.

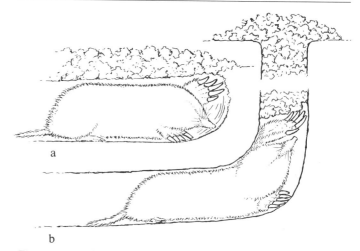

Figure 11 Mole tunnelling technique: (a) ridge construction, (b) mound construction

It extends its forearms forward, palms outward in the same manner as a swimmer using the breast stroke. Then with a powerful heave of the shoulders it pushes the hands sideways, and humps its body forward into the passageway formed. Though this method is adequate for the shallow surface burrows in loose soil, the deeper tunnels must be excavated from packed soil with its strong nails. Then the mole turns in the tunnel and pushes the loosened earth to the surface through a special ascending shaft. The mole remains hidden in the shaft while pushing the earth ahead of its large hands (Figure 11). A surface mound grows like a volcano, with fresh upheavals of earth pushed through the centre to cascade down the symmetrical slopes. Townsend's mole constructs the largest 'molehill' known to occur in America, which may be a foot in height and two feet in diameter. Eventually the mole progresses a considerable distance underground from the mound and so the shaft becomes filled and the mound abandoned, and the mole starts a new mound, two to six feet away from the previous one.

The more permanent deep tunnels (seven to twenty inches deep) are often constructed along fence rows or shrubby borders, where they will be less disturbed. There are several enlarged chambers containing damp grasses, which are used as resting spots. The shallow foraging tunnels form a maze of raised ridges just below the turf. Although the mole is essentially a solitary beast, its tunnels may occasionally be invaded by other members of the same species or a variety of other small mammals such as shrews and mice.

By quickly repairing breaches in their active tunnels, moles provide evidence of their activity. Experimentation has indicated that they are active throughout the twenty-four-hour period, with intervening periods of foraging and resting. They remain active all the year round.

Little information is available on sensory perception in this species. Eyesight is limited, the senses of smell and hearing are probably adequate, and the tactile sense in the vibrissae and snout is probably acute.

Moles find their food in regular patrols of their foraging tunnels. Many ground forms in insect larvae and pupae tumble into the tunnels, and earthworms crawl into them from their burrows. The diet of Townsend's mole has been found to consist of 76 per cent earthworms, 6 per cent fly larvae, and 1 per cent butterfly and moth pupae. Traces of centipedes, beetle grubs, grasshoppers, ants, and spiders also occur. This species consumes, too, an appreciable amount of vegetable matter (16 per cent), including wheat, corn, oats, peas, and bulbs. In some areas of the Pacific coast states, Townsend's mole has been found to be a menace to the intensive cultivation of bulbs such as tulips, tigridia, iris, lilies, and certain root vegetables such as potatoes, carrots, and parsnips. Individuals may acquire a taste for particular cultivated plants in spite of the local occurrence of their natural food. This species, which shows the typical high metabolic rate of the insectivores, has been known to eat 1.4 times its body weight in a single day.

Moles seem to have few natural predators and only

Map 13 Distribution of Townsend's mole, *Scapanus townsendii*

rarely fall prey to some predator such as a snake, weasel, or owl.

Habitat. Mole distribution in general is restricted to areas of loose, friable humus with little stone or gravel content. They are also found in light sandy soils. Townsend's mole prefers good humus under cultivated fields, in meadowlands and open forests.

Reproduction. Only one litter is born each year. Mating occurs in February, and the young are born in the latter part of March or early April. A rough nest of coarse grass lined with fine grass is built for the young in a chamber about six to nine inches in diameter in the lower permanent galleries. The nest, which usually has two or more entrances to facilitate escape in an emergency, is located off a main tunnel. The litter size varies from two to four (average 2.87). Such a low reproductive potential indicates that the species also has a relatively low rate of mortality. The young are pink and naked until they are ten days old, and then bluish up until twenty-two days, after which a fine, short plush coat develops. They abandon the nest after thirty-six days, before the end of May.

Economic Status. So restricted is the range of Townsend's mole in Canada that it is of insignificant economic importance. Elsewhere its predilection to bulbs and root vegetables does not add to its general popularity.

Distribution. This species is found on the humid Pacific northwest coast from northern California to the British Columbia border.

Canadian Distribution. Townsend's mole crosses the Canadian border only for a mile or two near Huntingdon, in the lower Fraser valley, British Columbia (see Map 13). The first Canadian specimens were secured by a National Museum expedition in 1927. The Canadian moles belong to the nominate race.

Scapanus townsendii townsendii (Bachman), 1839, Jour. Acad. Sci. Philadelphia 8: 58. Huntingdon, British Columbia.

REFERENCES

Kuhn, L.W., W.Q. Wick, and R.S. Pederson. 1966. Breeding nests of Townsend's mole in Oregon. Jour. Mamm. 47(2): 239–49.

Scheffer, T.H. 1949. Ecological comparison of three genera of moles. Trans. Kansas Acad. Sci. 52(1): 30–7.

PACIFIC COAST MOLE
Taupe du Pacifique. *Scapanus orarius* True

Description. The Pacific coast mole is a small edition of the larger Townsend's mole. Although it averages about $6^{1}/_{2}$ inches in total length, it is proportionally smaller and slimmer in all its parts than its larger cousin. The feet and skull are noticeably smaller, and there is no overlap in measurements of adults of the two species.

The pelage is a dark slate colour above, paler below: over all is a silvery sheen. The flesh-coloured snout, feet, and tail are practically naked.

Average measurements of eleven adult males: total length 163 (150–179), tail 34 (29–38), hind foot 21 (19–23) mm.

Habits. Very little attention has been paid to this species. What information is available is usually of a comparative nature in relation to the larger Townsend's mole. The Pacific coast mole is almost completely subterranean in its existence. Only the occasional remains of this species in owl pellets provide evidence that it sometimes ventures above ground at night. The mounds and surface tunnels of this species are smaller and less obvious than those of Townsend's mole. On the other hand, the Pacific coast mole seems to tunnel deeper than the larger species. The main labyrinth is frequently three to three and a half feet deep. On one occasion a mole tunnelled into a post hole seven feet deep; the observer speculated that it might have been seeking soil moisture during a prolonged dry spell.

There is also evidence that this species is less colonial than the larger one, and its population seems to be more scattered.

The diet of the Pacific coast mole shows the same emphasis on earthworms, which constitute about 70 per cent of its natural food; fly larvae make up about 25 per cent, butterfly and moth cocoons about 2 per cent, and traces of other insects such as beetles, ants, and grasshoppers have been found. Only a trace of vegetable matter has been found – a portion of a gladiolus bulb.

Habitat. It is in the choice of habitat that a differentia-

tion may be made between these two closely related moles. The Pacific coast mole is more tolerant of drier, sandy loams. It inhabits heavy coniferous forests and thickets on the edges of meadows. Occurring at much higher elevations than Townsend's mole, it has been trapped at elevations up to 5,500 feet in the Coast Range.

Reproduction. The reproductive period commences early in the year. Breeding activity has been observed in males in late January. The young, usually four in number, are born in late March or early April. There is only one litter born each year.

Economic Status. Since this species is more widely distributed in southwestern British Columbia than the previous one, it may be of more economic interest.

Under natural conditions, moles are beneficial in soil formation. Through their efforts in tunnelling, the soil is aerated, loosened, and turned over. They are also beneficial to plants in their destruction of white grubs and cutworms in the soil. However, in lawns and gardens their surface tunnels and mounds are unsightly and may locally kill the grass by lifting the roots from the substrate.

When moles attack cultivated fields, vegetable gardens, and nurseries, their efforts are more directly harmful. Their tunnels may heave seedlings out of the ground and cause them to die because of root damage or lack of moisture. Moles may even destroy seed beds of corn and peas. Their mounds may damage the cutting edge on harvesting equipment in the fields. It is entirely likely that much of the damage attributed to moles in the destruction of vegetable crops has, however, actually been done by mice travelling in mole tunnels, who, in relative safety underground, eat the roots exposed there. Moles have been branded by some researchers as potential carriers of plant diseases and pests.

Moles are wary of any tampering with their runways and are therefore difficult to trap, but there is one weak point in their natural caution, and that is the lack of suspicion of loose earth blocking the passageways. This is such a natural occurrence that the mole will push through the earth unsuspectingly. Special mole traps have been designed with a trigger in or on such a soil obstruction. These traps operate on three main principles: a choker-loop, diamond-jaws, or multiple spears. They are all effective and are recommended for use in mole control. It is practically impossible to trap moles using any other traps.

Moles may also be destroyed by opening the runways and inserting a volatile poison such as calcium cyanide or carbon disulphide and then making certain that all tunnel openings are closed. Such a method should be used with extreme caution, of course, especially if pets or children are in the vicinity. Poisoned baits such as thallium-coated peanuts have been effective in some areas tested.

Distribution. Pacific coast moles occur from northern California to southern British Columbia.

Canadian Distribution. This species is found in the lower Fraser valley of southern British Columbia north to Vancouver and Agassiz. It has not yet crossed Burrard Inlet (see Map 14). The Canadian population belongs to the interior subspecies.

Map 14 Distribution of the Pacific coast mole, *Scapanus orarius*

Scapanus orarius schefferi Jackson, 1915, N. American Fauna 38: 62. Fraser delta, British Columbia.

REFERENCES

Dalquest, W.W. 1948. Coast mole. *In* Mammals of Washington. Univ. Kansas Pub. Mus. Nat. Hist. 2: 127–30.

Glendenning, R. 1953. Does the Scheffer mole drink? Canadian Field-Nat. 67(3): 138–9.

HAIRY-TAILED MOLE
Taupe à queue velue. *Parascalops breweri* (Bachman)

Description. This is an average-sized mole (about 6 inches long) with a characteristic short tail, heavily covered with black stiff hairs. The body is typically fusiform and depressed. The forefeet are broad with long, flattened nails. The hind feet are relatively weak. The females possess eight mammae. The pelage forms a short dense pile, fuscous black with a coppery sheen, paler on the ventral surface. The flesh-coloured feet are sparsely covered with brown hairs. The slender pinkish snout, which has two lateral nostrils, is basally covered with short pale hairs. The minute eyes, generally hidden in the facial fur behind closed eyelids, may be protruded under conditions of extreme fear or pain. There are no external ear pinnae, but the auditory orifices are of normal size. Two groups of long, silvery vibrissae are prominent on each side of the face, and an additional pair is also located on the side of the head above each ear slit (Figure 12). The skull is illustrated in Figure 10b.

Frequently, an irregularly shaped, creamy coloured breast spot is found. The skin of the ventral surface from the base of the mandibles to the inguinal region is remarkably glandular. During the breeding season there is a light brownish secretion that stains the ventral fur of both sexes but is more extensive in the males. It gives a strong characteristic odour to the animals at that season.

The males average slightly larger than the females. The younger moles are usually browner. With increasing age, moles become more grizzled about the head, feet, and tail.

There are two moults during the year: the spring moult between the end of March and the end of May, and the autumn moult between the first of September and the middle of October. The moult sequences are the same during both seasons. The new fur first appears on the chest, soon to be followed by a second spot on the rump, and these two areas enlarge and eventually join along the flanks.

Average measurements of adults of both sexes: total length 158 (150–170), tail 27 (24–50), hind foot 19 (17–21) mm; weight 54 (40–64) g.

Habits. The hairy-tailed mole constructs two typical systems of tunnels. The surface network is pushed through the soft friable forest soil under the surface litter. There is often little evidence of molehills or ridged tunnels as found in the other species. The deeper permanent tunnels are constructed about ten to eighteen inches below the surface but may be up to thirty inches deep. The diameter of the tunnels varies from about one inch to almost 2 inches in main routes. The surface tunnel systems form a maze of crossing feeding tunnels with occasional openings. The permanent deep labyrinth varies from fifty to eighty feet in diameter. In its construction, much of the excavated soil is pushed to the surface to form small molehills about seven inches in diameter and three inches high. In the deep labyrinth, resting chambers and

Figure 12 Hairy-tailed mole

breeding and winter nests of dry grasses and leaves, about six to eight inches in diameter, are constructed. The nests are usually placed under a stone or stump for protection.

This animal spends the daylight hours in its tunnels but frequently forages about on the forest floor during the night, when it is sometimes captured by predators. This species exhibits no marked daily rhythm of activity, alternating feeding periods with rest periods throughout the twenty-four-hour period. It seems to be more active in its tunnels during the daylight hours, when it will usually repair a breach in a tunnel within an hour's time. It remains active throughout the winter months as well, but abandons the surface tunnels in frozen ground and retreats to the deeper labyrinth, which may extend below the frost line. There is little surface sign of mole activity during the winter months, but in early spring, during the month of April, there seems to be frenzied activity as many molehills appear overnight, an indication that these animals are rebuilding their tunnels and breeding nests. Again, in the autumn, increased digging activity indicates that the moles are preparing their deep tunnels for winter occupancy.

Like other moles, this species is extremely awkward above ground because of its short legs and rotated forefeet. However, it can dig through loose earth with considerable speed. The tactile sense in its vibrissae is acutely developed. It probably also receives information on the conditions on the roof of its tunnels from the vibrissae on the head. The stiff hairs on the wrists may serve as tactile organs as well. The striking reduction in the mole's sense of sight has long attracted attention. It is interesting to note that the little eyes appear to develop normally in the early embryos, but later, parts of the eye, including the lens, degenerate. Nothing is known of the acuteness of hearing or sense of smell of this species.

Hairy-tailed moles are usually solitary in habits, only one occupying a deep tunnel system, except during the mating season, when males invade the home ranges of females. The glandular secretions on the chest probably assist in locating mates. When irritated, this mole has been heard to utter high-pitched squeals. All nests excavated were found to be clean and free from defecations. The piles of faecal material found outside burrow entrances are evidence that these animals keep their nests and burrows in a sanitary condition.

In favourable locations, populations are estimated to average about 1.2 per acre, but populations as high as 11 per acre have been encountered in ideal habitats.

The hairy-tailed mole appears to place less emphasis on earthworms in its diet than do some other species of moles. In food analyses, worms have been found to constitute 34 per cent by bulk of the diet in comparison with 47 per cent insect material. The insects consumed included beetles, ants, and many larvae such as cutworms, white grubs, cocoons, and pupae. Small amounts of millipedes, centipedes, snails, and sowbugs were also consumed. This mole, which has the typical voracious appetite of the insectivores, has been known to eat three times its body weight of earthworms in a twenty-four-hour period.

Studies of tooth wear on trapped specimens have indicated that hairy-tailed moles may live to a ripe old age of four years, a fact which makes them, relatively, methuselahs of the insectivore clan. Among their natural enemies must be included red and grey foxes, owls, and large snakes.

Habitat. The hairy-tailed mole occupies the eastern hardwood forests and old pastureland where the soil is relatively dry and loose. It prefers moist sandy loams and avoids entering wet peats and clay soils. It does not mind sandy or rocky situations as long as the soil is not dry and compacted.

Reproduction. It was a common bit of European folklore that all moles were males until they were one year of age, after which half the population turned into females. Recent anatomical studies have shown that this is *apparently* the case, at least on the surface. The female genital opening is sealed during most of the year and opens only during the reproductive season. Only one litter is born each year, and shortly after birth the opening is sealed again until the following season. Besides that, the urethra discharges through a papilla that can be confused with the male organ. This unique reproductive system was first described for the European mole *Talpa europa* and later confirmed in the present American species.

The first signs of reproductive activity appear in both males and females in early spring. Mating usually occurs during the last week of March. At that time the young of the previous season are approximately ten months old, when they mature sexually. The exact gestation period is unknown, but it is between four and six weeks in duration. There are usually four young in each litter, which are born in a carefully constructed nest of dry leaves. Young nestlings are naked, with flesh-coloured wrinkled skin. The vibrissae on the snout appear at an early age. The eyes appear as black spots through the skin, and the ears as mere slits. The forefeet are characteristically broad with short, soft, blunt nails. The young moles grow rapidly but remain in the nest until almost fully grown. They first appear in the tunnels in mid-June, when they are about a month old. At that time they appear browner than the adults, with teeth not yet fully erupted.

Economic Status. These moles usually are found in woodlands and do not commonly come into contact with man's habitation. However, they may cause concern in gardens, lawns, and golf courses in close proximity to natural wooded areas. The damage is usually limited to the heaving of turf in their surface tunnels and to the construction of small molehills. Damage to garden vegetables should probably be attributed to the mice that occupy the mole tunnels.

Control methods have been discussed under the Pacific coast mole.

Distribution. This species occurs from southwest New Brunswick and central Ontario southward to North Carolina in the Great Smoky Mountains.

Canadian Distribution. The present species is monotypic, no geographical races having been described. Its occurrence in Charlotte County, New Brunswick,

Map 15 Distribution of the hairy-tailed mole, *Parascalops breweri*

lacks verification and rests on an old sight record. The hairy-tailed mole is common in southern Quebec and Ontario as far as Sault Ste Marie (see Map 15).

Parascalops breweri (Bachman), 1942, Boston Jour. Nat. Hist. 4: 32.

REFERENCE

Eadie, W.R. 1939. A contribution to the biology of *Parascalops breweri*. Jour. Mamm. 20(2): 150–73.

EASTERN MOLE
Taupe à queue glabre. *Scalopus aquaticus* (Linnaeus)

Description. The common mole of the eastern United States is anything but common in Canada. Its distribution barely reaches southwestern Ontario. This large mole (about 8 inches long) has a robust, depressed form with a short, slender, naked tail and very large, broad forefeet with stout, flat nails. Both the forefeet and the hind feet show indications of webbing between the toes. This fact led Linnaeus to believe that this mole was aquatic in habits, and so he gave it the specific name *aquaticus*. The females have only six mammae. The pelage is relatively long and dense and is rather woolly in texture. The colour is pale greyish brown with a golden sheen. The tail, feet, face, and snout are practically naked. The flesh-coloured skin carries sparse, fine greyish white hairs. The vibrissae are reduced to a few longer hairs on the snout and one or two on the side of the head above the ears. The wrists are lined with a row of short, stiff hairs. The chin and throat are often stained from the discharge of glands in that region. The skull is triangular: the first pair of incisors is greatly enlarged (Figure 10c) compared to other American species.

This is probably the most subterranean of all moles in America. The eyes, which are degenerate small black balls embedded in the skin beneath minute hairless eyelids, have moved forward out of the regular sockets to lie on the side of the snout. The ear orifice is an insignificant hole encircled by a ring of cartilage on the side of the head. The snout, which is moderately long and pointed, has terminal superior nostrils. It is also extremely mobile and sensitive and serves as the chief sensory organ, informing the animal of its environmental conditions.

There appear to be two annual moults: in spring and in autumn. The spring moult takes place in April and May, and the autumn moult in September and October. The sequence for the moults is similar. The fresh pelage first appears on the chest and progresses posteriorly until the abdomen and sides are covered with the new coat. It then progresses over the back and forward until the fur on the shoulders and head is replaced. During the moult there is a clear line separating the old and the new pelages.

The race found in Canada is the largest of the species. The males are slightly larger than the females. Average measurements of adult males: length 188–210, tail 30–40, hind foot 21–24 mm; weight 80–118 g.

Habits. The eastern mole spends practically all its life in its labyrinth of tunnels. It rarely exposes itself above ground, even when pushing soil to the surface or sealing a break in a tunnel. At most, the mobile pink snout will push through the loose soil at those times to explore the outside world. If food is detected on the surface some distance away, the mole will burrow to a spot under the food item and then drag it into its burrow without exposing itself.

The tunnelling behaviour of this species has been studied in great detail. The surface maze of tunnels is constructed immediately below the sod. The mole digs a tunnel with a deliberate sideways-and-upward stroke of one of its forefeet, each flattened nail acting as a small trowel to gouge out the earth. The loose earth is pressed against the upper side of the tunnel, causing the familiar raised ridge on the surface. During the operation the head is turned to the opposite side. When it is tired using one arm, it rotates its head to the other side and uses the opposite arm. The mole uses its sensitive snout to explore the surface of the tunnel for food. If the soil dries out and the earthworms retreat deeper, the mole will dig another tunnel, just below the former one, in the same manner. Then the fresh earth is pushed up into the old tunnel instead of being left to form raised ridges in the sod. During a prolonged drought the mole might form several galleries in this manner following its food downward to moist soil.

The deep permanent galleries that occur at depths of four to twenty-four inches are dug in a different manner; that is, the soil dug from the tunnel face is swept under the body with the front feet. As it accumulates under the mole, it is kicked backwards with the webbed hind feet. When a mound of loose earth has accumulated behind the mole, it turns around in its cramped quarters and pushes the earth before it with one enlarged palm. Each soil increment is pushed to the surface to cascade down the sides of the molehill from the central shaft. Since the earth plug is frequently quite long, the mole remains well concealed below ground while ejecting the earth.

The strength of the mole is quite prodigious. A 120-g mole has been known to move a mass thirty-five times its own weight. In comparison, a 150-pound man would have to move 4,800 pounds. Eastern moles have been observed digging surface tunnels at the rate of four yards an hour. Some main connecting tunnels may be a thousand yards in length.

As with other species, the eastern mole has been found to be active at irregular periods throughout the day-long period. It also abandons its surface tunnel system in the autumn and retreats to its deep galleries in winter. When these deep tunnels are accidentally cut in the frozen ground, they are quickly plugged with earth scraped from the tunnel sides, which freezes in place. The nest of dry leaves or grasses is built in a chamber up to eight inches in diameter, usually fairly deep underground. It is often under a stump or roots. Several passageways lead into it for escape routes.

Eastern moles, being intolerant of other members of their own clan, are solitary animals except during the mating season; at this time they will enter the tunnels of the opposite sex looking for mates. In the spring several moles may be taken from one set of tunnels.

This animal commonly sleeps in an upright hunched position with its nose tucked under its chest. Its sleep is deep, and it is sometime difficult to arouse. However, the sleep is never prolonged, and the mole awakens with a ravenous appetite.

Little direct information is available on the natural diet of this species. In one study of stomach contents, earthworms constituted 31 per cent, adult insects 23 per cent, insect larvae 29 per cent, and vegetable matter 13 per cent. Laboratory tests have indicated that this species shows only a slight preference for earthworms over white grubs and that such meat was chosen in preference to vegetable substances. However, certain seeds such as corn, wheat, oats, and squash were readily eaten as well as vegetables such as potatoes and tomatoes. Moles in captivity seldom drink water.

Undoubtedly much of their prey is seized when the moles are patrolling their tunnels. Other items are dug out of the soil. Beetles are slammed against the wall of the tunnel with the forepaw and then eaten. One observer reported that earthworms were eaten, head-first, after being pulled through the paws, by which action they were cleaned outside as well as inside before being swallowed.

However, other observers have noted that earthworms are often grasped in the middle and chewed up without much effort to line them up. Although mice carcasses are eaten, the blind mole seems to be unable to kill an active mouse even at close quarters. It is doubtful if the eastern mole can distinguish much more than light from darkness with its degenerate eyes. This species occasionally invades vegetable gardens but does not appear to burrow systematically down the rows, destroying the seeds and roots as it goes, as some species do. The potatoes or corn that are destroyed seem to have been discovered by accident.

These animals normally eat about one-third of their weight each day. One that was starved for twelve hours ate two-thirds of its weight in food in the following eighteen hours.

Little is known of the longevity or home range of this species. Its enemies consist of the lesser carnivores, the hawks, the owls, and perhaps the larger snakes.

Habitat. The eastern mole prefers moist friable loams in open woodlands and pastures. It seems to prefer hillsides to hilltops. Dry sandy or gravelly soils are avoided. If the surface becomes dry and compacted, the moles dig deeper. Sometimes river floodplains are colonized only to have the moles drown when the bottomlands flood.

Reproduction. As in other species of moles studied, the vaginal orifice remains sealed except during the reproductive period. The vagina opens at the onset of the mating season, which occurs in the latter part of March in the northern area of the species range. Most of the females are bred in a short three- to four-week period. Ovulation is thought to be induced by copulation. The exact gestation period is not known, but it is thought to be about four weeks, since most of the young are born in early May. The average number of embryos noted is 3.91 (3–5). Only one litter a year is produced. There is no evidence that young animals become sexually mature during the first calendar year of their lives.

As is true with all insectivores, the onset of the breeding season is accompanied by a tremendous growth in the reproductive organs. The testes of immature males (which are internally situated) increase to ten times their original weight between late summer and late winter, immediately prior to the breeding season.

The young moles are born naked in their nest, where they remain nursing for about a month. Even when a month old, their permanent teeth are loose and covered by a membrane. The deciduous teeth are thought to be lost before birth. However, the young moles grow rapidly during their nestling period and are almost adult size when they start to appear in the tunnels in June.

Economic Status. Although in the United States the eastern mole is considered a nuisance in parks, gardens, and lawns, and on golf courses, in Canada its range is too restricted to cause much concern. The damage it does is similar to that caused by other moles and is largely indirect, such as damage to plant roots by aeration. Destruction of garden produce is rather limited. Often damage

Map 16 Distribution of the eastern mole, *Scalopus aquaticus*

attributed to eastern moles has been actually done by pine voles or meadow voles.

Control may be exercised by means of the time-honoured trapping methods described under the Pacific coast mole. Recent experimental work has shown that this species may be effectively eradicated by using raw spanish peanuts treated with thallium sulphate or moistened earthworms coated with strychnine sulphate. The baits are inserted into the active surface runways at intervals. Care must be taken to cover the insertion holes but not to crush the tunnel. Control was accomplished in two or three days after application. The advantage of the described method is that the baits are available only to the occupants of the mole tunnels.

Distribution. The eastern mole occurs from Florida and the Gulf of Mexico northward to the Great Lakes region.

Canadian Distribution. This species is confined to Essex County, Ontario (see Map 16), where the northern race occurs quite commonly.

Scalopus aquaticus machrinus (Rafinesque), 1932, Atlantic Jour. 1: 61. Essex County, Ontario.

REFERENCES

Arlton, A.V. 1932. An ecological study of the mole. Jour. Mamm. 17(4): 349–71.
Conaway, C.H. 1959. The reproductive cycle of the eastern mole. Jour. Mamm. 40(2): 180–94.

STAR-NOSED MOLE
Condylure étoilé. *Condylura cristata* (Linnaeus)

Description. This is one of the really strange mammals of North America. It has been placed in a separate subfamily because of its anatomical differences from the other moles found on this continent (Figure 13).

Although the star-nosed mole measures about 8 inches in length, over one-third consists of a unique tail. The body is robust, but it is not as depressed as for most other moles. The head extends into a long snout, the tip of which is expanded into a naked, pink disc supporting twenty-two radially symmetrical finger-like tentacles, eleven on each side, surrounding the terminal nostrils. These sensory fleshy appendages give the species its name, 'star-nosed' mole. The eyes are minute (although relatively large for moles) and are hidden in the facial fur behind tiny eyelids. The ear orifices are remarkably large, although they lack external pinnae. The legs are somewhat longer than those of typical moles. The hind feet are black, scaly, and long, with well-developed claws. The forefeet are larger than the hind feet, although not as much as in typical moles. They are longer than broad. On the base of each digit is a series of two or three scales, and a row of short, stiff bristles surrounds the palm.

One might describe the star-nosed mole as being peculiar at both ends. The tail is long and fleshy with a noticeable basal constriction. It is moderately scaly and is covered with black hairs during the summer and autumn periods. In late winter the tail commences to thicken with stored fat. Eventually it grows to three or four times its original diameter during the reproductive period. The scales are separated, and the intervening pink skin is stretched tautly. The skin and hair become quite greasy to the touch. During the period of tail thickening, the basal constriction remains at about the original diameter, and the tail tapers to the tip like an arrow head.

The female has eight mammae.

Figure 13 Star-nosed mole

The pelage is noticeably shorter and thinner than the 'plush' of other moles. There is also some indication of a separation between a few longer white guard hairs and the fine silky underfur. The facial vibrissae are not noticeably pronounced. There are two or three longer grey 'eyebrows' on the side of the head. The colour above is black, with a greyish wash on limbs and underparts.

The spring moult of the star-nosed mole occurs later than in other species. It is at its peak in June and is generally completed by mid-July. The autumn moult takes place during October. The moulting sequence is irregular in this species. The new fur usually appears on the flanks and spreads first to the belly. A small posterior rump patch is almost invariably the last to moult. There is little difference between summer and winter pelages except that the latter is thicker.

Average measurements of adult moles: length 202 (189–211), tail 78 (71–84), hind foot 28 (26–30) mm; weight of males 53 (39–70) g. Females average slightly smaller in measurements and weigh 50 (35–77) g.

The skull of the star-nosed mole is very slender, with a long pointed rostrum. The zygomatic arches are very thin. The teeth are numerous and triangular. The ear conches are incompletely ossified, as found in the shrew mole *Neürotrichus* and in shrews (Figure 14).

Habits. The star-nosed mole is decidedly less fossorial than most other moles and spends a good deal of time foraging on the surface at night. It seems to occupy an ecological niche similar to the shrew-mole on the Pacific coast. However the resemblance seems to be more ecological than anatomical since there are many important skeletal differences, such as those found in the dentition.

This animal constructs a network of shallow tunnels in low, wet soil. The tunnels are usually only a few inches below the surface and vary from one and a half to three inches in diameter. Where the water table permits, deeper tunnels may be excavated. Then the wet soil is compacted into cylinders and pushed to the surface through an ascending shaft to form the characteristic molehills. These molehills may measure as much as twenty-six inches in diameter and six inches high. The ejected moist earth shows that it has been compressed in the passageway. The burrows often open to the banks of streams, or water may fill the deeper portions of the undulating tunnels. In burrowing, the star-nosed mole raises its forefeet to each side of its nose, and then with alternate strokes, or in unison, it

pushes the earth aside. The movement of the forelimbs is aided by a twisting movement of the body and the widely spread hind limbs. During digging the tentacles on the nose are folded over the nostrils to keep dirt from entering the nasal passage. Because of its longer limbs this mole can scuttle about the surface with greater ease than other species. It is unique, too, for its dexterity in swimming and diving. The forefeet paddle, and the hind feet kick independently, propelling the animal rapidly through the water. The tail is used as a rudder. When the animal dives, its tentacles are again folded over the nostrils to keep water out.

The eyesight of this mole is considered to be poor, but its hearing is thought to be excellent. However, it gets most of its information concerning the environment from its tactile nasal tentacles. It remains active throughout the twenty-four-hour period. It also remains active during the winter months, when it has been frequently observed along stream banks, under the shelf of ice, or even swimming under the ice of streams.

This species appears to be more congenial than most other moles and usually lives in colonies. Often several animals are trapped together. The home range is probably about an acre in extent, and populations as high as five moles per acre have been found in suitable habitat. No information is available on longevity.

The star-nosed mole lives primarily on aquatic insects, worms, crustacea, and molluscs. A quantitative study of the food habits has disclosed a diet of 49 per cent worms, of which aquatic forms composed 58 per cent, leeches 22 per cent, and terrestrial worms only 20 per cent. The 33 per cent insect remains in the diet were mostly aquatic larvae and nymphs. Crustacea composed 6.5 per cent and molluscs 2.2 per cent. Vertebrates, including small fish, similarly composed 2.2 per cent of the total diet.

Because of its unsavoury odour and protective habits, the star-nosed mole has few enemies. Remains have been found in the stomachs of red-tailed hawks and great horned owls. It is possible that a few fall prey to large fish such as pike and bass.

Habitat. As previously indicated, the star-nosed mole is the most aquatic of the American moles. It inhabits low-lying woods, meadows, and marshes where the soil is a wet mucky humus. It probably ranks with the shrew-mole for the title of poorest digger among the American moles. It is regularly to be found along lake- and stream-banks and spends considerable time hunting in the water. Specimens have frequently been taken in minnow traps as much as three feet below the surface.

Reproduction. The peculiar thickening of the tail in winter has been previously described. It has been suggested that this phenomenon may be associated in some way with the reproductive cycle. The first certain signs of the approach of the reproductive season is the enormous enlargement of the male testes and prostate gland in late January. These associated glands may grow to weigh 10 per cent of the total body weight at the height of the breeding season. They start to regress in May to the normal non-breeding condition. Mating probably takes place

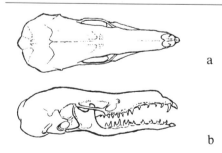

Figure 14 Star-nosed mole skull: (a) dorsal view, (b) lateral view (× 1)

Map 17 Distribution of the star-nosed mole, *Condylura cristata*, 1 *C. c. cristata*, 2 *C. c. nigra*

in late February, and the first litters appear in late March, though most are born in April. Some pregnancies, however, have been reported as late as July. Only one litter is born each year. The average number of young per litter is 5.4, with extremes of two to seven. The young moles mature the following spring, when they are approximately ten months old. The late litters are probably born to late-maturing young females or to females in secondary oestrus after unsuccessful first matings. The exact gestation period is not known.

In view of the dampness of the star-nosed mole's habitat, special efforts are often necessary to build a dry nest for the young moles. Nests have been found in some peculiar locations, such as manure piles, compost heaps, and stumps projecting from swamps. Others have been found under logs and roots of fallen trees, which provide refuges above the water table. The nest of straw, leaves, or grass is oval-shaped and is placed in an enlarged chamber about five inches in diameter.

The new-born moles are about 50 mm long and weigh about 1.5 g. At birth the skin is naked, pink, and crinkled.

The eyes appear as black spots under the skin. The short nasal tentacles are pressed against the snout. Later the back becomes dark with the growth of hair; the eyelids appear as mere slits over the eyes in the middle of a small white area; the ear orifices appear among the wrinkles on the sides of the head and the tentacles start to enlarge. The young grow rapidly. They weigh about 33 g in a month and may leave the nest shortly afterwards, usually in late May. By late summer the juveniles may weigh more than the adults.

Economic Status. Since the star-nosed mole normally frequents land too wet for cultivation, it rarely comes in competition with man's interests. It should be considered as beneficial in view of its insect diet.

Distribution. This species is the most northern mole on this continent, being found from near the treeline in northern Quebec and Labrador southward to the Allegheny Mountains in the Carolinas and to the Okefinokee Swamp of Georgia in the eastern United States.

Canadian Distribution. Two geographical races are recognized in Canada (see Map 17). The typical form is found over most of eastern Canada from Hamilton Inlet, Labrador, to the east coast of Hudson Bay, and westward to Lake Manitoba, Manitoba. A second geographical race has been described from Nova Scotia.

Condylura cristata cristata (Linnaeus) 1758, Syst. Nat., 10th ed., 1: 53. Eastern North America.

Condylura cristata nigra Smith, 1940, American Midl. Nat. 24: 218. Nova Scotia.

REFERENCES

Eadie, W.R., and W.J. Hamilton, Jr. 1956. Notes on reproduction in the star-nosed mole. Jour. Mamm. 37(2): 223–31.

Hamilton, W.J. Jr. 1931. Habits of the star-nosed mole, *Condylura cristata*. Jour. Mamm. 12(4): 345–55.

COLOUR PLATE

4

Comparison of Canadian squirrels: (a) hoary marmot, *Marmota caligata*; (b) woodchuck, *Marmota monax*; (c) Columbian ground squirrel, *Spermophilus columbianus*; (d) American red squirrel, *Tamiasciurus hudsonicus*; (e) Franklin's ground squirrel, *Spermophilus franklinii*; (f) northern flying squirrel, *Glaucomys sabrinus*; (g) Richardson's ground squirrel, *Spermophilus richardsonii*; (h) least chipmunk, *Eutamias minimus*; (i) thirteen-lined ground squirrel, *Spermophilus tridecemlineatus*; (j) golden-mantled ground squirrel, *Spermophilus lateralis*

a

b

c

d

e

f

g

h

i

j

5

6

COLOUR PLATE

5

Richardson's ground squirrel, *Spermophilus richardsonii*

6

Thirteen-lined ground squirrel, *Spermophilus tridecemlineatus*

Order **Chiroptera** / Bats

Bats have long been recognized as a distinct group of mammals because of their unique ability to fly. A few other mammals, such as the flying squirrels, flying lemurs, and gliding phalangers, may be thought to fly, but in reality those animals simply glide on furred membranes stretched between extended legs. Only three groups of terrestrial vertebrates have been known to achieve true sustained flight: the primitive reptilian pterosaurs, the birds, and the bats, and each group has developed a unique flight member.

The bat's wing consists of a double layer of skin stretched between the elongated fingers of the hand, and backwards to include the hind limb and tail. The clawed thumb is free of the wing (Figure 15). There are many other adaptations that fit bats for flight: the sternum is keeled to anchor the strong pectoral muscles, and the bones of the forelimbs are elongate and tubular to give a combination of strength and lightness. The hind limbs are weak; the pelvis is very narrow; the socket for the femur faces upwards so that the hind limb rotates backwards and the knee faces up. A cartilage called the 'calcar' extends back from the hind foot to strengthen the interfemoral membrane.

Bats generally have well-furred bodies, naked wing membranes, alert little faces with small weak eyes, but large ears, large chests, and narrow hips. Contrary to common folklore, they are not blind. They scuttle awkwardly on the ground on their wrists and hind legs with wings folded, but they are masters of twisting-turning flight, guided by echoes from their supersonic cries bouncing off obstacles in their way (radar). When resting, they hang by their tiny clawed hind feet upside-down from a twig or ledge. All bats are primarily nocturnal in activity.

ARTIFICIAL KEY TO FAMILIES OF CANADIAN CHIROPTERA

1   Tip of tail projects well beyond interfemoral membrane.
                                                    MOLOSSIDAE
1′ Tail included in interfemoral membrane.
                                              VESPERTILIONIDAE

Family **Vespertilionidae** / Smooth-faced Bats

Most families of bats are tropical in distribution and are highly adapted to some specialized mode of life. The members of this family are practically world-wide in distribution (except in the polar regions) and are rather difficult to characterize except in a negative way.

Vespertilionid bats have perhaps reached the highest perfection in flight adaptation. The forelimb shows the strongest modifications in the reduction of the ulna and in the complicated double articulation of the humerus on the scapula, which provides extra strength in flight. The long tail extends to the tip of the large interfemoral membrane. The face is smooth, and the ears are large and include a long tragus. (There are prominent subdermal cheek glands). All these characteristics aid these species in the vigorous pursuit of flying insects, their normal prey.

LITTLE BROWN BAT
Petite Chauve-souris brune. *Myotis lucifugus* (LeConte)

Description. It is appropriate to commence the description

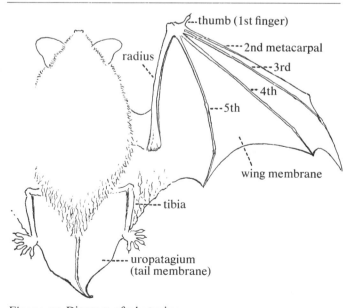

Figure 15 Diagram of a bat wing

thumb (1st finger)
radius
2nd metacarpal
3rd
4th
5th
wing membrane
tibia
uropatagium
(tail membrane)

of the bats in Canada with what is undoubtedly the most common species, the little brown bat. It is also a generalized vespertilionid type and, therefore, serves as a good basis for comparison with other species. Unfortunately it lacks a good vernacular name. Commonly called the little brown bat, it has so many close relatives that all the qualifying adjectives required to distinguish them make the whole nominal system unwieldy.

This small species is about 3½ inches in total length (including the tail), with a wing-spread of about 9 inches (Plate 1i). It is well covered with long, silky brown hair. On the back, the longer hairs are tipped with a burnished copper sheen, a characteristic of the species. Ventrally, the colour is buffy grey. There is a dark, dull shoulder spot. The forehead and nose are well covered with dull brown fur except around the eyes, lips, nostrils, and the moderately large ears (Figure 16c). The ears when laid forward do not project beyond the tip of the nose. The rather small eyes are shiny black. The wings are sparsely haired from the forearm to the knee, but the tail membrane is naked (Plate 1i). The young bats are dark grey-brown with shorter pelage. Nothing is known of moults in this genus. The skull is shown in Figure 18h.

Average measurements of adults of both sexes: total length 89 (79–93), tail 35 (31–40), hind foot 9.5 (8.5–10), ear from meatus 13–14.5 mm; weight 7.5 (5.5–12.0) g. The sexes are similar.

Habits. These little bats are a common sight over most of Canada, as they zigzag across the summer evening sky in pursuit of moths; however, to most observers the rest of their lives remains shrouded in mystery. Fortunately,

through the studies of naturalists, much of the bat's life has been pieced together to form a fascinating story.

The myotids are nocturnal or crepuscular in activity. They spend the summer daylight hours sleeping in a cave, mine, culvert, hollow tree, or attic, or behind a shutter or shingle, wherever they can find darkness and protection. After sundown, when dusk has gathered, they emerge to flit about in search of food. They do not necessarily fly all night, because they are known to return to favourite resting spots during the night. Just before dawn there is another surge of hunting activity before they return to their sheltered nooks about half an hour before dawn.

They are strong flyers and usually quarter back and forth at tree height over meadows and roadsides, occasionally dipping over a lake or stream to drink or pick up a floating insect. They fly at speeds of six to ten miles an hour (Figure 19).

The agility with which bats evade objects in their path in the darkness has always aroused human curiosity. Early naturalists performed the simple experiment of sealing the bats' eyes with soft wax and then marvelled at the facility with which they evaded walls and hanging objects in their path. More recently it was discovered that bats navigate by means of a specialized type of radar. In flight, they utter a

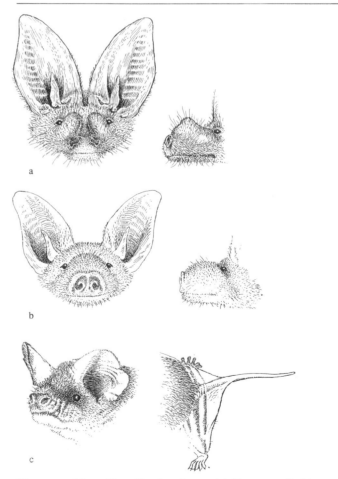

Figure 17 More Canadian bat faces: (a) Townsend's big-eared bat, *Plecotus townsendii*; (b) pallid bat, *Antrozous pallidus*; (c) big free-tailed bat, *Tadarida macrotis* (× 1)

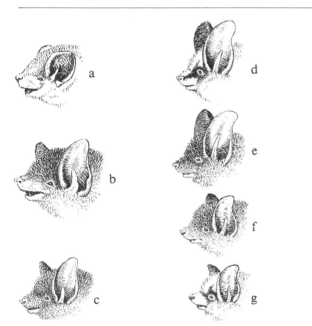

Figure 16 Some Canadian bat faces: (a) red bat, *Lasiurus borealis*; (b) big brown bat, *Eptesicus fuscus*; (c) little brown bat, *Myotis lucifugus*; (d) long-eared bat, *Myotis evotis*; (e) Keen's bat, *Myotis keenii*; (f) long-legged bat, *Myotis volans*; (g) small-footed bat, *Myotis leibii* (× 3/4)

rapid series of high-pitched cries up to 50,000 vibrations per second (far beyond human ken). They then catch the echoes reflected from walls, poles, wires, and trees, to guide their flight away from danger. Since they are able to pick up the echoes from flying insects, they are guided to their prey. They scan the air with a slow series of squeaks, and when a flying insect is detected, they increase the frequency and pitch of their calls and 'home in' on the echo from the insect's body.

The little brown bat is a gregarious species and usually occurs in colonies, which may number from a few individuals to several hundred. The sexes are generally segregated. The females usually congregate in favourable hideaways such as attics, church steeples, and mine shafts or behind the loose shingles of roofs. When nursery colonies are discovered in summer, they usually are made up of adult females, their young, and perhaps a few immature males. The summer roosts of the male adults have seldom been found, but evidence has been presented to indicate that some may join the females after parturition. Otherwise they roost in groups in secluded spots such as holes in trees or natural sink holes.

With the approach of autumn, Canadian conditions become quite unfavourable for bats. The animals seldom venture out on cold, windy, or rainy nights. Since in wintertime their insect food vanishes and since their ears and wings are quite unsuited to the season's environment, in early November the little brown bats seek caves in which to hibernate. Large caves or mine shafts are not always readily available, and some populations must migrate several hundred miles to their home cave. Rarely they have been observed migrating in clouds at dusk. Occasionally hundreds of bats have crashed in mid-town during a storm, or have hit lighthouses or aerial masts, but most find their home caves safely. Banding studies have indicated that they have strong homing instincts. Bats transported distances of up to 76 miles have returned to their own caves in five nights, and others have returned 180 miles over a period of two years. They are thought to follow broad river valleys in their normal movements and to recognize topographic features over a wide area.

Cave-dwelling bats have been shown to have poor thermoregulation systems. They remain homeothermic only while active. When they are resting the temperature of their bodies gradually drops from normal to that of the environment. Even in normal sleep, their body temperature drops, as is shown by the fact that they are cool to the touch. In order not to freeze to death in winter, little brown bats must find large caves where the temperature remains constant at about 40°F with a relative humidity of about 80 per cent. Here they hang from draftless, dark, vaulted ceilings, in packed masses, often totalling hundreds or thousands of individuals of both sexes each hanging by its toenails, as it were. The summer nurseries in church steeples and under roofs have to be abandoned during the winter because they do not offer protective temperatures maintained above 32°F.

The hibernation of cave bats is not as profound as that of some other mammals such as jumping mice or marmots, and is best described as 'dormancy.' The bats may

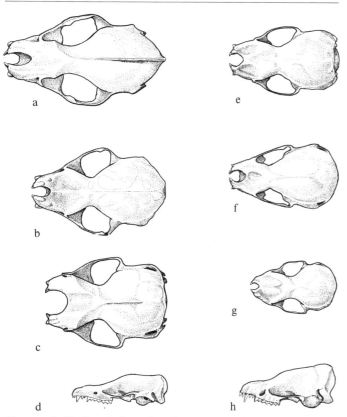

Figure 18 Skulls of Canadian bats: (a) pallid bat, *Antrozous pallidus*; (b) big brown bat, *Eptesicus fuscus*; (c) hoary bat, *Lasiurus cinereus*; (d) small-footed bat, *Myotis leibii*; (e) silver-haired bat, *Lasionycteris noctivagans*; (f) Townsend's big-eared bat, *Plecotus townsendii*; (g) eastern pipistrelle, *Pipistrellus subflavus*; (h) little brown bat, *Myotis lucifugus* (× 1³/₄)

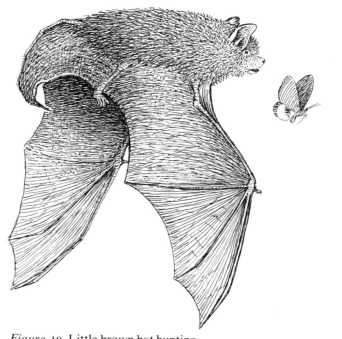

Figure 19 Little brown bat hunting

awaken at times and by a process of shivering raise their body temperatures enough to enable them to fly about or change positions. Banding studies have shown that hibernating bats may change position during the winter, or even change caves. Undoubtedly there is some movement during mild spells. However, the evidence points to the fact that they subsist on stored fat all winter long and do not feed, although they often drink when awakened. The low temperatures of their caverns assist in lowering their metabolic rates, thus conserving their fat. The relative humidity is often so high that the sleeping bats are bejewelled with droplets of dew.

Emergence from the caves usually takes place in late April or early May, and the sexes segregate and spread out across the country to their summer haunts.

Bats have few enemies. They seem to be relatively secure in their summer roosts and hibernating caves. A few fall prey to owls – screech owls, great horned owls, and barn owls. Shrews may enter caves and find a few asleep low down. Dogs and cats occasionally carry a bat home, but such victims are thought to be ill or at least 'grounded' ones. One of the strangest records of predation is that of a leopard frog catching a little brown bat. Rarely do bats get snagged in a burdock or a barbed-wire fence while flying low, or caught by a trout as they dip over the water. In comparison with similar-sized shrews, moles, and mice, bats live to a fantastic age. By checking banding returns it has been found that this species can live to an age of twenty-four years in the wild.

Bats are quite vocal and utter rasping chirps when disturbed.

There is little quantitative data on the food habits of this species. Its natural food appears to consist of moths, beetles, bugs, and some other soft-bodied flying insects. Its method of capturing insects is unique. The interfemoral membrane between the hind legs is used as a net, and the insects are trapped between the body and the membrane. If the insect is a large one, the bat will fly to a perch and dispatch the insect while holding it in its pouch, which is formed by the interfemoral membrane and sometimes the wings. It bites off the wings and discards them; then it chews up the food by lowering its head into the pouch between its hind feet. Small insects captured in flight are picked out of the pouch by lowering the head momentarily in the same manner. The little brown bat is quite an efficient insect catcher and, on an average, consumes easily one gram of insects per hour while hunting.

Habitat. The little brown bat is one of the cave-hibernating bats of Canada. In summer it is found in a wide choice of habitats. Originally it was probably a forest dweller, frequenting river banks and glades. However, with the advent of Europeans and their communities, this species has adapted to urban and village life during the summer months and 'hawks' for moths along lamplit tree-shaded streets.

Reproduction. The reproductive period is fairly long in this and other cave-dwelling bats. The adults enter the caves in November in a pre-breeding condition. The females are considered to be in a suboestrous stage. The

young of the year are probably sexually immature, but the adults may be receptive. Mating may occur in the late autumn or during the hibernating period, whenever the bats become aroused, or in spring before they leave the caves. Curiously, sperms have been found to remain viable in the female uterus for prolonged periods during winter hibernation. The females do not ovulate until April or May, just about the time they emerge from the caves. Only one egg matures at a time so that normally only one young is born after a gestation period of somewhere between fifty and sixty days, from mid-May to early July, depending on how early the female emerged from hibernation.

As the time for the birth of her young approaches, the female hangs, head upwards, by her thumbs. The interfemoral membrane is pursed to cradle the young bat, which is born in a breech delivery. The new-born bat soon scrambles up its mother's fur to find one of the two pectoral teats, shielded by the enveloping wings. At this early stage, the forearms and fingers are relatively short so that the young bat can scramble fairly well. Eventually it gets well anchored around its mother's broad chest by means of its clawed thumbs and hind feet. She can then clean herself and reverse her position to the normal one of hanging by her toes. At birth the young little brown bat measures about 48 mm in total length and weighs about 2.5 g (a sizable burden for its mother).

While in flight the female bat carries her young clamped to her breast for the first two or three days of its young life. Since there is only one young, it would disturb her balance if it hung on one side, so it hangs crossways across her chest, its mouth grasping one teat and its hind legs under the opposite armpit. The young bat grows rapidly so that after the first few days it can be left in the communal nursery during the mother's nightly forages. By the time its is three weeks old it learns to fly. It is believed that the young bats mature during the winter sleep and are ready to reproduce the next spring.

Economic Status. Bats have been subject to local superstitions throughout human history. In some cultures they are regarded as good-luck charms, and in others as evil omens. In Canada the favourite bit of folklore is that they fly low over a woman's head in order to become entangled in her hair. Rare occurrences of this incident have indeed been reported, but they are purely accidental.

On the other hand, some observers suggest that bats are beneficial because they destroy mosquitoes. However, stomach analyses have failed to confirm this. At our present state of knowledge concerning their food habits, bats must be ruled as neutral as far as man's interests are concerned.

These bats may become a nuisance because of their roosting habits in attics, under eaves, or behind shutters. They cause some annoyance by their squeaks and scampering feet, but the real nuisance is the accumulation of their faeces to form a malodorous bat guano, sometimes more than a foot deep, under their roosts. The control of bats under such conditions is difficult because of the extremely small crevice needed for them to gain entrance to

Map 18 Distribution of the little brown bat, *Myotis lucifugus*: 1 *M. l. alascensis*, 2 *M. l. carissima*, 3 *M. l. lucifugus*, 4 *M. l. pernox*

a chamber and the rarity of good bat roosts, which make such sites prime attractions to bats. Even after the first colony is destroyed, the site will attract new bats.

The only effective control method is to find out where the entrance is, to wait until autumn or winter when the young are on the wing or have left, to wait until the night when the bats have gone, and then to seal up the hole with wire or a wooden block. Bats can be encouraged to vacate a roost by the generous application of naphthalene or dichlorocide flakes, but this is only a temporary remedy. One might take the ultimate step of fumigating the building, but then one would have to deal with the removal of the bodies from the crannies where they might be wedged. If the colony is of long standing, bat guano will also need to be removed to wipe out all reminders of former occupancy.

In recent years the discovery of bat rabies has caused a drastic reappraisal in our attitude towards bats in Canada. The occurrence of rabies among the vampire bats of South and Central America has been known for about forty years. The vampire constitutes a reservoir of the disease,

which from time to time flares up in domestic animals and even in man. The first occurrence of a rabid bat in Florida, which was followed by isolated cases elsewhere in the United States, caused grave concern among public health authorities in that country. Eventually several records were obtained, scattered across the continent; a woman in California succumbed to rabies as the result of a bat bite. There were six determinations of rabies among bats in southwestern British Columbia between 1957 and 1960, and three cases in Ontario in 1961. These included three specimens of the little brown bat. Most of these identifications were obtained in special surveys of bat populations, but the first case, in 1957, arose when a boy in Vancouver was bitten by a bat. Fortunately prompt medical attention prevented serious consequences. The incidence of rabies in bats has increased during the last few years. There were twenty-eight positive identifications among Canadian bats in 1972. The big brown bat, *Eptesicus fuscus*, is the species most commonly infected.

How the disease reached the insectivorous cave-dwelling bats in Canada is not clear. It is possible that some of the migrating species became infected in Mexico, and these later infected the northern bats. The infection of the little brown bats causes concern because it is one of the species that associates closely with man in buildings.

In any event one is well advised to ward off any biting attempts by a crippled bat and, if bitten, to capture the assailant and seek medical aid. Even though the disease is extremely rare at present, it would seem wise to allay the apprehension about infection by speedily determining whether the bat is rabid or not.

Distribution. The little brown bat inhabits a broad belt across the middle of North America: from Georgia north to southern Labrador on the Atlantic coast, across southern Alaska and California on the Pacific coast.

Canadian Distribution. This species is remarkably uniform throughout an extensive part of its eastern range, but the western populations show some geographical variation. Four subspecies are recognized in Canada (see Map 18).

Myotis lucifugus alascensis Miller, 1913, N. American Fauna 13: 63. West of the Rocky Mountains of Alberta.

Myotis lucifugus carissima Thomas, 1904, Ann. Mag. Nat. Hist., ser. 7, 13: 383. A paler form, found in Canada only in the Okanagan valley, British Columbia.

Myotis lucifugus lucifugus (LeConte), 1831, *In* McMurtrie, The animal kingdom by Baron Cuvier, 1: appendix, 431. Canada, north and east of the Rocky Mountains.

Myotis lucifugus pernox Hollister, 1911, Smiths. Misc. Coll. 56(26): 4. A large form of uncertain status, known only from the vicinity of Jasper, Alberta.

REFERENCES

Cagle, F.R., and L. Cockrum. 1943. Notes on a summer colony of *Myotis lucifugus lucifugus*. Jour. Mamm. 24(4): 474–92.

Wimsatt, W.A. 1945. Notes on breeding behavior, pregnancy and parturition in some vespertilionid bats of the eastern United States. Jour. Mamm. 26(1): 23–33.

YUMA BAT
Chauve-souris de Yuma. *Myotis yumanensis* (H. Allen)

Description. The mouse-eared bats (genus *Myotis*) form a confusing array of similar species and subspecies that can be identified only by experts. Even in the hand they are difficult to identify because the trenchant characters are generally found in the skulls or indices of measurements.

The Yuma bat is a western species very similar to the little brown bat. However, it is generally smaller except for its relatively larger hind feet. The fur is shorter and woollier than in *lucifugus* and lacks the burnished tips of the dorsal hairs found in that species. The colour is a variable dull brown above and buffy grey below. The ears are about the same length, but the tips are narrower than in *lucifugus*. The brain-case rises abruptly from the rostrum.

Average measurements of Canadian adults: total length 86 (77–91), tail 37 (34–42), hind foot 9.5 (9–11), ear from meatus 11–12 mm. The sexes are alike.

Habits. Very little is known of the life history of this species. It occurs in summer nursery colonies in attics and behind chimneys in southern British Columbia, and probably migrates southward in winter. It is crepuscular and nocturnal in activity and feeds on flying insects. In captivity it has been found to eat the equivalent of approximately one-half its weight each day. Its general life history is probably much like that of *lucifugus*.

Habitat. The Yuma bat appears to show a preference for open clearings rather than forests. It is a characteristic species of the arid southwestern United States. It has also been taken in mountainous regions up to 11,000 feet.

Reproduction. Little information is available for this species. A single young is born in late June or early July in the nursery colonies.

Economic Status. The Yuma bat frequents the habitations of man as does the little brown bat. Its role is probably similar to that outlined for the latter species.

Distribution. This species occurs in western North America from central Mexico to southern British Columbia.

Canadian Distribution. Two easily differentiated subspecies occur in Canada. The coastal form is darker, the inland one much paler (see Map 19).

Myotis yumanensis saturatus Miller, 1897, N. American Fauna 13: 68. Coastal British Columbia, south of Prince Rupert, including Vancouver Island.

Myotis yumanensis sociabilis Grinnell, 1914, Univ. California Pub. Zool. 12: 318. Okanagan valley of British Columbia.

REFERENCE

Miller, G.S., and G.M. Allen. 1928. The American bats of the *Myotis* and *Pizonyx*. United States Nat. Mus. Bull. 144: 61–72.

KEEN'S BAT
Chauve-souris de Keen. *Myotis keenii* (Merriam)

Description. Keen's bat is essentially the same size and colour as the little brown bat, but its hair seems a little silkier and it has a brassy rather than coppery sheen. The colour below is buffy grey. The only good distinguishing characters are the long, rounded ears and the accompanying longer tragus (Figure 16e). The ears when laid forward extend about 4 mm beyond the nose. There is also a dull brown shoulder spot.

Measurements of adults: total length 84 (79–88), tail 42 (36–43), hind foot 8.5 (7–9.5), ear from meatus 14–18.5 mm; weight approximately 7 g. The sexes are alike.

Habits. Keen's bat appears to be less gregarious than most of its relatives. During the summer it hides under the loose bark of trees, in holes, in brush, or in rock crannies during the daylight hours. It sallies forth in early dusk, about fifteen minutes before the little brown bat, to capture insects on the wing. Although usually found alone, it is occasionally found in small groups.

Map 19 Distribution of the Yuma bat, *Myotis yumanensis*: 1 *M. y. saturatus*, 2 *M. y. sociabilis*

Keen's bat migrates in the autumn to its home hibernating cave. Transported away from home it has been known to return distances up to fifty-five miles in less than a month. It usually goes into hibernation about the end of October and comes out in early May.

In the hibernating caves, Keen's bat chooses dark, cool, moist passageways, where the temperature is about 40°F and where the relative humidity may be 90 per cent, such as is found above cave streams. It is often bejewelled with drops of glistening dew. It usually hangs alone, wedged into cracks or between stalactites.

From banding studies, Keen's bat has been known to live up to eighteen years. Its chief enemies are probably owls.

Habitat. This species shows a decided preference for forests, frequenting glades and rivers.

Reproduction. Little information is available on the reproduction of this species. The general pattern probably follows that of the little brown bat, described previously. A nursery colony was found under the shingles of a small shelter on a lakeshore in an Ohio State Forest. There were new-born bats on June 12. Two young bats fell from the ceiling on to the observer's sleeping-bag, where they squeaked loudly. For safe-keeping until morning, he placed them in a shoe. In the morning the shoe contained not only the two young bats, but an adult female nursing one of the young. During the period of observation the female nursed only one and always at the left teat, an indication that she recognized her own young and tried to succour it.

Economic Status. Keen's bat is probably of little economic importance because it seldom comes in contact with man.

Distribution. The species has a peculiar disjunct contribution. The eastern form is rather uncommonly distributed across central North America as far as Saskatchewan. The western population is confined to the Pacific coast from southern Alaska to Washington. Keen's bat is not often observed.

Canadian Distribution. The eastern subspecies is de-

46

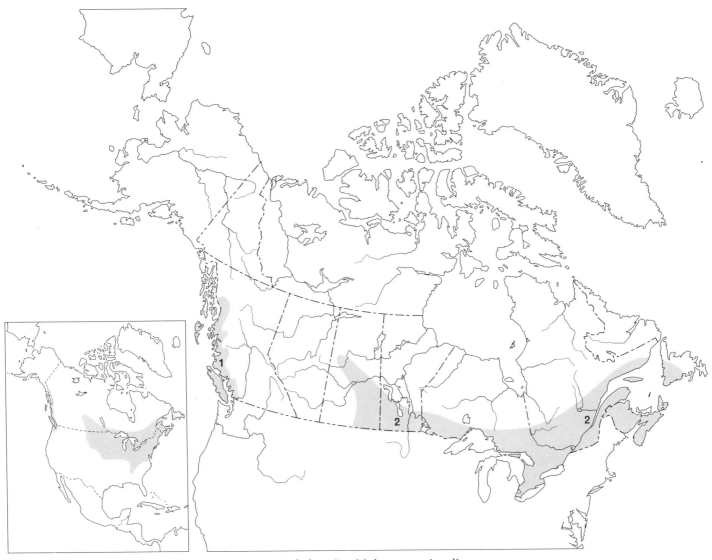

Map 20 Distribution of Keen's bat, *Myotis keenii*: 1 *M. k. keenii*, 2 *M. k. septentrionalis*

cidedly paler and is found from Newfoundland to Saskatchewan. The British Columbian coastal populations are rich brown with very dark ears and wing membranes (see Map 20).

Myotis keenii keenii (Merriam), 1895, American Nat. 29: 860. Coastal British Columbia.

Myotis keenii septentrionalis (Trouessart), 1898, Catalogus mammalium tam viventium quam fossilium, fasc. 1, p. 131. Eastern Canada.

REFERENCE

Brandon, R.A. 1961. Observations of young Keen bats. Jour. Mamm. 42(3): 400-1.

LONG-EARED BAT
Chauve-souris à longues oreilles. *Myotis evotis* (H. Allen)

Description. The long-eared bat is another of the confusing western mouse-eared bats. It is a little larger than average for the group. Its colour is generally paler than that of the little brown myotis, and the tail is longer. The light brown silky dorsal fur contrasts markedly with the dark brown (almost black) ears and wing membranes (Plate 1k). The unique characteristic of this species is the very large, rounded ears that extend 5 to 7 mm beyond the tip of the nose when they are laid forward. The tragus is similarly long and slender (Figure 16d). There is no sexual dimorphism. The skull is rather bulbous.

Average measurements of adults of the typical form: length 98 (92-103), tail 44 (42-47), hind foot 11 (10-11), ear from meatus 18 (17-19) mm; weight about 10 g.

Habits. Little is known of the life history of this bat in Canada. It is probably migratory, hibernating in caves farther south. It is nocturnal in habits and is reported to emerge later in the evening than *lucifugus*. It is found in small nursery colonies of females and young, in crevices between logs in cabins and behind brick chimneys and the loose bark of trees.

Habitat. This species appears to be another one of the

Map 21 Distribution of the long-eared bat, *Myotis evotis*: 1 *M. e. evotis*, 2 *M. e. pacificus*

forest-dwelling mouse-eared bats. It seems to favour rocky habitats on the British Columbia coast but has also been taken on the plains of Alberta.

Reproduction. The single young is born in July.

Economic Status. The long-eared bat is probably of little economic importance because it is an uncommon species.

Distribution. This bat inhabits western North America from Mexico to southern Alberta and British Columbia.

Canadian Distribution. Two well-differentiated subspecies of the long-eared bat are found in Canada (see Map 21). The interior form is much paler and a little larger than the darker coastal form.

Myotis evotis evotis (H. Allen), 1864, Smiths. Misc. Coll. 7: 48. Southern Rocky Mountain region of British Columbia and Alberta and the Alberta forested foothill region.

Myotis evotis pacificus Dalquest, 1943, Proc. Biol. Soc. Washington 56: 2. Coastal British Columbia including Vancouver Island, intergrading with the other subspecies in the interior.

FRINGED BAT
Chauve-souris à queue frangée. *Myotis thysanodes* Miller

Description. The fringed bat is closely related to the long-eared bat and to *Myotis nattereri* of the Old World. Its characteristic mark is a fringe of short brown hairs on the edge of the interfemoral membrane, particularly noticeable on each side of the tail. It is a medium-sized, pale buffy-brown bat with darker brown ears and wing membrane. The ears are large but not so large as in the previous species. When laid forward, they extend only 3 to 5 mm beyond the tip of the nose. The tail is also shorter.

Average measurements: length 89 (86–93), tail 38.5 (36–41), hind foot 10.5 (10–11), ear from meatus 16–18 mm. The sexes are alike.

Habits. Practically nothing is known of the life history of this species. It is thought to hibernate in caves, but most specimens have been secured from nursery colonies in deserted buildings during the summer months. The Canadian population is probably migratory. It is nocturnal in activity and hunts insects on the wing. The flight is

Map 22 Distribution of the fringed bat, *Myotis thysanodes*

fluttering and butterfly-like, and the bat often soars. It too has been known to eat the equivalent of one-half its weight in fly larvae each day in captivity.

Habitat. This species appears to prefer the arid yellow pine zone of the Pacific northwest.

Reproduction. Nothing is known for this species, but it is probably similar to other mouse-eared bats.

Economic Status. The species is too rare in Canada to be of any economic significance.

Distribution. This species inhabits western North America from Mexico to south-central British Columbia.

Canadian Distribution. The only Canadian specimens were secured from a summer nursery colony in a farm house near Vernon, British Columbia (see Map 22).

Myotis thysanodes thysanodes Miller, 1897, N. American Fauna 13: 80. Okanagan valley, British Columbia.

REFERENCE

Maslin, T.P. 1938. Fringe-tailed bat in British Columbia. Jour. Mamm. 19(3): 373.

LONG-LEGGED BAT
Chauve-souris à longues pattes. *Myotis volans* (H. Allen)

Description. The long-legged bat is a large, dark mouse-eared bat. The pelage is not as long as in some other species and is chocolate brown above and dark smoky brown beneath. The ears are relatively short, and when laid forward they barely reach the nose (Figure 16f). The wing membranes are sparsely furred on the ventral surface from the elbow to the knee, and the interfemoral membrane is also haired below, between the knees. There is a well-marked calcar supporting the interfemoral membrane, which carries a flat, projecting triangular keel on its outer surface (Figure 20). The bat derives its name from its relatively long tibia, but this is not too obvious without comparison with other species. The feet are relatively small.

Average measurements of adults: length 95 (88–99), tail 46 (38–54), hind foot 9 (8–10), ear 12 (11–14) mm. Average weight of pregnant females 9.8 (8.6–10.8) g.

Habits. Very little is known about this western bat. In California large nursery colonies have been found in June under the shingles of large deserted buildings. A few males have been found singly in groups of other species. In the northern part of its range it seems to occur in smaller groups or singly, and most specimens have been collected when flying over water or forest glades.

From Canada it is probably migratory to more southern climes in winter, where it may hibernate in buildings. It is a nocturnal insect feeder, as is normal for its clan.

Habitat. The long-legged bat appears to have a wide preference of habitat from forested regions to areas of open scrub.

Reproduction. This bat breeds about two weeks later than the little brown bat in the northern part of its range. The single young is usually born toward the end of July or in early August.

Economic Status. This bat is too rare in Canada to be of any economic significance. One observer reported that it is usually heavily parasitized by bat bedbugs, *Cimex pilosellus*. This is not the human parasite, which is *Cimex rotundatus*. Other parasites such as lice, fleas, and parasitic flies have also been taken from this species in California. Two specimens taken in 1972 were infected with rabies.

Distribution. The long-legged bat is found in western North America from Mexico to southern Alaska.

Canadian Distribution. The Canadian populations of this species belong to the northern geographical sub-

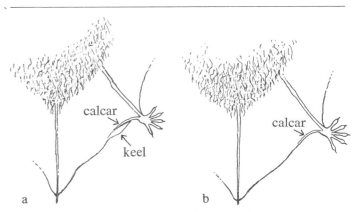
Figure 20 Calcar (a) with and (b) without keel (× 1)

Map 23 Distribution of the long-legged bat, *Myotis volans*

species (see Map 23). It is found sparingly from north-western British Columbia and central Alberta southward.

Myotis volans longicrus (True), 1886, Science 8: 588. Alberta and British Columbia.

REFERENCE

Dalquest, W.W., and M.C. Ramage. 1946. Notes on the long-legged bat (*Myotis volans*) at Old Fort Tejon and vicinity, California. Jour. Mamm. 27(1): 60–3.

CALIFORNIA BAT
Chauve-souris de Californie. *Myotis californicus* (Audubon and Bachman)

Description. The California bat is one of the smallest of the mouse-eared bats, measuring about 3 inches in total length and 8 inches in wing-spread. It is generally rich reddish brown above and buffy brown below. The dark ears are of moderate size and extend about 1 mm beyond the nose when laid forward. The thumbs are very small and delicate (5 mm), as are the hind feet. The calcar is strongly keeled.

The dorsal base of the interfemoral membrane is covered with fine hairs to a line one-third of the way down the tibia. The hairs on the under side of the wings are sparse and occur from the upper arm to the knee only.

Average measurements of adults of both sexes: length 80 (79–84), tail 36 (30–40), hind foot 6.5 (5.5–7.5), ear 13 mm.

Habits. This is one of the commonest small bats of the southern coastal region of British Columbia. It occurs in small summer nursery colonies in rock crevices and under loose bark or eaves of buildings. It is crepuscular and nocturnal, hiding during the daylight hours and emerging at dusk to hunt insects on the wing over lakes, rivers, meadows, and forest clearings. This bat's flight is particularly erratic as it zigzags and twists in pursuit of its prey.

Some California bats remain in the southern portions of the province to hibernate in mine shafts or caves where the temperature remains constantly above 32°F. Others probably fly farther south to their cave homes. Occasionally during mild spells they may emerge and fly about for an evening or two until a cold snap drives them to cover again.

Map 24 Distribution of the California bat, *Myotis californicus*: 1 *M. c. californicus*, 2 *M. c. caurinus*

In the southern United States this species hibernates in colonies, containing both sexes, in mine shafts and natural caves. Observation of these torpid bats has indicated that their body temperatures drop to an average of 53.5°F, while the average cave temperature is 53.2°F. When disturbed, they raise their body temperatures to a threshold of activity by shivering. Even when torpid, they become alarmed by the shrill cries of their neighbours.

Nothing is known of this species' longevity or of its predators, but they are probably similar to other cave-hibernating myotids.

Habitat. The California bats seem to have a wide tolerance of habitat. Although they appear to live in semi-arid regions of the southwest, they live as well in forested regions of the Pacific northwest.

Reproduction. The single young is born in July, as is typical for the group.

Economic Status. These little bats are probably neutral in man's scheme. Their consumption of insects must be balanced against the annoyance they could cause under the shingles of an old house.

The presence of rabies was detected in two specimens taken in 1970.

Distribution. The California bat occupies a wide range in western North American from central Mexico to the Alaskan panhandle.

Canadian Distribution. Two subspecies of the California bat occur in British Columbia. The one on the coast is darker than the one found in the Okanagan valley, which is more cinnamon brown in colour (see Map 24).

Myotis californicus californicus (Audubon and Bachman), 1842, Jour. Acad. Nat. Sci. Philadephia, ser. 1, pt. 2, 8: 285. Okanagan valley, British Columbia.
Myotis californicus caurinus Miller, 1897, N. American Fauna 13: 72. Western British Columbia, including Queen Charlotte and Vancouver islands.

REFERENCE

Reeder, Wm. G. 1949. Hibernating temperature of the bat, *Myotis californicus pallidas*. Jour. Mamm. 30(1): 51–3.

SMALL-FOOTED BAT
Chauve-souris pygmée. *Myotis leibii*
(Audubon and Bachman)

Description. The small-footed bat is probably the smallest mouse-eared bat found in America. It is quite similar to the California bat in appearance. The dorsal colour varies from a burnished coppery brown to a pale buffy grey in the various subspecies. The ears and wing membranes are contrastingly dark brown to dull black. As for the California bat, the base of the interfemoral membrane and the under surfaces of the wing membranes are sparsely furred, but in this species the furred areas are not so extensive. The hind feet and thumbs are similarly extremely weak and small. The ears when laid forward are slightly larger than the California bat's, extending about 1 mm beyond the nose (Plate 1g). The calcar has a pronounced keel. About the only external distinguishing mark is the black facial mask. In all other species of American myotids the sparsely furred facial areas around the eyes, cheeks, nostrils, and lips are natural brown, but in the masked bat these areas, including the ears and chin, are black (Figure 16g). There are other distinguishing characteristics in the skull, which is flattened with a broad cranium (Figure 18d). The sexes are alike, and there is no information available on seasonal moults.

Average measurements of adults: length 77 (72–84), tail 34 (30–38), hind foot 7 (6–8), ear 12 (11–13) mm.

Habits. The small-footed bat is another species of mouse-eared bat that characteristically hibernates in caves. In fact very little is known of this species other than its hibernation period. In eastern North America, it hibernates in a few caves in the Allegheny Mountains from West Virginia to Vermont and in the hills bordering the Ottawa valley in Quebec and Ontario. Nowhere is it common, and usually only a few individuals are found in caves that may shelter many thousands of individuals of other species of myotids. In fact, the largest number ever reported for the species (142) was found in a cave in the Ottawa valley, Ontario. Nothing seems to be known of its hibernating conditions in western North America, but it is thought to have a short hibernation period. It seldom enters its hibernation caves before the last of November, and at least in Pennsylvania it leaves them in early April. The hibernation period is probably longer in Canadian caves. It is also a unique bat in its ability to withstand low temperatures. It is usually found closer to the cave entrance than other species of bats, where it may be subject to cold draughts of dry winter air from outside. It usually picks small cracks in the cave ceiling in which to wedge itself, either alone or in small groups of both sexes of its own species. One interesting feature in suspended small-footed bats is the position of the forearms. In other species of myotids the forearms usually hang parallel in hibernation, but those of the small-footed bat diverge. There are also indications that this hardy bat is often active during the winter, shifting around in the hibernation cave during mild spells. When banded and removed to other near-by caves, it returns to its cave home.

Banding experiments have indicated that this species may live as long as nine years in the wild state.

Little else is known of the small-footed bat during the summer months as it has rarely been taken outside its hibernating caves. Its food habits, diurnal activity pattern, and predators are thought to be similar to those of other mouse-eared bats.

Habitat. In the eastern part of its range this species seems to show a preference for hilly country covered with coniferous forests. However, the choice of habitat of the western subspecies seems to be more towards arid sites.

Reproduction. The breeding habits of this species have not been studied in the same detail as those of the little brown bat. However, the evidence points to similar breeding habits among most of the cave-hibernating species.

Economic Status. The small-footed bat is too rare in Canada to have any economic significance.

Distribution. This species is uncommonly distributed across a broad belt of central North America from New Brunswick and the New England States to southern California.

Canadian Distribution. The range of the small-footed bat reaches Canada in three isolated regions, in each of which well-differentiated subspecies are found (see Map 25).

Myotis leibii ciliolabrum (Merriam), 1886. Proc. Biol. Soc. Washington 4(2): 1–4. An extremely pale form (the palest Canadian myotid): flaxen-coloured above, almost white below, known only from the southern prairies of Alberta.

Myotis leibii leibii (Audubon and Bachman), 1842, Jour. Acad. Nat. Sci. Philadelphia, ser. 1, 8: 284. The typical copper-brown form of southern New Brunswick, Quebec, and Ontario.

Myotis leibii melanorhinus (Merriam), 1890, N. American Fauna 3: 46. An orangy brown form, found in the Okanagan valley of southern British Columbia.

REFERENCES

Hitchcock, H.B. 1949. Hibernation of bats in southeastern Ontario and adjacent Quebec. Canadian Field-Nat. 63(2): 47–59.
Mohr, C.E. 1936. Notes on the least bat, *Myotis subulatus leibii*. Proc. Pennsylvania Acad. Sci., Harrisburg 10: 62–5.

SILVER-HAIRED BAT
Chauve-souris argentée. *Lasionycteris noctivagans*
(LeConte)

Description. After dealing with so many species that are difficult to identify it is a relief to find a species of bat that is easily identifiable in the hand by everyone. The silver-haired bat is of medium size, about 4 inches in total length, with a wing-spread of about 12 inches. The colour is deep

Map 25 Distribution of the small-footed bat, *Myotis leibii*: 1 *M. l. ciliolabrum*, 2 *M. l. leibii*, 3 *M. l. melanorhinus*

chocolate brown, almost black. The hairs of the back and belly are silver-tipped, giving the appearance of a silver-frosted cape. The head and neck lack this frosting (Plate 1h). The ears are black, short, and rounded, as is the blunt tragus. The wing membranes are dark neutral brown. Fine frosted hairs cover the interfemoral membrane for about three-quarters of its length towards the tip of the tail. The sexes are colored alike. The young are almost black, with silver frosting on their backs. The skull is depicted in Figure 18e.

The silver-haired bat is a monotypic species, unique to North America, most closely related to the previously mentioned mouse-eared bats of the genus *Myotis*.

Average measurements of both sexes: total length 103 (97–109), tail 42 (39–50), hind foot 10 (9–11), ear from meatus 14 (12–16), wing-spread 299 (281–312) mm; weight 7–9 g.

Habits. This was one of the first bats to be recognized as undertaking regular seasonal migrations, just as the birds do. In the northern part of its range it generally lives solitarily during the summer months. In late August and September it congregates in flocks containing both sexes to migrate towards its winter quarters in the southern part of its range. Its northward migration occurs in late May. During the autumn migration period silver-haired bats have been observed in large flocks at such out-of-the-way places as Mount Desert Rock, thirty miles off the coast of Maine, and Cape Cod, Massachusetts. A silver-haired bat was among the hundreds of birds that blundered into the Long Point lighthouse during a storm that swept over Lake Erie on September 25, 1929. They have also been observed migrating in flocks, far at sea, off the east coast of the United States, and have been blown as far as Bermuda in autumn storms. A few of these bats hibernate in caves, but most of them seek hiding places under the loose bark of trees, in abandoned woodpecker holes, or in unused sheds, wharves, and even in furled sails and cabins of ships in ports. They hibernate from about Vancouver and New York southward.

During the summer during the daylight hours, they seek

the seclusion of the forest in hollow trees and bulky bird's nests, or under loose bark, and soon after sunset they sally forth to hunt insects. They are the first bats to appear in the evening, and are often seen in broad daylight. At first they generally fly low over water to drink, but later they climb to tree-top level. Their flight seems rather feeble and jerky but at eleven miles an hour it is a little faster than the little brown bat's flight. Sometimes they may be batted-down with a branch rather easily as they course along a stream bank. It is reported that they are strong swimmers and will swim ashore if knocked into the water.

It is unfortunate that so little is known concerning the life history of this interesting species. At present many aspects of its life history and population fluctuations are riddles.

Habitat. The silver-haired bat is usually observed flying over rivers and lakes in the forests. Its food preference may be for emerging aquatic insects.

Reproduction. Little definite information is available on the breeding habits of this species. It is reported to mate in the autumn when the sexes congregate in migration. However, the twin or single young are not born until late June or early July. This suggests that the sperm may remain viable in the uterus during hibernation until ovulation occurs in the spring, as is found in closely related bats.

Nursery colonies of young silver-haired bats have been found in abandoned crow's nests and in piles of lumber. The young are born naked, blind, black, and wrinkled. They grow very rapidly and learn to fly when they are about three weeks old. At that time they are about 90 mm long and have a wing-spread of about 260 mm. At first their flight is rather hesitant and jerky, but by the middle of August they are fully grown and strong flyers, ready to accompany their parents on the southward migration.

Economic Status. The economic role of this bat is unknown. Although commonly distributed, it seldom comes in contact with men in its forest habitat. Single specimens infected with rabies were taken in 1971 and 1973.

Distribution. The silver-haired bat occurs in a broad belt across North America from the southern Maritime Provinces and South Carolina on the Atlantic coast to the Queen Charlotte Islands and northern California on the Pacific coast. The summer distribution is north of a line approximately from Pennsylvania across the Great Plains and the southern Rocky Mountains to Oregon. In winter it migrates from the northern portion of its range south of a line drawn from about New York City in the east across the southern plains to the Pacific coast. It is a winter straggler in Bermuda.

Canadian Distribution. This species is commonly distributed across southern Canada from Nova Scotia to Vancouver Island and northward to Moosonee, Ontario, the Peace River district, and the Queen Charlotte Islands (see Map 26). No variation among the various populations of this species has been recognized.

Lasionycteris noctivagans (LeConte), 1831, *in* McMurtrie, The animal kingdom by Baron Cuvier, 1: appendix, 431.

Map 26 Distribution of the silver-haired bat, *Lasionycteris noctivagans*

REFERENCE

Seton, E.T. 1909. Silvery-bat. *In* Life histories of northern animals, 2: 1166–76. Scribner's Sons, New York.

TOWNSEND'S BIG-EARED BAT
Oreillard de Townsend. *Plecotus townsendii* Cooper

Description. This species is not likely to be confused with any other bat in Canada because of its unusually long ears. The bat itself is about 4 inches long, with a wing-spread of about 11 inches, but the erect ears are fully 1 1/2 inches in length. The muzzle is naked and black, and bears a pair of grotesque lumps that cover the posterior portions of the crescentic nostrils. These lumps are composed of sebaceous glandular tissue covered by coarse skin (Figure 17a; skull Figure 18f).

This bat's rather short, silky pelage is pearly grey above and fades to a light tan beneath. The bases of the ears are covered with shorter, paler woolly hairs. The ears are supported by folded ridges, which are also haired for about half their length. The outer halves have about a dozen horizontal creases, which facilitate folding. The ears and wing membranes are dark and naked. The calcars are prominent, and the interfemoral membrane extends to the tip of the tail.

Adults have a single complete annual moult in August.

The new short hairs appear simultaneously all over the body. Immatures are darker and duller. The juveniles assume the adult pelage at about the age of one to two months in their first summer.

Average measurements of the typical race (as is usual for bats, females average slightly larger than males): females: total length 107 (100–112), tail 48 (46–53), hind foot 12 (11–12), ear from notch 33 (30–36), wing-spread 316 (310–321) mm; males: total length 100 (96–103), tail 46 (44–51), hind foot 11 (10–11), ear from notch 30, wing-spread 307 (300–314) mm.

Habits. Townsend's big-eared bat is another one of the cave hibernators, although it has been quick to occupy suitable man-made accommodation such as mine shafts. Townsend reported in 1839 that these bats occupied the Hudson's Bay Company's fur warehouses in the Columbia River district soon after they were built. They received protection by the fur traders because of their habit of eating the carpet beetles that abounded in the stored furs. In the southwest, where natural caves are rare, they roost in abandoned forts, missions, stage stations, and warehouses.

It is a sociable species and forms closely packed clusters of both sexes containing up to hundreds of individuals. It seems to prefer open ceilings, walls, or beams, and seldom crawls into a crevice. When it alights on a wall or ceiling to roost, it swoops up from below. Just before contact it folds its wings and agilely flips over so that its feet can grasp an anchorage. Asleep, the big-eared bat hangs by its feet, folds its wings over its body, lets its tail membrane droop to cover its posterior portions, and folds its long ears, accordion-like, along the side of its neck. The tragus, which remains erect, may be confused with the true ear until the latter unfolds. When disturbed, these bats unfold their wings and wave them about, a performance that gives the whole cluster of bats a weird appearance.

Townsend's big-eared bats generally hibernate in caves and mine shafts where the temperature is 37° to 62°F. Temperatures as low as 28.5°F have been measured near torpid bats, but the general body temperature of the cluster could be more. It is thought that if the temperature drops to 32°F the bats awaken and move to a better location. Variable humidity, drafts, and light conditions seem to be tolerated to some extent. It has been pointed out that the bats cluster in cool winter quarters to lower their metabolic activity and conserve their fat supply to make it last the winter season, so that high temperatures would be undesirable at that point.

The big-eared bat is easily aroused during its torpid period. Considerable movement in the caves in winter is probably quite normal. On awakening, the bat's temperature rises at a rate of about 1.8°F per minute from the environmental temperature. Flight becomes possible when the temperature reaches about 74°F. Flight speeds are six to twelve miles an hour.

In the southern portions of their range these bats become torpid during cold spells, but they remain active during warm periods. In the northern portion of their range, they enter their hibernating caves in mid-October and do not reappear until after mid-April. The males seem to hibernate less than the females.

During the summer months bands of females and young bats occupy temporary nursery roosts, while the males segregate and roost alone or in small groups. After the crepuscular forage, the bats return to temporary night roosts. During the summer they choose to roost in natural crevices, abandoned warehouses, and steeples. Although most observers report that this bat is late in emerging to hunt, some have reported that it flies high when first emerging in the evening and descends towards the ground as night approaches. Its flight is slow and cautious, with deep, measured wing-beats.

There is no evidence of long migrations in this species. Banded bats transported elsewhere have been known to return home from distances of up to twenty-eight miles. However, this bat seems to object to disturbances, usually deserting disturbed roosts. Populations in California have been estimated at one bat to every 419 acres, but densities are probably much less in its range in Canada.

The food of this species has not been studied in detail, but it is known to feed upon moths, which it pursues by echo location. It frequently utters a high-pitched grating squeak.

Habitat. Townsend's big-eared bat shows a wide adaptability to variations in terrain throughout its wide distribution. It seems to avoid deserts and prairies but inhabits cultivated valleys bordered by open deciduous forests, brush, or even coniferous forests.

Reproduction. The mating season extends from early October to late February. Most females have mated before entering the hibernating caves. Juvenile males probably do not reproduce in their first autumn. Mating continues spasmodically during hibernation in the southern roosts at least. Sperms are stored in the female uteri until spring. Spring matings have not been confirmed in this species. Ovulation occurs between February and April when the hibernation is broken. The exact period of gestation depends on the body temperature of the bat and on the period in which the female was lethargic after ovulation. It varies from 56 to 100 days in California populations. The young are born between mid-April and late July, the later date probably being closer to the parturition date in Canada. A single young is the rule for this species, and 98 per cent of the embryos are carried in the right horn of the uterus.

The birth of the young in captivity has been observed. The female hung suspended by her hind feet and thumbs. The wings and tail membrane were cupped to form a cradle for the young, which arrived in the normal breech presentation for bats. The youngster soon fastened itself both to a nipple and to the roof by means of its hind toes. Nursing proceeded in this upside-down fashion.

The new-born Townsend's big-eared bat has been described as a grotesque creature, pink, naked, and blind, with floppy ears and disproportionately large fingers and toes that give it a spider-like appearance. It weighs about 2.4 g at birth, but growth is rapid. Within a few hours it chirps. Short grey hairs cover the naked pink body in the

Map 27 Distribution of Townsend's big-eared bat, *Plecotus townsendii*: 1 *P. t. pallescens*, 2 *P. t. townsendii*

first week. At seven days the ears are erect, and soon afterwards the eyes open. It learns to fly when about three weeks old and at six weeks joins its mother on nightly forages.

Young big-eared bats are carried by their mothers for a very short period – perhaps only a day or so – and are then usually left hanging in the roost during routine flights. One observer remarked that upon disturbing a nursery roost all the adults took off in alarm, but to his amazement the cluster outline remained, formed by the tiny suspended young. On such occasions the mothers on their return unerringly find their own young in the cluster. Occasionally in the haste of exit a youngster may be transported dangling from a teat or dropped carelessly on the cavern floor. These miscues are usually quickly rectified, however, and the young bats are rescued. Weaning usually occurs at about the age of two months.

Economic Status. Big-eared bats have too restricted a distribution in Canada to have much economic importance. Their food habits are not known in enough detail to decide whether they are beneficial or not. Their mode of

life is such that they seldom come in contact with humans. When one recalls their early use as insect eaters in fur storage warehouses, perhaps they should be given the benefit of the doubt.

These bats do not seem to harbour such ectoparasites as ticks, lice, fleas, or bedbugs. They have, however, been found to be infested with peculiar parasitic wingless flies of the families Steblidae and Nycteribiidae, which infest many other species of bats as well. So far, this species has not been incriminated as a carrier of rabies.

Distribution. Townsend's big-eared bat is broadly distributed in western North America from Central Mexico to central British Columbia. There is an eastern offshoot of the range in the caves of the Allegheny Mountains in Virginia.

Canadian Distribution. Two geographical races of Townsend's big-eared bat are recognized in British Columbia (see Map 27). The typical form is found in the southwestern region of the province, and a paler form is found in the interior plateau as far north as Williams Lake, where it hibernates in mine shafts. The interior specimens are not considered typical of *pallescens* but rather inter-grade between that and the darker coastal race.

Plecotus townsendii pallescens Miller, 1897, N. American Fauna 13: 52. Central British Columbia, intergrading with next form.
Plecotus townsendii townsendii Cooper, 1837, Ann. Lyc. Nat. Hist. New York, 4: 73. Lower Fraser River delta and southeastern Vancouver Island, British Columbia.

REFERENCE

Pearson, O.P., Mary R. Koford, and Anita K. Pearson. 1952. Reproduction of the lump-nosed bat (*Coryno-rhinus rafinesquei*) in California. Jour. Mamm. 33: 273–320.

EASTERN PIPISTRELLE
Pipistrelle de l'Est. *Pipistrellus subflavus* (F. Cuvier)

Description. The pipistrelles constitute a group of little bats widely distributed in both the Old World and the New World. The present species is the only one that occurs in Canada. It is also probably the smallest bat in Canada, measuring about 3 inches in length, with a wing-spread of about 8 inches.

The general colour of the eastern pipistrelle is a grizzled yellowish brown, caused by tri-coloration of the individual dorsal hairs. The hairs are plumbeous at the base, next to which is a yellowish ring, followed by dark brown tips. Since the pelage is rather woolly in texture, the whole effect is a grizzled yellowish brown. The ventral surface is less grizzled and is a paler buffy brown. (Occasionally melanistic individuals occur.) The ears are relatively short, with a tapered, rounded tip; the tragus is also short but relatively slim. The wings are extremely delicate and rather shorter and broader than in the genus *Myotis*. The thumbs and hind feet are relatively large. The hind toes are covered with fine reddish hairs. The interfemoral membrane is similarly sparsely haired at the base of the dorsal surface. The calcar is prominent but is not keeled (the skull is depicted in Figure 18g). There is no information on moults.

In this species (as is true for many other species of bats) the females are slightly larger than the males. The males average: total length 86 (73–89), tail 40 (36–45), hind foot 9.9 (8–10), ear 13.9 mm; the females average: total length 89, tail 41, hind foot 9.7, ear 14.1, wing-spread 245 mm. The weight varies from about 3.5 to 6 g, depending upon sex and season.

Habits. Although the eastern pipistrelle is another one of the cave hibernators, it seems to be particularly sensitive to the cold. It enters the caves during the first autumn frosts, about mid-October, and remains until the warm weather returns in May. During the winter months it enters a state of profound torpor, from which it is seldom aroused until spring. In this feature it is unlike the mouse-eared bats of the genus *Myotis*, which are easily disturbed and easily awakened during hibernation. Since the pipistrelle selects the warmest (about 40–42°F), the most draft-free, and the dampest portions of the caverns in which to hibernate, it may be found at the most remote reaches of tunnels. The pipistrelle avoids other species of bats and hangs up either singly or in small clusters of both sexes in small crevices in cavern walls and ceilings, or it may hang suspended from a smooth ceiling.

In the southern portion of their range in Mexico, pipistrelles have been observed hanging among dead leaves in bushes. When captured they utter a high-pitched, rasping chirp.

During the summer months the sexes segregate, as is usual for bats. Seemingly sociable among their own kind, small nursery groups of females have been known to return for three years to a favourite attic colony.

The pipistrelle has a very weak fluttering flight and resembles a large moth at dusk. It is among the slowest flyers, at a speed of four to six miles an hour. It seeks shelter during the daylight hours in a cave, crevice, or attic, or in the foliage of a tree. It appears in the early evening to hunt flying insects such as flies, beetles, ants, and ichneumon flies, high in the tree-tops.

Banding studies have shown that this diminutive bat may live as long as ten years in the wild state.

Habitat. The pipistrelle prefers to flit across slow-moving rivers or to hunt among the bordering trees and pastures. Although it commonly associates with the red and silver-haired bats, it seldom is found among little brown bats.

Reproduction. With one or two notable exceptions, the breeding habits of the pipistrelle in broad outline follow the reproductive cycle of the cave-dwelling mouse-eared bats (*Myotis*). The pre-oestrous or receptive season of females in this species seems to be prolonged, as found in the myotids. Mating occurs regularly in October when the bats enter the caves and the sexes meet for the first time in five months. At that time probably only the individuals over one year old mate. The same phenomenon of the sperm remaining viable in the female uteri for periods over a month has been observed in this species as well. A second period of mating, which includes the yearlings, occurs in spring, just prior to the bats' departure from the caverns; ovulation then follows after the females emerge. Effective insemination probably results from the spring matings.

Pipistrelles differ from myotids in that a number of eggs are shed from both ovaries during ovulation. The usual number of young born is two, occasionally one. This means that there is a regular absorption of embryos *in utero*. The exact period of gestation is unknown. In Canada the young are born from late June to early July. Like the little brown bats, they are carried for the first two or three days of their lives by their mothers. When they get too heavy, they are deposited in the nurseries to await their mothers' return from the evening forages. They learn to fly for themselves when approximately one month old.

Economic Status. The pipistrelle is too rare in Canada to be of any economic importance. It has seldom been taken outside its hibernating caves.

Distribution. The eastern pipistrelle is found in eastern

Map 28 Distribution of the eastern pipistrelle, *Pipistrellus subflavus*

North America from the Yucatan Peninsula and Florida northward to the Great Lakes.

Canadian Distribution. In Canada this species is confined to small areas of southern Ontario and southeastern Quebec and in southern Nova Scotia (see Map 28). Although the northern populations are somewhat darker, they are thought to belong to the typical race of eastern North America.

Pipistrellus subflavus subflavus (F. Cuvier), 1832, Nouv. Ann. Mus. Hist. Nat. Paris 1: 17. Southern Ontario and southeastern Quebec.

REFERENCES

Davis, W.H., and R.E. Mumford. 1962. Ecological notes on the bat *Pipistrellus subflavus*. American Midl. Nat. 68(2): 394–8.
Guthrie, M.J. 1933. Notes on the seasonal movements and habits of some cave bats. Jour. Mamm. 14(1): 1–18.
– 1933. The reproductive cycles of some cave bats. Jour. Mamm. 14(3): 199–216.

BIG BROWN BAT
Grande Chauve-souris brune. *Eptesicus fuscus* (Palisot de Beauvois)

Description. The big brown bat probably exhibits the highest adaptability to civilization among North American bats. It and the little brown bat have been quick to move in to share man's accommodation. As a result of their broad American distribution and their occupation of buildings, these are the two species of bats that are most likely to come in contact with man.

Despite its name, the big brown bat is really only a medium-sized bat, about 5 inches long, including the tail, with a wing-spread of about 13 inches (Figure 21 and Plate 1j). The pelage of this species is rather oily in texture and rusty brown in colour. The underparts are greyish brown. The naked wing and tail membranes are almost black and are rather leathery in texture. The tip of the tail projects beyond the interfemoral membrane; the large hind feet have large claws; the calcar has a pronounced keel. Except for the forehead, the face is almost naked; the skin is blackish, and the lips are fleshy. The black ears are moderate in size and are rounded. The tragus is relatively short and broad. The bright black eyes are normal in size. There are a few vibrissae on the side of the nose (Figure 16b; skull Figure 18b). This bat moults in early summer. When disturbed, big brown bats utter a piercing, rasping cry.

Average measurements of adults: total length 120 (114–131), tail 50 (42–54), hind foot 12 (10–14), ear 18, wing-spread 335 (317–356) mm. The weight of the big brown bat varies with the season and the sex. It puts on a tremendous amount of fat before it goes into hibernation and loses a great deal of this weight during this period. Females enter hibernation weighing on the average 21.5 g and emerge weighing about 16.1 g. Males weigh an average of 20.6 g in the autumn and 13.7 g on emerging in the spring. The females gain weight more rapidly in the spring because they are pregnant.

Habits. Originally this species was a forest-dweller and during the warm months used hollow trees for daytime hideaways and nurseries. Many big brown bats still follow this mode of life, but large numbers have become civilized and during the summer months seek shelter behind shutters and loose boards, under shingles and eaves, and in attics and church belfries. During this period the sexes are

Figure 21 Big and little brown bat, big brown bat in flight

segregated, and most groups of roosting bats are nursery colonies of females with young. The males roost separately, and alone or in small bachelor groups. After the young have grown and are on the wing, the sexes reunite in late summer and autumn, when mixed roosts may be found.

The big brown bat is a strong flyer with deliberate wing beats and more direct flight than the smaller species. Its flight speed is eight to fifteen miles an hour. It often appears soon after sunset and may be seen flying high above the trees. Sometimes this species is seen about in broad daylight, particularly when looking for a place to hibernate in the autumn. Unlike the pipistrelle, the big brown bat is able to withstand severe winter conditions to an incredible degree. It enters hibernation late in the autumn, usually just when winter sets in in earnest, which may be as late as early December.

This species does not enter a very deep state of hibernation, and when a mild spell occurs in winter it may become fully active again and fly about in buildings or caverns. It is probably the first bat to emerge from hibernation in April. (I saw one on the wing in Ottawa on March 29, 1962.) When disturbed in hibernation, the bats awaken, raise their body temperatures by shivering, and after a period of about five minutes take to shaky flight about their winter quarters. If the disturbance ceases they soon regroup and return to their winter sleep.

Banding studies have shown that the big brown bat seldom wanders far from home. The average distance travelled is probably under twenty miles. One travelled sixty-one miles during the month of November and another thirty-three miles during the summer. They also show ability to return to their homes when transported distances of up to forty-five miles.

The big brown bat was originally a cave hibernator, and many still spend the winters in caves. They usually pick spots in the semi-darkness near the cave entrances to hang. If the cave shelters a large population of big brown bats, they hang in tightly packed clusters containing as many as a hundred or more individuals. If the colony is small, they may hibernate singly or in small groups, but they always avoid the company of other species. The ideal environmental conditions for hibernation seem to be a temperature of about 42°F with a relative humidity of about 80 per cent. They can, however, tolerate quite drafty conditions, and a wide range from the conditions ideal for hibernation. In the entrances and in drafty corridors of some caves in Canada the relative humidity may be quite low, and the temperature may be as low as freezing or even slightly below freezing. Bats can remain alive with a body temperature slightly below 32 degrees, although if it drops much lower, intercellular ice crystals form and they die. I have found big brown bats frozen to death in the entrance of LaFleche Cave, Gatineau County, Quebec.

Big brown bats also regularly hibernate in buildings, as well as in natural caverns and mine shafts. They have been found in frost-covered tunnels, hanging on cellar walls, and in crannies about windows, skylights, and attics. In Canada they are the commonest bat to hibernate in buildings. As mentioned previously, big brown bats enter hibernation in November in an extremely fat condition. The amount of fat may be as much as a third of the body weight. They do not feed during hibernation, however, but maintain their reduced metabolic rate by utilizing the stored fat. During hibernation the females lose approximately 30 mg of weight daily and the males drop about 38.5 mg a day. Upon emergence in spring, only about 10 per cent of the body weight remains as fat. It has been estimated that bats of average weight have enough fat to survive about 194 days in hibernation. Theoretically a prolonged winter could reduce some of the bats to the threshold of survival. Indeed, the fact that a few emaciated bodies of dead brown bats have been found in spring suggests that they entered hibernation without sufficient fat to survive and therefore perished of starvation before food was available again. Big brown bats, upon awakening from hibernation, have been noted to drink avidly. This thirst may be associated with dehydration connected with fat metabolism.

Big brown bats live upon flying insects captured in their pouched interfemoral membrane. An analysis of their food indicates that they eat the following orders of insects, in the order of abundance (by per cent) listed: Coleoptera (beetles) 36.1, Hymenoptera (flying ants, etc.) 26.3, Diptera (flies, craneflies) 13.2, Plecoptera (stoneflies) 6.5, Ephemeridae (mayflies) 4.6, Hemiptera (bugs) 3.4, Trichoptera (caddisflies) 3.2, Neuroptera (lacewing flies) 3.2, Mecoptera (scorpion flies) 2.7, Orthoptera (dragonflies, etc.) 0.6. They have been known to catch 2.7 g of insects per hour on the wing. In captivity they eat the equivalent of about a third their body weight in fly pupae each day.

Big brown bats probably have few natural enemies. Perhaps owls take a few on the wing, and grounded bats fall prey to skunks, opossums, and snakes. Banding records have indicated that this species may reach an age of over nine years in the wild, but these are thought to be exceptional cases. The average annual mortality is about 40 per cent, and few survive beyond seven years of age.

Habitat. Big brown bats have become quite urbanized. They are commonly observed at dusk flying along lamplit streets in our cities, towns, and villages, swooping after the insects attracted to the lights. They may be seen around farm buildings, meadows, and ponds.

Reproduction. Next to the breeding habits of the little brown bat, probably those of the big brown bat are best known. All male big brown bats reach breeding condition by late August, the older males ahead of the young. Since spermatogenesis ends in mid-October, mating probably occurs in the autumn. Females in hibernation have viable sperms in their uteri, which may survive three months. Spring matings have not been confirmed. Ovulation occurs about the first week in April, and the young arrive between mid-May and mid-June (the peak is between May 20 and 30). About a quarter of the young females do not mature early enough to bear young the first year of their lives. Usually four ova are released during ovulation, and the number of embryos implanted varies from one to four.

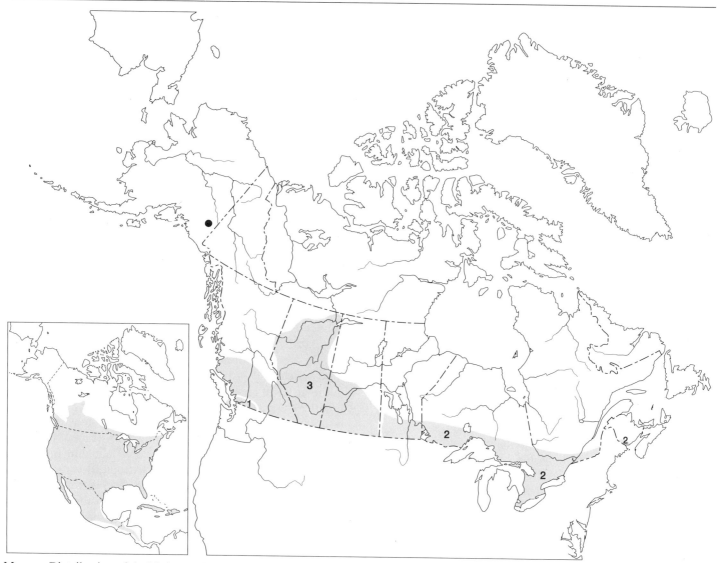

Map 29 Distribution of the big brown bat, *Eptesicus fuscus*: 1 *E. f. bernardinus*, 2 *E. f. fuscus*, 3 *E. f. pallidus*, ● extra-limital record

Since there are only two pectoral mammae, however, it is impossible for more than two to survive. A peculiar deviation in reproduction between eastern and western populations of *Eptesicus* has been noted. Western females usually bear yearly only one young, but those from eastern North America usually bear a litter of two young.

The young bats weigh about 2.5 g at birth, and grow very rapidly. The eyes open towards the end of the first week. The mother carries the young with her in flight during the first few days, but later she leaves them hanging in the nursery, which is often a hollow tree. When they are scarcely a month old, the young are weaned and learn to fly. The colony then may move to less secluded quarters such as shutters or behind loose boards and shingles. The young reach adult size by August, when there is much shifting among the colonies as the males join the group.

Economic Status. The big brown bat is one of the two most important Canadian bats because of its wide distribution and cohabitation with man. Whatever good the animal does in its destruction of insects is overbalanced by its nuisance value in occupying buildings. This bat freely enters open windows and doors to find suitable dark roosting areas both in summer and late autumn, and drastic steps are often required to rid one's home of the unwelcome guest. (For methods of controlling bats see section under the little brown bat.)

The big brown bat also constitutes a grave public health menace because it is the commonest rabies carrier. This species has been confirmed as a rabies vector in southern British Columbia, Quebec, and southern Ontario. The first known case of a rabid bat in eastern Canada was noted in the Toronto area in the autumn of 1961 and was attributed to this species.

Distribution. The big brown bat occupies most of Central and North America.

Canadian Distribution. This species is found across most of southern Canada from New Brunswick to British Columbia and northward as far as Wood Buffalo Park, northern Alberta. Three geographic races are recognized across the country (see Map 29).

Eptesicus fuscus bernardinus Rhoads, 1902, Proc. Acad. Nat. Sci. Philadelphia 53: 619. Southwestern British Columbia; a rich brown form.

Eptesicus fuscus fuscus (Palisot de Beauvois), 1796, Cat. raisonné du mus. de M. C.W. Peale, Philadelphia, p. 18. Eastern Canada west to eastern Saskatchewan.

Eptesicus fuscus pallidus Young, 1908, Proc. Acad. Nat. Sci. Philadelphia 60: 408. Western Prairies and south-eastern British Columbia.

REFERENCE

Phillips, Gary L. 1966. Ecology of the big brown bat (Chiroptera: Vespertilionidae) in northeastern Kansas. American Midl. Nat. 75(1): 168–98.

EVENING BAT
Chauve-souris vespérale. *Nycticeius humeralis* (Rafinesque)

Description. The evening bat is a more southern species, whose range barely reaches southwestern Ontario. It looks like a miniature big brown bat. The pelage is thin and short, muddy brown above and paler below. The ears are short and rounded; the tragus is blunt. The ears and wing membranes are black, hairless, and leathery. The skull is short, broad, and flat. The number of teeth is thirty.

Average measurements of both sexes: total length 93 (85–93), tail 37, hind foot 7–9, ear from notch 14 mm. Average weight of females 10.4 g.

Habits. The evening bat lives in small colonies, hiding in hollow trees and church steeples or behind shutters. The sexes are segregated during the summer months. Very little seems to be known concerning the life history of this species.

Habitat. This bat frequents cultivated and natural clearings in the southeastern hardwood forests.

Reproduction. It is thought that this species breeds after late August when the sexes reunite. Twins are born to the females in nursery colonies during the first week of June, all the females of a colony appearing to bear their young almost simultaneously. The young weigh about 1.6 to 1.8 g at birth, approximately 25 per cent of the weight of the mother. Many mothers have been seen carrying only single young, but twin embryos are the rule. The females carry their young on their hunting forages for a period of up to ten days after birth, and then they cache them in the nursery crèche.

Economic Status. This species is too rare in Canada to be of any economic significance.

Distribution. The range of the species is southeastern United States from the Gulf of Mexico to the lower Great Lakes (see Map 30).

Canadian Distribution. Only one Canadian specimen has been secured; it was taken at Point Pelee, Lake Erie, Ontario, in May 1911.

Nycticeius humeralis humeralis (Rafinesque), 1818, American Monthly Mag. 3(6): 445. Southwestern Ontario.

Map 30 Distribution of the evening bat, *Nycticeius humeralis*

REFERENCE

Gates, W.H. 1941. A few notes on the evening bat, *Nycticeius humeralis* (Rafinesque). Jour. Mamm. 22(1): 53–6.

RED BAT
Chauve-souris rousse. *Lasiurus borealis* (Müller)

Description. The red bat and the larger hoary bat exhibit enough important differences from the previously mentioned vespertilionid bats to separate them into a distinctive New World tribe. The red bat is our most handsome species (Plate 1f). It is of medium size, with the narrow pointed wings providing a wing-spread of about 11 inches. The fur is long and silky, completely lacking the oily texture of the big brown bat's. The male is a bright brick red above, a little paler below. The fur is actually tri-coloured: the base is black, the central portion is tawny yellow, and the tips are brick red. There are a pair of creamy shoulder flashes and frosting around the neck. A special feature is the heavy furring of the dorsal surface of the interfemoral membrane, of the hind legs, and at the bases of the wing membranes. On the under side, the interfemoral membrane is only furred at the base, but the short red fur extends along the forearm to include the wrist (Figure 22). The blunt face and the backs of the short, rounded ears are densely covered with short orange fur.

The eyes are small but bright. The thumbs are long and have a basal patch of buffy hairs (Figure 16a).

A unique feature of this species is the difference in the appearance of the sexes. Compared to the males the females are a paler, mahogany colour, much frosted by the cream-coloured tips to the dorsal hairs. They too have prominent creamy shoulder flashes. The female's head is more buffy than the male's. Otherwise the pelage is similar in extent. There is no information available on the moult.

The skull is short and broad with an inflated brain-case. The tooth formula is also distinctive.

Average measurements of adults of both sexes: total length 103 (95–112), tail 49 (45–62), hind foot 9 (8–10), ear from notch 10, wing-spread 330 mm; weight 9.5–15 g.

Habits. In marked contrast to the cave bats, the red bat is a solitary tree-dwelling species. During the daylight hours it hangs suspended by its hind claws in a favourite tree roost. It is perhaps not strictly solitary in that the young often cluster near their mother in late summer. They do not seem to be too particular concerning the species of tree used for roosting; although American elms are chosen most frequently, they also roost in Norway spruce, scotch pine, hard maples, fruit trees, and ornamental vines. The roost varies from five to forty feet from the ground, and is most often on the north side. They appear as dark objects suspended in a group of leaves or hanging from branches. Unless disturbed they return regularly to the same spot each morning.

In a special study of red bats in the town of Lewis, Iowa, 150 bats were estimated to inhabit its 1,650 trees. This population gave an estimated density of one bat to an acre and one family of bats to every 4.5 acres. Sometimes several bats roosted in a single tree.

Red bats occasionally roost in the entrances to caves, especially during migrations, but this habit is thought to be unusual.

These bats emerge from their daytime roosts early in the evening to hunt for flying insects. The flight is relatively

Figure 22 Red and silver-haired bat, red bat in flight

more direct and leisurely than that of the mouse-eared bats, and they fly most frequently at the height of the tree foliage. They are also about at dawn and seek the shelter of trees as the light increases.

There is little information on the diet of this species, though moths and tiny beetles have been identified as food remains. There is no information on longevity.

The red bat is another migratory species, commencing its southward migration in early September. Occasionally at this season it has been met in flocks, by ships far out at sea. This species reaches Bermuda with some regularity in October, usually remaining there a few weeks until the animals are strong enough to attempt the flight to the mainland. They have been found as far north as Long Island, New York, in December but generally migrate southward to the more southern areas from Washington, D.C., to the Gulf States where frosts occur only occasionally. In these areas they probably hibernate in hollow trees. The northward migration commences in April and reaches Iowa in early May and Canada towards the end of the month. During the migration periods they are occasionally observed flying in broad daylight.

Besides natural predators such as hawks and owls, red bats face a variety of other hazards. They have been found stuck to burdocks and snagged by barbed-wire fences. They have also been killed by lighthouses during migration; red bats were among the victims picked up at the Long Point lighthouse on Lake Erie in September 1929. Roosting bats are occasionally discovered by sharp-eyed blue jays and blackbirds and have been known to defend themselves and their young. Occasionally at dawn early-hunting hawks capture late-flying bats.

Habitat. The red bat was probably originally an inhabitant of the forest glades. With the advent of European culture, however, it quickly adapted to the village and town habitat where it found ideal hunting by hawking for insects attracted to the street lights.

Reproduction. Another feature that distinguishes the red bat and its relatives from the previously mentioned species is the possession of four teats and therefore larger litters. The young bats probably do not mature during the first summer. Mating takes place in August among adults. Several observers have reported aerial matings, and another observer saw a coupled pair fall to the ground. There must be some form of delayed fertilization or implantation since the young are not born until early June. The number of young in a litter varies from one to four, with an average of 2.3. The young are tiny at birth, weighing only 0.5 g. The female carries her young for a much longer time than the myotids do, leaving them behind only when they become such a burden that she can no longer safely navigate. Females have been caught carrying young whose combined weight was about three-quarters the weight of the adult. (Occasionally a female is 'grounded' by the excessive weight of the young.) After this stage, the young hang alone in the trees while their mother is away foraging, but they scuttle over to nurse when she returns. By midsummer they are strong enough to commence

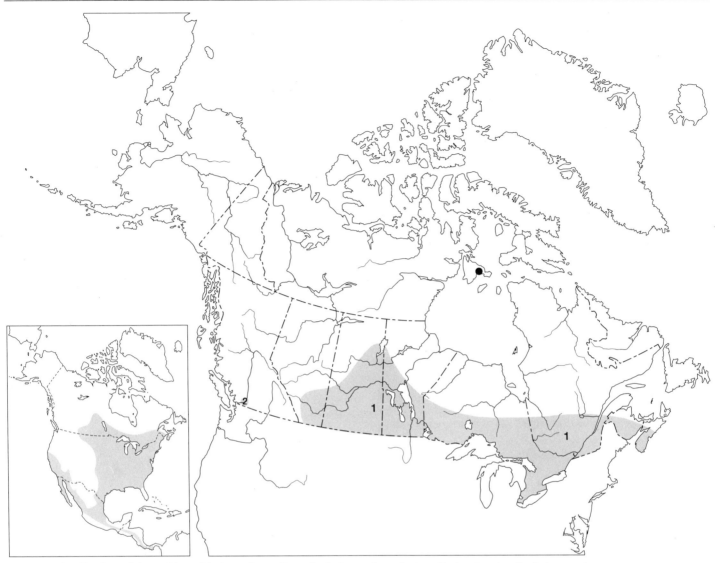

Map 31 Distribution of the red bat, *Lasiurus borealis*: 1 *L. b. borealis*, 2 *L. b. teliotis*, ● extra-limital record

flying and hunting, although they continue to roost beside their mother.

Economic Status. Lacking evidence on the feeding habits of these attractive and unusual creatures, it is difficult to appraise their economic importance. It was expected that they might become involved as carriers of bat rabies because of their migratory habits, but fortunately, they have not been incriminated in Canada so far. Perhaps their solitary behaviour lessens the risk of contact with other carriers. In any event their arboreal habits seldom bring them in contact with humans.

Distribution. The red bat enjoys a wide distribution across the continent from southern Canada to Central America and straying to Bermuda. However, it is absent from the central arid steppes of the United States. Closely related forms are also found in the Carribbean Islands and in Hawaii.

Canadian Distribution. The red bat is found across southern Canada from Nova Scotia to southern Alberta. It

has also been recorded in southwestern British Columbia. There are several unusual records of stray red bats: one at Coral Harbour, Southhamptom Island, Northwest Territories; and others miles at sea, southeast of Nova Scotia. These observations indicate that red bats are strong flyers and are frequently carried far across water during migration (see Map 31). Two geographic races are recognized in Canada.

Lasiurus borealis borealis (Müller), 1776, Des Ritters, Carl von Linne ... vollstandiges Natursystem ... Suppl., p. 20. Eastern and central Canada.
Lasiurus borealis teliotis (H. Allen), 1891, Proc. American Phil. Soc. 29: 5. Known only from one specimen from Skagit, British Columbia.

REFERENCE

McLure, H.E. 1942. Summer activities of bats (genus *Lasiurus*) in Iowa. Jour. Mamm. 23(4): 430–4.

HOARY BAT
Chauve-souris cendrée. *Lasiurus cinereus*
(Palisot de Beauvois)

Description. The hoary bat is the largest bat found in Canada, measuring almost 6 inches in total length, with a wing-spread of 17 inches. The common name gives a pretty good description of this bat (Plate 1e). The fur is long, dense, and silky. The individual hairs of the back have four different bands of colour; the base is slate-coloured, then comes a tawny-yellow band, followed by a dark brown band, and finally the silver tips. The over-all effect is a dark mahogany brown with a silver frosting over the back. The fur extends onto the bases of the wing membranes and completely covers the dorsal surface of the interfemoral membrane. On the ventral surface only the base of the interfemoral membrane has hair, but a tawny woolly covering extends out the arms to include bases of the fourth and fifth fingers. There is also a tawny patch at the base of the strong thumb as well as on the throat. The ears are thick and broad and are rimmed with black. The tragus is short and blunt. The face is foreshortened, and the muzzle is black (Figure 23). The sexes are coloured alike. Nothing is known of the moulting sequence. The skull is illustrated in Figure 18c.

Average measurements of adults: total length 136 (130–144), tail 60 (55–66), hind foot 12.5 (10–15), ear from notch 17.5, wing-spread 403 (384–415) mm; weight about 26 g.

Habits. The hoary bat, like its smaller relative the red bat, is a solitary, tree-dwelling species. Like so many generalizations in biology, both qualifiers must be explained. Hoary bats have been observed hunting in groups, and on rare occasions they have been found roosting in caves. The hoary bat normally roosts among the leaves of trees during the daylight hours. Since it emerges very late in the evening to hunt, it is seldom observed. My first contact with the hoary bat was on a museum expedition to northern Saskatchewan. I had been on the alert for bats on the shore of a lake at dusk. Finally the light was so

poor that I despaired of seeing one and returned to my tent to prepare some other specimens. Another member of the party was willing to remain and hunt, so I handed him the small shotgun. A few minutes later when it was quite dark I heard a shot, followed by his exclamation, 'I think I shot a night-hawk!' When the specimen was brought into the light of the tent it was found to be a large glistening hoary bat! The flight of the hoary bat is strong, swift (nine to thirteen miles an hour), and direct. The long, pointed wings also lend to the impression of a night-hawk in flight. Little is known of its particular insect prey. The fact that it has been observed on rare occasions pursuing smaller flying bats suggests it might eat smaller bats. When caught, the hoary bat utters shrill strident squeals.

This species is also migratory. During migrations it may be observed occasionally flying in daylight, roosting in leafless tall shrubs, or hiding in bulky squirrel's nests. The migration usually commences during the last week of August in the more northern portions of its range and extends through September, the last bats passing through southern Ontario in October. Hoary bats spend the winter in the southern states from coastal California to the Gulf States, and they are regular visitors to Bermuda during the winter months. The bats are also carried far out to sea by storms during migrations. The northward spring migration begins as early as the end of March in Kansas and continues through April and May in California. They reach Indiana in mid-May and southern Canada by the end of the month.

There is a marked segregation of the sexes during the spring and early summer. The males seem to wander erratically at that time and are never found in association with the females who are caring for their young. In mountainous states such as New Mexico the migration may be altitudinal, and the males may spend the summer in high boreal 'islands.'

Habitat. The hoary bat is a forest dweller, particularly of the northern coniferous forests. It also inhabits the more southern broad-leafed forests or shaded village streets. It is most frequently observed hunting over lakes or glades in the forest's canopy.

Reproduction. Very little is known of the reproductive cycle in this species. It is thought to mate in August, as does the red bat. The young are born in mid-June, most probably between the 12th and 20th. The female has four teats, and the litter size varies between one and four. Two young seems to be the usual number, however. The long period between mating and parturition suggests retention of viable sperm until spring ovulation, as found in females of other species. It is noteworthy that a female captured in Kansas on March 29 was apparently not pregnant. The birth of one young hoary bat has been observed. During parturition the female hung upside down and cradled the new-born young with her body and wings. Curiously, the birth observed was the second of twins, and during the process the first born had been temporarily cached on its mother's back. After the birth of the second, the first was transferred to a breast with the aid of one hind foot. The young hoary bat weighs approximately 4.5 g at birth. The young are carried by the female until they are about half-

Figure 23 Hoary bat

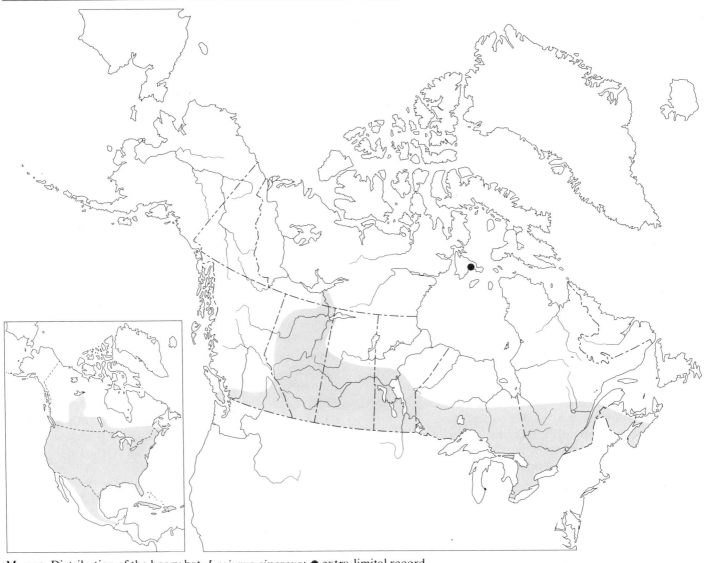

Map 32 Distribution of the hoary bat, *Lasiurus cinereus*: ● extra-limital record

grown. One observer has noted a female bat being 'grounded' by the weight of the young: the female weighed 20.8 g, and the immature bats weighed 13.9 and 14.2 g each, a combined weight of 25 per cent more than that of the female.

When they are older, hoary bats roost alongside their mother in a favourite tree. By the age of one month they learn to fly and fend for themselves.

Economic Status. The hoary bat is generally considered to be a rare species. It seldom comes in direct contact with man and is therefore of little economic importance. It is mainly of interest because it is a large, handsome inhabitant of the northern forests. There has been one confirmed case of rabies in this species in Ontario.

Distribution. The hoary bat is one of the most widely distributed of the smaller American mammals. It is found from northern South America to northern Canada and from the Atlantic to the Pacific. It is one of the few small mammals that show little geographical variation so that no subspecies are currently recognized.

Canadian Distribution. Though nowhere abundant in Canada, it has been reported from Halifax, Nova Scotia, to Vancouver, British Columbia. It also occupies the northern boreal forests as far north as Great Slave Lake. There is an extralimital record from Bear Island, Northwest Territories (see Map 32).

Lasiurus cinereus (Palisot de Beauvois), 1796, Cat. raisonné du mus. de M. C.W. Peale, Philadelphia, p. 18.

REFERENCES

Bogan, Michael A. 1972. Observations on parturition and development in the hoary bat, *Lasiurus cinereus*. Jour. Mamm. 53(3): 611–14.
Seton, E.T. 1909. The hoary bat or great northern bat. *In* Life histories of northern animals, 2: 1191–1200. Scribner's Sons, New York.

PALLID BAT
Chauve-souris blonde. *Antrozous pallidus* (LeConte)

Description. This is a large southwestern species, which barely reaches southern British Columbia on the fringe of its distribution. The pallid bat superficially resembles the big-eared bat, but there are important differences. The muzzle of the pallid bat terminates in a blunt, bare pad. The scroll-shaped nostrils are on a raised ridge. Behind the nostrils, on either side of the muzzle, are two flattened, sparsely haired glandular swellings, which are quite different from the large lumpy glands of the big-eared bat. These swellings emit a strong skunk-like odour. The eyes are remarkably large and alert for bats. The pale tan ears are large and broad; when laid forward they extend about 20 mm beyond the muzzle. The median edge is relatively simple and lacks the doubled edges of the big-eared bat. Along the lateral side there are nine to eleven horizontal creases, which permit the ears to be folded. The long tragus is pointed and serrated along the outer edge (Figure 17b; skull, Figure 18a).

The slate grey wings are broad, hairless, and relatively thick. The ample interfemoral membrane is supported by a weakly keeled calcar. The hind feet are broad and are armed with strong claws and covered with a few sparse hairs.

The pelage is short and sparse, particularly across the shoulders. The individual dorsal hairs have buffy bases and dusky tips. The ventral surface is almost white. There is an annual moult in the summer between May and August. The new hair first appears in two patches on the shoulders and breast and radiates outwards.

The females are slightly larger than the males. Average measurements of males: total length 116 (111–124), tail 40 (35–44), hind foot 13 (11–15), ear from notch 29 (27–31), wing-spread 383 (382–385) mm; weight 25 (21–29) g. Average measurements of females: total length 119 (107–130), tail 43 (37–49), hind foot 14 (12–16), ear 30 (26–33), wing-spread 380 (370–393) mm; weight 29 (24–35) g.

Habits. The life history of this species has been studied in detail in California. Over much of its range it appears to be a migratory species. During the spring, summer, and autumn periods from about April to October it occurs in mixed colonies of both sexes from a few individuals to about one hundred. These colonies occupy small caverns and rock crevices in cliffs and canyon walls. They also regularly use the roofs and attics of barns, sheds, and deserted cabins. Only occasionally do they occupy hollow trees. During the winter months they desert these summer quarters to hibernate in secluded spots, few of which have been found. A few individuals have been located in mine shafts and others in deserted cabins. When roosting, this bat does not hang suspended by its hind feet but lies with its ventral surface pressed against the rock face.

During their winter of torpor, these bats slowly lose weight by utilizing their fat reserves. Individuals kept under laboratory conditions for 144 days at temperatures between 40°F and 50°F lost an average of 27.6 per cent of their body weight, or 0.193 per cent per day per bat.

The various calls of this species are interesting: they emit an insect-like buzz when they are angered, rasping notes when squabbling, and a variety of chirping notes that are thought to be radar-like. Their strong wrists and hind feet aid them in crawling. Their flight is slow and laboured, with about ten or eleven strokes per second in ordinary flight. Their ultrasonic 'radar' cries are emitted in a narrow beam, ahead of the mouth, at an energy peak of about forty kilocycles per second. Pallid bats occasionally hover or glide short distances.

Besides the daytime roosts used during the warmer months, there are secondary nocturnal feeding roosts to which the bats return to eat their prey. This species is usually found alone and seldom fraternizes with other species of vespertilionid bats, but it does tolerate the company of the free-tailed bat *Tadarida*.

The pallid bats emerge from their roosts rather late in the evening when the illumination is less than a tenth of a foot-candle. In the autumn, they emerge soon after sunset, usually beginning their evening's activity by swooping over a stream or pond for a drink. The pallid bat has developed unique feeding habits among the vespertilionid bats. It sweeps back and forth over the canyons very close to the ground, often landing on the ground to catch ground-dwelling arthropods. From stomach analysis it has been found that such terrestrial forms as Jerusalem crickets and scorpions are its favourite prey. Other items taken include June beetles and grasshoppers. It is not known how this bat subdues the scorpions without being stung. So frequently does this bat land and scamper over the rocks that it has even been taken in mousetraps. Feeding experiments indicate that this species eats about a quarter of its weight in food each active day. Its natural enemies include owls, hawks, and snakes.

Habitat. Pallid bats appear to favour open arid plains or cultivated areas, but they also occur in coniferous forests and open brushland of the Pacific coast. They seem to require water surfaces near by to drink from.

Reproduction. Many of the details of the reproductive cycle of this species have been elucidated by the California study. Mating occurs during the months of October and November in active colonies. There may be occasional matings during the hibernation period, as has been found in other species. The females retain viable sperm in their uteri over the torpid period in winter. Ovulation, which usually occurs early in April, was induced in one case by placing the female in a warm room after December. The young are usually born between mid-May and mid-June after a gestation period of about nine weeks. The number of young in the litter varies from one to three with a 1.8 average. Since the female only has two teats, only two young can survive.

The females hang upright at the time of parturition, the young emerging in breech presentation. The young claw their way up the fur to fasten onto a teat, while the mother cradles them in her wings. When the mother reverses her position, the youngsters similarly are turned upside down. The young weigh about 3 g at birth; they are hairless and blind, and their ears are folded back against the head. The eyes open on the eighth day. The hair covering starts to appear after the fourth day and reaches full growth at the end of a month. They learn to fly at the age of seven weeks.

Map 33 Distribution of the pallid bat, *Antrozous pallidus*

The female carries the bats on her foraging trips when they are small, and they hang on so tightly they can scarcely be pulled off.

Economic Status. Although the diet of this species suggests that they may be beneficial in areas where they are abundant, they are so rare in Canada that they are economically insignificant.

Distribution. The pallid bat is found in southwestern North America from northern Mexico to extreme southern British Columbia (see Map 33).

Canadian Distribution. The only Canadian specimen was secured from under a slate in a rock talus slope three miles north of Oliver, British Columbia. The Canadian specimen belongs to the form:

Antrozous pallidus cantwelli V. Bailey, 1936, N. American Fauna 55: 391. South-central British Columbia (see Map 33).

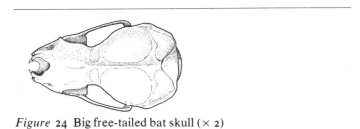

Figure 24 Big free-tailed bat skull (× 2)

REFERENCES

Orr, R.T. 1954. Natural history of the pallid bat, *Antrozous pallidus* (LeConte). Proc. California Acad. Sci., 4 ser. 28(4): 165–246.

Family **Molossidae** / Free-tailed Bats

The free-tailed bats constitute a large assemblage of insectivorous bats, widely distributed throughout the warmer parts of the world. The most apparent family feature is the thick, rat-like tail, which extends well beyond the restricted interfemoral membrane. The hind legs are short and powerful. The membranes and ears are rather leathery. These bats fly swiftly on pointed wings. The fur is short and has a peculiar velvet-like lustre. Many members of the family have a peculiar pungent musky odour, which may be detected about their roosts. Besides these external features there are trenchant skeletal characteristics that separate the molossid from the vespertilionid bats.

BIG FREE-TAILED BAT
Grand molosse. *Tadarida macrotis* (Gray)

Description. This is a very large bat, rivalling the hoary bat in size: more then 5 inches in total length, with a wing-spread of about 16 inches. The wings are long, pointed, and leathery. The interfemoral membrane is short, hairless, and creased. The tail extends an inch beyond the edge of the membrane. The pelage is fine and velvety, and the colour of the fur is mummy brown dorsally, paler beneath. When the dorsal hairs are parted, the whitish basis is exposed. The broad leathery ears almost join over the top of the head and, when laid forward, extend well beyond the muzzle. The tragus is short and blunt. There are several horny excrescences on the border of the ears. The muzzle is broad and blunt. The upper lip is full and wrinkled (Figure 17c; skull, Figure 24).

Average measurements of adults: total length 133 (129–138), tail 51 (48–54), hind foot 9 (9–10), ear from crown 25 (24–26), wing-spread 417 (407–432) mm.

Habits. This is an extremely rare bat in North America, and little is known of its life history. A closely related species (*Tadarida brasiliensis*) is more abundant in the southern United States, and certain deductions can be made from aspects of its life history.

The free-tailed bats are among the swiftest bats in flight. They are strongly colonial and migratory in habits. They remain active all year by migrating to warmer regions, and seem to lack the ability to store fat for hibernation. When chilled to temperatures of approximately 40°F for a period of one month, along with big brown bats (*Eptesicus fuscus*), they failed to survive, although the big brown bats resumed their activity after they were warmed.

During the summer months, the big free-tailed bat ranges northward erratically into the southwestern United States. It seeks shelter in rock crevices in canyon walls, caverns, and occasionally buildings. These bats show a

Map 34 Distribution of the big free-tailed bat, *Tadarida macrotis:* ● extra-limital records

remarkable ability to scamper about ledges and in crevices. The sexes are segregated during the summer months, the females forming typical nursery colonies during this period. If they roost in caverns during the day, they seek the warmest parts of the cave. The temperature amid clusters of *Tadarida brasiliensis* has been found to be slightly higher than that of the environment. Even when the broad clusters were disturbed and only the young remained, the cluster temperature remained higher.

Big free-tailed bats emerge from their hide-outs just before nightfall. No detailed data are available on their insect prey, but flying ants, beetles, midges, and small moths have been found in the stomachs of *Tadarida brasiliensis*.

Enemies include barn owls, great horned owls, red-tailed hawks, rat snakes, raccoons, and opossums.

Habitat. The range of the species in Mexico and in the southwestern United States seems to include largely deserts and steppes. The big free-tailed bat is, however, also found on the islands of the Caribbean and in tropical Central America.

Reproduction. The reproductive cycle of the free-tailed bats is quite unlike that of the hibernating vespertilionid bats. The reproductive cycle of *Tadarida brasiliensis* has been studied in some detail, and it is probably safe to assume that in general pattern the cycle of *Tadarida macrotis* is similar, in which case the bats become sexually mature at about the age of nine months. Mating occurs in the spring at the time of ovulation. There is no evidence of the storage of viable sperms over winter, as in the vespertilionids. The young are probably born in June after a gestation period of about twelve weeks. Only one young is born each season, although the females possess two pectoral teats. At birth the young bat does not have the same shelter as the vespertilionids, provided by the ample tail and wing membranes, but remains suspended by the cord until it can grasp a teat. Nor is the young bat carried by its mother when she forages for food but is cached in the brood cluster until it learns to fly in midsummer.

Economic Status. The big free-tailed bat is too rare in Canada to be of any economic significance.

Distribution. This species occurs in Central America, the West Indies, Mexico, and the southwestern United States. Erratic migrants have been found as far north as Iowa and New Westminster, British Columbia.

Canadian Distribution. The inclusion of this species in a list of Candian mammals is based solely on the capture of a single specimen in November 1938, when it flew into an open hospital window at Essondale, near New Westminster, British Columbia (see Map 34).

Tadarida macrotis (Gray), 1839, Ann. Nat. Hist. 4: 5–6.

REFERENCE

Borell, A.E. 1939. A colony of rare free-tailed bats. Jour. Mamm. 20(1): 65–8.

Order **Primates** / Primates

Although members of this order are the most intelligent mammals, the group retains many of the generalized physical characteristics of the primitive placental mammals. In fact the tree shrews (family Tupaiidae) are a link between the insectivores and the primates.

The order may be characterized as follows. They are plantigrade animals, that is, they walk on the heel. The clavicle is strong (most primates, being arboreal, need a stong clavicle for climbing). There are five digits on each foot, the inner digit of which is usually opposable and is furnished with a flattened nail (the big toe in man is not opposable). The terminal phalanges are flattened. The radius and ulna in the forearm are distinct. The orbits, which generally face forward, are surrounded by a bony ring. The teeth are varied; the third incisor and the first premolar are lacking, and the molars are more complex than the premolars. In the soft parts, the relatively larger brain is more developed, and the caecum (appendix) is present).

In habits, primates are usually gregarious, often having a social order, and are highly vocal, arboreal, and omnivorous; the young are altricial and require long maternal care.

Family **Hominidae** / Men

It is probably only because men have established the classification of animals that they have dignified their clan with a distinct family. The features that distinguish men from apes (Pongidae) are trivial compared to features that distinguish other allied families of mammals.

In man and his recognizable predecessors, the teeth are in an uninterrupted horseshoe-shaped series, and the canines are blunt. There is a decided chin on the mandibles, and there are projecting nasal bones. The cranium is highly arched; the brow ridges and occipital condyles are reduced. The forelimbs are shorter than the hind limbs. The hallux is not opposable. The vertebral column is bent into a sigmoid curve, and the femur is long and straight. The last two features are indicative of upright bipedal locomotion. The brain is relatively larger than in other mammals, and the cerebral hemispheres are enlarged and strongly convoluted. Men possess great manual dexterity, a sophisticated degree of intercommunication by means of speech, and the power of reason.

MAN
Homme. *Homo sapiens* Linnaeus

Man is included in the present list only to make the list of Canadian mammals complete. For information on this species in all its complexity, one should refer to anthropological texts. However, the relationships of the various races found in Canada are of some interest.

Homo sapiens afer Linnaeus, 1758, Syst. Nat., 10th ed., 1: 22. Negroes. Introduced to southeastern North America in the eighteenth century and now sparsely distributed over southern Canada.

Homo sapiens asiaticus Linnaeus, 1758, Syst. Nat., 10th ed., 1: 21. American Indians and Eskimos. Native races immigrated to Canada from eastern Asia, probably prior to the last glacial period (Wisconsin). The Indians and Eskimos are only poorly differentiated from other Asians. They probably immigrated in several waves. The Indians inhabited the forests and the plains areas of Canada, and the Eskimos the northern tundra regions.

Homo sapiens sapiens Linnaeus, 1758, Syst. Nat., 10th ed., 1: 20. Caucasians. Immigrated to eastern Canada in the sixteenth and seventeenth centuries from western Europe. Now widespread across southern Canada and sparsely distributed in northern Canada, Caucasians have assumed a dominant role in Canadian society.

COLOUR PLATE

7

Grey or black squirrel, *Sciurus carolinensis*

8

American red squirrel, *Tamiasciurus hudsonicus*

COLOUR PLATE

9

Northern flying squirrel, *Glaucomys sabrinus*

10

Eastern chipmunk, *Tamias striatus*

Order **Lagomorpha** /
Pikas, Hares, and Rabbits

For many years the lagomorphs were considered to be rodents because both groups were herbivorous, they were approximately the same size and shape, and they had in common a wide gap between the front and hind teeth. Recent studies have shown, however, that the lagomorphs have remained distinctive over a prolonged geological period and that the similarities are superficial and the result of similar habits. There are, on the other hand, many important anatomical differences that separate the two orders, and the general similarities are now considered to be a result of convergence.

The main characteristic of the group is the possession of two pairs of upper incisors (in adult life), the second pair behind the first. The incisors are completely covered with enamel, and the first pair are deeply grooved. A wide diastema separates the incisors from the cheek teeth. The latter are highly specialized: high crowned (hypsodont) and rootless, with transverse angular lophs. The fibula, which is ankylosed to the tibia, articulates with the calcaneum. The forefeet have five toes and the hind feet four.

There are several characteristics in the soft parts: the fur is soft and dense, the skin is paper-thin, the tail is extremely short or absent, and the large caecum is spiraled.

ARTIFICIAL KEY TO FAMILIES OF
CANADIAN LAGOMORPHA

1   Ears and hind feet long.   L E P O R I D A E
1′   Ears and hind feet not lengthened.   O C H O T O N I D A E

Family **Ochotonidae** / Pikas

These interesting little creatures well illustrate several important points in biology.

In the first place, they do not bear a close resemblance to their relatives the hares and the rabbits. At first glance, which is about all one gets of them in the wild, they appear to be more closely related to guinea pigs. But on closer examination their true relationship will become evident.

Secondly, they have a peculiar disjunct distribution – central Asia, Japan, and the mountains of western North America. The fact that there are many other animals with similar distributions supports the conclusion that they migrated to North America over a Bering Sea landbridge and have recently become separated by the present water barrier and the intervening inhospitable climate.

The living pikas belong to a single genus and form a close-knit group. They are all small robust mammals with short ears, short legs, and no external tail (the minute caudal vertebrae are enclosed in the body skin). The elongate skull, which lacks post-orbital processes, is flat and is constricted between the orbits. The teeth are, however, typically lagomorphic: the first pair of upper incisors are strongly grooved and notched. The third upper molar is lacking. The hind feet are not much longer than the forefeet.

AMERICAN PIKA
Pica d'Amérique. *Ochotona princeps* (Richardson)

Description. Pikas are small, stocky, tailless mammals, rather like guinea pigs in their normal hunched position. They are about 7 inches long and 3 inches high (Figure 25). Their short, rounded ears are dusky, edged with white.

Figure 25 American pika

Their alert eyes are relatively close to the Roman nose on the elongate skull (Figure 26). They have a small hare-lipped mouth, and their vibrissae are extremely long and numerous. Their legs are short, and their feet plantigrade, four-toed, with felt-padded soles and four small hairless oval pads under the toes.

The pelage is dense, long, and fine, and resembles that found on hares and rabbits. The long basal section is smoke-grey; the tips are greyish or buffy with a mixture of black, which gives an over-all salt-and-pepper appearance to the dorsal surface. The underparts are greyish. Two moults have been described in the pika. The summer moult is reported to commence in early July or August and to be completed within twenty days. The pika wears the full summer coat only a short period, and the autumn moult commences in late September. The new pelage appears first on the head and progresses evenly backwards over the shoulders and back. There is a prominent line of demarcation between the shorter, brighter new coat and the long, lax, faded old coat. However, the moult seems to be highly irregular in most cases, and all specimens secured from spring through fall seem to be in some stage of moult. Unfortunately the pika's habitat makes the winter collection of specimens extremely difficult.

The colour of the pika is very difficult to describe because of hair structure, moult, and individual variation. In general it is perhaps best described as cinnamon-buff. Certain geographical races are decidedly greyish, however, and others are blackish.

Average measurements of adults of the nominate race: total length 192 (181–204), hind foot 30.5 (29–33), ear from notch about 20 mm; weight 191 (175–234) g.

Habits. The pika is one of the characteristic mammals of the Rocky Mountains. It is of great interest because of its specialization for a particular habitat. It is diurnal in activity, appearing first very early in the morning and retiring soon after sunset. It spends considerable time sunning itself, hunched up on a prominent look-out rock. At other times its forages about for food. When frightened, the pika quickly drops off its look-out rock and scuttles between the rocks. It has a peculiar half-running, half-hopping gait. One of the most interesting features of the little creature is its call – a nasal bleat, which has a decided ventriloquial effect. As one approaches a pika's domain, the sharp

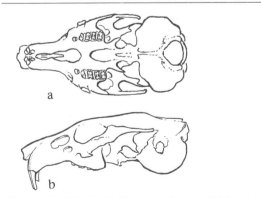

Figure 26 Pika skull: (a) ventral view, (b) lateral view (× 1)

bleats may be heard from several directions. It takes some time and effort to locate the little pika, perched on a rock some yards away, often in plain view. With each call its head jerks upwards convulsively, and its mouth opens momentarily to expose the curved needle-like lower incisors. Other pikas may answer from a distance. If the observer frightens the one nearest, it quickly drops out of sight with a chattering alarm call. Then follows a series of muffled calls as the creature steals away, out of sight, among the rocks. If the observer sits quietly and patiently, the pika often approaches and may quietly steal up to a near-by look-out rock for a better look at the intruder. However, because of the ventriloquial quality of its bleat, one is never sure of exactly where the animal will appear. So confident is the pika of its perfectly camouflaged coat's blending with the grey rocks that it often remains hunched and stilled, apparently staring ahead, down its arched nose, until the intruder almost reaches its look-out before it scuttles to shelter.

When one examines the pika's domain, the peculiar BB-sized dung and stains will identify its favourite look-outs and its well-travelled paths among the rocks. Of special interest are the pika's haystacks of cured fodder that it collects for the winter, for the little animal remains active throughout that season under the blanket of snow, tunnelling through the snow that has packed between the boulders. The haystacks may contain as much as a bushel of vegetation, cached under an overhanging rock to protect it from rain and snow. The grass-lined nest is hidden deep in rock crevices.

Few plants grow in the rocky domain of the pika, and when these have been consumed, the animal must venture away from the safety of its rock piles. It hurries to a tender plant, clips it off, transfers it crosswise in its mouth, and then moves on to another plant, and so on, until it has a bundle of plants held crosswise in its mouth. Then it hops back to the safety of the rocks. One can often observe the little foraging trails issuing from under a flattened rock and criss-crossing the adjacent meadow. The pika has a wide taste in its plant food, depending upon the various species that grow near at hand. Grasses and sedges usually predominate; also a wide range of tender flowering plants, such as lupine, golden-rod, paintbrush, fireweed, asters, penstemon, knotweed, saxifrages, cinquefoils, yarrow, phlox, mountain aven, pearly everlasting, and the pasque flower. It also eats the tender shoots of short woody shrubs such as bearberry, buffaloberry, blueberry, rose, aspen, willow, and dwarf birch, and service berries. During the late summer and autumn it commences its harvesting operations, bringing many mouthfuls of freshly cut flowers and grasses to its haystack, which continues to grow by layers, each cured and compacted, stopping only when the frost cuts down the plant life. By that time the pika has completed the task of obtaining sufficient cured hay to sustain it for the winter season. Pikas, like the hares, engage in reingestion.

Little is known of the social aspects of the life history of this little beast. It is known to be remarkably conscious of its home territory and to defend it against wandering

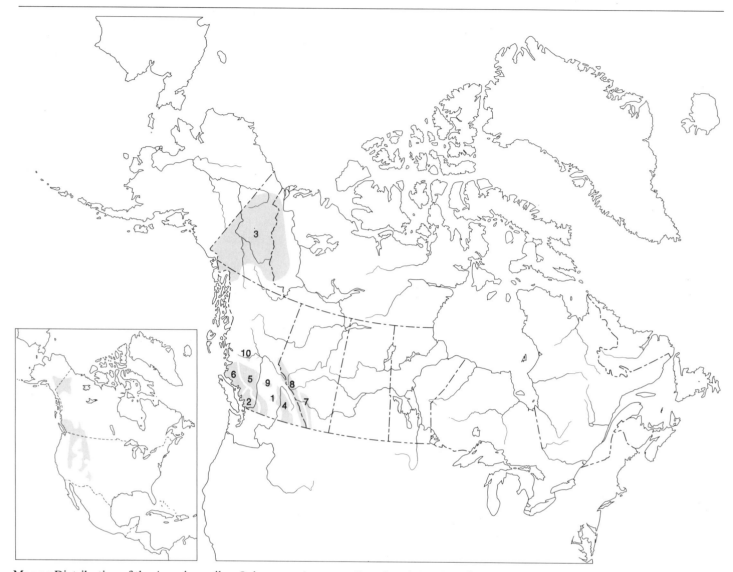

Map 35 Distribution of the American pika, *Ochotona princeps*: 1 *O. p. brooksi*, 2 *O. p. brunnescens*, 3 *O. p. collaris*, 4 *O. p. cuppes*, 5 *O. p. fenisex*, 6 *O. p. littoralis*, 7 *O. p. lutescens*, 8 *O. p. princeps*, 9 *O. p. saturata*, 10 *O. p. septentrionalis*

neighbours. It utilizes urine-anointed scent-posts, look-outs, and haystacks to delimit its territories, and it is believed that its normal calls are warnings to possible trespassers. It has been estimated that its territory may be as large as 750 square yards and that its population density may be in the order of six pikas per acre of rock slide.

The little pika spends much of its life evading predators. Avian predators, such as golden eagles and the large rodent-eating buteo hawks, are an important threat during the daylight hours when the pikas are basking in the sun. Mammalian predators such as the fox, marten, fisher, wolverine, lynx, and bears are also potentially dangerous, especially when the pikas are foraging away from their rock-bound retreats. However, they can often escape these by scuttling for safety into crevices between rocks too large for the carnivore to enter.

The pika's most dangerous predator is the ermine, *Mustela erminea*, which is slimmer than the pika and can follow it through its maze of rock tunnels. I have sat quietly on a rock pile and watched an ermine methodically

hunting through strewn boulders for a 'hot' pika trail. In the meantime the pikas could be heard chattering underground. Eventually the ermine emerged at the far end of the pile with a young pika clutched in its mouth, food for a litter of growing ermines somewhere near by.

Habitat. In the previous sections, mention has been made of the pika's restricted choice of habitat. These unique animals inhabit the rocky talus slopes formed by landslides in the mountains of western America. Typically they are found above treeline, up to the limit of vegetation, at about 9,000 feet elevation in the Canadian Rockies in the high alpine slopes. However, they occur less commonly on the west coast of British Columbia in rock piles in the forests and on lakeshores. Occasionally they may be found in odd sites such as log jams in rivers. There is one such notable colony at the outlet of Medicine Lake, Jasper National Park, Alberta. This lake was known to the Indians as Bad Medicine Lake, because it drained through a sink-hole, much below the former outlet of the Maligne River. The river-bed, which is dry for a distance of about a

74

mile below the lake where the water suddenly gushes up from its underground course, is composed of huge moss-covered boulders, which are now never reached by the river water. These boulders in the river-bed have provided shelter for generations of pikas.

Reproduction. Very little is known of the reproductive cycle in American pikas. A litter of three or four young (rarely five) is born during the summer from May to September after a gestation period of thirty days. They weigh approximately 8 to 9 g at birth, and are densely furred with short blackish hair. They are quite precocious and chirp and crawl about soon after birth. The mother is attentive and quick to retrieve her wayward young by the scruff of the neck. The adult coat first appears at about eight days of age, and the eyes open at ten days. Weaning commences at twelve days, and the young start to nibble vegetation. The youngsters are very playful, leaping and dashing about their nest. They reach about two-thirds adult size at the age of one month.

Economic Status. The pika inhabits such an isolated habitat that it has no economic importance to man. However, it has considerable aesthetic value because of its fascinating way of life and its history.

Distribution. The pika is widely distributed in the mountain ranges of western North America from northern New Mexico to western Alberta, British Columbia, Yukon, N.W.T., and Alaska. It is not found throughout this entire region but is restricted to locations with suitable habitat.

Canadian Distribution. Colonies of pikas are usually relatively isolated from others of their kind, because of their unique habitat requirements. The species also appears to be morphologically plastic. These factors have resulted in the evolution of a patchwork-quilt-like distribution of numerous local subspecies, only slightly differentiated by size and coat colour. Ten geographical races are currently recognized in Canada (see Map 35).

Ochotona princeps brooksi A.H. Howell, 1924, N. American Fauna 47: 30. Shuswap Lake area of south-central British Columbia.

Ochotona princeps brunnescens A.H. Howell, 1919, Proc. Biol. Soc. Washington 32: 108. Western slope of the Cascade Range, southwest British Columbia.

Ochotona princeps collaris (Nelson), 1893, Proc. Biol. Soc. Washington 8: 117. The collared pika inhabits the subarctic mountain ranges of extreme northwestern North America (Yukon, N.W.T., and Alaska). There is a broad corridor of about 400 miles in northern British Columbia, which separates the ranges of the collared and Rocky Mountain pikas, in which no pikas have been found. The collared pika is identical in form with its southern relatives, but there are slight differences in colour. The pelage is grizzled grey-brown above and white below. There is a pale grey band on each side of the neck behind the ears. The buffy tones found in the subspecies *princeps* are lacking in this race. The ears are darker, the inner edges are black, and the terminal light band is much subdued. In addition, the naked pads at the bases of the four toes are much smaller and are surrounded by a row of stiff hairs, which probably covers the pads in winter.

Ochotona princeps cuppes Bangs, 1899, Proc. New England Zool. Club 1: 40. Monashee and Selkirk ranges of southeastern British Columbia.

Ochotona princeps fenisex Osgood, 1913, Proc. Biol. Soc. Washington 26: 80. Eastern slope of the Cascade Range north to Chilcotin Plateau, central British Columbia.

Ochotona princeps littoralis Cowan, 1955, The Murrelet 35: 22. Western slopes of the Coast Range, western British Columbia.

Ochotona princeps lutescens A.H. Howell, 1919, Proc. Biol. Soc. Washington 32: 105. Eastern slopes of the Rocky Mountains of Alberta.

Ochotona princeps princeps (Richardson), 1828, Zool. Jour. 3: 520. Main ranges of the Rocky Mountains of eastern British Columbia and western Alberta.

Ochotona princeps saturata Cowan, 1955, The Murrelet 35: 23. Wells Gray Provincial Park, central British Columbia.

Ochotona princeps septentrionalis Cowan and Racey, 1946, Canadian Field-Nat. 60: 102. Itcha Mountains, central British Columbia.

REFERENCE

Millar, John S., and Fred C. Zwickel. 1972. Determination of age, age structure, and mortality of the pika, *Ochotona princeps* (Richardson). Canadian Jour. Zool. 50(2): 229–32.

Family **Leporidae** / Rabbits and Hares

So familiar are the rabbits and hares that an introduction to them is hardly necessary. Almost cosmopolitan in distribution, they were absent only from Madagascar, New Zealand, and Australia, until their introduction to New Zealand and Australia, with nearly disastrous results to agriculture. The typical form consists of a robust hunched body, powder-puff tail, narrow head with large eyes and elongate ears, long powerful hind limbs with furred soles, and plantigrade feet adapted for a hopping gait. The inside of the cheeks is characteristically haired.

Some of the diagnostic features of the skull include a laterally compressed rostrum, an arched cranium, large wing-shaped supraorbital processes, fenestrated maxillary bones, and a hard palate consisting of a narrow transverse bridge.

Rabbits differ from hares in that their young are born naked, blind, and helpless in underground burrows, while young hares are born eyes open and fully haired in a surface nest or form. Young hares are precocious and are able to run soon after birth. In contrast to the pikas, rabbits and hares are chiefly nocturnal in activity.

Leporids have a unique digestive process called reingestion or refection. Two types of material are eliminated from the alimentary tract. The first consists of normal brown faecal pellets, and the second of soft green pellets, composed of only slightly predigested plant food, which are passed mainly during the daytime rest period. These

75

are sorted out by the animal and reingested. The whole system recalls that found in ruminants, in which a cud of vegetation is returned to the mouth from the stomach and rechewed. Reingestion has been observed in a number of species and is probably characteristic of the whole group.

EASTERN COTTONTAIL
Lapin à queue blanche. *Sylvilagus floridanus* (J.A. Allen)

Description. Cottontails are the smallest native leporids and the closest relatives of the Old World rabbits on this continent. They have shorter hind feet and ears and their ears lack the black tips of the hares. Cottontails do not turn white in winter as do the native hares.

The pelage of the eastern cottontail is composed of a dense, silky slate-colored underfur and longer, coarser guard hairs, which are black-tipped and have a broad subterminal buffy brown band. The over-all dorsal effect is a dark buffy brown coat, washed with grey on the rump and flanks and sprinkled with black. There is a prominent rufous patch between the ears and shoulders. The legs and throat are pinkish buff on the inside, with dark brown anterior borders and buffy grey posterior borders. The powder-puff tail is brown above, but only the white ventral side is shown in running (Figure 27).

The skull of the cottontail may be distinguished from that of the snowshoe hare by the close proximity of the posterior lobes of the supraorbital processes to the skull, only a narrow slit separating them (Figure 28b).

There are two annual moults. The spring moult is prolonged over about four months, from April to July. The summer coat is short and brownish. The autumn moult occurs between the middle of September and the end of October. After that, the animals are in the longer and greyer winter pelage. Young cottontails go through three moults before they assume adult pelage. The nestlings have a fine, downy grey coat for the first five weeks. After that, they assume a thin, dark salt-and-pepper juvenile coat for another month. Finally, they reach the subadult

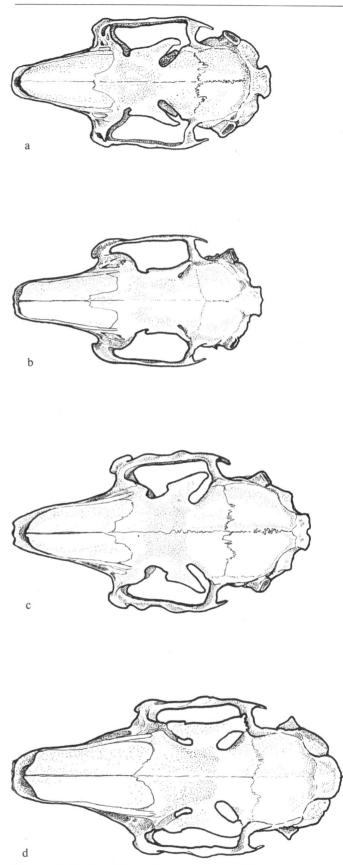

Figure 27 Eastern cottontail

Figure 28 Skulls of Canadian hares and rabbits: (a) snowshoe hare, *Lepus americanus*; (b) eastern cottontail, *Sylvilagus floridanus*; (c) arctic hare, *Lepus arcticus*; (d) white-tailed jack rabbit, *Lepus townsendii* (× 1)

stage, which is paler and buffier than the adults. During the moulting period the new hair grows through the old coat in sheets, usually appearing first on the back and then around the flanks to the belly. Rarely albino cottontails appear.

The adult sex ratio found in the wild population is close to 50 : 50. The average body temperature of the cottontail is 101.6°F.

Average measurements for the Canadian forms: total length 446, tail 60, hind foot 104 mm. The females are slightly larger than the males. The average adult weight class is between 1.1 and 1.2 kg (2½ pounds). Females may weigh over 1.5 kg. There is a progressive weight loss during the late winter months.

Habits. The cottontail, which is crepuscular and nocturnal in activity, makes its first appearance shortly after sundown and retires to its daytime hide-out after sunrise. It spends much of the daylight hours crouched in a favourite hollow under a shrub, log, or stump, or in a thicket or brushpile. Here, between naps, it grooms itself and stands on its hind legs with its forepaws pressed to its chest to take a brief look at its surroundings or to chew its reingested pellets. If danger threatens, say by the passing of a dog, the cottontail 'freezes,' ready for instant flight. If discovered, it explodes out of its shelter, bounds away in a straight path until it reaches cover, and then zigzags out of sight.

However, the cottontail never runs very far from its familiar thickets. Seton suggested that it remained within the area of an acre, but recent studies have indicated a larger home range, dependent to some extent on terrain and food supply, but in the neighbourhood of 8 acres. Individual estimates have varied from 1.2 to 22 acres. The does (as female rabbits are called) are thought to have smaller home ranges than the bucks, and they defend their territories against other trespassing does, particularly in the breeding season. On a 75-acre plot in Iowa, composed of 37 per cent cultivated crops, the breeding population of cottontails in June showed a density of 0.46 animal per acre. This increased to 1.65 per acre in late August, with the addition of the young, but dropped to 0.89 per acre in October because of dispersal and of hunting pressure.

Cottontails remain active all winter, finding shelter in thickets or usurping woodchuck and skunk burrows. They are particularly playful and sociable and have been observed gambolling about in moonlit fields.

There are two peaks of feeding activity: two to three hours after dawn and the hour after sunset. The summer diet consists of a variety of tender green grasses and herbs, grasses composing about 50 per cent and herbs 31 per cent. Among the plants eaten are golden-rod, plantain, chickweed, sheep sorrell, wild strawberry, smartweed, buttercup, cinquefoil, crab grass, barnyard grass, yellow foxtail, red top, and blue grass.

After the frost nips the green forage, the cottontail turns to the bark, twigs, and buds of shrubs and young trees. Among its favourites are the maples, birch, oaks, chestnut, hawthorn, red-osier dogwood, bittersweet, beech, wild apple, witch hazel, honeysuckle, viburnums, blueberry shrubs, staghorn sumac, wild rose, mountain ash, snowberry bushes, service berry, wild cherries, and pine. Its appetite for ornamental shrubs and garden produce is also well known.

The mammals of this family play an important role in the natural scheme of things by converting the vegetation of the meadows and thickets into meat for the sustenance of carnivorous birds and mammals. The cottontail is one of the chief prey species of its habitat and has a host of predators. These include the diurnal hawks (particularly the broad-winged hawks) and the larger nocturnal owls. Their terrestrial predators include the red fox and the grey fox, the coyote, and the long-tailed weasel. Man and his companions the dog and cat must also be counted among the list. The young rabbits have additional enemies to evade among the lesser predators such as snakes, shrikes, crows, and weasels.

It is therefore not surprising that the life expectancy of the cottontail rabbit is rather short. From the moment of birth, the life expectancy of the individual never rises above six months. The mortality rate from the age of four to twenty-nine months is relatively constant. About 25 per cent survive to live more than a year, and longevity tables indicate three years as a maximum possible longevity.

The cottontail is, however, not defenceless in the face of its enemies. It has keen senses of sight, smell, and hearing, and it is a quick, elusive runner. It is, however, the remarkable breeding potential that guarantees the survival of the species.

Habitat. The cottontail makes its home in meadows, orchards, and fence rows, and in weedy and shrubby areas and on the borders of woodlots. It has prospered with the development of agriculture in southern Canada because the deep forests are not to its liking.

Reproduction. The reproductive cycle of the cottontail has been studied in some detail. The male gonads begin to develop in the middle of January and reach breeding condition by mid-February. From then until September, when the gonads regress, the bucks are in active breeding condition. The does are polyoestrous and similarly come into heat first in late February, when the matings begin. Cottontails take part in an interesting mating dance, which, though usually occurring after dark, has occasionally been witnessed in daylight. In the preliminary stages the buck chases the doe in a lively pursuit around the meadow. Eventually she turns and faces the buck and spars at him with her front paws. As they crouch facing each other, a few inches apart, one of the pair suddenly leaps about two feet in the air, and the other runs nimbly underneath it. This performance is repeated several times by either cottontail before actual mating. The gestation period, though varying from 26 to 32 days, is usually given as 30 days. A few days before the arrival of the litter, the doe prepares a nest for the young. This is generally a grass-lined cavity in a small hollow, often beneath a shrub but as often in open tall grass. She carefully lines it with fur plucked from her abdomen. The litter may vary from two to seven young with an average of about 5.6. Communal nests of up to fifteen of two distinct sizes have been noted. The young rabbits are naked and blind and weigh about 25–35 g at

Map 36 Distribution of the eastern cottontail, *Sylvilagus floridanus*: 1 *S. f. mearnsii*, 2 *S. f. similis*, * introduced

birth. They receive a minimum amount of care from their mother, who nurses them only once or twice a day for anywhere from sixteen to twenty-two days. The remainder of the time she leaves them alone in the nest so as not to attract predators and is quick to lead enemies away from the nestlings. However, they grow rapidly, gaining about 2.5 g per day. Their eyes open somewhere between the fifth and the eighth day, and they leave the nest after about two weeks. At first the family stays together, but eventually at about the age of seven weeks the young become intolerant of each other and disperse.

The doe leaves the youngsters to fend for themselves long before the young disperse because she has new problems. The cottontail does mate again soon after the birth of their first litter, while they are nursing, and a second litter is soon on the way. In fact, three or more litters a year are usual, the last litters being born as late as September. The young cottontails mature rapidly and reach sexual maturity at the age of two to three months. It has been estimated

that 25 per cent of the production of young cottontails is contributed by juveniles.

Economic Status. The cottontail is one of the most important small game animals throughout its range. Rabbit hunting provides zestful sport and outdoor relaxation for hunters of both sexes and all ages. It is usually the first game hunted by youngsters and their dads. Small dogs are useful aids, but ordinary cross-country trampling techniques will produce 'bags.' Besides, the quarry provides an appetizing prize for the pot.

On the other hand, gardeners and nurserymen do not look on the lowly cottontail with as much appreciation. Local cottontails can do a great deal of damage in vegetable gardens in summer or among ornamental shrubs in winter. They will quickly girdle fruit trees, honeysuckles, and spindletrees. Chicken-wire fences probably offer the best protection for small gardens. There are rabbit repellents on the market now that provide some protection for short periods. These can be painted on the trunks and stems of small trees. However, valuable trees and shrubs should be provided with metal collars where cottontail damage is expected.

The cottontail is subject to a host of parasites and diseases, most of which are unimportant to man. One of these, tularaemia, is, however, dangerous. It is not easy for the casual hunter to identify the disease in rabbits and hares. It is therefore advisable not to handle any sickly rabbits discovered in the bush and to discard any carcasses that have abnormal organs or lesions noticed in preparing them. It is always reassuring to know that cooking the rabbit well will effectively kill the pathogenic organisms. One peculiar pathological condition occasionally met is the presence of facial 'horns.' These are really cornified growths, technically called papillomas, caused by a virus.

Distribution. The eastern cottontail inhabits a vast area of eastern and central North America from Central America to the Great Lakes and New England regions.

Canadian Distribution. Although investigations of pre-Columbian Indian village sites in southern Ontario indicate that the cottontail was a former inhabitant, it was absent from southern Canada at the time of European settlement. It first entered southwestern Ontario about 1867 or 1870, and was first noted at Niagara Falls about 1871. The first specimen taken at London, Ontario, was secured in 1883, and four were taken in the Toronto region between 1885 and 1890. The eastern cottontail reached Kingston about 1925 and Ottawa in 1931. It also reached Montreal Island about the same time, but has not spread very far inland from the Ottawa and St Lawrence river valleys.

Slightly later, the eastern cottontail appeared in southern Manitoba. The first specimen was secured near Treesbank in 1914. This species spread gradually northward to Morden in 1931 and finally reached the Dauphin area by 1940. It has recently been taken at Estevan, Saskatchewan. It is thought that agricultural practices have provided an ideal habitat for this species and permitted it to expand its range northward in Canada in the past hundred years (see Map 36).

Two geographical subspecies are recognized in Canada.

Sylvilagus floridanus mearnsii (J.A. Allen), 1894, Bull. American Mus. Nat. Hist. 6: 171. Southern Ontario, southeastern Quebec, and the Fraser delta of British Columbia, where it was introduced for hunting stock.

Sylvilagus floridanus similis Nelson, 1907, Proc. Biol. Soc. Washington 20: 82. Southwestern Manitoba and southeastern Saskatchewan.

REFERENCE

Lord, R.D. Jr. 1963. The cottontail rabbit in Illinois. Southern Illinois Univ. Press, Carbondale.

NUTTALL'S COTTONTAIL
Lapin de Nuttall. *Sylvilagus nuttallii* (Bachman)

Description. Nuttall's cottontail is a smaller, paler edition of the eastern cottontail, found in western North America. Above, it is a grizzled buffy brown with grey flanks and rump. The top of the tail is neutral grey, but the white undersurface predominates. The underparts are white, with a buffy brown collar across the throat. The nape, ankles, and forefeet are pale tawny. The hind feet are white above. The short ears are grey behind and pale grey inside with grey-brown anterior rims. The moults are not known to differ from those of the eastern cottontail. There are subtle differences in the skull, which are thought to distinguish the two species.

Average measurements of adults: total length 385 (350–390), tail 46 (44–50), hind foot 95 (88–100), ear 56 (55–56) mm. Weight of one male 678 g. Average weight of three females 928 (868–1032) g.

Habits. Nuttall's cottontail has not been studied in as much detail as the eastern cottontail. Its life history is probably similar to that of its eastern relative.

Habitat. This cottontail is an inhabitant of the arid sagebrush plains of western North America. More particularly it is found in the coulees and river bottomlands where it finds shelter in banks, and in the burrows of prairie dogs, ground squirrels, or badgers, or among the rocks. In the evening it ventures forth to feed on the open plains, but it is always quick to dash back to shelter at the first hint of danger.

Reproduction. The life cycle is not known to differ significantly from that outlined for the eastern cottontail.

Economic Status. Nuttall's cottontail is of less economic importance than the eastern species as it inhabits the short grass steppes, which are used more for cattle grazing or grain growing than for market-gardening. The populations of this form do not seem to be as dense as that of its relative, but undoubtedly it may occasionally be a local garden pest.

Its prime importance is probably as a buffer prey species for the local carnivores such as coyotes, foxes, badgers, the large buteo hawks, and the nocturnal owls.

Distribution. This species inhabits the western great plains region from Arizona to the southern Prairie Provinces.

Canadian Distribution. There are indications that Nuttall's cottontail has enlarged its Canadian distribution in the present century. The first record of its occurrence in the Cypress Hills of southwestern Saskatchewan was published in 1909. In 1917, it was taken near Steveville, Alberta. Later records followed: Cardston, Alberta, 1927; Eastend, Saskatchewan, 1921; Dollard, Saskatchewan, 1924; Johnston Lake, Saskatchewan, 1939. At present it is found fairly commonly on the third prairie steppe of southwestern Saskatchewan and southeastern Alberta. There is also an isolated Canadian population of the nominate race in the arid Okanagan and Similkameen valleys of south-central British Columbia (see Map 37).

Sylvilagus nuttallii grangeri (J.A. Allen), 1895, Bull. American Mus. Nat. Hist. 7: 264. Alberta and Saskatchewan.

Map 37 Distribution of Nuttall's cottontail, *Sylvilagus nuttallii*: 1 *S. n. grangeri*, 2 *S. n. nuttallii*

Sylvilagus nuttallii nuttallii (Bachman) 1837, Jour. Acad. Nat. Sci. Philadelphia 7: 345. Okanagan Valley, British Columbia.

REFERENCE

Anderson, R.M. 1940. The spread of cottontail rabbits in Canada. Canadian Field-Nat. 54(5): 70–2.

SNOWSHOE HARE
Lièvre d'Amérique. *Lepus americanus* Erxleben

Description. The snowshoe hare is commonly distributed throughout the forested regions of Canada from the Atlantic to the Pacific. It is one of the most familiar of the smaller mammals of Canada and also is an important source of food in parts of Canada that are remote from agricultural areas.

The snowshoe hare is medium-sized, weighing about 4 pounds, with very large broad hind feet and with larger ears than the cottontail rabbit. Its summer pelage is a grizzled rusty or greyish brown with a blackish mid-dorsal line, buffy grey flanks, and a white belly. The face, legs, and throat are cinnamon brown; the ears are brownish and are black-tipped behind and laterally edged with a creamy white border. The top of the tail is blackish, and the ventral surface white. The colour of the feet is variable: those of juveniles are brown, but those of adults retain many dirty white or buffy hairs all summer. The soles are densely furred with felt-like hairs (Figure 29).

Throughout most of Canada, with the exception of the southwestern corner of British Columbia, the snowshoe hare turns white in winter. At that time it is clothed in a long, silky white coat, which conceals the short greyish underfur. Only the eyelids, around the large luminous dark eyes, and the tips of the ears are black. The large hind feet are padded with thick stiff hairs, which give the animal its popular name – 'snowshoe' hare.

The coat appears to be composed of three layers: first, the short, dense, silky, slate-grey underfur; then a thin coat of longer buff-tipped hairs; and, finally, the long black-tipped (in summer) coarser guard hairs. It has been suggested that there are two sets of hair roots, one responsible for the vernal brown moult and the other for the white autumnal moult. These two sets of roots are thought to become active at different seasons and to regress in the off-season. This explains the two distinctive physiological colour periods. Hares plucked in early September will grow white hairs before there is any indication of regular autumnal moult to that colour, while hares plucked in January will grow brown hairs long before the regular vernal moult. Heredity, and physiological and environmental factors (particularly light), have been found to exert strong influences on the moulting period. Experimentally it has been demonstrated that increased length of periods of light (such as longer spring days) will activate the vernal moult, and that decreased periods of light (such as shorter autumn days) will activate the autumn moult.

The exact cause of the change of colour in the snowshoe hare was long debated. Some thought it was through whitening of the tips of brown summer hairs. Now we know that there are two distinct sets of pelage. The autumnal moult commences in late September and continues until the first of January, the average length of time for the moult being seventy-four days; females take less time to change coat than males and juveniles take, on an average, eleven days longer than adults. During the moult there is a gradual whitening, which commences on the legs, ears, and face, spreads to the flanks, and terminates on the back. This gradual change is caused by the continual growth of the new, long, white guard hairs and the shedding of the old brown ones. In early September, before the regular autumnal moult, there is a partial moult when the slate-coloured underfur is augmented by the growth of a much paler winter pile.

The vernal moult commences in early March and is 90 per cent complete in fifty days, although the average duration for the complete moult is seventy-two days. Again the females take slightly less time. At this period both the underfur and the guard hairs are completely replaced by the new brown coat, commencing on the mid-dorsal line of the back and progressing to the extremities. When the new coat matures, the old winter pelage drops out in patches in May. Generally the hind feet retain patches of white fur into the summer. Besides the normal colour, examples of melanistic (black) and albino (white) coats are occasionally met in wild populations.

The normal body temperature of the snowshoe hare has been found to be 102.3°F.

The skull of the snowshoe hare may be distinguished from that of the cottontail rabbit by the possession of well-marked posterior lobes of the supraorbital processes, which are separated from the frontal bones by a broad bay (Figure 28a).

Average measurements of adults from Manitoba: females: total length 483, tail 48, hind foot 139 mm; males: total length 472, tail 42, hind foot 125 mm. The range of specimens generally falls between the following measurements: total length 413–518, tail 39–52, hind foot 117–147, ear from notch 62–70 mm.

There is an annual fluctuation in the weight of adults, with two peaks in December and June. The average weight of females from Alberta in November was 1.55 kg, significantly more than that of the males, which weighed on the average only 1.43 kg.

Habits. The snowshoe hare, like the other leporids, is crepuscular and nocturnal in its activity pattern and remains active all winter as well. Its activity is governed by light intensity so that it is frequently active on cloudy winter afternoons. During the daylight hours it remains crouched under some sheltering bush, stump, or log. It dozes fitfully for short periods but is by no means immobile. It spends considerable time grooming itself by licking its fur. When grooming its long hind feet it assumes a grotesque pose, stretching them stiffly in front of its body. Or it may indulge in reingestion of its green faeces, as described for the cottontail. At all times the snowshoe hare remains alert. It may exhibit curiosity by sitting stiffly, bolt upright, with its forelegs pressed to its breast. When crouched, it keeps its forelegs back between the hind feet, ready for a quick bound away should danger threaten. Because of its protective coloration, the hare may 'freeze' to escape detection, or it may flee to escape its pursuer. As it grows older, it seems to rely increasingly upon flight. It travels with bounds, which may cover up to ten feet, and at speeds up to twenty-seven miles an hour. It is also very adroit at dodging and may make high clumsy leaps.

As evening approaches, snowshoe hares leave their coverts to feed. They follow familiar runways through their domains from shelter to feeding areas. These trails criss-cross in an intricate maze throughout their home range, and some runways swing in wide circles around favourite thickets or swamps. In summer their runways appear as well-padded trails, half-tunnelled through the fresh grass, and in winter they are well-marked padded trails through the snow. The hares are familiar with every turn, cross-over, thicket, and log shelter in the maze, as their lives often depend on this knowledge in a chase. In summer, they spend considerable time in clipping the growing vegetation from the runways to permit unim-

Figure 29 Snowshoe hare

peded travel, and in winter they pad down the trails in the fresh snow to allow speedy escape along well-known routes.

As would be expected, the hare's senses are extremely acute. It probably relies mostly on its sense of hearing, which includes the perception of vibration caused by footfalls. Hares are generally silent but indicate slight annoyance by snorting. When caught, they utter a high-pitched squeal of terror, which sometimes causes the surprised hunter to drop them. Much of their communication is conducted by thumping the hind feet rapidly against the ground. This may warn other hares of danger or may be indulged in in gambolling or in padding down the snow-covered runways.

Snowshoe hares are social animals, and often several inhabit the same thicket or swamp. They usually share the same forms, funk holes, and dusting spots. During the summer months they are very fond of rolling and spraying themselves with dust or sand. The forms are mere depressions in the grass at the base of a bush or beside a rock, log, or stump, under a low-growing branch, or in the entrance of another animal's den. During the winter, home may be under a snow-laden branch or even in a short tunnel in the snow scratched out by the hare itself. Generally, wind and light are the chief deterrents to the hare's widespread forages.

The snowshoe hare, however, is not unduly secretive in its movements. On still moonlit nights it frequently ventures into the forest clearings to gambol. As many as twenty-five have been observed flitting silently around a forest clearing on a frosty moonlit winter's night. Like small pale ghosts they appeared and disappeared in the shadows as they fed among the small spruces or chased each other in jerky spasms of movement.

Snowshoe hares occasionally swim across rivers or small lakes. They float quite high in the water and propel themselves with strong strokes of the hind feet. Upon reaching the opposite shore they hop into the brush without taking time to shake the water from their fur. If pursued by a predator, they may take to the water as a means of escape.

Like the cottontail rabbits, snowshoe hares may live their whole lives in a relatively small area. Live trapping and release experiments in Canada have indicated an average home range of about seven acres for females and eighteen acres for males. Other studies in the United States have indicated home ranges of the same order. However, the average daily range for each hare was found to be about four acres. During the breeding season the range of the bucks was determined by the number of local does they courted. Hares have also shown signs of possessing a sense of orientation and the ability to 'home' distances of up to three miles when transported to release sites as far as ten miles from their home ranges. When food becomes scarce in their home thickets, snowshoe hares may travel across, or feed in, open fields. This habit is particularly noticeable in late winter between February and April when 'snowshoes' have been tracked distances

of up to five miles across open prairies to distant wooded ravines.

During the parturition period, the home range of the doe is more restricted, and she becomes intolerant of the buck. On the other hand the range of the buck depends upon the availability of receptive does. The ranges of several bucks may overlap the ranges of the does they are courting. Therefore polyandrism (or several mates for each doe) seems to be indicated in this species.

The snowshoe hare is a classic example of a species that has tremendous oscillations in its population densities. Field studies indicate populations as low as 1 hare and as high as 3,400 hares to a square mile. In northern Canada populations as high as 10,000 to a square mile of favourable habitat have been estimated. Intermediate populations of 260 and 539 hares to the square mile have been encountered in increasing populations short of the peak. Since reproductive success is involved in population density, calculations have been made to determine ideal population densities to permit adequate reproduction. It has been found that a density of 32 hares to a square mile should allow for does to mate within an oestrous period of two weeks.

The amplitude of the population fluctuation varies across the range of the species. It is greatest in northwestern Canada and much lower in the United States and in the Rocky Mountain regions. Population peaks in the United States may be of the order of 20 : 1 to 25 : 1 as compared to 3,400 : 1 in northern Canada. It has been suggested that the fewer food chains and therefore fewer buffer species and simpler environmental conditions may be responsible for the more drastic fluctuations in the north.

Long-term research such as that undertaken by the Criddle brothers of Aweme, Manitoba (from 1895 to 1937), has indicated that the population fluctuations show remarkably uniform oscillations, with peaks spaced about six to thirteen years apart, with a mode of nine or ten years. There is a long build-up phase lasting several years after the population is minimal. The peak populations do not appear simultaneously across Canada. First, isolated foci of population increase appear; these coalesce and grow; then the area of peak population spreads across the country in a wave. It seems as though the migration of hares out of areas of abundance to marginal areas of low density may play an important role in the sequence of population peaks that sweep across the country. Indeed the migration of hares across Red Lake, Minnesota, has been reported.

During the summer months, snowshoe hares eat a wide variety of green grasses and forbs. Among the favourite food items may be listed the following: blue grass, brome, vetches, asters, jewelweed, wild strawberry, pussy-toes, dandelions, clovers, daisies, and horsetails. They also eat the tender leaves of trembling aspen, birches, and willows.

During the winter months they live on buds, twigs, bark, and evergreen leaves of woody plants. They often stand to clip the shrubs up to eighteen inches from the ground. As the snow deepens, the snowshoe hares are able to trim the shrubs and saplings higher and higher. After the spring thaw in March or April they are able to utilize the lower stems and evergreen ferns that had been buried by the snow. Among their favourite winter food plants are the following: willows, birches, hazelnut, silver willow, maples, trembling aspen, hawthorn, and such conifers as tamarack, white pine, hemlock, white spruce, balsam, fir, and white cedar (arborvitae). In winters of peak hare populations they may kill many young saplings and shrubs by girdling. These hares also exhibit cannibalistic tendencies in winter and do not hesitate to consume frozen carcasses of their less fortunate brethren.

As is so often the case in an abundant prey species, hares have a relatively short life-span. Of 454 hares live-trapped and released in one season, 70 were recaptured the next year, 52 during the second year, and 18 the third year – indicating a normal life-span in the wild of four to five years. In another study the crude survival rate for adults from one breeding season to the next was 14.7 per cent.

The snowshoe hare is an important link in Canadian food chains between the plants and the carnivorous animals. It has many predators, chief among which are the great horned, great grey, and barred owls, and the lynx, bobcat, red fox, coyote, wolf, and mink. In spite of these hazards hare populations may build up to the amazing levels mentioned previously. When the population finally crashes, disease, not predators, appears to be the most important mortality factor. Some of the pathogens implicated in local population crashes are *Salmonella*, *Pneumococcus*, ringworm, and *Pasteurella tularensis*. A paralytic syndrome resembling an opisthotonic seizure, characteristic of hypoglycaemia, was described in snowshoe hares as shock disease and implicated in a hare epizootic. Later research has shown that this was associated with live-trapping and holding the wild hares in cramped quarters. It is now called simply trap disease.

Habitat. Whereas the cottontail rabbit is characteristic of fields, fence rows, and overgrown meadows, the snowshoe hare inhabits forests, swamps, and riverside thickets. In the eastern part of its range it is most commonly found in cedar bogs or coniferous lowlands. In the prairie region it inhabits aspen 'bluffs' or copses. It also is found in mixed deciduous and coniferous forests and feeds among the raspberry canes in old burns. Generally it remains in the densest cover during the day and forages in the forest openings at night.

Reproduction. The reproductive organs of the bucks commence their annual growth cycle in late February, and courtship begins soon after. The breeding season starts about mid-March but varies by location and season. The male organs regress in July and August, and the breeding season is usually over in September. Occasionally winter leverets (young hares) have been recorded. Curious courtship parades have been observed with a doe in the lead, solemnly followed by several bucks, each drumming alternately in a series of hop-kicks as the procession pass-

es down a well-packed runway in the snow. At other times there is a wild chase: the doe dodging and leaping into the air and the buck running underneath. The females are polyoestrous, exhibiting their first period in late March as the duration of light increases. Embryos have been identified as early as March 24. Parturition occurs after mid-April, with the first batch of litters generally being born in May. The gestation period is thirty-six days. The first litters are usually smaller than the later ones but range from one to eight leverets. The average litter size in an Alberta study was found to be 3.82. The does breed again soon after parturition and may produce as many as four litters a year, the average figure found in the Alberta study being 2.75 litters a year. Juvenile hares do not breed in the first calendar year of their lives. However, the data indicate a tremendous breeding potential of 10.30 young per doe per year; or, since the normal adult sex ratio is 1:1, 5.2 young per hare per year. Studies continued during a fluctuating population in Alberta indicated that 4.11 leverets per litter were born during the rising population phase, but the litter size decreased to 2.20 when the population crashed. Also, there was a shift in sex ratio from an excess of females in the pre-peak year to 1:1 when the population was declining. Such is the raw material involved in the tremendous fluctuations in hare populations.

The young leverets are precocious at birth. They are born with a long coat of silky, grizzled brown hair, in their mother's simple grass-lined form, and their eyes open soon afterwards. The first day they crawl feebly, by the third day they can hop a bit, and by the sixth day they are alert enough to hop vigorously away from their nest. Although they weigh only 65–80 g at birth, they gain weight rapidly at the rate of about 9 g per day, so that by the eighth day of their young lives they have doubled their weight. About this time also they begin to eat greens on their own. The litters leave the nest and move around with the doe until they are weaned at two to three weeks of age. The doe is adept at leading predators away from her litter if danger threatens, and the youngsters usually escape detection by 'freezing.'

Economic Status. The snowshoe hare is undoubtedly the most important small game mammal of Canada. In remote sections it is often the mainstay in the winter larder of Indians, homesteaders, and trappers. Not suspicious by nature, it is easily snared in its well-marked runways. When it is abundant, it provides an appetizing and easily procurable source of food to the woodsman and frontier farmer. When the population is low, it is best ignored as a food item. A number of snowshoe hare pelts are sold each year as fur. In the 1971–72 trapping season 10,021 'rabbit' skins were sold for $1,002, at an average price of 10 cents a skin.

Because of the snowshoe's reluctance to leave its accustomed home range and well-known paths, it is a good quarry for the sportsman, particularly one with a small hound. The same warning about the risk of tularaemia mentioned for the cottontail rabbit holds for the snowshoe hare.

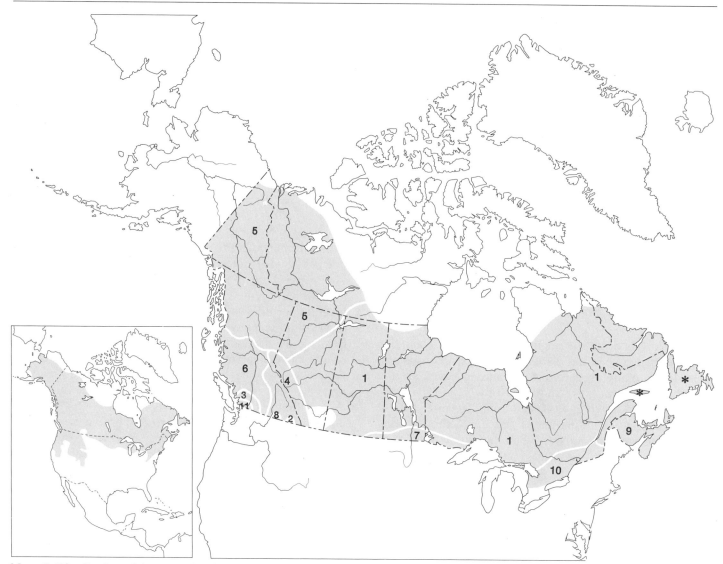

Map 38 Distribution of the snowshoe hare, *Lepus americanus*: 1 *L. a. americanus*, 2 *L. a. bairdii*, 3 *L. a. cascadensis*, 4 *L. a. columbiensis*, 5 *L. a. macfarlani*, 6 *L. a. pallidus*, 7 *L. a. phaeonotus*, 8 *L. a. pineus*, 9 *L. a. struthopus*, 10 *L. a. virginianus*, 11 *L. a. washingtonii*, * introduced

Unfortunately this hare shows the same predilection for vegetable gardens as does the cottontail. It is apt to be more troublesome about frontier homesteads near forests. The same control methods mentioned for the cottontail are equally applicable for the hare. Usually its depredations are viewed with a little more tolerance since it offers an appetizing addition to the northern larder.

Distribution. The snowshoe hare occupies a broad distributional belt across northern North America from Nova Scotia to Alaska. The southern boundary of the range includes the Allegheny Mountains of North Carolina and Tennessee, and the Rocky Mountains in northern New Mexico and California. The northern boundary is the treeline in Labrador, the Northwest Territories, and Yukon Territory.

Canadian Distribution. This widespread but fundamentally sedentary species is morphologically quite plastic. It has been segregated into eleven geographical subspecies,

which differ slightly in Canada in size and colour (see Map 38).

Lepus americanus americanus Erxleben, 1777, Systema regni animalis ..., 1: 330. Labrador, northern Quebec, Ontario, and the Prairie Provinces.

Lepus americanus bairdii Hayden, 1869, American Nat. 3: 113. Extreme southwestern Alberta and southeastern British Columbia.

Lepus americanus cascadensis Nelson, 1907, Proc. Biol. Soc. Washington 20: 87. Cascade Mountains of southwestern British Columbia.

Lepus americanus columbiensis Rhoads, 1895, Proc. Acad. Nat. Sci. Philadelphia 47: 242. Rocky Mountain region of eastern British Columbia and western Alberta.

Lepus americanus macfarlani Merriam, 1900, Proc. Washington Acad. Sci. 2: 30. Northwestern Canada, in the Northwest and Yukon Territories, northwestern

Alberta, and northern British Columbia.

Lepus americanus pallidus Cowan, 1938, Jour. Mamm. 19: 242. Central British Columbia.

Lepus americanus phaeonotus J.A. Allen, 1899, Bull. American Mus. Nat. Hist. 12: 11. Rainy River district of western Ontario, southern Manitoba, and southeastern Saskatchewan.

Lepus americanus pineus Dalquest, 1942, Jour. Mamm. 23: 178. Lower Okanagan valley, British Columbia.

Lepus americanus struthopus Bangs, 1898, Proc. Biol. Soc. Washington 12: 81. Maritime Provinces (introduced to Newfoundland about 1864) and Gaspé Peninsula of Quebec.

Lepus americanus virginianus Harlan, 1825, Fauna Americana, p. 196. Southwestern Quebec and southern Ontario.

Lepus americanus washingtonii Baird, 1855, Proc. Acad. Nat. Sci. Philadelphia 7: 333. Fraser River delta, British Columbia.

REFERENCES

Bider, J.R. 1961. An ecological study of the showshoe hare *Lepus americanus*. Canadian Jour. Zool. 39(1): 81–103.

Keith, Lloyd B., E.C. Meslow, and O.L. Rongstad. 1968. Techniques for snowshoe hare population studies. Jour. Wildlife Mngt. 32(4): 801–12.

MacLulich, D.A. 1937. Fluctuations in the numbers of varying hare (*Lepus americanus*). Univ. Toronto Biol. Studies 42.

Meslow, E.C., and L.B. Keith. 1968. Demographic parameters of a snowshoe hare population. J. Wildlife Mngt. 32(4): 812–34.

ARCTIC HARE

Lièvre arctique. *Lepus arcticus* Ross

Description. This large, heavy-bodied hare is found in the arctic regions of Canada, beyond the treeline, including the islands of the Arctic Archipelago. When fully grown, it weighs between 7 and 12 pounds. It seems to become larger and silkier the farther north it is found. In winter it is universally pure white with moderately long, black-tipped ears. In summer the pelage varies widely, however, depending on latitude. On the continental tundra, the summer pelage is bluish grey, with a frosting of white-tipped guard hairs on the face and back. The underparts are white; the ears are bi-coloured behind, grey-white on the lateral edges and black on the median edges; the throat is dark grey; the tail is silky white. On northern Ellesmere Island and Greenland the summer pelage is almost white, with a slight wash of cinnamon or grey on the face and back. Between these two extremes, the arctic hares on the intervening islands show intermediate amounts of cinnamon and pinkish-buff mottling on the face and back during the summer months. Occasionally, hares of a single group may be remarkably different, some having only a sugges-

tion of a grey cast to the pelage and others brownish faces and mottled ears and back (Figure 30).

The arctic hare's large feet are padded with a heavy, soiled-yellowish brush. Its curved claws are long and strong, especially those of the forefeet, and serve as effective digging tools in the crusted snow. Its pelage, which is composed of a dense, often kinky grey underfur and longer black-tipped guard hairs, is much longer, softer, and silkier than that of the snowshoe hare. Its eyes are large, brown, or yellowish brown with oval-shaped irises.

The skull of this hare is robust. The posterior lobes of the supraorbital processes stand prominently out from the skull. The anterior lobes are represented only by slight notches. The zygomatic arches have two distinct flattened dorsal planes (Figure 28c).

The exact method of moulting has not been studied in this species, but it is probably similar to that of the snowshoe hare. The new greyish or buffy coat may be seen under the worn winter coat in late May, before the June moult. Large amounts of woolly underfur may be seen clinging to vegetation at that time. The new summer coat appears first on the face, then on the ears, legs, and shoulders, with the back moulting last. The females appear to moult earlier. On Ellesmere Island the spring moult is later and carries on into July. The summer coat is carried only a very short time, however, for by mid-September the autumn moult to the silky white winter pelage has commenced. The ears seem to receive their silky white clothing first; then the white of the belly spreads onto the flanks, shoulders, and back. By the last of October, the face has lost its grizzled appearance and assumed its snow-white colour.

Average measurements of a series of adults from Banks Island: females: length 658 (605–711), tail 69 (40–101), hind foot 158 (146–178) mm; males: length 634 (600–800), tail 66 (50–75), hind foot 158 (153–174) mm. As is usual with hares and their allies, the female averages slightly larger than the male. The hares of Banks Island are about

Figure 30 Arctic hare

average for the species in size. The ear measures about 70–84 mm in length. The average weight of adults is 4.6 (4.0–5.4) kg.

Habits. Arctic hares appear unusually unwary or 'tame' upon first contact with man. They may often be approached to within a few feet without showing any alarm. If persistently followed, however, they soon become more wary and hop off short distances. They show remarkable ability in hiding behind rocks. It is often necessary to shout, throw stones, jump, or discharge a firearm to put the hares to flight. Their reaction to dogs, however, is remarkably different, and they immediately take flight when one approaches.

When resting, hares sit hunched behind a sheltering rock, ears laid back, eyes half-closed. When alarmed, they sit up, ears erect and turning to catch the slightest sound, nostrils quivering. If excited, they stand on tiptoes, beating the air with their short forelegs and peering at the unfamiliar object. Often they bound up and down on their hind toes to catch a better glimpse of an intruder. If they awaken leisurely from their rest, they stretch their limbs and necks deliberately, before hopping away to feed. Arctic hares are usually silent, but scream piteously when captured.

The normal gait is a series of four-legged hops, each hop carrying them about four feet. They normally run up a slope when fleeing. The southern populations use this gait almost entirely, but the northern races, found on the arctic islands from northern Baffin Island northward, use a very different gait. When first alarmed, the northern hare stands up on its hind feet and then bounds away, kangaroo-style on its hind toes, with its forelegs dangling loosely or pressed to its breast. After it has travelled some distance in this manner it lunges forward and resumes a normal four-footed hopping gait. If closely pursued, it will resume the two-legged hop.

These hares are also moderately gregarious. In the southern parts of their range they are usually met only as individuals or small family groups, but from northern Baffin Island northward they are often found in bands of up to 120 individuals. Most of the group usually occupy themselves in feeding or resting, but a few individuals are playful or alert. These animals may box each other or dance about on their hind feet with ears straining to catch the sound of danger. When alarmed, the group seems to lack leadership and much milling ensues before a general flight pattern is evident. As might be expected, these hares are nocturnal and crepuscular in their activity pattern, although one must keep in mind the annual cycle of daylight in their polar environment. They remain active all winter and sometimes huddle together for shelter in their snow forms. During the long daylight hours of summer they spend considerable time sunning themselves on slopes or on the sunny side of large boulders.

The winter form may be in a wreath of snow in the lee of a boulder, or the hare may excavate a snow den in a snowbank or become buried in a blizzard. Dens consist of a tunnel about four inches in diameter and one foot in depth, with an enlarged terminal chamber. As is true of

their relatives, arctic hares appear to have a small home range and a short daily range. Although their tundra environment may appear limitless and devoid of obstructions, they follow well-worn paths. In the northern parts of their range, where they are gregarious, the winter paths assume the appearance of well-padded highways.

Little is known of arctic hare population fluctuations. This hare seems to be rare for a number of years in one locality, and then it is suddenly common. There is no evidence that it indulges in mass migrations. Nor is there any information available on its longevity.

Arctic hares possess long, obliquely projecting incisors that operate like forceps in extracting dwarf tundra plants from the crusted snow. They may break the snow crust by pounding it with their forepaws and then dig with their claws and push the snow away with their noses. They clip off the twigs of willows or pull up short lengths of willow roots and clip them off with their incisors. When grazing on green summer grasses they crawl slowly forward in a crouched position. Their food consists of such summer greens as grasses, sedges, saxifrages, cinquefoils, campions, mountain sorrel, and the twigs and roots of arctic willows and crowberry. They are also fond of meat when they can get it, and are often attracted to bait in fox traps. They seem to be curious and often follow the trapper, inspecting his snowhouse and incidental piles of crusted snow. Along the sea-coasts they nibble on seaweed; even in winter they venture onto the sea-ice, searching for scraps of it.

The arctic hare is an important link in northern food chains. It is an important prey species for such carnivores as the arctic fox, the wolf, and the ermine (to a lesser degree). The avian raptores the snowy owl and the rough-legged hawk are also important predators.

Habitat. These hares are found only in the tundra zone beyond the treeline. They frequent rough Precambrian hillsides where the northern winds blow away the snow. They seldom occupy the low plains of glacial till where the winds firmly pack the snow, except during the summer. The Newfoundland race is also found on the high barren hills back from the coast.

Reproduction. The male gonads enlarge in April and regress to the non-breeding state in mid-September, indicating the over-all length of the breeding season. Young hares do not mature during the first year but take part in the breeding cycle as yearlings. Mating occurs during the bright days of April and May. The exact gestation period is not known, but well-grown foetuses have been observed on May 23. The first litter is born in June – as early as June 10 on the mainland, but not until the end of June in northern Greenland and Ellesmere Island. Probably most does bear only one litter a year, but the finding of lactating does as late as August 25 strongly suggests that a second litter may be born to some does. The litter may vary from two to eight leverets, with an average of about 5.4.

The young are born in a nest, which is a simple depression in the tundra among the mosses and grasses, sometimes in the protection of a boulder or shrub. The little leverets are born fully clothed in a dark grey coat even

86

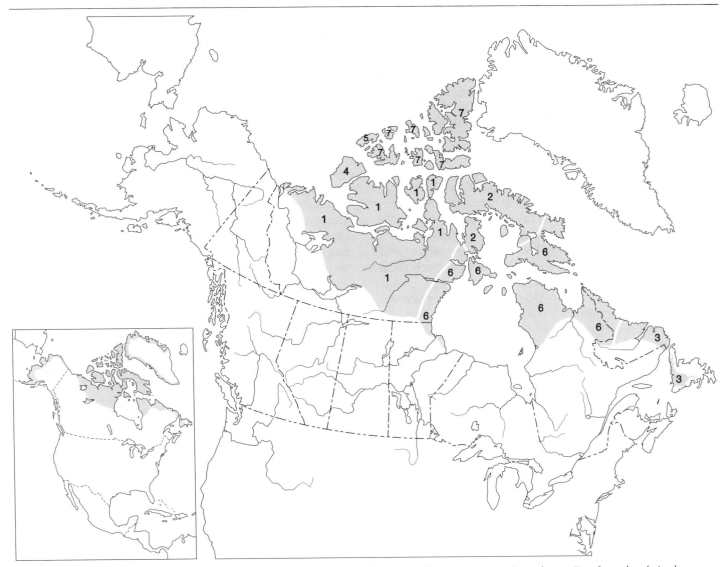

Map 39 Distribution of the arctic hare, *Lepus arcticus*: 1 *L. a. andersoni*, 2 *L. a. arcticus*, 3 *L. a. bangsii*, 4 *L. a. banksicola*, 5 *L. a. hubbardi*, 6 *L. a. labradorius*, 7 *L. a. monstrabilis*

on the arctic islands. They huddle together for warmth, pressed against the moss with their ears laid back across their shoulders. Soon after birth they measure about 175 mm and weigh about 105 g. By the age of nine days their weight increases to about 193 g. They are fully grown by early September.

Economic Status. The arctic hare constitutes an important faunal resource of northern Canada, providing food and items of clothing to the Eskimo residents and European travellers. The Eskimos take advantage of the hare's refusal to jump over a thong line stretched across its pathway. The hare invariably crawls under the line and is therefore easily captured in snares suspended from the line. They are also frequently taken in fox traps.

The meat of hares is white and well-flavoured. It is usually lean, and often it is necessary to add extra fat to make it attractive. Explorers have noticed that they were unable to eat hares when suffering from fat hunger. The Eskimos split the hind leg bones and suck out the marrow.

The skins are typically paper-thin, as found in all members of this order. Although the fur is exceedingly warm, the thin skin and the brittle, soft guard hairs lessen its value for clothing. The skins are usually made into stockings and hand towels, but in peeling the skins much care must be exercised not to tear them. The Eskimos use white wool for bandages.

Distribution. This species inhabits the tundra regions of Canada from Newfoundland and Labrador to the Mackenzie delta of the Northwest Territories. It also occurs on the arctic islands and in Greenland. A closely related species is found in northern Alaska. It has perhaps the most northern record of occurrence of all terrestrial mammals. Captain Markham of the H.M.S. *Alert* observed signs of these hares on the ice ten miles from the most northern land at latitude 83°10′ N. This species is closely related to the blue hare, *Lepus timidus*, of Eurasia.

Canadian Distribution. Seven geographical races of the arctic hare are recognized in Canada (see Map 39).

Lepus arcticus andersoni Nelson, 1934, Proc. Biol. Soc. Washington 47: 85. Central Keewatin and eastern Mackenzie districts; Victoria, King William, Prince of Wales, and Somerset islands; and Boothia Peninsula, Franklin District, Northwest Territories.

Lepus arcticus arcticus Ross, 1819, A voyage of discovery ..., 2nd ed., 2: appendix 4, p. 151. Melville Peninsula, northern Baffin Island and Bylot Island, Franklin District, Northwest Territories.

Lepus arcticus bangsii Rhoads, 1896, American Nat. 30: 253. Newfoundland and southern coastal Labrador. The 'mountain' hare was once plentiful in Newfoundland, and the meat was canned by the fishermen, who did not have to go far inland from the coastal villages to secure their supply. Hares seemed to decline after the introduction of the snowshoe hare about 1864, and competition from that species is thought to be the reason for the population decline.

Lepus arcticus banksicola Manning and MacPherson, 1958, The mammals of Banks Island, Arctic Inst. N. America Tech. Paper 2: 8. Banks Island, Northwest Territories.

Lepus arcticus hubbardi Handley, 1952, Proc. Biol. Soc. Washington 65: 199. Prince Patrick Island, Northwest Territories.

Lepus arcticus labradorius Miller, 1899, Proc. Biol. Soc. Washington 13: 39. Northern Ungava, southern Baffin Island, Southampton Island, and west coast of Hudson Bay.

Lepus arcticus monstrabilis Nelson, 1934, Proc. Biol. Soc. Washington 47: 85. Queen Elizabeth Islands (the islands north of Lancaster and Viscount Melville sounds) with the exception of Prince Patrick Island, Northwest Territories.

REFERENCE

Freuchen, P. 1935. The arctic hare. *In* M. Degerbøl and P. Freuchen, Mammals: Report of the Fifth Thule Expedition, 1921–24, vol. 2(4–5): 68–79. Gyldendalsk Boghandel Nordisk Forlag, Copenhagen.

WHITE-TAILED JACK RABBIT
Lièvre de Townsend. *Lepus townsendii* Bachman

Description. The first European travellers to the American prairies met a large, long-legged, long-eared prairie hare, which they promptly labelled the 'jackass rabbit.' Fortunately this name has mellowed over the years to its presently accepted form. It is a relatively slim hare with very slender legs, long ears (which the Canadian naturalist E.T. Seton thought were best fitted for shedding rain from the hare's back), and a relatively long white tail (Figure 31). Its average weight is about 7½ pounds, but it may weigh up to 12 pounds. The diagnostic features of the skull are the enlarged lobes of the elevated, supraorbital process. These lobes are anchylosed with the frontal bones behind and sometimes in front, to enclose four large openings on top of the skull (Figure 28d).

The summer coat is a uniform, grizzled buffy grey. The face is more hoary, and the tail has only a faint suggestion of a dark, mid-dorsal line. The ears are dark grizzled-grey in front with white outer rims, greyish white behind, and prominent black tips. The throat is greyish; otherwise the underparts and the hind feet are white. The forelegs are buffy. The whole pelage is rather thin and coarse. The underfur is pale grey; the long guard hairs have dark grey intermediate bands and long buffy tips.

The winter coat in Canada is pure white, with black-tipped ears. When the long guard hairs are parted, however, the buffy-grey underfur shows through. In the southern part of its range the white-tailed jack rabbit assumes a buffy winter coat. There are two annual moults: October to November, and April to May. After the snow has melted in late spring, white hares are occasionally seen squatting in bare, brown, ploughed fields.

Average measurements of adults: total length 545 (495–695), tail 90 (63–112), hind foot 150 (140–153), ear from notch 115 (100–125) mm; weight 3.35 (2.6–4.1) kg.

Habits. The white-tailed jack rabbit is predominantly nocturnal. It is seldom seen abroad during the daylight hours unless it is 'jumped' from its form. It is most frequently observed crossing the road in the beam of car headlights, its eyes glowing fiery-red. It is active all winter, as are all lagomorphs. It usually lies low in its form all day, ears pressed back over its back and eyelids half-closed over its strange yellow irises. It usually does not flush until the intruder is about to step on it; then it springs into the air. Occasionally if one passes near a hare, it will sneak off behind. When first flushed, the hare flees with long, high springs, its long legs dangling limply, head held high, ears erect, and white tail flopping from side to side. As soon as one or both hind feet touch the ground, its body is again propelled into the air. After this short burst of supreme effort, the hare settles down into a series of low gliding leaps, which may cover from four to seventeen feet of ground. It has been estimated that it may travel as fast as forty miles an hour in short bursts. It is also a strong

Figure 31 White-tailed jack rabbit

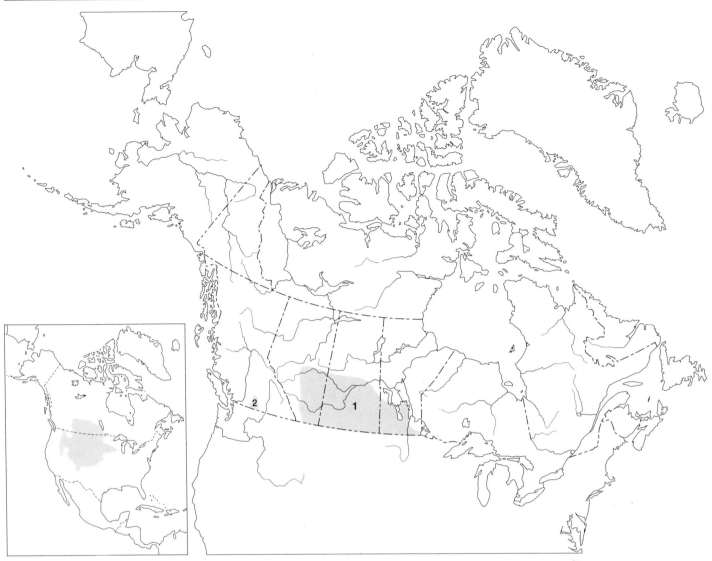

Map 40 Distribution of the white-tailed jack rabbit, *Lepus townsendii*: 1 *L. t. campanius*, 2 *L. t. townsendii*

swimmer and may plunge into a river when pursued and swim buoyantly with much splashing to the other side.

Jack rabbits are generally silent except for their shrill screams when wounded. A captured jack rabbit is not completely helpless and may inflict deep scratches with its long hind claws.

This species seems to be one of the least sociable of the group. The hares are generally solitary, but small groups of three or four may occasionally be observed in the mating season.

There is little information available on the home range of these hares. They appear to be more mobile than the snowshoe hares, but there is no evidence of any extensive migrations. Seton estimated that a single jack rabbit might range over an area approximately one mile in diameter. In the summer they crouch in slight depressions in the grass and travel along well-worn trails. In winter they burrow tunnels in snowbanks along drifted fence rows, or crouch in shallow depressions scratched in the snow, with only their backs, flattened ears, and eyes showing above the snow surface. They often return day after day to the same tunnels or forms, if not disturbed. They may seek shelter in badger burrows as well.

Their populations do not appear to fluctuate as dramatically as those of the snowshoe hare. Densities seem to be generally about 10 to 20 animals per square mile. If, however, the growing seasons are relatively dry, the populations may increase. In the peak year of 1951–52, in Minnesota, a density of 69 hares per square mile was estimated. Other local concentrations of 277 to 350 hares per square mile have been estimated on the basis of hunting drives. The clearing of forests and the cultivation of land appear to benefit the white-tailed jack rabbits. After such peak populations, declines usually set in. Diseases of several kinds, including tularaemia, Colorado tick fever, equine encephalitis, and fever caused by heavy infestations of *Cuterebra* (botfly) larvae have been found in connection with jack rabbit die-offs. Probably no single factor accounts for declining hare populations.

Jack rabbits eat a variety of green forage in summer,

including native grasses, clovers, cultivated grains, and alfalfa. They are also partial to vegetable greens such as lettuce and cabbage. In winter they browse on the twigs, buds, and bark of shrubs and trees including berry and fruit trees. They are also fond of haystacks and may gather there in small groups to shelter and eat stored hay.

Jack rabbits serve as prey for a number of the prairie predators including coyotes, wolves, and foxes. In the more southern mountainous areas of their range, bobcats and eagles are their predators. On the Canadian prairies they are hunted by day by the larger hawks and by night by the large owls. However, their great speed and their protective coloration as they crouch in their forms are great aids to their survival. They have been known to dodge under barbed-wire fences to escape the swoop of a hawk.

Habitat. These hares frequent pastures and cultivated grainfields, bordered by willow thickets and wild rose tangles, as well as the native short-grass sagebrush plains. They seldom penetrate wooded areas to any extent, except when seeking shelter from winter blizzards. In the mountainous western states, however, they are found high in the pine forests.

Reproduction. Very little is known of the breeding habits of this species. It mates in late April or early May. The young are born in June or early July. The litter of three to six averages about four. The leverets are born in a shallow nest, hidden in the grass or in an abandoned badger's burrow. They are heavily furred at birth and are born with their eyes open. New-born jack rabbits are remarkably precocious, even being able to run. They are nursed by their mothers (which possess eight mammae) until they are about a quarter grown, at the age of five to six weeks, about the end of July. It is not known whether one or two litters are born. The fact that lactating does have been observed as late as August 16 suggests that in Canada some may bear a second litter.

Economic Status. These hares are usually too sparsely distributed to cause much concentrated damage to grainfields and gardens. The black-tailed jack rabbit (a closely related, more southern species) does damage fields of barley. It has been found that this damage can be prevented if a sixteen-foot border of rye is planted around the barley. The hares eschew the rye and do not enter the field to find the barley. Most complaints against white-tailed rabbits arise because of damage to haystacks or girdling of fruit trees. In these instances wire screens or collars may be used for protection.

Jack rabbits make fine game animals because of their habit of lying close and then bounding off in a straight line. Their meat, which is quite flavourful, was a dietary staple in the pioneer days on the prairie. Because these hares are unfortunately subject to the usual variety of parasitic larval tapeworms and botflies, and to diseases such as tularaemia and equine encephalitis, the usual caution in preparing them for the table is necessary.

A peculiar horny skin condition, which produces facial 'horns,' has been occasionally noted in this species as well as in other Canadian hares and cottontail rabbits.

Distribution. This species inhabits the northern Great Plains regions of North America.

Canadian Distribution. This species is confined to the prairie portions of Manitoba and Saskatchewan and to a small pocket in the southern Okanagan valley of British Columbia. It was originally an inhabitant of the arid short-grass plains, but its range has spread northward with the advance of agriculture. It was unknown in Manitoba before about 1885, and Seton secured the first specimen north of the Assiniboine River at Carberry in 1892. It now occurs in the Interlaken district of Manitoba, the Prince Albert Park region of Saskatchewan, and north of Edmonton, Alberta. Two subspecies are recognized in Canada (see Map 40).

Lepus townsendii campanius Hollister, 1915, Proc. Biol. Soc. Washington 28: 70. Prairie Provinces.
Lepus townsendii townsendii Bachman, 1839, Jour. Acad. Nat. Sci. Philadelphia 8(1): 90, pl. 2. Found only in the arid Okanagan valley of British Columbia, where it is reported to be decreasing.

REFERENCE

Seton, E.T. 1909. Prairie hare, white-tailed jack rabbit or white jack. *In* Life histories of northern animals, chap. 1, pp. 654–73. Scribner's Sons, New York.

EUROPEAN HARE
Lièvre d'Europe. *Lepus europaeus* Pallas

Description. The European hare is not native to Canada but was successfully introduced to southern Ontario from Germany. It is a large, heavily built hare with moderately long ears and large feet, weighing on the average about 9 pounds.

The summer coat dorsally is grizzled rusty brown with greyish flanks and rump, ochraceous throat, white chin and belly, tail white below and black above, ochraceous forefeet, and buffy hind feet. The black-tipped ears are mostly brown, but greyish white inside. The face is grizzled brown with buffy eye-rings and prominent facial vibrissae. There are two annual moults: the spring moult is gradual and prolonged, and the autumnal moult is more complete and clear-cut. The winter coat is more greyish and less buffy. Occasionally individuals assume a pale grey dorsal and white ventral winter coat.

The pelage is composed of a dense pale grey underfur and long somewhat kinky guard hairs with a prominent black subterminal band and ochraceous tips. The guard hairs frequently part along the centre of the back to reveal dark patches and give the grizzled appearance.

The diagnostic features of the skull are the short, broad, heavy nasal bones, prominent anterior and posterior lobes of the supraorbital processes, carried clear of the braincase, and often prominent subcutaneous processes of the lachrymal bone that project from the anterior wall of the orbit.

Average measurements of adults: length 681 (640–700),

tail 92 (70–100), hind foot 153 (145–160), ear from notch 98 (79–100) mm; weight 4.2 (3.0–5.6) kg.

Habits. The European hare, like its relatives, is crepuscular and nocturnal and remains active all year. During the summer daylight hours it crouches in a shallow form in a clump of grass, weeds, or brush, only partially concealed, with its back showing. If detected, it bounds off across the open fields, avoiding thickets. It has great speed in the straightaway and also shows a tendency to dodge and double back if closely pursued. It has been timed at thirty-five miles an hour when bounding along a road. It is also a bold swimmer and will readily plunge into a stream to escape pursuit. During the winter months it may become buried by a snowstorm as it huddles in its form. It lies completely hidden there under the blanket of snow, but if it detects the footfalls of an intruder it will burst out of the snowbank as much as a hundred yards ahead of the observer.

These hares are usually solitary animals except during the breeding season. They have excellent sight and hearing as well as a keen olfactory sense. They are usually silent except for the low calls of does to their leverets and the piercing scream uttered when caught. There is little evidence that they occupy a restricted home range in this country as they have been tracked distances up to a mile or so in the snow. In England the home range is reported to be about twelve acres, and they are said to live up to twelve years of age.

The average population density in southern Ontario is about twenty-five hares to a square mile. However, populations of up to fifty to a square mile of ideal habitat are not uncommon, and the density may reach as high as one hundred under exceptional conditions. The population increased rapidly in Ontario from 1928 to 1940, declined from 1941 to 1948, and increased again between 1948 and 1950, before levelling off. The hare populations east of Toronto continued to increase, however, during the 1950s. This species has not lived in Canada long enough for us to ascertain whether it will assume a regular population fluctuation or whether the observed fluctuations are a result of the original population build-up. In its native Eurasia it is reported to show some fluctuation in densities.

European hares feed at night between 7 P.M. and 7 A.M. They eat grasses and herbs during the summer months and switch to the twigs, buds, and bark of shrubs and small trees in winter. The refection and reingestion of the green soft pellets occur during the daylight hours when the hares are resting in their forms.

Little is known of their predators in Canada. Undoubtedly red foxes, coyotes, and the larger hawks and owls are their chief enemies in this country.

Habitat. This species inhabits cultivated fields and meadowland.

Reproduction. In Europe the breeding season, which occurs between midwinter and midsummer, is thought to be terminated by summer drought (although rarely litters may be found at all seasons in England). During the breed-

Map 41 Distribution of the European hare, *Lepus europaeus*: * introduced

ing period the bucks appear to lose normal caution and career about the countryside chasing and fighting in broad daylight; after this period their gonads regress and remain dormant until midwinter. In spite of the unfavourable Canadian winter climate European hares appear to have maintained their reproductive cycle in this country. Several females taken between December and February in 1930 were either pregnant or lactating. A litter of new-born leverets was found frozen in the snow near Walkerton, Ontario, in early January 1929.

The gestation period is reported to be between thirty and forty-two days. The litter size varies between one and seven. The average number varies with the season in southern Russia, from 1.5 in the winter, 3.3 in the spring, 3.1 in the summer, to 2.0 in the autumn. The absorption of embryos *in utero* is quite high in this species and varies from 7 per cent in spring to 25 per cent in autumn. Near Moscow two litters a year for each adult doe seems to be the average. There is no comparable information for Canada.

The leverets are precocious at birth and are covered with long, silky grizzled fur. The white patches in the ears are characteristic of the species. Soon after they are born, the doe distributes the litter among several near-by forms to reduce the risk of total destruction by a predator. She visits the groups to nurse them regularly throughout the day. They do not mature until their second year.

Economic Status. European hares cause some damage to garden produce. Their greatest damage, however, is in orchards in winter, where they girdle the trunks of young apple trees. They have been known to girdle every tree in an orchard of 200 five-year-old apple trees. They seem to prefer apple to peach or cherry trees. In Duchess County, New York, damage by this species during the winter of 1915–16 amounted to an estimated $100,000. Control may be achieved by constructing collars of one-inch poultry mesh wire on two stake spreaders around the stems. An old-fashioned repellant, composed of a mixture of sulphur and lime, with glue added to provide adhesion, is effective if applied to the trunks with a paint brush two or three times during the winter months.

European hares are also prized as game animals. They run well before hounds and show remarkable talent in confusing them. Hares have been reported to run across recently manured fields, along railway tracks, in car tracks, and even over thin ice in order to throw the hounds off the scent. Often European hares are hunted in communal drives in southern Ontario. As many as 300 hares were killed in an area of six square miles during the early part of the winter of 1928–29. The meat is white and delicious.

Distribution. The natural distribution of this species includes Europe and Central Asia.

Canadian Distribution. The present Ontario population is derived from seven does and two bucks, which escaped from captivity on an island by crossing the frozen river in winter near Brantford, Ontario, in 1912. They spread very rapidly in southwestern Ontario, reaching Niagara Falls in 1921, Toronto in 1925, Kent County in 1928, Georgian Bay in 1928, and Kingston in 1948. They quickly occupied the parts of southern Ontario covered by Palaeozoic rocks, but did not invade the Precambrian Shield. More recently the hares crossed the narrow corridor of the Shield east of Kingston and reached the Ottawa valley, where a specimen was secured at Manotick in 1961. Several attempts were made to introduce these hares to the Lakehead near Fort William, Ontario, between 1941 and 1945. Survivors were seen until 1949, but the population has died out in that area (see Map 41). The introduced stock came from eastern Europe and belonged to the geographic subspecies:

Lepus europaeus hybridus Desmarest, 1822, Mammologie 2: 349. *In* Encyclopédie Méthodique, Paris.

REFERENCE

Dean, Paul B., and A. de Vos. 1965. The spread and the present status of the European hare, *Lepus europaeus hybridus* (Desmarest) in North America. Canadian Field-Nat. 79(1): 38–48.

Order **Rodentia** / Rodents

The rodents are the dominant order of mammals both in number of individuals and in number of species. They are practically cosmopolitan in distribution, being absent from only Antarctica. They are most easily identified by the two pairs of specialized incisors in the front of the mouth separated from the cheek teeth by a pronounced gap. The incisors grow throughout the life of the animal from persistent pulps. The enamel is restricted to the anterior face of the tooth. The softer dentine core of one tooth is continually abraded against its mate to form an efficient chisel-like blade for clipping vegetation. The lower jaw is specially articulated to permit only the incisors or cheek teeth to engage at one time. The animals chew with a side-to-side or rotary motion of the lower jaw. The hairy lips may be closed behind the front incisors to prevent debris from entering the mouth while the animal is cutting vegetation. The front feet usually have five digits, although the pollux is often vestigial. The hind foot usually has five clawed digits, but the number is less in some groups.

Rodents are primarily herbivorous in diet and therefore occupy an intermediate position in the food chain between vegetation and the carnivores. They are generally small in size, but some, such as the capabaras of South America, may weigh over 100 pounds.

ARTIFICIAL KEY TO THE FAMILIES OF CANADIAN RODENTIA

1	Quills on back and tail.	ERETHIZONTIDAE
1'	No quills on back and tail.	2
2	Aquatic rodents with webbed hind feet.	3
3	Tail flattened, paddle-like.	CASTORIDAE
3'	Tail long and round, fifth toe free of web.	CAPROMYIDAE
2'	Rodents without webbed feet (may be hair fringed).	4
4	Fur-lined pouches opening on cheeks.	5
5	Subterranean rodents with short, sparsely haired tails.	GEOMYIDAE
5'	Terrestrial jumping rodents with moderately long to very long tails with terminal tufts.	HETEROMYIDAE
4'	No fur-lined cheek pouches.	6
6	Stout, medium-sized, subterranean rodent, almost tailless, with flattened skull, found only in the lower Fraser valley of British Columbia.	APLODONTIDAE
6'	More slender, squirrel-like, or mouse-like, terrestrial rodents found across Canada.	7
7	Medium-sized, squirrel-like rodents, with bushy tails, rounded skulls with prominent post-orbital processes, mostly diurnal in activity (except the flying squirrel).	SCIURIDAE
7'	Small mouse-like, or rat-like rodents, mostly nocturnal.	8
8	Mice and rats with legs approximately the same size and tails short to medium in length.	MURIDAE
8'	Mice with hind feet enlarged for jumping, small forelimbs, and long wiry tails (no cheek pouches).	DIPODIDAE

Family **Aplodontidae** / Mountain Beaver

In rodent classification, the relationship of the masseter muscle to the infraorbital canal, which pierces the anterior wall of the zygomatic arch, is an important factor. In the mountain beaver, the masseter muscle has not modified the form of the infraorbital canal in any way. Because of this and other anatomical features it is considered to be the most primitive living rodent. The skull is very flat and triangular. There are no supraorbital processes. The lower jaw is powerfully built, particulary the angular processes. The cheek teeth are simplified in pattern and grow continuously through life. The auditory bullae are urn-shaped with an exceptionally long canal.

The external form of the single animal in this group is specialized for its fossorial way of life. The body is compact and heavy, and the legs, ears, and tail are short; the eyes are small; the feet are armed with strong claws.

MOUNTAIN BEAVER
Castor de montagne. *Aplodontia rufa* (Rafinesque)

Description. Since the mountain beaver is considered to be one of the living fossils it is one of Canada's really unique mammals. It has no living close relatives and appears to be related to the earliest known fossil rodents (Figure 32).

This species resembles a sort of tailless muskrat. It has a stout body, small, rounded ears, small brown eyes, short legs, and plantigrade feet with naked fleshy soles and long, pale curved claws. Its stubby tail is less than an inch long. When the thick hide has been removed it resembles a large mole with its short, thick neck, and the shoulder girdle so advanced that the heavily muscled forelimbs originate close behind the broad head (Figure 33). Its hind limbs are less robustly developed. It has two prominent anal glands, which emit a characteristic musky odour.

The pelage is grizzled brown and greyish beneath. It is composed of a thick undercoat, which is slate grey, except for the brown tips, and sparse, coarse guard hairs that are black-tipped dorsally and often white-tipped on the flanks and belly. The nasal vibrissae are long and coarse, and

Figure 32 Mountain beaver

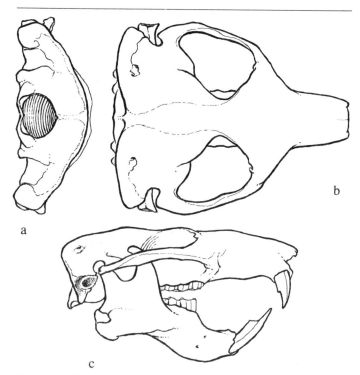

Figure 33 Mountain beaver skull: (a) hind view, (b) dorsal view, (c) lateral view (× 1)

there are a number of other long tactile hairs between the eyes and ears reminiscent of those found in the moles. Adult females possess prominent rings of darker fur about their three pairs of lateral mammae. There is one annual moult in midsummer. The new coat appears first on the shoulders and spreads irregularly to other parts of the body.

Average measurements of British Columbia males: length 357 (336–378), tail 33 (31–36), hind foot 59 (55–65), ear 15 mm. Average measurements of females: length 352 (350–358), tail 25 (22–32), hind foot 58 (56–60), ear 15 mm. Adult males weigh between 1 and 1.5 kg.

Habits. These animals are fossorial by habit and excavate a maze of tunnels about six inches in diameter and anywhere from less than a foot to six feet below the surface of the gound. The burrows are constructed in damp, porous soil, usually commencing in a stream bank and running fifty yards or more up the hillside. There are many entrances concealed in the undergrowth, and mounds of excavated earth and debris are scattered about. The animals also use an extensive network of runways through the bracken and salal connecting the entrances, which are not plugged like those of moles.

Mountain beaver are deliberate in their actions. They progress with a cumbersome gait above ground, frequently sitting hunched up to chew some tidbit. They seem to make little use of their eyes but use their sense of smell to detect food. Underground their well-developed vibrissae act as important sense organs. They whistle, squeal, and whine, and grate their teeth when cornered. They are generally shy animals but fight savagely when they have to.

Mountain beaver alternate active and rest periods throughout the full twenty-four-hour day. They have six or seven periods of activity of about ninety minutes' duration, principally about 3 A.M., 11 A.M., 3 P.M., and 10 P.M. The activity periods at night are about 50 per cent longer than those during the daylight hours. They do not hibernate but remain active throughout the winter. In severe weather they may plug their burrow entrances with vegetation and remain underground, utilizing their stored food. At other times they tunnel in the snow and peel the bark from saplings or clip off tender terminal shoots. They are occasionally observed running on top of the snow and even climbing into low bushes to feed on buds and tender twigs.

The mountain beaver appears to occur in loose colonies. Several may occupy the same extensive labyrinth of burrows. They do not, however, seem to be gregarious but rather are solitary in their behaviour. When penned, they do not huddle together but appear rather irritable. Most of the mature males bear scars, evidence of frequent fights.

These animals eat a wide range of plant materials in their habitat. During the summer months they show a preference for forbs and deciduous plants. Ferns and bracken seem to be high on their preferred list. They are also fond of the tender shoots and leaves of brambles and salmonberry and are known to eat such unattractive fare as skunk cabbage, nettles, and devil's club. During the winter they consume the needles, leaves, and tender twigs of such evergreens as salal, Oregon grape, cedar, fir, and hemlock.

Like the pikas, mountain beaver also sun-cure grass and fern fronds at the entrances to their burrows. Often the bundles are arranged neatly with all the stalks pointing in the same direction. This material is later dragged into the tunnels and stored for winter use near the nests.

Recently mountain beaver have been shown to reingest special green fæces, much as do the rabbits and their allies.

These large, sluggish rodents offer an attractive meal to some of the larger and stronger predators in their range. They are preyed upon by the cougar, lynx, coyote, fox, skunk, mink, and fisher, and during the hours of darkness quite a few fall prey to the great horned owl.

Although mountain beaver are fairly common in their favourite habitat, there is no information available on their longevity, home range, and populations. Unfortunately they are difficult to keep in captivity.

Habitat. The reference to beaver and muskrat in the description of this primarily fossorial animal is based upon its preference for a wet habitat. It inhabits a primarily riparian association in the forests. It frequently pads up small streams in preference to a dry land route and often blocks the streams with excavated soil and vegetable dirt. It digs its tunnels in porous damp soil in the stream's seepage areas. Often during the spring runoff, rivulets cascade down the mountain beaver's tunnels to pour out of the entrances in the banks and, rather than causing the mountain beaver to abandon the tunnels, this provides an atmosphere much to its liking.

The nest of leaves, grasses, and fern fronds is constructed in a chamber about fifteen to seventeen inches in diameter in a dry spot about two feet beneath a log, bank, stump, or overthrown tree. There is frequently clear water lying in a burrow a few feet below the nest.

The mountain beaver is found from the lower mountain valleys to the timberline and has been trapped at an elevation of 9,700 feet. Even when the climax forest is chopped down, the mountain beaver does well in the second-growth forest.

Reproduction. As is typical of many fossorial animals, this species has a low reproductive potential. Females do not mature until they are almost two years old. The species is monoestrous, which means that only one breeding cycle occurs each year. Oestrus occurs during a relatively short five- to seven-week period in February and March. Ovulation is spontaneous during this time. After a gestation period of twenty-eight to thirty days, the young are born sometime between mid-March and the end of April. The litter size varies from two to four, but two or three young are most frequently the rule. The young are born blind and helpless in the underground nest of dry grasses and bracken, but are soon covered with fine brown hair. They remain in the burrow for about two months, during which time they are suckled.

Economic Status. The mountain beaver is of consider-

Map 42 Distribution of the mountain beaver, *Aplodontia rufa*

able importance throughout its rather restricted range. Under natural conditions it inflicts heavy damage to the natural regeneration of young conifers by girdling the young trees and by stripping the leaders and side branches from them.

Unfortunately these animals also show a marked attraction to garden produce. They eat strawberries, raspberry canes, potatoes, cabbages, parsnips, cauliflowers, and pea vines. They not only eat the vegetables, but do quite a bit of damage in a market garden because of their size and their activity in tunnelling. This destruction includes tunnelling through irrigation ditches, plugging them with earth and vegetable debris, and muddying springs.

Mountain beavers are unwary and are easily trapped in steel traps or box traps. These methods are probably preferable to killing them by use of poison in such baits as apples or carrots, which may be eaten by pets or beneficial species about the garden.

In the early days the Pacific coastal tribes ate mountain beavers and also used their hides for robes. The Indian name of the robe is the basis of the common name 'sewellel.' The flesh and hides have no commercial value at present, however.

Distribution. This species is the sole living representative of a family unique to North America. Its distribution is confined to the Cascade Mountain range of the Pacific coast from east-central California north to southern British Columbia.

Canadian Distribution. The mountain beaver is confined to the moist coniferous forests of southwestern British Columbia south of the Fraser River (see Map 42). Two subspecies are recognized in Canada.

Aplondontia rufa rainieri Merriam, 1899, Proc. Biol. Soc. Washington 13: 21. Cascade Mountains of British Columbia, a slightly larger race than the typical form.

Aplodontia rufa rufa (Rafinesque), 1817, American Monthly Mag. 2: 45. Puget Sound lowlands of British Columbia.

REFERENCES

Lord, J.K. 1866. The naturalist in Vancouver Island and British Columbia, 1: 346–58. Richard Bentley, London.

Pfeiffer, E.W. 1958. The reproductive cycle of the female mountain beaver. Jour. Mamm. 39(2): 223–35.

Racey, Kenneth. 1922. The mountain beaver (*Aplodontia rufa*). Canadian Field-Nat. 36(2): 30–2.

Family **Sciuridae** / Squirrels

The animals that form this large family are among the best-known and best-liked small mammals. Almost cosmopolitan in distribution, they are absent only from Madagascar, New Guinea, Australia, New Zealand, and Antarctica. Squirrels are primarily diurnal in activity and have adapted to a wide choice of habitats from steppes to tropical jungles. Some are wholly terrestrial, others are arboreal, and a few are nocturnal gliders. All have large eyes, which serve as important sensory organs. Their fur is often varied and brilliant in colour: all have more or less bushy tails.

Structurally, the squirrels are primitive rodents – no part of the masseter muscle penetrates the infraorbital canal. The zygomatic arch is well formed with a slanting, flat anterior surface characteristic of the family. All squirrels possess prominent supraorbital processes on the frontal bones. The auditory bullae are well developed and rounded. The cheek teeth are ridged and rooted. The thumb is rudimentary, and the hind feet have five toes.

EASTERN CHIPMUNK
Suisse. *Tamias striatus* (Linnaeus)

Description. This perky little denizen of eastern Canadian woods, gardens, and fence rows is a favourite of young and old alike. When a chipmunk scampers across the path with its expressive tail held stiffly erect or inspects an intruder with sparkling eye, cocked head, and forepaws clasped to its breast, even the most urbane observer is charmed. Although alert and shy in its forest habitat, it soon becomes bold about the garden or cottage if unmolested and if offered handouts. The chipmunk offers little friendship in return, however, but imposes on its benefactor instead in order to satiate its extraordinary hoarding propensities (Plate 10).

Since almost everyone is familiar with a squirrel's

characteristic form, the chipmunk is best described as a diminutive ground-dwelling squirrel. Its face is rather longer than a squirrel's; it has short, rounded ears, a moderately long tail (about a third the total length) with a short, flattened 'brush,' flattened and hooked sharp claws, and large internal cheek pouches. Its skull is long, narrow, and delicate, with a relatively high cranium and sharp, slim supraoccipital processes pointing backwards.

The chipmunk's coat is quite distinctive. The pelage is short and fine. The muzzle and the top of the head are tawny or greyish brown; the cheeks are buffy, crossed by a tawny stripe from the vibrissae to below the ear, excluding a buffy eye-ring; the nape and shoulders are grey. Five prominent blackish stripes run down the back, the median one originating between the ears and running to the rump. Two lateral stripes occur on each side, separated by a creamy stripe from shoulders to rump. On each side of the median stripe is a grey stripe. The hips and rump are bright russet; the flanks and forefeet are buffy; the underparts are white. The upper surface of the tail is russet, with a fringe of mixed black and white-tipped hairs; below, the tail is tawny. The hind feet are ochraceous brown. There are apparently two annual moults. The midsummer one takes place in July and August, and there is evidence that a second moult occurs in late autumn or early winter when the chipmunks enter hibernation. The evidence is not conclusive, however, and exceptions seem to occur.

Average measurements of adults: length 268 (253–299), tail 101 (93–110), hind foot 37 (35–38), ear from notch 14 (12–16) mm; weight 97.0 (81.3–111.1) g.

Habits. Although chipmunks forage mainly on the ground, they also climb well. They are often seen harvesting berries in bushes and have been observed as high as sixty feet in a beech tree. They appear to depend a great deal on their eyesight and on their hearing. They can locate hidden foods that have a distinct odour but apparently not caches of dry nuts. Chipmunks are quite vocal. The normal call is an oft-repeated emphatic *chip* delivered with a jerk of the body. When alarmed they utter a sharp *chip* ending in a chatter – *chip p r r r* – before disappearing down their burrows. The chipmunk is strictly diurnal in activity. It appears above ground shortly after sunrise and returns to its burrow about sundown.

This species is frequently given as an example of a hibernator. True hibernators enter a prolonged state of torpor during the winter months when all their vital processes are lowered, but investigations have shown that the chipmunk remains in a state of torpor for only relatively short periods. When torpid, it rolls up in a ball with its head tucked between its hind legs and its tail pressed over its head and shoulders. Or it may assume a kitten-like position, lying on one side with its head turned sideways and its tail covering its face. It awakens from time to time in its winter nest to partake of some cached food or to perform its toilet in a special corner. When awakening, it trembles, stiffly unrolls, and staggers about, often with eyes shut. Chipmunks are very clean animals and keep their sleeping nests clear of shells, husks, and faeces, which they stuff into blind refuse tunnels. The eastern chipmunks awaken frequently during the late winter, and during mild spells in February or early March. They come out for a hasty reconnaissance, at which time one may often see their burrows and tracks on the late snowbanks in the woods.

In some areas such as New York State, the males first emerge from their winter quarters as early as March 7. The females appear about two weeks later, after March 23. They enter their burrows during the first cold spells of November, which may be as late as November 27 if the month is mild.

Chipmunks occupy an extensive burrow system, often more than twelve feet in length with one or two entrances. The burrows are excavated during the summer, and one burrow may be occupied permanently by the same chipmunk for its lifetime. Each year new storage tunnels or entrances are constructed and old ones closed until the galleries become extensive. The burrows are about two inches in diameter and lead tortuously to a central chamber about twelve inches in diameter and two to three feet underground.

In spite of all this tunnelling there is never any telltale pile of earth near the entrance, which is usually well concealed under a rock, root, or shrub. The tunnels appear to be excavated through a special 'work hole.' The dirt is either pushed out by the nose or carried in the cheek pouches and dumped some distance away. This loose dirt is sprayed about the vegetation by vigorous kicks as the chipmunk returns to its hole. The 'work hole' is eventually plugged, and the true entrance is left well camouflaged.

Chipmunks are solitary animals. The sexes fraternize only during the mating period. At other times they defend their territories vigorously against their neighbours. In ideal habitat the average home range of an adult male has been determined to be 0.37 acre and that of a female 0.26 acre. Chipmunks occupy these homes ranges, which broadly overlap others, more or less permanently. The males travel more during the breeding season in search of mates. Chipmunk populations varied between 4.14 and 15.23 animals per acre in a study conducted in New York State.

Chipmunks have been thought to aestivate during the summer months, but in fact they are merely quieter at that period. Many females are rearing their young then, and others are busy digging burrows. They are more obvious in the spring and even more so in the autumn when they are storing food for the winter.

Chipmunks may live up to five years in captivity, but in the wild three years seems to be about the maximum longevity. About 56 per cent of the adult population survives over winter, and about 45 per cent of the young survive their first winter.

Chipmunks eat a wide variety of seeds, fruits, and nuts as well as green vegetation, although this is of less importance to them. In spring they are particularly fond of the opening buds of American elms. Later they eat the samaras of maples and the seeds of herbaceous plants such as dog-toothed violets and wild geraniums. In the summer they eat a host of wild fruit – chokecherries,

pincherries, raspberries, partridge berries, and wintergreen berries. In the autumn the diet switches to the hard nuts – hickory, acorns, beech, and hazel. They are also fond of such domestic crops as corn and sunflower seeds. In the autumn they may store as much as six quarts of food underground for winter use, carrying loads of seeds and nuts crammed into their bulging cheek pouches (as many as thirty-two beech nuts or thirteen prune stones have been carried at one time). Much of this booty is stored in the nest chamber; other caches are laid in blind tunnels, stumps, and hollow logs. The animal's scientific name, *Tamias*, means 'steward' in Latin and seems to be particularly applicable.

The normal diet of the eastern chipmunk also includes a surprising array of animal food: slugs, worms, frogs, and salamanders. Most surprising are the eye-witness accounts of chipmunks pursuing and killing red-bellied and garter snakes up to two feet in length. Such a large snake is certainly a powerful antagonist for a chipmunk to tackle. Chipmunks drink a great deal of free water during their normal daytime activities. This they do by sucking up the water like a horse, rather than lapping it up like a dog.

The chipmunk must be perpetually vigilant against a host of predators, including the larger hawks, raccoons, foxes, and weasels. Probably the ermine and the long-tailed weasel are the most dangerous because they can follow it into its burrow. To evade these predators, the chipmunk may climb to the top of a tree. Cats are also important predators since the chipmunk's habitat so often lies close to suburban houses. There is also a record of a rat killing a chipmunk.

Habitat. Dry hardwood forests are the favourite haunts of the eastern chipmunk. The forests are particularly attractive if they provide suitable cover in the way of stumps, logs, rocks, banks, bushes, and woodpiles. The chipmunk will also inhabit more open country such as hedgerows, fences, stone piles, and gardens, if the earth is porous enough for tunnelling and if plenty of cover is available.

Reproduction. For the males, the annual breeding cycle commences in late February, while they are still in hibernation, and continues without abatement until July. The females have two annual oestrous cycles: the first from approximately mid-March to early April and the second from June 19 to July 10. Matings occur soon after the chipmunks appear in the spring. After a gestation period of thirty-one or thirty-two days, the first litters are born. These may number anywhere from one to eight, but the mode is three or four.

The young chipmunks are born in their mother's winter nest, which usually consists of dry leaf fragments on top of her winter cache of nuts and seeds. A litter of seven chipmunks born in captivity weighed a total of 21 g and averaged 66 mm in length. Their mother's weight dropped from 121 g before birth to 97 g after the event. At birth the young are naked, with wrinkled, reddish skin; they are also blind and completely helpless. They grow quite rapidly, however. At five days they measure about 80 mm in length, and the first reddish brown silky hair appears on

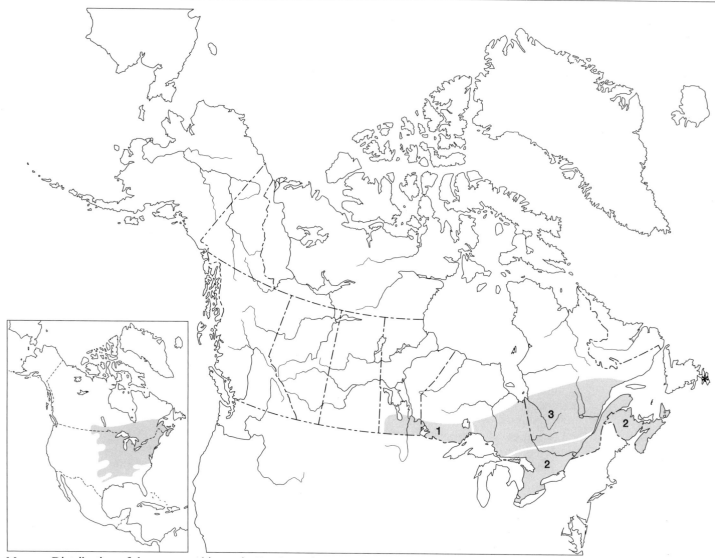

Map 43 Distribution of the eastern chipmunk, *Tamias striatus*: 1 *T. s. griseus*, 2 *T. s. lysteri*, 3 *T. s. quebecensis*, * introduced

their heads. At ten days the dorsal stripe appears, and the youngsters totter about the nest. At eighteen days the typical colour pattern is fully developed, and the chipmunks are clothed in short, silky hair. By the fourth week they behave like adults, scampering about the nest cavity and washing their faces, even though their eyes are still closed. Finally their eyes open on the thirty-first day after birth. The young chipmunks reach adult size after about eight weeks and weigh about 75 g. They first appear above ground at the age of five to six weeks, but stay with their mother in her burrow until they are two to three months old. By that time the mother is preparing for her second litter.

The young chipmunks of the spring litter moult their juvenile coats between late June and August. Although a few of the most advanced young females may mature during their first summer and bear litters in late summer, the males do not mature until late the following winter when their elders again become sexually active.

Those in the second litter, born in midsummer or later, do not moult to adult pelage until October or November,

and none of them mature until the following spring.

Economic Status. Very few complaints are ever registered against the eastern chipmunk. Usually householders willingly provide sunflower seeds or nuts in order to enjoy their company. About the only real damage they do is to eat the bulbs and corms of such ornamental plants as crocuses, tulips, and lilies. If the damage is not too extensive, they may escape with only an epithet hurled at them. One pleasant July evening while reclining in my garden admiring my favourite stand of tall, regal lilies, I was amazed to see one stalk suddenly collapse. I hurriedly picked up the stalk, which pulled freely out of the ground, revealing a hollow chamber in the soil underneath. As I peered down, the bright, saucy face of a chipmunk returned my gaze as it finished off the remainder of the lily corm from which it had cut the stalk.

Distribution. The eastern chipmunk is found in eastern North America from the states bordering the Gulf of Mexico north to the southern tip of James Bay.

Canadian Distribution. Three subspecies of this chipmunk are recognized in eastern Canada (see Map 43).

They occur from Cape Breton Island, Nova Scotia, to southern Manitoba and northward to Moosonee, Ontario, and Sept-Îles, Quebec, on the north shore of the Gulf of St Lawrence.

Tamias striatus griseus Mearns, 1891, Bull. American Mus. Nat. Hist. 3: 231. Southern Manitoba and northwestern Ontario.

Tamias striatus lysteri (Richardson), 1829, Fauna Boreali-Americana 1: 181. Southern Ontario and the Maritimes (except Prince Edward Island and introduced to Newfoundland).

Tamias striatus quebecensis Cameron, 1950, Jour. Mamm. 31: 347. Quebec and northeastern Ontario.

REFERENCES

Smith, L.C., and D.A. Smith. 1972. Reproductive biology, breeding seasons, and growth of eastern chipmunks *Tamias striatus* (Rodentia: Sciuridae) in Canada. Canadian Jour. Zool. 50: 1069–85.

Tryon, C.A., and D.P. Snyder. 1973. Biology of the eastern chipmunk, *Tamias striatus*: life tables, age distributions and trends in population numbers. Jour. Mamm. 54(1): 145–68.

LEAST CHIPMUNK
Tamia mineur. *Eutamias minimus* (Bachman)

Description. Whereas the genus *Tamias* contains only one well-marked species (the eastern chipmunk), the genus *Eutamias* contains a wide array of similar species in western North America, which are collectively referred to as western chipmunks. These species may be distinguished from the eastern chipmunk by their smaller size, slimmer body, longer tail (almost half the total length), pointed ears, greyer pelage, and narrower, longer dorsal stripes. They have other important anatomical features, such as an extra upper premolar (PM 3) and minute supraorbital processes. The closest relatives of the western chipmunks are found in Asia and not in eastern North America.

The eastern naturalist may be somewhat dubious of the recognition of so many almost indistinguishable species, some of which occur in the same locality. Close study will, however, show that the species have restricted ecological requirements so that they seldom meet except on the boundaries of their habitats. Often they are altitudinally separated in the mountains. One may also recognize behavioural and voice differences, which assist in segregating the species.

Four species of western chipmunks occur in Canada, of which the least chipmunk, though the smallest, has the widest distribution. Its forehead is brown. Three dark brown stripes cross the cheeks, the middle one running through the eye. Between these are two white lines running from nose to ears. The nape is grey. Dorsally, five black stripes (edged in brown) traverse the back. The median one, running from the forehead to the base of the tail, is the longest. The lateral dark stripes are short and

run only from the flanks to the hips. Between the dark stripes are four grey lines, the lateral ones paler than the medial ones. The shoulders are ochraceous, the rump and hind legs grey, and the underparts white from chin to tail. The flanks are buffy. The upper surface of the tail is dark brown sprinkled with buffy hairs. The under surface of the tail is fulvous with a submarginal black band and one of buffy-tipped hairs extending beyond it. The ears are lightly clothed with brown hair on the inside, blackish hairs on the anterior part of the back, and greyish hairs towards the posterior portion of the ear. There is a pronounced moult in July and August, when the animals assume a more ochraceous summer coat than the greyish winter pelage. There is a second, more gradual moult in late September and October, when the winter coat is assumed.

Average measurements of fifteen adult males of the widespread subspecies *borealis*: total length 221 (213–234), tail 100 (97–103), hind foot 30 (27–33), ear from crown 15 (15–16) mm. Fifteen adult females measured 229 (225–239), tail 103 (99–107), hind foot 30 (28–32), ear from crown 15 (14–16) mm. Average weight of both sexes was 42.9 (35.9–50.3) g.

Habits. This sprightly, diminutive squirrel is even quicker and more agile than the eastern chipmunk. It seems to spend most of its time in a frenzied preoccupation with gathering food. It is strictly diurnal and retires to its chamber to sleep before the sun has set. Although most of its activity takes place on the ground, it also spends considerable time climbing about the low branches of trees. It utters a wide variety of calls depending upon circumstances. There is a monotonously repeated low *wop-wop* and bird-like *chip-chip*. Finally it has its own alarm note *tsp p r r r* followed by a trill as it rushes for cover. The chipmunk is always alert for the warning sounds of other species and is quick to give warning itself when a hawk or carnivore appears. Although extremely shy by nature, it becomes very bold about a camp-site if unmolested and is soon pilfering tidbits from the fireplace or larder.

The least chipmunk, like its close relatives, enters a state of torpor during the winter months. Its hibernation is not complete, however, as it awakens fitfully to take food from the store pile and to attend to its toilet. The dates at which it enters and terminates hibernation vary with the district. In southern Manitoba a few are seen as late as early November and most become active again by the first week of April. However in Wood Buffalo Park in Alberta and the Northwest Territories it disappears by early October and does not reappear until the end of April.

The winter nest is carefully constructed of dry shredded grass or bark and often lined with rabbit hair, cut-up feathers, or silky fibres of poplar or willow catkins. It is placed in a chamber about six inches in diameter on top of a store of nuts, seeds, acorns, and cherry pits, usually situated between eighteen and thirty-six inches below the surface. The chamber is reached by a tunnel about an inch and a half in diameter and four or five feet long. The tunnel is carefully constructed through a 'work hole,' through which the earth is removed and dumped, and which is then loosely plugged, so that there are no signs of fresh earth about the true entrance. The western chipmunks appear to dig only one entrance to their burrows. Although it is probable that they could escape through the plugged work holes in an emergency, many are probably trapped when a weasel or large snake enters the burrow. The winter dens are usually situated in forests, where the ground is heavily mulched with leaves, which provide further frost protection.

During the summer months the least chipmunk may occupy a nest in an abandoned woodpecker cavity, hollow log, or stump or may even build a bulky nest of grass and leaves in the branches of a tree.

The diet of the least chipmunk includes a wide range of seeds, berries, and nuts of native plants in its environment. Among its favourite foods are blueberries, raspberries, thimbleberries, and strawberries. The chipmunk does not eat the whole fruit, as one might think, but cuts it open, eats the seeds, and rejects the pulp. Neat little piles of fruit pulp on rocks are mute evidence of the presence of these little squirrels. They are also fond of cherry pits, acorns, rose hips, and crabapple pips, and eat the seeds of a wide variety of grasses, sedges, and weeds, such as smartweed and cranesbill.

The least chipmunk stores away a great deal of its food in caches. Some stocks have been found to contain as many as 478 acorns and 2,734 cherry pits, and one contained 167 hazel nuts and several thousand cherry pits. The chipmunks cram their ample cheek pouches to carry their booty. One pouch examined contained as many as 3,700 blueberry seeds, another 86 smartweed seeds, another 800 timothy seeds, and still another 66 red-osier dogwood pits. Green vegetation is only rarely eaten.

Besides their vegetable diet, these chipmunks eat a wide variety of invertebrates, including grasshoppers and their eggs, beetles, caterpillars, and fly larvae. They seem to eat fewer large vertebrates than the larger eastern chipmunks, but they may occasionally take birds' eggs or young birds in the nest.

Little information is available on population densities for this species, although it is known that their population fluctuates from year to year. Densities of six chipmunks per acre have been recorded. In captivity, individuals have lived as long as six years, but their longevity in the wild is probably much less. The home range has been estimated to be about a quarter of an acre.

The little animals are beset by a host of predators: snakes and hawks, and also carnivores from the ermine weasel to the mighty grizzly bear – although the grizzly would hardly obtain enough nourishment from one least chipmunk to merit the energy required to dig one out of its nest or the stump in which it took refuge.

Habitat. The least chipmunk occupies a wide variety of habitats from alpine tundra and evergreen coniferous forest to sagebrush plains. Although it is a characteristic mammal of the boreal forest region, which spans Canada in a broad belt, this species seldom inhabits the dense climax coniferous stands. It occupies the forest edges, openings, stream valleys, and lakeshores wherever sunlight breaks through the coniferous canopy. It is particularly abundant in open stands of jackpine on sandy ridges and in second growth after fires and lumbering operations. It likes tangles of logs, rocks, and underbrush and proximity to water, although it prefers dry to damp situations.

It also may be found on the alpine tundra in the shrubby growth beyond the timberline and in river banks and coulees on the arid sagebrush plains wherever there is adequate cover.

Reproduction. Breeding commences soon after the chipmunks emerge from hibernation in early spring. At that period there are frequently lively chases across the forest floor. By May things have quieted down considerably as the females become involved in family matters. After a gestation period of twenty-eight to thirty days, the young are born. The litter size varies from four to seven and averages about 5.5. The earliest litters arrive after mid-May. There is usually only one litter a year, but if the first litter is lost the female experiences post-partum oestrus and a second litter is born in late June.

At birth the young are naked, with pinkish, transparent skin. Their eyes are closed, and their ear orifices are also closed by a thin membrane. They measure about 50 mm in length and weigh about 2.25 g. They stay with their mothers for about two months, during which period the latter have been observed carrying their young about by the scruff of the neck and teaching them to forage for themselves.

Economic Status. These little chipmunks, though quite fond of domestic grain seeds, are seldom numerous enough to create any appreciable damage. Their role in forest regeneration is not known in any detail; but they do 'plant' many tree seeds in their caches. They also destroy many insects. However, these drawbacks are seldom considered when the camper watches with pleasure as a bold chipmunk stuffs bread crusts into its cheek pouches, for it is generally agreed that this species has a high aesthetic value.

Distribution. This species is the most northern of western chipmunks and occurs in a broad belt across Canada from the central Yukon Territory to Noranda, Quebec. It also occurs southward in the Rocky Mountain region as far as Arizona and New Mexico.

Canadian Distribution. The least chipmunk is a plastic species, which shows considerable geographical variation in size and colour over its range. Seven subspecies are currently recognized in Canada (see Map 44).

Eutamias minimus borealis (J.A. Allen), 1877, *in* Coues and Allen, Monogr. N. American Rodentia, p. 793. Central Canada from northeastern British Columbia and southern Mackenzie District to James Bay, Ontario. The typical race, as described.

Eutamias minimus caniceps Osgood, 1900, N. American Fauna 19: 28. Southern Yukon Territory and adjacent northwestern British Columbia. Greyer than *borealis*, under side of tail a pale buff; hind foot longer.

Eutamias minimus hudsonius Anderson and Rand, 1944,

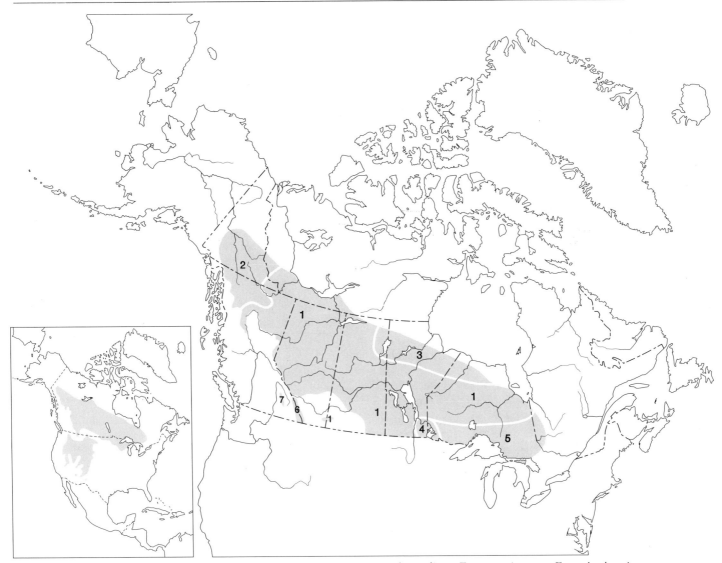

Map 44 Distribution of the least chipmunk, *Eutamias minimus*: 1 *E. m. borealis*, 2 *E. m. caniceps*, 3 *E. m. hudsonius*, 4 *E. m. jacksoni*, 5 *E. m. neglectus*, 6 *E. m. oreocetes*, 7 *E. m. selkirki*

Canadian Field-Nat. 57: 133. Northeastern Saskatchewan, northern Manitoba, and northwestern Ontario; greyer.

Eutamias minimus jacksoni A.H. Howell, 1925, Jour. Mamm. 6: 53. Southeastern corner of Manitoba and the Lake of the Woods area of western Ontario. Smaller and more brightly coloured than other subspecies.

Eutamias minimus neglectus (J.A. Allen), 1890, Bull. American Mus. Nat. Hist. 3: 36. Central Ontario and the Noranda-Rouyn area of northwestern Quebec. A dull race. This race of the least chipmunk has shown a marked eastward expansion of its distribution in the past thirty-five years. In 1928, Lake Abitibi, Lake Nipissing, and the French River appeared to be the eastern limits of its range. Recently it has spread into northern Quebec and southward to the Parry Sound district and Algonquin Park in southern Ontario. Over much of its range in central Ontario the least chipmunk and the eastern chipmunk occur together. The present species prefers coniferous woods, and the eastern species hardwood forests.

Eutamias minimus oreocetes Merriam, 1897, Proc. Biol. Soc. Washington 11: 207. Alpine tundra of the Rocky Mountain watershed from the international boundary north to southern Banff National Park, Alberta, and British Columbia at elevations of 6,800 to 7,500 feet. Small, pale, with short tail.

Eutamias minimus selkirki Cowan, 1946, Proc. Biol. Soc. Washington 59: 113. Small, dark, with short tail. Known only from the Selkirk Mountains of British Columbia.

REFERENCE

Sheppard, D.H. 1969. A comparison of reproduction in two chipmunk species (*Eutamias*). Canadian Jour. Zool. 47: 603–8.

YELLOW PINE CHIPMUNK
Tamia amène. *Eutamias amoenus* (J.A. Allen)

Description. The yellow pine chipmunk is very similar to the least chipmunk in size and colour, but there are sufficient differences to distinguish between them in the few areas where their distributions overlap. This species tends to be larger than the other, and the markings differ. This species has the same distinctive pattern of black and pale grey stripes that is characteristic of all western chipmunks, but the coloration is richer. There is a general ochraceous wash to the pelage that differs from the greyish tones found in *E. minimus*. The flanks are a pronounced cinnamon colour. The dorsal surfaces of the ears are black, with a more prominent white posterior edge and similar whitish areas on the back of the head behind the ears. The undersurface of the tail is more ochraceous brown than the tawny yellow colour found in *minimus*. In several races the belly is buff, however, but unfortunately this is not the rule. The rump is more olive-brown than that of the least chipmunk.

There are two annual moults. The males assume their brighter summer coat in late June and July, followed by the females in late July and August. There is usually a prominent dividing line between the old pelage and the new one, which occurs on the head and shoulders and works gradually backwards. The greyer winter coat comes in gradually in patches. The males commence their autumn moult in September and October, and the females in October and November.

Average measurements of fifteen adults of the northern race *septentrionalis*: length 223 (214–230), tail 95 (89–100), hind foot 33 (31–35), ear 17 (16–18) mm. Average weight of adults in August, 51 (46–62) g.

Habits. This species has the same bright, nervous energy as the least chipmunk. When foraging on the ground it always moves in short rushes. When sitting it may wave its tail from side to side, and when running it may hold it erect or horizontally. The yellow pine chipmunk also climbs trees in short spurts. It climbs about the lower shrubs freely and when the pine cones are opening in late summer it may climb over a hundred feet and stay aloft for as long as thirty minutes feeding on the seeds. It is as reluctant to swim as are its relatives, which may explain why large rivers frequently mark the boundaries of chipmunk ranges.

As may be expected, these chipmunks are strictly diurnal in activity. They appear shortly before sunrise and are very active for the first few hours. Few are seen from about nine in the morning until three in the afternoon during the heat of summer. They become more active again in the evening but normally retire within thirty minutes after sunset. They usually stay under cover during heavy rainstorms and periods of strong wind. After a shower, however, they seem to become very active and 'chip' incessantly.

They have a variety of calls from a soft *whoit* to a shrill chatter of fright. They have keen hearing and keen sight. Chipmunks quickly identify a hawk threading through the trees and immediately spread the alarm. They are clean little animals and spend considerable time brushing their fur, washing their faces, and taking dust baths. They are not very sociable, however, and live solitary lives on the whole, except for their brief period of family responsibilities.

102

COLOUR PLATE

11

Woodchuck, *Marmota monax*

12

Hoary marmot, *Marmota caligata*

COLOUR PLATE

13

American beaver, *Castor canadensis*

14

Muskrat, *Ondatra zibethicus*

The various species of western chipmunks appear to be light hibernators. Two facts support this conclusion: they do not put on an excessive layer of fat in the autumn, and they store seeds in their winter nests. They have labile body temperatures: 38°c with moderate activity, 34°c sleeping, and 4.6°c in deep hibernation. They become lethargic even in cold spells during the summer. In eastern Washington State these animals are active through the early snowfalls of October but disappear before mid-November. Farther north, at Banff, Alberta, they enter their winter dens by mid-October The first chipmunks usually appear in early April, but it is not until later in the month that many are seen.

This species excavates its own burrow, which is, on an average, about twenty-seven inches in length (ranging from fifteen to thirty-nine inches) and about one and a half to two and a half inches in diameter. It leads to a chamber about six inches in diameter and, on an average, eleven inches (ranging from seven to nineteen inches) below the surface. About ten inches from the entrance there is usually an enlargement or blind tunnel, which is thought to be a turning area. There is no loose earth about the entrance, and the existence of plugged side branches suggests that the burrow is constructed through a 'work hole,' as with other chipmunks. The nests are composed of an outer shell of dried grasses, containing a mixture of seeds and nuts in the autumn, and are lined with thistle down or rabbit fur.

Yellow pine chipmunks eat a wide array of seeds, fruit, fungi, and corms found in their environment. Some of the more important plant seeds eaten include knotweed, yarrow, thistle, yellow pine, Douglas fir, larch, huckleberries, grass, and sedge. They are also reported to eat subterranean fungi and underground parts of plants such as corms. Apparently nuts are not as important in the diet of this species as they are in that of some other chipmunks. Animal food in the form of insects is also taken less frequently.

Predators include the rattlesnake, the diurnal pigmy owl, the goshawk, Cooper's hawk, and weasels, coyotes, badgers, and bobcats. In spite of the array of predators, 65 per cent of one population sampled survived over one winter. Marked chipmunks of this species have been known to live at least five years in the wild state. No information is available on population density.

Habitat. This species is characteristic of the open, dry yellow pine–Douglas fir forests where they inhabit the stumps, logs, brush, and rock outcroppings. Although they occur at intermediate altitudes in Canada (from about 2,500 to 6,000 feet), they are found as high as 14,000 feet on Mount Rainier in Washington State. There they inhabit brushy zones beyond the dense subalpine forests on the border of the open alpine tundra.

Reproduction. There seems to be only one annual breeding season, in early spring. The males are in reproductive condition upon emergence, but the gonads regress by the middle of May. There is no information on the oestrous cycle of the females. Mating probably occurs in April, and the young are born between mid-May and early June. The

103

Map 45 Distribution of the yellow pine chipmunk, *Eutamias amoenus*: 1 *E. a. affinus*, 2 *E. a. felix*, 3 *E. a. ludibundus*, 4 *E. a. luteiventris*, 5 *E. a. septentrionalis*

litter size varies between four and eight, with an average of 5.8. There are four pairs of mammae: one pectoral, two abdominal, and one inguinal. The average weight at birth is 2.65 g and the total length about 50 mm. The young are born and cared for in the female's winter burrow. The ears unfold at about seven days of age, the dorsal black-and-white stripes appear at about ten days, and the eyes open at thirty to thirty-three days. Weaning is a gradual process and is completed when the young are about six weeks old. The young first appear above ground in late June. They reach adult size by autumn but do not mature until the following spring.

Economic Status. There is no quantitative information available on the role of these animals in forest regeneration. Although they eat many coniferous tree seeds, they also cache many seeds, which they then lose, so that in a sense these are planted. This species appears to be less destructive to young trees than some other small mammals.

Above all, their attractive ways lend much interest to the mountain forests.

Distribution. The yellow pine chipmunk is found in the Rocky Mountain region of western North America from northern California to central British Columbia.

Canadian Distribution. Five geographical races are recognized in the Rocky Mountain region of Canada (see Map 45). British Columbia west of the Continental Divide is the heart of the range of the species in Canada, but it has crossed the Divide to the eastern slope of the Rockies in Alberta through several low passes north to the Yellowhead Pass in Jasper National Park.

Eutamias amoenus affinis (J.A. Allen), 1890, Bull. American Mus. Nat. Hist. 3: 103. The palest race, found in south-central British Columbia.

Eutamias amoenus felix (Rhoads), 1895, American Nat. 29: 941. The darkest race, found in coastal southwestern British Columbia.

Eutamias amoenus ludibundus Hollister, 1911, Smiths. Misc. Coll. 56: 1. The brightest race, with white belly and rufous under side of the tail. East-central British Columbia and Jasper, Alberta.

Eutamias amoenus luteiventris (J.A. Allen), 1890, Bull. American Mus. Nat. Hist. 3: 101. Buffy underparts. Southeastern British Columbia and the east slope of the Rocky Mountains of Alberta from the Kicking Horse Pass in Banff National Park southward. The lower Bow valley in Banff Park separates the ranges of *E. a. luteiventris* (on the west) from *E. m. borealis* (on the east). Only in the immediate vicinity of the Lake Louise and Banff bridges has this species captured a foothold on the eastern bank.

Eutamias amoenus septentrionalis Cowan, 1946, Proc. Biol. Soc. Washington 59: 110. Rather drab colouring with paler under surface of tail. Central British Columbia.

REFERENCE

Broadbooks, H.E. 1958. Life history and ecology of the chipmunk *Eutamias amoenus* in eastern Washington. Mus. Zool. Univ. Michigan Misc. Pub. 103.

TOWNSEND'S CHIPMUNK
Tamia de Townsend. *Eutamias townsendii* (Bachman)

Description. This is the largest of the western chipmunks. The pelage is washed with warm brown, which masks the colour contrasts of the dorsal stripes found in other western chipmunks. The black stripes are more brownish (particularly the lateral ones), and the intervening 'pale' stripes are tawny brown. The forehead is dark brown; the cheeks are buffy, crossed by two brown stripes. The shoulders, flanks, and rump are dark ochraceous to olive brown. The medial line of the unusually bushy tail is rufous, bordered by a submarginal black band and grey hair tips. The under side of the tail is bright rufous red bordered in black. The underparts are whitish.

There are two annual moults, and in each case the males moult before the females. The males commence the summer moult in late June and complete it in July, while the females moult in August and early September. The males assume the paler winter coat in late September and October, while the females moult even later. There are indications of two colour phases in this species, independent of sex and moult: one is dull olivaceous, and the other is more tawny.

Average measurements of ten adult males from British Columbia: length 254 (246–263), tail 113 (104–119), hind foot 37 (34–40) mm. The average measurements of females are slightly larger: length 271 (265–280), tail 124 (120–130), hind foot 38 (37–39) mm. Average weight of both sexes 85 g.

Habits. This species appears to be more shy and secretive than its relatives. It usually stays well hidden in dense undercover. Its movements are more deliberate, and it seems to call less frequently. The usual note is a slowly

Map 46 Distribution of Townsend's chipmunk, *Eutamias townsendii*, ∗ introduced

repeated *chuck chuck chuck*, and the alarm note is a brisk *kivis*. This species climbs regularly in bushes and in the lower branches of trees, occasionally to heights of forty or sixty feet. It is most active after dawn and in late afternoon, and few are abroad after 6 P.M. Like its relatives, it stays under cover during rainy spells.

Hibernation is shorter in this species than in the other chipmunks considered. It is usually active from March to late November, and remains dormant only through the most inclement winter weather. Torpid Townsend's chipmunks have been found in nests under stumps and in one case in a stump five feet above the ground. Some have been seen during mild spells in February. Chipmunks living at higher elevations in the mountains have longer hibernation periods.

This species also excavates burrows mostly near the bases of trees where the nest is protected by the large roots. One excavated burrow, which was about four feet long with a single entrance and a turning point, led to a sedge- and lichen-lined nest in a chamber about a foot underground among the roots of a tree.

The home range of this species is about 1.7 acres, and its longevity is seven years.

The food of this species consists of nuts (hazelnuts), seeds, fruits, insects, bulbs, and roots.

Habitat. Townsend's chipmunk is an inhabitant of the

dense Pacific coast forests of Douglas fir and red cedar. It is confined to the coastal lowlands and to the dense montane hemlock forests of the Cascade Mountains. Since much of its natural habitat has been logged over, it now lives amid a tangle of logs and subclimax brush. Populations in this habitat, however, seem to be lower than in the remaining islands of climax forest.

Reproduction. The reproductive cycle of this species has not been studied in detail, but it is unlikely that it differs much from that of the other western chipmunks.

Economic Status. Unknown.

Distribution. The Pacific coast of North America from California to southern British Columbia between the Cascade Mountains and the ocean.

Canadian Distribution. Townsend's chipmunk is found only in extreme southwestern British Columbia, where two races are recognized (see Map 46).

Eutamias townsendii cooperi (Baird), 1855, Proc. Acad. Nat. Sci. Philadelphia 7: 334. Cascade Mountains in the Hope–Princeton area, British Columbia.

Eutamias townsendii townsendii (Bachman), 1839, Jour. Acad. Nat. Sci. Philadelphia 8: 68. Fraser River delta lowlands, British Columbia. Introduced to Esquimalt, Vancouver Island.

REFERENCE

Larrison, E.J. 1947. Notes on the chipmunks of west central Washington. The Murrelet 28: 23–30.

RED-TAILED CHIPMUNK
Tamia à queue rousse. *Eutamias ruficaudus* A.H. Howell

Description. The red-tailed chipmunk is quite similar in appearance to the least and yellow pine chipmunks, but it is a little larger and more brightly coloured. There are three prominent black dorsal stripes – the central one running from between the ears to the tail – between which are two medial grey stripes. The two lateral pale stripes are whitish, and the lateral dark stripes are brownish and less prominent. The forehead is grizzled brown. The cheeks are crossed by two prominent white stripes separated by three brown stripes. The posterior surfaces of the ears are black anteriorly and posteriorly. The shoulders and flanks are rufous brown, the rump is olive brown, the feet are cinnamon, and the underparts are white. The dorsal side of the tail is rufous, with a black submarginal band and yellowish tips to the hairs. The central portion of the ventral surface of the tail is brick red.

Average measurements of adults: length 225 (211–235), tail 95 (90–102), hind foot 35 (34–36) mm; average weight 60 g.

Habits. Little has been written concerning the life history of this species. In Waterton Lakes National Park, Alberta, I found these animals to be much more arboreal than other chipmunks. They spent much of their time in the low branches of coniferous trees. They were also particularly lively and uttered quick chattering calls reminiscent of small-scale red squirrels.

Map 47 Distribution of the red-tailed chipmunk, *Eutamias ruficaudus*

Habitat. The two subspecies of this chipmunk seem to have very different habitats. The nominate race occupies the spruce–fir forests of the Continental Divide and may frequently be observed at the timberline in the scrubby alpine fir. It occurs in an altitude range of from 5,800 to 7,000 feet. The second subspecies occurs in open valley stands of yellow pine.

Reproduction. No details are known.

Economic Status. This chipmunk is too scarce in Canada tomze of any economic significance.

Distribution. The red-tailed chipmunk is found in the central Rocky Mountain region of Montana, Idaho, Alberta, and British Columbia.

Canadian Distribution. This chipmunk barely reaches southwestern Alberta and the East Kootenay valley of British Columbia. Two subspecies are recognized (see Map 47).

Eutamias ruficaudus ruficaudus A.H. Howell, 1920, Proc. Biol. Soc. Washington 33: 91. The Continental Divide in extreme southwestern Alberta and southeastern British Columbia, as described above.

Eutamias ruficaudus simulans A.H. Howell, 1922, Jour. Mamm. 3: 179. Smaller and paler form found in the open, dry East Kootenay valley of British Columbia.

WOODCHUCK
Marmotte commune. *Marmota monax* (Linnaeus)

Description. The marmots form a group of large, robust ground-dwelling squirrels. They have thickset bodies, broad, flat heads, hardly any necks at all, short, rounded ears, short, powerful limbs, and tails only about a quarter of the body length. Their skulls are similarly broad and flat. The supraorbital processes projecting from the frontals at right angles are strongly developed. The tips usually project slightly forward in this species (Figure 34). The first digit on the forelimb (pollex) is rudimentary and covered by a flat nail, but the hind foot has five well-developed digits. All the other digits are armed with flattened, curved claws. A large woodchuck may measure 2 feet in length and weigh 14 pounds (Plate 11).

Of the American marmots the woodchuck or groundhog is the best known. The common name is believed to be a corruption of an Indian name used by trappers in northern Canada. This mammal is the focal point of a fanciful piece of folklore: it is supposed to come out of its burrow each year on February 2 and to forecast the weather for the following six weeks. If it sees its shadow it becomes frightened and returns to the protection of its burrow and by so doing forecasts another six weeks of winter. If, however, it is cloudy, it remains active and thus forecasts an early spring. Although there are a few records of woodchucks being active in mid-winter, it would be a hardy specimen indeed that would venture forth on February 2 during our Canadian winters.

The woodchuck's pelage is composed of two coats of fur. The underfur is dense and woolly on the flanks and back, but absent on the ventral surface; it is dark grey at the base and tipped by a buff or cinnamon band. The guard hairs project beyond the underfur. These guard hairs have a dark brown or blackish subterminal band and pale buffy tips, which give the animal its over-all grizzled appearance. The relatively short bushy tail is dark brown or black. The feet are black. The ventral surface is covered with sparse tawny or rufous hairs. The shoulders and forelegs are rufous. The cheeks and throat are tawny; the forehead is brown; the facial vibrissae are black and bristle-like; the small eyes are black. There is one annual

moult from late May to early September, which begins on the tail and rump and progresses forward. When the animals reappear in the spring, the fur is long and thin and is often soiled until the new coat appears. Albinos and melanistic individuals are not uncommon. Even a 'woolly' specimen that lacked guard hairs has been described.

The woodchuck possesses three nipple-like anal glands, which disperse its characteristic 'musky' odour. This seems to be a means of communication between individuals.

Examples of malocclusion of the incisors are frequently observed in this species, although this lesion may occur in any rodent. In these cases the front incisors have failed to meet and wear properly, with the result that the teeth continue to grow in a perfect arc. The upper incisors occasionally grow around to pierce the rostrum behind their roots, while the lower incisors circle upwards over the muzzle. Such cases appear in about 1 per cent of a population of woodchucks.

Average measurements of adults: length 576 (457–654), tail 131 (105–163), hind foot 79 (65–89) mm. Males are slightly larger than females. Average weight of males, 2.85 kg. The weight follows a well-marked annual cycle, the animals being much heavier in the autumn just before they hibernate. At that time males average about 3.50 kg in weight.

Habits. To most rural Canadians the woodchuck is a familiar mammal of field and fence row. It does not seem to be very bright since it is among the easier mammals to trap. Its normal gait is a slow walk, but when caught far from its den it runs with a loping gallop that equals the best speed of a farm boy over rough pasture – about ten miles an hour. It has a curious nature and frequently sits at the entrance of its burrow to watch intruders. When the intruder gets too close, it dives down it with a shrill whistle. As well as being a good swimmer the woodchuck is a good climber, frequently going as high as ten or twelve feet in maple and cherry trees. It occasionally climbs a fence post to observe the countryside. Although quick to retreat to its den, the woodchuck shows desperate courage when cornered and often attacks its adversary with chattering teeth. A large male is more than a match for a small terrier. It shows great strength and a great tenacity to live when wounded.

The woodchuck is generally solitary, but pairs may share the same den during the summer, and females and their young may stay together over the winter. It has a number of calls: a short piercing whistle, a muffled *phew*, and the previously mentioned grinding of teeth in terror or anger.

Like most squirrels, the woodchuck, with some exceptions, is diurnal in activity. When it first appears in early spring, it is most active about noon when the chill has left the ground. In the heat of summer, however, it is most active shortly after dawn and in the evening twilight hours. There is some evidence that when food is scarce in early spring it may even feed at night.

In common with the other ground squirrels, wood-

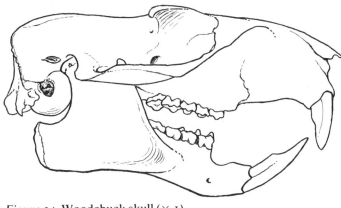

Figure 34 Woodchuck skull (× 1)

chucks excavate burrows for shelter. These are of two main types: hibernating dens, which are usually located in woods or fence rows, and summer dens in fields. The woodchuck usually chooses well-drained soil, such as that on a hillside or stream bank, or under a rock or stump, so that the den remains dry. The burrow usually leads upwards to the nest chamber or has an intermediate low sump so that the rain runoff will not drain directly into the chamber. An occupied burrow may be recognized by the pile of fresh earth at the entrance. The woodchuck always keeps its burrow clean and well padded. Faeces are seldom found, for they are buried in a blind passageway or in the soft earth at the entrance. The woodchuck digs with alternate strokes of its powerful foreclaws and kicks the loose earth backwards with its hind feet. It turns in the tunnel and pushes out loads of fresh earth with its broad muzzle or flat head; indeed, it pushes out sizable stones as well. The diameter and length of the burrow depend on the size of the occupant. A young woodchuck may dig a burrow, about five feet long and four inches in diameter, to a simple sleeping chamber in a single day. But the den of an established adult usually has from two to five entrances and tunnels about ten inches in diameter, which lead to several dens three or four feet below the surface. Tunnel systems as much as forty-two feet in length have been excavated. Usually the main entrance with the telltale pile of earth is about twelve inches in diameter. Near by is a second, hidden entrance or 'plunge hole' with a small diameter and a vertical drop of about two feet in the main tunnel. There are enlarged turning areas near the entrances as well. The nesting chambers are about fifteen inches in diameter and are usually sparsely lined with dry leaves, but about a third of the dens have no lining whatsoever.

Woodchucks are usually cited as true hibernators – that is, they enter a prolonged state of torpor with lowered body processes. But this statement must be made with reservations. It is true that, instead of storing food in the autumn as chipmunks do, they lay on a tremendous store of abdominal and subcutaneous fat. There are, however, scattered records in Ontario of individuals seen above ground during mild spells as early as January 4 and on many other dates in February and March. The remainder of the population, including the females, appears during the first mild spells of early April. Often the first animals out have to dig through the crusted snowbanks over their burrows. In August and September, they accumulate fat and become increasingly lethargic so that the early frosts of October drive them to their hibernating dens, usually before the 26th.

The causes of hibernation are not known, but the coming of colder weather, the increasing length of darkness, the cutting off of green food, the low oxygen content in the den, and the lethargy resulting from storage of fat are cited as contributing factors. In any event the woodchuck seals itself into a hibernating chamber in the autumn. These chambers are seldom found; indeed the only one described was discovered when a tree was being bulldozed. The hibernating chambers are thought to be usually located under the roots of a tree. In hibernation the woodchuck rolls itself into a ball, its head tucked between its hind legs, and enters a state of torpor in which the body temperature sinks as low as 8°C to 17°C and in which respiration can only be detected by instruments. In this condition the animal is slow to respond to stimulation and awakens slowly over a period of hours through a process of shivering. During the winter period of torpor the body slowly utilizes the stored fat for vital processes. By spring the animal has lost 17 to 55 per cent of its weight (average about 30 per cent). Juveniles amass their fat more slowly than adults and seem to be under greater stress from loss of weight in spring.

Little precise information is available on population densities. In optimum habitat the population of woodchucks may run as high as five per acre. Probably one woodchuck for every six acres would be a good estimate, or a hundred to a square mile. There is no evidence of regular population fluctuations. These animals are restricted in their normal movements, seldom venturing more than a hundred yards from their dens. In the spring, particularly, the males show a wanderlust, having been reported to travel up to an eighth of a mile from their dens.

Woodchucks are primarily grazing animals and eat green vegetation. They often sit on their haunches and pull plants over with their forepaws. Some of the most important food plants are clover, alfalfa, buckwheat, buttercups, dandelions, plantains, asters, goldenrod, and soybeans. When they first emerge, no green leaves are available, and so they turn their attention to the bark and twigs of cherry trees, sumac, and dogwood. Unfortunately woodchucks are also fond of green crops. Fruits and vegetables, such as corn, carrots, beets, beans, celery, lettuce, cabbage, turnips, strawberries, and melons, are eaten. The normal diet also includes a few insects and the young birds of ground-nesting species blundered upon in forages.

With the extermination of some of the larger predators in the east, such as the cougar and the wolf, and the great reduction of some of the others such as the bobcat and the coyote, the woodchuck has lost many of its important predators. Its population has increased until it is undoubtedly the most abundant mammal of its size group throughout its range. Larger buteo hawks and rattlesnakes are known to eat a few young groundhogs, but the red fox is undoubtedly its greatest predator at present.

Woodchucks live up to six years in the wild and up to ten years in captivity.

Habitat. The woodchuck is one of a small group of mammals that has prospered as a result of agricultural and forestry practices. Originally it was an uncommon denizen of the climax forests and forest glades. As a result of the deforestation of eastern North America and the maintenance of the land in cultivated fields and pastures, the woodchuck has thrived and multiplied, making the present population many times greater than the original natural population. Man has been an unintentional ally of the woodchuck in that he has changed the landscape to suit himself and in doing so has suited the woodchuck as well.

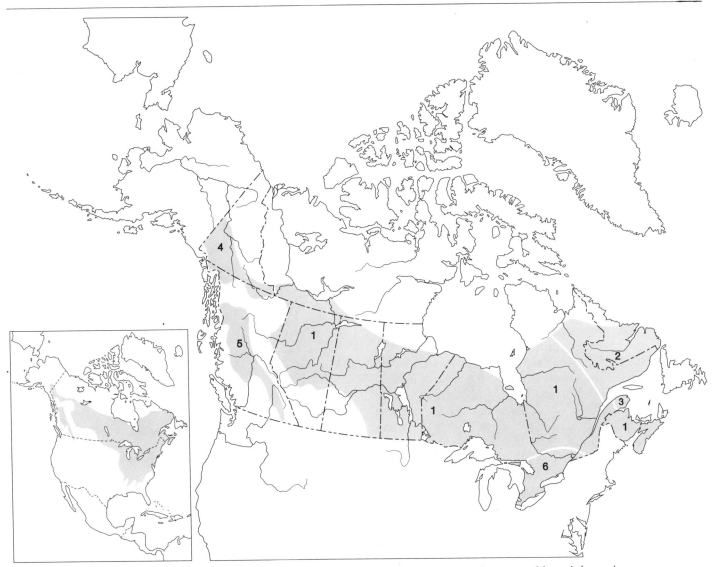

Map 48 Distribution of the woodchuck, *Marmota monax*: 1 *M. m. canadensis*, 2 *M. m. ignava*, 3 *M. m. johnsoni*, 4 *M. m. ochracea*, 5 *M. m. petrensis*, 6 *M. m. rufescens*

Today the animal prefers rolling land with mixed wood-lots, pastures, and fence rows, studded with stumps and large boulders.

Reproduction. The males are sexually active upon emergence from hibernation in March. There is considerable fighting among them at this time, and the oldtimers are heavily scarred about the head and shoulders. The females are monoestrous and mate soon after they emerge in April. Only a few of the yearling females mature and breed at the age of eleven months; the remainder breed for the first time as two-year-olds. After a gestation period of thirty-one to thirty-two days, the young are born in May. The litter size varies between one and eight, with an average of 3.45 in Pennsylvania and 4.07 in northern New York.

The young are born naked, pink, and wrinkled, and blind and helpless, in the sparsely lined nest. At birth they weigh an average of 26.5 g and measure about 105 mm in length. The total weight of the litter is about 100 g. At the age of one week their skin becomes pigmented, at two weeks they have acquired a covering of short black hair, and at three weeks they begin to crawl. Between the twenty-sixth and twenty-eighth day their eyes open, and soon after that they start to feed on green material. At five weeks of age they look like sleek miniature woodchucks and can whistle and grate their teeth. They emerge from the burrows at this age to romp and play at the entrance. The female is reported to stand while she nurses her litter. She has four pairs of teats: two thoracic, one abdominal, and one inguinal. The young are weaned at about six weeks of age. As yearlings they are subadult in size, and late in the second year of life their growth is complete.

Economic Status. Woodchucks are serious agricultural pests. Their burrows are a hazard to mowing since the mounds of earth or stones dull sickle bars. Besides, horses occasionally stumble into the burrows and break their legs. Woodchucks trample young grain down near their burrows and eat oats and also young corn. A woodchuck can create havoc in a small vegetable garden practically overnight.

On the credit side, woodchucks perform a useful duty in turning over the soil and in providing shelter for a variety of game animals, from foxes, skunks, raccoons, and cottontails to small fry such as chipmunks, salamanders, and snakes. They also provide sport hunting throughout the year for small-bore rifle enthusiasts. Indeed shooting is considered the best means of controlling their populations on agricultural lands and the best time is spring. At this time they are most active; the young have not yet arrived; and the vegetation has not grown enough to provide protective cover in the fields. A 22 or 25 calibre rifle and high-velocity shells are recommended and of course a telescope to spot them. Woodchucks may also be easily trapped, but they are very strong and often are able to pull out of light traps. They may also be destroyed in their burrows by the use of carbon bisulphide or calcium cyanide. The first should be poured on cotton waste and then poked down the burrow by means of a long stick. Best results for this method are achieved after a rainfall. Calcium cyanide is a powder and should be pushed down the burrow in a container; best results occur if the ground is dry. In both cases, all entrances should be plugged with earth after the application of the gas. So great is the woodchuck population, however, that after a couple of months the treated fields will be reoccupied by immigrants.

Distribution. The woodchuck occurs over a broad part of eastern North America and across the Prairie Provinces to British Columbia, Yukon Territory, and central Alaska.

Canadian Distribution. The woodchuck occurs in every province and territory with the exception of Prince Edward Island. Six geographical subspecies are recognized across the country (see Map 48).

Marmota monax canadensis (Erxleben), 1777, Systema regni animalis ..., 1: 361. The typical form, found from peninsular Nova Scotia to southern Mackenzie District and northeastern British Columbia.

Marmota monax ignava (Bangs), 1899, Proc. New England Zool. Club 1: 13. A larger and darker race, found in the Hudsonian zone of southern Labrador and central Quebec.

Marmota monax johnsoni Anderson, 1943, Ann. Rept. Provancher Soc. Nat. Hist. Quebec 1942: 53. Gaspé Peninsula, Quebec.

Marmota monax ochracea Swarth, 1911, Univ. California Pub. Zool. 7: 203. Smaller; more ochraceous, particularly the tail. Yukon and northwestern British Columbia.

Marmota monax petrensis A.H. Howell, 1915, N. American Fauna 37: 33. Central British Columbia.

Marmota monax rufescens A.H. Howell, 1914, Proc. Biol. Soc. Washington 27: 13. A large and brightly coloured race, found in southern Ontario.

REFERENCE

Grizzell, R.A. 1955. A study of the southern woodchuck *Marmota monax monax*. American Midl. Nat. 53(2): 257–93.

110

YELLOW-BELLIED MARMOT
Marmotte à ventre jaune. *Marmota flaviventris* (Audubon and Bachman)

Description. This species possesses the typical stout body and short legs of the marmots. It is similar in size to the woodchuck, but its coloration is quite distinctive. The underfur is long and banded; the basal portion is dull grey, followed by a broad terminal buffy band. The long, sparse guard hairs, which are brown with prominent buffy or silvery tips, project through and give the animal's back a grizzled, buffy-brown appearance. However, the rufous tones of the woodchuck are lacking. The sides of the neck, hips, and belly are buffy-yellow. The short bushy tail is grizzled brown; the feet are pale brown. The pattern of colour on the head is quite distinctive. The top of the head and muzzle are olive-brown with a creamy coloured bar across the bridge of the nose and a similar coloured area about the lips. There are prominent bristle-like facial vibrissae. The ears and claws are much shorter than those of the woodchuck.

There are some other important anatomical differences. The females are reported to have five pairs of mammae normally, and the skull has some peculiarities. The cheek tooth rows diverge slightly anteriorly, and the tips of the supraoccipital processes project more posteriorly.

The sequence of moults is thought to be similar to that found in the woodchuck.

Average measurements of males: length 546 (495–660), tail 159 (133–178), hind foot 78 (76–80), ear from notch 20 mm; weight approximately 2.5 kg.

Habits. In marked contrast to the woodchuck, little has been written concerning the life history of the yellow-bellied marmot. Casual observations suggest that their life histories are very similar. This species is more gregarious than the woodchuck. Many family groups often live together as a colony in their specialized habitat. Though home ranges overlap, contacts are avoided. There is a preference for a burrow in the centre of the colony. The marmot utters short, sharp whistles or a metallic chirp. On approaching a colony one sees sentinels sunning on the rocks, while other animals are making short excursions to feed. When the alarm is raised, they all gallop back to the safety of the rock pile with tails flopping from side to side. Nothing is known of their den construction. They are active from sunrise to thirty minutes after sunset.

The yellow-bellied marmot hibernates from the second week of August to April, but like its relative the woodchuck it lays in no winter supply of food. The natural food consists of native forbs, grasses, sedges, clovers, and stonecrop (*Sedum* sp.).

Habitat. If its eastern relative is called the 'woodchuck' because it burrows in the woods, this species should be called the 'rockchuck' because it inhabits rocky talus slopes. In Canada it lives at low elevations in such slopes on the sides of mountains, under cliffs, and in rocky flats or rock piles. It invades the forest edge only near rocky shelter. It lives in the rock crevices, and somewhere deep among the rocks it builds its nest.

Map 49 Distribution of the yellow-bellied marmot, *Marmota flaviventris*: 1 *M. f. avara*, 2 *M. f. nosophora*, ● extra-limital record

Reproduction. Mating probably occurs as soon as the animals break their hibernation. The young are born in early May. The litter may number between three and eight, but the usual number is four or five.

Economic Status. Since the yellow-bellied marmot generally inhabits inhospitable terrain, it is of little economic significance. Occasionally it invades marginal fields of alfalfa or clover situated near rock slides.

This marmot is one of the favourite hosts of the tick *Dermacentor andersoni*, which transmits Rocky Mountain spotted fever, a virus disease that is a local threat to both man and domestic animals.

Distribution. The yellow-bellied marmot inhabits the central Rocky Mountain region from northern New Mexico to southern Alberta and British Columbia.

Canadian Distribution. The heart of the range of this species lies south of our borders. Two subspecies reach Canada on the northern fringe of their distribution (see Map 49).

Marmota flaviventris avara (Bangs), 1899, Proc. New England Zool. Club 1: 68. Dry interior of south-central British Columbia.

Marmota flaviventris nosophora A.H. Howell, 1914, Proc. Biol. Soc. Washington 27: 15. Specimens of this form have been taken in only three locations near the southern boundary of Alberta: Waterton Lakes National Park, the Milk River valley, and Lake Newell. All the evidence points to the spread of this marmot into Alberta within the past twenty years. There are no recent signs of the species in the Waterton Lakes Park rock slide, where the first specimen was secured.

REFERENCE

Armitage, K.B. 1962. Social behaviour of a colony of the yellow-bellied marmot (*Marmota flaviventris*). Animal Behaviour 10(3,4): 319–31.

HOARY MARMOT
Marmotte des Rocheuses. *Marmota caligata* (Eschscholtz)

Description. The hoary marmot is the largest American

marmot. It may grow to about twice the size of the woodchuck and weigh up to 30 pounds. It was known as 'the whistler' by the early English explorers to the far west and by the name of 'siffleux' to the Canadian voyageurs.

The hoary marmot has a grizzled-grey mantle over the shoulders and foreback. The lower back and rump are grizzled-brown, which is the result of the buffy-tipped underfur being half-hidden by the long, stiff black-tipped guard hairs. Its short bushy tail is brown also, frequently banded with black-tipped hairs. Its feet are black. It has grey cheeks, grey underparts, and a grey band across the bridge of the nose. The muzzle, head, and, usually, a stripe behind the ears are black (Plate 12).

This species has the usual midsummer moult. The summer colours are a little more brown in tone, and the winter pelage is more hoary.

The skull of this marmot is ruggedly constructed. There is a pronounced interorbital construction behind supraorbital processes, the tips of which point backwards. The cheek tooth rows diverge anteriorly as in *M. flaviventris*. There are also ten teats in this species, as opposed to eight in *M. monax*. The short, round ears are pressed against the head.

Average measurements of adults of the race *oxytona* (which is the one with the widest range in the Canadian Rockies): length 716 (680–750), tail 213 (177–230), hind foot 100 (91–102), ear from notch 25 mm; weight 5.87 (4.98–6.80) kg.

Habits. Unfortunately, so remote are the areas inhabited by the hoary marmot that very little has been written concerning its life history. On first impression it seems extremely wary. The first sign of its presence is the long shrill whistle, almost exactly the same pitch and duration as the familar police whistle. This always has a startling effect upon the visitor, who immediately assumes he is being called by someone in an apparently lonely land. Since the whistle has a tremendous carrying quality and reverberates around the empty cirque, it is difficult to locate the whistler. Eventually it is seen at some distance as it gallops clumsily across the alpine tundra to its burrow. Unfortunately that is about the last one usually sees of the hoary marmot unless one follows it to its burrow entrance. Its den may be found under the border of a rockslide, but more commonly it is on open hilly ground under some huge boulder or in the loose shale talus under some cliff. Large boulders provide protection against the grizzly bear's efforts to dig out the marmot. The nest, hidden deep in the crevice, is composed of grasses. In the spring the winter nest is frequently thrown out of the burrow and replaced by a new one of fresh grasses. Characteristic of the hoary marmot's territory is the observation post, which is usually a high boulder; here the marmot crouches to watch for danger. It also frequently stretches out on a smooth rock surface to sun itself. At such a time it assumes a pose characteristic of all the squirrel family – flat on its belly with legs fully extended diagonally out from the body. There are well-beaten trails extending from the burrow entrance to favourite look-out posts and across the greensward to feeding locations.

Hoary marmots seem to live in loose colonies. They are thus able to take advantage of their neighbours' watchfulness. If danger approaches, they pass the warning whistle along the valley, and those feeding at considerable distances from shelter gallop for home. They also take note of the alarm calls of some of their lesser neighbours such as pikas and ground squirrels. These marmots are of such a size that only the largest and strongest predators hunt them. These include grizzly and black bears, wolves, and golden eagles, eagles being probably their main predator.

Hoary marmots are diurnal in activity and spend about eight months of each year in hibernation. They are seldom observed above ground after the first of September and do not reappear until late April. They are, however, active during a considerable part of the year.

As grazing animals they eat a large variety of green alpine grasses and forbs. Often the area about their dens appears heavily grazed, and they may travel several hundred yards to feed. They store no food for winter but become excessively fat in late summer prior to hibernation. In the Arctic the mosquitoes are such a scourge that they may keep the marmots underground during warm, windless days.

Habitat. The hoary marmot dwells in the alpine tundra zone beyond the treeline as far as the limit of vegetation. Here it finds the rolling alpine meadows, rocky taluses, and cliffs to its liking. In the Rocky Mountain region this area lies between 6,800 and 8,000 feet in elevation. Far to the north in the Yukon Territory the area may lie as low as 2,500 feet, and it is said that this species almost reaches sea level in some parts of Alaska. Occasionally hoary marmots are found at lower elevations in the forest edge where rock piles and clearings provide the proper food and shelter for the species.

Reproduction. The marmots probably mate as soon as they emerge from hibernation. The young are born towards the end of May or in early June. Litters of four or five seem to be the average. The young marmots first appear at the entrance to the den in late July. Their growth is relatively slow. As yearlings they appear only half-grown, and they probably do not breed until the second year.

Economic Status. The hoary marmot fortunately does not come into conflict with man's economy. It remains one of the spectacular and interesting inhabitants of the wilderness. Few people other than mountain climbers and those living in the arctic mountain wilderness of our Northwest ever reach its native haunts.

Indians and Eskimos used to make fur garments from hoary marmot skins, and its flesh was also eaten. Little use is made of the animal now, however.

Distribution. The hoary marmot is found in the northern Cordilleran region of North America.

Canadian Distribution. This species is quite variable in colour and size throughout its distribution, and six geographical subspecies have been described from Canada (see Map 50).

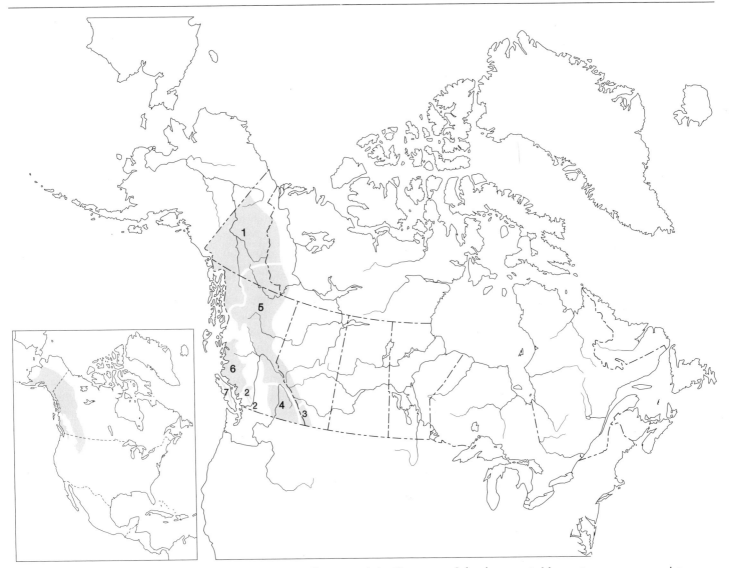

Map 50 Distribution of the hoary marmot, *Marmota caligata*, and the Vancouver Island marmot, *Marmota vancouverensis*: 1 *M. c. caligata*, 2 *M. c. cascadensis*, 3 *M. c. nivaria*, 4 *M. c. okanagana*, 5 *M. c. oxytona*, 6 *M. c. raceyi*, 7 *Marmota vancouverensis*

Marmota caligata caligata (Eschscholtz), 1829, Zool. Atlas, pt. 2, p. 1, pl. 6.

Marmota caligata cascadensis A.H. Howell, 1914, Proc. Biol. Soc. Washington 27: 17. A larger and darker race, found in the Cascade Mountains of southwestern British Columbia.

Marmota caligata nivaria A.H. Howell, 1914, Proc. Biol. Soc. Washington 27: 17. A large, pale race, found in the Rocky Mountains of southwestern Alberta.

Marmota caligata okanagana (King), 1836, Narrative of a journey to the shores of the Arctic Ocean ... 2: 236. Southeastern British Columbia.

Marmota caligata oxytona Hollister, 1912, Smiths. Misc. Coll. 56: 1. A large race, brightly coloured with light and dark areas; found in the Rocky Mountain region from southeastern Yukon Territory to near Banff, Alberta.

Marmota caligata raceyi Anderson, 1932, Nat. Mus. Canada Bull. 70: 112. Lacks brown tones on the rump; underparts dark grey; found in Itcha and Chilcotin mountains of west-central British Columbia.

REFERENCES

Bailey, V. 1918. The mammals. *In* Wild animals of Glacier National Park, pp. 50–3. Nat. Parks Serv., Dept. of Int., Washington.

Dixon, J.S. 1938. Birds and mammals of Mount McKinley National Park. Nat. Parks Serv., Washington, Fauna Ser. 3: 169–73.

VANCOUVER ISLAND MARMOT

Marmotte de l'île Vancouver. *Marmota vancouverensis* Swarth

Description. The Vancouver Island marmot is closely related to the hoary marmot, but its exact relationship is not known. It is a little smaller than the continental races of

113

hoary marmots, but its coloration is distinctive. In its fresh coat this marmot is a uniformly rich, glossy, chocolate brown. It has a dirty white patch on the muzzle and a scattering of white hairs on the back, a blackish sheen on the rump, and sometimes white spots on the abdomen.

This species moults into its fresh coat in July. Prior to that the old coat is faded to a wood brown colour.

Average measurements of seven adult males: length 674 (632–710), tail 221 (200–300), hind foot 98 (90–102) mm; weight 3.5 kg.

Habits. Very little is known of the life history of this species. It was described as extremely vigilant and unapproachable by its discoverer, who correlated its extreme wariness with the observation that its brown coat made it conspicuous against the grey rocks and the greensward of its habitat. It also seemed to be much quieter than the hoary marmot.

These marmots live in burrows dug in rocky ground. Since the snow lies so long in their habitat, it is thought that they hibernate for a longer period than other marmots.

Habitat. Treeline and beyond, as well as in forest openings on the mountains of Vancouver Island.

Reproduction. No details are known.

Economic Status. Of no economic importance.

Distribution. This species inhabits mountainous parts of western Vancouver Island. It is believed that it became isolated on Vancouver Island during the withdrawal of the last Cordilleran Wisconsin glaciation about 10,000 to 12,000 years ago. There is a closely related form in the Olympic Mountains south of the Straits of Juan de Fuca (see Map 50).

Marmota vancouverensis Swarth, 1911, Univ. California Pub. Zool. 7: 201.

REFERENCE

Swarth, H.S. 1912. Report on a collection of birds and mammals from Vancouver Island. Univ. California Pub. Zool. 10(1): 89–90.

RICHARDSON'S GROUND SQUIRREL
Spermophile de Richardson. *Spermophilus richardsonii* (Sabine)

Description. This ground squirrel is one of the most familiar small mammals of the Canadian prairies, though it is not known by this name. Locally it is most commonly called the 'gopher,' which comes from the French word for honeycomb (*gaufre*) – an appropriate reference to its burrows. Unfortunately, the name 'gopher' has been applied to a variety of burrowing animals including a tortoise, a snake, four species of Canadian ground squirrels, and another distinct group of fossorial rodents, which have been named 'pocket gophers.' Richardson's ground squirrels are commonly seen as one drives along secondary roads across the prairies. The road banks are virtually 'honeycombed' with their burrows, and individual

squirrels scamper along the crest or scurry across the road with flopping tails. Occasionally one may be seen sitting bolt upright in the middle of the road surveying an approaching car. With a sinking feeling the driver sees it suddenly disappear under the hood of the car; surprisingly, however, the rear-view mirror reveals no quivering body. And on stopping the car to investigate, one would probably discover a burrow entrance in the centre of the gravelled road (Plate 5).

Richardson's ground squirrel is a plump-bodied species about 12 inches long, with short legs, armed with long, slightly curved claws (the vestigal pollex carries a flattened nail), and a stubby tail about a third of the body length. It has short, broad ears and small internal cheek pouches. Its skull is sturdy and rounded, the rostrum is short, the zygomatic arches spread posteriorly, and the supraoccipital processes are prominent (Figure 35). These ground squirrels possess three anal scent glands similar to those of the larger marmots.

The short pelage is warm buffy-grey dorsally, deepening to yellowish on the cheeks, shoulders, flanks, and thighs. The crown is cinnamon brown; the rump is dappled with brownish transverse bars. The brown tail has an indistinct submarginal black band on top and is the colour of clay underneath. The underparts and feet are grey or buff-coloured. There is one annual moult in summer.

Average measurements of adults: total length 285 (277–306), tail 74 (65–83), hind foot 45 (43–47), ear from crown 2–4 mm. Average weight in the spring, 405 g, which increases to 485 g in the autumn before hibernation.

Habits. These squirrels live in loose, straggling colonies, although they do not seem to be individually very sociable. Each squirrel benefits, however, from the continued vigilance of its neighbour. This species seems to live quite amicably with other rodent neighbours such as

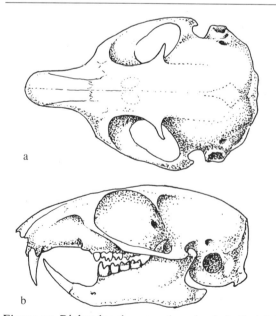

Figure 35 Richardson's ground squirrel skull: (a) dorsal view, (b) lateral view (× 1½)

the black-tailed prairie dog and the meadow vole. On the western boundary of its range it comes into contact with a larger relative, the Columbian ground squirrel, and has been observed occupying the same territory. The relationship between these two species in the area of overlap is, however, not known. Occasionally one sees a ground squirrel living alone at some distance from a colony. These are quite often large bachelor males.

Like most of its relatives, Richardson's ground squirrel is strictly diurnal in activity. It has three peaks of activity during the daylight hours: about two hours after dawn, 10 A.M. to 2 P.M., and 4 P.M. to sunset. It is most active on warm, sunny days but stays below ground when it is excessively hot or when it rains. When alert it sits on its heels and stretches its body to full height with its forelegs on its chest. In this position on the short grass prairie it resembles stakes used to restrain feeding horses and has so earned its other common name 'picket pin.' Its call is a short, shrill whistle, always accompanied by a jerk of the tail. When thoroughly alarmed it plunges down its burrows with shrill chatter. It also utters a variety of other soft chattering notes and squeals when fighting. It does not show much speed when running, and a small dog or a fast boy, or both, can easily catch one. It gallops with flopping tail, every now and then giving a series of short hops on the hind feet and quickly dodging its pursuers.

The Richardson's ground squirrel excavates complicated burrows, which consist of a maze of galleries, blind passages with various entrances, and several chambers. The winter burrows are usually deeper, and the hibernation chamber is plugged so that its entrance from the tunnel is difficult to locate. The burrows, which are about three inches in diameter, vary between twelve and forty-nine feet in length and between two and a half and six feet in depth. There are, on an average, eight entrances. The main one is easily recognized by the mound of fresh earth; others, dug from inside the tunnel, have hidden 'plunge holes.' The nest is lined with grass and oat hulls and placed in a chamber about nine inches in diameter. The mounds of fresh earth serve as observation posts, from which radiate trails beaten down in the natural vegetation or crops. The squirrels may feed at distances up to a hundred yards from their burrows but are usually much closer to a familiar 'funk-hole.'

These ground squirrels hibernate for about seven months of the year and emerge, as a rule, during the first mild spell, which on the Canadian prairies is some time during the second half of March. One report from North Dakota stated that they were out on March 10, and I saw them frequently south of Calgary, Alberta, on March 15, 1951. It may be as late as mid-April, however, in Manitoba. A prolonged mild spell in late February will sometimes encourage a few to make their first appearance. However, once they have awakened, even a late blizzard will not discourage them, as their tracks are often seen on fresh snow. The onset of hibernation seems to be more irregular. Few are observed after the middle of August. 'Last squirrels' have been reported on September 1, 2, and 14, and on October 12. Probably the first cold snaps of late

September or early October drive the late stragglers to their hibernation dens.

These squirrels increased dramatically across the prairies with the first breaking of the natural grassland for agriculture. They became a serious burden to the pioneer western farmers as early as 1894. Seton estimated their populations to be about five per acre, or 5,000 to the square mile. Brown and Roy have divided their population estimates according to land use: virgin prairie, eight per acre; grassland, six per acre; abandoned land, five per acre; cultivated fields, three per acre; and irrigated lands, two per acre; with an average population in Alberta of 3,200 to a square mile. The home range is probably not over a hundred yards in diameter.

The food of ground squirrels consists of the roots, leaves, and seeds of native grasses and forbs. Sage, bindweed, pigweed, wild sunflowers, and wild onions are among the favourites. They are also fond of domestic crops, particularly oats and wheat. In the spring, when green vegetation is scarce, they dig up and eat the drilled seed; later they cut the succulent growing stems. At harvest time they pull down the stalks and cut off the heads of grain.

In the late summer they begin to store seeds. Counts of cheek pouch loads reveal as many as 240 grains of wheat, 264 grains of oats, or 1,000 seeds of wild buckwheat (a weed). Seton dug up a store of two quarts of sprouted wheat in a winter den in October. It is not certain, however, how important these winter stores are, since the ground squirrels are thought to be profound hibernators. It may be that they are utilized in the spring when food is scarce. These ground squirrels are also carnivorous (they eat grasshoppers), and even cannibalistic. Many a careless ground squirrel is crushed by a car while dining on the remains of a neighbour who met a similar fate.

Richardson's ground squirrel must maintain constant vigilance lest it fall prey to a host of predators. It is the chief prey of several large buteos such as the ferruginous rough-legged hawk, Swainson's hawk, the red-tailed hawk, and the prairie falcon. Burrowing owls, which use the ground squirrels' burrows to raise their young, also consume young ground squirrels. Among the four-footed predators are the ermine and the long-tailed weasels, the black-footed ferret, the badger, the red fox, the kit fox, and the coyote. Rattlesnakes and bullsnakes also eat ground squirrels, but since they are rare in Canada they are of little importance as predators.

It is a pity that man has harried many of those carnivorous species such as the hawks, the ferret, and the kit fox to the verge of extinction when they could have assisted in maintaining a biological control of the ground squirrel population, which constitutes an important agricultural scourge.

Habitat. Richardson's ground squirrel inhabits the open prairie but prefers high rolling hills of gravelly or sandy soils in which to burrow. It is quick to move into cultivated fields and avoids wet lands.

Reproduction. The ground squirrels mate upon first emerging from their hibernation in late March or early

Map 51 Distribution of Richardson's ground squirrel, *Spermophilus richardsonii*

April. There is evidence that the gestation period may be as short as eighteen days, but twenty-seven days seems more likely. Parturition occurs generally after April 29. The litter size may vary from five to eleven, with an average of 7.5. The females are monoestrous so there is only one litter a year. The young squirrels mature as yearlings. The nestlings weigh about 6 g at birth and measure 46 mm in length. They first appear at the burrow entrances to romp or sun themselves in late June when they are about six weeks old. They are about a third grown at that time and reach full size by the beginning of September.

Economic Status. Richardson's ground squirrel is one of the most serious agricultural pests in Canada. Its role in agriculture was recognized early in the colonization of the prairies. Bounties of three cents a tail were paid in Manitoba as early as 1889, and bounties and the distribution of free 'gopher' poison were instituted in Alberta in 1911. It is doubtful that the bounties had any extensive effect on the ground squirrel population. In 1890, bounties were paid for 40,000 ground squirrel tails in one Manitoba

municipality without any appreciable continuing effect. It must be admitted, however, that it provided entertainment and pocket money for the youngsters.

Ground squirrels cause damage by trampling the grain and by burrowing, which causes local destruction of grain, and, of course, eat a considerable amount (estimated to be a bushel per animal per year).

Besides the depredations upon crops, Richardson's ground squirrel has proved to be a public health menace. A mink farmer at Stanmore, Alberta, died of bubonic plague in 1937. In 1939 it was confirmed that the local ground squirrels were infected with sylvatic plague (the wildlife form of bubonic plague, which is usually fatal to the squirrels as well). The squirrels are hosts to at least two species of fleas, which are recognized transmitters of bubonic plague caused by the bacillus *Pasteurella pestis*. The danger was recognized, and to discourage the handling of ground squirrels the bounty on squirrel tails was removed in 1940. The plague area is considered to be about 2,000 square miles of prairie east of Drumheller, Alberta.

Besides being carriers of the plague, these squirrels

116

have been shown to be reservoirs of tularaemia and Rocky Mountain spotted fever, which are transmitted by the tick *Dermacentor andersoni* in the Lethbridge–Medicine Hat region of southeastern Alberta. Tularaemia is caused by infections of the bacillus *Pasteurella tularensis*, while Rocky Mountain spotted fever is caused by one of the near virus *Rickettsia*. One or two local cases of these diseases among humans have been reported.

Several methods of controlling these ground squirrels are commonly employed. They are easily trapped in number 'o' steel traps, placed in the entrances to their burrows. The favourite method used by two generations of western boys was to snare them with strong twine. After a squirrel was chased into his burrow, the noose was carefully laid around the entrance. Then the hunter retired about ten yards away and lay down on the soft prairie with the end of the string in his hand. In a few moments the squirrel would emerge cautiously, and then with a quick tug it would be captured. If it was tardy in reappearing, it could often be 'squeaked' up.

The most effective control of these squirrels is by carrying out extensive poison programs in early spring. One may distribute spoonfuls of strychnine-treated wheat or oat grains by hand into all the active entrances. Another method uses Cyanogas powder, which is poked down the burrows, followed by a turn of the heel in the soft earth to seal all entrances.

Distribution. The central plains of North America.

Canadian Distribution. The typical race is distributed across the southern portions of the three Prairie Provinces (see Map 51). It is scarce in the Red River valley of southern Manitoba. Only scattered colonies occur in the Emerson area, though they are more abundant on the second and third prairie steppes in Saskatchewan and Alberta. In 1912, the distribution in Alberta reached only as far north as Battle Creek valley, but there has been a continued northwestward advance since then, and they now occupy the southern part of the province as far as Whitecourt and Athabasca. In the Medicine Hat–Manyberries area of southeastern Alberta they have greatly decreased in numbers over the past twenty-five years. Indeed many observers report a general decline in populations across the prairies since 1950. It is difficult to say whether this is a fact, possibly resulting from ground squirrel control programs, or whether the apparent decline is a result of fewer squirrels' being observed from the new, raised black-topped highways.

The race in Canada is the typical form.

Spermophilus richardsonii richardsonii (Sabine), 1822, Trans. Linn. Soc. London 13: 589.

REFERENCE

Brown, J.H., and G.D. Roy. 1943. The Richardson ground squirrel, *Cittellus richardsonii* Sabine, in southern Alberta: its importance and control. Sci. Agri. 24(4): 176–97.

COLUMBIAN GROUND SQUIRREL
Spermophile du Columbia. *Spermophilus columbianus* (Ord)

Description. This is one of the larger ground squirrels. It has the typical robust form of the group, and the short legs, ears, and tail. The tail is moderately bushy. The skull is more elongate than that of *S. richardsonii*. The rostrum is longer, the zygomatic arches are narrower, and the skull is flatter in lateral aspect, particularly in the interorbital region (Plate 4c).

The pelage is short and fine. The underfur has three bands: grey base, buffy intermediate zone, and black tips. The guard hairs have a prominent, tawny subterminal band and black tips, a combination that gives a black-and-tan dappled effect to the back. The nose is rufous: there is a buffy eye-ring; the head and neck are frosted slate grey; the forefeet are ochraceous; the hind feet are cinnamon, while the flanks and underparts are tawny. The base of the tail is rufous; the brush is peppered brown with a buffy-white terminal band. Altogether this is a very attractively coloured squirrel. There is a single annual moult in June and July.

Average measurements of adults: length 350 (327–377), tail 100 (83–116), hind foot 51 (48–55), ear 10 mm. Average weight of adult males in hibernation 492 (435–571) g.

Habits. This ground squirrel is colonial. It is generally alert, suspicious, and quick to warn its neighbours of an intruder. It has keen eyesight and hearing. When alarmed it scurries to the closest burrow. After an appropriate time interval, it slowly emerges again. At first only the nose and eyes appear, then it emerges in a crouch, and finally it stretches up to the familiar 'picket pin' stance. From this position it utters its characteristic clear, metallic chirp, repeated three or four times, which may carry several hundred yards. Each chirp is accompanied by a convulsive jerk and flick of the tail. If the animal is thoroughly alarmed, it vanishes with a *churr*. It runs in a series of bounding leaps or scurries through the grass, and seldom walks. It assumes a hunched position to eat.

The Columbian ground squirrel is strictly diurnal in activity. Each day it appears about twenty minutes after sunrise and disappears about ten minutes after sunset. If the day is extremely hot, it may retire to its burrow for protection from the blazing noon sun. It also shrinks from rain, but sprawls indolently on its belly on the warm earth beside its burrow to soak up the sun's rays in the late afternoon. It is primarily terrestrial but climbs clumsily in low bushes for berries. It is a reluctant swimmer.

This species excavates an extensive tunnel system for summer occupancy. The burrows are situated unprotected on open ground or in banks, usually under boulders, stumps, or logs. From the main entrance the burrow leads downward at a forty-five-degree grade and then levels off between two and three feet beneath the surface. The tunnels (three to four inches in diameter) vary between ten and sixty feet in length and may have an average of eleven entrances (from two to thirty-five). Piles of loose earth appear at the main entrance, but there are many hidden plunge-holes. There is a central chamber about thirty inches in diameter lined with cottony anemone down or grasses, from which tunnels radiate towards different feeding grounds. Some tunnels lead to feeding grounds; others are 'blind' and serve as toilet areas.

In late summer the hibernating den is constructed separately off the summer burrow system. It is usually deeper (sometimes up to six feet in depth down to hardpan). It consists of a hibernation chamber with a basal dust mulch and a complete lining of dried grasses. Immediately off the entrance to this chamber is a sump, which varies from one to five feet in depth. This sump drains off any water that might flood the chamber. A plug about two feet long, tamped into place with the squirrel's forehead, seals off the entrance to the hibernation den from the summer burrow. The earth used for the plug comes from the construction of the sump. Leading upwards is a short section of the escape hatch. In spring the emerging squirrel digs directly upwards to the surface, and uses the fresh earth to fill up the sump. The squirrel does not remove the plug to enter the old burrow system.

During the period of hibernation the squirrel rolls up in a ball, its head buried between its hind legs, its tail over its head, resting on its rump, facing the entrance to the den. It is completely surrounded by grassy nesting material. The average hibernation period for squirrels in eastern Washington State is 208 (192–220) days for males. Before hibernation the squirrels develop thick layers of intestinal and subdermal fat. While dormant, the body temperature drops from approximately 98°F to close to the environmental temperature. The squirrels remain dormant for many months, but they are not immobile throughout the whole period, arousing themselves naturally at least every nineteen days.

The adult males appear first (about April 6), about ten days ahead of the females. Those Columbian ground squirrels that live on the north slopes of hills, where snowbanks persist in spring, emerge, mate, bear their litters, and enter hibernation about ten days after their neighbours on the south-facing slopes. Those at higher elevations are even more delayed. Near the timberline they may not emerge until June; then they remain active until the beginning of October. At one time the term 'aestivation' was used to account for the midsummer disappearance of ground squirrels at lower elevations. It is now thought that summer drought and the resultant parched vegetation drive the ground squirrels to their winter dens.

The food of the Columbian ground squirrel consists of a wide variety of roots, bulbs, stems, leaves, and flowers, and the seeds of grasses, sedges, and forbs. Some of the favourites are strawberry, whortleberry, willow, buttercup, dandelion, beargrass, balsamroot, lupine, penstemon, ragweed, rose, camas, wild onion, glacier lily, gooseberry, thimbleberry, and serviceberry. When they are close to cultivated crops they also eat clover, oats, rye, and barley, and vegetables such as potatoes, vines, lettuce, and carrots.

It has been estimated that the Columbian ground squirrel feeds for an average of only 130 days each year, consuming possibly 17.2 per cent of its body weight in one day. It also eats a certain amount of animal food such as grasshoppers, cicadas, beetles, caterpillars, dead fish, and mice. Very little is stored in the burrow, but the old males may store seeds and bulbs for spring in the lining of their nests to sustain them when they emerge, which is so early (they often tunnel through a foot of snow) that no fresh vegetable food is available.

Columbian ground squirrel populations may be as high as six animals per acre on agricultural lands, but 1.7 per acre is average. Individual squirrels have lived as long as four years in captivity.

A wide variety of predators prey upon this ground squirrel. Among the four-footed predators are weasels, badgers, coyotes, foxes, bobcats, cougars, and grizzly bears. The grizzlies, particularly in the autumn after the ground squirrels have hibernated, spend much time and effort digging the ground squirrels out of their dens. The diurnal avian predators, such as the golden eagle and large buteo hawks, also repeatedly quarter across clearings and alpine meadows looking for an unwary squirrel. One agitated female ground squirrel was watched dispersing her young in all directions when a long-tailed weasel entered the colony. After the weasel departed, she called her young together again but kept them away from the old home burrow.

Habitat. Columbian ground squirrels inhabit open country, from high grass plateaus and sagebrush plains to alpine meadows, old burns, avalanches, and stream banks from 700 feet to 8,000 feet in elevation. They prefer friable or light sandy soils but stay away from clays or packed hardpan.

Reproduction. The males are sexually active upon emergence, but their gonads regress and are withdrawn into the abdominal cavity about six weeks later. Mating occurs soon after the females emerge. Dates cannot be given since the time of emergence varies a great deal depending on slope and altitude. The females are monoestrous, but, if they are not impregnated the first time, a second oestrus occurs about fifteen days later. The gestation period is twenty-four days. The litters vary between two and seven, and average four. The parturition date varies from early May at low elevations to late June at high elevations.

The young are born naked and blind, with the auditory meatus closed. They weigh about 9 g each at birth. At the age of nineteen days they are covered with short, silky hair. Their eyes open between twenty-one and twenty-three days of age, and they are weaned at thirty days. They emerge from the burrow between the ages of twenty-one and twenty-nine days. This may be as early as June 27 in the valleys, but the date of emergence may be delayed one day for each additional one hundred feet of elevation. At the treeline, they may be only two-thirds grown by August 22. When they first appear, they creep about in a group near the burrow entrance. Within a week

Map 52 Distribution of the Columbian ground squirrel, *Spermophilus columbianus*

they sit up on their haunches and nibble green vegetation. They appear almost fully grown by hibernation time but do not reach full growth or sexual maturity until they are yearlings.

Economic Status. This species is an agricultural pest in some parts of its range, particularly in Washington State where it inhabits the open plains. There it damages wheat and alfalfa crops. In Canada, however, it is confined to mountain pastures and foothill ranges, where it is less destructive. Its natural distribution at present reaches the margin of the Peace River district, and it will be interesting to see if it spreads out over those agricultural lands.

This species plays an important role in the food chains of the Rocky Mountain region of Canada and is responsible in no small part for the wide array of carnivores present in the area. It also provides a point of interest in camp grounds, where it is quick to learn to seek handouts from the picnic tables.

In the United States this species is known to be a reser-voir for such diseases as Rocky Mountain spotted fever and bubonic plague. It has been shown to serve as an intermediate host for the tick *Dermacentor andersoni* in southwestern Alberta. However, it does not serve as an important agent for those diseases in Canada.

Distribution. The Columbian ground squirrel is found in the central Rocky Mountain region of western North America.

Canadian Distribution. Only the typical subspecies is found in Canada (see Map 52), and that subspecies occurs along the eastern flanks of the Rocky Mountains from the international boundary north to near Wembley, Alberta. In British Columbia it occurs westward to the Ashnola River and northward to the Parsnip River.

Spermophilus columbianus columbianus (Ord), 1815, *in* Guthrie, A new geography, history, and comm. grammar ... , Philadelphia, American ed. 2: 292. Eastern British Columbia and western Alberta.

REFERENCES

Shaw, W.T. 1924. The home life of the Columbian ground squirrel. Canadian Field-Nat. 38(7): 128–30; 38(8): 151–3.

– 1925. The hibernation of the Columbian ground squirrel. Canadian Field-Nat. 39(3): 56–61; 39(4): 79–82.

– 1925. Breeding and development of the Columbian ground squirrel. Jour. Mamm. 6(2): 106–13.

– 1925. Duration of the aestivation and hibernation of the Columbian ground squirrel (Citellus columbianus) and sex relations of same. Ecology 6(1): 75–81.

– 1945. Seasonal and daily activities of the Columbian ground squirrel at Pullman, Washington. Ecology 26(1): 74–85.

ARCTIC GROUND SQUIRREL
Spermophile arctique. *Spermophilus parryii* (Richardson)

Description. The arctic ground squirrel is the largest of the American ground squirrels and also the most northern in distribution. Its range is quite isolated from other American members of the group. Although it resembles the Columbian ground squirrel in colour, there are some significant differences. It has a large, broad, rugged skull. The wide zygomatic arches are twisted and flattened in the horizontal plane. The strong supraorbital processes, which are posteriorly located, are depressed. The interorbital region is broad and concave. The skull, which is strongly arched in lateral aspect, resembles the skull of the prairie dog in some ways. The tail is also relatively longer than that of *S. columbianus* and has a bushy tip.

The head, cheeks, and shoulders of this species are cinnamon or tawny coloured. There is a buffy eye-ring. The nape and back are greyish or buffy brown, dappled with white spots. The flanks, legs, and underparts are ochraceous or tawny coloured. Dorsally, the tail is a mixture of buffy browns and black-tipped hairs, the black being concentrated towards the terminal brush. Below, the tail is mostly clear tawny except for the terminal brush, which is blackish.

There are two annual moults compressed into the short five months in which the squirrels are active. In late June, the spring moult commences on the head and progresses posteriorly with a noticeable moult line. It may be quite irregular on the flanks and rump. The autumn moult progresses rapidly in the reverse direction without a moult line. The summer coat tends to be more ochraceous and the winter coat greyer.

Measurements of a series of males of the average-sized northern Yukon race: (males) length 403 (377–435), tail 118 (105–126), hind foot 65 (60–68), ear 14 (10–17) mm; weight 791 g (greatest weight 907 g); (females) length 385 (348–425), tail 111 (88–135), hind foot 61 (55–64), ear 15 (12–19) mm; weight 698 g.

Habits. This species is colonial. Individual squirrels appear to enter several burrows, and do not seem to defend any particular territory against their neighbours. One adult male, closely observed all summer, occupied a home range of about ten acres. Other individuals have been seen wandering as much as a mile from their burrows. In their travels they wear trails through the sparse arctic vegetation. They usually crawl carefully through the low heaths when they are feeding but make a run for their burrows if alarmed. They also swim voluntarily across small streams in their paths. On warm days considerable time is spent in sunning and sand-bathing. They avoid cold and rainy days by remaining in their dens. Upon first appearance in spring they are usually silent but soon become quite vocal. Their usual note is a double *keek keek*, which has led to their Eskimo name *sik sik*, and their Russian name *suslik*. They also utter other calls: a bird-like *chir chir* and a scolding chatter.

The arctic environment has introduced several problems into this ground squirrel's normal routine. For instance, there is continuous daylight for most of this species' active period during the year. The arctic ground squirrel remains conventionally diurnal in its activity pattern, however, being abroad between the hours of 4 A.M. and approximately 9.30 P.M. It is believed that lowered light intensity and temperature restrict its activity, even though the midnight sun might be shining when it retires.

Permafrost also seriously restricts the burrowing habits of this squirrel. It excavates an extensive maze of tunnels, which are usually less than three feet deep and are often under only the turf. The colony area is usually honeycombed with burrows, which are used year after year. Individual tunnels, which may be up to sixty feet long, may have as many as fifty-six entrances in an area fifty yards square. During the summer, short 'bachelor' burrows may be dug for temporary shelter. These may only be six feet long with a small chamber. One burrow over ten yards long was dug in a twenty-four-hour period. The diameter of the burrow varies between two and eight inches depending on the size of the occupant.

The hibernation dens are specially constructed side tunnels off the main burrows. They are situated twenty-four to thirty inches below the surface. The chamber is about ten inches in diameter and is completely lined with grasses, lichens, leaves, and sometimes the hair of caribou or ground squirrel.

The arctic ground squirrel spends about seven months in hibernation. Rolling up in a ball with its back uppermost, its head tucked into the ventral surface and its tail covering its head and shoulders, it enters a prolonged and deep torpor. During hibernation, its body temperature drops from a normal 36.4°C to 17°C. Handling the squirrel during torpor need not awaken it, although there are natural arousals every few weeks.

Adult males first appear in late April or early May, about a week ahead of the females. The exact date of emergence depends upon altitude, latitude, and local weather conditions. Those higher and farther north emerge later. When the squirrels first appear, snow still covers the land, and the animals must burrow up through it. At first the animals stay near the burrow entrance, but once the snow starts to

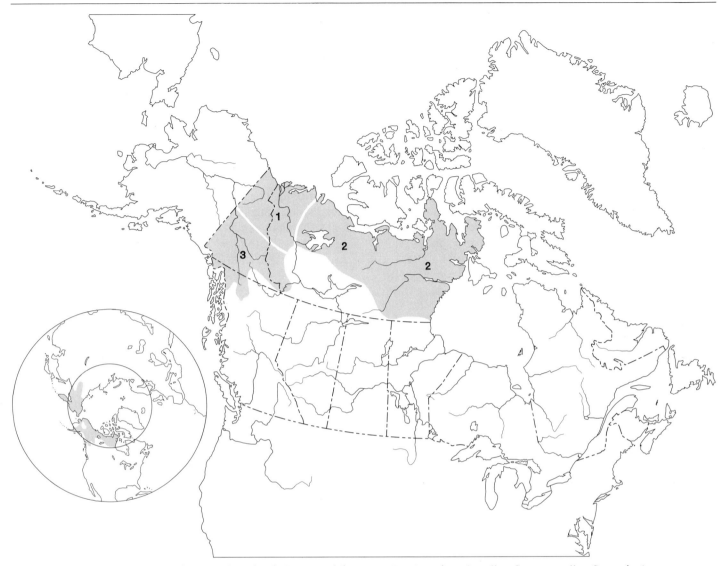

Map 53 Distribution of the arctic ground squirrel, *Spermophilus parryii*: 1 *S. p. kennicottii*, 2 *S. p. parryii*, 3 *S. p. plesius*

melt they wander a little farther afield. They have been seen active in April when the air temperatures were as low as 22°F.

In the autumn, the adults first enter hibernation about mid-September, but the young are usually active until about October 6. Both adults and young must put on sufficient fat to tide them over the long hibernation period. Arctic ground squirrels have been known to be active in November and even as late as December 3.

Arctic ground squirrels eat a wide variety of native trundra vegetation. They consume the leaves, seeds, fruit, stems, flowers, and roots of many grasses, forbs, and woody species. Plants eaten include mushrooms, grasses, sedges, cottongrass, bog rush, knotweeds, bearberry, bilbery, milk-vetch, oxytropis, lousewort, saxifrages, mountain cranberry, mountain avens, and willows.

In late summer, seeds and leaves are cached in the hibernation den or in the passages leading to it. The cache may amount to about four pounds of willow leaves, grass seed heads, and bog rush capsules. The squirrels feed upon these stores after they emerge in early spring before the new vegetation grows.

Arctic ground squirrels, like their relatives, will also eat meat from the carcasses of lemmings, ground squirrels, birds, or caribou. There is a record of one having carried away two pounds of caribou meat during a single day.

This species is an important food item for arctic carnivores such as ermine, wolf, arctic fox, and grizzly bear. Bears often tear up great patches of tundra turf hunting for ground squirrels, which provide an important food source in the spring and autumn when the green vegetation has been killed by frost.

Habitat. Permafrost is an important factor in limiting the distribution of this species. It occupies tundra regions beyond the treeline and clearings within northern forests. However, in these regions it is restricted to gravel or sandy hillocks where good drainage prevents permafrost from occurring near the surface. Typical habitats include eskers, moraines, river banks, lake shores, and sandbanks. Farther south it occupies more extensive open meadows where permafrost is limited to the bogs and dense coniferous forests.

Reproduction. The arctic environment places a severe restriction on the reproductive period available for northern animals. The arctic ground squirrel, like many arctic birds, has a shortened breeding period. Upon emergence in spring the testes of the males are probably still abdominal but descend to the scrotum in the first week of activity. The animals are then in breeding condition for a short period of three weeks in May. Regression begins in early June and the testes are withdrawn into the abdomen by the middle of the month. The females are similarly monoestrous and are bred during the last half of May. After a gestation period of twenty-five days, the young are born after mid-June. The litter size varies between five and ten. The young are altricial, but they develop rapidly. Skin pigmentation appears on the fourth day, and hair on the head on the eighth day. At the end of fourteen days the dorsal spotting occurs. The eyes open after twenty days, and the young emerge from the burrows soon after, in mid-July. At first they romp and sun themselves close to the entrance, but after a week they venture farther afield. They are weaned about this time. Growth of the young is very rapid. In a captive litter of nine, the average weight at birth was 10.8 g, at twenty-four days 141.2 g, at thirty-eight days 463.8 g, and at fifty-three days 785 g. By the beginning of September they appear almost full-grown. In late summer they abandon the natal burrow and occupy an empty one or dig a new one on the boundary of the colony. There is considerable mortality of young during the first winter because the sites chosen may become flooded or enveloped in permafrost. The young squirrels remain active longer than the adults because they must lay on sufficient fat to overwinter. They mature the following spring and reach mature weight during their second spring.

Economic Status. Eskimos use arctic ground squirrels as food and their pelts for the lining of winter parkas. Occasionally the pelts are made into attractive summer parkas.

Distribution. The arctic ground squirrel is closely related to the Asian species *Spermophilus undulatus*. It is distributed from eastern Siberia to Hudson Bay and southward as far as northwestern British Columbia.

Canadian Distribution. Three geographical subspecies are recognized in Canada (see Map 53).

Spermophilus parryii kennicottii (Ross), 1861, Canadian Naturalist and Geologist 6: 434. Northern Alaska, northern Yukon Territory, and the lower Mackenzie River valley, Northwest Territories.

Spermophilus parryii parryii (Richardson), 1825, *in* Parry, Journal of a second voyage ..., p. 316. A large, dark race found on the continental tundra of the Mackenzie and Keewatin districts from the Anderson River to Melville Peninsula and Hudson Bay.

Spermophilus parryii plesius Osgood, 1900, N. American Fauna 19: 29. A smaller race found in southern Yukon Territory and northwestern British Columbia. Melanis-

tic individuals predominate in the population in certain parts of southern Yukon.

REFERENCE

Mayer, W.V. 1953. A preliminary study of the Barrow ground squirrel, *Citellus parryi barrowensis*. Jour. Mamm. 34(3): 334–45.

THIRTEEN-LINED GROUND SQUIRREL
Spermophile rayé. *Spermophilus tridecemlineatus* (Mitchell)

Description. The thirteen-lined ground squirrel is one of the smaller species of the group and distinctly slimmer in build than the other Canadian species. The tail is about half the body length, and the fur forms a pencil-thick covering rather than a brush. Compared to that of its relatives the skull of this species is also relatively long and narrow and weakly constructed. The zygomatic arches are not expanded; the interorbital region is long and flat, and the small supraorbital processes are posteriorly placed (Plate 6).

The striking coloration of this species has earned the animal its common name. It is prominently striped dorsally with seven wide, dark brown stripes, each enclosing a row of buffy squares. The brown stripes are separated by six narrow buff stripes. The crown is speckled brown and buff. The nose, eye-ring, cheeks, feet, and underparts are buff-coloured. The central portion of the tail is tawny, and on each side there is a submarginal black band, tipped with beige hairs.

There are two annual moults, one in June and the second in late summer. During the spring moult the new hair first appears on the crown and progresses backwards with a prominent moult line. During the autumn moult, the new coat appears on the rump and works forward. Its progress is more irregular, and there is no moult line. The summer pelage, which is worn for only about two months, is more buffy. The winter coat, assumed just prior to hibernation, is greyer with more contrasting stripes. Throughout the year, however, the pelage is much shorter and more brittle than in the other Canadian species, and the underfur is less prominent.

Average measurements of a series of Manitoba males: length 275 (257–298), tail 101 (91–111), hind foot 39 (38–42), ear 7 mm. Female measurements: length 265 (257–272), tail 95 (90–100), hind foot 37 (35–40) mm. Average weight of males, 164 g, and of females, 140 g.

Habits. This slim little ground squirrel appears quicker in movements and more elusive than its more clumsy larger relatives. It is more solitary in behaviour than the others and lives alone or in isolated family groups. Often one can camp in its habitat for some time before catching sight of it. It utters a high-pitched trill, which has ventriloquistic qualities and does not reveal the location of the camouflaged caller. It is diurnal and on bright warm days is most active between 10 A.M. and 1 P.M. It is a fairly strong swimmer and occasionally climbs into low shrubs.

The thirteen-lined ground squirrel excavates relatively simple burrows. It scratches out the dirt with its long, clawed forefeet, kicks it out from under its body with its hind feet, and sprays the loose dirt around the entrance so as not to leave a telltale distinctive pile. The squirrel uses its forehead to pack the roof of its burrow. The main burrow is about five yards long and leads to a chamber about six feet beneath the surface. When the nesting chamber and storage areas are completed, the ground squirrel starts to dig a second tunnel to the surface from about halfway along the first tunnel. The earth that is pushed out through the first entrance may be used later on to plug the original entrance. Eventually the new entrance is completed from the inside so as to leave neither fresh earth nor an enlarged mouth to reveal its presence. Only a simple hole about two inches in diameter, hidden in a clump of grass, serves as entrance to the den. The sharp bend in the finished burrow discourages the digging of one of the squirrel's arch predators, the badger, because it would have difficulty in throwing the earth out of an L-shaped excavation. Occasionally the original work-hole is not filled, leaving the squirrel with two entrances. It usually digs several other short, shallow burrows about its home range during the summer months, all connected by well-travelled runways through the vegetation. When a squirrel seeks sanctuary in one of its temporary burrows, it usually plugs the entrance.

The hibernation chamber is constructed off the deeper burrow, but no sump similar to those excavated by the Columbian ground squirrels has been described. The nest chamber is an oval about seven inches in diameter. The nest is lined with dried grasses and well sprinkled with seeds and grain. After plugging the burrow, the hibernating squirrel assumes the typical rolled-up pose, propped on its haunches, its head tucked between its hind feet and its head and shoulders covered by its tail. In this condition it is stiff and cold to the touch and irresponsive to external stimuli. It does not remain immobile all winter, however. Laboratory studies have shown that natural arousal periods occur at least every twelve days.

The hibernation of this species has been studied in the laboratory by Dr G.E. Johnson and his associates. They have reported various differences between the active and hibernating states. The normal respiration rate varies between 45 and 340 per minute, the lower figure representing a sleeping animal and the higher figure an agitated one. The respiration rate for a hibernating ground squirrel at 40°C varied between 1 and 15 per minute, the lowest rate being recorded for a live animal in deep torpor being 1 to 2 per minute. The normal heart beat is 100 to 200 per minute, but for a torpid animal below 10°C the pulse rate is 5 to 20 with an average of 17.4. The normal temperature of active squirrels fluctuated between 35.5°C in a cold room and 38.4°C in a warm room. Ground squirrels have poor thermoregulation mechanisms, and under heat stress their temperature has risen as high as 42.3°C. In hibernation the temperature of the torpid animal falls to one or two degrees above the environmental temperature. It may fall to 0.5°C, but the animals do not survive if the body temperature drops below 0°C. The greatest weight loss during hibernation was 39 per cent, which amounted to 0.29 per cent a day.

In Manitoba, most thirteen-lined ground squirrels enter hibernation at about the end of September, but exceptionally late animals have entered on October 20, November 2, and November 8. They usually reappear in early April, the males about a week before the females. March 29 is the earliest date for Manitoba, but farther south, in Kansas, they appear about mid-March. Upon first emergence, they feed upon their cached seeds and kernels of grain, clean out their burrows, and replace their soiled nests.

The home range may vary between 1.62 and 11.7 acres. Males have larger home ranges than females. Some individuals are known to travel several hundred yards to grainfields. Studies of populations in an abandoned field in Michigan have found 2.18 squirrels per acre.

This species is probably more insectivorous than most other species of ground squirrels. A study of the contents of eighty stomachs revealed that 54 per cent was composed of insects and 44 per cent of vegetable matter, 2 per cent being unidentifiable. The thirteen-lined ground squirrel is very fond of grasshopers, crickets, and caterpillars. In early spring, it consumes fresh green foliage and later a number of weed seeds such as thistles, goosefoot, knotweed, ragweed, clover, native grasses, dandelion, vetch, and nightshade berries. Unfortunately, it is also fond of domestic grains and garden produce.

From the middle of summer onwards this species carries its harvest produce, packed in its cheek pouches, to storage caches in the grass lining of its nest and side passages of its burrow. Pouches have been found to contain as many as 196 seed pods of sleepy catchfly (*Silene antirrhina*) or 362 grains of wheat. Excavated caches have contained as many as 23,000 oat kernels and 2,000 to 3,000 wheat kernels. Burr oak acorns and crabapples have also been noted. The squirrels do not cache all their stores underground; they may hide grain in clumps of grass or in shallow holes. Often the squirrels forget these seeds, which, undisturbed, take root and sprout naturally. During the summer months the squirrels will daily visit available water supplies to drink.

The thirteen-lined ground squirrel must maintain constant vigilance for a host of predators, the most important of which are the large buteo hawk, the badger, the coyote, the fox, and the weasel. Even crows have been observed killing young squirrels.

Habitat. This species does not inhabit the open grasslands as do so many other ground squirrels. Instead, it is found in abandoned overgrown fields, shrubby areas, poplar bluffs, and swales. This species, which seems to be local in distribution, is often abundant in aspen parklands but rare or absent in certain Great Plains areas.

Reproduction. Some male squirrels may be sexually mature upon first emergence in the spring; others attain their peak in sexual activity a couple of weeks later. Mating takes place during a brief two to three weeks' flurry

Map 54 Distribution of the thirteen-lined ground squirrel, *Spermophilus tridecemlineatus*: 1 *S. t. hoodii*, 2 *S. t. tridecemlineatus*, 3 *S. t. pallidus*

during the last half of April and early May. By June the male gonads regress and by the beginning of July they are withdrawn into the abdomen. During the mating season males explore widely for females, and there is considerable scrapping when two males meet.

The females are similarly sexually inactive during most of the year, and their vaginal orifices are then sealed. They are monoestrous and are receptive soon after emergence in mid-April. Ovulation is stimulated by coitus. The oestrous period lasts about two weeks. If the females are not fertilized, or if they lose the first litter, they may mate later. Very small embryos have been found in a female shot as late as June 8. Normally the female's genital system regresses in June.

After a gestation period of twenty-seven to twenty-eight days, the litters are born in late May or early June. The litter size may vary between three and thirteen, with an average of 8.06 young. Since the female has only ten teats, there is occasionally some mortality soon after birth.

Females have been known to eat one or two of their young while raising the remainder successfully.

At birth the young weigh about 6 g apiece. They are altricial in development. Dark pigmentation develops on the eighth day; on the twelfth day the stripes appear and the young first utter their characteristic trill. When they are twenty-six to twenty-eight days old, their eyes open, and soon after they appear at the burrow entrance, by about the beginning of July. The young squirrels are weaned at about the twenty-ninth day, and although they have only reached about a third of their full growth they start to fend for themselves. After they have been above ground about ten days, they leave the natal burrow and dig their own dens close by. These burrows are usually shallow and only about three feet in length and an inch in diameter. By the end of July the young weigh 100 to 150 g and are about three-quarters grown. They do not reach full size or sexual maturity until they emerge in spring at the age of eleven months.

Economic Status. On the Canadian prairies this species is not as destructive to agriculture as is Richardson's ground squirrel. It usually lives at some distance from cultivated fields, and its forays are more confined to a few rows on the edge of a field. They are, however, particularly destructive in spring before their natural food has appeared, and at that time they dig up newly planted seed. They eat and carry away kernels of wheat, corn, and oats in particular. They are often a nuisance about vegetable gardens, which are usually closer to favourable cover under shrubs and trees. They eat peas, beans, cucumbers, squash, beets, and strawberries.

In spite of their depredations, however, one should not lose sight of the fact that the thirteen-lined ground squirrel destroys great numbers of grasshoppers in late summer.

This species is most effectively controlled by poison campaigns as described under Richardson's ground squirrel. If the damage is caused by a local family, as is often the case, trapping at their burrows would provide adequate control.

Occasionally this species is the cause of considerable damage to golf courses. It is not its burrows, which are only a slight nuisance, that cause large-scale damage but the excavations made by badgers hunting them.

Distribution. The thirteen-lined ground squirrel has the distinction of being the most easterly distributed ground squirrel, occurring as far east as Michigan and Ohio. It occupies a wide range in the central Great Plains region of North America north of the Gulf of Mexico.

Canadian Distribution. Three geographical subspecies are recognized in the Prairie Provinces of Canada (see Map 54).

Spermophilus tridecemlineatus hoodii (Sabine), 1822, Linn. Soc. London Trans. 13: 590. Northern aspen parklands from western Manitoba to central Alberta. A slightly larger and darker race.

Spermophilus tridecemlineatus pallidus J.A. Allen, 1874, Proc. Boston Soc. Nat. Hist. 16: 291. The arid short grass steppe of southwestern Saskatchewan and southeastern Alberta. A small, pale race.

Spermophilus tridecemlineatus tridecemlineatus (Mitchell), 1821, Medical Repository (n.s.), 6(21): 248. The typical form, found on the plains of southern Manitoba, Saskatchewan, and Alberta.

REFERENCES

Criddle, Stuart. 1939. The thirteen-striped ground squirrel in Manitoba. Canadian Field-Nat. 53(1): 1–6.
McCarley, H. 1966. Annual cycle, population dynamics and adaptive behavior of *Citellus tridicemlineatus*. Jour. Mamm. 47(2): 294–316.

FRANKLIN'S GROUND SQUIRREL
Spermophile de Franklin. *Spermophilus franklinii* (Sabine)

Description. Named in honour of the famous English explorer Sir John Franklin, who lost his life in the Canadian Arctic in 1846, this species bears a closer resemblance to the tree squirrels than the other ground squirrels do because of its long, bushy tail, which makes up two-thirds of its total length. Its skull is also relatively long, particularly the rostrum, with narrow zygomatic processes and a narrow, flat cranium.

The pelage is short and wiry. The underfur is sparse, particularly in the summer coat. There is one annual moult is early summer.

Dorsally the animal is olive brown, checked with numerous short black bars. The head is smoke grey with a frosting of silver-tipped hairs. There is a white eye-ring. The ears are a little larger then those of other Canadian ground-squirrels. The underparts are covered with sparse buff-grey hairs. The feet are hoary grey. The proximal portion of the tail is olive brown, but the distal portion is a mixture of light and dark grey, with a prominent light grey border (Plate 4e).

Average measurements of Manitoba males: length 388 (363–430), tail 144 (120–155), hind foot 55 (51–68), ear 15 mm. The adult females are a little smaller: length 387 (367–408), tail 139 (128–155), hind foot 55 (52–57) mm. The males are also slightly heavier, up to 473 g on the average; the average for females is 426 g.

Habits. Franklin's ground squirrel is very secretive in its habits. It lives either solitarily or in small family groups, but not in large colonies. During the summer months it is active only during the daylight hours, from dawn to dusk. On cold, rainy, or windy days it may not venture from its burrow at all. It has been estimated to be active above ground for only 10 per cent of its lifetime; the rest is spent underground in its burrow hibernating, sleeping, or seeking shelter from the weather or from predators. When above ground it scampers along well-beaten runways in the vegetation between burrows. It climbs considerably better than other ground squirrels and indulges in lively chases through the branches of trees. It is also a strong swimmer. Its call is a remarkably clear musical whistle.

Populations of this squirrel fluctuate dramatically. They may be abundant one year and rare a few years later in the same locality. The peaks in abundance in southern Manitoba since about 1910 have occurred every four to six years. Average populations are about 4 to 5.2 animals per acre of good habitat.

Franklin's ground squirrel emerges from hibernation about two weeks later than Richardson's ground squirrel. The date of first appearance in Manitoba between 1939 and 1947 varied from April 14 to 26, depending on local weather conditions. The males emerge about a week ahead of the females. They start to disappear in late August, and only a few younger animals are about after mid-September. Late dates of observation of active Franklin's ground squirrels are October 2 and 7.

This ground squirrel is an omnivorous feeder. Animal material composes about a third of its diet; the remainder is vegetable matter. Favourite plant foods include sow thistle, beach pea, chokecherry, elderberry, white clover, and unidentified seeds and roots. In early spring it first

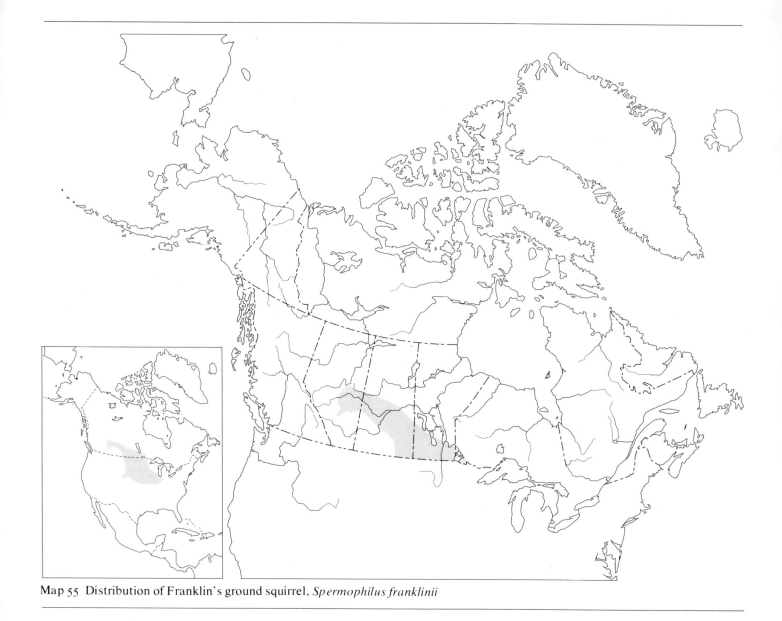

Map 55 Distribution of Franklin's ground squirrel, *Spermophilus franklinii*

feeds on cherry stones, roots, and nettle and grass shoots; later it eats dandelion and wild cucumber; and as the small fruits mature in early summer it transfers its attention to them. It is also fond of domestic grains such as corn, oats, and wheat. In late summer it stores oats, berry stones, and grass seeds in its burrows for autumn and early spring use.

The animal food eaten by this species includes beetles, larvae, crickets, grasshoppers, caterpillars, and ant eggs. It also eats small ground-nesting birds' eggs and young, as well as frogs and toads. A special study of its predation on duck's nests near Delta, Manitoba, indicated that these ground squirrels destroyed about 19 per cent of the vulnerable duck nests within their range. They also kill young ducklings that have strayed from their broods.

Because of this ground squirrel's limited availability, it constitutes a less important item in the diet of predators than other local rodents of the same size. The red-tailed hawk and the marsh hawk are known to prey upon it to some extent, but they are seldom about when the larger owls are hunting. Probably the carnivores, such as the

badger, red fox, coyote, skunk, and weasel, are the more important predators.

Habitat. Franklin's ground squirrels inhabit wooded areas and the edges of woods. They are abundant in poplar bluffs of the aspen parkland that lies between the Great Plains and the coniferous forest. They have even penetrated the coniferous forest belt along the alder banks of streams and the patches of poplars in the evergreen forests, and frequently hunt in marshy areas that lie close to wooded ridges.

Reproduction. The males are reported to be in breeding condition upon emergence from hibernation. The actual breeding period is determined by the appearance of the females, and lasts about three weeks. During this period there is much scrapping among the males in pursuit of the females. The young are born about the beginning of June. The litter size varies from four to eleven, with an average of 7.5.

Although born naked, wrinkled, and helpless in their mother's grass-lined den, about three feet underground, the young grow rapidly and are well furred by the sixteenth day. Their eyes open on the twentieth day, and soon after they emerge to explore. They are weaned when about thirty-nine days old, in early July, and set out to establish their own homes. They do not mature sexually until the following spring.

Economic Status. An ideal habitat is provided for Franklin's ground squirrels in the poplar bluffs near farm homes on the Canadian prairies. It is this species that does the most damage to gardens. Carrots, peas, string beans, tomatoes, and potatoes are frequently damaged. It is also a menace about the hen-house and will kill chicks as well as nearly half-grown fowl.

Since the damage is usually done by a few animals, the best means of control is probably trapping. Control in marsh areas for protection of duck eggs is probably not feasible. One should keep in mind that the ground squirrel numbers fluctuate drastically and that significant damage is probably limited to the one year in four or more when they are abundant.

Distribution. Franklin's ground squirrel is found along the eastern border of the Great Plains from western Illinois and Kansas to central Alberta.

Canadian Distribution. The species is monotypic, and no subspecies have been described. In Canada it is found from the Rainy River region of western Ontario to the Edmonton area of Alberta. It is absent from the short-grass prairie (see Map 55).

Spermophilus franklinii (Sabine), 1822, Trans. Linn. Soc. London 13: 587.

REFERENCE

Sowls, Lyle K. 1948. The Franklin ground squirrel, *Citellus franklinii* (Sabine), and its relationship to nesting ducks. Jour. Mamm. 29(2): 113–37.

GOLDEN-MANTLED GROUND SQUIRREL
Spermophile à mante dorée. *Spermophilus lateralis* (Say)

Description. The golden-mantled ground squirrel is one of the most attractive Canadian small mammals. It is sometimes called the big chipmunk because of its striking coloration and bold, winsome ways. Its stocky form, its moderately short bushy tail, about a third of the body length, and its three anal papillae indicate, however, that it belongs to the ground squirrel group. It possesses certain unique features such as relatively large ears (for a ground squirrel) and a diamond-shaped glandular area of thickened skin between the shoulders. The skull is narrower and more delicately formed than that of some larger species.

This species is easily identified by the two broad whitish lateral stripes running from shoulders to rump, each bordered by narrower black stripes. The centre of the back is grizzled grey, and the flanks are buffy. The head, neck, and shoulders are covered in a mantle that varies from golden-brown to russet-brown. Above and below the eyes

are white crescents. The feet and legs are ochraceous-buff. The tail is blackish above, and ochraceous below with buffy-tipped hairs. The pelage is soft and dense. The guard hairs are augmented by a layer of underfur, which has a dull grey base and beige tips (Plate 4j).

There is one annual moult each year, in June and early July for the males, and as late as early August for the females. The new coat is richly coloured, the old coat in spring being much paler.

Average measurements of adults of both sexes: length 287 (270–315), tail 102 (95–115), hind foot 43 (40–45), ear 17 mm; weight 231 (167–275) g. The males on the average weigh a little more than the females.

Habits. The golden-mantled ground squirrel is more deliberate in its movements than the smaller and slenderer western chipmunks, with which it often associates. It is more strictly a ground dweller and only occasionally climbs among the low shrubs. It will occasionally swim across small brooks. When it runs, its tail is elevated at an angle of approximately forty-five degrees from the ground. It spends much of the day stretched out full-length sunning on a rock, or standing alert like a small bowling pin on a stump or log. It has good hearing and eyesight and quickly recognizes potential danger. Although the population is usually evenly dispersed over the suitable habitat, individuals will travel several hundred yards and congregate at camping grounds and cabins where they can expect handouts. Ordinarily the golden-mantled ground squirrel is a rather silent animal, but it has a shrill, high-pitched, two-noted whistle, *trp-trp*, the second note being lower than the first. It also utters an explosive alarm note, *tsp*, or a buzzing chatter if cornered.

Like its relatives, this species prefers warm, sunny weather and is active only between sunrise and sunset or shortly afterwards. If the morning is chilly, it may not appear until the dew has evaporated. It may be inactive during the heat of noon. Cold, windy, or rainy days also cause it to remain in the shelter of its burrow.

This ground squirrel constructs short, simple burrows, with entrances located under a rock, stump, log, or bush. There is never any telltale pile of earth near by to betray its presence. The entrance is usually about three inches in diameter but rapidly narrows to two inches in the tunnel. The burrows average about four feet long but may be up to fifteen feet in length. There may be two or more entrances. The average depth of the burrow is about eighteen inches, and it leads to a chamber about six inches in diameter and to one or two blind passages that serve as toilet or storage areas. The nest is composed of a mat of shredded leaves, grasses, and pine needles on the floor of the chamber. After entering for the night the squirrel often plugs the entrance with loose earth.

The golden-mantled ground squirrel often builds its den near the edge of a rock pile or occasionally in a hollow log or deserted cabin. Several burrows or shelters are connected by a series of well-travelled trails over rocks or along logs to favourite reconnaissance points on stumps or boulders.

Individual squirrels have been observed to range 100 to 300 yards. A female with young in a nest under a log was observed driving off all intruders for distances up to 10 yards from her nest. Populations vary between 2.5 and 5 squirrels per acre. Individuals have lived up to eleven years in captivity, but the turnover in nature is probably much quicker.

In late summer these ground squirrels pack their cheek pouches with seeds and carry them to their burrows or cache them in various shallow pits. The booty is packed in with their forepaws until the pouches project as if the squirrel had the mumps. Nesting material is transported in the same way. One squirrel carried off four pounds of shelled peanuts to a den 100 yards away. This species becomes excessively fat at this season – a squirrel that weighed 225 g in the spring might weigh up to 275 g in the autumn. This species enters hibernation in early September in Canada (usually after the Columbian ground squirrel). In California they may remain active as late as November 25. The lean females and young animals are the last to hibernate.

In Canada the adult males are the first to reappear, about mid-April. In California they may reappear as early as March 24. Those squirrels at higher elevations appear later, often tunnelling through a foot of snow to reach the sunshine. In hibernation this species assumes the typical rolled-up position with its head tucked into its lower abdomen and its tail curled over its head and shoulders. It is relatively insensitive when in torpor. It does not maintain one position uninterrupted all winter, however. Experimental study in the laboratory has shown that there are rhythmical arousals every five days or so, these being more frequent at the beginning and end of the hibernation period. No animals remained torpid at 0°c for periods longer than sixteen days. Adult males were found to arouse more frequently than females or juveniles, and animals held at higher temperatures had more frequent arousals. The natural arousals usually lasted from a few hours up to twenty-four, during which time only traces of food and water were taken. It was found that urination took place during each arousal, and it was indicated that most of the urine voided was formed during the brief active period when the animal's body temperature approached the normal active level of 32° to 35°c. It is suspected that the accumulation of metabolic end-products might be the stimulus to arousal.

The food of the golden-mantled ground squirrel consists of a wide array of seeds, fungus, leaves, flowers, fruits, and roots of native vegetation. In one study of the contents of 273 stomachs, underground fungus was found to be the most important food item, amounting to 65 per cent by volume of the summer food and 90 per cent of the autumn food. Among the other plants eaten are pine and fir seeds, rose hips, serviceberries, thimbleberries, gooseberries, chokecherries, lupine seeds, milk vetch, clover, smartweed, penstemon, mullein, grasses, strawberries, fireweed, and dandelions.

They also eat an appreciable amount of arthropods, amounting to 16 per cent of the summer diet. These include grasshoppers, beetles, caterpillars, flies, ants, and butterflies.

Their predators include large snakes, bobcats, foxes, coyotes, weasels, skunks, grizzly bears, and such avian raptores as the red-tailed hawk and the goshawk.

Habitat. This species is an inhabitant of the mountain slopes and foothills. It occupies open, sunny forests where there is an abundance of fallen logs, exposed rock, and underbrush of bearberry or Oregon grape. Stands of yellow pine, Douglas fir, or Englemann spruce are favoured sites, where this squirrel occurs in association with the western chipmunk and the Columbian ground squirrel. It is also found on the alpine tundra beyond the treeline, and particularly in rock slides, where it associates with pikas, bushy-tailed woodrats, and hoary marmots. In Canada it is usually found in the altitudinal range of 5,000 to 8,000 feet, but it occurs up to 13,000 feet on Pikes Peak in Colorado.

Reproduction. Very few details are known concerning the reproduction of this species. The males emerge first in spring, but are not in breeding condition for about two weeks. The females appear towards the end of April, and mating occurs soon after. The females are monoestrous; only one litter is born each year. The reproductive period ends in early July. The litter varies between two and eight, and usually consists of four to six. The number of teats is variable: eight, nine, or ten.

The initial appearance of the young above ground during early July marks the weaning time. At first the females are solicitous and push the young down the burrow at the first sign of danger, but by mid-July the young animals are on their own and leave the natal burrow. At that time they appear half-grown. They do not reach mature size until the following spring, when they attain sexual maturity.

Economic Status. The golden-mantled ground squirrel seldom comes into contact with agriculture. Only occasionally is the species in a position to raid marginal oat or wheat fields to supplement its larder. More often concern is expressed concerning the role of this species in connection with reforestation practice. It is known that they destroy young planted seedlings and they feed on conifer seeds. It has been shown that the natural regeneration of conifer seedlings is, however, dependent upon special conditions such as an abundant seed crop, generous rains, and the removal of the ground duff so that the seeds can root in mineral soil. When the conditions are favourable for reproduction, the effects of ground squirrels and chipmunks are immaterial. In the meantime these ground squirrels may 'plant' many seedlings in their caches and not return to eat them.

This species has also been shown to serve as an intermediate host of the Rocky Mountain spotted fever tick *Dermacentor andersoni*, and as such must be considered a minor public health hazard; however, it has provided endless pleasure to campers and woodsmen with its bold antics around campsites and cabins in the mountains.

Distribution. The central Cordilleran region of western North America.

Canadian Distribution. Two geographical subspecies

Map 56 Distribution of the golden-mantled ground squirrel, *Spermophilus lateralis*: 1 *S. l. saturatus*, 2 *S. l. tescorum*

are found in the mountains of Alberta and British Columbia from Mount Selwyn south to the international boundary (see Map 56).

Spermophilus lateralis saturatus (Rhoads), 1895, Proc. Acad. Nat. Sci. Philadelphia 47: 43. A large, pale grey race in which the dorsal striped pattern is much subdued. The lateral white stripes have only vague dark borders, and the cinnamon mantle is restricted to the cheeks and sides of the neck. This subspecies is confined to the eastern slopes of the Cascade Mountains of southwestern British Columbia south and west of the Similkameen and Tulameen rivers. It was originally given species status because of its present isolated range.

Spermophilus lateralis tescorum (Hollister), 1911, Smiths. Misc. Coll. 56(26): 2. The typical form, found in the Rocky and Selkirk mountains, western Alberta, and eastern British Columbia.

REFERENCES

Gordon, K. 1943. The natural history and behavior of the western chipmunk and the mantled ground squirrel. Oregon State Univ. Monogr., Studies in Zool. 5.

Pengelley, E.T., and K.C. Fisher, 1961. Rhythmical arousal from hibernation in the golden-mantled ground squirrel, *Citellus lateralis tescorum*. Canadian Jour. Zool. 39(1): 105–20.

BLACK-TAILED PRAIRIE DOG
Chien de prairie. *Cynomys ludovicianus* (Ord)

Description. The early explorers to the Great Plains of North America were much impressed by the antics of this common and conspicuous inhabitant of their route along the upper Missouri River. Their journals contain many references to its peculiar bark-like call and its dense colonies, which they called dog-towns. It was called the prairie dog, *petit chien*, or barking squirrel; indeed its scientific name means Louisiana dog-mouse, since the Mississippi basin was then known as Louisiana.

The prairie dogs are closely related to the ground squirrels, from which they may be distinguished by their larger

129

size, stouter bodies, and shorter tails. Their ears are extremely short, often hidden in the fur. Adults may reach 16 inches in length and weigh up to 3 pounds. There are many anatomical features that set them apart as a distinct genus. These include the rudimentary cheek pouches, the well-furred wrist and heel with a tuft of hair on the sole of the hind foot, the short pollux that carries a typical curved claw (in place of the rudimentary flattened nail found in *Spermophilus*), and the eight mammae in the females. The skull is broad and angular and heavily built (Figure 36). The molar teeth are much larger than in the ground squirrels, and the tooth rows converge prominently behind. The antero-orbital canal terminates in a pronounced tubular prominence. The pelage is uniform in colour and lacks the striking patterns found in the genus *Spermophilus*. In the black-tailed prairie dog the dorsal colour is a uniform pale cinnamon-buff, lined with scattered black hairs towards the rump, forehead, and cheeks. The lower part of the face and the underparts are pale buffy white; the feet are creamy in colour. The basal two-thirds of the tail is pinkish cinnamon; the tip is grizzled black. The claws and vibrissae are black.

There are two annual moults separating a thin, wiry summer pelage and a longer, softer, heavily underfurred winter pelage. The spring moult occurs in June and July and progresses from chest and underparts to the back, head, and, finally, to the rump and tail. The autumn moult proceeds in the opposite direction, starting on the rump in September and progressing anteriorly. This autumn moult excludes the tail, which receives only one annual renewal. In the northern part of the prairie dog's range the summer coat is worn for only a short period, and the two moults seem to run together.

Average measurements of adult males: length 388 (360–415), tail 86 (75–98), hind foot 62 (61–63) mm. The females are slightly smaller. Average weight of males, 1.36 kg, and of females, 1.14 kg.

Habits. Black-tailed prairie dogs are strongly gregarious and are colonial in distribution. Very few stragglers are found away from the densely populated dog-towns. These towns may be only six or seven acres in extent, but they usually occupy several hundred acres. In the early days the Staked Plains of western Texas, an area approximately 100 miles in width and 250 miles in length, was considered to be one huge dog-town, harbouring 400 million prairie dogs. The burrows are situated twenty-five to fifty yards apart, and the populations have been estimated to be as low as five or six animals per acre in Saskatchewan and up to thirty animals per acre in dense colonies in the United States. One of the early pieces of lore concerning prairie dogs was that they lived amicably with rattlesnakes and burrowing owls and derived some mutual benefit from these strange bedfellows. This has been shown to be pure legend. Prairie dogs do provide homes for rattlesnakes and burrowing owls, but the advantage is decidedly one-sided since those animals prey upon young prairie dogs and the dogs soon evacuate the burrows occupied by the unwelcome neighbours. Only Richardson's ground squirrels share the same site occasionally with the larger prairie dogs with no apparent ill-effects.

Topographic and vegetative features divide a typical dog-town into semi-isolated wards. The individuals in each ward are organized into discrete social units called 'coteries.' The average number of individuals in a coterie was found to be 8.5 (2–35). All the prairie dogs in a coterie are socially integrated. There seems to be no social hierarchy, and all are nearly equal in social status. The group is co-ordinated through social activities such as muzzling, grooming, and playing, and by vocal communication. The average area occupied by a coterie in the dog-town studied was 0.70 acre and that was the mean home range for each member of the coterie. This area was defended by all members against outsiders.

Only during the breeding season is there some intra-coterie strife; at this time the females defend individual territories about their burrows. The colonies expand in summer when adult males move out to new areas with fresh food supplies, and the females follow and so form new coteries. The young animals do not form the new towns.

This species is also strictly diurnal. It first appears about fifteen minutes after sunrise and feeds steadily for about two hours. Most of the warm daylight hours are spent in grooming, dust-bathing, stretching spread-eagled in the sun, or visiting neighbours. Friends meet and recognize one another by mouth nuzzling ('kissing'). Strangers are

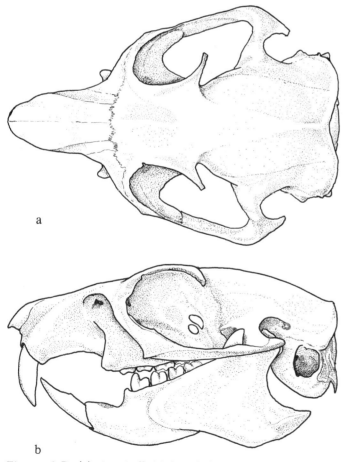

a

b

Figure 36 Prairie dog skull: (a) dorsal view, (b) lateral view (× 2)

repelled by lively chases among the burrow entrances. The prairie dogs feed cautiously, crawling on all fours for five to ten seconds, and then sit on their haunches for three to four seconds for a brief reconnaissance. When alarmed they stand straight up, and even rise on their toes. The alarm note is a loud explosive bark, given with a leap or an emphatic tail twitch. The other animals in the colony are quick to respond to the general alarm, all scuttling towards their burrows. Those already at their burrows echo the alarm with leaping and barks. If the danger is near, they drop down their burrows with chattering squeals.

There is a noontime siesta in the heat of the day when few animals appear above ground. Feeding activity increases in late afternoon and continues till sundown. Stormy weather is not to their liking, and they remain underground until the sun reappears.

The prairie dog burrow is unique. Soil from the excavation of the burrow is heaped around the entrance like a crater. The mounds usually measure about a foot high and three to four feet wide at the base. Occasionally the mound is even higher in an established burrow. It is not clear how the animal brings up the soil from the burrow; probably it uses its forehead to push it. The animal is not satisfied with the amount of soil excavated from the burrow, however, and kicks up on the mound soil from the area surrounding the burrow. All this material is compacted with vigorous bunts of the forehead. The mound serves as a dam to keep the runoff of showers from flooding the burrow, and also as a look-out. The burrow itself, which is about four inches in diameter, falls away in a vertical plunge for ten to fourteen feet. Three to five feet from the surface is a small side chamber, which provides a turning point. At the bottom of the plunge, the tunnel levels off and proceeds another ten to forty feet. It has one or two short side entrances to nesting chambers and one or more side tunnels that may either be used as toilet areas or be blocked with old nesting material or fresh earth. The main tunnel may connect with other entrances so that there could be some underground traffic between burrows. The chambers, which measure about eight to twelve inches in diameter, contain a bed of dried grasses and weed stalks. Defecation takes place either on the mound or in special passages so that the nest remains clean.

The black-tailed prairie dog does not seem to be a true hibernator. It does not hibernate in the southern portion of its distribution, and even in northern areas it is seen regularly on fine winter days. One was observed feeding on sagebrush in a foot of snow after a night when the temperature dropped to −25°C. Others were active near Livingston, Montana, on January 28, 1914. This species does, however, remain in its burrow for prolonged periods of inclement weather during the winter. The depth of the burrow is such that it may be below the frost line. Strange to say, prairie dogs are not known to carry food in their cheek pouches or to store food. They must, therefore, live off their excess autumn fat during the winter or feed occasionally above ground.

The food of the black-tailed prairie dog consists primarily of the leaves, stems, and roots of grasses, weeds, and forbs. In a study of 249 stomachs, vegetable matter formed 98.4 per cent of the identifiable remains and animal matter only 1.4 per cent. Of the vegetable matter, grasses such as grama grass, wheatgrass, fescue, bluegrass, and brome grass formed 61 per cent of the diet. Forbs of the goosefoot family, including Russian thistle, formed 12 per cent, and other plants such as prickly pear, mustard, and sage were also noted. The animal matter eaten includes grasshoppers, cutworms, beetles, and bugs. The prairie dog does not need to drink free water since it gets its water requirements from the moisture in plants. Since practically all the green grasses and forbs are clipped in a dog-town, the animals spend much of their time grubbing for roots.

The predators of prairie dogs include the badger (one with two young dug out fourteen dogs in six days' work in one colony), the coyote, the black-footed ferret, and the prairie rattlesnake. The avian raptores include golden eagles, ferruginous rough-legged hawks, red-tailed hawks, and the previously mentioned burrowing owl.

Habitat. This species occupies a relatively restricted range on the open, level, arid short-grass plains. It is particularly fond of river flats and coulee bottomlands where sagebrush, greasewood, and prickly pear grow. It shuns wetlands or shrubby areas.

Reproduction. Very few details of this species' reproduction are known. The females are monoestrous. In Canada, mating probably takes place in mid-April, and the young are probably born in late May. The gestation period of a closely related species is thought to be between twenty-seven and thirty-three days. The litter size varies between two and eight, with an average of four or five. The dark red, wrinkled young measure about 82 mm in length at birth and weigh about 55 g. They are altricial and develop relatively slowly. The vibrissae appear at eleven days; the bulbous eyes and ear apertures are closed at birth but are apparent at thirteen days; they are well haired at twenty days, and can crawl about at twenty-six days. Their eyes open at thirty-three to thirty-seven days, and they soon learn to walk, crawl, and bark. They appear above ground at the age of about five to six weeks (July 6 in Saskatchewan) and weigh between 114 and 147 g at this age. They are weaned at about seven weeks of age but stay together in and about the natal den for two to three weeks before they disperse. Usually there is no need to dig a new burrow because natural mortality makes vacant ones available. It appears that only some of the females mature as yearlings, and these bear smaller litters than their seniors.

Economic Status. Before the advent of Europeans to this continent, the populations of these large ground squirrels were kept in check by their natural predators. They were also hunted by Indian boys, as they provided a useful addition to the larder. The latter part of the nineteenth century saw the great westward migration of Europeans and the destruction of the prairie dog's competitors (bison and antelope) and predators alike, with the result that by the early twentieth century the population of prairie dogs on the southern and central plains had grown tremendously. They destroyed crops of corn, wheat, alfalfa, and

Map 57 Distribution of the black-tailed prairie dog, *Cynomys ludovicianus*

hay; they dug up sorghum, beans, potatoes, and cantaloupes; they girdled newly planted fruit trees. In addition, they competed with the cattle and sheep for the range. It was estimated that 32 dogs ate the forage of one sheep, and 256 ate the grass required for one cow. Their mounds were a hazard to horses and riders as well. During the first half of this century a constant war was waged against the prairie dog by poison, trap, and gun until now it is much reduced over its range in the United States.

Distribution. The black-tailed prairie dog occupies a narrow band of dry plains stretching from central Texas north to the Canadian boundary, west of the 100th parallel of longitude.

Canadian Distribution. In spite of continuing rumours, it was not until 1927 that the first dog-town, about six miles north of Val Marie, Saskatchewan, was discovered in Canada. At the same time specimens were secured. This was a small town containing only about twenty-five occupants, which were later flooded out by a dam. In 1929, a much larger town was discovered six miles southeast of Val Marie in the Frenchman River flats. This one was estimated to contain about a thousand animals. In 1937, this town at Prairie Dog Butte included 700 acres and contained an estimated 8,700 animals. I visited the area in 1939 and collected further specimens and learned of other colonies near by. By 1958, a total of eleven towns were

reported along the eleven miles of river flats between the butte and the international boundary.

Fortunately the prairie dogs inhabit an extremely isolated valley where their damage to human interests is minimal. This is the only location of this interesting species in Canada, and it is to be hoped that they are permitted to continue to occupy the area (see Map 57).

The race occurring in Canada is the nominate one.

Cynomys ludovicianus ludovicianus (Ord), 1815, *in* Guthrie, A new geography, history, and comm. grammar ..., Philadelphia, American ed. 2: 292, 302. Frenchman River, Saskatchewan.

REFERENCES

King, John A. 1955. Social behavior, social organization and population dynamics in a black-tailed prairie dog town in the Black Hills of South Dakota. Contrib. Lab. Vert. Biol. Univ. Michigan 67.

Soper, J.D. 1938. Discovery, habitat and distribution of the black-tailed prairie dog in western Canada. Jour. Mamm. 19(3): 290–300.

– 1944. Further data on the black-tailed prairie dog in western Canada. Jour. Mamm. 25(1): 47–8.

GREY OR BLACK SQUIRREL
Écureuil gris ou noir. *Sciurus carolinensis* Gmelin

Description. This familiar inhabitant of eastern Canadian woodlots and city parks greatly influences our impression of the squirrel family, much to the disadvantage of its ground-dwelling relatives. It is a large, slim-bodied, arboreal squirrel with a long, flattened tail and moderately long, lightly haired ears (Plate 7). The first digit of the forefoot is vestigial and carries a vestigial flattened nail. The remaining digits carry short, sharp claws, which are flattened and curved, reminiscent of a cat's claws. They are a powerful aid in tree-climbing, and, since they are fixed, they can be hooked into the bark with no muscular exertion. Adult squirrels are about 20 inches long, including 10 inches of bushy tail, and weigh up to 1½ pounds. Their skulls are narrower than those of ground squirrels. The rostrum is relatively narrow, the interorbital region is broad and flat, and the cranium slopes away behind.

The soft, dense pelage of this squirrel is composed of a thick, lead-coloured underfur and longer, banded guard hairs. The typical colour is grizzled grey above with a long, white-tipped, black-banded, grey-brown tail. The face, feet, and flanks usually have a stronger mixture of browns. The underparts are white. Besides this normal colour phase there is a common black (melanistic) phase (the black squirrel), a rare red (erythristic) phase, and occasionally mixtures such as black squirrels with reddish tails. The black colour gene must carry with it some unknown northern adaptation because most grey squirrels are black in the northern part of their distribution. Albinos are occasionally met as well.

The winter coat is long and dense. The soles of the feet

Map 58 Distribution of the grey or black squirrel, *Sciurus carolinensis*: 1 *S. c. hypophaeus*, 2 *S. c. pennsylvanicus*, *introduced

are haired at this season, and the outer surfaces of the ears are covered with creamy hair. There is also a prominent grizzled-brown dorsal stripe in the northern populations at this period. The summer pelage shows more brown on the flanks and feet. The spring moult commences on the head in early May and progresses posteriorly; the tail often is quite ratty before the new fur appears in mid-June. The autumn moult commences in late September and continues to early November. It appears first on the rump and progresses forward. There is no moult of the tail at this time, however.

Average measurements of adults: length 487 (430–500), tail 235 (210–240), hind foot 68 (60–70), ear 30 mm; weight of males 526 g, and of females 520 g.

Habits. The grey squirrel is a socially tolerant species. Often several adults may feed in close proximity, or occupy the same den. Only the females show decided territoriality and drive intruders away from the den tree. Occasionally they carry their half-grown young to a new den or nest and will deposit them temporarily along the

route to drive off an intruder. Within each local population is a well-established order of dominance or peck-order with a large old male usually lording it over his inferiors. The social hierarchy is decided in sham battles during brief encounters when the squirrels sidle up to each other, growling. Brief flurries of pushing usually decide the issue.

The relationship between the grey and the smaller red squirrel is an interesting one. The red squirrel is highly territorial in behaviour and drives all intruders from its territory, including the grey squirrel. The latter species, being indifferent to the defence of territory, readily gives ground, though it is not intimidated by the incident. If food is available in the area, the grey squirrels will gather to feed there, much to the frustration of the outnumbered and smaller red squirrels on whose territory the harvest lies.

Grey squirrels are arboreal and run and jump through the trees with great facility. They climb down the tree trunks, head-first. They come to the ground to feed, cache food, or reach an isolated tree. On the ground they walk slowly if feeding but bound away if frightened. The call-note is a rasping *whick,* often delivered with a flick of the tail.

The species is diurnal in activity with two peaks of feeding activity, the first between 7 and 8 A.M. and the second between 3 and 6 P.M. Activity decreases during inclement weather, such as rain or snow. Grey squirrels remain active all winter but usually 'hole up' during blizzards.

Grey squirrels occupy two types of homes. The first is the permanent tree den, which may be in a natural cavity or in an abandoned woodpecker's hole. The second type is a bulky nest of fresh leaves and twigs, woven onto the crotch of a limb thirty to forty-five feet above ground. Usually conifers such as white pine or hemlock are chosen for the leaf nests, but they may be in large elms, maples, or oaks as well. They are usually built and occupied only during the summer.

During the pioneer days in southern Ontario, spectacular hordes of emigrating squirrels were occasionally seen in the autumn. There is a report of hordes of squirrels swimming across the Niagara River near Buffalo in the early nineteenth century. Food shortages do not seem to have been involved in the mass movements, and the squirrels never returned. One can only speculate as to the cause of these emigrations. The squirrels appear to have abandoned this practice in recent years, and the species is now relatively static.

Investigations have shown that the females occupy home ranges of approximately five to fifteen acres while the males travel much more widely, especially during the summer, when they range over fifty to fifty-five acres. Populations vary between 21 and 117 squirrels per hundred acres, but the average population is 30 to 75 animals per hundred acres. Grey squirrels transported distances of up to two miles have been unable to find their way home in three days.

The food of this species varies with the season. In early spring it feeds upon the swelling buds of the American elm, the maples, and the oaks. The palatability of these buds changes dramatically with their development. Next, in June, it feeds on maple flowers and samaras and elm seeds. The summer is a time of plenty; it is then that it lives on a wide variety of fruits and seeds of wild grapes, hazelnuts, cherries, blueberries, apples, and mushrooms. In autumn these squirrels turn their attention to their favourite hard nuts, including oak acorns, butternuts, walnuts, beech nuts, and pine seeds. At this season they individually cache a great number of nuts in shallow holes under the ground litter to be dug up later. The winter time may be a period of stress if there has been a mast failure. Then, until spring arrives they live under conditions of starvation on pine seeds, and on elm, maple, and sumac twigs and bark. Individual food requirements have been measured to be 470 g per week. They also eat a few insects and caterpillars, and an occasional clutch of birds' eggs if it comes their way.

Whether these squirrels are on the ground or in the trees, they are besieged by a host of predatory animals. Their mammalian predators include the weasel, mink, red

15

Comparison of some Canadian mice and voles: (a) northern bog lemming, *Synaptomys borealis;* (b) meadow vole, *Microtus pennsylvanicus;* (c) heather vole, *Phenacomys intermedius;* (d) heather vole, *Phenacomys intermedius mackenzii;* (e) western jumping mouse, *Zapus princeps;* (f) Gapper's red-backed vole, *Clethrionomys gapperi;* (g) chestnut-cheeked vole, *Microtus xanthognathus;* (h) long-tailed vole, *Microtus longicaudus;* (i) prairie vole, *Microtus ochrogaster;* (j) deer mouse, *Peromyscus maniculatus;* (k) brown lemming, *Lemmus sibiricus;* (l) Ord's kangaroo rat, *Dipodomys ordii;* (m) northern grasshopper mouse, *Onychomys leucogaster;* (n) sagebrush vole, *Lagurus curtatus;* (o) Richardson's water vole, *Arvicola richardsoni*

16

17

fox, raccoon, skunk, and bobcat. Their avian predators include an array of forest-dwelling hawks such as the red-shouldered, the broad-winged, Cooper's, and the goshawk. Occasionally an early-hunting great horned or barred owl will capture a late squirrel.

Habitat. The grey squirrel is an inhabitant of the eastern hardwood or mixed forests. It prefers the deep forest to the brighter forest edges. Although most of its food comes from deciduous hardwoods, it seeks the cover of scattered hemlocks and white pines.

This species has adapted readily to the protection provided in town and cities and has become a characteristic inhabitant of tree-shaded parks and lawns in suburban areas.

Reproduction. Two breeding seasons occur in this species. The females are thought to be polyoestrous, having two distinct oestrous periods, one in January and another in June and July. From about the first of August to the first of December the females are in anoestrus, and the vaginas are imperforate. The males are similarly in breeding condition from early December to February and in June and July. Between periods, the gonads regress and are withdrawn into the abdomen.

During the mating periods the squirrels engage in lively ritualistic chases. When a female enters the breeding condition, she begins to call incessantly with a characteristic call that attracts all the responsive males within hearing distance. Soon a large retinue gathers, and fights ensue to establish priority in the stag line. In the next phase the female becomes agitated and begins to race through the trees and across the intervening ground pursued by her amorous retinue 'chucking' and jockeying for position. Eventually, in her own good time, she yields to the dominant buck while the others stay restively in the wings. Happily for the others there are other chases, and the dominant role changes hands frequently.

Although there are two litters annually in the population, only about 20 to 40 per cent of the females have two litters. These females are thought to be adults. In years of good survival, as many as 40 per cent may produce two litters. The young females probably bear only one litter as yearlings so that the average number in a population is about 1.4 litters per year. Female squirrels have been reported to carry bones to their nests to eat during pregnancy, possibly because of a deficiency in calcium.

After a gestation period of about forty-four days, the young are born in March and July, usually in tree dens. Sometimes the summer litter may be born in a leaf nest. The litter may contain from one to six young, with an average of 2.72, with the summer litter usually the larger (3.23 versus 2.50) because of the abundance of food. The young squirrels are born pink, wrinkled, and toothless with scarcely visible indications of eyes or ears. They measure about 109 to 119 mm in length and weigh 15 to 18 g. They are altricial in development.

The care of the young is the sole responsibility of the mother, and she is very solicitous. In the young the lower incisors erupt and the back is fully haired at twenty-one days; the ears open at twenty-four to twenty-eight days;

135

the eyes open gradually between the thirty-second and thirty-seventh days. At first the eyes are cloudy blue; later they clear and become black. At four weeks, the tail is sleekly furred with silvery hair and it begins to accelerate in growth at five weeks. Weaning begins at seven weeks when the youngsters weigh about 150 g. They gradually switch to solid food between the tenth and twelfth week, by the end of which time they have achieved full independence. The first moult takes place after weaning in June and October, and the respective litters go into the appropriate summer or winter coat. In the southern part of the distribution, 10 per cent of the young female grey squirrels of the spring litter may breed in the autumn at the age of thirty to thirty-six weeks, but farther north in Canada this is unlikely, and the whole reproductive season is a little later. Many of the small, loose-looking leaf nests, built in late summer, are constructed by newly independent young squirrels.

Economic Status. Throughout much of its range, the grey squirrel is classified as an important small game resource, and the hunting of it is regulated by law. Investigations have shown that populations of more than forty-seven squirrels per hundred acres are required to provide a bag of one squirrel per hunter per day. Since the squirrels become exceedingly wary after the fourth or fifth day of the open season, few are observed. About 13 to 19 per cent of the population is usually taken by legal hunting operations. Still, it is a popular sport, and many a squirrel reaches the table in squirrel pie.

Most urban squirrels never have to face the hunter's gun and recognize humans only as a soft touch for peanuts or bread crusts. Occasionally the squirrel becomes a garden pest by digging up and eating freshly planted tulip and crocus bulbs or becomes objectionable by denning in an attic. At these times it is best to take up arms against the individual offender with a small gun or a live trap, after first checking with the local game authorities to ascertain how they view the planned assault.

Distribution. The grey or black squirrel is found in eastern North America from Florida and the Gulf of Mexico north to the Great Lakes region and southeastern Manitoba.

Canadian Distribution. Two geographical races occur naturally in southeastern Canada (see Map 58) from southeastern New Brunswick, southern Quebec, and Ontario to western Ontario and southern Manitoba.

Sciurus carolinensis hypophaeus Merriam, 1886, Science 7: 351. Western Ontario and southeastern Manitoba. Strays are occasionally reported from Saskatchewan cities, but these undoubtedly are escaped pets.

Sciurus carolinensis pennsylvanicus Ord, 1815, *in* Guthrie, A new geography, history, and comm. grammar ..., Philadelphia, American ed. 2: 292. Native to southwestern New Brunswick, southern Ontario, and Quebec. Introduced to Stanley Park, Vancouver, British Columbia, prior to 1914. Escaped pets occasionally seen in Nova Scotia.

REFERENCE

Robinson, D.J., and I.McT. Cowan. 1954. An introduced population of the grey squirrel (*Sciurus carolinensis* Gmelin) in British Columbia. Canadian Jour. Zool. 32(3): 261–82.

FOX SQUIRREL
Écureuil fauve. *Sciurus niger* Linnaeus

Description. Although the distribution of the fox squirrel extends to the southern boundary of Ontario and over a considerable area, this species is established only on Pelee Island, in Lake Erie, where it was introduced.

The fox squirrel is a large diurnal tree squirrel, larger than the grey squirrel. Although in certain colour phases the two species look superficially alike, they are distinct species with no known hybrids. The diagnostic feature in this species is the absence of the third upper premolar (the

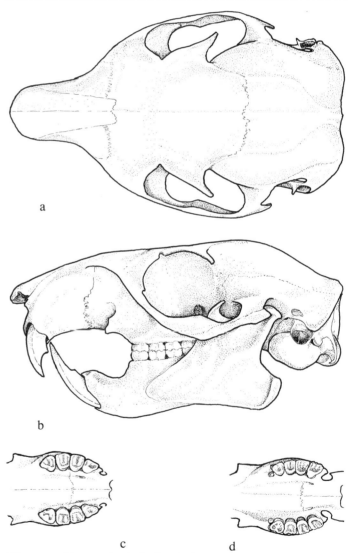

Figure 37 Fox squirrel skull: (a) dorsal view, (b) lateral view. Also comparison of dentition of (c) fox squirrel, *Sciurus niger*, and (d) grey squirrel, *Sciurus carolinensis* (× 1^1/$_2$)

first cheek tooth in *Sciurus carolinensis*) (Figure 37). A comparison of the life histories also shows several subtle differences.

As in the grey squirrel, there are at least three well-marked colour phases: red, black, and grey, and combinations of these. Each phase is, however, somewhat different from the equivalent phase in the grey squirrel. There is also a geographical pattern of distribution of the colour phases, and the grey phase is dominant in the northern fox squirrel population. In this form, the back is grizzled grey. The over-all effect is produced by the guard hairs, which have buffy bases, black subterminal bands, and grey tips. The ears, cheeks, feet, and underparts are strikingly pale fulvous to cinnamon-coloured. Dorsally the bushy tail is banded black and buff; the tail underneath is rufous with a subterminal black border and cinnamon tips. The soles of the feet are black and naked. The prominent facial vibrissae and claws are also black.

Only one annual moult is reported for the fox squirrel. This usually occurs in April and May and progresses from the head backwards. Adult females that have a litter of young usually moult two or three months later. A moult line is usually found, but in some squirrels the hair is replaced irregularly.

Average measurements of adult squirrels: length 535 (500–565), tail 244 (217–265), hind foot 74 (62–80), ear 28 mm. The average weight is 790 g. The females weigh a little more than the males, and both lose weight in the winter. The heaviest squirrel in a Michigan study weighed 1.23 kg.

Habits. The fox squirrel is a little more deliberate in its movements than the grey squirrel. It can jump distances up to one yard between trees and sometimes leaps from the high branches to the ground without injury. It may travel as fast as fifteen miles an hour in long bounds along the ground, and it swims tolerably well.

These squirrels are fairly tolerant socially; they frequently pair up in the winter and occupy a single den. The home ranges of several squirrels may overlap without friction, and the only sign of territoriality is the defence of the den tree. The females drive the males away before the birth of the young. This species is non-migratory. An individual squirrel occupies at least ten acres in one season and may range over forty acres during the course of a year. Males travel more widely than females, especially during the breeding season. There is a pronounced autumn population shuffle, especially among juveniles. Tagged juveniles have been known to travel forty miles. These squirrels also have a remarkable homing instinct, and tagged squirrels have returned as far as forty-six miles in a three-month period.

The population densities vary considerably with the forest type. Upland oak associations may maintain populations of up to one squirrel per acre, while beech-maple forests can support about one squirrel to two acres. Maximum populations of two squirrels per acre are found in oak–hickory forests. These populations are subject to fluctuations, dependent upon mast yields as well as on predation, disease, and forest cutting.

The fox squirrel is most active about two to four hours after sunrise and again between 1 and 2 P.M. Rain, sleet, and snow, as well as summer heat, restrict its activity. It often lies sprawled on a horizontal limb, with its ample tail held over its back as a sun shade; in fact its generic name *Sciurus* comes from this habit, as it means 'shade-tail.' The fox-squirrel may remain holed up during prolonged winter cold snaps if it is sufficiently fat, but it does not hibernate.

This species has two types of home. Leafy nests are built during the summer months in forks of deciduous trees about thirty feet from the ground. The leaves and twigs are cut from the tree, approximately one to two feet in diameter, in which the nests are found. They are snug and dry even in wintry gales, and the squirrels may occupy them in winter if there is a scarcity of good tree dens. Tree dens are, however, preferred for winter and the rearing of young. Natural cavities are developed when the lower limbs of forest trees die because of shading, and the limbs eventually break off and a hole develops in the stub. Woodpeckers, such as flickers, also provide cavities, which are usurped by the squirrels and then lined with dry oak leaves.

Fox squirrels have been known to live as long as seven and a half years in the wild.

The food habits of the fox squirrel are similar to those of the grey squirrel. In spring it feeds on the developing buds of maples, elms, basswood, willows, and oaks. Later it eats the flowers, catkins, seeds, and samaras. In summer it eats green corn and fleshy fruit such as serviceberries, strawberries, raspberries, blackberries, elderberries, blueberries, wild grapes, and cherries. At that time of year it also eats a few insect grubs and caterpillars as well as eggs and young birds. The autumn is the time of plenty for these creatures, for then they gather the mast harvest of shagbark hickory, oaks, butternuts, walnuts, beech, and hazelnuts. The fox squirrel does not amass a cache of nuts but buries each nut or acorn singly in the soft forest earth about one inch beneath the surface, covering it with duff. Sometimes it retrieves almost a hundred per cent of the harvest. As long as the soil is moist, the fox squirrel can locate the nuts by smell when needed. In the winter it digs up its buried food supply; or if the mast crop fails, it lives on such persistent seeds as hackberry, bittersweet, rose hips, haws, and wild grapes.

The enemies of the fox squirrel include the red-tailed hawk, the red fox, the grey fox, the raccoon, and the dog. Occasionally an early hunting great horned or barred owl will capture a late fox squirrel.

Habitat. Originally the western fox squirrel inhabited the clumps of burr oak that interlace the eastern edge of the prairies. It never did favour the deep forests but lives more on the forest edges. Today farm woodlots and shady urban streets are much to its liking, and it has become a common denizen of the suburbs of many midwestern cities.

Reproduction. Like its close relative the grey squirrel,

Map 59 Distribution of the fox squirrel, *Sciurus niger*: ● extra-limital record

this species has two reproductive periods each year. The winter breeding takes place in January and February, and the spring breeding season is May and June. After the breeding season the male testes regress and may remain withdrawn until December. The occurrence of several age classes, however, complicates the picture.

After a gestation period of approximately forty-five days, the spring litter appears in late February or March, and the summer litter in July. The adult females are polyoestrous, but the yearling females usually bear only one litter the first year. Occasionally food scarcity may cause the failure of one breeding season.

The average litter size is 3.02 (one to six young). Since only approximately a third of the population is adult and the remainder are juveniles (which bear only one litter), the average annual production is four squirrels per female.

The young are born naked, blind, deaf, and helpless in the leaf nests or dens. They weigh 13 to 17 g at birth, and only their claws seem well developed at that time. Their development is altricial. They are well covered with hair at two weeks; their eyes open during the fifth week, and they begin to climb about the nest. They venture forth to see the light of day between the seventh and eighth weeks, but they do not leave the den to forage about the ground until they are about three months old. The juveniles usually disperse in September or October, although they may den together or with their mother the first winter.

The female yearlings mature at the age of ten to eleven months; the males mature more slowly.

Economic Status. The fox squirrel, an important small game species in the United States, is also hunted on Pelee Island during the autumn.

Distribution. The natural distribution of the fox squirrel is eastern North America, from the Gulf of Mexico to the southern shores of the Great Lakes.

Canadian Distribution. Fox squirrels were introduced to Pelee Island about 1890 by Charles Mills of Sandusky, Ohio. The stock came from southern Ohio. Although the squirrels at first thrived, they were decimated by excessive hunting about 1925, but they are now firmly established and are common in the drier, wooded areas of the island (see Map 59). The local race is:

Sciurus niger rufiventer G. St-Hilaire, 1803, Cat. des Mamm. du Mus. Nat. d'Hist. Nat., Paris, p. 176.

REFERENCE

Allen, D.L. 1944. Michigan fox squirrel management. Game Div., Dept. Conservation, Lansing, Michigan.

AMERICAN RED SQUIRREL
Écureuil roux. *Tamiasciurus hudsonicus* (Erxleben)

Description. By his constant scolding from the safety of a low limb, this rough-and-ready rogue is quick to make his presence known to any intruder into his forest domain. The forest traveller is torn between his enjoyment of the red squirrel as a companion and his annoyance at its thieving along the trapline and in the larder as well as its destruction of blankets and mattresses in his cabin.

The red squirrel, which is much smaller and chunkier than the grey squirrel, seldom exceeds 15 inches in total length. Its tail, which is about three-quarters the length of the body, is also slimmer. Its head is relatively short and broad. There is a thickened glandular area surrounding the anus, which secretes a musky discharge through two minute orifices. The black vibrissae are prominent on the side of its nose, eyebrows, and cheeks. A few other long tactile hairs are to be found on the forearms and abdomen. It has a relatively shorter, broader, and more rounded skull than that of the genus *Sciurus* (Plate 8). The red squirrel has been segregated from the other tree squirrels because of certain unique anatomical features of the reproductive system, including the vestigial os penis (baculum), which is prominent in other members of the group. Females possess the normal eight mammae.

The summer and winter pelages are quite different in the red squirrel. The summer coat is glossy olive brown above, flecked with black. The backs of the ears and of the limbs are cinnamon. There is a prominent white eye-ring and a black flank stripe. The underparts are white. The tail is rufous red above, with a black submarginal band and tawny tips; underneath, it is grizzled grey.

In winter the fur is much longer and silkier. There is a thick leaden grey, buffy-tipped undercoat, but the general coat colour is much brighter. A clear orange-red stripe runs from head to tail. And at this time of year the flanks are more reddish brown, the flank stripe is obscure, and the underparts are grey. Silvery hair covers the soles of the feet, and the ears have prominent red or black tufts (depending on subspecies).

Besides these normal pelages, albinos, partial albinos, and melanistic (black) squirrels are occasionally seen. In the partial albinos the general tone may be pale grey, or perhaps only the tail will be white.

The spring moult takes place between late March and early July, and progresses from nose and feet to the rump. Most squirrels moult for two months in April, May, or June, but the moult of the pregnant females takes place later. The autumn moult commences on the tail (which is renewed only once annually) and progresses to the rump, crown, back, belly, and finally the feet. It occurs during the period from late August to early December, but most squirrels moult between mid-September and mid-November.

Average measurements of adults: length 310 (282–336), tail 124 (105–145), hind foot 48 (44–52), ear 25 mm. There is no difference between the sexes. Males average a little heavier than non-pregnant females: 193 g for the former and 188 g for the latter.

Habits. The red squirrel's behaviour is remarkable when one considers that it is a small, diurnal, edible rodent. Instead of being secretive, it is bold, curious, noisy, and rapacious. The animal's speed, agility, and seemingly boundless energy are sources of contant amazement. Fundamentally the red squirrel is solitary in habits and intolerant of strange individuals of its own species as well as of birds and other small mammals. It exhibits territorial behaviour in the vicinity of its feeding stations and den sites. It is occasionally tolerant towards its neighbours; it may form a loose attachment with its mate over a period of months and shares the same den with its partner or half-grown young. It usually reacts with vigour, however, to drive off grey squirrels and birds such as jays and crows.

The red squirrel is quick to spread the alarm if an intruder enters the forest community. The alarm note is an oft-repeated metallic *chick-chick-chick*, uttered with an emphatic jerk. If the intruder approaches, the call changes to a frenzied chatter *tcherrr*, given with stamping feet. There is also a less emphatic note, *whuck-whuck*.

This species is more arboreal than the grey squirrel and seldom ventures far from trees to feed, as the grey squirrel occasionally does. It is extremely agile in trees, often running along the underside of limbs; it may leap ten feet between branches or as much as thirty feet to the ground. When leaping, it extends its legs and flattens its body and tail to maximize the body surface. Occasionally one may fall from a tree when pursued by a predator or when engaged in a scuffle, and in falling, it will grasp at branches. It has been known to fall as much as 120 feet from the top of a tree without injuring itself. It also scampers along logs, rail fences, and stone walls. It swims strongly, with head, shoulders, and tail above the surface.

It may frequently venture to cross lakes and rivers as wide as Lake Champlain. If met by a canoe in mid-stream, it will frequently climb up an offered paddle to rest in the boat.

Red squirrels are most active for the first two hours after sunrise and again just before sunset. In summer they rest during the middle of the day, often basking in the sun on stumps, logs, or limbs. During cold winter days, however, they often restrict their outside activity to the warmest part of the day. Strangely, they are occasionally active during moonlit nights in late summer and early autumn. They do not hibernate but may remain inactive in burrows or nests for two or three days during winter storms. A few have been noted active in Alaska when the temperature was −30°F.

The home range of a single squirrel varies between 2.73 and 6.03 acres. Populations vary from a low of 0.28 squirrel per acre to a high of 1.85 per acre, depending upon the habitat. In the early days there were reports of migrations of red squirrels from areas of excessive populations to areas of less dense populations. This species has been known to live ten years in captivity.

This squirrel may make its home in a wide variety of situations depending upon what is available. It may use tree cavities, woodpecker holes, leafy nests, bark nests, fallen trees, artificial bird boxes, rock piles, underground burrows under tree roots, or its own food cache. The leafy nests are more common for winter occupancy in the southern parts of its range, and burrows are more generally used in the northern parts. The leaf nests, situated anywhere from six to sixty feet up in a conifer, are usually placed near the trunks of the trees. Occasionally they may be in an abandoned crow or hawk nest, in a grape vine, or in the 'broom' at the top of a conifer created by the removal of the leader. The leaf nests are composed of twigs, leaves, and bark, approximately a foot in diameter, with a cavity five inches in diameter lined with pine needles or duff from the forest floor. These are only for summer occupancy in northern Canada and Alaska. In winter the northern red squirrels occupy a labyrinth of tunnels up to five yards long under stumps or tree trunks and in their food caches. There are needle-lined chambers and stores of cones in the passageways. Often snow tunnels are dug to join separate caches; the snow is pressed against the walls, not thrown out.

One reason for the success of this squirrel is its wide taste in food. In Canada the most important food items are undoubtedly the cones of conifers such as white, red, scotch, jack, and lodgepole pines, and white and red spruce, balsam fir, Douglas fir, hemlock, larch, and cedars. In hardwood forests it likes the nuts relished by the grey and fox squirrels. It also eats buds, flowers, fleshy fruits, bark, mushrooms, and sap in season. In spring it feeds upon the swelling buds, flowers, and catkins of deciduous trees. At this season it slashes the bark of the sugar maple to lap up the sap, or drives off the sapsucker from its tapped holes. In summer it eats fleshy fruit, seeds, and a wide variety of insects, birds' eggs, fledglings, and mice. It is very fond of mushrooms, which it carefully cuts and hangs in trees to cure, or stores in underground chambers. It even eats the deadly fly amanita with no apparent ill-effects.

The red squirrel is far more carnivorous than the other tree squirrels and will eat practically anything it can catch that will not eat it. It has been known to eat deer mice, meadow voles, young cottontails, robins, bluebirds, orioles, and ruffed grouse. One boldly entered a cavity occupied by a sawwhet owl and ate the cached mice.

By midsummer the red squirrel turns its attention to the swelling cones at the tops of conifers. It climbs about the high branches for periods up to two hours at a time, cutting the terminal twigs that bear the clusters of green cones. This squirrel may cut anywhere from ten to a hundred cones before it descends to carry the cones to its cache. It may bury the cones in the damp earth below the forest floor, or in underground chambers, or it may pile them at the base of stumps or logs. By early autumn the squirrel spends much time caching its cones. These caches may contain less than a bushel of cones, or they may contain many bushels; they may measure up to four yards in diameter and one yard in height. Referred to as 'middens,' they are characteristic signs of red squirrel territory. By spring, middens consist of refuse dumps of conifer cone scales. Favourite localities, which are used year after year, become prominent features of the coniferous forest floor. The fact that the cones are cut green and stored in damp places prevents the scales from opening and the seeds from dispersing.

The red squirrel is also an important link in the boreal forest food chains. As an abundant herbivore it forms an important prey of a number of predators and raptores. The occasional red squirrel falls to large fish while it is swimming, or to a rattlesnake or black snake while it is crossing rocky territory. Its more common predators, however, are forest-dwelling birds of prey, including the red-tailed, the red-shouldered, and the broad-winged hawks, the Cooper's hawk, and the goshawk. Even the little sparrow hawk has been known to kill young squirrels, and the marsh hawk occasionally catches one. Barred and great horned owls catch more red squirrels than the more strictly diurnal grey squirrels. The mammalian predators include the tree-climbing marten, fisher, bobcat, and lynx, while the long-tailed weasel, coyote, and wolf are predators during the squirrel's excursions on the ground. The red squirrel is quick to observe a passing hawk, and at such times it silently 'freezes' on the limb where it is perched. Forest fires and vehicles also take their toll.

Habitat. This species seems to be more versatile in its habitat requirements than the grey squirrel. It is a characteristic inhabitant of the boreal coniferous forest, which stretches across Canada. Indeed it is one of the few mammals that make their homes in climax conifer forests. It also lives in the eastern hardwood deciduous forests, although it prefers a mixed forest containing white pines and hemlocks on the cool northern slopes.

Reproduction. In the more southern parts of their distribution, mature female red squirrels are polyoestrous and usually bear two litters per year. Oestrus occurs in February and March and again in June and July. Studies in northern Canada suggest that only a single litter is born each year. The males' testes develop in late February and remain in active breeding condition until August; then they regress to remain withdrawn between September and December in each year. Mating is accompanied by the same type of mating chases described for the grey and fox squirrels.

In the south the litters are born in April and May and again in August and September after a gestation period of approximately forty days. The average litter size is 4.5, but it may vary from one to eight. The young at birth are pink, wrinkled, naked, blind, and deaf; only the claws seem well developed. They measure about 70 mm long and weigh about 6.7 g.

The development of this species is altricial. After a week the hair begins to appear, and by ten days it is well defined. The external meatus of the ear opens after eighteen days, and the eyes open between twenty-seven and thirty-five days. At thirty-eight days, the young play together, staging chases and mock fights about the nest or tree cavity. They are weaned between seven and eight weeks and appear outside at ten weeks, when they are about a third grown. There is a period of training with their mother, who may carry them to a new nest if disturbed. The young generally remain with their mother until the age of about eighteen weeks, after which time they disperse.

The young squirrels are clothed in a soft, long rufous coat. They moult at the age of eleven months and breed as yearlings. Young born during the summer are thought to breed for the first time at the next midsummer oestrus.

Economic Status. Not surprisingly, the red squirrel is a controversial figure in forest management. On the debit side of the ledger, red squirrels do considerable damage to plantations of young trees near the shelter of larger trees. They clip the leaders of the seedlings to eat the tender buds. In the forest they consume much of the seed harvest of the conifers. On forest homesteads they are occasionally agricultural pests, stealing corn and grain from cribs and granaries. Occasionally a red squirrel is caught killing young chicks and ducklings in poultry yards.

On the credit side, one must consider that the red squirrel may play no small part in reforestation by leaving tree seeds in misplaced caches. It may be an important factor in the control of forest insect pests, and it most certainly serves as a useful buffer prey species, removing predator pressure from some more desirable species.

The red squirrel has some minor economic value as a fur-bearer. Originally its skin was used by the Indians for the linings and trim of winter fur garments, particularly for children. Now it performs a useful role in providing 'pin money' for Indian women and children who often trap squirrels around their camps while the menfolk are off on distant traplines. In the 1971–72 trapping season, 390,884 squirrels were taken across Canada at an average value of 56 cents, for a total value of $217,971.

Distribution. The red squirrel occupies a broad forested

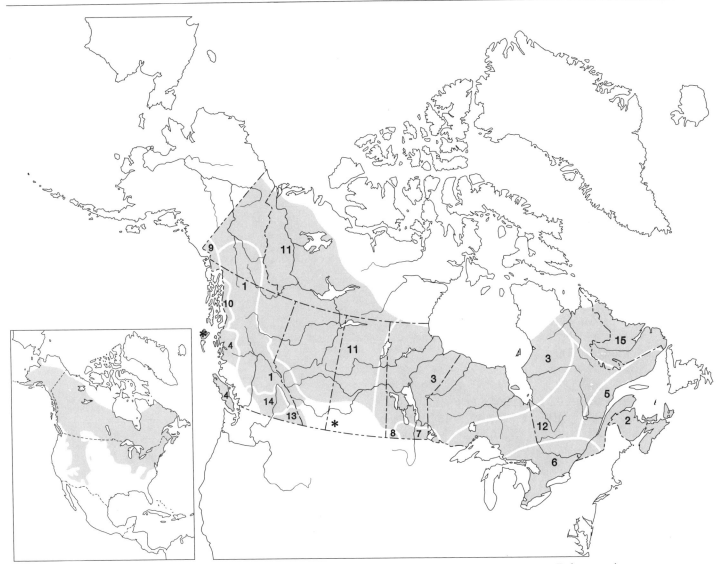

Map 60 Distribution of the American red squirrel, *Tamiasciurus hudsonicus*: 1 *T. h. columbiensis*, 2 *T. h. gymnicus*, 3 *T. h. hudsonicus*, 4 *T. h. lanuginosus*, 5 *T. h. laurentianus*, 6 *T. h. loquax*, 7 *T. h. minnesota*, 8 *T. h. pallescens*, 9 *T. h. petulans*, 10 *T. h. picatus*, 11 *T. h. preblei*, 12 *T. h. regalis*, 13 *T. h. richardsoni*, 14 *T. h. streatori*, 15 *T. h. ungavensis*, *introduced

belt across central North America from the Atlantic to the Pacific ocean, and southward in the Rocky Mountain region.

Canadian Distribution. This is a highly plastic species which has been divided into fifteen geographical subspecies across its Canadian range. The various races differ in size, and relative length of tail, and in colour, which ranges from pale to dark (see Map 60).

Tamiasciurus hudsonicus columbiensis A.H. Howell, 1936, Proc. Biol. Soc. Washington 49: 135. Southern Yukon Territory, central British Columbia, and west-central Alberta.

Tamiasciurus hudsonicus gymnicus (Bangs), 1899, Proc. New England Zool. Club 1: 28. Maritimes (excluding Newfoundland) and Quebec (south of the St Lawrence River).

Tamiasciurus hudsonicus hudsonicus (Erxleben), 1777,

Systema regni animalis ..., 1: 416. Northern Manitoba and Ontario.

Tamiasciurus hudsonicus lanuginosus (Bachman), 1839, Proc. Zool. Soc. London 1838: 101. Vancouver Island, central coast of British Columbia, and introduced and thriving on Graham and Moresby islands, Queen Charlotte Islands.

Tamiasciurus hudsonicus laurentianus Anderson, 1942, Ann. Rept. Provancher Soc. Nat. Hist. Quebec 1941: 31. North shore of the Gulf of St Lawrence.

Tamiasciurus hudsonicus loquax (Bangs), 1896, Proc. Biol. Soc. Washington 10: 161. Southern Ontario and western Quebec.

Tamiasciurus hudsonicus minnesota J.A. Allen, 1899, American Nat. 33: 640. South-central Manitoba.

Tamiasciurus hudsonicus pallescens A.H. Howell, 1942, Proc. Biol. Soc. Washington 55: 13. Southwestern Manitoba.

Tamiasciurus hudsonicus petulans (Osgood), 1900, N. American Fauna 19: 27. Southwestern Yukon Territory.

Tamiasciurus hudsonicus picatus (Swarth), 1921, Jour. Mamm. 2: 92. West of the northern coast range in British Columbia.

Tamiasciurus hudsonicus preblei A.H. Howell, 1936, Proc. Biol. Soc. Washington 49: 133. Northern parts of Alberta and Saskatchewan, Northwest Territories, and northern Yukon Territory. The northern boundary of the red squirrel's distribution is the treeline.

Tamiasciurus hudsonicus regalis A.H. Howell, 1936, Occas. Papers Mus. Zool., Univ. Michigan 338: 1. Central Ontario and Quebec.

Tamiasciurus hudsonicus richardsoni (Bachman), 1839, Proc. Zool. Soc. London 1838: 100. Southwestern Alberta and southeastern British Columbia.

Tamiasciurus hudsonicus streatori (J.A. Allen), 1898, Bull. American Mus. Nat. Hist. 10: 267. South-central British Columbia.

Tamiasciurus hudsonicus ungavensis Anderson, 1942, Ann. Rept. Provancher Soc. Nat. Hist. Quebec 1941: 33. Labrador and northern Quebec.

REFERENCE

Zirul, D.L., and W.A. Fuller. 1971. Winter fluctuations in size of home range of the red squirrel (*Tamiasciurus hudsonicus*). Trans. N. Amer. Wildlife and Natural Resource Conf. 35: 115–27.

DOUGLAS'S SQUIRREL
Écureuil de Douglas. *Tamiasciurus douglasii* (Bachman)

Description. This species, which is closely related to the red squirrel, is found in Canada only along the southwest coast of British Columbia. The ranges of the two species meet but do not overlap. No intergrades have been recognized.

In summer the pelage of Douglas's squirrel is dark, grizzled olive-brown above with blackish ear-tufts, black flank stripe, and bright orange feet, eye-ring, and underparts. The tail is dark reddish brown, with a black subterminal band and prominent buffy-white tips.

The winter coat is a little longer and softer. There is an indistinct grizzled reddish brown mid-dorsal stripe, and the flanks are more greyish than in the summer coat. The ears are black-tufted; the tail is coloured as it is during the summer; and the black flank stripe is indistinct. The most noticeable change is on the underparts, which turn pale yellowish grey in winter. The spring moult occurs in May and June, and the autumn moult commences in late August and continues into September and early October.

Average measurements of adults: length 304 (290–318), tail 121 (113–136), hind foot 48 (31–55), ear 20 mm.

Habits. The habits of Douglas's squirrel do not appear to differ significantly from those of the red squirrel. It is diurnal and active throughout the year. Mostly arboreal, it lives in hollow trees or constructs nests of twigs high in

Map 61 Distribution of Douglas's squirrel, *Tamiasciurus douglasii*

coniferous trees. Its food consists primarily of the cones of pine, spruce, fir, and hemlock. At other times it eats various seeds, nuts, maple samaras, fleshy fruit, alder catkins, and mushrooms.

It is territorial in behaviour, but information is lacking on home range or populations. It is reported to be shy and silent in the spring but noisier in summer.

Habitat. Although this squirrel is confined mostly to the dense coniferous forests of the south Pacific coast forest section, it may venture out into logged-over areas as well.

Reproduction. This species is thought to produce only one litter per year, in late May. Although four is the average litter size, up to eight young have been observed.

Economic Status. This species has been accused of eating conifer seeds and clipping leaders of seedlings, but it also serves in dispersing and planting conifer seeds.

Distribution. Douglas's squirrel is found on the Pacific coast from central California to southwestern British Columbia.

Canadian Distribution. Only one subspecies is found in Canada (see Map 61), along the British Columbia mainland from the Fraser delta north to Rivers Inlet, west of the Coast Range.

Tamiasciurus douglasii mollipilosus (Audubon and Bachman), 1841, Proc. Acad. Nat. Sci. Philadelphia 1: 102. British Columbia.

REFERENCE

Bailey, V. 1936. Douglas's squirrel. *In* The mammals and life zones of Oregon, N. American Fauna 55: 119–25.

SOUTHERN FLYING SQUIRREL
Petit polatouche. *Glaucomys volans* (Linnaeus)

Description. Flying squirrels are among the most interesting and attractive of our small mammals, for they are our only nocturnal squirrels and our only gliders. The present species is small and delicately built, measuring less than 10 inches in total length (half of which is tail). It has large black luminous eyes, a characteristic of nocturnal animals. The skin of the flank is pulled out into a loose fold, which extends between the wrist and the ankle. A cartilaginous spur at the wrist supports this flight membrane even beyond the extent of the forearm. Its tail is relatively long, and its thick fur is flattened laterally. It has relatively long, pointed naked ears. So reduced is the thumb that it is practically non-existent. The digits possess minute, sharp, curved claws.

The skull of this species is small and delicate. The rostrum is narrow and flat; the cranium is inflated but strongly bent downwards behind the orbits; and the zygomatic arches are flattened laterally.

The pelage is soft, silky, and dense. Although attractive, it is too soft to withstand wear, and the hides therefore have no commercial value. The fur is dull slate grey at the base with wood-brown tips above. The over-all effect is a soft grey-brown. The flanks are darker, the upper surface of the flight membrane being almost black, while the under surface is a striking pinkish buff. The cheeks and sides of the neck are buffy grey; the underparts are clear white, even to the base of the fur; the tail is smoke-grey and buffy grey beneath; the feet are pale grey above and whitish below.

There is only one annual moult, which occurs in September or October. The new fur appears first on the flanks and then spreads over the back; the shoulders and the head are the last to be renewed. In this species the tips of the hind feet are whitish in winter.

Measurements of adults: length 232 (211–257), tail 100 (81–120), hind foot 30 (26–33), ear 20 mm. The average weight of adults varies between 52 and 69.5 g.

Habits. The flying squirrels are more strictly arboreal than the other American squirrels. They are extremely agile in the trees but clumsier on the ground when they descend to feed. Their best running speed is about twenty-five yards in twelve seconds. They do not attempt to dodge, and if pursued they try to hide in the grass rather than flee. When surprised at some distance from a tree, they may be caught by hand. They are masters at gliding, however. One was observed gliding fifty yards from the top of a tall oak tree to the ground. Another glided even farther down a hillside. When about to launch itself, this squirrel faces head-down on the tree trunk, gathers its feet under its body, and then springs out into space. As soon as it leaves the tree, it stretches out its legs and brings its tail downwards to a horizontal plane. In flight the membranes hang rather loosely, providing a parachute-effect as the squirrel quickly weaves its way among the branches or banks to one side. The angle of planing varies from forty to thirty degrees, depending upon the height and the wind velocity. As the squirrel approaches a landing on another tree trunk, it banks steeply upwards and comes gently to rest against the tree trunk. It usually scrambles upwards a short distance before resting. The squirrel exercises easy control over its direction and slope of glide in flight by manipulating its tail and feet.

Flying squirrels are highly sociable. Several may feed together or occupy the same den; as many as twenty have been removed from a winter den. They do not appear to exercise territorial defence. One squirrel occupies a home range of approximately four acres. Tagged specimens have returned home from release sites a mile away, crossing treeless areas en route. Populations may vary from 1.1 to 2.2, and more, squirrels per acre. Although seldom seen because of their nocturnal habits, flying squirrels may outnumber the diurnal grey squirrels in the same locality.

Flying squirrels sleep in their dens all day and are active from about sunset to sunrise. They are thought to have peaks of activity about 10.45 P.M. and 3.30 A.M. They may, however, appear in the late afternoons of cloudy days. They are not active during windy nights. They make a bird-like chipping sound, which may be recognized in the darkened woods if one is familiar with it.

This species usually constructs its nest of shredded bark, leaves, and grass in abandoned woodpecker holes. Although it seems to be particularly fond of downy woodpecker holes in poplar trees, it may also build nests during the summer, measuring about a foot in diameter, of shredded bark and moss in hemlocks, cedars, firs, or oaks. Frequently it occupies bird boxes, attics of houses, or outbuildings in the forests.

Although flying squirrels are not true hibernators, they may be inactive for prolonged periods during the severest part of the winter. Few range very far from their dens during the months of January to March in the northern part of their distribution.

Hickory nuts and white oak acorns are the favourite food of the southern flying squirrel. Besides these items it eats serviceberries, other fleshy fruits, seeds, and nuts. It is insectivorous and eats moths and junebugs that gather about lights. It has also been known to eat small birds' eggs and fledgings.

Unlike grey and fox squirrels, flying squirrels store great hoards of hickory nuts and acorns in their dens or other cavities in trees. It is this store of food that enables them to remain inside during cold spells. Only occasionally do they bury individual nuts under the forest duff.

The night-flying owls are the flying squirrel's main predators, but occasionally one falls prey to a hawk foraging at dawn or dusk. On the ground the domestic cat is the most important predator in suburban and rural areas.

Habitat. The southern flying squirrel inhabits eastern

Map 62 Distribution of the southern flying squirrel, *Glaucomys volans*

deciduous forests. Highest populations are found in mature beech–maple stands. Oak, hickory, and poplar stands are also favourite habitats. A few may be found in almost any mature farm woodlot or wooded surburban area. The cutting of dead hollow trees is probably an important factor in reducing the possible number of den sites.

Reproduction. The females are polyoestrous and usually bear two litters per year. Oestrus occurs during late February and early March and again in June. After a gestation period of approximately forty days the litters are born in April and May and again in July and August. The litter may contain anywhere from one to six young, with an average of 3.4. The females have eight mammae.

The young are born in tree dens, undeveloped, blind, and naked. Even at birth their lateral folds are visible, and there can be no doubt that the young are flying squirrels. One young squirrel weighed 3.4 g at birth, and grey hair was visible on its head at fifteen days. The young first appear outside the den at the age of seven weeks. If the female decides to transfer them to another den, she carries them one at a time, holding each by the skin of its belly,

while the youngster rolls up like a ball around her head. She may even glide while carrying a youngster. By eight weeks of age, when they are gradually being weaned, they become very active in climbing and exploring their environment. Their first calls are shrill and piping.

The juveniles first moult at the age of ten to twelve weeks. They seem to mature a little earlier than some other species, and young females born of summer litters may bear young the following spring at the age of nine months.

Economic Status. Flying squirrels are completely harmless. They may occasionally make nuisances of themselves by romping about an attic during the night hours to the annoyance of other occupants of the building, but this situation can usually be quickly remedied.

Flying squirrels are very gentle and make interesting, friendly pets. However, they are sleepy and listless during the daylight hours and only show off to best advantage at night, and it is not often that one can enjoy their antics. They are extremely clean in habits.

Distribution. The southern flying squirrel is found in

Mexico and eastern North America from the Gulf of Mexico to the Great Lakes.

Canadian Distribution. Only the nominate race is found in southern Ontario (see Map 62).

Glaucomys volans volans (Linnaeus), 1758, Syst. Nat., 10th ed., 1: 63. Ontario.

REFERENCE

Sollberger, D.E. 1940. Notes on the life history of the small eastern flying squirrel. Jour. Mamm. 21(3): 282–93.

NORTHERN FLYING SQUIRREL
Grand polatouche. *Glaucomys sabrinus* (Shaw)

Description. Although the two species of flying squirrels are very similar in colour, there are important anatomical and behavioural differences. Although the distributions of the two species partially overlap, there is no evidence of hybridization between the two.

The northern flying squirrel, which measures up to 18 inches in total length, is much larger and more heavily built than the southern species. The dorsal colour is more cinnamon brown. The cheeks and underparts are grey or blotched with pinkish cinnamon, and the basal portion of the belly fur is lead grey rather than white as in the smaller form. The broad, flattened tail is grey above (darker towards the tip) and pale buffy grey beneath. The feet are grey above and whitish beneath (the soles are well furred in winter) (Plate 9).

The skull of the northern form is more ruggedly constructed, with a longer cheek tooth row. However, the trenchant feature is found in the bacula of the males. That of this species is short and broad, averaging 6.8 mm in length and 1.8 mm in width. The baculum of *Glaucomys volans* is a long, slender, twisted shaft, measuring about 12.6 mm in length and 1.0 mm in width.

Average measurements of adult northern flying squirrels: length 305 (245–368), tail 145 (108–180), hind foot 39 (34–45), ear 22 mm. The weight may vary between 75 and 139 g.

Habits. This species is just as sociable as its smaller relative, the southern flying squirrel. Several adults may feed and play together, although the adults usually dominate the juveniles at a feeding tray. The paired adults usually occupy near-by nests, even when the female is rearing her young. As many as nine adults have been found in communal winter nests. Their voice may be described as a 'chuckling' sound. They forage quite a bit on the ground, either walking or hopping. The flight membrane does not seem to get in the way of its squirrel-like movements. This species is nocturnal and makes its appearance about halfway between sunset and darkness. Occasionally it meets a late-foraging red squirrel that shares its habitat, and it always gives it a wide berth.

The northern flying squirrel is hardier than the southern species, and the winter weather seems to curtail its activity but little.

It lives in tree cavities in the winter, but in the summer it seems to prefer bark and twig nests or 'drays.' Measuring about twelve to sixteen inches in diameter, the nest may be built of twigs, shredded bark, moss, or lichens and is situated anywhere from three to thirty feet up in coniferous trees. Young spruces and cedars are often chosen, and the nest is usually situated close to the trunk. The young are frequently born in these drays.

The food of this species consists of arboreal lichens and the buds, leaves, seeds, fleshy fruits, and nuts of many trees and shrubs. It is also fond of insects, birds, and birds' eggs, and may scavenge on carcasses found in the forests. Seton reported that flying squirrels have been found drowned in maple sap buckets in spring.

The northern species also caches nuts and cones in hollow trees. Its nut middens may occasionally be observed on stumps or in piles about tree trunks in the forest.

Its predators are about the same as those of smaller species but probably include more northern fur-bearers.

Habitat. The northern flying squirrel inhabits the boreal forest belt, which is composed primarily of coniferous species. The hemlock–yellow birch association is a favourite habitat in the east.

Reproduction. It seems that only one litter a year is normally produced in this species, although under ideal conditions a few mature females may carry second litters. Mating is thought to occur in late March and early April, and the young are usually born in May. Three young seems to be the average litter size.

At birth this young squirrel is naked and pink in colour, with a dark spot over each eye; the lateral fold is evident, and the feet are webbed. It measures about 70 mm in length and weighs 6 g. At six days of age the vibrissae appear, and by eighteen days the young squirrel is well furred. Its eyes open after thirty-two days. At first, the black-furred tail is cylindrical, but after the thirty-fifth day it becomes flattened. The young squirrels crawl at first but walk freely after the forty-first day. They sample solid foods about the forty-seventh day but are not weaned until after sixty-five days. They first learn to glide at three months, and at four months are proficient at gliding, climbing, and running.

Economic Status. A fondness for meat often leads the northern flying squirrel to steal the bait from traps set in cubbies for marten. Trappers consider it a nuisance because it so often gets caught in the traps set for fur-bearers. The squirrels themselves are valueless, because the fur is too soft.

Distribution. The northern flying squirrel's distribution crosses North America from Labrador to Alaska. Its range also includes southern spurs in the eastern Appalachians and western Rocky Mountains.

Canadian Distribution. This is another plastic species whose populations may be divided into a number of subspecies, depending upon variations in colour and size. Fourteen subspecies are currently recognized in Canada (see Map 63).

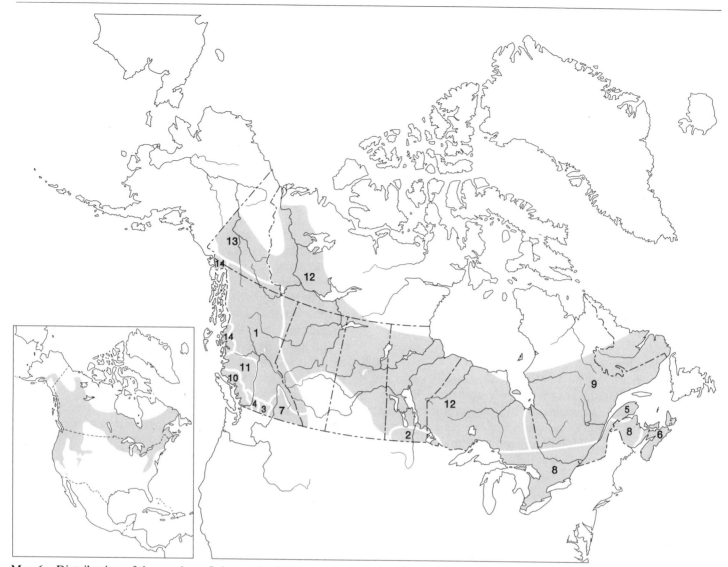

Map 63 Distribution of the northern flying squirrel, *Glaucomys sabrinus*: 1 *G. s. alpinus*, 2 *G. s. canescens*, 3 *G. s. columbiensis*, 4 *G. s. fuliginosus*, 5 *G. s. goodwini*, 6 *G. s. gouldi*, 7 *G. s. latipes*, 8 *G. s. macrotis*, 9 *G. s. makkovikensis*, 10 *G. s. oregonensis*, 11 *G. s. reductus*, 12 *G. s. sabrinus*, 13 *G. s. yukonensis*, 14 *G. s. zaphaeus*

Glaucomys sabrinus alpinus (Richardson), 1828, Zool. Jour. 3: 519. Northern and eastern British Columbia and the central Rocky Mountain region of Alberta.

Glaucomys sabrinus canescens A.H. Howell, 1915, Proc. Biol. Soc. Washington 28: 111. South-central Manitoba.

Glaucomys sabrinus columbiensis A.H. Howell, 1915, Proc. Biol. Soc. Washington 28: 111. Okanagan valley, south-central British Columbia.

Glaucomys sabrinus fuliginosus (Rhoads), 1897, Proc. Acad. Nat. Sci. Philadelphia 49: 321. West slope Cascade and Coast ranges, southern British Columbia.

Glaucomys sabrinus goodwini Anderson, 1943, Ann. Rept. Provancher Soc. Quebec 1942: 55. Gaspé Peninsula, Quebec.

Glaucomys sabrinus gouldi Anderson, 1943, Ann. Rept. Provancher Soc. Quebec 1942: 56. Nova Scotia.

Glaucomys sabrinus latipes A.H. Howell, 1915, Proc. Biol. Soc. Washington 28: 112. Rocky Mountains of southeastern British Columbia and southwestern Alberta.

Glaucomys sabrinus macrotis (Mearns), 1898, Proc. United States Nat. Mus. 21: 353. New Brunswick, southern Quebec, and Ontario.

Glaucomys sabrinus makkovikensis (Sornborger), 1900, Ottawa Nat. 14: 48. Labrador.

Glaucomys sabrinus oregonensis (Bachman), 1839, Jour. Acad. Nat. Sci. Philadelphia 8: 101. Southwest coast of British Columbia.

Glaucomys sabrinus reductus Cowan, 1937, Proc. Biol. Soc. Washington 50: 79. Coast Range and Cariboo Parklands of western British Columbia.

Glaucomys sabrinus sabrinus (Shaw), 1801, General Zool. 2: 157. Northern parts of Quebec, Ontario, Manitoba, Saskatchewan, Alberta, and the Mackenzie District, Northwest Territories.

Glaucomys sabrinus yukonensis (Osgood), 1900, N.

American Fauna 19: 25. Central Yukon Territory.
Glaucomys sabrinus zaphaeus (Osgood), 1905, Proc. Biol. Soc. Washington 18: 133. Northwest coast of British Columbia, and southwest corner of Yukon Territory.

REFERENCES

Booth, E.S. 1946. Notes on the life history of the flying squirrel. Jour. Mamm. 27(1): 28–30.
Coventry, A.F. 1932. Notes on the Mearns flying squirrel. Canadian Field-Nat. 46(4): 75–8.
Cowan, I. McT. 1936. Nesting habits of the flying squirrel *Glaucomys sabrinus*. Jour. Mamm. 17(1): 58–60.

Family **Geomyidae** / Pocket Gophers

The pocket gopher family is restricted to southern and western North America. Although most of the species are found farther to the south, two species have reached the Canadian prairies. The pocket gophers constitute the third family of Canadian mammals that is modified for a fossorial life, the other two families being the moles and the mountain beaver.

Pocket gophers are rat-sized rodents with thickset bodies, no apparent neck, broad, flat heads, and short, strong legs. The forelimbs are armed with four long, strong, curved claws (the thumb is vestigial). The short tail is either naked or sparsely covered with tactile hairs. Additional fossorial adaptations include small eyes and ears and short, fine fur. The incisors are large and protruding, and behind them are external openings to large fur-lined cheek pouches, which characterize the family.

The skulls are rugose: the rostrum is long and rectangular, the occiput is large and square, the zygomatic arches are strong and angular, the auditory bullae are relatively small, and the mandibles are massive. The cheek teeth are ever-growing and have reduced enamel surfaces.

The animals get their name from the fur-lined external cheek pouches and from their labyrinths of tunnels that honeycomb the earth (French *gaufre*, honeycomb). Since they are fossorial in habits, they are rarely observed, and their excavations and mounds on the dry plains of Manitoba, Saskatchewan, and Alberta are erroneously credited to moles although no moles occur in these areas.

NORTHERN POCKET GOPHER
Gaufre gris. *Thomomys talpoides* (Richardson)

Description. The northern pocket gopher is a thickset, short-tailed rodent about 9 inches long. It has a blunt face, small eyes, extremely small, round ears, short legs, and a short, thick tail which is sparsely covered with short, stiff white hairs. The most unusual feature is the ample, fur-lined cheek pouches which open on the side of the face (not into the mouth as squirrels' pouches do). These pouches, which extend backwards to the shoulder region, are large enough to accommodate a thumb or index finger.

The large, prominent incisor teeth, which protrude in front of the mouth, facilitate the cutting of roots without permitting the soil to enter the mouth. The forefeet are only slightly larger than the hind feet. The naked soles are surrounded by a row of short bristles. The four main toes are armed with sharp, narrow scythe-shaped claws. The skin is very tough and loose fitting.

The skull of this species is rugose, flat, and angular in outline. The palate is extremely narrow (Figure 38). The incisors lack grooves and exhibit a phenomenal growth rate. It has been shown that the upper incisors grow 0.056 mm per day, and the lower incisors 0.099 mm per day. Over a period of a year this means that the lower incisors would grow 3.65 cm or over 1.4 inches. They are, however, abraded away at the tips by the gopher's constant gnawing of roots and obstacles in its tunnels. Although all rodents' incisors grow constantly, the gopher sets a record.

This gopher's pelage is soft, dense, and short, and has a silky sheen. The back is generally a pale brown, the flanks are grey, and the belly is pale buffy grey. The chin is usually white, and there may be irregular white blotches on the throat and chest. There is a dark grey patch about each ear, and the dorsal surfaces of the feet are white. Pocket gophers exhibit a wide range of coloration among local populations. Some may be much darker brown than described. Albinos are rarely seen, but melanistic indi-

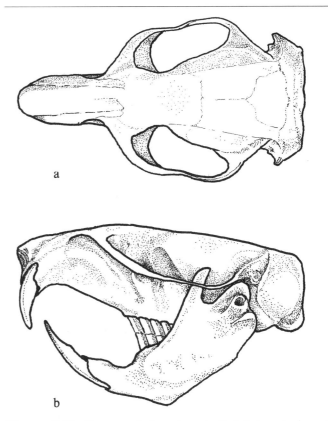

Figure 38 Northern pocket gopher skull: (a) dorsal view, (b) lateral view (× 2)

viduals are quite common. Some geographical races are known only in the melanistic form.

Gophers appear to be moulting most of the year. The fur is prime only between November and April. The spring moult begins in mid-April, starting on the face and continuing backwards over the shoulder with a prominent moult line. The moult seems to progress in waves so that two or more moult lines may occur on the body at the same time. The thinner summer coat seems to be only transitory because when, in late summer, the winter coat appears on the head there may still be spring moult lines on the rump.

Average measurements of adult males: length 234 (191–257), tail 66.5 (47–77), hind foot 26.5 (25–32), ear 6.2 mm. The average female is smaller: length 220, tail 65.5, hind foot 27 mm. Average weight of males 150 g (heaviest 209 g); average weight of females 127 g.

Habits. Pocket gophers are generally solitary creatures except during the mating season. They usually avoid meeting other gophers by plugging connecting tunnels. In the mating season, however, the males enter the burrows of females, which seem to be tolerant of this intrusion into their domains. The young gophers occupy their mother's burrow for about two months. Gophers are quarrelsome and cannot be kept together without fighting except during the breeding season. When cornered they are pugnacious and can inflict serious wounds. They have a keen sense of smell and fair hearing, but their sight is poor. Probably the tactile sense in the silvery vibrissae, the wrist bristles, and the tips of their tails gives them most information about their underground environment. They are generally silent in nature but squeal and grind their teeth in captivity.

Pocket gophers are active all year in their burrows. They seldom venture far from the burrow entrance during the day but may travel farther afield at night. They are primarily subterranean. Their tunnel system may be divided into two parts: the deep permanent galleries and the shallow feeding tunnels. The deep galleries, which may be situated at a depth of three to nine feet, with an average depth of about six feet (below the frostline in winter), contain several nesting chambers and storage chambers about eight to ten inches in diameter. The nests are composed of finely shredded grasses, and the chambers are situated at the end of short side tunnels, usually with only one entrance. One set of deep tunnels excavated was 165 feet in length. From the central fortress the shallow feeding tunnels radiate. They are about two inches in diameter and are situated at a depth of five to eighteen inches. Unlike moles, pocket gophers do not leave a raised ridge in the turf.

The gopher uses its powerful front claws to excavate tunnels. These it thrusts forward and downward, with alternate strokes of the forelimbs. It piles earth beneath its body and then uses its hind feet to kick it backwards. The gopher then turns, and, with chest and forefeet extended, bulldozes the earth to the surface with powerful thrusts of its hind feet. Gopher 'mounds' are low piles of earth containing anywhere from a couple of quarts of earth to over a bushel. The gopher pushes the earth out from the entrance in a fan shape, eventually blocking the entrance with a firm earth plug. The mounds may be distinguished from molehills by the lower relief and fan shape, with the earth plug on the side rather than at the centre as in the molehill. The mounds are located off short lateral burrows from the main tunnels. Not all the earth excavated from new tunnels is brought to the surface; much is used to refill disused tunnels. The moist earth mounds are frequently used as daytime refuges by tiger salamanders.

During the late winter and early spring, when the ground has thawed but is still snow-covered, the pocket gopher displays a unique habit in that it burrows quite freely through the snow to feed. As an added protection it lines the snow tunnels with earth excavated from its underground tunnels. When the snow melts in late spring these peculiar earthen casts of tunnels are found lying about on the ground many yards from the burrow entrances. The casts soon crumble, and the spring rains wash them away.

Pocket gophers are reported to run backwards in their burrows using their sensitive tails as probes. Occasionally adults may leave their burrows to migrate overland to new sites. One was observed swimming across the Assiniboine River in Manitoba, a distance of about three hundred yards.

Although pocket gophers are solitary animals and although their burrows and mounds are usually randomly distributed, in favourable localities the population may be so concentrated that it seems to form a colony. These animals are remarkably sedentary. Individual home ranges may occupy only 150 to 200 square yards. The animals often occupy the same area for their whole life-span, but some individuals may wander a thousand yards searching for a better area. Population densities of twenty-one to fifty-two animals per acre have been encountered in favourable sites.

The average life expectancy of a pocket gopher is about 2.9 years. The oldest ones found in a tagging program were four years old. There is a rapid population turnover each year. At the breeding season the population consists of about 75 per cent yearlings and 25 per cent two-year-olds and older animals.

The roots of perennial forbs form the bulk of the diet of these pocket gophers. During the summer months they turn their attention to the green parts of plants – leaves and stems. They secure their food during brief nocturnal forays above ground, or they burrow under the plant, cut the root, and then pull the plant down into the burrow. The summer diet consists of 70 to 90 per cent forbs and the rest grasses. About 70 per cent of their food is made up of leaves and 30 per cent roots. During feeding trials, individuals ate an average of 83 g of dandelion and 80 g of peavine each day. This would amount to approximately 1,460 pounds per acre per year for an average population of twenty-two gophers on one acre of land. Among the favourite plants eaten are dandelion, peavine, artemisia, clover, anemone, golden-rod, yarrow, and penstemon. Gophers are also partial to many domestic crops such as alfalfa, potatoes, carrots, parsnips, artichokes, turnips, beets, radishes, peas, and beans.

This species cuts roots and stems of plants into 50-mm

lengths and uses its forefeet to stuff them into its cheek pouches. It empties its cheek pouches by placing its forepaws at the back of the pouch and pushing forward.

During the autumn, from August to October, the gophers are very active, tunnelling and throwing up new mounds while they collect roots for winter storage. In spring, they are also active cleaning out their tunnels, but in summer they are less so when they are raising their young and feeding on green stuff.

The pocket gopher forms the prey for a number of predators, including the badger, weasel, skunk, coyote, and fox. The number of remains of pocket gophers found in the pellets of great horned, great grey, and long-eared owls is an indication that gophers must be quite active above ground at night.

Habitat. Pocket gophers inhabit natural grasslands, cultivated fields, roadsides, and river banks. They prefer a deep, heavy, moist soil. When the higher soils dry out during the summer months, fresh mounds may be found on the edges of sloughs, poplar buffs, and river banks.

Reproduction. The northern pocket gopher has only one breeding season each year. The male gonads start to swell in December, and they descend to the scrotum or lie in lateral inguinal canals during the breeding season. They regress and become small and flabby afterwards from mid-June to late November. The female organs commence their growth in December and reach maximum size in May. The females are monoestrous. In Canada mating occurs in April and early May, but the breeding season may be delayed in the mountains to July and early August. The gestation period has been determined to be nineteen days for the closely related southern pocket gopher (*T. umbrinus*). The young gophers are born in late May and early June. The female has four pairs of mammae. A special hormone secreted during pregnancy dissolves the pubic symphysis so that parous and non-parous females can be easily recognized by the possession of open or closed pubic bones. The litter size varies between one and eight young, and the average litter size between 6.4 and 3.2, according to latitude and altitude. The Canadian litter size is nearer the lower figure.

The young gophers are born blind and toothless, with naked, transparent pink skin. They have chubby little bodies. Within a couple of days the cheek pouches appear as shallow depressions. The natal chamber is usually well stocked with green shoots and roots so that the female will not have to forage for some time. The young remain with the female for six to eight weeks. They leave home in August when they are about the size of field voles and about 45 g in weight. These juveniles often travel above ground for some distances before they dig their own shallow temporary burrows. They suffer heavy mortality from predators during this period. At the same time they shed their silky juvenile grey pelage and assume the adult winter coat. They reach adult weight at about five to six months, and become sexually mature the following spring at the age of eleven or twelve months.

Economic Status. Under natural conditions pocket gophers perform a useful role in the ecology of grasslands.

They help keep the soil porous and friable by bringing up subsoil and scattering it on the surface. It has been estimated that they turn over 3.6 to 7 tons of soil per acre per year. At the same time they enrich the soil by burying the stubble to form humus. Their consumption of forbs assists the establishment of the grass turf.

On agricultural lands, however, they are serious pests. They are particularly destructive in vegetable gardens, where they burrow down the rows of vegetables, consume the roots, and even drag the tops through the holes. In orchards they trim the roots off young cherry trees. In grainfields they consume planted corn or alfalfa, or bury sprouting grain under their mounds. The mounds themselves are hazards in mowing, because they dull the blades of the machines. Their tunnels in irrigation embankments may cause local flooding as well. They also eat many ornamental plants, including the roots of perennials such as the iris and the corms and bulbs of tulips, gladioli, and freesias, as well as the roots of such hedges as caragana or even young pines.

Pocket gopher populations are often excessive on overgrazed range lands. However, it is the pioneer forbs and not the natural grasslands that attract them to the area, and they do not actually destroy the natural grasslands. The original damage is usually caused by overstocking.

A unique way in which pocket gophers cause serious damage is by gnawing through lead and copper sheeting on underground cables. They are not particularly attracted to the cables, but gnaw them when they block their tunnels. Poisons and repellents are useless deterrents because the gopher uses only its incisors in gnawing and the chips therefore do not enter its mouth. Steel hardware cloth and aluminum basket-woven sheeting have proved to be effective barriers.

Control of pocket gophers is usually effected on a large scale by the dispersal of poisoned grain such as strychnine-treated oats and milo maize. The baits should be distributed when the gophers are most active, in May or August to September. A new bait dispenser has been devised, which consists of a funnel to hold the bait and a blunt probe to locate the feeding tunnels. After the probe pierces the tunnel, the bait follows the probe into the burrow. Another method of bait distribution is through the medium of an artificial burrow digger, which is a peculiar plough with a torpedo. This digs an artificial burrow of the correct diameter and depth. The poisoned baits follow the torpedo, and two large wheels close the turf over the tunnel. Many free-tunnelling gophers will eventually break into the artificial tunnel and travel along it to the baits. The local control of gophers in gardens is usually undertaken with Macabee traps, which consist of a treadle-plate and two spread hooks that spring together when the gopher pushes earth against the vertical plate. The traps are set in opened burrows, which the gophers will attempt to close with fresh earth.

Distribution. Central plains and western mountain regions of North America.

Canadian Distribution. Northern pocket gophers are commonly distributed across the Prairie Provinces from

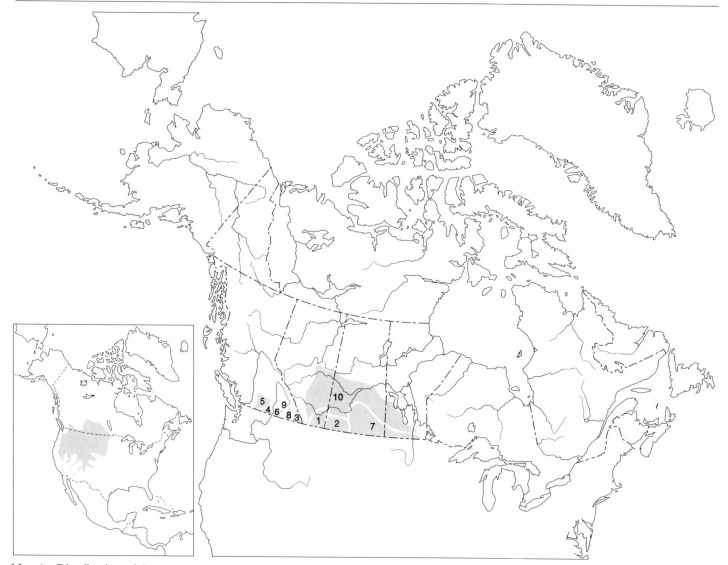

Map 64 Distribution of the northern pocket gopher, *Thomomys talpoides*: 1 *T. t. andersoni*, 2 *T. t. bullatus*, 3 *T. t. cognatus*, 4 *T. t. fuscus*, 5 *T. t. incensus*, 6 *T. t. medius*, 7 *T. t. rufescens*, 8 *T. t. saturatus*, 9 *T. t. segregatus*, 10 *T. t. talpoides*

southwestern Manitoba to the Rocky Mountains of Alberta. They are also found in the mountain valleys of south-central British Columbia (see Map 64).

A great deal of racial variation is exhibited in the sedentary populations of pocket gophers. About fifty-eight geographical subspecies are recognized in North America, of which ten occur in Canada.

Thomomys talpoides andersoni Goldman, 1939, Jour. Mamm. 20: 235. Southeastern Alberta.

Thomomys talpoides bullatus V. Bailey, 1914, Proc. Biol. Soc. Washington 27: 115. Southwestern Saskatchewan.

Thomomys talpoides cognatus Johnstone, 1955, Canadian Field-Nat. 68: 163. Crowsnest Pass and Flathead valley areas of southeastern British Columbia.

Thomomys talpoides fuscus Merriam, 1891, N. American Fauna 5: 69. Okanagan valley of southern British Columbia.

Thomomys talpoides incensus Goldman, 1939, Jour. Mamm. 20: 240. Thompson River valley of southern British Columbia.

Thomomys talpoides medius Goldman, 1939, Jour. Mamm. 20: 241. Kootenay valley, British Columbia.

Thomomys talpoides rufescens Wied-Neuwied, 1839, Nova Acta Phys.-Med. Acad. Caes. Leop.-Carol. 19 (pt. 1): 378. Southwestern Manitoba and southeastern Saskatchewan.

Thomomys talpoides saturatus V. Bailey, 1914, Proc. Biol. Soc. Washington 27: 117. East Kootenay and Moyie River valleys, British Columbia.

Thomomys talpoides segregatus Johnstone, 1954, Canadian Field-Nat. 68: 155. Near Wynndel, British Columbia.

Thomomys talpoides talpoides (Richardson), 1828, Zool. Jour. 3: 518. Central Plains, western Manitoba to Alberta.

REFERENCES

Criddle, Stuart. 1930. The prairie pocket gopher. Jour. Mamm. 11: 275–80.

Tryon, C.A. Jr. 1947. The biology of the pocket gopher (*Thomomys talpoides*) in Montana. Montana State Coll., Agr. Expt. Sta. Bull. 448.

PLAINS POCKET GOPHER
Gaufre brun. *Geomys bursarius* (Shaw)

Description. The plains pocket gopher is much larger than the northern pocket gopher, measuring up to 12 inches in total length. The forefeet are noticeably larger and carry four exaggerated scimitar-shaped claws. The short claws of the hind feet are rather flat by comparison. Otherwise it has the typical stout gopher body and the small eyes and ears. The skull is also much more heavily built. The upper incisors carry two longitudinal grooves, a broad lateral one and a narrow medial one. The upper incisors have been found to grow at a rate of 0.035 mm per day and the lower incisors at 0.067 mm per day, a rate somewhat less than for the northern pocket gopher.

The pelage of this species is short and glossy, slate grey underneath, and brown-tipped. Dorsally, the colour is rich cinnamon brown or liver brown, pale ventrally. The forefeet are white, and the hind feet are a soiled white. The moderately long tail is sparsely covered with white hairs and may be almost naked at the tip.

The males are larger than the females. Adult Canadian male specimens average: total length 290 (285–298), tail 89 (85–94), hind foot 37 (36.5–38.5) mm; weight 268.5 (226.5–343.0) g. Canadian females average: total length 260 (241–272), tail 80 (72–84), hind foot 34 (33.5–35) mm; weight 228.3 (220–260.7) g.

Habits. This species has not been studied as intensively as the northern pocket gopher, but its habits appear to be similar. It is generally a solitary, intolerant, pugnacious animal, which relaxes its antipathy towards others of its kind only during the breeding season. Only at that time, between February and June, may two or more gophers be found in one burrow.

It is active throughout the year, and all day exhibits short bursts of activity of an average duration of a little over half an hour, separated by rest periods of an average of about one hour. Most mound-building appears to take place at dawn and dusk, especially after a rain. On an average 1.77 mounds are built per day.

In Canada there seems to be little to differentiate the mounds of this species from those thrown up by the northern pocket gopher. Farther south, however, in river-bottom habitat, this species constructs huge mounds, which may be up to six feet in diameter and eighteen inches high. In such mounds the nest and storage chambers are constructed for protection from flooding when the water table is near the surface. From these mounds the feeding tunnels radiate. The tunnels are approximately three inches in diameter and lie usually between six and eight inches below the surface, though occasionally they

Map 65 Distribution of the plains pocket gopher, *Geomys bursarius*

are as much as thirty inches deep. The nest, which is composed of shredded grass, may be found as deep as sixteen inches in well-drained soil.

The population density of plains pocket gophers depends a great deal upon the nature of the soil. Under ideal conditions it may be as high as 6.8 per acre, but under average conditions it is about 4.5 animals per acre. A high percentage of the population survives the winter to establish territories; on the average they live at least two years.

The food of this pocket gopher consists of roots, stems, and leaves of grasses, forbs, shrubs, and trees. It stores large caches of sectioned roots, bulbs, and root stalks. Its favourite plants include grasses, clovers, mullein, plantain, bull nettle, dock, vetch, acorns, ragweed, and black-eyed susan.

Among the predators of this species may be listed the king snake, the great horned owl, the weasel, the skunk, and the badger.

Habitat. The plains pocket gopher prefers a deep, fine sandy loam and avoids silty clays and sandy gravels. It occurs in bottomlands, in natural meadows lightly covered with shade trees, and in cultivated land. In Canada it is confined to areas of suitable rich loam.

Reproduction. The females are monoestrous; they reach breeding condition about the beginning of March and taper off in June. The males become fertile about two months before the females and continue in breeding condition about one month after the females. Fertile males have been recorded from December through July, but the peak of breeding in Colorado was found to be February to April.

The gestation period is unknown. The peak of litter production occurs between mid-April and late May; in Minnesota late litters have been found as late as August. The litter size varies between one and eight, with an average of 3.4 young. The young gophers measure about 40 mm long at birth and weigh 5.1 g on the average. Little is known of their subsequent growth. The young start to disperse from the parental burrows in July, when they are about a third grown. Mutual intolerance seems to be an important factor in this dispersal.

Economic Status. Plains pocket gophers are too restricted in distribution in Canada to be of any economic importance, but elsewhere they may be a menace to agriculture. Controls effective for the northern pocket gopher would also be suitable for this species.

Distribution. This species occupies the eastern Great Plains region of North America from the Gulf of Mexico to the Canadian boundary.

Canadian Distribution. The species occurs in Canada only in the Roseau River valley, north of the international boundary, east of Emerson, Manitoba (see Map 65). The nominate race occurs in Canada.

Geomys bursarius bursarius (Shaw), 1800, Trans. Linn. Soc. London 5: 227. Manitoba–Minnesota boundary.

REFERENCES

Vaughn, T.A. 1962. Reproduction in the plains pocket gopher in Colorado. Jour. Mamm. 43(1): 1–13.

Wrigley, Robert E., and John E. Dubois. 1973. Distribution of the pocket gophers *Geomys bursarius* and *Thomomys talpoides* in Manitoba. Canadian Field-Nat. 87(2): 167–9.

Family **Heteromyidae** / Pocket Mice and Kangaroo Rats

This is another unique North American family of rodents, closely related to the previous family, the Geomyidae or pocket gophers. Both families share a number of anatomical and skeletal characters including the external fur-lined cheek pouches. The members of this family, however, are rather mouse-like or rat-like in form and, unlike the pocket gophers, are not modified for a fossorial existence. In this family there is a progressive tendency for the forelimbs to become weaker and the hind limbs more powerful, culminating in the kangaroo rats, which are highly modified for a bipedal saltatorial mode of locomotion.

In this family the skull, unlike the heavy geomyid skull, is light, papery-thin, and flat. The nasal bones project noticeably beyond the incisors; the lower mandibles are small and weak. The most remarkable feature is the inflation of the tympanic bullae and the mastoid bones, which form part of the top of the skull.

In all species the ears are rather small, the tail is moderately to markedly long, and the hallux and pollex are reduced.

These creatures are typical of the arid western plains, where they live in burrows but emerge at night to feed on seeds. They show many physiological adaptations to desert conditions.

OLIVE-BACKED POCKET MOUSE
Souris à abajoues des Plaines. *Perognathus fasciatus* Wied-Neuwied

Description. The olive-backed pocket mouse, perhaps the most diminutive of Canadian rodents, was discovered by Maximilian, Prince of Wied-Neuwied, in 1833. This gentle 'mouse' measures only about 5 inches in length, of which slightly less than half is slender tail. It is one of the easiest mammals to keep in captivity as it will live for many months in a large jar with a sand floor on a diet of bird-seed alone. It has rather large hind feet and small forefeet. It crouches on its centrally placed hind feet with its body held horizontally, propped by its tail. This position frees the forefeet for manipulating its food. The eyes are relatively large and provide a dorsal field of vision. The ears are small; the cheek pouches are prominent.

The pelage is short, stiff, and shiny. The back is a grizzled olive grey; the flanks are light grey, and the underparts are white, bordered by a buffy-yellow stripe that runs from the cheek to the thigh. There is a similar buffy spot behind each ear. The feet are white, and the heel is lightly covered with silvery hairs for about half the length of the foot. Melanistic individuals have been observed.

Average measurements of adults: total length 130 (115–143), tail 60 (57–67), hind foot 17 (16–18), ear 6–7 mm; weight 9.4 (8.9–9.9) g.

Habits. This is a solitary, relatively mild-mannered creature, which is often beaten in chance encounters with other small mice. It is strictly crepuscular or nocturnal in activity. Pocket mice may be observed with the aid of a flashlight or in the beam of the headlights of a car as they dart across narrow, weed-grown dirt roads in the short-grass prairies at night. They are relatively slow-moving in comparison with some of the other species of mice. They use all four feet in a gallop. Their strong hind legs propel them three or four feet at one bound in a series of long leaps. When they are cornered or when they encounter another animal, they make high evasive leaps, quickly changing direction after each landing.

Pocket mice are very fond of sand baths, and their dusting bowls, covered with minute tracks, may sometimes be found. They spend much time brushing their fur and even evert their cheek pouches with the forepaws and brush them clean. Their pouches are automatically retracted by muscular action upon the appearance of danger.

The temperature regulation of a closely related species, *P. longimembris*, has been studied in great detail, and some of the findings are undoubtedly referable to our species as well. The thermoregulation mechanism of pocket mice seems to be highly adapted to living under desert conditions with seasonally restricted food supplies, and the body temperature varies between 35° and 38°C, often under the influence of the ambient temperature. It decreases whenever the pocket mice are asleep. Ambient temperatures near freezing tend to depress the body temperature of active pocket mice, and only by remaining active and eating can they continue to regulate their body temperature. If food supplies are limited, they become drowsy and finally torpid. Pocket mice held at temperatures of between 0° and 9°C all entered hibernation before the ninth day in spite of the availability of a food supply. Under natural conditions it seems that pocket mice remain dormant for short periods of about a week's duration when food caches are available. They do not lay on a supply of fat in the autumn, as do marmots and ground squirrels.

Even during the summer, when the temperature is 20° to 25°C, individual pocket mice often permit their body temperatures to drop and enter a dormant period. From a physiological point of view it would seem that in these animals hibernation and aestivation are very similar. In Canada it appears that this species remains in its burrows during the winter months, between mid-October and mid-April. During this time, dormant periods probably alternate with active periods when it consumes food from winter caches.

Pocket mice excavate a network of small tunnels close to the surface during the summer months. There are usually several small entrances, close to a clump of weeds, cactus, or sagebrush. Near by are small piles of sand. The 'mice,' like dogs, excavate the burrows with their forepaws. Then they rapidly propel the sand backwards with vigorous kicks of the hind feet. They bulldoze the loose sand out of the burrow entrances with their noses and then 'tap' the piles firmly with rapid vibrations of the forepaws. These tiny burrows may honeycomb furrowed fields, sand banks, or level range land for an area seven yards in diameter. The summer nests and storage chambers are at a depth of about twelve to eighteen inches, but the winter nests are much deeper. In the autumn they burrow down about six feet. Storage chambers are also constructed off the deep burrow. In winter the entrances are closed either with a plug by the mice, or by loose soil, ice, or snow.

Pocket mice are also able to live for a long time without free water, obtaining metabolic water from the digestion of dry seeds. They are primarily weed-seed eaters, although they do eat insects during the early summer months. They sit on their hind legs, sifting the soil with their paws and filling their cheek pouches with seeds. These they carry to their storage chambers, and quickly empty from their pouches by a rapid forward stroke of the paws. Among their favourite foods are the seeds of foxtail grass, bugseed, knotweed, Russian thistle, blue-eyed grass, and tumbleweed.

Pocket mice must be on the alert for a wide array of predators, including rattlesnakes, burrowing owls, weasels, badgers, skunks, foxes, coyotes, and mice such as deer mice and grasshopper mice.

Habitat. The olive-backed pocket mouse is found in loose sandy soils on arid, open, thin grasslands. It generally avoids cover, though it may be found on the edge of aspen parklands. The distribution is not continuous since the species is found only in the lightest soils and is absent from intervening areas of rich humus soil.

Reproduction. Few details of reproduction are known for this species. The females have six mammae, two inguinal pairs and one pectoral pair. The breeding season commences in April, and the young are born between mid-May and mid-July. The gestation period is unknown, but the length of the parturition period suggests that the females are polyoestrous and may bear two litters in a season. The males also appear to be sexually active as late as early July. The average litter size is about four young, but may be as high as six.

Economic Status. The olive-backed pocket mouse is too sparse in Canada to be of much economic significance. Preliminary food studies indicate it may exert a small beneficial effect by destroying weed seeds.

Distribution. This species inhabits the central Great Plains of North America.

Canadian Distribution. A few years ago this was considered to be a rare species in Canada, but recent studies have indicated that it is sparsely distributed on the short-grass plains of the second prairie steppe in southern Manitoba, Saskatchewan, and Alberta. Two subspecies occur in Canada (see Map 66).

Perognathus fasciatus fasciatus Wied-Neuwied, 1839, Nova Acta Phys.-Med. Acad. Caes. Leop.-Carol. 191: 369. The typical form found in Manitoba and southeastern Saskatchewan.
Perognathus fasciatus olivaceogriseus Swenk, 1940, Missouri Valley Fauna 3: 6. A smaller and paler race found in southeastern Alberta and adjacent Saskatchewan.

REFERENCES

Criddle, Stuart. 1915. The banded pocket mouse, *Perognathus fasciatus* Wied. Ottawa Nat. 28(10): 130–4.
Nero, R.W. 1957. The pocket mouse in Saskatchewan. Blue Jay 15(4): 172–3.
– 1957. Behaviour of a captive pocket mouse. Blue Jay 15(4): 173–6.
– 1958. Additional pocket mouse records. Blue Jay 16(4): 176–9.

GREAT BASIN POCKET MOUSE
Souris à abajoues des pinèdes. *Perognathus parvus* (Peale)

Description. In spite of its specific name this species of pocket mouse is much larger than the previous one. It has the typical pocket-mouse form: a stout body; a tail about the same length as the body, grey above, white below, tufted at the tip; hind feet slightly enlarged (only the heels are haired, the remainder of the sole being naked); small haired ears; external fur-lined cheek pouches; and a horizontal bipedal stance.

Map 66 Distribution of the olive-backed pocket mouse (A), *Perognathus fasciatus*, and the Great Basin pocket mouse (B), *Perognathus parvus*: 1 *P. f. fasciatus*, 2 *P. f. olivaceogriseus*, 3 *P. p. laingi*, 4 *P. p. lordi*

The pelage is wiry and glossy. Dorsally it is buffy grey with a dominant mixture of black-tipped hairs, which gives it a superficial peppered effect. The underparts and the feet are white. There is an indistinct narrow, lateral buffy line. The paler ear spots are indistinct. There is one annual moult in late summer, the males moulting in late August and the females somewhat later. The juvenile coat is slate grey.

The characteristic feature in the skull is the junction of the inflated tympanic bullae on the median line.

Since the two subspecies found in Canada differ significantly in size, the measurements will be found under each subspecies. The males are larger than the females in this species.

Habits. The life history of the Great Basin pocket mouse does not differ significantly from that of the olive-backed pocket mouse. It is a solitary species: only during the breeding season may more than one animal be found in a single network of tunnels. It is also crepuscular and nocturnal in activity.

In summer it constructs a shallow network of tunnels in the loose soil with several entrances and underground storage and nesting chambers. Leading off from this system is a deeper tunnel that descends between three and six feet to a deep winter nest. The nest cavities are circular and about three inches in diameter and are lined with dry shredded grasses, weed stalks, and flower heads. Characteristic of the burrows of this species are the small, packed piles of earth near the entrances. These are often used as dusting bowls, as the numerous small tracks testify.

This animal is active only eight or nine months of the year, although activity varies from individual to individual. Few are observed between November and March. The males emerge in early April before the females. During the winter months this species does not enter a profound state of torpor but rather is dormant in its nest for periods of varying length. In between these dormant periods it eats some of its stored seeds. The unutilized burrow entrances gradually fill in during the winter, and there is little evidence of activity.

During the summer months pocket mice keep busy sifting the dust soil with their forepaws while propped on their large hind feet and tail. It was first thought that they were largely seed-eaters since they pack seeds into their pouches for underground storage, but recent studies have shown that insects play a significant role in their summer diet as well. They consume a large number of caterpillars on the spot. Plant foods include Russian thistle, pigweed, wild mustard, and bitterbrush. On agricultural lands they will also consume grain and the tender green parts of sprouting grain. They can live for long periods without free water.

Natural predators include rattlesnakes, burrowing owls, short-eared owls, badgers, skunks, weasels, and foxes.

Habitat. This species inhabits arid, sandy short-grass steppes, and brushland covered with sagebrush, bitterbrush, and rabbit brush. It also infests wheat fields on arid marginal lands.

Reproduction. Mating occurs soon after emergence in April. The gestation period is between twenty-one and twenty-eight days. The first litter is born in May, and late litters appear in August. This fact, along with the occurrence of two age classes of juveniles, strongly suggests that the females are polyoestrous and that two litters may be born in a single season. The average number of foetuses has been determined at 5.2, with a range of two to eight.

Economic Status. The Great Basin pocket mouse is an agricultural pest in the Pacific northwestern United States. It damages wheatfields on arid marginal land by destroying the sown seed, growing seedlings, and ripened grain. Even the accidental sprouting of seedlings from shallow pocket mouse larders is a nuisance in the spring. Often the populations of pocket mice reach enormous sizes in infested fields.

The distribution of poisoned grain is the most reliable method of control.

Distribution. This species occurs in the intermontane Great Basin, which lies between the Rocky Mountains and the coastal ranges of western North America.

Canadian Distribution. In Canada the species is found in the arid interior of south-central British Columbia, where two races occur (see Map 66).

Perognathus parvus laingi Anderson, 1933, Nat. Mus. Canada Bull. 70: 100. A small, dark race occupying the open grasslands plateau at 3,000 feet elevation on Anarchist Mountain, eight miles east of Osoyoos Lake, British Columbia. Average measurements of adult males: length 174 (166–180), tail 90 (84–101), hind foot 22 (22–23), ear 9 mm. Females: length 166 (156–174), tail 88 (84–91), hind foot 22 (21–23), ear 8–9 mm.

Perognathus parvus lordi (Gray), 1868, Proc. Zool. Soc. London 1868: 202. A larger, paler race, occupying the low arid valleys of the Similkameen, Okanagan, and Thompson rivers, British Columbia, at elevations between 1,000 and 1,500 feet. Average measurements of adult males: length 187 (173–202), tail 101 (91–112), hind foot 24 (23–25), ear 9 mm; weight 19.7 g. Females:

length 175 (166–183), tail 92 (86–100), hind foot 23 (21–24), ear 7–9 mm; weight 14.4 g.

REFERENCE

Scheffer, T.H. 1938. Pocket mice of Washington and Oregon in relation to agriculture. United States Dept. Agri. Tech. Bull. 608.

ORD'S KANGAROO RAT
Rat kangourou d'Ord. *Dipodomys ordii* Woodhouse

Description. The kangaroo rats exhibit the most pronounced adaptations to the bipedal saltatorial gait and to a desert economy found in the family. Ord's kangaroo rat is the most generalized of the many species found in western North America and the only one found in Canada. It has a robust body, shortened neck, small, delicate forelegs, and long, strong hind legs. Its tail is considerably longer than its body and is well-furred and tufted. It has large, luminous eyes, and since these are dorsally placed it is doubtful if the animal can see what it is handling. It has the characteristic furred cheek pouches and the short, rounded ears. Between the shoulders is a thickened holocrine skin gland, composed of modified sebaceous glands, which produces a crusted secretion to keep the fur oiled. This animal measures up to 12 inches in length, including the long tail. The hallux and pollex are present but are reduced in size (Plate 3).

The skull is flat and triangular, from the slender projecting nasal bones to the broadly inflated mastoid and tympanic bones on the back (Figure 39). The maxillary roots

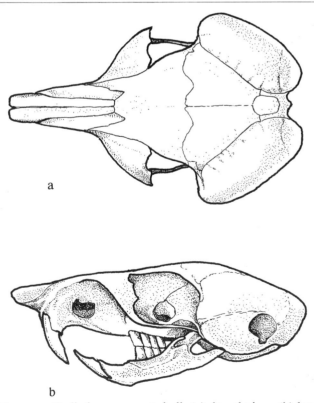

Figure 39 Ord's kangaroo rat skull: (a) dorsal view, (b) lateral view (× 2)

of the zygomatic arches are broad and flat, but the jugal components are thread-like. The cheek teeth are simple, columnar, and ever-growing; the upper incisors are grooved; the lower incisors are awl-like. It is thought that the inflated auditory region is associated with the need for delicate balance in connection with the bipedal saltatorial gait.

The pelage is long and silky. The upper parts are rich tawny, with a scattering of black hairs along the mid-dorsal line, particularly in the glandular region. The upper lip, a spot over each eye, the area behind each ear, and lines across the hips are white, as are the underparts and the feet. The vibrissae are prominent and arise from a black patch on the side of the nose. The tail has two grey lines, above and below, and the sides are white. The terminal tuft is soft grey. The soles of the long hind feet are completely covered with soft felt-like hair, which is grey at the heels and white at the toes. The claws are thin and delicate.

Average measurements of adults: total length 273 (265–282), tail 155 (143–157), hind foot 43 (40–44), ear 13 mm; weight 81 (55–96) g. There is no significant difference between the weights of the sexes, but there is a considerable annual variation in the animal's weight, which reaches a peak at the breeding season and declines afterwards.

Habits. Although kangaroo rats are easily handled and make interesting pets, they are belligerent, solitary creatures in the wild. They are quick to defend their burrows and food caches against all intruders, whether of their own species or another. Only during the mating season is this intolerant behaviour relaxed briefly, and then only towards a mate. Among its own species it engages in aerial combat during brief encounters, two animals leaping into the air together and slashing at each other with strong hind feet. Towards more dangerous foes such as rattlesnakes it uses the technique of turning its back on the intruder and vigorously kicking sand in its face. (This technique was once used on me when I was in a sleeping-bag.)

The kangaroo rat is alert and quick in its movements, and possesses a keen sense of sight even in the dark, as well as keen senses of hearing and smell. When travelling normally it progresses with slow quadripedal hops, briefly touching its forefeet to the ground, but when speed is required it travels in long bipedal hops covering six feet or more at each leap. The forefeet are tucked into the chest, and the body is carried horizontally, propelled by strokes of the powerful hind legs moving in unison. The long, tufted tail floats behind, serving as a balance. The closely related species *D. heermanni* has been clocked at twelve miles an hour in full flight, and captive animals have been known to run as much as sixteen miles on exercise wheels in a single night. When pursued it may make a series of high, erratic escape-hops.

Many of the kangaroo rat's habits are similar to those of the smaller pocket mouse. It sand-bathes regularly; indeed, deprived of sand its fur becomes matted and oily. It feeds in a hunched position, the small forepaws gathering seeds and packing them into its cheek pouches, while the luminous dorsally placed eyes are alert to catch a movement that might signify danger. Not very vocal, it utters only soft chuckles and squeals. It has, however, another interesting means of communication. When examining the burrows one often hears an underground thumping or drumming. This is made by a vibration of the hind feet on packed sand when the animal crouches with forefeet on the ground.

Ord's kangaroo rat is strictly nocturnal in activity and does not appear until complete darkness has fallen. Even bright moonlight discourages outside activity. It is most active between about midnight and 4 A.M. It is not known at present whether it hibernates during the winter months. Kangaroo rats in general seem to have poor internal thermoregulation mechanisms. Their body temperatures are labile, and the animals show distress at temperatures below 70° and above 80°F. Field evidence suggests that they have periods of dormancy below ground during the winter months.

Ord's kangaroo rat is a poor digger because of its weak forelegs and slender claws, and digs shallow burrows in loose sand. Many species of southwestern kangaroo rats build their burrows in large mounds of loose sand, but our species excavates its burrow in the sides of natural sand dunes, river banks, or road cuts. There is one central burrow with trails radiating to feeding areas, and for temporary protection from aerial attacks there are also a number of shallow 'funk-holes' on the borders of the home range. The tunnel entrances are approximately three inches in diameter, and small mounds of fresh, damp sand outside the entrance indicate an active burrow. During the daylight hours the entrances are, as a rule, blocked with a plug of sand. The hot, drying winds of summer usually erase the previous signs of activity, but each morning the sand reveals the tracery of many tracks and the snake-like imprint of the dragged tail. The burrows generally lead only eight to twenty-four inches below the surface to a chamber lined with grass stalks and seed hulls. There are also storage chambers filled with seeds and root sections and long connecting tunnels just under the surface. The nests are often so shallow as to be turned up by a plough or disc.

Ord's kangaroo rat forages as far as twenty-five yards from its burrow entrance. The population density may be about 1.4 to 7.0 animals per acre, as determined for *D. merriami*.

Kangaroo rats eat primarily the seeds of grasses and forbs; however, during the summer they also eat many insects such as grasshoppers and moths. In Canada the distribution of the kangaroo rat appears to be closely associated with that of the grey-green leguminous plant *Psorelea lanceolata*. Kangaroo rats exhibit a physiological adaptation to desert conditions in that they can live for prolonged periods on dry vegetation by using metabolic water for their vital requirements. They are also able to reabsorb water from their urine. Actually they obtain adequate free water from succulent plants. Ord's kangaroo rat will drink free water, but some species will not. Under

Map 67 Distribution of Ord's kangaroo rat, *Dipodomys ordii*

prolonged drought stress, they will nibble their own faeces for moisture and lick urine from moist surfaces.

Ordinarily they live at least two years in the wild, although they must be constantly on guard for predators such as rattlesnakes; burrowing, short-eared, and horned owls; badgers; black-footed ferrets; skunks; foxes; coyotes; and weasels.

Habitat. This species is confined to open, sandy areas with a sparse vegetation of sagebrush, snowberry, rose, creeping juniper, and buffaloberry. An increase in perennial grass cover leads to a decrease in its population. The kangaroo rat is one of our few typical desert mammals.

Reproduction. Reproduction in Ord's kangaroo rat, which has not been studied in great detail in our latitude, appears to be complex. The species is seasonally polyoestrous, but the breeding time seems to follow favourable growing seasons. Following a drought, few females breed, but after a favourable moist season, most females breed, and the young females mature quickly so that several litters are born and the population builds up very rapidly. The oestrous cycle is about five to six days in duration. During the receptive period the female's genital region becomes swollen and inflamed. At this time the sexes lose their usual animosity and actively pursue each other in playful chases. The actual breeding periods may last from February to June in New Mexico, or from August to February in Texas and Oklahoma. In Utah there seem to

be two breeding periods, in spring and in autumn, with anoestrous periods in summer and winter. Spring is the normal breeding season in Canada.

The gestation period is between twenty-nine and thirty days. The litter size averages 3.5 young and may vary from one to six. There may be two or more litters in one year. The young are born in grass-lined nests, naked and helpless, with eyes and ears closed and with shallow facial folds representing the pouches. Growth is rapid, and the eyes and ears open about the sixteenth day. The young remain in the nest for a period of four to five weeks. During a favourable breeding period, females of the first litter may become sexually mature at the age of two months.

Distribution. Ord's kangaroo rat occupies the Great Plains, the Great Basin, and the Mexican Highlands of western North America from central Mexico north to the Canadian border region.

Canadian Distribution. These rats are found in Canada only in the Great Sand Hills area of southwestern Saskatchewan and adjacent southwestern Alberta. They are locally quite plentiful, however, and the population has been estimated at several thousand animals (see Map 67). The race that occurs in Canada is:

Dipodomys ordii terrosus Hoffmeister, 1942, Proc. Biol. Soc. Washington 55: 165. Alberta and Saskatchewan.

REFERENCE

Nero, R.W., and R.W. Fyfe. 1956. Kangaroo rat colonies found. Blue Jay 14: 107–10.

Family **Castoridae** / Beavers

Beavers are among the larger rodents. Adult Canadian beavers have been known to weigh as much as ninety pounds and are exceeded in size only by the South American capabaras. The living beavers, however, are babies compared to the giant beaver *Castoroides*, which inhabited North America at the end of the last glacial period, perhaps 10,000 years ago. That species was as large as a black bear.

The beaver family is distantly related to the squirrel family. Most of its unique characteristics are adaptations to its aquatic mode of life. The body is robust, the head is broad and blunt, the neck and limbs are short, and the tail is uniquely paddle-shaped and covered with scales. The feet have five well-developed digits. The forefeet are delicate and dextrous; the hind feet are large and webbed and serve as powerful paddles when swimming.

The skull of the beaver is ruggedly constructed. The rostrum is broad; the zygomatic arches are strong and laterally compressed. Behind the arches are two pits on the side of the cranium. The auditory canal is elongate. The incisors are remarkably large; the cheek teeth are high-crowned with numerous enamel folds, which act like a washboard in chewing and never seem to wear out during the animal's lifetime (Figure 40).

AMERICAN BEAVER
Castor. *Castor canadensis* Kuhl

Description. The beaver is the national emblem of Canada. It was the first natural resource to be exploited, and it played a leading role in the exploration and settlement of New France and the vast northern territories of the Hudson's Bay Company. The beaver pelt, which had been held in high esteem among the Indians before the arrival of the Europeans, quite naturally became the unit of currency in the new land. Indian wars and bitter feuds between the traders were fought over the rights to beaver trapping territory, and fortunes were made and lost in the fur trade.

To the Europeans the beaver was a familiar animal. European beavers had been considered a valuable resource since Grecian times because of their glandular secretion known as castoreum. Their pelts were used primarily in the manufacture of felt hats, or 'beavers.' The introduction of American beaver to areas in Europe and Asia where the native beaver was depleted has resulted in the production of a hybrid population. This indi-cates that the American and European beavers are closely related species.

As a result of its popularity a great amount of folk-lore has been built up around this interesting species. It is difficult even now to filter fact from fancy. The more one studies the beaver the more one realizes that the truth is indeed 'stranger than fiction.' Although numerous accounts have been written of the beaver since Samuel Hearne's time, many aspects of its life history are still unknown.

Most of the beaver's features are adaptive. The well-furred lips meet behind the incisors, permitting the beaver to cut and peel branches under water. The nostrils and ears possess valvular flaps, which may be closed when the beaver dives, sealing these orifices to water. The small delicate forepaws have elongate digits and slender claws to facilitate the handling of wood, and the claws on the hind feet are remarkably specialized. Under the first two claws are horny pads, and the claws themselves, particularly the one on the second digit, have sharp serrated edges. These are used to comb, and the beaver is known to spend much of its leisure time carefully grooming its coat with these special claws. The remaining claws on digits 3, 4, and 5 are flat and blunt.

The beaver's unique tail is well furred at the thick base but only sparsely haired on its murky-grey 'paddle.' The caudal vertebrae are flattened and surrounded by a somewhat gelatinous cortex. Beaver-tail soup is considered a delicacy by most Indians. Functionally, the tail is very important to the beaver. It serves as a rudder in swimming, a prop in walking and standing, and a lever in dragging logs, but never as a trowel. Two sets of glands are found in the anal region of both sexes. Lateral to the anus are two large castor glands, which discharge the musky castoreum into the common cloaca. Behind the anus is a pair of smaller oil glands. These discharge oil through many fine pores onto the hair. The beaver carefully brushes this oil onto its pelage with its forepaws in the preliminary grooming process, before the final combing with the hind feet. A sleek, oiled pelage is most important to an aquatic mammal (Plate 13).

The rich, dense pelage of the beaver makes it an important pelt for the furrier. The undercoat is long, dense, slightly wavy, and dull brown in colour. Growing through the undercoat is the outer coat of long rich brown guard hairs. The head and shoulders are brighter brown than the back, and the underparts are dull chestnut-brown. There are two annual moults in late autumn and spring. The kits, or young beaver, are duller in colour. Occasionally albino beaver are found.

Measurements of adult males: total length 104.7 (98–113), tail 44.2 (38–53), hind foot 17.3 (16–19) cm. Females: total length 103 (95–114), tail 44.4 (40–51), hind foot 17.5 (15–19) cm. Weights of beavers are highly variable, dependent upon age, sex, and season. The weights of adults usually vary between 15 and 35 kg, with an average of about 20 kg.

Habits. Beavers have an elaborate society in which the family is the basic unit, and the female is the central figure.

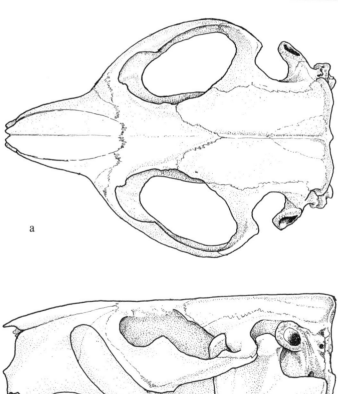

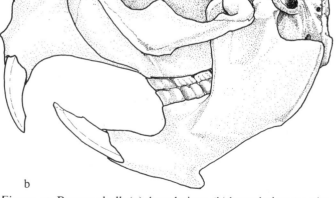

Figure 40 Beaver skull: (a) dorsal view, (b) lateral view (× 3/4)

158

It is usually the female that establishes the home site. If her mate is lost, she remains with her family, and another male joins her in the mating season. If the female is killed and leaves no daughters, the males will usually abandon the site. All members of the family perform co-operative work about the site. There is a well-developed social hierarchy, based on size and a system of communication in the clan.

One often comes upon the soft 'mud pies' constructed by beaver along their trails or canals, which serve as a means of communication. Upon close examination, fresh paw marks may be seen, and often the oily deposit of musky castoreum may be detected on fresh piles. Beavers also have a system of auditory signals in their low whines and bellows and in the startling tail-whack on the surface of the still water that serves as an alarm.

Beavers are most active between sunset and sunrise, but are often about during the late afternoon on dull or quiet days. On land they have a slow, awkward, ambling gait, but they are much more at home when they slip quietly into the water. They swim with only the blunt head above water, the back and tail awash, trailing an ever-widening ripple across the black waters. They do not swim fast – about two to three miles an hour – but can swim under water as quickly as on the surface. With forepaws pressed close to their flanks, they are propelled by rapid strokes of their hind legs. They use their tails only as rudders or to give a quick flip in a crash dive when danger threatens.

Beavers do not hibernate but remain active all winter beneath the ice and in their lodges. Occasionally they may be seen in the open water that frequently is found near the dam overflow. Rarely are their trails seen across the ice to a new cutting on shore, and regular outside feeding activity occurs only if the colony is faced with starvation beneath the ice. Then they may cut their way out of the top of the lodge.

Almost every Canadian is familiar with the work of the beaver. It is one of the few mammals, aside from man, that can profoundly change its own habitat, and for this reason it has earned the title 'engineer of the wild.' Probably the dam is the first feature of a beaver colony to be constructed. It is composed of sticks, stones, roots, sod, and mud, carefully located at a narrow point in the river, where the banks are firm and there is a quicker flow than elsewhere, and where the resulting pond will provide access to a food supply. The dam is started by laying parallel sticks and branches in the stream-bed, the butt ends facing upstream so that the current anchors the spreading branches more securely in the bottom. The first layer is then plastered with stones, roots, and mud. Again the current aids in packing the silt into the spaces between the twigs and leaves. So the dam grows: row upon row of poles, branches, sods, and mud. As the impounded water creeps higher, the dam is continued along the banks, often incorporating large boulders, stumps, and trees. Although the dam frequently has the ideal engineered concave crown, this is only accidental because it is built only on the highest ridge and never across low spots. The dam is built up high enough to hold back a pond six to ten feet deep – deep enough to permit swimming under the thickest winter ice, which may be three feet deep. The leading edge of the dam is then plastered with a thick layer of mud to seal it, which often results in the dredging of a deep channel just behind the dam edge. The wings of the dam are completed by the construction of a mud bank into the forest. The current also helps to settle the silt that seals the dam. The water is permitted to spill over only at the central position of the old stream-bed, greatly lessening the risk of a washout, since the current is swiftest at that point. When the dam requires repairs, which is fairly often, the male is usually the first to work on it, but others may assist if extensive work is required.

The finished dam is usually about fifty yards in length, six feet high, and about nine feet through the base, but it may be as much as one hundred yards in length. Below the main dam are subsidiary ones, which flood other feed beds and may provide back pressure to support the main dam.

The beaver lodge may be situated in the middle of the pond, or it may be on the bank. The lodge is usually six to nine feet high and ten to twenty feet in diameter. Constructed on a base of sunken poles and brush (perhaps the remains of a former feed bed), it is either situated on the edge of deep water or has deepened underwater channels leading to its base. It is usually constructed in a month during the autumn and may be occupied for many years. Gradually the base is raised until it is about six inches above the water line. A firm platform of mud, twigs, and bark is laid down at this level. The lodge continues to grow, with a layer of poles on the outside and lighter brush on the inside, until the dome is reached. Then the central chamber and entrances are gnawed out. The central chamber is about five feet wide and two feet high. There are two or more plunge-holes from the floor to the deep channels on different sides of the lodge. The finished chamber has a sloping floor of dry shredded willow bark, so that dry sleeping quarters are situated higher than the eating area around the main plunge-hole. The main water-filled entrance tunnel may be fifteen inches in diameter in order that branches may be dragged into the lodge for food. The apex of the lodge above the chamber is usually the thinnest spot and is composed of looser branches to permit ventilation. In the autumn the sides of the lodge are plastered with mud, which washes into the cracks and freezes to make the lodge secure from the attacks of powerful predators.

Besides the lodges, a beaver colony has bank burrows. These are reached by channels about three feet under the surface, and the rising tunnel leads back three to five yards under the bank to a cavity about a yard in diameter, usually situated about two feet under the roots of a tree or a clump of shrubs, or under a large rock. These bank burrows may be used as retreats when the lodges are attacked or flooded out. But some beaver that inhabit lakes and large rivers may not build lodges and may live completely in bank burrows.

Besides the dam and lodge there are other constructions which form part of a beaver colony. The deepened channels have been mentioned. Beavers may dig canals in low terrain as much as one hundred yards long to facilitate reaching their logging areas. Often they deepen and widen a small spring or freshet flowing through the forest. The canal may be interrupted by 'locks' to maintain an adequate depth of water in the upper reaches. The beaver climbs over the locks in its path. The actual area of tree-felling is reached along well-beaten paths from which the vegetation has been cut on each side to facilitate the dragging of branches.

The food of the beaver consists of the bark of certain trees cut from the soft cambrium layer, and leaves, twigs, and buds, as well as much herbaceous pond vegetation, including submerged root stalks. Its favourite food is undoubtedly the trembling aspen; then willows, white birch, balsam poplar, cottonwood, rowanwood, maples, ash, hawthorns, cherries, and apple trees. Conifers such as pines are occasionally cut, but spruce bark is considered starvation diet. In summer, eelgrass, duckweed, pondweed, water-lilies, and cattails are eaten as well.

The beaver cuts down complete groves of aspen for food, felling trees up to fifteen inches in diameter. Usually a single beaver cuts a tree, but occasionally two may work on a large one. The beaver stands beside the stump, propped by its tail and clasping the tree with its forepaws at shoulder height, and cuts two horizontal grooves about three inches apart with its incisors. Next, it pries out the intervening wood in the form of large chips, which fall beside the stump. The beaver works to right and left, gradually cutting the trench wider and deeper. Then it moves around to the opposite side of the tree and connects up the trench, usually at a slightly higher level. The beaver never cuts directly through the trunk, but always leaves a central column, which splinters when the wind and the weight of the tree topple it. The beaver possesses no special faculties to ensure that the tree will fall the desired way. The trees are usually on a gentle slope towards the river or pond and fall that way. Examination of a cut-over area, however, usually reveals a tangle of logs and the occasional 'hung-up' tree. Beavers themselves are occasionally trapped beneath a falling tree.

After the tree has been felled, the branches are trimmed into convenient lengths for dragging to the pond. The beaver does its feeding in the water or in the lodge. It trims off all the leaf-bearing branches, leaving only the main trunk on the ground. Whole saplings are dragged to the water's edge.

The distance the beaver will work away from water depends upon the safety of the site. Where large predators are absent, they have been known to work over 150 yards from the pond, dragging the branches over a slight rise. In Riding Mountain National Park, Manitoba, there was, however, a definite cutting line about twenty-five yards back from the shore. Since the park contained an array of beaver predators, such as the coyote and lynx, travel away from water was a risky matter.

The daily food consumption of one beaver has been estimated to be 662 g of woody vegetation. It has also been estimated that one beaver will cut 216 trees in a year and that one acre of aspen trees will support one beaver for a year.

In September and October beavers lay aside a store of winter food in the form of feed piles. They drag branches to deep water close to the lodge entrance, and then pile them, one on top of another, until the whole mass sinks to the bottom with the accumulated weight. The presence of these feed piles and of freshly plastered lodges in the autumn indicates an active colony.

The beaver colony is normally composed of an adult pair, the kits, and the yearlings of the previous year, bringing the normal family group usually to ten or twelve by autumn. Other colonies, however, might consist of only a pair of young adults or even a single beaver, so that the average colony size has been found to be approximately 5.7 animals. Individual beavers have been known to live as long as twelve years. The established colony is sedentary, but the two-year-olds may travel far before settling down. They generally travel downstream, but some may take off across the land to other watersheds. Tagged beaver have been known to travel up to 150 miles by water, but most travel less than six miles from the natal lodge.

Since the beaver is a powerful antagonist at bay, only the strongest of carnivores will tackle one. The bear, wolf, coyote, fisher, wolverine, otter, and lynx are listed as beaver predators. Most of these are terrestrial predators and must capture a beaver either when it is cutting trees in the forest or when it is in its lodge. During the winter the predator can reach the lodge in the ponds only by crossing the ice. However, the frozen sticks and mud usually defy the attacks of claw and tooth. During the summer months black bears will occasionally try to break into the top of an occupied bank lodge. Even then, however, the tangle of inwoven sticks and baked mud is such a barrier that the beaver have plenty of time to escape through the plunge-hole.

A more serious predator is the otter, which also inhabits the water and can enter the lodge freely, summer or winter, through the underwater tunnel. The relationship between otters and beavers is not well understood. There is some evidence that otters occasionally kill young beavers and maim adult females, but it is probable that a family of beavers in their lodge would be a little too much for an otter to handle. Of course the second tunnel offers a handy exit. In any event the two species seem to have lived together in the same habitat without the otter seriously reducing the beaver population.

Habitat. Beavers inhabit slow-flowing streams, lakes, rivers, and marshes. They do not colonize swift-flowing mountain brooks, which are subject to flash floods. They usually live in forested regions but occasionally in streams on the prairies, in muskegs, or in tundra or alpine meadows. Although aspen groves are preferred for food, they can live where only shrub willows, alders, or water plants provide food.

Reproduction. Surprisingly, very little is known of the breeding habits of the beaver. In the first place it is difficult to tell the sexes apart, since both genital systems dis-

Map 68 Distribution of the American beaver, *Castor canadensis*: 1 *C. c. acadicus*, 2 *C. c. belugae*, 3 *C. c. caecutor*, 4 *C. c. canadensis*, 5 *C. c. labradorensis*, 6 *C. c. leucodontus*, 7 *C. c. michiganensis*, 8 *C. c. missouriensis*, 9 *C. c. sagittatus*, * introduced

charge into a common cloaca. The male organs can be palpated with some difficulty, keeping in mind the existence of the castor glands. The females have four pectoral teats, which are prominent in parous adults but insignificant in juveniles, and are monoestrous. The male gonads develop in the late autumn and regress in size towards the end of April. Mating takes place in January and February; the males are monogamous. The gestation period is of three and a half months' duration, and the kits are born between late April and late June. The average litter size is about 3.9 (1–8). Embryonic absorptions are known to account for about 27 per cent of prenatal mortality.

Shortly before the birth of the kits the female drives the adult male from the lodge, and he takes up temporary quarters in an old lodge or in a bank burrow. The young are born in a relatively late stage of development. They measure about 125 mm long and weigh about 450 g. They are fully furred with lustrous, dark brown fur, and their tails are only slightly flattened. Reports are at variance

concerning the condition of their eyes at birth – whether they are open or closed. In any event they seem to open at a relatively early age. If the lodge is threatened, the female will carry the young in her mouth, under water, to some other retreat.

The young grow rapidly. The first summer they do not work. The second season as juveniles they remain in the lodge but assist with the many colony chores such as cutting food, repairing the dam and lodge, and digging channels and canals. During their second winter they mature sexually, and when spring comes the adults drive them out of the colony before the arrival of the new litter of kits. They venture forth to establish new colonies either alone or paired with their litter-mates. There seems to be a relatively high degree of inbreeding in this species.

Economic Status. The early importance of the beaver in the fur trade has already been mentioned. Because of heavy exploitation, the beaver population was almost wiped out by 1930. Unfortunately beavers refuse to breed

161

in cages, and the natural destruction of the two-year-olds by adults in larger enclosures discouraged the development of beaver farming along the lines of mink and fox farming. Fortunately the conservation of beaver by the regular harvest of only surplus beaver from counted lodges was developed by James Watt of the Hudson's Bay Company in the early thirties. This practice was successful and quickly spread across the country, with the result that the beaver population quickly increased until it has again assumed its role of leadership in the wild fur market. During the 1971–72 season, 390,884 beaver were taken in Canada at an average value of $17.80 for a total value of $6,445,201.

Unfortunately, with the increase in the beaver population, the problem of the nuisance beaver appeared. They plugged culverts, and flooded roads, bridges, railroads, and agricultural lands. They cut ornamental trees on the edges of towns, cities, golf courses, and parks. As a result, provincial game departments have been forced to maintain regular programs of live-trapping and moving the offending beaver to unstocked areas.

Beavers may also occasionally constitute a public health menace because they may fall victims to such diseases as tularaemia and rabies. In the broad picture, however, they remain one of our most valuable and interesting mammals, serving many useful secondary purposes such as maintaining water levels and providing habitat for fish and waterfowl. Deprived of the activity of the beaver, forest streams would lose much of their variety and life.

Distribution. North America from the Mexican boundary to Alaska.

Canadian Distribution. The beaver is found from coast to coast and north to the treeline in the Yukon Territory. It was naturally absent only on Anticosti and the Queen Charlotte islands. It has been exterminated on Prince Edward Island and introduced to the Queen Charlotte Islands in 1950. It is sparse in the prairies and extends but a short distance into the arctic tundra region, although stragglers have reached the mouth of the Coppermine River in the Northwest Territories. Nine subspecies of beaver have been described from Canada (see Map 68).

Castor canadensis acadicus V. Bailey and Doutt, 1942, Jour. Mamm. 23: 87. The Maritime Provinces and Quebec.

Castor canadensis belugae Taylor, 1916, Univ. California Pub. Zool. 12: 429. Coastal British Columbia mainland north of Rivers Inlet and the Yukon Territory.

Castor canadensis caecutor Bangs, 1913, Bull. Mus. Comp. Zool. 54: 513. Newfoundland.

Castor canadensis canadensis Kuhl, 1820, Beitr. Zool. u. vergleich. Anat. Abth. 1: 64. Central Canada from the western Quebec border to the Mackenzie delta, Northwest Territories, and the Peace River district of northeastern British Columbia.

Castor canadensis labradorensis V. Bailey and Doutt, 1942, Jour. Mamm. 23: 86. Labrador.

Castor canadensis leucodontus Gray, 1869, Ann. Mag. Nat. Hist. Ser. 4, 4: 293. Southern British Columbia

including Vancouver Island.

Castor canadensis michiganensis V. Bailey, 1913, Proc. Biol. Soc. Washington 26: 192. Reported only from the Sault Ste Marie region of Ontario.

Castor canadensis missouriensis V. Bailey, 1919, Jour. Mamm. 1: 32. Extreme southwestern Saskatchewan and southeastern Alberta.

Castor canadensis sagittatus Benson, 1933, Jour. Mamm. 14: 320. Central British Columbia.

REFERENCES

Aleksiuk, M., and I. McT. Cowan. 1969. The winter metabolic depression in Arctic beavers (*Castor canadensis* Kuhl) with comparisons to California beavers. Canadian Jour. Zool. 47: 965–79.

– 1969. Expenditure in the beaver (*Castor canadensis* Kuhl) at the northern limit of its distribution. Canadian Jour. Zool. 47: 471–81.

Dugmore, A. Radclyffe. 1914. The romance of the beaver. William Heinemann, London.

Green, H.U. 1936. The beaver of the Riding Mountain, Manitoba. Canadian Field-Nat. 50: 1–23, 36–50, 61–67, 85–92.

Family **Muridae** / Rats, Mice, and Voles

This family includes a large group of small- to medium-sized cosmopolitan rodents that usually pass as 'rats and mice.' They are variable in form and habitat; most are terrestrial, but a few are arboreal, aquatic, or fossorial in adaptation. All have a moderately developed v-shaped infraorbital canal, through which a strand of the masseter muscle passes. The anterior part of the zygomatic arch is a tilted plate, and there are no supraorbital processes. The cheek teeth are universally reduced to three molars. These may be low-crowned and tuberculate (as in rats and mice), or high-crowned, open-rooted, and prismatic (as in most voles). If the teeth are tubercular, the tubercules occur in two or three parallel rows. The number of toes on the forefeet is usually four, rarely five; five toes occur constantly on the hind feet.

WESTERN HARVEST MOUSE
Souris des moissons. *Reithrodontomys megalotis* (Baird)

Description. The western harvest mouse rivals the olive-backed pocket mouse for the title of smallest rodent in Canada. Both are about the size of the larger shrews. This species is a small, slim, long-tailed mouse, slightly over 5 inches in length. It has prominent, naked ears, a slender, sparsely haired tail, grey above and whitish below. It has four toes on the forefeet and five on the hind feet.

The pelage of this species is grey brown above with a dark mid-dorsal stripe from the forehead to the tail. The flanks and cheeks are buffy brown. The underparts and feet are greyish white. The harvest mouse is easily confused with the house mouse, *Mus musculus*. However, the harvest mouse is more buffy, and the longitudinal grooves

Map 69 Distribution of the western harvest mouse, *Reithrodontomys megalotis*: 1 *R. m. dychei*, 2 *R. m. megalotis*

on its upper incisors distinguish it from the house mouse with certainty.

The harvest mouse has three pelages: juvenile, sub-adult, and adult. The juvenile pelage is rather woolly and dull grey. The adult pelage is the brightest. Moulting starts on the ventral surface and spreads over the flanks to meet on the back; then the new fur spreads fore and aft. A second point of origin is on the muzzle, the new coat spreading back to form a moult-line behind the ears. There is one annual moult each summer.

Average measurements of adults: length 133 (120–152), tail 68 (61–78), hind foot 17 (16–18), ear 14 (12–15) mm. Average weight of Californian specimens 11.2 g; northern specimens are slightly lighter.

Habits. The information on the sociability of this species is rather conflicting. It has been described as 'ferocious,' 'cannibalistic,' 'not gentle,' and 'nervous,' and it has been reported that it dislikes being handled. In colonies, harvest mice appear rather sedentary and spend much of their time clustered together. On the other hand, they are remarkably compatible in mixed colonies of house mice and deer mice, *Peromyscus maniculatus*. They often cluster together with these other species and even form integrated social hierarchies in the mixed group.

The harvest mouse is terrestrial in habit and nocturnal in activity. It is active between sunset and sunrise but less so on bright, moonlit nights. The peak in activity is between 7 and 9:30 P.M. Minimum activity occurs between 6 A.M. and noon. It is active the year round.

These mice utilize the hidden trails or runways through the grass built by the field vole, *Microtus pennsylvanicus*, and its relatives. They may have one or more nests situated in their home range. The nests are small balls of grass about the size of a baseball (about three inches in diameter) hidden in a clump of grass or weeds or under a small bush. There is a tiny entrance on the under side, which leads into a golfball-sized chamber, lined with the finest of plant material such as cattail down or dandelion fluff.

Populations in California have reached twelve per acre in good habitat, only to decline to one per acre before the spring breeding season. Harvest mice seem to range over distances of about seventy-five yards. There is a rapid population turnover as none have been known to live a year.

The summer food of this rodent consists of green vegetation: grasses and herbs such as blue grass, fescue, brome grass, oats, vetch, and clover. Small caches of sectioned grass blades and stems may be found in runways occupied by harvest mice. In late summer and winter its diet changes to the seeds of grasses and forbs. No large stores of seeds are apparently gathered. Harvest mice also eat insects such as moths and grasshoppers. The average food consumption has been found to be 1.63 g of oats per day.

A rodent as diminutive as the harvest mouse must be on guard against a host of possible predators. These may include the larger shrews, snakes, larger mice, squirrels, owls, and shrikes, and the lesser carnivores, such as weasels, skunks, and foxes.

Habitat. The western harvest mouse inhabits grassland with scattered clumps of taller forbs and small shrubs. The shrubby borders of lakes, streams, and salt-marshes are also favoured locations.

Reproduction. The breeding season of this species includes most of the year, with the exception of late winter. Towards the northern limits of its range, where the seasons are pronounced, it breeds in late spring and summer. In California, however, it has two peaks in breeding activity: April and May, and September and October.

The female is seasonally polyoestrous, but there is no post-partum oestrus. There are three pairs of mammae: one pectoral and two inguinal. The gestation period is twenty-three to twenty-four days. Several litters are born each year, the average size of which is 2.6, but the number of young varies from one to nine.

The young harvest mice weigh approximately 1.0 to 1.5 g at birth. They are pink, naked, and blind. Their lower incisors appear at four days; the pelage is visible at five days; the eyes open between the tenth and the twelfth day, and they begin to walk at about the same time. They are weaned at nineteen days. They continue to develop rapidly, and mature sexually when slightly over four months old.

Economic Status. In Canada the western harvest mouse is too rare and local in distribution to be of any economic significance.

Distribution. This species occurs widely in the arid regions of western North America, from the central plateau of Mexico northward to the Canadian boundary.

Canadian Distribution. The harvest mouse was first discovered in the Okanagan valley of British Columbia in 1942. Ten years later it was found in southeastern Alberta. The two restricted populations (see Map 69) represent two geographical subspecies.

Reithrodontomys megalotis dychei J.A. Allen, 1895, Bull. American Mus. Nat. Hist. 7: 120. Known only from specimens taken at Medicine Hat and the Milk River, Alberta.

Reithrodontomys megalotis megalotis (Baird), 1858, Mammals, *in* Repts. Expl. Surv. ... Rail. to Pacific 8(1): 451 (Washington). Okanagan Valley, British Columbia, northward as far as Okanagan Landing. It appears that the mouse has only recently reached Okanagan Landing.

REFERENCES

Brant, D.H. 1962. Measures of the movements and population densities of small rodents. Univ. California Pub. Zool. 62(2): 105–84.
Smith, C.F. 1936. Notes on the habits of the long-tailed harvest mouse. Jour. Mamm. 17: 274–8.

DEER MOUSE
Souris sylvestre. *Peromyscus maniculatus* (Wagner)

Description. The deer mouse derives its name from its bi-coloured coat, rufous above and white below, which resembles the coat of a deer. This is the ubiquitous native mouse. Away from city centres it may be found practically everywhere in Canada from Nova Scotia to Vancouver Island and from the international boundary north to Yukon Territory and Hudson Bay. Because of its diminutive size and nocturnal habits, one may not be aware of its presence; yet wherever one walks in its domain, whether striding across the open prairie or scuffling through the leaves of the forest carpet, one passes, unseeingly, the hidden crouched forms of deer mice. To many, the deer mouse may be only a repulsive vermin to be crushed under heel, but its bright inquisitive face with its shining beady-black eyes, twitching vibrissae, and alert ears, coupled with its light, quick movements and trusting manner, make it an interesting, lively companion in many a lonely cabin.

The form of the deer mouse is typically murine, with a slender body, well-developed hind legs, and a moderately long tail. The length of the tail is quite variable in this species. In some subspecies the tail may be only about half the body length, but in others it may be longer than the body. Those with the longer tails are usually semi-arboreal and use the tail as a semi-prehensile organ to brace against twigs, or as a balance. The subspecies with

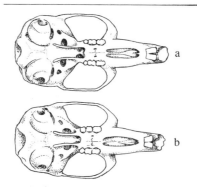

Figure 41 Comparison of skulls of (a) deer mouse, *Peromyscus maniculatus*, and (b) white-footed mouse, *Peromyscus leucopus* ($\times 1\frac{1}{2}$)

the shorter tails usually live on plains or in fields, and seldom climb. The deer mouse has a moderately long nose, very long vibrissae, and large membranous ears. The pollex is vestigial, but the hallux is well formed. The digits are slender, and the claws are delicate. There are internal buccal pouches for food storage (Plate 15j).

The deer mouse's skull is light and delicate. The rostrum is long and slender; the cranium is rounded. The anterior incisive foramina are long and rectangular (Figure 41). The lateral maxillary prominences are reduced, and in lateral aspect the infraorbital foramen is hidden by the zygomatic plate.

The pelage of this species is soft and dense. The undercoat is lead-coloured at the base and tipped with brown on the back and with white on the underparts. The colour above is extremely variable, from greyish to rufous brown. The longer dark-tipped guard hairs of the dorsum usually form a dark brown mid-dorsal stripe. The sides are greyish or rufous and are sharply divided from the white flanks and underparts. The tail, which is well-haired with a terminal 'pencil' of hairs, is sharply bi-coloured, blackish above and white below. The feet and heels are covered with fine white hairs. The cheeks are rufous. The ears are covered with fine grey hairs. There is usually a tuft of whitish hairs at the anterior base of each ear. The upper lips are white; the eyelids are black. The pelage of the throat is white-tipped, but when it is parted the lead-coloured base is plainly evident.

This species has three coats during its lifetime. The juvenile coat is dark lead grey above and white below. The subadult coat is more brownish. The rufous tones appear in the adult coat, as described. During each moult, the new coat appears first along the flanks as a brighter band and then over the back. There is one annual moult in the autumn when a longer, denser, and glossier coat is grown. There seem to be other vague coat changes in later winter, after which the coat often assumes more rufous tones. Both melanistic and albino specimens are occasionally observed.

The deer mouse is so variable in size that average measurements are meaningless. The larger subspecies are about twice the size of the smaller. The total length varies from 121 to 222, the tail from 46 to 123, the hind foot from 17 to 25, and the ear from 12 to 20 mm; the weight varies from 12 to 30 g.

Habits. The deer mouse is a sociable little creature. During most of the year, individuals are highly tolerant, regardless of age and sex, and particularly during the winter months, when groups of up to thirteen mice may huddle together to conserve heat. These winter aggregations usually consist of family units and unrelated mice, but they may also include other species such as the white-footed mouse, the harvest mouse, or jumping mice. The female expels the male from the nest shortly before the birth of the young but accepts him a little later. He usually assists in raising the young mice by washing them, maintaining the nest, and later taking them on foraging excursions.

Although this species is generally more placid and gentle than the white-footed mouse, there is considerable variation among the various subspecies. The semi-arboreal *gracilis* is placid and deliberate in its actions while the terrestrial *bairdii* is tenser and more apt to 'freeze' under stress. Easily tamed, deer mice soon cease to bite when handled. They make engaging pets with their bright inquisitive ways and are easy to accommodate.

Deer mice climb well, walk deliberately, or hop on all four feet, leaving four tiny footprints in the snow and an occasional tail side-swipe. Mainly nocturnal, they are seldom active during daylight hours. When alarmed they drum with the forepaws on some resonant object. If a watcher sits patiently in the forest at dusk, he is usually rewarded by seeing a deer mouse scamper across the leaves, along a log, or perhaps about the trunk of a tree. Deer mice may use tiny beaten paths under logs in the forest or runways through the prairie grass. The grassland forms usually nest in short burrows, often those constructed by other species. The nests are spheres of grass about four inches in diameter, containing a cavity lined with dandelion or thistle down, or some other fine material. Often bits of odd material such as bone, fur, cloth, or paper may be worked into the nest. The nests are hidden in a wide variety of locations: in a clump of grass, in the abandoned den of a larger mammal, under a board, log, stump, or stone, in a natural cavity of a tree, stump, or log, or in a tin can.

Deer mice are active all winter, and the tracery of their tracks may be seen on newly fallen snow. In the autumn months, September to November, they are busy building up a store of seeds for the winter. Packed in their cheek pouches, the seeds are carried great distances to the cache in a chamber near the nest. The seeds are carefully segregated into species and the total volume of the cache may total three quarts. Seeds eaten include those of ragweed, panic grass, sorrel, tick trefoil, apple, cherry, Douglas fir, and oak acorns. These caches are usually completely used up by the following March.

Deer mice are usually sedentary, and the average home ranges have been calculated to be 2.31 acres for adult males and 1.39 acres for adult females. Individuals, however, occasionally travel more widely, perhaps up to a thousand yards. They also exhibit a remarkable homing instinct; one returned to its home after being transplanted over two miles. Usually, once a home has been established and young have been produced, the adult spends the rest of its life in that area. There is little evidence of territorial defence. The home ranges of individuals often broadly overlap. Only the female with young defends the vicinity of the nest. Even that territoriality may be relaxed, and communal broods with two females in attendance have been observed.

Deer mouse populations show regular annual fluctuations from a minimum in spring to a maximum in late autumn. The normal fluctuation is of the order of one to twenty-two mice to two acres. Occasionally, under favourable conditions of food supply, the population may

165

be larger. At such times they may overflow from their normal habitat to less desirable locations, where the overflow mice are at a considerable disadvantage and usually succumb. The populations of this species, however, do not show the spectacular explosions so typical of the meadow vole and its relatives.

These small herbivores resemble the shrews in their rapid population turnover. Few mice survive from one year to the next. In natural populations, individually tagged specimens have been known to live as long as thirty-two months, but in the laboratory individuals have lived as long as eight years, four months.

The deer mouse is primarily a seed-eater. During the summer it eats the seeds of a wide variety of grasses and forbs, and such fruit as strawberries, raspberries, cranberries, cherries, wild apple, and the fruit of hawthorns, as well as mushrooms. It climbs into trees and shrubs to eat buds. In spring, deer mice eat maple and elm samaras. It also eats the tender buds and swelling leaves of shrubs and trees. Besides this vegetable diet, deer mice are very fond of insects, eggs, larvae, cutworms, caterpillars, and spiders.

This small herbivore is an important link in many food chains between vegetation and the carnivores. It is preyed upon by such diverse creatures as snakes, large fish, short-tailed shrews, ground squirrels, tree squirrels, weasels, skunks, mink, raccoons, bears, foxes, coyotes, and wolves. Probably owls, weasels, and foxes are its most important predators. The red fox often catches several mice at a time and caches their bodies in a snowbank during the winter for later consumption. Since deer mice are active at night, the day hunters, such as hawks, seldom catch them, but they are the mainstay of the diet of most owls, from the saw-whet to the great horned. During the winter months when the deer mice scramble about over the snow, they become much more vulnerable to owl predation than the field vole, which continues to travel along its runways under the blanket of snow.

Habitat. Few other mammals exhibit such a broad tolerance for different habitats as does the deer mouse. It may be found from the arid short-grass steppes to the deep, dark coniferous forests. One factor alone seems to remain constant: the habitat must be dry. Deer mice seldom occur in low, wet habitats. There are sharp differences, however, in the habitats selected by the various races: *gracilis* is found in the cool northern hardwood forest association of hemlock, white pine, yellow birch, and hard maples, while *bairdii* occurs on sandy beaches and in meadowlands and cultivated fields. The two races, which may be found in contiguous areas with minimal overlaps, are good examples of ecological isolation.

Reproduction. The deer mouse is an ideal laboratory animal and has therefore provided investigators with significant information on its life cycle and breeding potential. Females are seasonally polyoestrous. The vulva is sealed in the winter anoestrous period but becomes perforated with the onset of oestrus in March. There are numerous oestrous cycles between then and October, when the breeding season usually ceases (unless there is

166

an unusual food supply such as unharvested grain in the fields). The females also exhibit a post-partum oestrus shortly after the birth of their young. The gestation period varies from twenty-two to thirty-five days. The first litter is carried for twenty-two to twenty-seven days. Lactation delays later conceptions, which may last between twenty-two and thirty-five days. If the females are nursing the first litter, implantation of the early embryos may be delayed. The litters are usually born between the end of April and early October. There are peaks of production in the spring and autumn and a lull in the summer. The average litter size is 4.04, but the number of young may vary from one to nine. The largest litters, which occur at the height of the breeding season, are born to adult females. There may be as many as four to eight litters in a year under ideal laboratory conditions, but probably the lower number is near the maximum in the wild state.

The male deer mouse shows seasonal changes in the genital organs. The testes of fecund males descend to the scrotum in late March and measure about 8 mm in length. They are much smaller and abdominal in position in the non-breeding period from late October onwards.

The deer mouse has a tremendous breeding potential. Theoretically, four generations could be produced in one year, and if maximum litters survived, the offspring of one pair could number 10,000 in a year. Of course this does not occur in nature, but it does indicate the dimensions of the excess population available to support the carnivores.

At birth the young mice have wrinkled, bright pink, transparent skins and weigh approximately 1.72 (1.1–2.3) g. The vibrissae are about 3 mm long. The eyes are closed, the ear pinnae are folded over the orifices, and the toes are not completely divided. Dark pigment appears dorsally after the second day, and the juvenile hair starts to grow. The pinnae unfold on the third day. The eyes open between the twelfth and seventeenth days. The youngsters are weaned between twenty-two and thirty-seven days (the same as the gestation period). Before the arrival of the second litter, the female drives off the youngsters, and these may take up new quarters near by with the father.

If the female deer mouse is disturbed with her young in the nest, she may flee with her brood clinging to teats; or if she has more time, she will carry them singly in her mouth to a new hide-out.

The young juvenile females may mature sexually at as early an age as thirty-two to thirty-five days. The males mature a little later at the age of forty to forty-five days. The juveniles scatter just before sexual maturity, but there seems to be a high degree of natural inbreeding in the species, particularly if one of the adult pair is lost.

Economic Status. In the animal community the deer mouse performs an important role in providing a staple food supply for the small carnivores such as the fur-bearers.

Unfortunately this mouse is also somewhat of a menace in natural forest regeneration and reforestation practice because of its destruction of tree seeds, especially of conifers. Deer mice have been estimated to consume between two and three hundred Douglas fir seeds daily. Field

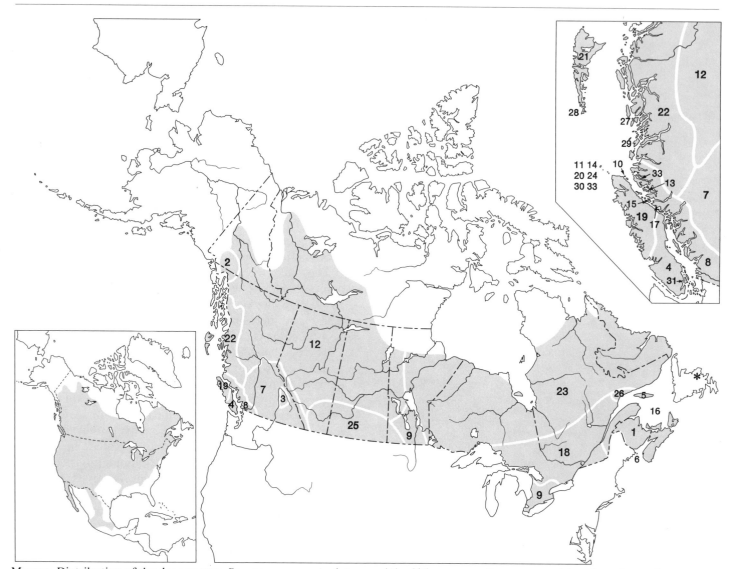

Map 70 Distribution of the deer mouse, *Peromyscus maniculatus*, and the Sitka mouse, *Peromyscus sitkensis*: 1 *P. m. abietorum*, 2 *P. m. algidus*, 3 *P. m. alpinus*, 4 *P. m. angustus*, 5 *P. m. anticostiensis*, 6 *P. m. argentatus*, 7 *P. m. artemisiae*, 8 *P. m. austerus*, 9 *P. m. bairdii*, 10 *P. m. balaclavae*, 11 *P. m. beresfordi*, 12 *P. m. borealis*, 13 *P. m. cancrivorus*, 14 *P. m. carli*, 15 *P. m. doylei*, 16 *P. m. eremus*, 17 *P. m. georgiensis*, 18 *P. m. gracilis*, 19 *P. m. interdictus*, 20 *P. m. isolatus*, 21 *P. m. keeni*, 22 *P. m. macrorhinus*, 23 *P. m. maniculatus*, 24 *P. m. maritimus*, 25 *P. m. osgoodi*, 26 *P. m. plumbeus*, 27 *P. m. pluvialis*, 28 *P. sitkensis prevostensis*, 29 *P. m. rubiventer*, 30 *P. m. sartinensis*, 31 *P. m. saturatus*, 32 *P. m. saxamans*, 33 *P. m. triangularis*, * introduced

studies have similarly shown that they were the chief agents (along with western chipmunks) in destroying 92 per cent of the seed of ponderosa pine sown at the rate of 75,400 seeds per acre. Some hope for controlling such damage by mice is offered by the practice of pelleting seeds, which consists of coating them with an inactive adhesive agent such as feldspar or china clay to which has been added fertilizers, fungicides, insecticides, or rodent repellents, and then pelleting them by a machine similar to the ones which make medicinal pills.

On the credit side, one must mention the deer mouse's predilection for insects, including such injurious forest insects as the larch sawfly pupae. Studies have shown that the deer mouse makes a significant contribution to the control of this insect.

This is the only native mouse that regularly enters

houses and sheds. It often enters cottages and homes in the country, particularly in the autumn. Here it raids larders for stored grain, vegetables, or meat. It also attacks mattresses, trunks, and drawers of linen or clothing – shredding the material for its nest. Deer mice in such situations are easily controlled by the distribution of poisoned grain or mouse traps, but it is also good practice to hang mattresses over wire lines when leaving a cabin or cottage.

Distribution. The deer mouse occurs from the Mexican plateau northwards to the vicinity of the treeline in Labrador, Hudson Bay, and Yukon Territory. In Canada its distribution stretches from Nova Scotia to the Queen Charlotte Islands, British Columbia. It is notably absent only in Newfoundland and in the arctic zone beyond the treeline.

Canadian Distribution. The deer mouse is a highly plastic species, occupying many ecological niches. It is divided into a large number of geographical forms that differ in size, colour, and relative length of appendages. Thirty-two subspecies have been described in Canada (see Map 70); many of these are restricted to islands.

Peromyscus maniculatus abietorum Bangs, 1896, Proc. Biol. Soc. Washington 10: 49. A rather grey, long-tailed race found in the Maritime Provinces, westward to the St Lawrence River.

Peromyscus maniculatus algidus Osgood, 1909, N. American Fauna 28: 56. Another grey, long-tailed race, found in southwestern Yukon Territory and the northwestern corner of British Columbia.

Peromyscus maniculatus alpinus Cowan, 1937, Proc. Biol. Soc. Washington 50: 215. A large dark race from the northern Selkirk Mountains, south of the big bend in the Columbia River, British Columbia.

Peromyscus maniculatus angustus Hall, 1932, Univ. California Pub. Zool. 38: 423. Southern and eastern coast of Vancouver Island, British Columbia.

Peromyscus maniculatus anticostiensis Moulthrop, 1937, Sci. Pub. Cleveland Mus. Nat. Hist. 5(3): 11. A dark race with pronounced dorsal stripe, restricted to Anticosti Island, Quebec.

Peromyscus maniculatus argentatus Copeland and Church, 1906, Proc. Biol. Soc. Washington 19: 122. A shorter-tailed form found on Grand Manan Island, New Brunswick.

Peromyscus maniculatus artemisiae (Rhoads), 1894, Proc. Acad. Nat. Sci. Philadelphia 46: 260. A medium-sized race with pale coloration, found in southeastern British Columbia and southwestern Alberta.

Peromyscus maniculatus austerus (Baird), 1855, Proc. Acad. Nat. Sci. Philadelphia 7: 336. A medium-sized dark race, inhabiting the British Columbia coast south of Kingcome Inlet.

Peromyscus maniculatus bairdii (Hoy and Kennicott), 1857, *in* Kennicott, Agricultural Rept., United States Comm. Patents, 1856, p. 92. A small, grey short-tailed subspecies inhabiting fields, plains, and beaches in southern Manitoba and southern Ontario. This race invaded southwestern Ontario prior to 1907 and rapidly spread northeastwards along the shores of lakes Erie and Ontario, reaching London in 1912 and Toronto in 1924. More recently it has spread eastwards to Orono in Durham County, and northwards to Port Elgin in Bruce County.

Peromyscus maniculatus balaclavae McCabe and Cowan, 1945, Trans. Royal Canadian Inst. 25: 197. Balaclava and Hope islands, north of Vancouver Island, British Columbia.

Peromyscus maniculatus beresfordi Guiguet, 1955, Ann. Rept. British Columbia Prov. Mus. 1954: B71. A very large race, found on Beresford Island, north of Vancouver Island, British Columbia.

Peromyscus maniculatus borealis Mearns, 1911, Proc. Biol. Soc. Washington 24: 102. An average-sized buffy race with short, strongly bi-coloured tail, found over an immense area of Yukon and Northwest Territories and the northern parts of British Columbia, Alberta, Saskatchewan, and Manitoba.

Peromyscus maniculatus cancrivorus McCabe and Cowan, 1945, Trans. Royal Canadian Inst. 25: 195. A pale ochraceous form found on Table Island, off the coast of British Columbia.

Peromyscus maniculatus carli Guiguet, 1955, Ann. Rept. British Columbia Prov. Mus. 1954: B72. Occurs on Lanz and Cox islands, off the north end of Vancouver Island, British Columbia.

Peromyscus maniculatus doylei McCabe and Cowan, 1945, Trans. Royal Canadian Inst. 25: 197. Confined to Doyle Island, between Vancouver Island and the mainland of British Columbia.

Peromyscus maniculatus eremus Osgood, 1909, N. American Fauna 28: 47. A dark form with medium-length tail, found on Grindstone Island, Magdalen Islands, Quebec.

Peromyscus maniculatus georgiensis Hall, 1938, American Nat. 72: 453. Occurs on Savary, Texada, Lasqueti, Thormanby, and Bowen islands in Georgia Strait, British Columbia.

Peromyscus maniculatus gracilis (LeConte), 1855, Proc. Acad. Nat. Sci. Philadelphia 7: 422. A medium-sized mouse of average colour, widely distributed in central Ontario and western Quebec.

Peromyscus maniculatus interdictus Anderson, 1932, Nat. Mus. Canada Bull. 70: 110. A dark, long-tailed race found on the northern half of Vancouver Island, British Columbia.

Peromyscus maniculatus isolatus Cowan, 1935, Univ. California Pub. Zool. 40: 434. A large, dark, long-tailed race restricted to Pine Island off the northern tip of Vancouver Island, British Columbia.

Peromyscus maniculatus keeni (Rhoads), 1894. Proc. Acad. Nat. Sci. Philadelphia 46: 258. An average-sized, greyish race found on the larger islands of the Queen Charlotte group including Graham, Moresby, Louise, and Lyell, but not Kunghit Island.

Peromyscus maniculatus macrorhinus (Rhoads), 1894, Proc. Acad. Nat. Sci. Philadelphia 46: 259. A large, dark race inhabiting the coast of British Columbia north of Rivers Inlet.

Peromyscus maniculatus maniculatus (Wagner), 1845, Arch. Naturgesch. Jahrg. 1: 148. A smoky-coloured race found in northeastern Canada from Labrador to northern Manitoba.

Peromyscus maniculatus maritimus McCabe and Cowan, 1945, Trans. Royal Canadian Inst. 25: 199. Known only from the largest of the Moore Islands, in Hecate Strait, British Columbia.

Peromyscus maniculatus osgoodi Mearns, 1890, Bull. American Mus. Nat. Hist. 2: 285. A pale, short-tailed form found on the southern arid plains of Alberta and Saskatchewan.

Peromyscus maniculatus plumbeus C.F. Jackson, 1939, Proc. Biol. Soc. Washington 52: 101. A dark form with greyish underparts found on the north shore of the Gulf of St Lawrence from Pigou River to the Bay of Seven Isles.

Peromyscus maniculatus pluvialis McCabe and Cowan, 1945, Trans. Royal Canadian Inst. 25: 199. A large reddish form from the Goose Islands off the coast of British Columbia.

Peromyscus maniculatus rubiventer McCabe and Cowan, 1945, Trans. Royal Canadian Inst. 25: 196. A large, dark race with the underparts streaked with rufous, found on the coastal islands off Bella Coola, British Columbia.

Peromyscus maniculatus sartinensis Guiguet, 1955, Ann. Rept. British Columbia Prov. Mus. 1954: B69. A large race found only on Sartine Island off the north tip of Vancouver Island, British Columbia.

Peromyscus maniculatus saturatus Bangs, 1897, American Nat. 31: 75. A richly coloured form found on Saturna Island, Strait of Georgia, British Columbia.

Peromyscus maniculatus saxamans McCabe and Cowan, 1945, Trans. Royal Canadian Inst. 25: 198. Found on Duncan, Heard, Hurst, and Bell islands, between the northern end of Vancouver Island and mainland British Columbia.

Peromyscus maniculatus triangularis Guiguet, 1955, Ann. Rept. British Columbia Prov. Mus. 1954: B69. A large race with white blaze on the forehead, grey underparts, white only in inguinal region; found only on Triangle Island in Queen Charlotte Sound, British Columbia.

REFERENCES

Criddle, Stuart. 1950. The *Peromyscus maniculatus bairdii* complex in Manitoba. Canadian Field-Nat. 64(5): 169–77.

Howard, W.E. 1949. Dispersal, amount of inbreeding and longevity in a local population of prairie deer mice on the George Reserve, southern Michigan. Contrib. Lab. Vert. Biol. Univ. Michigan 43.

King, J.A. (ed.). 1968. Biology of *Peromyscus* (Rodentia). The American Soc. Mamm. Spec. Pub. 2.

CASCADE DEER MOUSE
Souris des Cascades. *Peromyscus oreas* Bangs

Description. The deer mice of the Cascade Mountains of the Pacific coast have only recently been recognized as a distinct species. It appears likely that this species survived the last Vashon Glaciation about 12,000 to 30,000 years ago in relative isolation in southern Washington State. There it developed certain reproductive and ecological barriers, which have prevented assimilation with the more widespread *Peromyscus maniculatus* when the two species subsequently expanded their ranges.

It is a large, pale grey deer mouse, characterized by a long tail and large hind feet. Its skull is relatively long and narrow, compared to near-by races of *Peromyscus maniculatus*.

Average measurements of adults: length 204 (194–211), tail 109 (101–117), hind foot 23 (22–24) mm.

Habits. The life history of this species is probably very similar to that of the deer mouse. It appears to be more active and nervous than the deer mouse and frequently performs an 'escape jump.'

Habitat. The Cascade deer mouse prefers the deep, damp, subalpine forest of Engelmann spruce and lodgepole pine. It inhabits dense ground vegetation. Though occasionally found at sea level, it is more common at higher elevations.

Reproduction. The breeding period is restricted from April to the end of July. The litters appear to be a little larger than those of *Peromyscus maniculatus*, the average number of embryos observed being 6.1.

Economic Status. Unknown.

Distribution. This species is found only in the Cascade Mountains of Washington State and the southern Coast Range of British Columbia. It occurs sympatrically with certain races of *Peromyscus maniculatus* in narrow ecological belts on the boundary of its range without general intergradation. Only occasionally are local hybrids produced.

Canadian Distribution. This species is found on both flanks of the Coast Range from the international boundary north to Rivers Inlet. It is absent from the lower Fraser valley and canyon (see Map 71).

Peromyscus oreas Bangs, 1808, Proc. Biol. Soc. Washington 12: 84. British Columbia.

REFERENCE

Sheppe, Walter. 1961. Systematic and ecological relations of *Peromyscus oreas* and *P. maniculatus*. Proc. American Phil. Soc. 105(4): 421–46.

SITKA MOUSE
Souris de Sitka. *Peromyscus sitkensis* Merriam

Description. The Sitka mouse is a large, dusky deer mouse, with large ears and a bi-coloured tail as long as the body. It has brown sides, a broad, dusky, dorsal stripe, and a brown face with dusky orbital ring and spot at the base of the vibrissae. The ears are greyish and narrowly edged with white. The legs are brownish to the wrist and ankle, then greyish on the feet. The underparts are greyish white, occasionally streaked with chestnut patches. Black, melanistic individuals are very common in some populations.

The skull is large and heavy: the rostrum is long. Two elongate, slit-like posterior palatine foramina distinguish this species from the deer mouse.

Average measurements of adults: total length 219 (205–229), tail 104 (96–113), hind foot 26 (24–27), ear from notch (dry) 16 (14–16) mm; weight 41 (34–46) g.

Habits. Little is known of the life history of this species, but it is undoubtedly similar to that of the deer mouse. They are chiefly nocturnal and remain active all year.

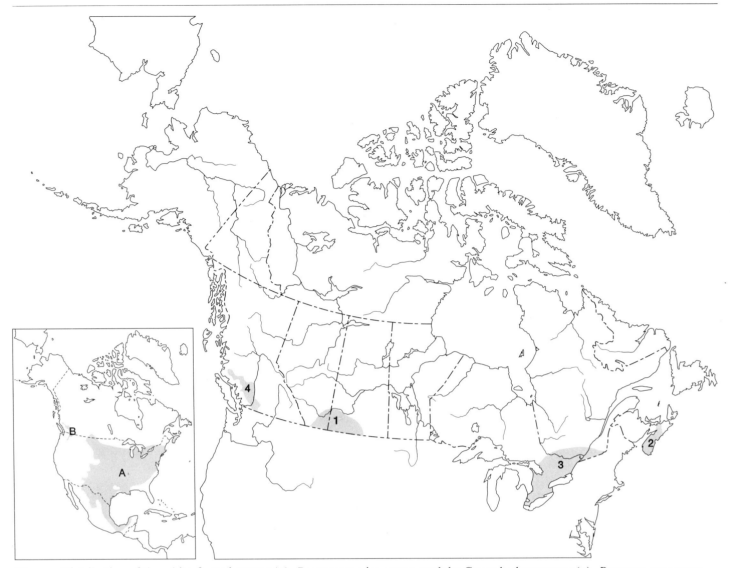

Map 71 Distribution of the white-footed mouse (A), *Peromyscus leucopus*, and the Cascade deer mouse (B), *Peromyscus oreas*:
1 *P. l. aridulus*, 2 *P. l. caudatus*, 3 *P. l. noveboracensis*, 4 *Peromyscus oreas*

They are found under logs on the beach and must prey upon small mollusks and Crustacea along with their diet of berries and seeds of coniferous trees.

Habitat. This species inhabits the edge of the dense, moss-hung Sitka spruce–western cedar forests of the coastal islands, where it lives among the rotting logs, stumps, and rock crevices.

Reproduction. The breeding and development of young is probably similar to that of the deer mouse.

Economic Status. The Sitka mouse is too rare and local in distribution in Canada to be of any economic significance.

Distribution. The Sitka mouse has a peculiar peripheral distribution on several outer islands off the southern coast of Alaska and in the Queen Charlotte Islands group of British Columbia.

Canadian Distribution. In Canada it occurs on Frederick, Hippa, Gordon, Anthony, Hotspring, and Ramsay islands. It was originally discovered on Kunghit Island,

but since the introduction of roof rats, *Rattus rattus*, to the whaling station at Rose Harbour, the native Sitka mice seem to have disappeared.

Sitka mice probably reached the many outer islands which they occupy upon natural rafts of tangled tree trunks carrying sections of the forest floor entangled in their roots. Numerous scars along the precipitous coasts show where landslides have frequently carried small sections of the forest into the sea. The peripheral distribution of the Sitka mouse on the outer islands of the Queen Charlotte group, while the larger islands – Graham and Moresby – are occupied by the deer mouse *P. m. keeni*, also strongly suggests that the larger species is less competitive than the deer mouse and has been supplanted on the larger islands by the deer mouse. The two species never occur together and the Sitka mouse is now found only on the smaller outer islands, probably the ones not yet reached by the deer mouse. The subspecies found in Canada is (see Map 70):

Peromyscus sitkensis prevostensis Osgood, 1901, N. American Fauna 21: 29. Outer Queen Charlotte Islands, British Columbia.

Thomas (1973) also considers the subspecies *carli, doylei, isolatus*, and *triangularis* from islands north of Vancouver Island, previously assigned to *P. maniculatus*, to be subspecies of *P. sitkensis*.

REFERENCES

Cowan, I. McT. 1935. A distributional study of the *Peromyscus sitkensis* group of white-footed mice. Univ. California Pub. Zool. 40(13): 429–38.
Thomas, Barry. 1973. Evolutionary implications of karyotypic variation in some insular *Peromyscus* from British Columbia, Canada. Cytologica 38: 485–95.

WHITE-FOOTED MOUSE
Souris à pattes blanches. *Peromyscus leucopus*
(Rafinesque)

Description. The white-footed mouse resembles the deer mouse very closely. It may occur in the same locality, but in different habitats, and it may require the attention of a specialist to distinguish the two species. In spite of their close resemblance, study has shown that they have many behavioural differences, and that no hybrids are produced even in laboratory experiments. The white-footed mouse is more southern in distribution and reaches Canada in only three isolated areas.

The form is typically murine: a pointed nose, long vibrissae, large luminous eyes, large parchment-like ears, delicate feet, and a slim tail which is as long as the body. The general colour on the head and back is cinnamon brown with a dark dorsal stripe caused by the strong mixture of black-tipped hairs. The underparts and feet are clear white. The greyish base of the ventral fur may be seen when the belly fur is parted, but the hair of the throat is clear white to the skin. There is a black spot at the base of the vibrissae and black eyelids. The practically naked grey ears are outlined faintly by a white rim, but the preorbital tuft of white hair, so characteristic of *maniculatus*, is lacking. The tail also offers some distinguishing marks: in *leucopus* it is much more thinly haired and less contrastingly bi-coloured, being brownish above and cream-coloured below (Plate 17).

The skull of *leucopus* is shorter and broader, with a shorter rostrum that carries prominent lateral bumps. The anterior incisive foramina are shorter with more bowed lateral margins than those of *maniculatus*. The infraorbital canal entrance appears ahead of the zygomatic plate in lateral aspect more clearly than in the deer mouse (Figure 41).

The white-footed mouse also has three distinct pelages during its lifetime. The first juvenile pelage, which is slate grey above and white below, is worn until the mouse is about forty days old; then it assumes a brownish subadult pelage. The new coat first appears as a patch or narrow line on the flank, just above the edge of the white underparts and in front of the hind legs. The line of rufous new fur spreads forwards to the shoulders and gradually broadens over the back. The last parts to moult are the forehead and the base of the tail. The whole process takes about three and a half weeks. The final adult pelage, characterized by a rich, glossy cinnamon brown coat, is assumed at the autumn moult in October.

Average measurements of adults: 170 (157–189), tail 76 (60–92), hind foot 21 (18–23), ear 17 (15–19) mm; weight 16–28 g.

Habits. The white-footed mouse is more excitable and more difficult to handle than the deer mouse. It does not seem to be quite as sociable as the other species. During the breeding season females are very antagonistic towards other females and defend territories about their nests. The males appear to be a little more tolerant and are frequently found in the company of other mice. During the winter months, white-footed mice form aggregations of family groups and other acceptable individuals, which huddle together to conserve body heat. The huddle has a social structure in that the dominant mouse is usually in the middle, and the less aggressive ones are on the outside. These winter aggregations forage over a group territory and attack interlopers to their areas. In March, at the commencement of the breeding season, these aggregations break up and the mice pair off. Considerable inbreeding seems to take place within families. White-footed mice are active only from sunset to sunrise during most of the year, when they scamper over the forest floor or climb about stumps and low bushes.

They construct nests composed of balls of shredded grass, about seven inches in diameter, which are placed in a variety of places: under logs, stumps, and brush piles, or in deserted squirrels' nests, birds' nests, or hollow trees. Since the mice are not particularly sanitary, new nests are frequently required. When white-footed mice enter cottages, which they frequently do, their nests may be found in the most embarrassing places, such as in mattresses, pillows, drawers, boxes, and shoes. On one occasion a white-footed mouse built a nest and bore a litter of young in a rubber boot between 7 P.M., when the owner took it off, and 10 P.M., when he picked it up to put it on again.

White-footed mice are quite sedentary. Once they have established a home, they remain in the area for the rest of their lives. It is the young animals that disperse to colonize new territory. They have a well-developed homing instinct, however, and individuals transported away from their home ranges have returned distances of up to one mile. Preliminary studies indicate that these mice occupy minimum home ranges of approximately a quarter (0.27) of an acre. The populations show a regular annual fluctuation from a spring low to an autumn high as a result of the addition of the year's offspring. Populations may vary from between 1.8 to 12.0 mice per acre, depending upon the season and the habitat. Aside from the annual fluctuations in population, there are long-term fluctuations depending upon local weather conditions and mast yield.

White-footed mice populations are, however, not usually considered as exhibiting any regular 'cycles' as do the populations of voles and lemmings.

There is virtually a complete annual turnover of these mice. The average life-span of white-footed mice that reached the age of five weeks has been found to be only 17.4 weeks. The oldest mouse in a 'field live-trapping and tagging' program lived twenty-two months.

The white-footed mouse is primarily a seed-eater. It lives on a wide variety of seeds, fleshy fruits, and nuts in season, starting with maple samaras in spring and ending with oak acorns and hickory nuts in the autumn. During the summer months it also consumes insects and other invertebrates. In the autumn it stores seeds and nuts, carrying its booty in bulging cheek-pouches to caches under logs or in hollow trees, which may contain as much as two quarts of peeled acorns, beechnuts, or weed seeds. During the winter months it augments its supplies by hunting for weed seeds, conifer cones, and winter buds.

It is unlikely that any white-footed mouse lives long enough to die of old age. Rather, its short life probably comes to a quick close as an item of food for one of the many carnivores that share its habitat. Large snakes such as the fox and milk snake are 'mousers,' and the humble white-footed mouse is a mainstay in the diets of many owls and small carnivores such as weasels, mink, foxes, skunks, and raccoons.

Habitat. The white-footed mouse is a typical inhabitant of the dry eastern deciduous hardwood forest. It prefers stands of oak–hickory–basswood, where it finds shelter in the abundance of fallen logs, stumps, shrubs, and debris. It also occupies brushy fence-rows but seldom ventures into open fields and pastures.

In the Prairie Provinces this mouse occurs locally in the shrubby river valleys that cut through the arid short-grass plains.

Reproduction. To hold its own in nature a small mammal with such a short life-span must be prolific, and for this the white-footed mouse is well equipped. The females are seasonally polyoestrous. Mating starts about mid-March, and by the first of April almost all the females are pregnant. The gestation period is normally about twenty-two to twenty-five days. After parturition there is a post-partum oestrus, and mating occurs again. The implantation of the second set of embryos is, however, usually delayed during the lactation period. The second gestation period may last as long as thirty-seven days. The earliest litters are born in early April, and the second litters are weaned about the end of June or early July. This period of breeding activity is followed by a summer lull until late August, when mating begins again. Usually two more litters are born before breeding is completed in early October.

In the laboratory there may be as many as ten litters in a year, but in the field the normal number is probably four. The litter size is on the average about 4.1, but may vary between one and nine. Even though the female has only six teats she may raise seven young successfully. Experimental pairs of animals have raised up to forty-five young per season in the laboratory.

The males show a similar annual sexual cycle. The testes enlarge and descend to the scrotum in early March, where they remain until the close of the breeding season, about the beginning of October, when they are withdrawn into the abdominal cavity. The male takes part in bringing up the youngsters after they have been weaned, and they accompany him on foraging trips.

Young white-footed mice are similar in appearance and development to the closely related deer mice. They weigh about 1.87 (1.4–2.4) g at birth. The ear pinnae unfold on the third day, and the eyes open between the tenth and fifteenth day. The young are usually weaned at about three weeks of age, but should no second litter arrive, they may continue to nurse up to the age of thirty-seven days. The female may often abandon her young in the nest at this time and build a new nest to receive the next litter.

Young females mature sexually at the age of seven or eight weeks. The juveniles born in the spring bear young during the following autumn, but those born in the autumn wait until the following spring to breed.

Economic Status. Because of its more southern distribution, the white-footed mouse is less of a menace to forestry practice than the deer mouse is. It is still a nuisance, however, about granaries and storehouses on farms and in cottages. The same control methods mentioned for the deer mouse may be applied to the white-footed mouse.

Distribution. This mouse is found in eastern North America from the Gulf of Mexico northward to southern Nova Scotia, and from the Great Lakes region westward to the southern border of Saskatchewan and Alberta.

Canadian Distribution. This species is found in three isolated areas in Canada. Each population is a distinctive subspecies. Two of the areas are contiguous with the main distributional area in the United States, but the population in the southern part of Nova Scotia is completely separated by sea from the closest range in southern Maine (see Map 71).

Peromyscus leucopus aridulus Osgood, 1909, N. American Fauna 28: 122. Short-grass plains of southwestern Saskatchewan and southeastern Alberta. A pale form found in river valleys.

Peromyscus leucopus caudatus Smith, 1939, Proc. Biol. Soc. Washington 52: 157. An isolated population in southern Nova Scotia.

Peromyscus leucopus noveboracensis (Fischer), 1829, Synopsis mammalium, p. 318. Southern Quebec and Ontario.

REFERENCES

Burt, Wm. H. 1940. Territorial behavior and populations of some small mammals in southern Michigan. Mus. Zool. Univ. Michigan Misc. Pub. 45: 16–42.

Nicholson, Arnold. 1941. The homes and social habits of the wood mice (*Peromyscus leucopus noveboracensis*) in southern Michigan. American Midl. Nat. 25: 196–223.

Snyder, Dana P. 1956. Survival rates, longevity and population fluctuations in the white-footed mouse, *Peromyscus leucopus*, in southern Michigan. Mus. Zool. Univ. Michigan Misc. Pub. 95.

NORTHERN GRASSHOPPER MOUSE
Souris à sauterelles. *Onychomys leucogaster*
(Wied-Neuwied)

Description. Maximilian, Prince of Wied-Neuwied, discovered this mouse in the Mandan Indian village along the Missouri River in 1833. He reported that this species entered the villages in winter and ate the stored grain. The grasshopper mouse resembles the deer mouse in a general way, but the body is stouter, the legs are shorter, and it has a peculiar short, fleshy, tapering tail. The ears are smaller, and are more pointed and more heavily furred. The forefeet are slightly larger and have longer claws. Occasionally one notices a pungent body odour. The stomach has a specialized brown glandular swelling midway along the greater curvature (Plate 15 m).

The skull resembles the skulls of *Peromyscus* but is more sturdily built; the rostrum is short and the cranium is broad. The mandibles are similarly more sturdily constructed. There are no cheek pouches.

The adult pelage is dense, long, and fine but tends to be slightly oily and ruffled. The upper parts are brownish tawny on the flanks and greyish on the forehead and back. The cheeks, nose, feet, underparts, lower surface, and tip of tail are greyish white. The tail is covered with fine hairs, which are greyish above; there are whitish tufts of hair around the ears; the nose is pink. There are three pelage changes during the lifetime of the mouse: the juvenile pelage, worn from birth to about three months of age, which is dark slate grey above and white below; the sub-adult pelage, worn until the animal is five or six months old, which is a paler grey-brown coat; and the annual autumnal moult.

Average measurements of adults of the subspecies *missouriensis*: length 150 (141–161), tail 39 (29–45), hind foot 21 (20–22), ear 14 (13–16) (dry) mm; weight 46 (41–52) g. The typical form is a little larger.

Habits. The unique feature of this little rodent is that it is highly carnivorous. Most rodents appreciate a little meat in their diet once in a while, but this mouse lives largely on animal matter, only about 11 per cent of its diet being vegetable matter. In the Great Plains region, where short-tailed shrews and moles are absent, the grasshopper mice take their place as insect-eaters.

The grasshopper mouse is a solitary wanderer that seems to shun the company of its kind. It does not follow regular runways or dig its own burrow, but usurps the burrows of other small animals. It is an alert, active little hunter with large, sparkling eyes and expressive ears and tail. It does not seem to be very nervous or timid, but it does not become tame if caged. It eats grasshoppers readily from the hand but shows its objection to being held or petted by squirming and trying to bite.

It is quite vocal, uttering a variety of calls. The most interesting one is a long, shrill, insect-like whistle at about 10,000 vibrations per second, which is just about the limit of the human auditory range. The mouse sits on its haunches, sometimes placing its paw on its prey, and throws its head back to call, much like a miniature wolf or coyote. Although most observations have been made on captive mice, naturalists have reported hearing the call in the field. It also utters a series of short, bark-like squeaks. Its senses are keen: the rapidity with which it pounces on insects suggests that it may even hear their movements. Compared to other species such as deer mice or meadow voles, it is not swift in its movements because its limbs are short. It is primarily terrestrial but has been reported to swim across small streams and to climb clumsily.

The grasshopper mouse is chiefly nocturnal in activity and has rarely been seen during the daylight hours. It does not hibernate but becomes rather fat in the autumn and lives to some extent on stored seeds. Since it lacks large internal cheek pouches, it has only a limited carrying capacity. Pet mice have been observed carefully carrying two sunflower seeds in their mouths to their cache.

As has been mentioned previously, the diet of the grasshopper mouse during the open seasons consists primarily of insects. It quickly pounces upon a grasshopper, grasps it firmly in its forepaws, and bites its head. Then it sits on its haunches and consumes its prey, head-first. Occasionally it is bowled over by the desperate kicks of its prey, but it seldom loses its grip. Stomach analysis has shown that its summer diet consists of 39 per cent Orthoptera (crickets, grasshoppers, 'Jerusalem' crickets, and camel crickets), 21 per cent Coleoptera (ground beetles, darkling beetles, dung beetles, adults, and larvae), 17 per cent Lepidoptera (caterpillars, pupae, and adult moths), and about 3 per cent other insects such as Hymenoptera, Hemiptera, and Diptera (ants, flies, and bugs as eggs, larvae, cocoons, and adults). Besides these insects, other invertebrates such as spiders, harvestmen, and scorpions are eaten, but to a lesser extent. Mammals such as deer mice, pocket mice, and meadow voles formed 3 per cent of the stomach contents. Grasshopper mice are known to prey upon other mice, particularly the young. They corner their prey, seize it, and bite through the base of the skull with their sabre-sharp lower incisors.

About 11 per cent of this species' summer diet consists of plant seeds such as native grasses and grains (wheat and barley). Seeds of wild forbs such as climbing buckwheat, lamb's-quarters, geranium, and spurge are also eaten. It is possible that seeds form a larger percentage of the winter diet when insects are less available.

Little is known of the natural predators, which probably include rattlesnakes, ground squirrels, weasels, ferrets, badgers, foxes, coyotes, and owls.

Habitat. The grasshopper mouse inhabits the western Great Plains region. It is nowhere very common, however.

Reproduction. Few details of the reproductive cycle of the grasshopper mouse are known. The female has six mammae: one pectoral pair and two inguinal pairs. The breeding season probably lasts from March to August.

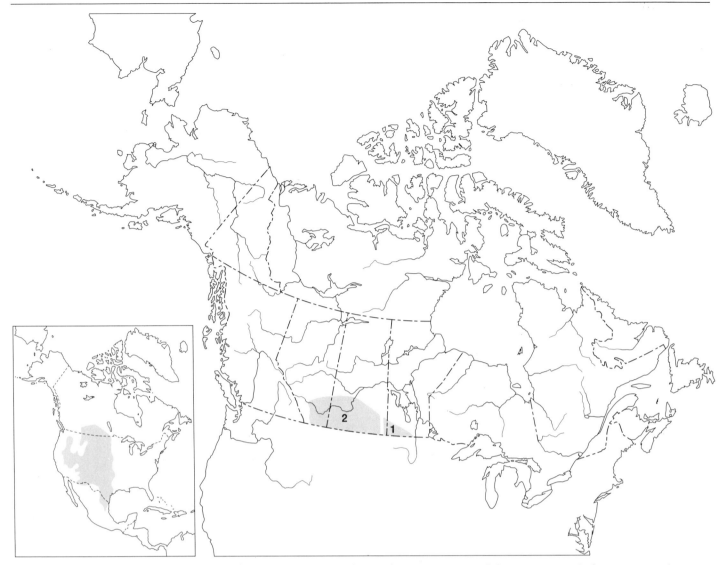

Map 72 Distribution of the northern grasshopper mouse, *Onychomys leucogaster*: 1 *O. l. leucogaster*, 2 *O. l. missouriensis*

The gestation period is thirty-two days for non-lactating females and thirty-three to forty-seven days for lactating females. There are probably two litters a year, averaging about three young.

The young weigh on an average 2.2 (1.7–2.7) g at birth. They are pink, naked (except for vibrissae), and blind, and have blunt, thickened tails and folded ears. Their backs are darkly pigmented, and their ears unfold on the third day. The incisors appear on the eleventh day. They are covered with silky, dark grey fur by the twelfth day, and their eyes open between fifteen and twenty days of age. They are weaned at the age of about twenty-four days and quickly evicted from the nest to fend for themselves. Juvenile females mature sexually at the age of three months, while they are still wearing the grey juvenile coat. Young of the first spring litter may breed by August and bear young the first year.

Economic Status. Aside from the earlier reference to the eating of stored grain by grasshopper mice in the Mandan villages, there have been very few reports of their depre-

dations on agricultural produce. Occasionally individual mice will get into a roothouse and eat stored vegetables, but such occurrences are now rare. This rodent is probably unique in that its feeding habits are largely beneficial to man's interests. It has even been reported that a pet grasshopper mouse, given the freedom of a kitchen at night, soon extirpated the resident cockroaches. Each day the mouse voluntarily returned to its cage.

Distribution. This species is found in the Great Plains region of North America from the Gulf of Mexico to the Canadian prairies.

Canadian Distribution. There are two subspecies of the northern grasshopper mouse, which occur sparingly in the southern parts of the Prairie Provinces (see Map 72).

Onychomys leucogaster leucogaster (Wied-Neuwied), 1841, Reise in das innere Nord-America 2: 99. A larger, darker race found on the first prairie steppe of south-western Manitoba.

Onychomys leucogaster missouriensis (Audubon and

Bachman), 1851, The viviparous quadrupeds of North America 2: 327. A smaller, more cinnamon-coloured form, found in southern Saskatchewan and Alberta.

REFERENCE

Bailey, Vernon, and Charles C. Sperry. 1929. Life history and habits of grasshopper mice, genus *Onychomys*. United States Dept. Agr. Tech. Bull. 145.

BUSHY-TAILED WOOD RAT
Rat à queue touffue. *Neotoma cinerea* (Ord)

Description. This is the only native rat found in Canada. Its long, bushy tail distinguishes it from the introduced Old World rat. It is a large squirrel-like rodent measuring up to 20 inches in total length. Its black eyes are prominent; its long vibrissae extend well beyond the large ears, which are covered with fine grey hairs. The pollex is rudimentary and clawless, but all the other digits carry sharp, curved claws, which are concealed in the stiff white fur that covers the heels and dorsal surface of the feet. The long tail is covered with long fur. The males have prominent mid-ventral musk glands, which emit a strong, sweet musky odour. The glands are covered with stiff hairs, which are stained, greasy, and matted. These glands are vestigial in the females (Plate 16).

The skull of this species is long and narrow. The rostrum is long and rectangular; the incisive foramina are long; the interorbital region is constricted; the brain-case is rounded and tapered anteriorly; there are two prominent temporal ridges with an intervening depression; the auditory bullae are large. The cheek teeth are rooted and moderately high-crowned.

The adult pelage is long, soft, and dense – quite different from the short, stiff pelage of the Old World rats. There is a short, dense underfur and longer, sparse guard hairs. The cheeks, shoulders, and flanks are a rather tawny brown, while the profusion of black-tipped guard hairs on the dorsum gives it a grizzled brown appearance. The tail is dark grey above and white beneath. The ventral surface is greyish white, stained with creamy patches. The feet are white with grey ankles and wrists.

The wood rat has three coats during its lifetime. The juvenile coat is grey, soft, and woolly; the tail is pencil-like, covered with short grey fur. The post-juvenile moult starts when the youngsters are between the ages of forty and forty-five days and ends between the ages of fifty-four and 134 days. It occupies most of the animal's first summer. The subadult coat appears first on the belly and spreads laterally over the flank and around the rump. The nape of the neck is the last area to moult. This coat has browner tones on the flanks and includes the growth of the long, dark-grey guard hairs on the tail so that it assumes its normal bushy appearance. This coat is moulted during the first autumn. The annual autumn moult to the adult pelage first appears as a tawny lateral line and follows the same general pattern.

Average measurements of adult females: length 412 (379–435), tail 210 (178–222), hind foot 48 (43–52), ear

approximately 30 mm. The adult males are about 8 per cent larger. Average weight of females is between 379 and 392 g.

Habits. These are primarily solitary rodents. They pair up only during the breeding season, and at that time the female dominates the male, who is driven out of the nest during the period when the young are suckling. They are strongly territorial in behaviour, and the males distribute scent around their territories by rubbing their ventral musk glands on toilet posts, nests, middens, and food caches. They also fight among each other with claws and teeth. Many old males have shredded ears and bobbed tails.

Wood rats are alert and quick in their actions. Their senses are keen, particularly the tactile sense in their long vibrissae and other tactile hairs on the cheeks and wrists. They are swift runners and dodgers among rocks, logs, and rafters, and are excellent climbers. They are particularly noisy and quarrelsome – squealing, whining, and chattering their teeth. They also thump their hind feet to produce a drumming sound. One expects wild animals to be stealthy, but wood rats seem to be almost clumsy. If one is unfortunate enough to share a cabin with a wood rat, one gets little rest because of the continual disturbance caused by the rat's knocking objects over or dropping things it is carrying.

This species is most active during the half hour after sunset and dawn, but is occasionally observed during the day. It is active the year round, although most of the winter activity is under a blanket of snow. Occasionally its tracks may be observed to cross 200 yards of snow cover. Although this rat is generally rather sedentary, some wander widely to occupy isolated habitats. There is rarely more than one family in a rock talus slope covering two to five acres. One rat to twenty acres is given as an average population density in its habitat.

Characteristic of the wood rat's habitat are its large bulky dens of sticks, bones, foliage, debris, and human artifacts. These bulky piles, which may contain one to three bushels of material, are not the true nests. The nests are much smaller and are constructed of shredded bark, grasses, moss, and often shredded cotton batting, cloth, or oakum. They are open or domed and are placed in the stick pile. The bulky dens serve a number of purposes: as a platform for the nest (a defensive maze to ensure time to escape from a predator), as an eating platform, and as a drying rack for the food cache. The dens are built in caves and rock crevices, under cliffs, and in cabins and mine shafts. The nest itself is clean, but near by are regular toilet areas where the faeces accumulate in crevices or hollows and where the rocks become encrusted and stained from the accumulation of urine.

The habit of collecting and hoarding objects is so strong in these rodents that they have earned the name 'pack rats.' Many small items such as silverware, string, clothing, oakum, paper, watches, razors, tooth brushes, and matches have been stolen from cabins and camps and piled among the sticks and bones of their dens or woven into the nests.

Map 73 Distribution of the bushy-tailed wood rat, *Neotoma cinerea*: 1 *N. c. cinerea*, 2 *N. c. drummondii*, 3 *N. c. occidentalis*, ● extra-limital record

Wood rats show a dietary preference for the foliage of a wide variety of trees, shrubs, and forbs, but not grasses. The leaves of aspens, cherries, roses, snowberries, currants, elderberries, and willows are preferred, but the twigs and needles of such conifers as western white pine, Douglas fir, Engelmann spruce, alpine fir, and junipers, and the seeds and fruits of Douglas fir, anemones, fireweed, gentians, honeysuckle, cinquefoils, gooseberries, raspberries, and elderberries are also eaten.

In the autumn, cuttings are gathered and cured in loose piles near the den. Then they are packed into crevices or under large boulders, much like the haystacks of pikas. Four winter caches were found to contain two gallons of alpine fir twigs, one pint of Engelmann spruce, five gallons of chokecherry cuttings, and one gallon of goldenrod.

There is no information available on the longevity of the bushy-tailed wood rat, but an eastern relative, the Allegheny wood rat, has been known to live at least four years.

The bushy-tailed wood rat must constantly be on the alert for a large number of predators, which include rattlesnakes, great horned owls, weasels, skunks, martens, wolverines, foxes, coyotes, and wolves.

Habitat. The bushy-tailed wood rat is found from sea level to mountain-tops up to 14,110 feet high. Although it occupies a variety of life zones from the Arctic–Alpine to the desert Sonoran, it seems to be most at home in the transitional zone. It inhabits cliffs, rock talus, caves, river canyons, and rock outcrops in open forests of Douglas fir and ponderosa pine. It may wander quite far in the forests to deserted buildings and mine shafts, which it finds much to its liking.

Reproduction. The female of the species is seasonally polyoestrous; some experience a post-partum oestrus and breed within twenty-four and forty-eight hours after parturition, but others do not breed until after the first litter has been weaned. There are two pairs of inguinal teats. The males are in breeding condition from February to August. The males pursue the receptive females and indicate their interest by nuzzling and purring. The peak of the breeding season is between March and June. The gestation period lasts between twenty-seven and thirty-two days, and lactation does not appear to extend it. The litter size is on the average 3.5, but may vary from one to six. In the laboratory a female may have up to seven litters in one year, but in the wild, under favourable conditions, two litters are born during the year, about two months apart. In the northern part of the range, probably only one litter is born each year.

The young wood rats weigh an average of 13.5 (12.0–17.3) g at birth. They are naked, and their tails are quite short. They spend much of their early lives attached to their mother's teats, which results in high mortality in litters of more than four. The instinct to assemble under the mother and to hold one of the teats is strongly developed. When disturbed, the female wood rat dashes from her nest to another den with her young firmly attached to her teats. The ears unfold within seventy-two hours; the incisors appear between twelve and fifteen days of age; and the eyes open between the fourteenth and fifteenth day. The young rats grow rapidly and gain an average of 2.2 g per day during the nursing period. They venture out of the nest at twenty-two days and are weaned between twenty-six and thirty days of age. At that time the males weigh between 118 and 150 g, and the females between 85 and 132 g. The scent glands appear on the males at the time of the post-juvenile moults when they are about fifty days old. The young wood rats do not mature, however, until they are about eleven months old.

Economic Status. Wood rats are of no agricultural significance because of their rocky habitat and foliage diet. Their attraction to deserted buildings, however, makes them a nuisance of some economic importance. Given sufficient time they can wreck the interior of a cabin and render it almost uninhabitable. They will construct their large bulky dens of sticks, rags, bones, silverware, and debris on the bunks or in the stove. Everything movable is shredded and cached – mattresses, bedding, oakum insulation, firewood, clothes. The rafters are streaked with urine, and piles of faeces are everywhere: in drawers, on eating utensils, and on tables and the floor. Everywhere the strong musky odour of the wood rat pervades.

Distribution. The Cordilleran region of western North America from the Yukon Territory southward to Arizona and New Mexico.

Canadian Distribution. Three subspecies of the bushy-tailed wood rat are recognized in Canada (see Map 73).

Neotoma cinerea cinerea (Ord), 1815, *in* Guthrie, A new geography, history, and comm. grammar ..., Philadelphia, American ed. 2: 292. A grey form found in southwestern Saskatchewan (Govenloch), southern Alberta (Milk River, Banff), and southeastern British Columbia (Newgate).

Neotoma cinerea drummondii (Richardson), 1828, Zool. Jour. 3: 513. Foothills and Rocky Mountains of Alberta (Dunvegan) and eastern British Columbia northward to southeastern Yukon and southwestern Northwest Territories (Fort Liard).

Neotoma cinerea occidentalis Baird, 1855, Proc. Acad. Nat. Sci. Philadelphia 7: 335. A darker form with dusky rings about the ankles; found in western British Columbia.

REFERENCES

Esoscue, H.J. 1962. The bushy-tailed wood rat: a laboratory colony. Jour. Mamm. 43(3): 328–37.

Finley, R.B. 1958. The wood rats of Colorado: distribution and ecology. Univ. Kansas Pub. Mus. Nat. Hist. 10(6): 213–552.

Howell, A.B. 1926. Anatomy of the wood rat. Williams and Wilkins Company, Baltimore.

NORTHERN RED-BACKED VOLE
Campagnol à dos roux boréal. *Clethrionomys rutilus* Pallas

Description. A number of features distinguish voles from mice. They have plump bodies, blunt noses, small eyes, short ears that barely extend beyond the fur, and a short tail. Their legs appear much shorter because the upper portions of each limb are enclosed in the loose body skin. The cheek teeth are relatively long and are characterized by prismatic occlusional surfaces (Figure 43).

The northern red-backed vole is a small, relatively slender, brightly coloured vole. It has rounded, well-furred ears, which extend well beyond the pelage. Its short tail is covered with dense, bristly fur. The forefeet have four toes, and the relatively large hind feet five. The males have small flank glands of thickened skin covered by denser hair. The body fur is long and silky. The small, light skull is rounded, the zygomatic arches are slender, and the mandible is weak. The palate terminates between the posterior molars in a thin-edged shelf, which is characteristically interrupted in this species. Only about 34 per cent of the second-year adults and none of the first-year voles have complete bony palatine shelves. In adults the molar teeth bear twin roots.

In the summer pelage, there is a bright rufous dorsal stripe, extending from the forehead to the tail. The flanks, cheeks, and feet are ochraceous, and the belly is buffy or creamy white. The ears are rufous-tipped. The tail is tawny below and rufous above, tipped with blackish hairs. The winter pelage is longer and silkier, and the dorsal stripe is more contrastingly cinnamon-coloured. Besides the normal coloration there is a grey phase in which the rufous colour is lacking and the dorsal stripe is sepia grey. About 13 per cent of the population is so coloured. There is also a rare yellow-brown colour phase.

There are three pelage changes during the lifetime of the vole. The juvenile coat is composed of fine, soft, thin, dark grey underfur. This is followed by a subadult coat for the early litters, but later litters may not go through this phase. The subadult pelage is more brownish, particularly on the back. Each moult starts on the flanks and spreads over the back; the face is the last area to moult.

There are also two annual moults, in autumn and in spring. Juveniles born late in the season may moult di-

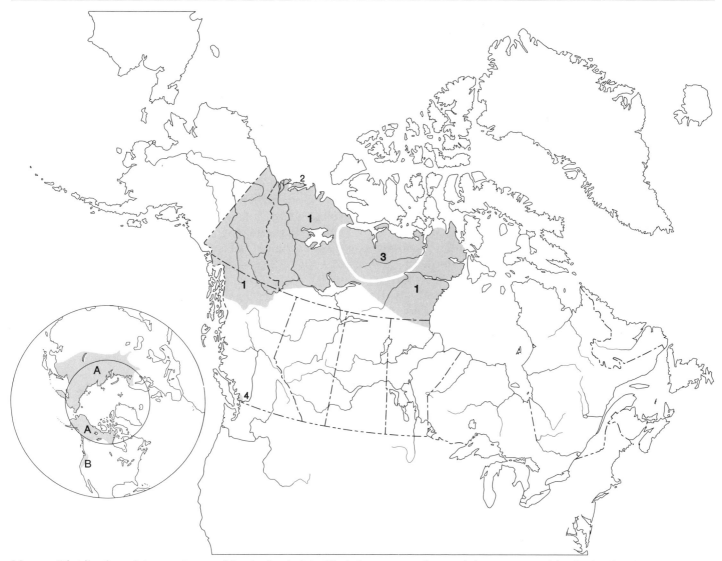

Map 74 Distribution of the northern red-backed vole (A), *Clethrionomys rutilus*, and the western red-backed vole (B),
Clethrionomys occidentalis: 1 *C. r. dawsoni*, 2 *C. r. platycephalus*, 3 *C. r. washburni*, 4 *Clethrionomys occidentalis*

rectly to the winter coat, which takes place from September to late October. The spring moult, starting in May, is more irregular, and appears in patches first on the throat and cheeks. It does not seem to be a complete change of coat, and much of the darker summer pelage appears to be derived from the wear and the shedding of the long buffy guard hairs.

Average measurements of adults: total length 146 (137–161), tail 41 (33–48), hind foot 20 (19–21), ear 15 (14–17) mm; weight 21.9 (17.8–29.6) g.

Habits. This species is less well known than the next, Gapper's red-backed vole. It is mainly nocturnal or crepuscular but is of necessity about during the prolonged arctic daylight season. It is active all winter and constructs long tunnels under the snow. It utilizes surface runways through the vegetation, and builds its nest in a short underground burrow or under some protective object such as a rock or root. Winter nests are placed on the ground.

The northern red-backed vole eats the leaves, buds, twigs, and fruit of a wide range of shrubs; it also eats forbs,

such as bunchberries, louseworts, golden-rod, bilberries, blueberries, milk vetch, cloudberries, geranium, dwarf birch, twin-flower, and wintergreen. It occasionally eats heaths such as crowberry but does not eat mosses or lichens.

Habitat. This species is characteristic of a northern shrub vegetation, or an open taiga forest of scattered spruce, fir, or birch. It is not usually found on the tundra far from shrubby growths of alders, willows, and birches. In the absence of shrubs it inhabits rock fields and rock talus. In winter it frequently invades Eskimo houses.

Reproduction. The females have four pairs of mammae: two pectoral and two inguinal. The breeding season extends from May to August. The males are sexually active during the same period, and the testes are withdrawn into the abdominal cavity after mid-August. The females are polyoestrous, and there is probably post-partum oestrus, resulting in the birth of two or three litters during the short northern season. From data available on embryo counts the average litter size would appear to be 5.93 (4–9).

179

The first litters are usually born in late May or early June. The young at birth are like most young rodents: naked, greyish pink, blind, and deaf. The average weight is about 1.75 g. The dorsal hair appears at three to four days, and the ears open at ten to eleven days. Young red-backed voles, in common with many other mammals, have poor thermoregulatory mechanisms at birth, and are unable to regulate their temperature successfully until about the eighteenth day. By this time they are weaned and leave the nest.

There is little growth during the winter months because of the restricted food supply. Only about 20 per cent of the females from the first litters breed during their first summer. The offspring of the later litters mature the following May.

Economic Status. These voles are of little economic significance, except as a food supply for northern fur-bearers. They may damage stored meat and vegetables in cabins and root cellars in winter. Some carried off about forty pounds of rolled oats stored in the attic of a cabin during a three-week absence of the owner. Upon his return some of the booty was found cached in the pockets of a coat hanging downstairs.

Distribution. The northern red-backed vole is one of the holarctic species distributed from northern Scandinavia across the Soviet Union and into North America from Alaska to Hudson Bay.

Canadian Distribution. Three geographical subspecies have been described from Canadian territory (see Map 74).

Clethrionomys rutilus dawsoni (Merriam), 1888, American Nat. 22: 650. A greyish form found in the forested parts of Yukon and the Northwest Territories and northwestern British Columbia, and apparently on the Keewatin tundra as well.

Clethrionomys rutilus platycephalus Manning, 1957, Nat. Mus. Canada Bull. 144: 50. A bright, tawny race from the tundra near Tuktoyaktuk, Northwest Territories, and possibly farther along the Arctic coast.

Clethrionomys rutilus washburni Hanson, 1952, Jour. Mamm. 33: 500. Central tundra of Mackenzie and Keewatin districts, south of Coronation and Queen Maud gulfs.

REFERENCES

Fuller, W.A. 1969. Changes in numbers of three species of small rodents near Great Slave Lake, N.W.T., Canada 1964–1967, and their significance for general population theory. Ann. Zool. Fennici 6: 113–44.
Manning, T.H. 1957. The northern red-backed mouse *Clethrionomys rutilus* (Pallas), in Canada. Nat. Mus. Canada Bull. 144.

GAPPER'S RED-BACKED VOLE

Campagnol à dos roux de Gapper. *Clethrionomys gapperi* (Vigors)

Description. This is the common red-backed vole found in forested and brushy areas across the country. It is a rela-

tively small, slender vole with small eyes, prominent, rounded ears, slender feet, and a moderately short, slim tail, scantily covered with short hairs (Plate 18). The male has small flank glands. The skull of this species is delicate and rounded (Figure 42f); the mandible is weak; the molars are slender and have double roots (Figure 43); the palatine bridge is completely ossified during the juvenile period and is straight-edged.

There is a bright chestnut dorsal stripe from the forehead to the base of the tail; the face, flanks, and rump are buffy grey; the feet and underparts are pale grey. The vibrissae are delicate and silvery, and the ears are clothed in fine brown hair. The feet are only sparsely haired, the soles being practically naked. The tail is faintly bi-coloured, grey below and brown above, with a black tip. Besides the normal rufous phase, a varying proportion of the population in any locality may be in the grey phase with a sooty dorsal stripe replacing the rufous dorsum.

There are two annual moults, in autumn and in spring. The winter coat is the longer, silkier, and brighter of the two. There are also the usual juvenile and subadult coats. The juvenile carries a thin coat when it first leaves the nest, brownish above and slaty grey below.

It is difficult to provide average measurements for this species because it varies considerably in size throughout its range. The extremes in external measurements of adults are: length 120–164, tail 30–58, hind foot 16–21, ear 12–16 mm; weight 13–42 g. The average measurements reported for *C. g. loringi* males are: length 129, tail 34, hind foot 18, ear 13 mm; weight 13.6 g; and for *C. g. phaeus* the average measurements are: length 156, tail 51, hind foot 20, ear 16 mm; weight usually between 20 and 28 g.

Habits. The red-backed vole is a highly nervous species and far from docile when captured. It chatters its teeth and attempts to bite its captor in panic. It seems to be rather delicate and may faint or even succumb on being handled. These voles seem to live rather solitary lives during the summer months, except for the female and her litter, but during the winter they congregate in family groups. Although primarily terrestrial in activity, scampering over the forest litter, they also climb well and frequently have been observed climbing trees. They are not particularly vocal but squeal occasionally when captured or when fighting among themselves. The males seem to be particularly pugnacious.

Although the red-backed vole is most active from sunset to sunrise, it is often about during the daylight hours as well. If one sits quietly in the woods, one may be rewarded by seeing one of these small creatures scampering along a log or foraging among the leaves of the forest floor. They have even been observed sunning themselves on the limb of a tree. They do not hibernate but remain active throughout the year.

Generally these voles construct no special runways of their own but often use those of other species such as the bog lemming and the meadow vole. In their forest habitat they utilize fallen logs, stumps, trees, and brush piles for shelter during their travels. Tunnels in the soft litter under

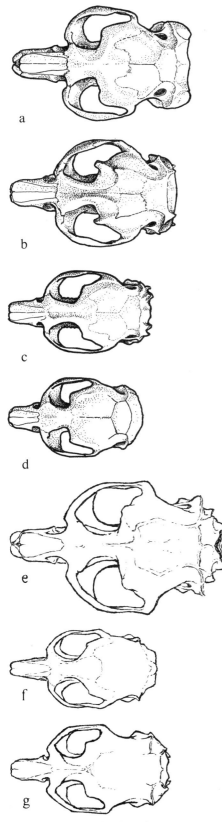

Figure 42 Skulls of microtine rodents: (a) brown lemming, *Lemmus sibiricus*; (b) collared lemming, *Dicrostonyx torquatus*; (c) heather vole, *Phenacomys intermedius*; (d) southern bog lemming, *Synaptomys cooperi*; (e) Richardson's water vole, *Arvicola richardsoni*; (f) Gapper's red-backed vole, *Clethrionomys gapperi*; (g) meadow vole, *Microtus pennsylvanicus* (× 1½)

fallen logs or through the deep sphagnum moss are favourite passageways. They construct spherical nests of grasses, mosses, lichens, or shredded leaves, which are hidden under the roots of stumps, logs, or brush piles. They may also build their nests in holes in trees or in the crotch of a branch twenty feet above the ground. They may use the abandoned burrows of other rodents or during the winter months may place their globular nests of grass directly on the ground under the snow. Tunnels radiate from the nests under the snow.

Red-backed voles may utilize a home range as large as 3.56 acres in summer, and there may be much overlapping of neighbouring home ranges. When foraging is restricted by a blanket of snow, winter home ranges may be as small as 0.35 acre. The population of this species fluctuates widely from year to year, but there does not seem to be any periodicity associated with these fluctuations. Measured population densities have varied between 0.17 and 4.42 per acre. Red-backed mice have been known to live at least twenty months in the wild state, but like so many small rodents and shrews they are primarily an annual crop.

This species of vole is practically omnivorous in diet. Its favourite food seems to be the petioles of broad-leafed forbs and shrubs, as indicated by the piles of sectioned petioles often found near its den. Its diet is varied, however. In spring it grazes on the tender shoots of growing plants. In summer it augments its petiole diet with a broad variety of berries, starting with strawberries, blueberries, chokecherries, and bearberries. In the autumn it turns its attention to seeds: beechnuts, hazelnuts, and weed seeds. During the winter it feeds upon the petioles, twigs, and winter buds of a number of biennial and perennial plants; on blueberries, bearberries, evergreen, and silverberries; and on heaths that remain green under the snow cover. After such food has been utilized, it eats the bark of roots and the stems of a variety of shrubs and trees such as the Manitoba maple, the white ash, and cherries. Red-backed voles are also carnivorous and readily devour mouse carcasses. Insects, however, do not seem to play an important role in their diet. These voles do not lay aside any large stores of food for the winter months.

The red-backed vole is also an important prey species for a wide variety of carnivorous animals, which include red-shouldered and rough-legged hawks; long-eared, great-horned, barred, and screech owls; and raccoons, weasels, red foxes, coyotes, skunks, martens, minks, and black bears. Even the short-tailed shrew and the red squirrel are potential predators upon these voles.

Habitat. Gapper's red-backed vole prefers forests where mossy rotten logs, stumps, and brush provide cover for foraging among the plant cover of the forest floor. Coniferous forests are preferred, but hardwood forests are also inhabited. The availability of water is also important to this species, and they seldom wander far from springs, brooks, or bogs. They may inhabit white cedar swamps and bogs as well as shrubby forest edges. On the prairies they usually are found in aspen bluffs and shrubby vegetation in coulees.

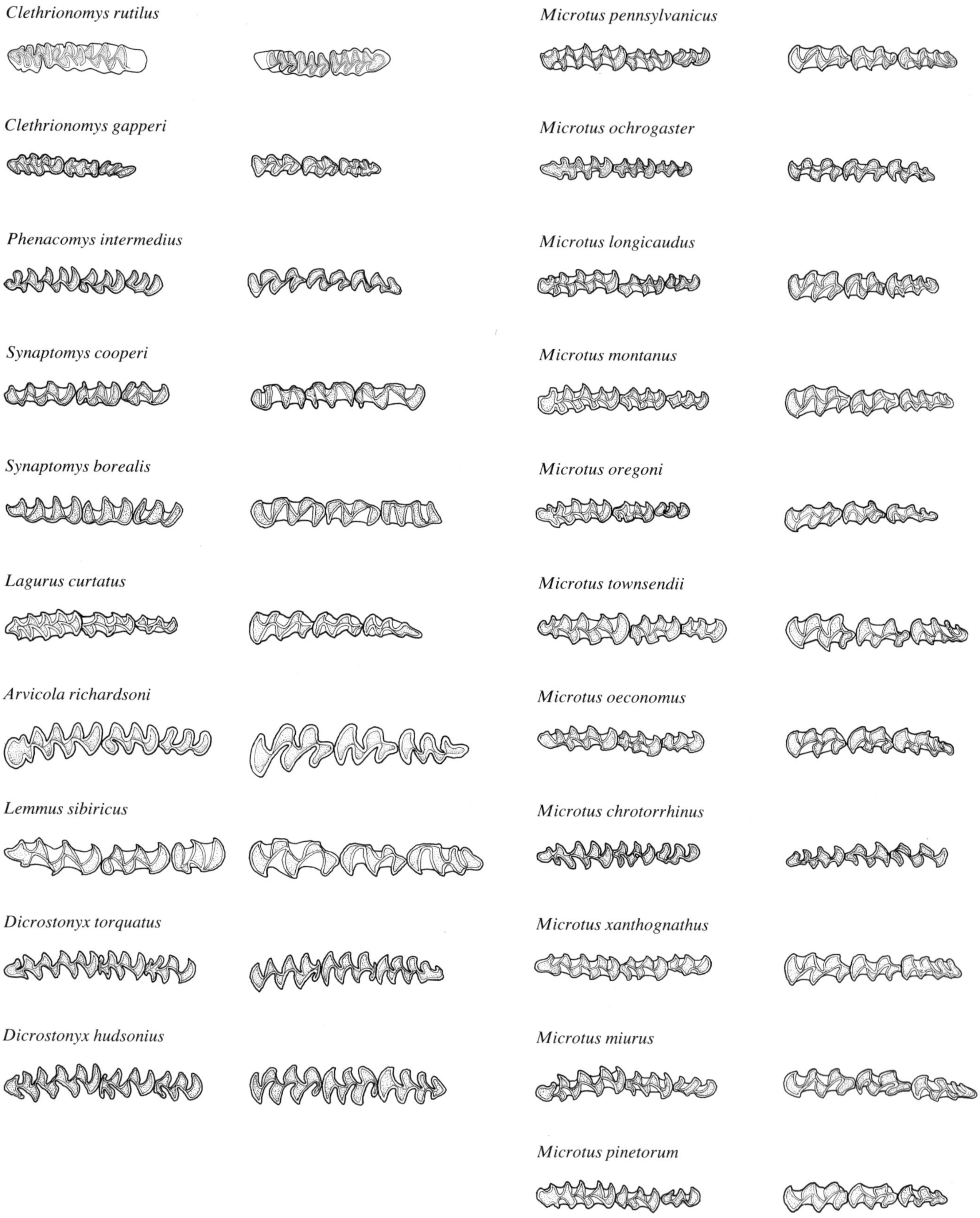

Clethrionomys rutilus

Clethrionomys gapperi

Phenacomys intermedius

Synaptomys cooperi

Synaptomys borealis

Lagurus curtatus

Arvicola richardsoni

Lemmus sibiricus

Dicrostonyx torquatus

Dicrostonyx hudsonius

Microtus pennsylvanicus

Microtus ochrogaster

Microtus longicaudus

Microtus montanus

Microtus oregoni

Microtus townsendii

Microtus oeconomus

Microtus chrotorrhinus

Microtus xanthognathus

Microtus miurus

Microtus pinetorum

Figure 43 Dentitions of microtine rodents: right upper tooth row at right, front end to left (×5)

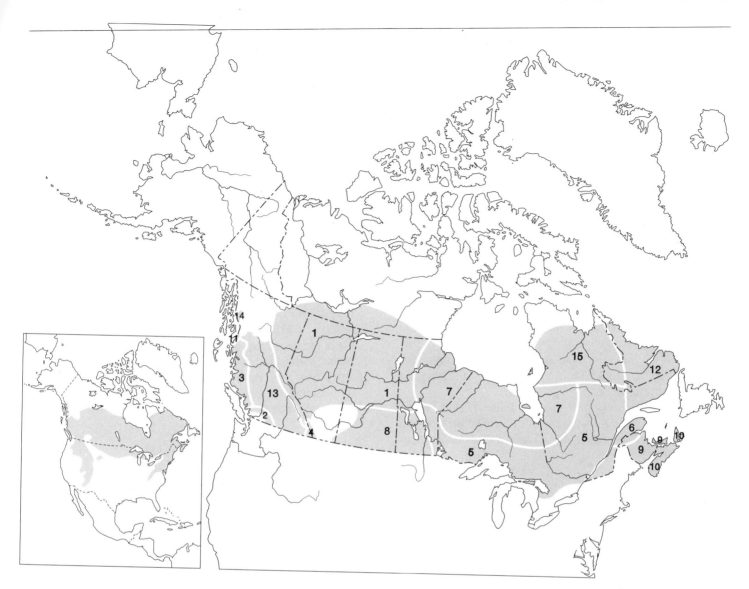

Map 75 Distribution of Gapper's red-backed vole, *Clethrionomys gapperi*: 1 *C. g. athabascae*, 2 *C. g. cascadensis*, 3 *C. g. caurinus*, 4 *C. g. galei*, 5 *C. g. gapperi*, 6 *C. g. gaspeanus*, 7 *C. g. hudsonius*, 8 *C. g. loringi*, 9 *C. g. ochraceous*, 10 *C. g. pallescens*, 11 *C. g. phaeus*, 12 *C. g. proteus*, 13 *C. g. saturatus*, 14 *C. g. stikinensis*, 15 *C. g. ungava*

Reproduction. This vole is one of the more prolific small rodents. The female is seasonally polyoestrous and breeds immediately after oestrus without any increase in gestation period because of lactation. The breeding season is prolonged – from April to early October. There seem to be three peaks in litter production during this period: in May, July, and September. Probably three or four litters are borne by a female during this period. The gestation period is between seventeen and nineteen days. The litter size has been found to average 5.47 but may vary from one to eight. The variation is considerable from year to year, depending upon the population density, and is lowest (3.12) when the population is densest.

The young voles are born in a grass-lined nest. They are blind, deaf, hairless, and helpless at birth and weigh about 1.9 (1.7–2.3) g. At the age of five days they crawl about feebly; at six days they hold fast to the mother's nipples and may be dragged about in that way; at seven days the incisors appear; at eleven days they wash their faces and

totter about. Their eyes open between the ninth and the fifteenth day, and they begin to run about and groom themselves soon afterwards. The young are weaned between the seventeenth and twenty-first day, and after that they are on their own. The juveniles of the spring litter mature during the first season and bear their first young when they are about four months old.

Economic Status. Generally speaking, red-backed voles are of little economic significance in agriculture because of their forest habitat. In western Canada, however, they may inhabit shelter belts and orchards, where they may girdle fruit trees such as the crabapple and the cherry. They also occasionally enter root houses and eat stored vegetables such as carrots, parsnips, potatoes, and turnips. They will also enter cabins and eat bagged grains. In forestry practice, red-backed voles have been found to girdle young plantations of Scotch pine.

The depredations of this species can best be controlled by wrapping orchard tree trunks with tarpaper or metal collars and also by removing litter, brush piles, and tall grass from the fence rows. In buildings they are controlled by the distribution of strychnine-coated grain.

Distribution. The red-backed vole inhabits northern North America from Labrador to British Columbia and from the Great Slave Lake region south to the Great Smoky Mountains in the east and the southern Rocky Mountains in the west.

Canadian Distribution. This species is found across central Canada with the exception of Newfoundland, and Anticosti, Vancouver, and the Queen Charlotte islands. It is also absent from southern Ontario. This is another plastic species in which at least fifteen subspecies are recognized in Canada (see Map 75).

Clethrionomys gapperi athabascae (Preble), 1908, N. American Fauna 27: 178. A greyish race, found in the southern part of the Northwest Territories and in the northern parts of British Columbia, Alberta, Saskatchewan, and Manitoba.

Clethrionomys gapperi cascadensis Booth, 1945, the Murrelet 26: 27. dusky race, found in the southern Cascade Mountains of British Columbia.

Clethrionomys gapperi caurinus (V. Bailey), 1898, Proc. Biol. Soc. Washington 12: 21. A dull form with brown dorsum and olive-grey flanks, found on the British Columbia coast.

Clethrionomys gapperi galei (Merriam), 1890, N. American Fauna 4: 23. A pale form from the southern Rocky Mountains of Alberta and British Columbia.

Clethrionomys gapperi gapperi (Vigors), 1830, Zool. Jour. 5: 204. The typical form of central Ontario and southwestern Quebec.

Clethrionomys gapperi gaspeanus Anderson, 1943, Ann. Rept. Provancher Soc. Nat. Hist. Quebec 1942: 57. A grey-sided race, found in the Gaspé Peninsula of Quebec and in northern New Brunswick.

Clethrionomys gapperi hudsonius Anderson, 1940, Ann. Rept. Provancher Soc. Nat. Hist. Quebec 1939: 73. A large, richly coloured race, found in the boreal forests of central Quebec, northern Ontario, and eastern Manitoba.

Clethrionomys gapperi loringi (V. Bailey), 1897, Proc. Biol. Soc. Washington 11: 125. A small, brightly coloured race from the southern parts of the Prairie Provinces.

Clethrionomys gapperi ochraceous (Miller), 1894, Proc. Boston Soc. Nat. Hist. 26: 193. A dull-coloured form from southern New Brunswick and the Eastern Townships of Quebec.

Clethrionomys gapperi pallescens Hall and Cockrum, 1952, Univ. Kansas Pub. Mus. Nat. Hist. 5: 302. A pale form from Nova Scotia.

Clethrionomys gapperi phaeus (Swarth), 1911, Univ. California Pub. Zool. 7: 127. A rich red form, from Alaska and from Port Simpson, British Columbia.

Clethrionomys gapperi proteus (Bangs), 1897, Proc. Biol. Soc. Washington 11: 137. Found in southern Labrador and on the north shore of the Gulf of St Lawrence,

Quebec. The grey colour phase predominates in this race.

Clethrionomys gapperi saturatus (Rhoads), 1894, Proc. Acad. Nat. Sci. Philadelphia 46: 284. A large, brightly coloured race, which occupies central British Columbia.

Clethrionomys gapperi stikinensis Hall and Cockrum, 1952, Univ. Kansas Pub. Mus. Nat. Hist. 5: 305. A medium-sized dark form from the Stikine River area of northwestern British Columbia.

Clethrionomys gapperi ungava (V. Bailey), 1897, Proc. Biol. Soc. Washington 11: 130. Northern parts of the Quebec peninsula.

REFERENCES

Criddle, Stuart. 1932. The red-backed vole (*Clethrionomys gapperi loringi* Bailey) in southern Manitoba. Canadian Field-Nat. 46(8): 178–81.

Manville, R.H. 1949. A study of small mammal populations in northern Michigan. Misc. Pub. Mus. Zool. Univ. Michigan 73: 44–51.

Svihla, A. 1930. Breeding habits and young of the red-backed mouse, *Evotomys*. Papers Michigan Acad. Sci., Arts and Letters 11: 485–90.

WESTERN RED-BACKED VOLE
Campagnol à dos roux de l'Ouest. *Clethrionomys occidentalis* (Merriam)

Description. The western red-backed vole is much more sombrely coloured than Gapper's red-backed vole; it also has shorter ears and a slightly longer tail. Its ears, feet, and tail are very sparsely haired. Its skull is shorter, broader, and more angular in construction than that of Gapper's. The auditory bullae are inflated and crowded together over the basioccipital bone. The post-palatine bridge, which is completely ossified in juveniles, carries a median spine. The last upper molar and the first lower molar have fewer enamel prisms than found in *C. gapperi*.

The pelage of this species is a dull, dark, chestnut-brown above. There is no well-defined dorsal stripe, the brown extending vaguely onto the flanks, which are dusky grey with a mixture of buffy hairs. The ventral surface is silvery grey with the dull grey underfur showing through. The face and feet are dusky; the tail is vaguely bi-coloured, dark grey above and light grey beneath.

Average measurements of adults: length 146 (121–165), tail 45 (34–53), hind foot 18.3 (18–21), ear 11 (10–13) mm.

Habits. The habits of this species have been little studied. Undoubtedly its life history is very similar to that of the other species. It is primarily terrestrial, active both day and night throughout the year. It does not follow set runways but scampers over the forest floor. Its specific food habits are unknown, beyond the fact that it feeds on seeds and green vegetation.

Habitat. The western red-backed vole inhabits dense coastal coniferous forest as well as subclimax clearings in the forest. It is found from sea level to 2,500 feet in the coastal mountains.

Reproduction. Since the females are polyoestrous and experience a post-partum rut as well, two or more litters are born to a female in a season. The breeding season extends from May to October. The gestation period is eighteen days, and the average number of young in a litter is three, but it may vary from two to four.

The young are similar to other voles at birth. Within a week they are covered with dark grey hair. Their eyes are open at fourteen days, and they are weaned soon after that. When the family of mice is disturbed, the mother is very solicitous and carries or drags her young to a new nest, but when disturbed in captivity, the mother may eat her young.

Economic Status. The western red-backed vole is too restricted in Canada to be of any economic significance.

Distribution. The species is restricted to the Pacific coast of North America, from California to southern British Columbia (see Map 74).

Canadian Distribution. The species is represented by the nominate race in Canada, which occurs only in the lower Fraser valley south of Burrard Inlet.

Clethrionomys occidentalis occidentalis (Merriam), 1890, N. American Fauna 4: 25.

REFERENCE

Svihla, Arthur. 1931. The Olympic red-backed mouse. The Murrelet 12(2): 54.

BROWN LEMMING
Lemming brun. *Lemmus sibiricus* Kerr

Description. Our brown lemming is closely related to the Scandinavian lemming, *Lemmus lemmus*, which is famous for its sporadic mass emigrations. Lemmings are small 'schmoo-like' creatures with large heads, no apparent neck, fat bodies, short, furry feet, and stubby tails. Their eyes are beady, and their small ears are hidden in their long, soft fur. Their forefeet have specialized claws; the thumb is reduced but carries a long, flat nail (Figure 44). The claw on the second digit is not remarkable, but those on the lateral three digits are short, broad, and curved. The sole and toes are covered with long, stiff bristles. The toes of the hind feet have regular, narrow, curved claws and four reduced plantar tubercules hidden under the fur. The females have eight teats: two pectoral pairs and two inguinal pairs (Plate 15k).

The skull of the brown lemming is massive, broad, and rectangular (Figure 42a). The rostrum is short and depressed; the cranium is flat and rectangular; the zygoma are massive and rectangular. The short intraorbital isthmus is constricted and ridged, and the squamosal bones

Figure 44 Forefoot of brown lemming (× 2)

are crested. The auditory bullae are inflated and filled with spongy cells. The mastoid processes are peg-like. The dentition is heavy; the upper incisors bear shallow longitudinal grooves; the rootless cheek teeth diverge posteriorly. The enamel pattern is characterized by deep bays on the outer side of the upper teeth and on the inner side of the lower molars. These bays are so deep that the central isthmus connecting the enamel-enclosed triangles is carried over to the opposite side of the tooth, not in the middle as is characteristic of *Microtus* (Figure 43).

The long, silky pelage of this species is grizzled buffy grey over the head and shoulders and chestnut brown on the lower back. The cheeks and flanks are tawny, the chin is grey, the belly is buffy grey, and the feet are silvery grey. The first grey juvenile pelage grows from the back around to the ventral surface. Two other coats have been described: post-juvenile and preadult, which are produced by the growth of new hair starting along lateral lines and then proceeding over the back and finally the belly. The bright adult pelage appears first at the autumn moult. It develops from irregular patches along the lateral line and spreads over the back. The winter coat is longer and greyer than the summer coat, which grows after the spring moult. Albino and melanistic individuals have been reported.

Average measurements of adult males from Alaska: length 151 (132–168), tail 21 (16–26), hind foot 21 (18–23), ear 10 (9–13) mm; weight 78.3 (48–113) g. Adult females: length 145 (133–161), tail 21 (17–25), hind foot 20 (19–22), ear 10 (8–11) mm; weight 67.8 (41–105) g.

Habits. Lemmings are gregarious rodents and are usually found in colonies. They are scrappy little creatures, which hunch up, box, and squeal at their assailant or flip onto their backs and try to bite. They are often observed walking very deliberately over the tundra or scuttling on their short legs into their burrows. They also swim freely, floating high in the water like grey powder-puffs, buoyed up by their long, dense fur. They are active throughout the total twenty-four-hour period but more so on dull or cloudy summer days than in bright sunshine. They remain active all winter under snowbanks. Spring and autumn are critical periods for them: spring because the melting snows reveal their nests and tunnels under the snow, and autumn because the first winter blizzards may strike before an insulating blanket of snow covers the vegetation.

During the brief summer, brown lemmings excavate short, shallow tunnels and sunken runways through the moss. The tunnels are about ten (4–40) inches in length, situated about two to twelve inches below the surface. They lead to two or three adjoining chambers about six inches in diameter, which usually rest on the permafrost line. One of the chambers, which is used for a nest, is lined with dry grass and lemming fur; the others are usually bare and are used as resting places or as toilet areas. A network of about thirty-five yards of runways generally connects a nesting site and several other 'funk holes.' Occasionally nest are found in the ruins of Eskimo huts and in stranded whale skulls. Winter nests are hollow balls of dried grass, about six inches in diameter, lined with lemming fur and

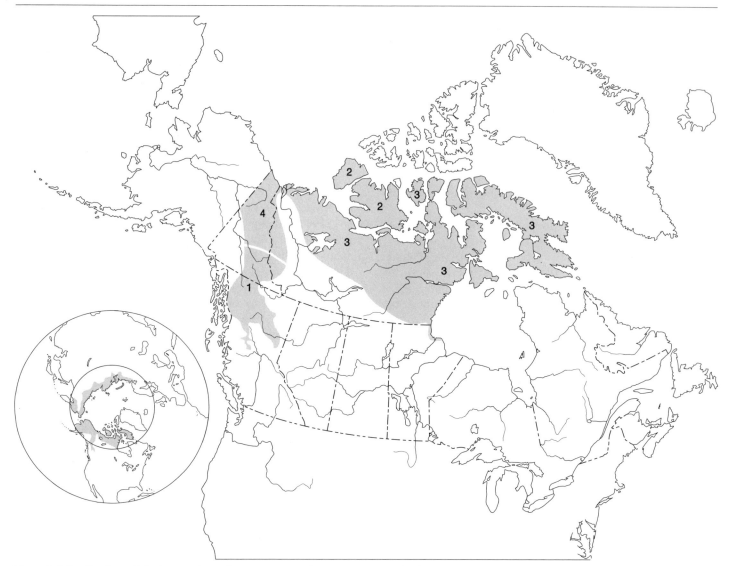

Map 76 Distribution of the brown lemming, *Lemmus sibiricus*: 1 *L. s. helvolus*, 2 *L. s. phaiocephalus*, 3 *L. s. trimucronatus*, 4 *L. s. yukonensis*

placed on the surface of the tundra. A succession of nests is built during the winter and each one is abandoned when it becomes soiled. When the snow melts directly above the nest because of the lemming's body heat, the resulting air space provides increased insulation. Numerous grass-canopied subnivial trails radiate from the winter nests to feeding areas.

The home range occupied by a single lemming may be as small as three and a half square yards in a crowded winter community, but it is thought to be of the order of thirty-six square yards for normal populations. Population densities may vary from 20 to 130 lemmings per acre in an expanding population. Lemmings show regular fluctuations, reaching peak numbers every two to five years. The population slowly builds up over a period of two to four years provided climatic, vegetative, and intrinsic factors are favourable. Eventually the high breeding potential produces an excess population, which may overutilize the food supply and force the lemmings to emigrate in order to

survive. The breaking point usually seems to be reached in June, when the flooding of their winter quarters forces them to move to higher ground. Then they become more vulnerable to predation by the great numbers of avian raptores that congregate in areas of high lemming populations. The emigration may carry lemmings into townsites, across lakes and bays, and out over the frozen sea, where their carcasses have been observed more than ten miles from land. On other occasions, intrinsic factors appear to govern the build-up, and great mortality occurs among the juveniles at the population crash.

The brown lemming has been known to live fourteen months in the wild.

This species lives primarily upon tender grass shoots and, later, on the tender blanched bases of the leaves of both grasses and sedges. It consumes forbs to a lesser degree and eats the bark and twigs of willows and dwarf birch in winter. The following plants have been reported as part of its diet: sedges, cottongrass, blue grass, other northern grasses, and buttercups. Brown lemmings do not seem to store any food in winter. Instead, they clip the bases of the grass sward which is blanketed by snow. In spring, this cut hay may cover the wet tundra in windrows piled up by wind and waves. In some local areas of concentration, 95 per cent of the previous year's growth of grasses and sedges have been cut in this manner. Lemmings are not above cannibalism in times of stress.

A host of arctic carnivores and raptorial birds live on lemmings. Among the most important predators are the snowy owl, the short-eared owl, the glaucous gull, the raven, the gyrfalcon, the rough-legged hawk, the pomarine, and the parasitic and long-tailed jaegers. The jaegers quarter over the tundra at low level and pounce on any lemming caught in the open. The carnivores include the least weasel, ermine, arctic fox, red fox, wolf, wolverine, and grizzly bear.

Habitat. Wet tundra swales are the favourite habitat of the brown lemming. It prefers areas covered with grasses and sedges to those covered by dry lichens or shrubs. It also inhabits stream banks, lakeshores, and grassy slopes. In winter it retreats to the wet meadows, where the snow lies fluffy among the dry stalks, and seeks shelter under the crests of ridges, where snowbanks will form. In June the melting snow becomes pockmarked with lemming holes and eventually discloses the swale honeycombed with their runways.

The brown lemming also occurs in alpine tundra, rock talus, and stream banks in the subalpine forests of the northern Rocky Mountains. During years of peak populations it may descend to the valley floors to occupy sphagnum bogs.

Reproduction. Under ideal conditions the breeding season may continue all winter under the snow, but there is usually a pause from mid-May to mid-June when the dramatic population upheaval takes place. In other years the breeding season is restricted to the summer period from mid-June to September. The females are seasonally polyoestrous and may bear from one to three litters a year. Normally the males are sexually active from early June to about mid-August. The gestation period is twenty-three days, and the average litter size is 7.3, but it may vary from four to nine.

The young lemmings weigh about 3.3 g at birth. Their eyes open on the eleventh day, and they scramble about the burrow at fifteen to seventeen days of age.

Economic Status. Lemmings are of great economic importance because they constitute the main food supply of many arctic fur-bearers. They may also supply an emergency source of food for humans in dire necessity.

Distribution. The brown lemming occurs in Siberia and across northern North America from Hudson Bay to Alaska and southward in the Rocky Mountains to central British Columbia. It also occupies the lower tier of arctic islands from Baffin to Banks islands.

Canadian Distribution. Four geographical subspecies of the brown lemming are recognized in Canada (see Map 76).

Lemmus sibiricus helvolus (Richardson), 1828, Zool. Jour. 3: 517. A bright rufous form, found in the mountains of southern Yukon and British Columbia, as far south as Mount Brilliant in the Rainbow Mountains.

Lemmus sibiricus phaiocephalus Manning and Macpherson, 1958, Arctic Inst. N. America Tech. Paper 2: 27. The lemming of Banks and Victoria islands, characterized by a greyer head and shoulders.

Lemmus sibiricus trimucronatus (Richardson), 1825, *in* Parry, Journal of a second voyage ..., appendix, p. 309 (London). The typical form of continental Northwest Territories, and Prince of Wales, King William, Baffin, and Southampton islands.

Lemmus sibiricus yukonensis Merriam, 1900, Proc. Washington Acad. Sci. 2: 27. Northern Yukon Territory.

REFERENCES

Krebs, Charles J. 1964. The lemming cycle at Baker Lake, Northwest Territories, during 1959–62. Arctic Inst. N. America Tech. Paper 15.

Sutton, G.M., and W.J. Hamilton, Jr. 1932. The mammals of Southampton Island. Mem. Carnegie Mus. 12(2), sect. 1: 53–8.

Watson, Adam. 1956. Ecological notes on the lemmings *Lemmus trimucronatus* and *Dicrostonyx groenlandicus* in Baffin Island. Jour. Animal Ecol. 25(2): 289–302.

SOUTHERN BOG LEMMING
Campagnol-lemming de Cooper. *Synaptomys cooperi* Baird

Description. Bog lemmings are very difficult to distinguish from meadow voles, *Microtus pennsylvanicus*, in external appearance. The diagnostic features are found in the skull. Bog lemmings are small, plump microtine rodents. They have very small eyes and short tails, scarcely longer than the hind feet (Figure 45a). The rims of the moderately long ears are only scantily haired, and there is a buffy patch of fur at the base of each ear. Their feet are small and delicate; the pollex is vestigial but bears a nail; the remaining claws are slender; the heel is sparsely haired, and there are six plantar pads on the naked sole. Males have prominent flank glands, which expand during the breeding season, and in older animals these sometimes possess tufts of white hairs. The females have six teats: one pectoral pair and two inguinal pairs.

For a microtine rodent, this lemming's skull is small and delicate (Figure 42d). The rostrum is very short and depressed. The upper incisors bear characteristic shallow, lateral, longitudinal grooves (Figure 46). The upper molars have deep re-entrant angles on the outside, and the lower molars have similar deep bays on the inner side. The last upper molar has four simple transverse loops, and the lower molars have closed triangles on the outer side (Figure 43).

The pelage of this species is longer and shaggier than

that of the meadow vole. It is bright brown dorsally and silvery grey ventrally. The face is greyer, and the feet are dark brown. Albinos have been encountered.

The juvenile pelage, which is fuzzy and dark grey in colour, is worn during the first month. The subadult pelage grows in along the lateral line, commencing at about twenty-four to twenty-eight days of age; this lasts for the next two months. It is darker and duller than the brown adult coat, which develops from irregular dorsal areas. There are two annual moults: autumnal from October to December and vernal from June to August. The winter coat is greyer and longer than the summer coat.

Average measurements of adults: length 125 (112–139), tail 20 (14–24), hind foot 19 (17–20.5), ear 12 (11–14) mm; weight 28.3 (18.7–39.6) g. The sexes are similar in size.

Habits. Bog lemmings are an uncommon species with a discontinuous distribution restricted to suitable habitats. They appear nervous and in captivity often quickly suc-

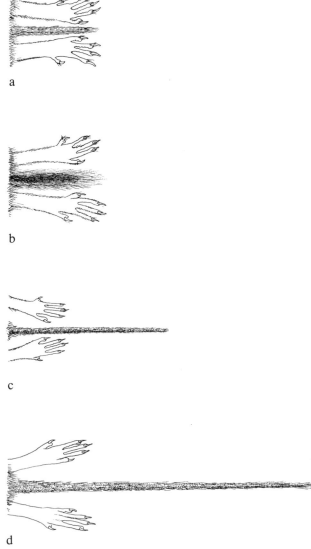

a

b

c

d

Figure 45 Hind feet and tails of microtine rodents: (a) southern bog lemming, *Synaptomys cooperi*; (b) singing vole, *Microtus miurus*; (c) meadow vole, *Microtus pennsylvanicus*; (d) long-tailed vole, *Microtus longicaudus* (× 1)

cumb to shock. When reared successfully, they seem to have a moderately mild disposition with only average strife among themselves. They are noisy, chattering when threatening, and uttering musical clicks when courting or low sounds when calling their young. They often move slowly and deliberately when feeding but can quickly scamper along their runways, swim with ease, or climb about low shrubs. They are continuously active night and day, with peaks of activity at dawn and dusk.

Throughout the severest winter weather they move about, but they may migrate at this time from their marsh habitat to dryer wooded slopes.

They dig shallow underground burrows, about an inch and a half in diameter, through the forest leaf mould, and a maze of sunken runways under sphagnum moss and through grass tussocks. Their nests, which are usually hidden in hollows under sphagnum mounds, logs, and stumps, or in grass tussocks, are constructed of dry shredded grasses and sedges and are about four to six inches in diameter. There are one or more entrances leading to sunken runways. Besides the nests, there may be several resting and feeding chambers in the lemmings' territory.

This species' home range varies from a fifth to half an acre. The males usually travel more extensively than the females. Although bog lemmings defend the territory about their nests, two occupied nests have been found less than three yards apart. Population densities vary from 2.3 to 14 animals per acre. The populations show regular annual cycles of abundance from a low in the spring to an autumn peak. There are also irregular fluctuations in the density from year to year. Individuals have lived a year in captivity and could have lived longer if they had not been sacrificed at that time.

The food of the bog lemming consists primarily of the leaves and bases of sedges, grasses, and beak rush. It cuts the sedges up into short (one- to three-inch) sections and piles them in its runways and at the entrances to feeding chambers. Bundles of whole sedge leaves, one to two feet long, are often stacked in the runways.

In summer, blueberries and huckleberries are eaten avidly, and in winter the leaves and twigs of leather-leaf. Bog lemmings are also noteworthy because of their consumption of an underground fungus, *Endogone*. Beetles and snails form a very small part of their diet. There does not seem to be any storage of winter food other than the bundles of sedge clippings. The presence of bog lemmings can usually be detected by the piles of bright green faeces (those of the *Microtus* are brown).

Bog lemmings are preyed upon by a number of carnivorous animals that inhabit bogs and swamps, including

Figure 46 Grooved upper incisors of bog lemmings (× 2)

Map 77 Distribution of the southern bog lemming, *Synaptomys cooperi*

opposums, short-tailed shrews, raccoons, grey and red foxes, long-tailed weasels, striped skunks, red-tailed, broad-winged, and marsh hawks, great horned and barred owls, crows, and black, king, water, and pine snakes.

Habitat. As the name indicates, the bog lemming is found mostly in bogs where sphagnums and heaths predominate. It also occurs in grassy marshes and damp mixed forests surrounding bogs.

Reproduction. The breeding season usually lasts from April to September but may extend to include the winter months under ideal conditions of food and cover. The females are seasonally polyoestrous and experience post-partum oestrus within twelve hours after the birth of their young. It is not known whether lactation prolongs the gestation period. The male gonads descend from April to mid-November, after which they ascend to the abdomen. The gestation period is twenty-three days. Most litters are born between May and September, with a decided spring peak. The litter size is three on the average, but may vary from one to seven. One female in captivity bore six litters in twenty-two weeks, but in the field females probably bear litters every sixty-seven days through spring and summer.

Young bog lemmings are like other small rodents at birth: blind and deaf, wrinkled and pink, and weighing about 3.7 g. Their incisors erupt on the fourth day, and by the seventh day they have acquired a covering of light yellowish-brown fur. Their ears open on the eighth or ninth day, and their eyes between the tenth and twelfth days. The youngsters start eating sedge leaves soon after their eyes open, and weaning takes place between the sixteenth and twenty-first days. Juvenile males mature at about five weeks of age.

Economic Status. The bog lemming is of no economic importance.

Distribution. The southern bog lemming is found in east-central North America.

Canadian Distribution. This species is widely distributed in southeastern Canada from the Maritime Provinces (absent on Prince Edward Island, Anticosti Island, and Newfoundland) to southeastern Manitoba (see Map 77). The typical form occurs in Canada.

189

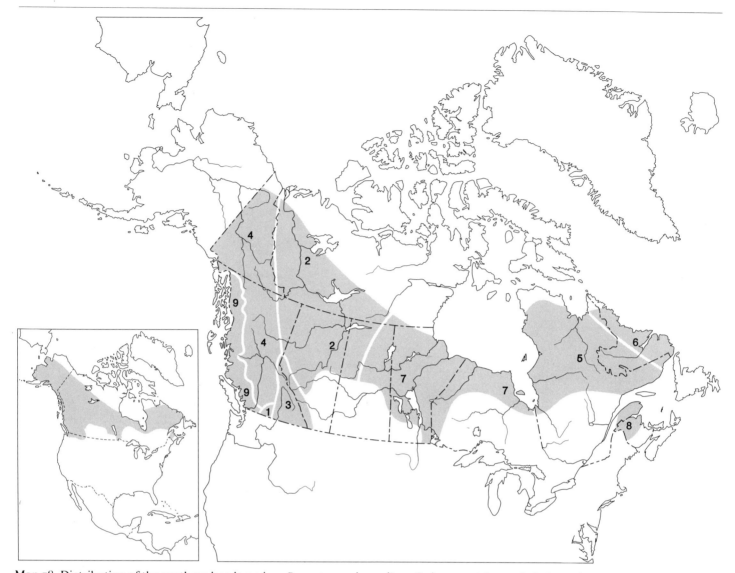

Map 78 Distribution of the northern bog lemming, *Synaptomys borealis*: 1 *S. b. artemisiae*, 2 *S. b. borealis*, 3 *S. b. chapmani*, 4 *S. b. dalli*, 5 *S. b. innuitus*, 6 *S. b. medioximus*, 7 *S. b. smithi*, 8 *S. b. sphagnicola*, 9 *S. b. wrangeli*

Synaptomys cooperi cooperi Baird, 1858, Mammals, *in* Repts. Expl. Surv. ... Rail. to Pacific, 8(1): 558.

REFERENCE

Conner, Paul F. 1959. The bog lemming *Synaptomys cooperi* in southern New Jersey. Pub. Mus. Michigan State Univ., Biol. Ser. 1(5): 161–248.

NORTHERN BOG LEMMING

Campagnol-lemming boréal. *Synaptomys borealis* (Richardson)

Description. Northern bog lemmings are superficially similar to southern bog lemmings. They can be identified with certainty only through the combination of a number of dental characteristics. The centres of distributions of the two species are generally widely separated, although the two species overlap in southeastern Manitoba, in the Allegheny Highlands region of Quebec, and in northern New Brunswick. Although they may occur in the same region, there is no intergradation in their dental characters.

The northern bog lemming is one of the lesser-known Canadian mammals. It is a small microtine rodent with a stubby tail. Its ears are sparsely haired along the rims, with buffy orange fur at the base, and project beyond the general body fur. The flank glands of the adult males are often clearly marked by a patch of white hair. In contrast to *S. cooperi*, the females possess eight teats: two pectoral pairs and two inguinal pairs (Plate 15a).

The skull has the very short rostrum typical of the genus *Synaptomys*. The trenchant dental characters include the projections on the upper incisors, outside the median longitudinal grooves, which extend beyond the medial edges of the teeth; the thin, pointed mandibular incisors; and the absence of closed triangles on the outer sides of the mandibular molars (Figure 43).

The pelage colour varies from greyish brown to chestnut brown in the various subspecies. The middle claws of this species are reported to enlarge in winter.

Average measurements of adults from the Rocky Mountains: length 129 (122–140), tail 23 (20–27), hind foot 19 (18–21) mm; weight about 33 g.

Habits. The habits of the northern bog lemming seem to be similar to those of the southern species. It digs short underground burrows and also uses runways through the vegetation. It constructs globular nests of grasses, which are placed underground in the summer and on the surface during the winter. It is active all winter and also during most of the twenty-four-hour period.

The food of these lemmings consists of grasses and sedges, which they cut into short sections and pile along their runways.

Habitat. This bog lemming frequents primarily sphagnum–Labrador tea–black spruce bogs, but it may also be present in deep mossy spruce woods, wet subalpine meadows, and alpine tundra. One subspecies inhabits dry sagebrush hillsides.

Reproduction. The breeding season extends from May to August; litters average about four but may vary from two to eight.

Economic Status. The northern bog lemming is too rare to be of any economic significance.

Distribution. This species occurs across northern North America from Labrador to Alaska. There is an isolated population south of the St Lawrence River in the northern Appalachian Mountains.

Canadian Distribution. This species is uncommon in northwestern Canada and rare in eastern Canada; its distribution has not yet been fully elaborated, however. A large number of poorly differentiated subspecies have been described, many of which are represented by only a handful of specimens (see Map 78). Further study may reduce the number of valid subspecies.

Synaptomys borealis artemisiae Anderson, 1932, Nat. Mus. Canada Bull. 70: 104. A small, pale subspecies that occupies the dry sagebrush slopes of the southern Okanagan valley in British Columbia.

Synaptomys borealis borealis (Richardson), 1828, Zool. Jour. 3: 517. A rich mahogany brown subspecies from the Mackenzie District and northern parts of Alberta, northeastern British Columbia, and northwestern Saskatchewan.

Synaptomys borealis chapmani J.A. Allen, 1903, Bull. American Mus. Nat. Hist. 19: 555. A greyish brown form, found in the southern Rocky Mountains of Alberta and British Columbia and in the Selkirk Mountains of British Columbia.

Synaptomys borealis dalli Merriam, 1896, Proc. Biol. Soc. Washington 10: 62. The northern interior of British Columbia.

Synaptomys borealis innuitus (True), 1894, Proc. United States Nat. Mus. 17: 243. A bright brown subspecies, found in northern Quebec.

Synaptomys borealis medioximus Bangs, 1900, Proc. New England Zool. Club 2: 40. A dark form from Labrador.

Synaptomys borealis smithi Anderson and Rand, 1943,

Canadian Field-Nat. 57(6): 101. A large, dull subspecies, distributed from central Saskatchewan to the foot of James Bay and north to southern Keewatin District.

Synaptomys borealis sphagnicola Preble, 1899, Proc. Biol. Soc. Washington 13: 43. Found in the Gaspé Peninsula of Quebec and in northern New Brunswick.

Synaptomys borealis wrangeli Merriam, 1896, Proc. Biol. Soc. Washington 10: 63. A variable form, found in the Coastal Range of western British Columbia.

REFERENCE

Harper, Francis. 1961. Land and fresh-water mammals of the Ungava Peninsula. Univ. Kansas Mus. Nat. Hist. Misc. Pub. 27: 57–60.

HEATHER VOLE
Phénacomys. *Phenacomys intermedius* Merriam

Description. Until 1953 the heather vole was considered one of the rarest North American mammals. Only eighty-five specimens had been collected in eastern Canada since its discovery in 1889; however, in 1953 at least ninety-five specimens were collected, and within the next two years the total had reached more than three hundred, in an unprecedented increase of these small rodents. So closely does the species resemble the ubiquitous meadow vole that it was not until Dr G.M. Dawson, former Director of the Geological Survey of Canada, sent a specimen to Dr C.H. Merriam in Washington in 1889 that it was first recognized. Merriam gave the name *Phenacomys*, meaning 'cheat' or 'deceiver' mouse, to the new genus because 'the external appearance of the animal gave no clues as to its real affinities.' This species, being unknown to the layman, has no common name. Only recently the name 'heather' vole has come into common usage in the scientific literature.

The plump-bodied heather vole has small eyes, short, rounded ears that barely extend beyond the fur, four toes on the manus, a short, wire-thin tail, and white feet. Its skin is loose and paper-thin, and its pelage is long and silky. The pelage colour is difficult to describe because it is quite variable across the country. Dorsally, heather voles are grizzled buffy brown. The eastern races are mostly a grizzled ochraceous brown; the western forms are a grizzled greyish-brown. In several of the eastern races there is a prominent tawny nose and a tawny rump, and the tips of the ears are also tawny; in some races the nose is more orange-brown; in others it is simply grey. The tail is bicoloured – dark grey above, white below – and sparsely haired. The underparts and feet are silvery grey (Plate 15c and d).

The truly diagnostic features are found in the cheek teeth of an otherwise rather typical microtine skull (Figure 42c). The prismatic surfaces of the mandibular molars are characterized by deep inner (lingual) re-entrant angles, and the outer (buccal) bays are much shallower. The high-crowned teeth continue to grow during the juvenile period until the root cavities occlude. The rooted adult

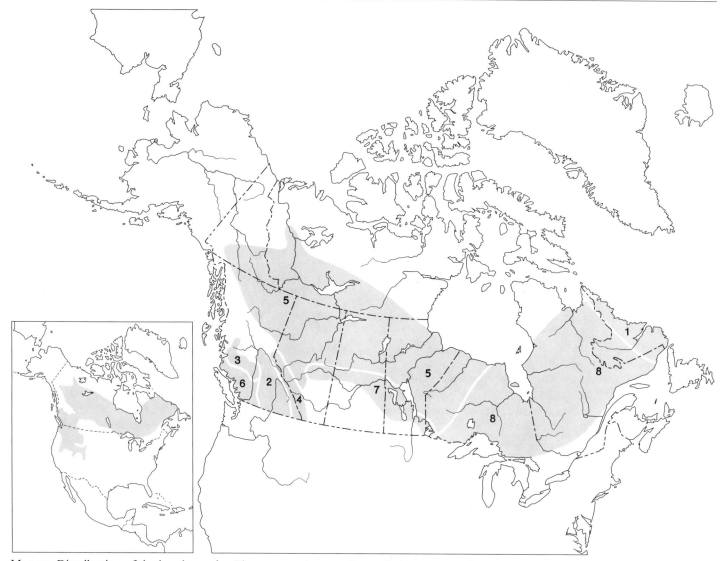

Map 79 Distribution of the heather vole, *Phenacomys intermedius*: 1 *P. i. crassus*, 2 *P. i. intermedius*, 3 *P. i. laingi*, 4 *P. i. levis*, 5 *P. i. mackenzii*, 6 *P. i. oramontis*, 7 *P. i. soperi*, 8 *P. i. ungava*

molars of the heather vole resemble those of the red-backed vole. There is no post-palatine shelf in the heather vole, and the cheek teeth are usually black (Figure 43).

There are three typical pelages: juvenile, subadult, and adult. The juvenile coat is brown and particularly thin on the belly. The subadult pelage is grizzled brown above and white-tipped below with a faint suggestion of orange-brown on the nose in the eastern races.

Average measurements, which vary between subspecies to some extent: length 138 (122–155), tail 33 (26–41), hind foot 18 (17–21), ear 12 (11–17) mm; weight 25–40 g.

Habits. The heather vole is the most docile vole: it never tries to bite and seems to take capture and captivity rather casually. It is not particularly wary and is occasionally observed in the wild state. This lack of caution may explain why its remains turn up frequently in owl pellets. During the summer months these voles lead solitary lives except for contact during the breeding season, when the

males fight viciously. The care of the young seems to be left to the female, and she will defend her nesting territory against intruding red-backed or other heather voles. During the winter months, however, the family groups huddle together in communal nests.

The heather vole is less diurnal in activity than the red-backed vole and is active mostly during the northern twilight hours. It is most active on dark, cloudy, stormy nights, and is active all winter beneath the blanket of snow. Though terrestrial, this species swims occasionally. It has a variety of squeaks.

Two types of nests are constructed. The winter nest, which consists of a hollow sphere of heather twigs and lichens about six inches in diameter, is lined with grass and placed on the ground under the protection of a shrub or wedged between rocks. Tunnels under the snow radiate out from the nest site. The summer nest, which is made of shredded moss, lichens, dried leaves, or grass, is built about four to ten inches underground, under a log, root, or stump, or at the base of a bush. Short tunnels (about three feet long) radiate from the nest to the surface. In one of these tunnels, close to the nest, the toilet area is located.

Little is known of the home range and population density of this vole, although tagged individuals have been known to travel at least two hundred yards. This species has irregular population fluctuations, and a population peak seems to flood all the local habitats.

In winter the heather vole lives on the bark and buds of shrubs and heaths including willow, dwarf birch, blueberry, bilberry, and bearberry. In summer it turns its attention to the green foliage of shrubs, heaths, and forbs, also to the berries and seeds of these plants, which include the blueberry, bearberry, soapberry, willows, dwarf birch, crowberry, bog-rosemary, mountain cranberry, sheep laurel, cinquefoil, fireweed, and baked-apple. Less attractive to it are lichens, licorice-root, and Labrador tea. Grasses and sedges it seldom touches.

The heather vole differs from the red-backed vole in that it prepares caches of food for the winter. These caches may contain about two quarts of twigs, and have been found to include 68 per cent blueberry, 9 per cent soapberry, 9 per cent dwarf birch, 6 per cent bearberry, 1 per cent crowberry, and 1 per cent fireweed. In summer these voles drag stores of cut foliage to the entrances of their burrows to eat in safety.

Hawks and owls, such as the rough-legged hawk and the short-eared, snowy, and hawk owls, seem to be the most important predators. Undoubtedly weasels and martens take their toll as well. There is even one instance of a heather vole's falling prey to a speckled trout.

Habitat. The heather vole seems to inhabit a wide range of habitats from sea level to the treeline in the Rocky Mountains at about 7,200 feet. Most have been taken in dry, open coniferous forests of pine or spruce with an understory of heaths such as blueberry, sheep laurel, dwarf birch, and soapberry, usually near water. Another favourite habitat seems to be shrubby vegetation on the borders of forests and in moist, mossy meadows. Usually shrubs in the form of willows, blueberry, or soapberry are near by.

Reproduction. The females possess four pairs of mammae: two pectoral and two inguinal. They are seasonally polyoestrous. The breeding season extends from May to August, and the litters are born between mid-June and early September after a gestation period of nineteen to twenty-four days. The average litter size is 4.8 (2–8), or, if only the adult females are considered, 5.9. The juvenile females bear smaller litters (average 3.8) the first season.

Young heather voles are typically pink, wrinkled, naked, blind, and deaf at birth and weigh approximately 2.4 (2.0–2.7) g. Pigmentation appears on the back, and the vibrissae are noticeable within the first twenty-four hours. They squeak feebly the second day. They are covered with satiny fur by the sixth day; they crawl on the eighth day and walk on the eleventh day; their eyes open on the fourteenth day; and weaning begins on the seventeenth day. They start to wander out of the nest by the time they are three weeks old, and after that they are on their own.

The juvenile females become sexually mature within four to six weeks and bear their first young three weeks later. The juvenile males, however, do not mature until the following spring.

Economic Status. This rare and interesting rodent is probably of no real economic significance in forestry or agriculture. It has been known, however, to succumb to listeriosis, a virus disease of some public health significance.

Distribution. The heather vole is found across northern Canada from Labrador to the Yukon Territory and southward in the Rocky Mountains to northern New Mexico.

Canadian Distribution. Eight subspecies are currently recognized from Canada (see Map 79).

Phenacomys intermedius crassus Bangs, 1900, Proc. New England Zool. Club 2: 39. A brown race with a dull orange-brown nose, found in coastal Labrador.

Phenacomys intermedius intermedius Merriam, 1889, N. American Fauna 2: 32. A dark, grizzled brown subspecies, found in central British Columbia.

Phenacomys intermedius laingi Anderson, 1942, Canadian Field-Nat. 56(4): 59. A grey race from the Coast Range of west-central British Columbia.

Phenacomys intermedius levis A.B. Howell, 1923, Proc. Biol. Soc. Washington 36: 157. A grizzled greyish-brown race from the Rocky Mountains of Alberta and British Columbia.

Phenacomys intermedius mackenzii Preble, 1902, Proc. Biol. Soc. Washington 15: 182. A grizzled buffy brown race with orange nose, found in the boreal forests of the northern parts of the Prairie Provinces, southern Yukon, and the Northwest Territories as well as the Peace River district of British Columbia.

Phenacomys intermedius oramontis Rhoads, 1895, American Nat. 29: 941. A large, dark, dull race, found in the Cascade Mountains of southwestern British Columbia.

Phenacomys intermedius soperi Anderson, 1942, Canadian Field-Nat. 56: 58. A grizzled ochraceous brown race with an orange nose, found on the edge of the coniferous forest in central Manitoba, Saskatchewan, and Alberta.

Phenacomys intermedius ungava Merriam, 1889, N. American Fauna 2: 35. An ochraceous brown subspecies with a tawny nose and rump, distributed from western Labrador to western Ontario. Some mammalogists believe the eastern forms constitute a distinct species, *P. ungava*.

REFERENCE

Foster, J.B. 1961. Life history of the phenacomys vole. Jour. Mamm. 42(2): 181–98.

COLLARED LEMMING
Lemming variable. *Dicrostonyx torquatus* (Pallas)

Description. This is the only rodent that turns white in winter. The Eskimos then call it *kilangmiutak*, which means 'that which drops from the sky.' This animal turns white about the time of the first autumn blizzards. It is frequently seen scurrying about on the new snow searching for winter quarters. The early Eskimos presumed that it dropped from the skies with the snowflakes. When it has its brown summer coat, some Eskimos do not distinguish it from the brown lemming, the tundra vole, or the northern red-backed vole, and simply call them all *avingak*.

The collared lemming, which shows a greater adaptation to the arctic environment than any other rodent, occurs on the most northerly tip of Greenland. It has the typically chunky lemming form; its eyes are moderately large and bright; its ear conch, which is vestigial, is hidden in the body fur; it has a mere stub of a tail. Its feet are much broader than those of the brown lemming and are more heavily furred on the soles. The stiff hairs that surround the toes give the impression that the lemmings are carrying wisps of straw in their feet. The plantar pads are vestigial under the fur. Its fur is dense, long, and silky. In its winter coat the lemming looks like a large cotton ball.

The most remarkable external feature of the species is the foreclaws in winter. The pollex is vestigial and carries a strap-like nail. The remaining four claws are not remarkable in summer, although there is a prominent pad at the tip of each toe. In the autumn, however, the pads on the third and fourth digits begin to bulge. They grow into compressed, cornified paddles, fifteen millimetres long. At the same time the claws, which are situated above them, lengthen. The two parallel growths are separated by a groove and a deep notch at the tips. This seasonal growth results in the appearance of two paddle-like bifid claws on each forefoot, measuring about fifteen millimetres in length. The claw on the fifth digit is a much smaller replica, but that on the second toe remains a single long scimitar-shaped claw. These special claws are used to dig burrows through wind-packed snowbanks. When growth stops in spring, the bifid claws are gradually worn back, the terminal pad softens, and the regular claw returns to its natural shape (Figure 47). The claws on the five digits of the hind feet are not remarkable.

The skull of the collared lemming is sturdily constructed. The nasals are flat and depressed. The zygomatic arches are oval in outline (rather than rectangular as in *Lemmus*). The interorbital borders are ridged, but there is a narrow dividing groove. Two prominent squamosal pegs project into the orbits from behind. The cranium is short and broad. The small auditory bullae are filled with spongy cells. The incisive foramina are long and broad (Figure 42b).

The cheek teeth are long and complex. The re-entrant angles are of equal depth on each side, leaving a central column and many lateral, enclosed enamel triangles. The first and second upper molars have small, posterior, internal enamel folds, and the last lower molar has a similar small anterior internal fold. The incisors are narrow and smooth (Figure 43).

This species' pelage is composed of long, dense, slate-coloured pile and longer, silky guard hairs. The winter coat is white with a greyish cast caused by the slate-coloured base of the hair. The flanks are often stained yellowish in late winter. The adult summer pelage is distinctive and colourful: the nose is black; the forehead is grizzled; the cheeks are grey; the ear spots are tawny or chestnut brown with a grey crescent behind; the shoulders, chest, and flanks are tawny to chestnut-coloured; the back is grizzled, with a variable black median stripe from ears to tail; the lips, flanks, and belly are buff or tawny-coloured; the tail is brownish at the base with a brush of stiff tawny or creamy hairs; the feet may be tawny to silvery white.

The juvenile pelage is woolly and grey above, with a prominent median dorsal black stripe from ears to tail, buffy below, and on the face, feet, and tail. The black median stripe persists in the adult coats of some populations but not in others.

There are two annual moults for the adults. The vernal moult takes place in May. The summer coat first appears on the head and progresses posteriorly and ventrally. The autumn moult begins in early October on the lateral line and progresses both ventrally and dorsally. The head is the last part to assume the white winter coat.

The juvenile coat is worn for the first twenty-five to thirty days, after which the preadult coat appears on the lateral line and spreads over the whole body. It is more tawny than the juvenile coat, and the black median line continues. The preadult pelage may be worn for a variable period of two weeks to three months, depending upon the season. Litters born in the spring moult into the summer adult coat, but those born in the autumn progress through a grey subadult phase into the winter adult coat. The moult is tied up with the reproductive cycle and influenced by the length of daylight, much as described for the snowshoe hare. Females may breed in the winter coat, but they moult into the summer coat before the birth of the young.

Average measurements of twenty-seven adults from Adelaide Peninsula, Northwest Territories: length 145 (132–162), tail 14 (12–18), hind foot 19 (17–22) mm; weight, 73 (56–112) g.

Habits. Collared lemmings are reported to be less colonial than brown lemmings. The family bonds are strong, however, and both sexes care for the young. The family often stays together until sexual maturity is reached, so that fathers mate with their daughters. The two species

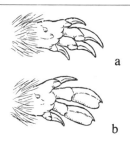

Figure 47 Forefoot of collared lemming showing growth of winter claws: (a) summer, (b) winter (× 1½)

often occur together in common runways under the snow in winter. This species has many of the same habits as the brown lemming, such as hopping about and shadow-boxing when cornered, or flattening itself when moving cautiously across the exposed tundra.

Under various light conditions, the frequency of activity during the twenty-four-hour period remains about the same, but the average duration of activity increases during periods of darkness. There is no significant nocturnal rhythm of movement, but activity may increase under arctic night conditions.

During the summer months these lemmings occupy shallow burrows under the tundra sod. The tunnels may be nine feet in length, four to eight inches deep, and two to three inches in diameter. There are usually small, bare resting chambers and toilet areas. The tunnels are generally deeper than those of the brown lemmings. The burrows lead to subterranean summer nest chambers, which are about four to six inches in diameter and lined with dry grasses and sometimes feathers, muskox hair, or wool. The chambers are located on the permafrost, often in a grass hummock or under a stone. Faint runways may be observed in permafrost crevices or among low heaths, but this species is less restricted to runways. The nesting burrows of this species are defended against interlopers.

In winter, these lemmings place their grass nests on the surface of the ground under a snowbank or even in the centre of a snowbank. They dig their tunnels through the heart of the snowbank with their winter claws. Occasionally they drill through the walls of igloos.

Populations of this species fluctuate just as dramatically as brown lemming populations, but the fluctuations are not always synchronized with those of that species. Peak populations have occurred at Churchill, Manitoba, in the years 1929, 1933, 1936, 1940, ——, 1949, 1954, 1958, and 1960, illustrating a periodicity of two to five years (no figures are available for the war years). The population fluctuations are thought to be controlled to some extent by weather and intrinsic factors. Mild winters, deep snow, and good food supplies encourage winter breeding, while extreme cold and windy, snowless winters result in high mortality. Densities vary between 0.6 animal per hectare at a population minimum to 400 per hectare at a peak. The mean longevity in captivity is 694 days, and the maximum 3 years, 3½ months. Probably few lemmings live beyond a year in the wild.

The summer food of collared lemmings consists of sedges, cottongrass, grasses, and bearberries. In winter they eat the buds, twigs, and bark of many species of willow. Clumps of willows may appear completely stripped in spring after a winter of high lemming numbers. They also indulge in cannibalism during periods of population stress.

Among the predators of this species are ermines, arctic foxes, wolves, and wolverines, snowy and short-eared owls, rough-legged hawks and peregrine falcons, glaucous gulls, and parasitic, pomerine, and long-tailed jaegers. Migrating herds of caribou are reported to eat the lem-mings they dislodge from runways, but I have never been able to confirm this. Migrating caribou herds in summer may, however, trample considerable areas of lemming habitat.

Habitat. The collared lemming is restricted to the arctic tundra zone. In summer it occupies higher, dryer, rockier tundra than the brown lemming, but much depends upon the moisture conditions. During exceptionally dry years it may remain on lower peaty tundra, but if there is sufficient moisture it will burrow in high gravel eskers in summer. In winter it retreats to lower sedge and cottongrass meadows where it is protected by a blanket of snow.

Reproduction. The breeding season usually extends from early March to early September, with a pause from mid-May to mid-June when the spring break-up causes such a dramatic population shift. Under ideal winter conditions, breeding may commence in January. The females are seasonally polyoestrous and experience post-partum oestrus. Ovulation is spontaneous. The males' gonads usually shrink about mid-August. The females possess eight mammae: two pectoral pairs and two inguinal pairs. The females are very aggressive during the mating season, often causing bloodshed among their male suitors. In captivity they frequently kill smaller males at this time. The gestation period is nineteen to twenty-one days in duration but may extend from twenty-two to twenty-six days by delayed implantation as a result of lactation.

The normal period of parturition is between early March and mid-September, but births have occurred as early as January 29. The average litter size in the wild is 4.53, but litters may vary from one to seven. Usually fewer are born in captivity, and the litter size seems to decrease when the age of the mother is over one hundred days. Up to five litters may be born in captivity, about a month apart, from April to September. Probably two or three litters are born in the wild during the summer.

The young weigh on the average 3.8 (2.7–4.8) g at birth. By the third day the grey juvenile pelage with the mid-dorsal black line is evident. The incisors erupt between the fourth and fifth days. When the female leaves her young, she covers them with nesting material. The ears open between the ninth and eleventh day, and the eyes between the twelfth day and the fourteenth. By that time they have full juvenile pelage, and they start to wander out of the nest. They are weaned at sixteen days and appear above ground for the first time. At this period the toe pads on the third and fourth digits of the forefeet are very prominent. If the litter is born in the autumn, the winter claws begin to grow at this age. By twenty-five days of age the autumn youngsters will have well-formed winter claws and will begin to moult into the pearly grey preadult winter pelage. At forty days old the subadults weigh approximately 42 (28–56.3) g. The juvenile females become sexually mature at twenty-seven to thirty days of age, when they weigh about 30 g. The males mature later, at about forty-six days of age, when they are in full subadult pelage.

Economic Status. The collared lemming is of great importance in the arctic biotic community, supporting a

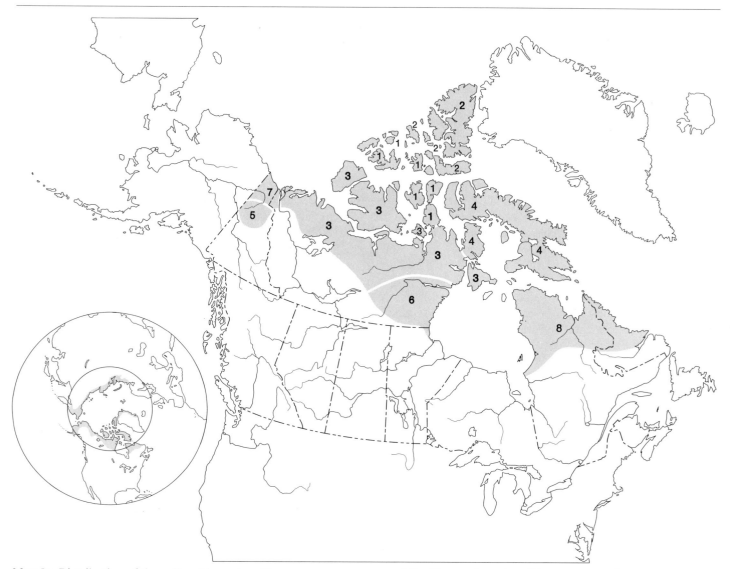

Map 80 Distribution of the collared lemming, *Dicrostonyx torquatus*, and the Ungava lemming, *Dicrostonyx hudsonius*:
1 *D. t. clarus*, 2 *D. t. groenlandicus*, 3 *D. t. kilangmiutak*, 4 *D. t. lentus*, 5 *D. t. nunatakensis*, 6 *D. t. richardsoni*,
7 *D. t. rubicatus*, 8 *Dicrostonyx hudsonius*

number of economically important fur-bearers such as the ermine and the arctic fox. This species also influences the tundra vegetation, scattering willow seeds and fragmenting the heaths during periods of excessive population.

The collared lemming may be of some adverse public health significance since it has been found to be host to the bacterium *Listeria monocytogenes*.

Distribution. The collared lemming is found in the tundra zone of Alaska, Yukon, and the Northwest Territories of Canada, and of northeast Greenland. The same species occurs as well on the Siberian tundra, and on Novaya Zemlya and the New Siberian Islands in northern Asia.

Canadian Distribution. Seven geographic subspecies of the collared lemming are currently recognized in Canada (see Map 80).

Dicrostonyx torquatus clarus Handley, 1953, Jour. Washington Acad. Sci. 43: 197. Borden, Prince Patrick,

Melville, Bathurst, Prince of Wales, and Somerset islands of the Arctic Archipelago, Northwest Territories.

Dicrostonyx torquatus groenlandicus (Traill), 1823, *in* Scoresby, Journal of voyage to the northern whale fishery ..., p. 416. A grizzled grey form, found on Greenland, Ellesmere, Devon, and Axel Heiburg islands, Northwest Territories.

Dicrostonyx torquatus kilangmiutak Anderson and Rand, 1945, Jour. Mamm. 26: 305. Banks, Victoria, Southampton, and King William islands of the Arctic Archipelago and the mainland tundra from the Mackenzie delta to Wager Bay.

Dicrostonyx torquatus lentus Handley, 1953, Jour. Washington Acad. Sci. 43: 198. Baffin Island and Melville Peninsula, Northwest Territories.

Dicrostonyx torquatus nunatakensis Youngman, 1967, Proc. Biol. Soc. Washington 80: 31–4. Isolated greyish form in Ogilvy Mountains of central Yukon.

Dicrostonyx torquatus richardsoni Merriam, 1900, Proc.

Washington Acad. Sci. 2: 26. A dark brownish form from the southern tundra west of Hudson Bay.

Dicrostonyx torquatus rubicatus (Richardson), 1839, *in* The zoology of Captain Beechey's voyage ..., p. 7. The brightest rufous-sided subspecies of Alaska, found on the Yukon tundra and as far east as the Mackenzie delta.

REFERENCES

Hansen, R.M. 1957. Development of young varying lemming (*Dicrostonyx*). Arctic 10(2): 105–17.
– 1959. Aspects of coat color in young varying lemmings. Jour. Mamm. 40(2): 205–13.
Manning, T.H. 1954. Remarks on the reproduction, sex ratio, and life expectancy of the varying lemming, *Dicrostonyx groenlandicus*, in nature and captivity. Arctic 7(1): 36–48.
Shelford, V.E. 1943. The abundance of the collared lemming (*Dicrostonyx groenlandicus* (Tr.) var. *richardsoni* Mer.) in the Churchill area 1929–1940. Ecology 24: 472–84.

UNGAVA LEMMING

Lemming d'Ungava. *Dicrostonyx hudsonius* (Pallas)

Description. Although the Ungava lemming is very similar to the collared lemming, trenchant dental characteristics mark it as a distinct species. The discovery of a skull of this species in western Pennsylvania, dating from the late Wisconsin glacial stage about 11,000 years ago, leads to the conclusion that it was the species trapped south of the Laurentian Ice Sheet, which has migrated northward to its present location in the Ungava–Labrador Peninsula. The collared lemming, on the other hand, is thought to have immigrated into northwestern Canada from a glacial refuge in Alaska and western Yukon territory.

This species is similar in external appearance to the previous one. The first and second upper molars, however, lack the rudimentary posterior internal enamel loop, and the third lower molar lacks the rudimentary anterior internal loop, both of which characterize the collared lemming (Figure 43).

The summer pelage is grizzled grey above with a faint black mid-dorsal stripe; it has tawny ear spots and a pale collar. The flanks and throat are buffy or tawny, and the underparts are grey. The feet and tail are silvery grey. The winter pelage is white, and the characteristic winter claws develop on the third and fourth digits.

Average measurements of adults: length 150 (134–167), tail 16 (10–20), hind foot 21 (20–23), ear 9 mm.

Life History. The habits, food, predators, reproduction, and economic status are not known to differ significantly from those of the collared lemming.

Distribution. The Ungava lemming is restricted to the tundra zone of the Quebec–Labrador Peninsula. It also occurs on offshore islands in eastern Hudson Bay, including the Belchers. Along the coasts it occurs as far south as Hamilton Inlet on the east and as far as Kakachischuan Point at the top of James Bay on the west. Inland, these lemmings inhabit the tundra hilltops near Schefferville and Michikamau Lake (see Map 80). The species is monotypic.

Dicrostonyx hudsonius (Pallas), 1778, Novae species quadrupedum e glirum ordine ..., p. 208. Northern Labrador and Quebec.

REFERENCE

Harper, Francis. 1961. Land and fresh-water mammals of the Ungava Peninsula. Univ. Kansas Mus. Nat. Hist. Misc. Publ. 27: 53–7.

MUSKRAT

Rat musqué. *Ondatra zibethicus* (Linnaeus)

Description. The muskrat is the largest of the North American rats, mice, and lemmings, measuring about 2 feet in total length and weighing about 3 pounds. It is modified for an aquatic life and is one of the important North American fur-bearers. It has a robust form, small beady eyes, and short ears, which are hidden in the fur. Its fleshy, furred lips, close behind the incisors, enable it to gnaw under water without getting water in its mouth. It has short legs, and small, delicate forefeet, which are used for grasping objects (the short pollex has a well-developed claw). Its large hind feet are rotated slightly; the soles are bare and have five plantar pads. The five toes, which are partially webbed, carry strong claws. There are also stiff fringes of hair on the edges of the feet and toes. The long, scaly tail is laterally compressed and only sparsely covered with hair on the sides, but it has prominent dorsal and ventral fringes of hair. Both sexes have prominent anal glands, which enlarge during the breeding season and emit a powerful musky discharge. The waterproof fur is composed of dense, soft underfur and longer guard hairs. The nostrils, the tail, and the soles of the feet are black. The females possess six teats: one pectoral pair and two inguinal pairs (Plate 14).

The skull is large and massive for a microtine rodent. The rostrum is long and stout; the zygoma is flaring; the interorbital region is narrow and ridged; the squamosal bones bear prominent ridges. The dentition is similarly massive and is characterized by rooted molars in the adults.

The dorsal coat colour is glossy mahogany brown, darkest on the head and rump. The flanks are chestnut to hazel-coloured. The underparts are olive grey or tawny, shading to silvery grey on the throat and hips. The dorsal surfaces of the feet are covered with short, sleek mouse-grey fur. The chin is black, and the lips are straw-coloured. Besides the normal coat there are a number of colour mutations: black, white, maltese grey, fawn, and albino (pink-eyed).

Although much has been written about primeness in muskrat pelts, little is known about the moult. Young muskrats have two distinct moults, but adults appear to shed their fur more or less continuously throughout the year. The bluish-black colour on the flesh side of the unprime pelt is caused by the concentration of pigment granules in deep-seated hair roots of the new coat. As the new hair grows, the pigment migrates into the hair, and the roots themselves move towards the surface. These processes result in the flesh side of the pelt becoming creamy white when it is prime. The adult autumn and spring moults are characterized by the blotched pattern of the pelt. Subadults and kits show a more regular moult pattern. The new hair first appears on the nape of the neck and on two narrow lateral lines. This black horseshoe pattern gradually spreads over the back, the belly usually being the last to become prime. The young kit muskrats have a darker, woollier pelage.

Average measurements of adult male northern muskrats: length 572 (496–616), tail 256 (222–282), hind foot 76 (70–81) mm; weight 1.13 (0.75–1.16) kg. Females: length 562 (513–596), tail 250 (195–278), hind foot 74 (68–80) mm; weight 1.05 (0.80 –1.37) kg.

Habits. The muskrat is an amphibious rodent that spends most of its time in the water. It is an excellent swimmer, using its hind feet as propellers and its tail as a rudder. It can swim a hundred yards underwater and remain submerged for seventeen minutes under stress, but two to three minutes is the usual period of submergence. When loafing along, the muskrat often holds its tail out of the water. When surprised it dives quickly with a splash of its long tail. In winter its progress under thin ice may be followed by the line of bubbles it leaves. It has been reported that it refreshes the air in its lungs by pausing to breathe in large air bubbles trapped under the ice. It is chiefly nocturnal or crepuscular in activity but may often be seen feeding during daylight hours, especially on cloudy days.

Muskrats live in family units occupying a house, several feeding platforms and canals, or tunnels through the cattails. The diameter of their home territory during the summer, autumn, and winter is about sixty-seven yards. They are very quarrelsome among themselves and defend their home territory against neighbours. Muskrats are vicious fighters and dangerous when cornered or captured. They have been known to attack people walking along roads.

During the autumn there is a population shift, with some muskrats abandoning dried-out ponds that would endanger winter survival. Again in early spring an even more pronounced population dispersal occurs, particularly among the males and young. The females take possession of the closest denning sites and force the excess females and males to move elsewhere in search of dens and mates. Muskrats seem to be monogamous during the breeding season. There is a great deal of strife at this period, and most adults become torn and ragged. Many are killed in spring fights. Tagged muskrats have been known to migrate as much as eight miles.

Population densities may vary from three animals per acre of open pond to thirty-five per acre of cattail marsh. Quantitative analyses of food supply have shown that Manitoba marshes may carry as many as twenty-three to twenty-six animals per acre. Excessive populations cause local 'eat-outs' of cattails around the houses. Muskrat harvests have been as high as eight muskrats per acre in

Ontario, and such high densities usually result in much intraspecific strife and epizootics. Muskrat populations show dramatic long-term fluctuations. These seem to follow an approximate ten-year periodicity in northern Canada but a shorter six-year periodicity in Saskatchewan. Climatic fluctuations, epizootics, fur prices, and marsh management schemes affect the harvest.

No exact data are available on longevity, but it is thought that muskrats live about three years in the wild and up to ten years in captivity.

Muskrat houses constitute a familiar feature of our marshes. They are usually constructed of broad-leaved cattails or bulrushes and are plastered with mud and pond weeds. House construction, which commences in August or September, is completed in October. Houses are usually destroyed in the spring by flooding and are not repaired. The muskrat builds its house on a log or stump or in a clump of willows, usually located near the edge of the emergent vegetation zone and near deep water. Initially a platform is built, and then a dome is arched over a central chamber. When completed, it may rise four feet above the water level, with a bed of dry grass for each muskrat.

Muskrats also use bank dens, if there is any firm ground around their ponds. The entrance to the dens is under water, and the tunnels lead upwards for a distance of from one to ten yards to dry chambers. If the bank den has been occupied for several years, there may be a number of entrances and tunnels leading to two or three chambers. Muskrats prefer to bear their young in bank burrows. In rivers and lakes many muskrats live in bank burrows all winter as well. If no dry land is available, the young are born in reconstructed houses in the marsh.

If the pond becomes shallow in the summer because of evaporation and growth of vegetation, the muskrats construct water-filled canals and tunnels in the mud, radiating from the houses.

A characteristic feature of the northern muskrat in winter is the construction of 'push-ups,' i.e. domes of frozen vegetation covering a plunge-hole in the ice, in which the muskrat feeds in winter. The muskrat starts the process in the autumn when the pond first freezes over by chewing a hole through the thin ice (often using an air bubble or the location of escaping marsh gas). It then pulls up submerged vegetation such as pondweed, bladderwort, or water milfoil, and constructs a dome over the hole. The vegetation freezes and eventually becomes covered with snow, which insulates the feeding station from the cold. Constant visits by the muskrat break the thin ice and circulate the water. The plunge-holes are kept open even though the ice may become as thick as three feet. The push-ups are constructed about twelve yards apart in straight lines from the house or bank den to the feeding grounds. Gradually during the winter the number of active push-ups diminishes because of damage to the insulation, muskrat mortality, or abandonment.

The summer food of muskrats consists primarily of readily available emergent vegetation. Among the most important species are broad-leaved cattail, bulrush, stovepipe reed, sedge, sweet flag, water lily, arrowhead, and other pond weeds. Muskrats also eat a considerable amount of animal matter, among which fresh-water mussels are the most important. Piles of discarded shells of the following species are often found on their feeding rafts: *Quadrula pustulosa*, *Crenodonta costata*, *Pleurobema cordatum*, *Lampsilis ovata*, *Lampsilis radiata*, *Anodonta grandis*, *Anodonta cataracta*, *Tritogonia verrucosa*, *Lasmigona complanata*, and *Actinonaias carinata*. They also are reported to eat small turtles, frogs, salamanders, and slow-moving catfish.

The winter food consists of submerged vegetation including pondweeds, coontail, water lily tuber, water milfoil, water weed, bladderwort, and bur reed. It is not thought that muskrats store any significant amount of food for winter use, but sections of stovepipe reed have been found in bank burrows.

The amphibious muskrat must always be on the alert for predators. Pike and snapping turtles attack young muskrats while they are swimming. The mink is probably the most serious predator, particularly in the autumn and spring when many muskrats are travelling or when young muskrats are in the dens and houses, but an adult muskrat, cornered in his house or den, has been known to defend himself effectively and to chase mink out. Otters, though more interested in other game, occasionally kill a muskrat under special circumstances. Muskrats travelling on the land fall easy prey to foxes, coyotes, and wolves. In the early autumn these same carnivores may capture a few muskrats in the newly formed push-ups. Later in the season, however, the push-ups freeze too solidly to be opened. Black bears and lynx would not pass up a wandering muskrat either! Some of the larger avian raptores also kill muskrats when they are exposed in the marshes; these include great horned owls, gyrfalcons, goshawks, and bald and golden eagles.

Caribou, domestic reindeer, and wapiti create a special hazard in winter. They cross the frozen ponds and paw the frozen push-ups to eat the green vegetation. This action may result in the freezing up of the plunge-holes unless the muskrat can repair the damaged push-up.

Habitat. The muskrat is found in a wide range of aquatic environments: lakes, rivers, ponds, sloughs, and marshes. Ideally the water should be about four to six feet deep so that it will not freeze to the bottom. It should not be over twelve feet in depth, or there will be no submerged vegetation on the bottom.

Many of the shallow cattail marshes inhabited in the summer must be abandoned during the winter if the water and the bottom freeze, for then the muskrat can neither travel nor feed.

Reproduction. Female muskrats are seasonally polyoestrous. The oestrous cycle averages 6.1 (2–22) days in length. Ovulation is spontaneous. Post-partum oestrus occurs in the southern part of the range, but northern litters tend to be farther apart. The muskrat may breed throughout the whole season in the south, but in Canada the breeding season is confined to the period between March and September.

The male testes enlarge in late February, descend into the scrotum in March, begin to shrink in late August, and are withdrawn into the abdomen in November or early December. Active spermatogenesis has been observed from March 19 to late August. The gestation period is between twenty-five and thirty days. The first litters are born between mid-May (in Manitoba) and early June (in the Mackenzie Delta). The last Manitoba litter was reported on September 20. The litter size varies with latitude and may average as low as 2.4 in the south and 7.1 in the north. The total range of litter size is from one to eleven young. The number of litters produced in a year also varies with latitude, but conversely to litter size. In Louisiana three to six litters may be born in a year, but two litters is the norm in northern Canada.

Young muskrats are naked, blind, and helpless at birth and weigh about 22 g. At five days of age they are covered with coarse sooty hair and are able to move about the nest. Their eyes open between fourteen and sixteen days, at which time their coats are grey and fine. Weaning takes place between the twenty-first and twenty-eighth day, and the young muskrats are on their own by the time they are a month old.

The juveniles (kits) may mature at the age of six months in the south, but in the north they do not mature until they are yearlings. The yearling females experience their first oestrus in mid-May, usually later than the adults. The first litters are also smaller, averaging 4.9 young. There is some evidence that they have only one litter during their first breeding season.

Economic Status. The muskrat is one of the more important Canadian fur-bearers, from one to four million skins having been taken annually for many years. During the 1971–72 trapping season 1,794,544 skins were taken and sold at an average value of $1.76 for a total value of $3,160,480. In previous years the value of muskrat pelts has been higher (up to $2.75 in 1945) and the gross has been almost five million dollars. Muskrats are normally trapped at their push-ups during the winter months when the skins are prime, but sometimes they are trapped in their houses or shot in the open water in spring, although their pelts may be torn from fighting at that time. Good management practice ensures that muskrats are harvested in early winter as soon as the pelts are prime and before winter losses occur from freeze-outs and epizootics.

Muskrats are also good to eat and have been marketed in several large American cities in the past. Care should be taken not to rupture the musk glands in skinning and to keep the fur from touching the flesh. Soaking in brine lessens the 'gamey' taste. They are best during the autumn and winter months when the musk glands are reduced.

Muskrats are susceptible to tularaemia, which causes periodic die-offs. Care should be taken not to handle sick muskrats in view of the risk of contracting the disease. As a result of their tunnelling activities, muskrats are a nuisance in irrigated districts.

Distribution. The muskrat inhabits practically all of North America from the Gulf of Mexico to Alaska, with the exception of portions of the arid Southwest and the arctic tundra.

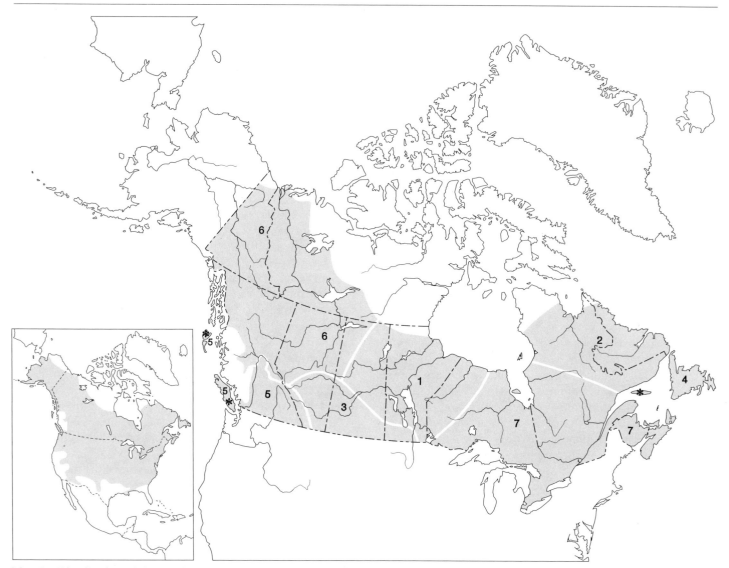

Map 81 Distribution of the muskrat, *Ondatra zibethicus*: 1 *O. z. albus*, 2 *O. z. aquilonius*, 3 *O. z. cinnamominus*, 4 *O. z. obscurus*, 5 *O. z. osoyoosensis*, 6 *O. z. spatulatus*, 7 *O. z. zibethicus*, * introduced

Canadian Distribution. The species is widely distributed across Canada from Newfoundland to coastal British Columbia and northward to include most of Yukon Territory and Mackenzie District. It has been introduced to Vancouver, Anticosti, and the Queen Charlotte islands. It is absent from the tundra zone. It is a fairly plastic species, and seven subspecies are recognized in Canada (see Map 81).

Ondatra zibethicus albus (Sabine), 1823, *in* Franklin, Narrative of a journey to the shores of the Polar Sea ..., p. 660. A pale form, found southwest of Hudson Bay, including much of the Prairie Provinces.

Ondatra zibethicus aquilonius (Bangs), 1899, Proc. New England Zool. Club 1: 11. A small, dark race from Labrador and northern Quebec.

Ondatra zibethicus cinnamominus (Hollister), 1910, Proc. Biol. Soc.Washington 23: 125. A pale form from the southern prairies.

Ondatra zibethicus obscurus (Bangs), 1894, Proc. Biol. Soc. Washington 9: 133. The muskrat of Newfoundland, characterized by a weaker skull and shorter tooth row.

Ondatra zibethicus osoyoosensis (Lord), 1863, Proc. Zool. Soc. London, p. 97. A large, dark race, found in southern British Columbia.

Ondatra zibethicus spatulatus (Osgood), 1900, N. American Fauna 19: 36. A medium-sized dark subspecies, found throughout most of northwestern Canada and Alaska.

Ondatra zibethicus zibethicus (Linnaeus), 1766, Syst. Nat., 12th ed., 1: 79. The nominate race, found in eastern Canada.

REFERENCES

Butler, L. 1940. A quantitative study of muskrat food. Canadian Field-Nat. 54(2): 37–40.

Fuller, W.A. 1951. Natural history and economic impor-

Map 82 Distribution of the sagebrush vole, *Lagurus curtatus*

tance of the muskrat in the Athabasca-Peace delta, Wood Buffalo Park. Wildlife Mngt. Bull., ser. 1, no. 2. Canadian Wildlife Serv., Ottawa.

McLeod, J.A., and G.F. Bondar. 1952. Studies on the biology of the muskrat in Manitoba. Part 1. Oestrous cycle and breeding season. Canadian Jour. Zool. 30: 243–53.

Stevens, W.E. 1953. The northwestern muskrat of the Mackenzie delta, Northwest Territories, 1947–48. Wildlife Mngt. Bull., ser. 1, no. 8. Canadian Wildlife Serv., Ottawa.

SAGEBRUSH VOLE
Campagnol des armoises. *Lagurus curtatus* (Cope)

Description. The sagebrush vole's closest living relative is the steppe lemming, *Lagurus lagurus*, of Central Asia. Our species is a moderately sized, robust vole with a tail scarcely longer than the hind foot. Its ears are also short.

The soles of the feet are quite well furred. There are usually five indistinct plantar pads. The males have flank glands, and the females have eight mammae: two pectoral pairs and two inguinal pairs (Plate 15n).

This vole's skull is flat and broad; the rostrum is short; the incisive foramina is long and broad; and the post-orbital squamosal crests are prominent. The auditory bullae are enlarged and filled with spongy cells. The dental pattern is quite distinctive. The molars are delicately constructed with tightly enclosed triangles and wide intervening re-entrant angles. The upper last molar has two medial closed triangles and a slender posterior loop. The first lower molar has five closed triangles (Figure 43).

The pelage of the sagebrush vole is long and lax. The dorsal colour is pale buffy or ash grey; there are clear buffy areas on the nose, ears, and flanks; and the underparts and feet are soiled white. The tail is heavily furred, mostly soiled white with a narrow, dark grey dorsal stripe and a terminal 'pencil' of hairs. There are two annual moults.

201

The winter pelage is lighter than the summer one. The first juvenile coat is marked by long dusky hairs.

Average measurements of adults: length 128 (112–130), tail 20 (18–21), hind foot 18 (17–18) mm; weight 31.5 (26–38) g.

Habits. The sagebrush vole is generally found in isolated colonies. The populations may fluctuate from year to year, being abundant in a given locality one year and scarce there a few years later. They are active both day and night and show little fear of exposing themselves even on sunny days. They are also active all year around.

This species excavates a shallow network of burrows in light sandy soils. The burrows are seldom more than four to twelve inches deep and may be as short as two feet in length (although they are usually longer) before the nesting chamber (seven to ten inches in diameter) is reached. The burrow system usually has a number of entrances under sagebrush clumps, although the holes may also be in the open. The tunnels are often paved with grass cuttings. The nests, which are located underground, are constructed of shredded sagebrush bark and lined with dry grass. The voles scamper between the burrow entrances, darting from one clump of sagebrush to another over well-beaten trails across the arid ground. Since the vegetation is sparse, their runways are not canopied like those of the meadow voles.

The summer food of this species consists of green leaves and the soft seed heads of blue grasses, cheat grass, wild onion, sagebrush, tumbling mustard, and blazing star. In winter these voles consume the bark and cambium layer of sagebrush and the underground roots of several plants. They are not known to store food supplies.

The short-eared owl has been cited as a predator. Undoubtedly other predators, including snakes, hawks, weasels, ferrets, badgers, fox, and coyotes, prey upon these voles.

Habitat. Sagebrush voles are found on high, arid sagebrush steppes. In California they also occur at an elevation of 12,000 feet in high, grassy ridges, road borders, and stone walls.

Reproduction. This species breeds all year in the southern part of its distribution, but only from March to early December in the northern part. Litters have been born between April 11 and December 2. The average litter size is 6.1, but embryo counts have varied from two to eleven.

Economic Status. The sagebrush vole in the United States has been found to carry fleas that were infected with the sylvatic plague bacillus, *Pasteurella pestis*, although there was no evidence of an epizootic among the voles.

Distribution. The sagebrush vole inhabits the arid steppes and mountains of central North America.

Canadian Distribution. In Canada the species is found only on the arid, short-grass plains of southwestern Saskatchewan and eastern Alberta, as far northwest as Drumheller (see Map 82). The Canadian form is:

Lagurus curtatus pallidus (Merriam), 1888, American Nat. 22: 704.

REFERENCE

Soper, J.D. 1931. Field notes on the pallid meadow mouse, *Lagurus pallidus* (Merriam). Canadian Field-Nat. 45(9): 209–14.

RICHARDSON'S WATER VOLE
Campagnol de Richardson. *Arvicola richardsoni* DeKay

Description. Recent anatomical studies have shown that this species is closely related to the Eurasian water vole, or water rat, *Arvicola terrestris*. Richardson's water vole has a robust body and is the largest of the American voles; it has a moderately long, well-covered, bi-coloured tail; short, furred ears; and large feet armed with long, curved claws. The pollex is vestigial and carries a flattened nail; the soles of the feet are naked, and the number of plantar tubercules is usually reduced to five. There are eight mammae: two inguinal pairs and two pectoral pairs. Both sexes have prominent flank glands about ten millimetres in diameter and an anal gland that secretes a musky discharge. As might be expected from the name, this species has slight amphibious adaptations. Its body is fusiform, the underfur is dense, and there are faint fringes of stiffened hairs on the edges of the hind feet (Plate 150).

The skull is massive and angular, for a vole. The widespread zygomatic arches are strongly developed, and there are post-orbital crests on the squamosal bones for the attachment of powerful muscles. The auditory bullae are reduced, and they are not filled with spongy bones like those found in *Microtus*. The rostrum is slender; the incisive foramina are laterally constricted and not noticeably enlarged anteriorly. The paraoccipital processes are well developed, and the mandible is similarly ruggedly constructed (Figure 42e).

The dentition is robust: the incisors are noticeably protruding. The last upper molar has two or three closed medial triangles followed by a crescentic posterior loop. The lower first molar has five closed median triangles (Figure 43).

The dorsal colour is a mixture of dark reddish brown and black-tipped hairs; the underparts are smoky grey; the feet are dark grey in colour; and the tail is dark brown above and pale grey beneath. There are two annual moults: vernal and autumnal. The juvenile pelage is rather woolly and dark greyish brown.

Average measurements of adults: length 252 (234–274), tail 83 (66–98), hind foot 30 (27–34), ear 15 mm.

Habits. The water vole is semi-aquatic in habits. It lives along stream banks and lakeshores and is an excellent swimmer and diver. It often takes to water to escape predators. It is colonial in behaviour, and is active throughout the total twenty-four-hour period as well as throughout the winter months beneath the snow.

It constructs large burrow systems (up to five inches in diameter) along stream banks, sedge meadows, and alder and willow banks. At times the banks may be honeycombed with their burrows, while broad runways criss-

Map 83 Distribution of Richardson's water vole, *Arvicola richardsoni*

cross the wet meadows. After the snow has melted in the spring, the ground may be quite cluttered with abandoned nests, caches, and runways strewn with vegetative debris.

The populations of this large vole fluctuate dramatically from abundance to scarcity. Population peaks occurred in southern British Columbia in 1919, 1927, 1949, and 1958.

The water vole feeds on a number of herbs such as valerian, lousewort, arnica, sneezeweed, and lupine as well as on the twigs and buds of willows.

Habitat. This species is found primarily in alpine meadows and along mountain streams from about 5,200 feet to 6,500 feet in elevation. Occasionally it occupies the stream-bank habitat in the alpine forest or in forest glades. Occasionally it also reaches the upper limit of the vegetative zone at about 7,500 feet.

During periods of peak populations water voles descend from the mountains to overrun valley farms as low as 600 feet in elevation.

Reproduction. Few details are known of the reproduction of this species. The breeding season occurs between mid-June and early September. The females are polyoestrous and usually bear more than one litter per season. The juvenile females of the spring litter mature in about five weeks to bear small litters in midsummer. The average litter size is five, but there may be from two to eight young.

Economic Status. Usually this species is of little economic significance, but about once each decade the population explodes, and these large voles descend upon isolated valley homesteads. They infest alfalfa fields and potato crops, and damage turnips and potatoes stored in root houses.

Control methods outlined for the meadow vole should be effective against this species as well.

Distribution. Richardson's water vole occurs in the central Rocky Mountain region of North America.

Canadian Distribution. Canadian water voles appear to belong to a single geographical subspecies. They inhabit the Cascade Mountains of southwestern British Columbia and the southern Rocky Mountains of southeastern British Columbia and southwestern Alberta (see Map 83).

Arvicola richardsoni richardsoni DeKay, 1842, Zoology of New York, Mammals, p. 91.

REFERENCES

Anderson, R.M., and A.L. Rand. 1943. Status of the Richardson vole (*Microtus richardsoni*) in Canada. Canadian Field-Nat. 57: 106–7.

Racey, K. 1960. Notes relative to the fluctuation in numbers of *Microtus richardsoni richardsoni* about Alta Lake and Pemberton Valley, B.C. The Murrelet 41(1): 13–14.

WOODLAND VOLE
Campagnol sylvestre. *Microtus pinetorum* (LeConte)

Description. The woodland vole is another isolated rodent species that has adopted the subterranean way of life and, like the western creeping vole, *M. oregoni*, exhibits a few fossorial adaptations. These include minute eyes; very small ears, which are hidden in the general body fur; a short tail; and soft, glossy, plush-like fur, which lacks the usual longer guard hairs. The woodland vole is a small, slender vole with a relatively large head. Its feet are small and delicate; the naked soles carry five plantar pads on the hind feet; the heels are well-furred. There are no flank glands, but anal glands are prominent. The skin is thin and tears easily. The females possess only four inguinal teats.

The skull of this vole is short, broad, and flat and has the same dental prismatic pattern as found in the prairie vole (Figure 43).

The pelage is sleek and silky, dark chestnut above, rather tawny on the flanks, and silvery or buffy grey beneath. The feet are grey, and the sparsely haired tail is bi-coloured. There is sometimes a mixture of blackish hairs on the face and rump. Pale tawny specimens are occasionally seen.

These voles have two annual coats: the winter coat, which is darker, is replaced in May or June by the light chestnut summer coat, which is moulted in November. The new fur seems to appear first around the forelimbs and then on the chest and head. A moult line usually develops over the shoulders and moves rapidly back to the rump. The first juvenile coat is short and thin and is slate grey in colour. This is shed at about five weeks of age, when the subadult coat with more brownish tones appears. After the age of about seven weeks the moult to adult pelage begins.

Average measurements of adults: length 121 (113–132), tail 21 (16–24), hind foot 17 (14–18) mm; weight 25.6 (22–37) g, exclusive of pregnant females.

Habits. This species is generally gregarious. Woodland voles are fairly placid individually, but are rather quarrelsome in colonies. If one of their number dies, its companions quickly turn to cannibalism. They are quite vocal, uttering a double-note alarm call, soft chatterings, and teeth gnashing when fighting. They are mostly fossorial in activity and seldom venture above ground. They are active throughout the twenty-four-hour period and show a slight preference for the twilight hours of dawn and dusk.

They scamper slowly along their burrows and swim and climb clumsily. Their eyesight is poor, but their hearing and tactile senses are acute.

The woodland vole threads a network of shallow burrows across the forest floor, just below the carpet of leaves. It is not a powerful digger and usually tunnels in rich humus or sandy soils, rarely below four inches in depth. It digs with its teeth and forefeet and kicks the loose earth out behind with the hind feet, leaving little piles of earth scattered on the forest floor. In heavier soils it uses mole and short-tailed shrew tunnels.

The globular nest of shredded grass or maple or birch leaves is usually constructed in a small hollow under a log, board, or stone, but it may be located in a chamber a foot deep under the roots of a stump. Occasionally the woodland vole excavates much deeper burrows (up to three feet) beneath the roots of orchard trees.

The woodland vole is very sedentary and occupies a home range about fifteen yards in diameter or a quarter of an acre in area. Forest populations fluctuate from year to year, never reaching plague proportions, but populations in orchards may reach a density of 100 to 200 per acre. Woodland voles live about a year in the wild.

As might be expected from the subterranean habits, the woodland vole's food consists largely of bulbs, tubers, and rhizomes. In the summer it eats green leaves and in the autumn considerable amounts of seeds and nuts. Among its favourite food plants are clover, quack grass, wild morning glory, dock, barnyard grass, witch grass, and the nuts of hickory, hazel, white oak, and burr oak. It caches tubers of violets, dutchman's breeches, and squirrel corn in the underground chambers along its tunnels.

Because of the subterranean habits of this species, few are taken by hawks and owls. However, they are hunted by foxes, raccoons, opossums, mink, weasels, dogs, and cats. The short-tailed shrew is a suspected predator.

Habitat. The woodland vole occupies a variety of habitats, all of them wooded. The most common habitat is the dry deciduous forest of beech, maple, and oak, although it also occurs in mixed forests and stands of pure hemlock. Less typical sites are scrubby sand dunes and orchards.

Reproduction. The females are polyoestrous, and the prolonged breeding season extends from January to October. The male gonads regress in early October, but spermatogenesis commences again in early January. The females are quite aggressive and may initiate mating. The males are often injured in mating encounters. Parturition occurs as early as February 11. The average litter size is 3.9, although one to eight embryos have been counted. There may be four to six litters born during a season.

The young weigh about 2.2 g at birth and soon fasten on to their mother's four teats. At three days of age the dorsum is leaden-coloured; the ear pinnae unfold at eight days. The young are well furred at nine days, and between nine and twelve days their eyes open and they begin to crawl out of the nest. Young woodland voles are weaned before they are seventeen days old.

Economic Status. In the United States the woodland

Map 84 Distribution of the woodland vole, *Microtus pinetorum*

vole has short legs and tail and small eyes and ears. Normally there are only five plantar pads on the hind feet, and the flank glands are obscure or lacking in the males. The females possess only six teats: one pectoral pair and two inguinal pairs (Plate 15i).

The skull is small and light: the incisive foramina are relatively short and are not pinched posteriorly. The auditory bullae are not enlarged. The dental pattern has trenchant differences that distinguish it from the meadow vole. The middle upper molar lacks the internal posterior loop, and the last upper molar has only two closed medial triangles rather than three. The first lower molar has three closed and two open triangles (Figure 43).

The dorsal colour of the prairie vole is grizzled grey, rather than brownish as in the meadow vole. This is caused by a mixture of light buff and black hair. The underparts, though usually a buffy grey, are sometimes a silvery grey. The well-furred tail is bi-coloured: dark brown above and light grey beneath. The feet are greyish above with well-furred wrists and heels. Occasionally individuals with white spotting on the back are seen, and a pure white specimen has been reported.

Three pelages have been described. The juvenile pelage is worn until the third or fourth week, and then the animal moults into the subadult pelage, which it wears until it is two or three months old before assuming the adult pelage. In each moult the new coat appears first on the chest, spreading anteriorly to the chin and posteriorly to the tail, then laterally to the flanks. The bands of new fur meet on the back and rump. The crown is the last spot moulted. The whole process takes about three weeks.

Average measurements of adult males: length 143 (121–167), tail 32 (25–42), hind foot 20 (17–22) mm. Adult females: length 150 (131–170), tail 33 (31–41), hind foot 19 (17–21) mm. Average weight of adult males 43 (38–55) g, and adult females 45 (38–58) g.

Habits. The prairie vole is more colonial and socially tolerant than the meadow vole. Small colonies (up to nine individuals) live together during the winter months, huddling in the same nest, travelling through the same burrows, and eating from the same food caches. These are probably family groups containing parents and late litters. During the severest winter weather these voles remain active beneath the surface, venturing forth in surface runways only during mild spells. When spring arrives the small colonies disperse, and the voles use surface runways and thick clumps of vegetation for cover.

Prairie voles may be active during any period of the day or night, but they are basically nocturnal creatures with two peaks of activity – one between sunset and midnight and a lesser peak at dawn. Seventy-five per cent of their activity takes place at night, the remaining activity being irregular food gathering.

These voles excavate an elaborate system of shallow underground feeding burrows, which are two inches in diameter, two to four inches below the surface, and as long as 120 yards. Most of the burrows are excavated in the autumn after rains have made the soil friable. The voles also use mole and pocket gopher tunnels as avenues.

vole is a serious orchard pest. It may burrow along the roots of apple trees, clipping off rootlets and stripping the bark from the main roots. It also girdles young trees. It frequently tunnels under fallen fruit and eats the apples from beneath. Fortunately this vole is uncommon and occupies a restricted range in Canada.

Distribution. The woodland vole is found in eastern North America from the Gulf of Mexico to the Great Lakes. It has a relative in southern Europe and central Asia.

Canadian Distribution. This species is found in southwestern Ontario north of Lake Erie and in the Eastern Townships of Quebec (see Map 84). The Canadian race is:

Microtus pinetorum scalopsoides (Audubon and Bachman), 1841, Proc. Acad. Nat. Sci. Philadelphia 1: 97. Southern Ontario and extreme southern Quebec.

REFERENCE

Benton, A.H. 1955. Observations on the life history of the northern pine mouse. Jour. Mamm. 36(1): 52–62.

PRAIRIE VOLE
Campagnol des Prairies. *Microtus ochrogaster* (Wagner)

Description. The prairie vole is quite similar in appearance to the meadow vole, *Microtus pennsylvanicus*. This small

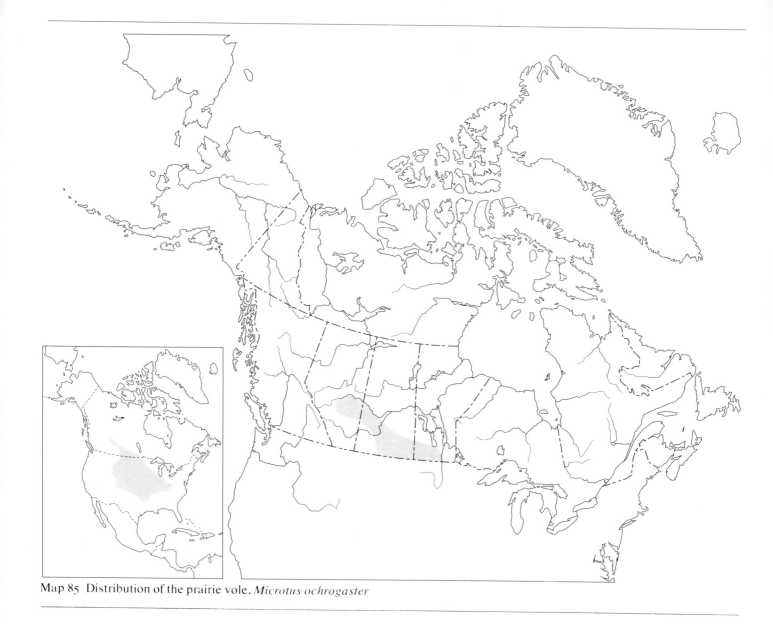

Map 85 Distribution of the prairie vole, *Microtus ochrogaster*

During the summer months they utilize a network of canopied surface runways.

The winter nests are placed in large underground chambers measuring as much as eight inches in diameter and located anywhere from six to eighteen inches below the surface. The globular nest is composed of shredded grass or sedge. Summer nests may be found in clumps of vegetation or grann stocks, under boards, or in pocket gopher burrows.

Populations of prairie voles fluctuate, but one cannot say that they show regular cycles of abundance. The normal annual cycle from abundance in the autumn to scarcity in the spring is regular, and longer fluctuations are often the result of moisture and food supply conditions and the prevalence of competitors. Population densities of 25.2 to 145.8 animals per acre have been measured.

The average home range of both sexes over a ten-month period was 0.24 acre, but it has been found to be as small as 0.02 acre for a female in another study.

Most individuals live less than a year: those born in the autumn as a group live longest. Most of the mortality is among the young, and well established adults may live twenty-two months in the wild or thirty-five months in captivity.

The food of the prairie vole consists of a wide variety of green forbs and grasses in summer and stored bulbs, rhizomes, and seeds in the autumn. Plants eaten in summer include alfalfa, sweet clover, quack grass, brome, wild lettuce, blue grasses, sage, and golden-rod. Winter stores consist of horse nettle fruit, dandelion seeds, ragweed seeds, prairie lily, wild onion, sunflower, pasque flower and avens, tubers, and bulbs.

Prairie voles excavate very large storage chambers up to three feet in length and eighteen inches in height and sometimes only an inch below the surface. In the autumn they pack these chambers with stored bulbs, tubers, rhizomes, and seeds. One cache inventoried in Manitoba contained 1,176 lily bulbs, 678 onion bulbs, 583 sunflower rhizomes, and 417 pasque flower tap-roots, which weighed a total of six pounds.

Predators of the prairie vole are short-eared and long-eared owls, hawks, badgers, skunks, foxes, coyotes, and weasels. The least weasel is perhaps the greatest menace, because one will usurp a winter nest and gradually dispatch the whole colony.

Habitat. The prairie vole inhabits the dry grassland plains. It requires considerable cover and evades bare areas, but it often inhabits shrubby borders. It will not enter wooded regions, however, and it will also leave the damper locations to the meadow vole.

Reproduction. This species may breed throughout the year in the more southern parts of its range under favourable conditions of food, moisture, and cover, but in Canada the breeding season appears to be confined to the period between April and September. The males are polygamous, and the females polyandrous. The gestation period lasts for about twenty-one days. The females are polyoestrous, and post-partum oestrus occurs a few days after the birth of each litter. In Canada as many as five litters may be born between the beginning of May and the end of September. The average litter size is 3.37, but there may be one to seven young. Subadult females produce smaller litters (2.9) on the average than do adults (3.4).

The young voles weigh about 2.9 g at birth. The female is very solicitous of her young and will defend them against other marauding adult voles, which would eat them if the opportunity arose. The suckling young cling to their mother's teats, and the mother drags them about if she leaves the nest. As mentioned previously, female prairie voles possess only six teats in contrast to the meadow vole's eight. Since the pectoral pair appear to be poorly supplied with milk, the young voles invariably cling to the inguinal teats. It is doubtful if more than four young could successfully be raised; this probably accounts for the lower litter size in comparison with that of the meadow vole.

The growth of the young voles is comparable to other species. Their eyes open at the age of nine to ten days. Juvenile females mature at thirty-six to forty days.

Economic Status. In Canada the prairie vole is much less common than the meadow vole, and therefore this species does less damage. Local colonies, however, may be quite damaging to ornamental and vegetable gardens because of their more subterranean habits.

Distribution. This species occupies the Great Plains region of North America.

Canadian Distribution. The prairie vole is found in southwestern Manitoba, southern Saskatchewan, and eastern Alberta as far northwest as Edmonton (see Map 85). The Canadian subspecies is:

Microtus ochrogaster minor (Merriam), 1888, American Nat. 22: 600. Prairie Provinces.

REFERENCES

Krebs, C.J., B.L. Keller, and R.H. Tamarin. 1969. *Microtus* population biology: demographic changes in fluctuating populations of *M. ochrogaster* and *M. pennsylvanicus* in southern Indiana. Ecology 50(4): 587–607.

Martin, E.P. 1956. A population study of the prairie vole (*Microtus ochrogaster*) in northeastern Kansas. Univ. Kansas Pub. Mus. Nat. Hist. 8(6): 361–416.

SINGING VOLE
Campagnol chanteur. *Microtus miurus* Osgood

Description. This vole was first discovered in Canada in 1943 during the construction of the Alaska Highway. Dr C.H.D. Clarke collected the first specimen in the St Elias Mountains of the Yukon Territory and called it the singing vole because of its habit of coming to the entrance of its burrow and uttering a high-pitched trill.

It is a medium-sized vole with small ears and a very short tail. The flank glands are prominent on the males during the breeding season. The wrists and heels are well furred. The pollex is suppressed, but the hallux is prominent. There are five plantar pads on the hind feet. The claws are relatively long and narrow. The female has the normal microtine pattern of eight mammae. The long soft fur gives the vole a robust, lemming-like appearance (Plate 19).

The diagnostic features are found in the skull, which is light, narrow, long, and flat. There is a prominent interorbital keel in the adults, and this region is also depressed. The cranium is relatively small and narrow; the auditory bullae are large. The tooth enamel pattern is illustrated in Figure 43.

This species is quite variable in colour throughout its distribution. Some specimens are pale tawny grey above, while others are grizzled greyish brown. The characteristic markings include a buffy or tawny ear spot and a short, heavily furred tail, which is grizzled above, clear buff or tawny beneath, and tipped with stiff buffy or tawny hairs (Figure 45b). The flanks may be tawny or grey, and the underparts clear grey or heavily suffused with an ochraceous tint. The feet are clear grey or buffy grey. There is frequently a buffy patch at the base of the fine, long vibrissae.

Four pelages have been reported: juvenile (nestling), post-juvenile, preadult, and adult. The juvenile pelage first appears on the back and works around to the belly. Other moults start first on the flank and gradually work both dorsally and ventrally, usually ending up on the rump. There are two annual moults: autumnal (September–October) and vernal (May–June). The winter coat is longer and paler than the summer coat.

Average measurements of adults from the Alaskan Brooks range: males, length 155 (147–161), tail 30 (21–35), hind foot 20 (19–21), ear 13 (11–14) mm; females, length 147 (134–161), tail 29 (25–32), hind foot 19 (18–21), ear 13 (11–14) mm. Average weight of adult males, 48 (40–60) g; and of adult, non-pregnant females, 43 (32–52) g.

Habits. The singing vole is colonial in behaviour. It swims well and climbs among the low willows and heaths of the tundra. It is probably the most vocal of the voles, uttering a series of high, thin, pulsating chirps whenever danger threatens the colony. It is active throughout the twenty-four-hour period and throughout the year as well.

Map 86 Distribution of the singing vole, *Microtus miurus*: 1 *M. m. andersoni*, 2 *M. m. cantator*

This species excavates short, shallow burrows about an inch in diameter and four to eight inches below the surface. These burrows, which may be as short as eight inches, seldom exceed three feet in length. They lead directly to a nesting and storage chamber of considerable size (up to twelve inches in length), whose roof is often within two inches of the surface. The voles carry the excavated soil to the surface in their mouths and dump it at the burrow entrance, so that it accumulates to form a readily observed pile of fresh earth. They construct their nests of shredded, dry vegetation at the back of these chambers. Although the surface runways are not so pronounced as those of the meadow vole, they may be traced through the moss in the vicinity of the burrows.

The singing vole's food consists of forbs such as lupine, arctic locoweed, horsetails, knotweed and sedge, and leaves and twigs of dwarf arctic willows. In autumn it caches large amounts of food for winter use. The knotweed and sedge rhizomes are stored underground, but much green vegetation is cut and piled around the stems of low willows and birches to cure. Individual stacks contain-

ing as much as two quarts of willow leaves and green forbs may be piled up in three days. Large stacks may stand as high as eighteen inches and contain half a bushel of forage.

Populations fluctuate greatly: one season they may be the most abundant small mammal in their habitat; another year in the same locality it may be impossible to find a single specimen. They seem to be sedentary, and the home range of one isolated individual was estimated to be not more than twenty square yards.

Their predators include grey jays, short-billed and herring gulls, jaegers, short-eared owls, grizzlies, wolves, red foxes, arctic foxes, ermines, and least weasels.

Habitat. The singing vole occupies the alpine tundra of arctic and subarctic mountain ranges from about 1,000 to 6,000 feet elevation. It occurs on dry open tundra, in willow thickets, and along river banks, lakeshores, and gravel beds. Usually it occurs on dry ground near water but leaves the wet swale habitat to the tundra vole.

Reproduction. Little is known of the reproduction in this species. Its breeding season extends from the end of May to September. The male gonads usually regress after mid-August. The female is seasonally polyoestrous, because up to three litters may be born in a season. The average litter size is 8.2 at the height of the breeding season, but may vary from four to twelve.

Economic Status. The Alaskan Eskimos raid the winter caches of these voles for the tubers, which they use as vegetables.

Distribution. The singing vole is found in northern Alaska, Yukon Territory, and western Mackenzie District, Northwest Territories. A closely related species is found in northern Asia.

Canadian Distribution. Two forms of this species have been described for northern Canada (see Map 86). At present too few specimens are available to make an adequate appraisal of the distribution of the species in Canada.

Microtus miurus andersoni Rand, 1945, Nat. Mus. Canada Bull. 99: 42. Ogilvy Mountains, Yukon Territory.

Microtus miurus cantator Anderson, 1946, Nat. Mus. Canada Bull. 102: 161. St Elias Mountains, Yukon Territory.

REFERENCE

Bee, J.W., and E.R. Hall. 1956. Mammals of northern Alaska. Mus. Nat. Hist., Univ. Kansas Misc. Pub. 8: 136–56.

MEADOW VOLE
Campagnol des champs. *Microtus pennsylvanicus* (Ord)

Description. This is the ubiquitous 'field mouse' of most of Canada. It is a medium-sized, stout-bodied vole, with small, beady eyes, rounded ears that barely appear beyond the fur, and a short tail about twice the length of the hind foot. The thumb is vestigial (Figure 48); the hind feet have six tubercles on the sole; the males have a pair of thickened glandular areas on the hips; the females have four pairs of teats, two pectoral and two inguinal (Plate 21).

The skull of the meadow vole is relatively rectangular and is heavily constructed for a vole (Figure 42g). The palate is vacuolated with a median ridge; the incisive foramina are long. The roots of the lower incisors extend laterally and behind the molars. The upper incisors are not grooved. The cheek teeth are rootless and ever-growing. The re-entrant angles are of equal depth on each side of the teeth. The diagnostic feature of the dentition is the possession of a fifth internal enamel loop behind four triangular enamel prisms on the middle upper molars (Figure 43).

The pelage consists of a dense slate grey underfur and long, buffy-banded, black-tipped guard hairs. The summer coat is short and rough, grizzled rusty brown above, clouded greyish white beneath. The winter coat is longer and silkier and a little greyer than the summer coat. The feet are grey, and the tail is sparsely haired and faintly bi-coloured, dark above and paler below (Figure 45c).

Virtually nothing has been written concerning the moults in this species. The juvenile pelage is short and very dark; the feet are almost black. The subadult pelage is similar to the adult pelage. There are probably two annual moults, vernal and autumnal. Albino, melanistic, and spotted individuals have been reported.

The size of these voles varies considerably depending on geography, available food, and population structure. A series of twenty adult males from Manitoba measured: length 163 (151–197), tail 43 (40–46), hind foot 18 (17–21), ear 10–16 mm; weight 37.2 (30.2–45.5) g. A series of twenty adult females measured: length 159 (144–178), tail 45 (41–51), hind foot 18 (17–21) mm; weight 35.9 (30.2–49.9) g. The maximum length may be over 200 mm and the maximum weight over 71 g. There is a loss of weight throughout the winter months.

Habits. Meadow voles are usually found in extensive colonies, but they are far from co-operative among themselves. They are socially aggressive and pugnacious and strange voles usually scrap when they meet. The males fight viciously during the mating period, and the females generally dominate the males. Only among family units does one find maternal concern for the young and juvenile playfulness. The voles are clean creatures and spend much time in grooming, washing their faces, and combing their flanks. They use a communal toilet area some distance form the nest.

Primarily terrestrial, meadow voles scuttle across the ground on tiny blurred feet. They are also quite at home in the water and swim with ease, buoyed up by air bubbles trapped in their fluffy fur. They have been known to swim across small lakes and to dive when pursued.

Meadow voles are most active during the first three hours after dawn and during a two- to four-hour period before sunset, with lulls in activity around noon and midnight. Individuals usually exhibit a short-term, two- to three-hour periodicity of activity associated with their digestion period. They do not hibernate and are active all winter.

If one parts the rank grasses in an overgrown meadow, one will find a labyrinth of criss-crossing mouse paths. These are vole highways, which are constructed first by gnawing off the grass stems and then by trampling down the paths. The grass growing on each side eventually arches over the runways and provides added security. The runways lead to short, shallow burrows, toilet bays, or to the cover of boards, rocks, logs, or shrubs. In winter the runways continue to be utilized under a blanket of snow. The voles construct globular nests of woven grass about six inches in diameter. During the summer months they

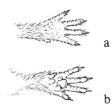

Figure 48 Forefoot of meadow vole: (a) dorsal view, (b) ventral view (× 1)

209

place them under boards or rocks, in a shallow abandoned burrow of a chipmunk or ground squirrel, or in a grass tussock. During the winter months they place them on the ground under a blanket of snow. The combined body heat of the occupants melts the snow to form a miniature chamber about the nest. The melting snows of spring disclose the open chimneys and grass nests before the ground becomes bare. The voles are quick to abandon any old soiled nests and can construct a new dry one in less than a day.

The home range of a meadow vole has been calculated to be between 0.08 and 0.23 acre. It varies with habitat and season, being at a minimum under the snow of late winter and at a maximum after the breeding season in the autumn. Transplanted voles have been known to return to their home ranges from distances of up to about 250 yards, but they do not show the pronounced homing instinct of deer mice. Meadow voles defend small territories, no more than seven yards across, around their nests. The females show a higher degree of territoriality than the males.

This is another Canadian mammal that exhibits dramatic fluctuations in populations. However, the fluctuations have a much shorter periodicity than those of the snowshoe hare, the peak populations usually appearing every three or four years. It is the tremendous breeding potential of the vole that is largely responsible for the shorter periodicity. At normal population levels, meadow voles have been observed at densities of 15 to 45 animals per acre of old field habitat and 45 to 150 animals per acre of marsh habitat. There is a normal annual cycle of population density from a low point at the end of winter to a high point towards the close of the breeding season in the autumn. During population peaks the density may go as high as 400 per acre.

Of the mammals studied, the meadow vole has one of the shortest life-spans, if not the shortest. The maximum life-span in the wild is thought to be about sixteen months. In a Michigan field study, the maximum longevity was about eleven to twelve months, but the average life-span of the voles in the study was less than a month. The greatest mortality (88 per cent) was in the first month. After that time there was a constant specific rate of survival; no animal, therefore, ever reached senility. The average time adults remained in the habitat was two months. In this study the voles were essentially a semi-annual crop: the spring young bore an autumn crop, which survived until the next spring to breed.

Meadow voles live primarily upon grasses and sedges and to a lesser degree on the forbs of the fields. In spring they feed on tender growing grass shoots, in summer they cut the grass stems into match-length sections to reach the succulent leaves and seed-heads, and in winter they eat the basal green portions of the grass beneath the snow. The summer diet is augmented by the flowers, leaves, and fruit of forbs. In the winter, they eat seeds, underground roots, and bulbs. When food supplies are scarce, they strip the bark from roots, stems, and twigs of woody shrubs and saplings. They augment their normal vegetable diet with a few insects and snails, and frequently resort to cannibalism, eating their own kind, especially the nestlings.

This vole stores supplies of seeds, tubers, and grain in winter. The tubers of the three-flowered avens are a favourite food on the prairies as well as the seeds of brome and crested wheat grass.

The predators of the field vole are legion. They include garter, black, fox, and milk snakes, as well as rattlesnakes; pickerel, pike, bass, and speckled and lake trout (the voles are captured while swimming across lakes and rivers); short-tailed shrews (which prey particularly on nestlings), least weasels, ermines, long-tailed weasels, marten, mink, skunks, badgers, opossums, foxes, coyotes, bobcats, and bears. The avian predators include hawks, owls, crows, magpies, jays, shrikes, gulls, and herons. Voles are less vulnerable than deer mice to avian predation in winter, because they spend more time under the snow.

Habitat. The preferred habitat of the meadow vole is wet meadows, but the species may inhabit any grassland habitat, small or large, such as salt marshes, abandoned fields, prairies, vacant lots, and edges and openings in woods, where there is a protective carpet of grasses, sedges, or mosses. It avoids deep forests and high, dry grassland, where it is replaced by the prairie vole.

Reproduction. The rabbit is generally considered to have reached the acme of fecundity, but it is not even in the same league as the meadow vole. These creatures meet, mate, and multiply almost before rabbits can get started.

The breeding season commences in April under the influence of the new green vegetation and usually terminates in October with the curtailment of vegetative growth. Under ideal conditions, such as when unharvested grain is standing in the fields and there is a protective blanket of snow, breeding may continue during the early winter months until February. If the summer is hot and dry, there may be a drop in reproduction at that season.

The females are polyoestrous, and mating is performed in a perfunctory manner. Outside the oestrous period, females usually bite any inquiring male on the nose, but when receptive they accept mates promiscuously. The females attract males from a considerable distance by squeaking. There seems to be no pairing when the young are in the nest.

The gestation period is of twenty to twenty-one days' duration, and post-partum oestrus occurs immediately after the birth of the litter. The average litter size is 6.3 but the number varies between one and eleven. The first litter is usually about four and the size of the litter increases as the mother grows older. The litter size also increases when food conditions are favourable and when the population density is rising, but it falls dramatically at the population peak. In the laboratory as many as seventeen litters have been born to a single female in one year, but the average in the field is about 3.5 litters per year. If all the young of a laboratory pair lived to bear young, who also lived to reproduce, and so on, the population would total over a million voles in one year.

The young voles at birth weigh approximately 2.1 (1.6–2.9) g and are blind, deaf, naked, and helpless. They soon cling to their mother's teats, and if the female has to flee from her nest she drags her young to another sanctuary. If one loses its grip, she will return and pick it up in her mouth. The young grow rapidly, gaining 0.2 to 0.5 g per day. After five or six days they are clothed in velvety fur, and the incisor teeth appear. Their eyes open on the ninth day, and the youngsters start to wobble about. They are weaned on the twelfth day at an approximate body weight of 14 g. Soon afterwards they scatter from the natal nest. Throughout the suckling period the female has to protect her young from being eaten by roving voles.

The young females mature quickly and mate at approximately twenty-five days of age. They bear the first young at forty-five days, when they are about half-grown and weigh approximately 20 g. The young males do not mature until the age of about forty-five days, when they weigh 20 to 25 g. Males born after midsummer probably do not mature until the next season.

Economic Status. The meadow vole is one of the most important small mammals of Canada because of its role as a food resource for fur-bearers and because of its depredations on forest and agricultural crops.

Before the advent of Europeans to this continent, these voles served the Mandan Indians of the Great Plains region well because their autumn caches of ground beans and 'artichokes' provided the Indians with vital food. Indian women gathered the grain, beans, and rhizomes by the bushel from the 'bean mouse' caches.

Nowadays these voles are considered serious agricultural pests. It has been estimated that a moderate population of voles would eat as much as a ton of hay off one hundred acres of alfalfa. In a vole eruption in Nevada in 1907, individual ranches estimated their losses from mouse damage at $8,000 to $28,000, and the total loss in the valley was estimated at $300,000. The most serious damage done by the voles arises from the girdling of fruit trees in orchards under the snow in winter. They also girdle ornamental shrubs and eat underground bulbs and vegetables. In forest nurseries they girdle the bark of Scotch and jack pine seedlings and even mature trees, but they neglect red pine and spruce. They also chew the waxed casing of underground telephone cables.

The best means of control is by distributing cracked corn coated with 2 per cent zinc phosphide. The corn should be dyed green with methyl to protect seed-eating birds, which ignore coloured grains. The poisoned grain may be distributed in a garden seeder (from which the furrow opener and closer have been removed) at a rate of ten to twenty kernels per foot (two pounds per acre) between the rows of fruit trees. The toxicity lasts only about a week, but good control is usually obtained by that time. It is also important to remove rank weed growth along the fence-rows and in the orchards where the voles find shelter. The trunks of orchard trees or ornamental trees should be wrapped with hardware cloth or tar paper in winter to prevent damage by voles.

Distribution. The meadow vole enjoys one of the broadest distributions of North American small mammals from the Atlantic to the Pacific and from Georgia to Alaska.

Canadian Distribution. This species is found all across Canada from Newfoundland to British Columbia east of the Coast Range and north to the Mackenzie delta, but it does not occur on Vancouver or the Queen Charlotte islands, British Columbia (see Map 87). It is a plastic species and is divided into thirteen subspecies in Canada.

Microtus pennsylvanicus acadicus Bangs, 1897, American Nat. 31: 239. A pale buffy race, found in Nova Scotia, Prince Edward Island, and southern New Brunswick.

Microtus pennsylvanicus alcorni Baker, 1951, Univ. Kansas Pub. Mus. Nat. Hist. 5: 105. Southwestern Yukon territory.

Microtus pennsylvanicus aphorodemus Preble, 1902, N. American Fauna 22: 52. A large, grizzled race, found along the western coast of Hudson Bay in Manitoba and southern Keewatin District.

Microtus pennsylvanicus arcticus Cowan, 1951, Jour. Mamm. 32: 353. Known only from Richards Island at the mouth of the Mackenzie River, Northwest Territories.

Microtus pennsylvanicus copelandi Youngman, 1967, Jour. Mamm. 48(4): 579–88. A large, dark race, found on Grand Manan Island, New Brunswick.

Microtus pennsylvanicus drummondii (Audubon and Bachman), 1853, The viviparous quadrupeds of North America 3: 166. A widespread race found in western Canada from northern Ontario to the eastern flank of the Coast Range, British Columbia, and from the southern Prairie Provinces north to the treeline in the Yukon and Northwest Territories.

Microtus pennsylvanicus enixus Bangs, 1896, American Nat. 30: 1051. A dark race found in the central Ungava Peninsula from James Bay to southern Labrador and the Straits of Belle Isle.

Microtus pennsylvanicus insperatus (J.A. Allen), 1894, Bull. American Mus. Nat. Hist. 6: 347. A pale form found on the short-grass prairies of southeastern Alberta and southwestern Saskatchewan.

Microtus pennsylvanicus labradorius (V. Bailey), 1898, Proc. Biol. Soc. Washington 12: 88. A race characterized by protruding incisors and found in extreme northern Labrador and the northwest corner of the Ungava Peninsula west of Ungava Bay.

Microtus pennsylvanicus magdalenensis Youngman, 1967, Jour. Mamm. 48(4): 579–88. A large, reddish brown form, found on the Magdalen Islands, Quebec.

Microtus pennsylvanicus modestus (Baird), Mammals, in Repts. Expl. Surv. ... Rail. to Pacific, 8(1): 535. A large, robust form from extreme southern British Columbia.

Microtus pennsylvanicus pennsylvanicus (Ord), 1815, in

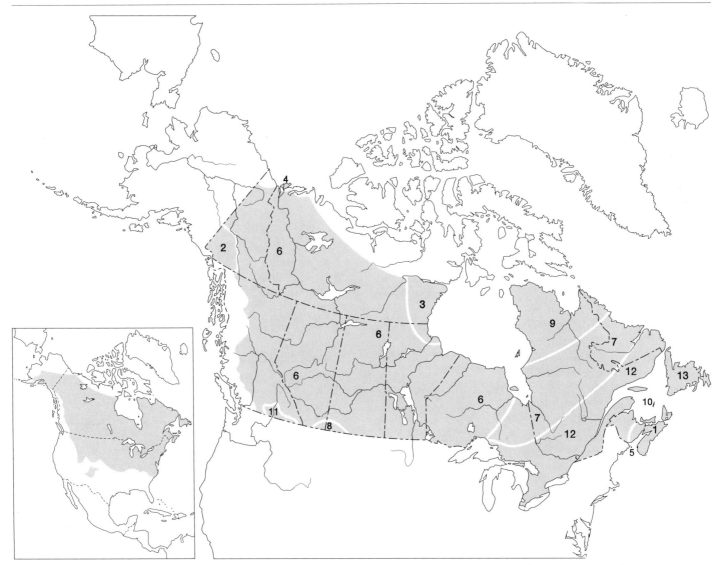

Map 87 Distribution of the meadow vole, *Microtus pennsylvanicus*: 1 *M. p. acadicus*, 2 *M. p. alcorni*, 3 *M. p. aphorodemus*, 4 *M. p. arcticus*, 5 *M. p. copelandi*, 6 *M. p. drummondii*, 7 *M. p. enixus*, 8 *M. p. insperatus*, 9 *M. p. labradorius*, 10 *M. p. magdalenensis*, 11 *M. p. modestus*, 12 *M. p. pennsylvanicus*, 13 *M. p. terraenovae*

Guthrie, A new geography, history, and comm. grammar ..., Philadelphia, American ed. 2: 292. The typical race found in southern Ontario, Quebec, and northern New Brunswick.

Microtus pennsylvanicus terraenovae (Bangs), 1894, Proc. Biol. Soc. Washington 9: 129. A very pale grey form, found on the island of Newfoundland.

REFERENCES

Getz, L.L. 1960. A population study of the vole, *Microtus pennsylvanicus*. American Midl. Nat. 64(2): 392–405.

– 1961. Home ranges, territoriality, and movements of the meadow vole. Jour. Mamm. 42(1): 24–36.

Golley, F.B. 1961. Interaction of natality, mortality and movement during one annual cycle in a *Microtus* population. American Midl. Nat. 66(1): 152–9.

Krebs, C.J. 1970. *Microtus* population biology: behavioral changes associated with the population cycle in *M. ochrogaster* and *M. pennsylvanicus*. Ecology 51(1): 34–52.

Thompson, D.Q. 1965. Food preferences of the meadow vole (*Microtus pennsylvanicus*) in relation to habitat affinities. American Midl. Nat. 74(1): 76–86.

MONTANE VOLE

Campagnol montagnard. *Microtus montanus* (Peale)

Description. The montane vole is very similar to the previously described meadow vole, but there are several trenchant characters that distinguish the two voles in the hand. The adult pelage in this species is grizzled greyish rather than brownish. The feet are silvery grey, and the tail is distinctly bi-coloured, dark above and pale grey below. The underparts are silvery grey.

The skull of the montane vole is similar to that of the

meadow vole. The middle upper molar is diagnostic: it is a short tooth with four enclosed prisms lacking the posterior internal loop of *M. pennsylvanicus*. The incisive foramina are constricted posteriorly as well (Figure 43).

This species has two annual moults: autumnal and vernal. The winter pelage is longer, and the underparts are white, whereas in summer the underparts are more greyish. The juvenile pelage is uniformly grey ventrally and brown dorsally. The subadult pelage is decidedly bi-coloured, silvery grey beneath and dark grey above. The adults are more grizzled, with the ventral and dorsal colours blending on the flanks.

Average measurements of adults from British Columbia: length 152 (134–165), tail 38 (31–45), hind foot 19 (18–20), ear 10 mm. Adults weigh more than 35 g; subadults weigh between 20 and 30 g.

Habits. Montane voles have not been studied in as much detail as meadow voles, but their life history and habits are thought to be similar. This species seems to be more sociable. It is active both day and night and throughout the year. It occupies shallow surface burrows and travels in surface runways. Population densities up to 100 per acre have been estimated. This species also exhibits dramatic population explosions between periods of scarcity.

Montane voles live on the leaves, stems, and roots of a wide variety of meadow forbs, including nettles and pigweed, but grasses, sedges, and rushes form the dietary staples.

This species is also preyed upon by a wide range of animals: hawks, owls, ravens, crows, magpies, gulls, herons, foxes, skunks, weasels, badgers, and coyotes.

Habitat. The distribution of this species exhibits the phenomenon of an altitudinal cline found in other species such as the least chipmunk. In the southern part of its range it occurs on mountain-tops in alpine meadows, but northward its habitat is at lower elevations, until in Canada it is found only in the valleys. It seems to prefer arid short grassland.

Reproduction. The reproductive cycle is similar to that of *M. pennsylvanicus*. Since the females are seasonally polyoestrous and experience post-partum oestrus, two or three litters are born in quick succession. The breeding season, however, seems to be confined to the period between April and October, with no winter activity. The average litter size for mature females is 5.8, but may vary from two to ten. Mean litter sizes increase from the first to fifth litter, and then decline. The litter size seems to be inversely proportional to the population density: high during a sparse expanding population and low during the crash period.

The juvenile females mature sexually at a weight of 22 to 26 g for spring and 29 to 32 g for autumn litters. The males mature at an approximate weight of 35 g.

Economic Status. The montane vole has been an important agricultural pest in some parts of the western United States, but its importance in Canada is limited because of its distribution. The control methods described for the meadow vole would be equally applicable for this species.

Map 88 Distribution of the montane vole, *Microtus montanus*

Distribution. Central Cordilleran region of western North America.

Canadian Distribution. The montane vole is found only in a limited area of south-central British Columbia including the Okanagan, Kettle, Thompson, and Fraser valleys north to the Caribou district (see Map 88).

Microtus montanus canescens V. Bailey, 1898, Proc. Biol. Soc. Washington 12: 87. A small, grey race found in the valleys of central British Columbia.

REFERENCES

Anderson, Sydney. 1959. Distribution, variation, and relationships of the montane vole, *Microtus montanus*. Univ. Kansas Pub. Mus. Nat. Hist. 9(17): 415–511.
Negus, Norman C., and A.J. Pinter. 1965. Litter sizes of *Microtus montanus* in the laboratory. Jour. Mamm. 46(3): 434–7.

TOWNSEND'S VOLE
Campagnol de Townsend. *Microtus townsendii*
(Bachman)

Description. Townsend's vole is larger and has a longer tail than the common eastern meadow vole. Its ears stand out prominently above the thin, harsh coat. The sparsely haired tail is two to three times as long as the large hind feet. Adult males possess prominent hip glands. The dor-

Map 89 Distribution of Townsend's vole, *Microtus townsendii*: 1 *M. t. cowani*, 2 *M. t. cummingi*, 3 *M. t. laingi*, 4 *M. t. tetramerus*, 5 *M. t. townsendii*

sal colour is dark brown, with a strong mixture of black hairs; the ventral surface is dusky grey; the feet are dusky; the tail is uniformly brown. The juvenile coat is dark brown with almost black feet. The winter coat is longer with more silvery grey underparts.

The adult skull is heavily constructed and heavily ridged. The long incisive foramina are posteriorly constricted. The middle upper molar has four closed enamel sections, as in *M. montanus* and *M. longicaudus* (Figure 43).

Average measurements of adults: length 191 (170–222), tail 57 (48–72), hind foot 24 (22–25) mm.

Habits. Very little has been written concerning the life history of this species. It seems to be more subterranean than most voles and digs long, shallow tunnels in friable soil. These voles may also use the tunnels of Townsend's mole to feed upon underground rootstocks and on vegetables such as potatoes.

Habitat. This species is a characteristic denizen of salt marshes and most lowland fields and meadows, but it is

also occasionally found on mountain slopes up to the treeline.

Reproduction. Few details are known of the reproduction of this species. Embryo counts have averaged seven (5–8).

Economic Status. Townsend's vole has been responsible for some of the damage to vegetable gardens wrongly blamed on Townsend's mole because the voles use the moles' tunnels as highways.

Distribution. This species occupies a restricted range on the Pacific coast west of the Cascade Mountains from northern California to Vancouver Island.

Canadian Distribution. Five subspecies are recognized in the Vancouver Island–Fraser delta region of British Columbia (see Map 89).

Microtus townsendii cowani Guiguet, 1955, Ann. Rept. British Columbia Prov. Mus. 1954: 67. The largest race, found only on Triangle Island off the north tip of Vancouver Island.

214

Microtus townsendii cummingi Hall, 1936, The Murrelet 17: 15. Occurs only on Bowen and Texada islands in Howe Sound.

Microtus townsendii laingi Anderson and Rand, 1943, Canadian Field-Nat. 57(415): 74. A large race from the northern part of Vancouver Island south as far as Sayward and Beaver Creek. Also occurs on Hope, Hurst, and Nigei islands off the northeast tip of Vancouver Island.

Microtus townsendii tetramerus (Rhoads), 1894, Proc. Acad. Nat. Sci. Philadelphia 46: 283. A small, dull form found on the southern part of Vancouver Island north to Alberni and Comox, also on Saltspring Island in the Straits of Georgia.

Microtus townsendii townsendii (Bachman), 1839, Jour. Acad. Nat. Sci. Philadelphia 8: 60. A richly coloured race found in Canada only in the lower Fraser delta from Hope to Vancouver south of Burrard Inlet.

REFERENCE

Anderson, R.M., and A.L. Rand. 1943. Townsend vole (*Microtus townsendi*) in Canada. Canadian Field-Nat. 57(45): 73–4.

MM

ROOT VOLE

Campagnol nordique. *Microtus oeconomus* (Pallas)

Description. The root vole is another Canadian species with a holarctic distribution. It is medium-sized, with short ears and a short tail. The ears are hidden in the pelage, and the well-furred tail is bi-coloured, dark brown above and pale grey beneath. The pelage is long and lax, grizzled brown above and buffy grey beneath. There is a strong suffusion of yellowish brown, particularly on the flanks and rump, and a mixture of blackish hairs, particularly on the dorsum. The feet are grey, and the heels and wrists are well covered with stiff silvery hairs in winter. Melanistic specimens have been reported.

This vole's skull is strong and angular: the incisive foramina are only moderately long and are constricted to a slit posteriorly. The upper middle molar has four closed enamel triangles, and the first lower molar has four lingual closed triangles. The fifth prism is open and confluent with the posterior loop (Figure 43).

There are two annual moults: autumnal and vernal. The winter pelage is long and silky. The juvenile coat is plumbeous; the dorsal surfaces of the feet are blackish. The post-juvenile and preadult pelages are like the adult coat in autumn.

Average measurements of adults: length 174 (153–188), tail 50 (44–54), hind foot 20 (19–21), ear 13 mm. Adult males weigh between 33 and 45 g. Adult females weigh between 25 and 80 g (near parturition).

Habits. The general life-history pattern of the root vole is very similar to that of the meadow vole. It is active at all times of the day and throughout the year. It is a particularly good swimmer, freely crossing brooks and ponds. It digs shallow burrows in loose soil and in tundra vegetation above the permafrost. Using dried vegetation it constructs bulky nests about six inches in diameter and lines them with grasses and sedges. The nests are placed in chambers immediately under the roots of heaths, in tussocks, in banks, or in such artificial sites as under a whale skull and among sod blocks of collapsed Eskimo huts. Often little piles of dirt are evident at the entrances to its burrow. Like the meadow vole the tundra vole travels across the wet tundra in a network of runways, which are often located in frost cracks. The runways may be so persistent as to furrow the soil, particularly along the banks of streams. There are neat little toilet areas off the main traffic arteries.

The summer food consists of clipped sections of sedges and grasses. The root voles store grass seeds and forb rhizomes in their burrows in the autumn, particularly rhizomes of liquorice root and knotweed. It was this habit that suggested their specific name – the economic vole.

This species is an important source of food for many northern carnivorous birds, mammals, and fishes, including snowy owls, rough-legged hawks, duck hawks, gyrfalcons, jaegers, gulls, shrikes, ermines, arctic foxes, and wolverines. Even lake trout manage to capture a few.

Habitat. The root vole prefers damp tundra areas around lakes, stream banks, or sedge and cottongrass marshes. If its runways are flooded in spring, it may move temporarily up the slopes. It also occurs on alpine tundra at higher elevations towards the southern part of its distribution. At times it moves into townsites to occupy the rank growth of grasses around outbuildings or long-abandoned sod hut ruins.

Reproduction. Little information is available on the reproduction of this vole in North America, but it is probably very similar to that of the meadow vole. The breeding season lasts from May to early September. The females are seasonally polyoestrous and ovulate spontaneously. Post-partum oestrus occurs occasionally but not generally. Two or three litters are born during the breeding season. The breeding season in males terminates about August 22 with the withdrawal of the testes into the body cavity. The litters are large, averaging 7.5 young, but may vary from five to eleven.

Economic Status. Alaskan Eskimos used to train special dogs to locate the voles' caches of liquorice root in the autumn, which the Eskimos would then add to their own winter larders.

Distribution. The root vole occurs in Scandinavia, the northern part of the Soviet Union, Alaska, and northwest Canada.

Canadian Distribution. The Canadian distribution is limited to the Yukon Territory, the northwest corner of British Columbia, and the Mackenzie District eastward along the arctic coastal tundra to Bathurst Inlet. Two subspecies are recognized in Canada (see Map 90).

Microtus oeconomus macfarlani Merriam, 1900, Proc. Washington Acad. Sci. 2: 24. The typical form of the Yukon and Northwest Territories.

Microtus oeconomus yakutatensis Merriam, 1900, Proc. Washington Acad. Sci. 2: 22. A greyish race found on

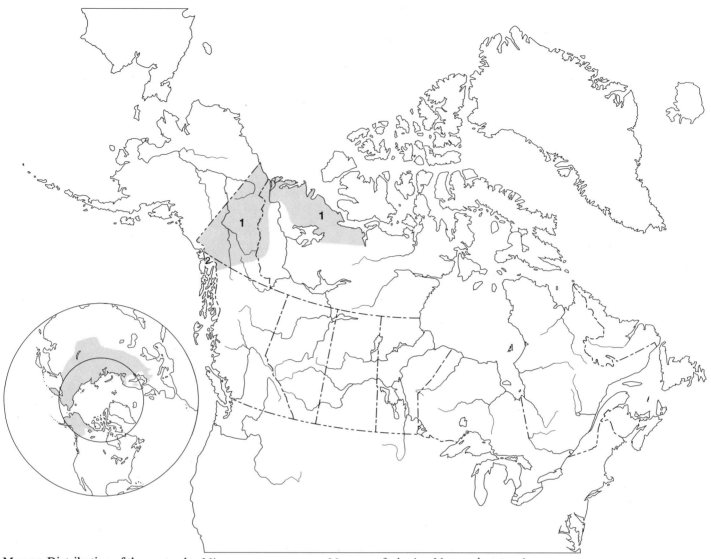

Map 90 Distribution of the root vole, *Microtus oeconomus*: 1 *M. o. macfarlani*, 2 *M. o. yakutatensis*

the coastal slope of the St Elias Mountains in the north-west corner of British Columbia.

REFERENCES

Barkalow, F.S. 1952. Life history and ecologic observations on the tundra mouse (*Microtus oeconomus*) and lemmings (*Lemmus trimucronatus* and *Dicrostonyx groenlandicus*) at Barter Island, Alaska. Jour. Elisha Mitchell Sci. Soc. 68(2): 199–205.

Hoyte, H.M.D. 1955. Observations on reproduction in some small mammals in arctic Norway. The oestrus cycle in *Microtus oeconomus*. Jour. Anim. Ecol. 24: 212–25.

LONG-TAILED VOLE
Campagnol longicaude. *Microtus longicaudus* (Merriam)

Description. This species is quickly recognized by its tail, which is relatively long for a vole, being over half the combined length of the head and body (Figure 45d). Otherwise it is an average-sized vole with rather sparse,

harsh fur, which varies dorsally from greyish to dark brown. Usually the flanks are predominantly greyish, and the brown tones are confined to a narrow dorsal ribbon. The underparts are silvery grey; the feet are dull grey; the tail is sparsely furred and is only slightly paler beneath. There are six tubercules on the hind feet, and the hip glands of the males are rarely found (Plate 15h).

The skull is rather long, flat, and smooth. The second upper molar has four closed triangles without the posterior loop, and the the first mandibular molar has five median closed triangles (Figure 43). The incisive foramina are long and gradually narrow behind.

There are the usual autumnal and vernal moults; the winter pelage is longer and greyer than the summer pelage; the juvenile coat is darker. Specimens with an unusual diluted pelage colour have been noted.

Average measurements of adults of the most widespread race *vellerosus* are: length 180 (167–192), tail 64 (60–70), hind foot 20 (19–22). Adult males weigh between 40 and 60 g; adult females, 36 to 58 g.

Habits. This species has not been studied in detail, but

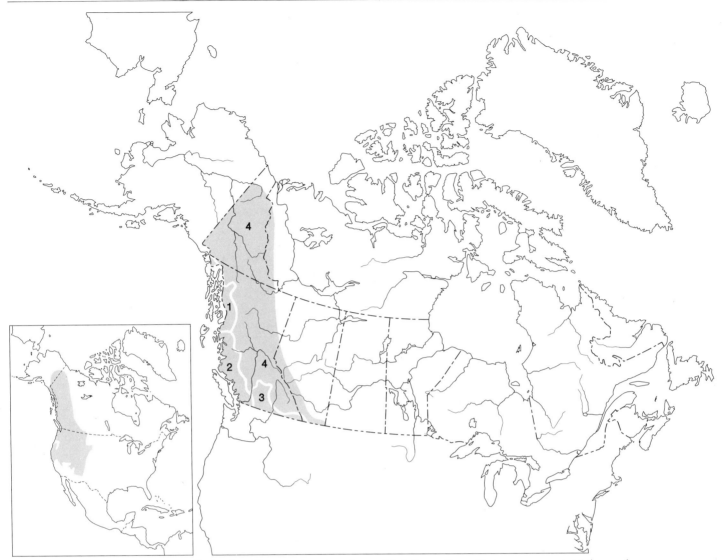

Map 91 Distribution of the long-tailed vole, *Microtus longicaudus*: 1 *M. l. littoralis*, 2 *M. l. macrurus*, 3 *M. l. mordax*, 4 *M. l. vellerosus*

its habits are not thought to differ significantly from those of the meadow vole. It is known to be diurnal in activity and active all winter under the blanket of snow. It seems to be less prone to construct runways, although it does this in some areas. Populations also fluctuate widely from year to year.

Habitat. The long-tailed vole exhibits a very broad choice of habitat selection. It may be found from sea level to over 9,000 feet. In my experience this species is commonest in small, isolated grassy plots in the forest and along the banks of alpine streams. It has also been reported from alpine tundra, rock fields, open dry grasslands, forest edges, marshes, and sagebrush plains. It usually occurs in small isolated colonies.

Reproduction. Little has been written concerning the reproduction of this species. The females have eight mammae, are probably polyoestrous, and bear more than one litter a year. Embryo counts average 5.4, but vary from two to eight.

Economic Status. This species seldom comes in contact with agriculture in Canada.

Distribution. The long-tailed vole inhabits much of the Cordilleran region of western North America.

Canadian Distribution. This vole is found in the Rocky Mountain region from northern Yukon Territory to the international boundary in British Columbia and Alberta. Four subspecies are currently recognized in Canada (see Map 91).

Microtus longicaudus littoralis Swarth, 1933, Proc. Biol. Soc. Washington 46: 209. A reddish brown race, found along the northwest coast of British Columbia and adjacent Alaska.

Microtus longicaudus macrurus Merriam, 1898, Proc. Acad. Nat. Sci. Philadelphia 50: 353. A large, dark brown form, found along the southern coast of British Columbia and the coastal islands north to Princess Royal Island.

Microtus longicaudus mordax (Merriam), 1891, N. American Fauna 5: 61. A grizzled grey race from south-central British Columbia.

Microtus longicaudus vellerosus J.A. Allen, 1899, Bull. American Mus. Nat. Hist. 12: 7. A grey-flanked brownish-backed race, found in the Rocky Mountains of eastern British Columbia and western Alberta northward to Rampart House, Yukon Territory, and Glacier Lake, Nahanni Valley, Northwest Territories. An isolated population occurs on the Sweetgrass Hills on the international boundary in Alberta.

REFERENCE

Anderson, R.M., and A.L. Rand. 1944. The long-tailed meadow mouse (*Microtus longicaudus*) in Canada. Canadian Field-Nat. 58(1): 19–21.

ROCK VOLE
Campagnol des rochers. *Microtus chrotorrhinus* (Miller)

Description. The rock vole is one of the rarer Canadian small mammals. It resembles the meadow vole rather closely. Its ears are moderately large; its tail is rather sparsely haired and of average length for a vole. Its smooth skull is lightly constructed; the incisive foramina are relatively short, broad anteriorly, and slightly tapered behind (not constricted). The key character for the species is found in the upper third molar, which has five closed triangles (*M. pennsylvanicus* has three) (Figure 43).

The summer pelage of the rock vole is short and soft. Dorsally, the colour is dark brown or bistre with a strong mixture of black-tipped hairs. Ventrally, the colour is dull grey to silvery grey. Its feet are dull grey, and its tail is slightly paler below. The orange or dull rufous colour of the face, which is brightest about the vibrissae and spreads backwards to include the ears, is the identifying mark in the hand. It has also a touch of fulvous on the rump. The young are slightly greyer with paler faces. Their winter coat is longer and glossier.

Average measurements of adults: length 165 (152–185), tail 47 (42–53), hind foot 20 (19–23), ear 13 mm; weight 30–40 g.

Habits. The rock vole occurs in small isolated colonies throughout its range. Relatively few specimens have been collected, and its life history has not been studied in detail. Dense populations of this species have never been found.

It lives in the forest, and its pathways threading between rocks are indistinct but may be traced to shallow burrows. Small piles of partly eaten stems and leaves of false mitrewort, violet, bunchberry, and mayflower provide mute evidence of its presence. It is mostly active during the daylight hours.

Habitat. This species has received its common name from its choice of habitat – damp, mossy, rocky talus slopes under cliffs or frost-fracture rock outcrops in the forest. It is usually located near forest springs or rivulets. It also occurs among the bracken in small clearings in spruce–birch–balsam fir forests. One colony was found under a tangle of logs in a recently cut-over area. It is found on the mountaintops from 1,500 to 4,500 feet in the southern part of its distribution and at sea level towards the northern limit.

Reproduction. The females are polyoestrous, and post-partum oestrus occurs so that two or more litters are born each year. The average litter size is 3.56, with a range of two to five.

Distribution. The rock vole is found in the Allegheny Mountain region of North America, from the Great Smoky Mountains of western North Carolina northward to the Gaspé Peninsula and the north shore of the Gulf of St Lawrence. It also occurs in the Precambrian Highlands of central Quebec and Ontario, westward as far as Lake Superior.

Canadian Distribution. Two subspecies are currently recognized in eastern Canada (see Map 92).

Microtus chrotorrhinus chrotorrhinus (Miller), 1894, Proc. Boston Soc. Nat. Hist. 26: 190. The typical dark brown race found in northern New Brunswick, the Gaspé Peninsula, the north shore of the St Lawrence River, central Quebec, and Ontario.

Microtus chrotorrhinus ravus Bangs, 1898, Proc. Biol. Soc. Washington 12: 188. A smaller, greyer race, known only from southern Labrador (Straits of Belle Isle).

REFERENCE

Goodwin, G.G. 1929. Mammals of the Cascapedia Valley, Quebec. Jour. Mamm. 10(3): 244.

CHESTNUT-CHEEKED VOLE
Campagnol à joues jaunes. *Microtus xanthognathus* (Leach)

Description. This vole is an enigma among American microtine rodents. Very few mammalogists have captured specimens, but that fact does not signify that the species is rare. Indeed, very large series have been taken by some scientists, who found the species locally abundant. Others who returned to the areas where the specimens were taken have been unable to find a single specimen. It seems that the species was more abundant during the early years of this century than it is at present. The National Museum of Canada had only two specimens of the chestnut-cheeked vole until recently, when a large series was secured in the Yukon Territory.

This species resembles the rock vole in colour, but its known distribution is restricted to northwestern America, whereas the rock vole is restricted to eastern America. These two facts have led some writers to express the opinion that the two forms belonged to a single widely distributed boreal species. The two species are, however, quite distinct in size, cranial characters, dental pattern, and habits. The most recent discovery of chestnut-cheeked voles is a very ancient one. Numerous skeletal remains were found in cave deposits in Virginia and Pennsylvania, dating from late Pleistocene times, about 11,000 years ago. The specimens were identified by their cranial characteristics and, what is more important, were as-

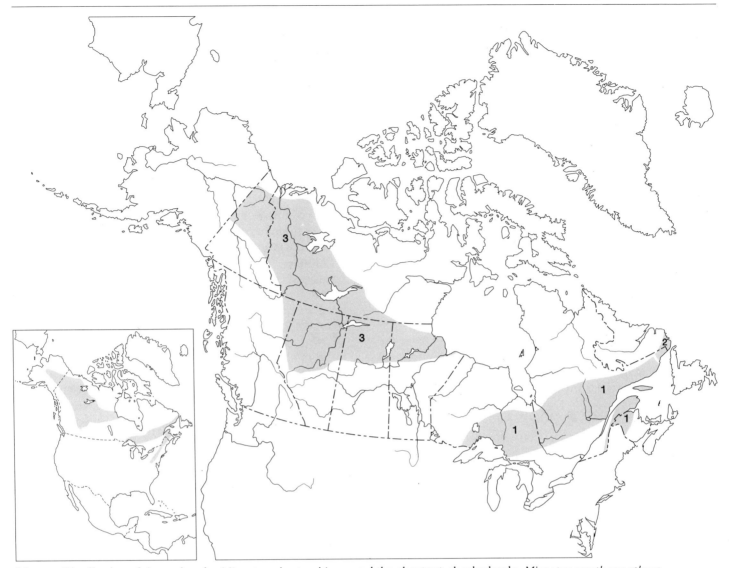

Map 92 Distribution of the rock vole, *Microtus chrotorrhinus*, and the chestnut-cheeked vole, *Microtus xanthognathus*: 1 *M. c. chrotorrhinus*, 2 *M. c. ravus*, 3 *Microtus xanthognathus*

sociated with equally identifiable specimens of the rock vole. Pollen samples from the matrix in which the bones were preserved indicated a boreal pine forest cover. It therefore appears that the chestnut-cheeked vole once enjoyed a much broader distribution, which included southeastern North America at the close of the last glacial period, and it has slowly migrated northwestward to its present range following the migration of the northern boreal forest.

The chestnut-cheeked vole is one of the larger microtines. The upper parts are dark sepia brown, heavily interspersed with black-tipped hairs; the underparts are smoky grey. The short ears, which are concealed in the fur, have a rusty tint to their edges. The tail, which is of average length, is distinctly bi-coloured. The feet are relatively large, and are dark brown above. There is a prominent chestnut or rusty yellow patch on the nose. The juveniles are darker, more reddish brown (Plate 15 g).

The skull is large, rugose, and relatively narrow. The long incisive foramina are tapered posteriorly. The upper incisors of adults bear a longitudinal groove. The molars are distinctly heavier than those of *M. chrotorrhinus*. The dental pattern is rather variable, but the last upper molar usually has only three closed medial triangles (Figure 43).

Adult males bear two hip glands, which are farther forward than in other voles of this genus.

Average measurements of adults: length 213 (186–226), tail 50 (45–53), hind foot 25 (24–27). Adult males may weigh up to 170 g. The average weight of five females was 135 g.

Habits. Little is known of the life history of this species. It is colonial in behaviour. It digs deep burrows in the friable forest earth, depositing large piles of earth (one to three yards in diameter) at the entrances. From these holes, wide well-trodden runways radiate fifty to seventy-five yards. Sometimes the colonies are small and isolated; at other times they may cover extensive areas of forest. The voles are active both day and night, but the peak of activity occurs at dusk. They are very vocal and chirp when intruders approach the colony.

219

Chestnut-cheeked voles seem to depend a great deal on horsetails and lichens for food. Predators include marten and great grey owls. The populations of this species fluctuate dramatically from local abundance to rarity over the span of a few years.

Habitat. This species appears to be primarily a forest dweller, but extends its runways to sphagnum bogs. One colony was, however, located on a willow-covered island in the Mackenzie River, and others were found on the edge of a forest bordering marshes. They do not inhabit rocky taluses as the rock vole does.

Reproduction. No details of reproduction are known beyond the fact that these moles breed in early summer and that the females may carry as many as seven to eleven embryos. There are eight teats, as is normal in the genus.

Economic Status. This species is too rare and too remote to be of any economic significance.

Distribution. The present known distribution of the chestnut-cheeked vole is confined to northwestern Canada and central Alaska.

Canadian Distribution. The species occurs across the northern forested parts of the Prairie Provinces from the west coast of Hudson Bay to the Rocky Mountains and northward across northern Yukon Territory. No subspecies have been described (see Map 92).

Microtus xanthognathus xanthognathus (Leach), 1815, Zool. Misc. 1: 60.

REFERENCES

Guilday, J.E., and M.S. Bender. 1960. Late Pleistocene records of the yellow-cheeked vole, *Microtus xanthognathus* (Leach). Ann. Carnegie Mus. 35(14): 315–30.

Preble, E.A. 1908. A biological investigation of the Athabaska–Mackenzie region. N. American Fauna 27: 188–90.

CREEPING VOLE
Campagnol d'Orégon. *Microtus oregoni* (Bachman)

Description. The creeping vole is a small, slender mouse with dense, short, plush-like underfur; the longer guard hairs are compressed. The eyes and ears are small; the tail is short. The plantar tubercules on the hind feet are reduced to five. The males bear inconspicuous flank glands; the females have the normal eight mammae.

The short skull of this vole is depressed with elliptical brain-case and narrow rostrum. The incisive foramina are long and are not posteriorly constricted. The molars are short. The upper third molar has two or three closed triangles, and the lower first molar has five closed triangles. The auditory bullae are small and globular (Figure 43).

The pelage is dusky brown above, produced by a mixture of black and buffy hair tips. The ventral surface is smoky grey with a buffy wash. The ears barely show their blackish tips through the body fur. The feet are clear grey. The tail is darker grey above than below.

Average measurements of adults: length 138 (125–153), tail 35 (29–39), hind foot 18 (16–20) mm; weight 19.2 g.

Habits. This vole is semisubterranean in habits. It constructs a labyrinth of shallow, narrow burrows through the friable forest soils. Even when it travels on the surface, it prefers to force up a ridge of duff on the forest floor so that its runways are protected by a canopy of leafy litter. It frequently uses the burrows of the coast mole as highways. Little is known concerning other details of its life history.

Creeping voles may live at least 320 days in captivity. They exhibit the usual small rodent annual turnover in the wild state. The autumn population consists primarily of young of the year with only an occasional yearling. The food is thought to consist primarily of underground rootstalks, but green forage is also consumed.

Habitat. This vole typically inhabits the humid coniferous forest of the Pacific coast, utilizing the mellow woodland soils and rotting bogs to burrow in. Densest populations are usually found on the forest edges or in abandoned brushland, from which the voles are quick to invade near-by cultivated fields. Although the general area is predominantly moist, they generally prefer relatively dry conditions.

Reproduction. Fortunately many of the details of reproduction are known for this species. The creeping vole enjoys a relatively prolonged annual breeding season under the mild climatic conditions of its environment. In extreme cases it may last from mid-February to early November, but most of the breeding takes place between March and September. During the winter anoestrous period, the female's vulva is closed, and the male's gonads are withdrawn. Mating usually commences in early March, and the first litters are born in early April, after a gestation period of between twenty-three and twenty-four days. The first litters are smaller in size on the average than later litters (2.3 as compared with 4.5 young). The average litter size throughout the season is 2.95, with a range of one to five. The females are polyoestrous and also experience post-partum oestrus, without lactation anoestrus, so that the litters follow in quick succession. In the laboratory, females may produce six litters in a single season, but the maximum in the field is probably four or five, and the average is probably three.

The young at birth weigh an average of 1.7 (1.6–2.2) g. They are tiny, pink, wrinkled creatures with eyes and ears closed and pinnae folded. But growth is very rapid. Within the first day vibrissae and dorsal pelage appear, and by eight days the young voles are well furred. The incisors erupt after five days. The external auditory canals open by the tenth day, and the eyes open between the tenth and twelfth days. Soon the youngsters start to explore beyond the nest and to eat solid food. They are weaned at thirteen days. The average daily weight gain is 0.7 g between the fifth and twentieth day. The average adult weight is reached between the ages of forty and fifty days.

The juvenile males mature between forty and fifty days of age, and the females between the ages of twenty-two and twenty-seven days.

Map 93 Distribution of the creeping vole, *Microtus oregoni*

Economic Status. The creeping vole is too restricted in distribution in Canada to be of much economic importance. Its depredations are insidious, however, because of its subterranean habits. It injures root vegetable crops, ornamental shrubs, perennials, and bulbs, but its use of mole tunnels may result in the transfer of blame to the mole.

Distribution. This vole occupies a restricted distribution on the Pacific coast west of the Cascade Mountain range, from northern California to southern British Columbia.

Canadian Distribution. In Canada this species is confined to a narrow strip along the international boundary of southwestern British Columbia (see Map 93). The Canadian population belongs to:

Microtus oregoni serpens Merriam, 1897, Proc. Biol. Soc. Washington 11: 75.

REFERENCE

Cowan, I.McT., and Margaret G. Arsenault. 1954. Reproduction and growth in the creeping vole, *Microtus oregoni serpens* Merriam. Canadian Jour. Zool. 32(3): 198–208.

ROOF RAT
Rat noir. *Rattus rattus* (Linnaeus)

Description. The rats and mice of this group (Murinae) are native to the Old World. They are considered to be more advanced than the rats and mice (Cricetinae) or the voles and lemmings (Microtinae) of the New World. They are distinguished by the three longitudinal rows of rounded cusps on their molar teeth (Figure 49). Three species of this group have been accidentally introduced to the Western Hemisphere. They are commensal species, which thrive in association with man and have become serious agricultural and public health pests.

The roof rat is a large, slim rat with a very long, naked scaly tail and large parchment-like ears. It has two colour phases: one is sooty black above and slate grey below with a black tail; the other is grizzled brown above and light grey below with a brown tail. In both cases the fur is soft.

The roof rat's skull is long and slender with slight brow ridges. The first upper molar tooth has distinct notches on the first row of cusps.

Average measurements of adults: length 397 (372–430), tail 214 (195–231), hind foot 37 (35–39) mm.

Habits. This rat receives its common name from its climbing ability. It first reached our shores on the sailing ships of the early explorers and settlers and has remained on our coasts without securing a toehold in the interior. Although usually found about human habitation, it has been able to establish feral populations on the edges of the coastal forests of British Columbia. There it builds its nest of twigs and leaves in a log or stump, or in the crotch of a tree. It lives on seeds, nuts, insects, and small birds and mammals. Where rats become established on small islands, the native small rodents are usually extirpated, as has occurred on Langara and Kunghit islands of the Queen Charlotte group in British Columbia.

Habitat. Cities, farm buildings, or forest edges.

Reproduction. The females possess ten mammae. The reproductive cycle is similar to that described for the species that immediately follows. They are polyoestrous and bear several litters during a single year. The gestation period is approximately twenty-one days.

Economic Status. The black rat is less of a pest than the Norway rat because it is less aggressive. It has been largely displaced by the latter species.

Distribution. This species originally lived in southern Asia as a wild animal, but commensal forms have become cosmopolitan in distribution along with man.

Canadian Distribution. The species is at present established only in coastal British Columbia – the Fraser River

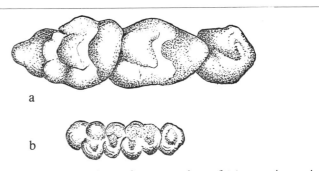
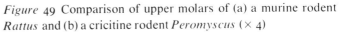
Figure 49 Comparison of upper molars of (a) a murine rodent *Rattus* and (b) a cricitine rodent *Peromyscus* (× 4)

delta and southern Vancouver Island – and on the Queen Charlotte Islands.

Rattus rattus rattus (Linnaeus), 1758, Syst. nat., 10th ed., 1: 61. The two colour phases of this species were originally described as distinct species, although it is now known that mixed populations occur together in many parts of the Old World. Since the accidental introduction to America was often of very small groups, occasionally pure local stocks are found of only one colour phase. The 'black' rat is found around Victoria and Vancouver, and on the Queen Charlotte Islands. Two mummified carcasses of black rats were also found on Charlton Island, James Bay, in 1920.

The 'Alexandrian roof rat' is the common name often applied to the brown colour phase (*R. r. alexandrinus*). Populations of this colour phase are found on Langara Island, Queen Charlotte Islands, and individual specimens are occasionally met elsewhere.

On February 23, 1927, when a case of trees from France was being unpacked at Strathroy, Ontario, about twenty rats of both colour phases were discovered in the packing. Fortunately authorities were able to kill all of them. This species also was established in Halifax, Nova Scotia, during the early nineteenth century but was exterminated prior to 1861.

NORWAY RAT
Rat surmulot. *Rattus norvegicus* (Berkenhout)

Description. The Norway rat is a larger and stockier animal than the roof rat, but it has a decidedly shorter tail (less than the body length). Its pelage is coarse, grizzled brown above and yellowish grey below; it has a thick brown scaly tail (Figure 50); and its ears are decidedly smaller than those of the roof rat. White, black, or mottled specimens are occasionally met. The juvenile coat is grey and woolly.

The skull of the Norway rat is heavier and broader than that of *R. rattus*, and the lateral brow ridges are prominent from the interorbital constriction to the back of the skull. The first upper molar lacks notches.

Figure 50 Norway rat

Average measurements of adults: length 316–460, tail 122–215, hind foot 30–45, ear 15–20 mm; weight 195–485 g.

Habits. The Norway rat is a commensal species, living in association with man. It is colonial, and each colony has a highly organized social hierarchy. Usually the largest males are dominant and maintain harems and territories. The social rank of an individual is of basic importance in determining its living quarters, food, and reproduction. If the population increases in the rat 'ghetto' to densities causing strife, the weakest individuals will be starved, killed, or forced to emigrate. Curiously, there is an anti-social caste, which takes no interest in establishing homes or in mating and is permitted to wander through the colony, always giving way to the socially conforming aggressors.

This rat is noisily active at all times of the day and is a vicious fighter. It is an excellent burrower and often digs extensive tunnel systems with nesting cavities, but it is a less agile climber than the black rat. It also builds bulky nests of twigs, leaves, and scrap in shelters of packing boxes and building materials, or under buildings.

Rats are relatively sedentary and generally occupy home ranges of approximately twenty-five to fifty yards in diameter. Population densities of Norway rats in Baltimore in the United States varied from about 25 to 150 rats per block, and the rural populations on a Maryland farm fluctuated from about 75 to 300 rats. It has been estimated that the rat population for the United States is about 123 million.

Rats eat a wide variety of food: stored grains, vegetables, fruit, meat, and by-products such as butter, cheese, and soap. They are carnivorous and kill chickens, ducks, and even lambs and piglets. Most of their food in cities is made up of what they can salvage from garbage.

In spite of the numbers of rats killed by cats, dogs, and certain wild predators such as the great horned, barred, and snowy owls, long-tailed weasels, foxes, and coyotes, none of these predators make serious inroads into the population of rats.

Habitat. Most rats are concentrated in cities and towns, but many others live on farms. During the summer they may move out into the fields, but the majority return to the shelter of the buildings during the winter. Rats occupy barns, haystacks, silos, warehouses, garbage dumps, dock areas, alleyways, stores, and private houses.

Reproduction. Rats are very prolific. The females are polyoestrous; heat lasts for about twenty hours, and the oestrous cycle from four to six days. The breeding season may last all year, but there are usually spring and autumn peaks in breeding. The gestation period is twenty-one to twenty-two days. The number of young in the litter may vary from six to twenty-two, with an average of about nine. The average number of litters born per year is five (from three to twelve). The litter size decreases with the age of the female after the second litter, and those born in the autumn and winter are smaller. Post-partum heat occurs within eighteen hours after the birth of the litter.

The young rats are born naked and blind, and their

development is altricial. The young juveniles mature at approximately fifty-two days of age.

Economic Status. The Norway rat is probably man's worst animal pest. It subsists largely upon food produced by man. A rat eats the equivalent of 50 g of corn or 35 g of wheat per day. It was estimated in 1941 that the annual loss from rat damage on the farm was $10 to $35 per rat each year.

Besides the destruction and soiling of food, rats also damage property. This includes the chewing of electric and telephone cables, lead water pipes, leather goods, packages, boxes, and furniture. The annual losses caused by rats in the United States were estimated at approximately $200 million. The losses in Canada on the same basis would have been approximately $20 million a year.

Furthermore, the rat is a serious public health menace. It serves as a reservoir and source of infection for a number of serious human diseases including bubonic plague (*Pasteurella pestis*), typhus fever, spirochetal jaundice (*Leptospira icterohaemorrhagiae*), food poisoning (*Salmonella* sp.), tularaemia (*Pasteurella tularensis*), and trichinosis (*Trichinella spiralis*).

Rats may also act as direct predators, attacking helpless babies and sleeping children and adults. There have been several cases of rats attacking babies in Canada, including one case in Ottawa in 1961.

Since the level of the rat population is primarily determined by environmental factors such as availability of food, cover, and nesting sites, the first step in any rat control program is sanitation. Such programs should include the regular collection and disposal of garbage, the removal of debris and dilapidated buildings, and the rat-proofing of food storage areas. After these steps have been taken, an active poison campaign, as discussed under the control of meadow voles, *Microtus pennsylvanicus*, would effectively reduce the population to a low level. In 1952 Norway rats arrived in Field, British Columbia, by way of railway grain cars, but before they became established the distribution of warfarin baits eradicated them.

Distribution. The Norway rat was originally a native of central Asia, but it has followed man to most other parts of the world. It reached western Europe about 1700, England by 1730, and North America about 1775. In northern areas it quickly drove out the black rat, *Rattus rattus*. In more southern areas it often dominates the ground level and restricts the black rat to the trees and higher stories of buildings.

Canadian Distribution. These rats are widely distributed in most settled areas of Canada in the cities and in more southerly rural areas. Most of British Columbia and Alberta, the Yukon and Northwest Territories, and the northern parts of Quebec, Labrador, Ontario, Manitoba, and Saskatchewan remain relatively free of rats. The commensal subspecies is:

Rattus norvegicus norvegicus (Berkenhout), 1769, Outlines Natural History of Great Britain and Ireland, 1: 5. Cosmopolitan.

REFERENCES

Calhoun, J.B. 1966. The ecology and sociology of the Norway rat. United States Dept. Health, Education and Welfare, Washington.
Chitty, Dennis, and N.H. Southern (eds.). 1954. Control of rats and mice. 3 vols., Oxford Univ. Press, London.
Davis, David E. 1953. The characteristics of rat populations. Quart. Rev. Biol. 28(4): 373–401.

HOUSE MOUSE
Souris commune. *Mus musculus* Linnaeus

Description. The house mouse is familiar to almost everyone. It is a small mouse with a pointed head, large ears, and a long scaly tail. The dorsal colour is ochraceous-brown, and the ventral colour is dark grey. The tail is only slightly paler below than above. The last joints of the toes are whitish. The house mouse may be easily distinguished from native white-bellied deer mice, *Peromyscus* sp., but is more difficult to separate from the western harvest mouse, *Reithrodontomys megalotis*, which has buffy, whitish underparts and a distinctly bi-coloured tail. The grooved incisors of the harvest mouse are the trenchant characteristic (Figure 51).

The molars of the house mouse have the typical murid three rows of tubercules. Otherwise the skull is rather undistinguished.

Average measurements of adult males: length 172 (168–177), tail 85 (81–90), hind foot 19 (16–21) mm.

Habits. House mice are colonial, social little beasts. (The white mice used as laboratory animals and pets are albino house mice.) They are chiefly nocturnal in activity. They build nests of grasses in trash, under buildings, or in boxes, cupboards, and mattresses. Though chiefly terrestrial they often burrow in the fields and use microtine runways.

Their food consists of grains, fruit and vegetables, stored food, and refuse. They are preyed upon by cats,

Figure 51 House mouse

dogs, snakes, hawks, owls, weasels, opossums, skunks, raccoons, and foxes.

Habitat. Originally, in the wild, this species lived on dry, arid steppes. The commensal form lives primarily in human dwellings, particularly in forested, wet, or cold regions. In dry grasslands and farmlands, however, it may live in feral communities.

Reproduction. The breeding cycle of the house mouse is much like that of the rat. It is polyoestrous, breeding throughout the year under ideal conditions. The length of the oestrous cycle varies from three to nine days; ovulation is spontaneous. The gestation period is twenty-one days. Post-partum oestrus occurs within twenty-four hours after parturition. The average litter size varies from 4.5 to 7.4, the extremes being one and twelve. There are several litters each year. The young are altricial in development. Sexual maturity is reached at thirty-five days of age.

Economic Status. Probably everything written concerning the damage done by the rat is applicable to the house mouse. However, the depredations of this little kitchen brigand do not seem quite so vicious. Usually a few well-placed mousetraps will bring the situation under control in a short time.

Distribution. The form found in Canada is a commensal race of the wild subspecies *Mus musculus wagneri*, which is native to Russian Turkestan. Commensal races evolved in that region, where early agriculture promoted the growing of grain, and then migrated along the caravan routes to the eastern Mediterranean, North Africa, and Spain. The commensal race *M. m. domesticus* invaded western Europe from northern Spain and eventually reached North America in the baggage and stores of the early explorers and settlers.

Canadian Distribution. House mice inhabit human settlements throughout southern Canada, north as far as the Mackenzie delta, Northwest Territories. They also occur in feral populations in fields across southern Canada. The race found in Canada is:

Mus musculus domesticus Rutty, 1772, Essay Nat. Hist. County Dublin 1: 281.

REFERENCE

Schwarz, E., and H.K. Schwarz. 1943. The wild and commensal stocks of the house mouse, *Mus musculus* Linnaeus. Jour. Mamm. 24(1): 59–72.

Family Dipodidae / Jumping Mice and Jerboas

This family consists of small rodents adapted to a saltatorial mode of locomotion. The birch mouse, *Sicista betulina*, of northern Europe is a primitive member of the group without enlarged hind legs. Our species, however, have greatly elongated hind feet, toes, and tail, although their forefeet are shorter than average for mice of comparable size. Jumping mice assume a kangaroo-like stance,

squatting on their hind feet and using their forefeet when eating.

In general body form, jumping mice resemble the Heteromyidae (pocket mice and kangaroo rats) but they lack cheek pouches. Jumping mice have separate metatarsals, but jerboas have increasingly united central metatarsals.

The skulls of jumping mice are narrow; the oval infra-orbital foramen permits the passage of a slip of the masseter muscle along with its nerve. The zygomatic arches are depressed and slender. The upper incisors are short and grooved. The cheek teeth are rooted and moderately high crowned. The upper fourth premolar is present in the genus *Zapus* but absent in the genus *Napaeozapus* (Figure 52). There is a closely related jumping mouse in China, *Eozapus setchuanus*, whose upper premolar is much larger than in the American species.

Jumping mice are small, slender nocturnal rodents that hibernate. The females have four pairs of mammae: one pectoral, two abdominal, and one inguinal.

PACIFIC JUMPING MOUSE
Souris sauteuse du Pacifique. *Zapus trinotatus* Rhoads

Description. The Pacific jumping mouse is considered to be the most primitive of the three species in its genus because of its relatively large and functional upper premolar at the front of the cheek tooth row. The basic colour patterns are similar in all three species, and the differences are subtle. The trenchant characters are found in the skulls, particularly the dentition. The three species are thought to have been isolated in three different refugia, south of the ice-sheet during the last glacial period, and to have gradually migrated northward following the retreating glacier to occupy their present ranges. They now overlap in a few areas, but no hybridization has occurred, suggesting that there may be some subtle, as yet undiscovered, ecological separation in their requirements.

This species is the brightest of the three. It has a broad, dark olive brown band extending from nose to rump. The cheeks and flanks are ochraceous or tawny, streaked with black hairs and bordered on the ventral side by a narrow orange stripe. The underparts are white, with buffy spots on the chest. The prominent ears are clothed with short, dark brown fur. The very long, thin tail is bi-coloured, brown above and creamy white below, and is sparsely covered with short hairs so that the scale annulations

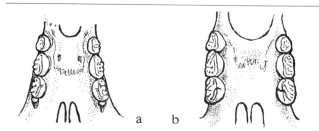

Figure 52 Comparison of cheek teeth of (a) *Zapus* and (b) *Napaeozapus* (× 3)

show prominently. The soles of the feet are naked, and the long hind feet are covered with short buffy grey hairs.

The skull is relatively stout, and the zygomatic arches, though more flaring than in the other species, are thread-like and lack anterior shelves. The cranium is relatively high; the coronoid process of the mandible is elongate. The dentition is relatively heavy; the premolar has an occlusal surface with a labial re-entrant fold forming a crescentic loop. The male baculum is long and spatulate.

The pelage is short and wiry. There is one annual moult during the summer. The new coat appears simultaneously on the crown and shoulders, progresses anteriorly first to include the head, and then spreads laterally and posteriorly over the body until the rump is finally renewed.

Average measurements of adults: length 238 (223–249), tail 143 (129–155), hind foot 32 (31–35) mm.

Habits. The life histories of the three closely related meadow jumping mice are very similar, but since the eastern species, Z. hudsonius, has been studied in much more detail than the others, additional information may be obtained by referring to the section on it.

The Pacific jumping mouse is primarily nocturnal in activity. It progresses either by crawling on all fours or by leaping on its hind legs. Its long, wiry tail acts as a balancing organ, and if it loses its tail by accident the animal tumbles about. Though relatively quiet, it drums the ground with its tail. It is an excellent swimmer. In captivity it is reported to be delicate and shy.

Pacific jumping mice store fat in late summer and hibernate towards the end of September. They are sometimes found in a semi-torpid state during cold snaps in the early autumn, but they become more active as they warm up during the day. Two hibernating jumping mice were discovered rolled up in nests of shredded paper, four inches apart, about thirty inches underground in February. Another, which aroused itself in the warm sunlight but became dormant again when the temperature dropped to 45°F, was found hibernating under a stump in April. This species finally emerges when spring is well advanced.

The food of the Pacific jumping mouse consists of the seeds of grasses, dock, and skunk cabbage, as well as blackberries (occasionally its chin is stained with the juice of these berries). It cuts down the grass in long sections to reach the seed heads but stores no grain for winter use.

Owls, weasels, skunks, and badgers are important predators of these nocturnal mice.

Habitat. This jumping mouse inhabits alpine meadows, the shrubby borders of streams, marshes, and sphagnum bogs.

Reproduction. It is thought that these mice bear a single litter in June or early July of from four to eight young. The new-born jumping mice are unusually small, averaging 0.8 (0.7–0.9) g in weight. The tails are longer than those of deer mice of comparable size.

Economic Status. This mouse is of no known economic significance.

Distribution. This species is restricted to the Pacific coast region, from California to southern British Columbia.

Map 94 Distribution of the Pacific jumping mouse, *Zapus trinotatus*

Canadian Distribution. The nominate subspecies is found in Canada, but only in extreme southwestern British Columbia eastward as far as Okanagan Lake (see Map 94).

Zapus trinotatus trinotatus Rhoads, 1895, Proc. Acad. Nat. Sci. Philadelphia 1894: 42.

REFERENCE

Svihla, A., and R. Svihla. 1933. Notes on the jumping mouse, *Zapus trinotatus trinotatus* Rhoads. Jour. Mamm. 14(2): 131–4.

WESTERN JUMPING MOUSE
Souris sauteuse de l'Ouest. *Zapus princeps* J.A. Allen

Description. The western jumping mouse is larger and more robust than the eastern species, Z. hudsonius. Its head and back are olive brown; its flanks are yellowish buff, streaked with black hairs; it has white underparts; the lateral line is yellowish. The feet are grey, and the ears are dusky with buffy rims. The tail is brown above, pale grey below, without a white tip (Plate 15e).

The skull of this species is larger than that of Z. hudsonius. The zygoma lack any small anterior ventral shelf. Its diagnostic feature is the heavier dentition (cheek teeth measuring over 3.8 mm in length).

There is one annual moult, in summer. The new coat

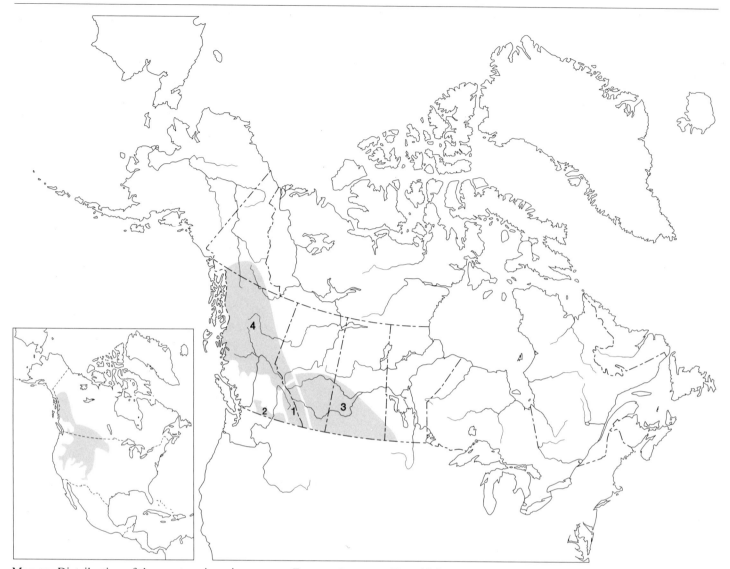

Map 95 Distribution of the western jumping mouse, *Zapus princeps*: 1 *Z. p. idahoensis*, 2 *Z. p. kootenayensis*, 3 *Z. p. minor*, 4 *Z. p. saltator*

appears first on the shoulders and gradually spreads anteriorly, laterally, and posteriorly. The rump is the last area to moult.

Average measurements of twenty adults from northern British Columbia: length 248 (235–265), tail 150 (140–158), hind foot 33 (31–34) mm.

Habits. The western jumping mouse may be quite abundant in suitable habitat. It is primarily nocturnal in activity and creeps along hidden trails or leaps about when pursued. It is an excellent swimmer and takes to water readily. Its nest is constructed of woven grasses in shallow depressions among grass clumps.

During July this jumping mouse begins to lay on fat, and in September it hibernates and does not emerge until late May.

The food of this species consists of grass seeds and summer berries.

Among the western mouse's enemies are garter snakes, large fish, hawks, owls, weasels, foxes, and coyotes.

Habitat. The western jumping mouse is found in mountain meadows, along stream banks, and in alder and willow groves, as well as in coulees and swales on the prairies.

Reproduction. There is perhaps only one litter born during the season, between mid-June and the end of July. The average litter size is five, with a range from two to seven.

Economic Status. These mice seldom come in contact with agriculture in Canada.

Distribution. The western jumping mouse occupies the Rocky Mountain region of North America from New Mexico to southern Yukon Territory and eastward to include the Canadian prairies. It probably spread northward from the southern Rocky Mountains following the retreat of the glaciers.

Canadian Distribution. Four geographical subspecies based upon slight colour differences are recognized in Canada (see Map 95).

Zapus princeps idahoensis Davis, 1931, Jour. Mamm. 15: 221. A large, buffy-flanked race with the tail only indistinctly bi-coloured (brown above and tan below) and with lateral line faint. Found in the southern Rocky Mountains of southwestern Alberta and southeastern British Columbia.

Zapus princeps kootenayensis Anderson, 1931, Nat. Mus. Canada Bull. 70: 108. A yellowish-flanked race with a distinctly bi-coloured tail, from extreme south-central British Columbia.

Zapus princeps minor Preble, 1899, N. American Fauna 15: 23. A small race with bright contrasting back, flanks, and belly colour pattern, found in the southern portions of the Prairie Provinces.

Zapus princeps saltator J.A. Allen, 1899, Bull. American Mus. Nat. Hist. 12: 3. A large greyish race from northern British Columbia and southern Yukon Territory.

REFERENCE

Krutzsch, Philip H. 1954. North American jumping mice (genus *Zapus*). Univ. Kansas Pub. Mus. Nat. Hist. 7(4): 394–420.

MEADOW JUMPING MOUSE
Souris sauteuse des champs. *Zapus hudsonius* (Zimmermann)

Description. The first glimpse a farm lad usually has of this mammal is of a small creature bounding erratically ahead of a clattering mower. At first it is difficult to decide whether it is a frog, a grasshopper, or a mouse. If captured and examined in the hand, it will be found to be a small, slim mouse, with long, spindly hind legs and an exceptionally long, wire-like tail. It has a small head, large ears covered with fine fur, small, delicate forelegs, a vestigial pollex, and five very long hind toes. Its bi-coloured, scaly tail is much longer than the body and scantily haired. The soles of its feet are naked (Figure 53). The male baculum is less than 5.1 mm long. The skull is narrow and high crowned. The narrow zygomatic arches have a small in-

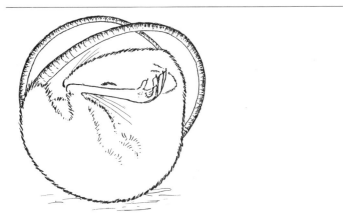

Figure 53 Hibernating meadow jumping mouse

ternal shelf on the anterior ventral surface. The short upper incisors are longitudinally grooved. The cheek teeth are very small (the upper tooth row being less than 3.7 mm in length), and there is a small peg-like upper premolar in front of the molar series, with a shallow re-entrant fold (Plate 20 and Figure 52).

The pelage is short, thick, and wiry. There are three types of hair: guard hair, overhair, and underfur. The dorsal surface is marked by a broad olive brown band from nose to rump. The flanks are ochraceous, and heavily lined with black hairs. The underparts are buffy white. There is usually a clear pale yellow stripe separating the belly from the black-lined flanks. Juveniles are paler on the dorsum, which lacks the blacker hairs, and the result is the olive brown band. Spotted or pale specimens have been noted, but are rare.

The one annual moult in adults commences after mid-June and takes about three weeks. The juveniles begin to moult in August. The new pelage appears on the nose and shoulders and spreads ventrally and posteriorly.

Average measurements of adult males: length 215 (188–236), tail 127 (112–134), hind foot 30 (28–31), ear 13 (11–15) mm. Females may be slightly larger. Average summer weight: males 16 (11.5–19.2) g, females 18.9 (12.5–24.8) g.

Habits. Jumping mice appear to be solitary animals, although they are not aggressive and mix easily with others of their kind. They are gentle and seldom bite, and therefore are easily tamed. They utter few sounds: the young squeak, and the adults utter a rasping sound, chatter their teeth, or drum the ground with their tails. Their normal locomotion is by a series of short hops. They also creep along vole runways, but when frightened they bound off in a series of erratic leaps, each about a yard long, using their long tails for a balance. After a few leaps they crouch, pressing their white bellies to the ground and exposing only their olive brown backs in the hope of escaping detection.

They are excellent swimmers and often cross small streams or enter them simply to frolic. They float high in the water and progress with jerky pattering of their hind feet. They also dive and swim under water as deep as four feet. Occasionally individuals are observed climbing in low shrubs.

Jumping mice are mostly nocturnal in activity but may appear on damp, cloudy afternoons. Summer nests are hollow spheres of woven grass or leaves about four inches in diameter, placed under a log, board, or root, or in a tussock of grass on the surface of the ground. There is a short tunnel or runway leading to the nest. They travel across open ground or creep through rock crevices or along runways.

This species enters hibernation during the last part of September or early October. The hibernacula are situated about one to three feet below the surface in a moist but well-drained location such as a river bank or hill of earth. Jumping mice may dig their own burrows or use deep burrows excavated by other mammals such as wood-

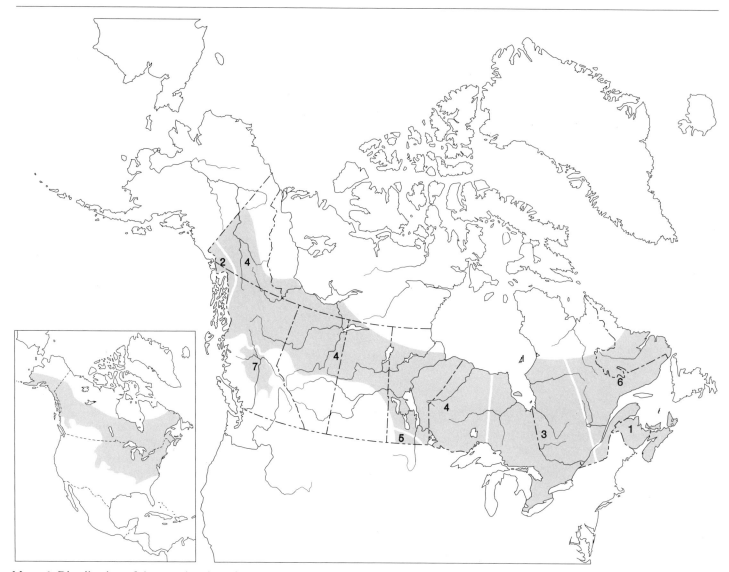

Map 96 Distribution of the meadow jumping mouse, *Zapus hudsonius*: 1 *Z. h. acadicus*, 2 *Z. h. alascensis*, 3 *Z. h. canadensis*, 4 *Z. h. hudsonius*, 5 *Z. h. intermedius*, 6 *Z. h. ladus*, 7 *Z. h. tenellus*

chucks. The hibernating jumping mouse is invariably found rolled into a ball, its head tucked between its hind feet and its long tail curled like a watch-spring around its body (Figure 53). The hibernacula are lined with dry leaves. The animals enter hibernation gradually, and are lethargic for a few days before final withdrawal. Once they have hibernated, they appear to enter a state of profound torpor characterized by slow respiration, slow heart beat, and depressed body temperature.

For several weeks before entering hibernation, jumping mice accumulate a layer of subdermal and visceral fat. At that period those animals ready for hibernation weigh about 26 g, while the non-hibernators weigh approximately 16 g. The adults hibernate first, and the juveniles later, when they have accumulated sufficient fat. In the first two weeks after entering the torpid state, the animals lose considerable weight, but the weight loss then levels off.

Jumping mice emerge from hibernation relatively late in spring. The males emerge about the beginning of May, and the females towards the end of May, about the time when the leaves are unfolding.

These mice are not as sedentary as some other species. They seem to be more nomadic, and there is a significant turnover in local populations during the summer. Tagged animals have been known to move about a thousand yards. The mean home range for males in Minnesota was found to be 2.70 acres and for females 1.57 acres. There is a considerable overlap of home ranges for different individuals. They do not exhibit any strong homing instinct. Population densities vary from about 1.81 to 11.91 animals per acre. The populations of meadow jumping mice fluctuate considerably from year to year in the same locality. There is an almost complete annual turnover in population, only a few individuals surviving two years.

Jumping mice are primarily seed eaters. They cut down the grasses in sections in order to reach the seed heads. In summer they also eat a wide selection of fruit such as blueberries, raspberries, strawberries, currants, and red baneberries. They are carnivorous to some extent and eat larvae and adult insects. They do not store food for winter use.

Their predators include bullfrogs, green frogs, pike, snakes, owls, and weasels. Mortality is confined mostly to the summer months, and they are relatively secure in hibernation.

Habitat. Meadow jumping mice prefer to occupy moist grassland. They are often found along grassy stream banks, marsh borders, alder–willow borders, and low fields, and occasionally on the borders of woods and fence rows.

Reproduction. The breeding season commences as soon as the females emerge from hibernation. In the north most of the litters are born between mid-June and the end of August. The females are polyoestrous and bear two, or occasionally three, litters per year. The gestation period is approximately eighteen days, but is prolonged in lactating females. The average litter size is 5.3 (2–8) young.

The young are born pink, naked, blind, and deaf. They are relatively small and weigh only about 0.78 g. During the first week, the ear pinnae unfold, the backs become clothed with grey fur, and the young begin to crawl. Tawny hair appears during the second week. The incisors erupt on the thirteenth day, the auditory canal opens on the nineteenth day, and the eyes open between twenty-two and twenty-five days. In the fourth week the adult pelage appears and the young mice are weaned, and when they are twenty-eight to thirty-three days old they are independent.

Juvenile females born in the spring reproduce when they are about two months old. Those born in late summer are thought to produce their first litter about a month after the first adults produce theirs in the following spring.

Economic Status. This attractive and interesting rodent is not known to be of any economic significance. Its populations never reach levels that affect the harvest.

Distribution. The meadow jumping mouse has the widest distribution of all jumping mice. It occupies a broad belt across North America from the Atlantic coast to western Alaska and occurs from northern Georgia to the arctic treeline.

Canadian Distribution. The species is plastic, and seven geographical subspecies are recognized in Canada (see Map 96), based upon slight variations in size and colour.

Zapus hudsonius acadicus (Dawson), 1865, Edinburgh New Phil. Jour. 3: 2. A relatively large ochraceous form, found in the Gaspé Peninsula, the Eastern Townships of Quebec, and the Maritime Provinces (except Newfoundland).

Zapus hudsonius alascensis Merriam, 1897, Proc. Biol. Soc. Washington 2: 223. A relatively large, dark-backed, pale-flanked race, found in southwestern Yukon Territory and extreme northwestern British Columbia.

Zapus hudsonius canadensis (Davies), 1798, Trans. Linn. Soc. London 4: 157. A dull form, found in eastern Ontario and western Quebec.

Zapus hudsonius hudsonius (Zimmermann), 1780, Geog. Geschichte d. Menschen u. vierfussigen Thiere, 2: 358. The typically coloured, small subspecies, which occupies a large area of the western boreal forest in northwestern Ontario; northern Manitoba, Saskatchewan, Alberta, and British Columbia; southern Mackenzie District; and most of the Yukon Territory.

Zapus hudsonius intermedius Krutzsch, 1954, Univ. Kansas Pub. Mus. Nat. Hist. 7(4): 447. A medium-sized yellowish subspecies found in southwestern Manitoba.

Zapus hudsonius ladus Bangs, 1899, Proc. New England Zool. Club 1: 10. A relatively dark race with a less distinct dorsal band, found in northeastern Quebec and Labrador.

Zapus hudsonius tenellus Merriam, 1897, Proc. Biol. Soc. Washington, 11: 103. A subspecies characterized by its darker, less distinct dorsum and more olivaceous flanks, found in central British Columbia.

REFERENCE

Quimby, Don C. 1951. The life history and ecology of the jumping mouse, *Zapus hudsonius*. Ecol. Monogr. 21: 61–95.

WOODLAND JUMPING MOUSE
Souris sauteuse des bois. *Napaeozapus insignis* (Miller)

Description. This mouse is one of the most attractive of the small denizens of our eastern woods. It is a larger edition of the meadow jumping mouse but is somewhat stouter and may be quickly identified by the white tip on its extremely long tail. Although the basic colour patterns are similar to those of the meadow jumping mouse, the present species is much brighter than the genus *Zapus*. The head and broad dorsal band are buffy brown; the nose and base of the long vibrissae are black; the prominent ears are covered with short brown hair, and the rims are tipped with buff. The cheeks and flanks are golden yellow, lightly streaked with black hairs; the underparts are white. The long, wiry tail is bi-coloured, brown above, creamy white below, and tipped with white. The covering is sparse, and the scale annulations show prominently. The soles of the long hind feet are naked, and the dorsal surfaces are covered with short grey fur. The pelage is short, thick, and somewhat harsh to the touch. No information is available on the moult sequence.

The skull of this jumping mouse is typically zapodid: the infraorbital foramina are large; the zygoma are narrow, slender, and depressed; the interorbital construction is broad and flat; the cranium is high and narrow. It has short bright orange incisors, which are longitudinally grooved. Its cheek teeth are large, broad, and flat, with complicated folded occlusal surfaces; the fourth premolar is missing (Figure 52). The palate is broad, the incisive foramina are wide, and the auditory bullae are small.

Average measurements of adult males: length 234 (230–253), tail 147 (132–160), hind foot 31.5 (30–33), ear 15 (13–16) mm; non-hibernating weight 21.5 (16.3–26.8) g. Adult females: length 240 (231–259), tail 149 (138–159), hind foot 31 (30–33), ear 14 (13–15) mm; non-hibernating weight 23.4 (18.3–31.5) g. The females are, on the average, a little larger than the males. Prior to hibernation both sexes weigh approximately 31 g.

Habits. Woodland jumping mice are sociable and appear to be colonial. They often feed together, and there is some indication that the pairs travel together. An occurrence of a woodland jumping mouse being captured in a box trap with a deer mouse, *Peromyscus maniculatus*, indicates that these two species occupy the same habitat harmoniously. This species of jumping mouse can leap distances up to three to four yards. It seems to burrow more than the meadow jumping mouse and frequently uses the shallow tunnels and runways of other species of small mammals. It also swims well, floating high in the water with its tail kinked so as to keep it out of the water. It can climb in small shrubs as well. It is primarily nocturnal in activity.

During the summer months this species excavates shallow burrows about a yard long, two inches in diameter, and four inches below the surface. The nest of leaves or grass is placed in a chamber about four to six inches in diameter. Here the young are born and nursed. The adult carefully plugs the entrance with earth after entering for the daylight hours so that the nest is extremely difficult to find. Nests have also been located under logs or in brush piles.

Woodland jumping mice accumulate a layer of fat during the late summer and early autumn before they enter hibernation. The adults disappear before the juveniles, towards the end of September and early October. Only exceptional individuals are active after mid-October. They emerge from hibernation during the first week of May. The yearling males seem to emerge earliest, probably because they have utilized all their fat reserves; the adult males and females follow. The hibernacula of the woodland jumping mouse have rarely been found. Animals kept in experimental outdoor cages dug individual burrows and gathered nesting material of wood shavings in a cavity about eight inches below the surface. When the entrances were plugged, the animals became torpid and rolled up into a ball. Animals kept in indoor colonies remained active all winter and became torpid only fitfully for short periods. Jumping mice emerge from hibernation much later than marmots and ground squirrels – late enough to find their food readily available again, so that they do not have to live off their accumulated fat for a month or so as marmots do.

Woodland jumping mice are relatively nomadic. The average home range for an adult male is 8.96 acres and for an adult female 6.55 acres. There is much overlapping: many individuals cover the same territory. These mice may become very abundant and overrun the wooded environment. At such times they may be the most abundant small mammal and outnumber the deer mice and red-backed voles. I found this to be the case in Algonquin Park, Ontario, in 1939, and in the Gaspé Peninsula, Quebec, in 1962. At other times, however, they may be quite rare, as they were in Algonquin Park during the summer of 1941. Tagged individuals have lived over one

COLOUR PLATE

22

Coyote, *Canis latrans*

23

American porcupine, *Erethizon dorsatum*

24

25

year in the wild state, but little information on longevity is available.

The food of this species consists of subterranean fungi (*Endogone* and *Hymenogaster*), herbs, roots, seeds, and fruit. Plants eaten include buttercups, iris tubers, mitrewort, May apples, fruits of alders, wintergreen berries, raspberries, blackberries, strawberries, and huckleberries. They also eat a number of insect larvae, pupae, and adults, such as butterflies, caterpillars, grasshoppers, dragonflies, beetles, and fly grubs. They have internal cheek pouches and may carry a few seeds in them, but they store no food.

Predators include owls, hawks, mink, weasels, and skunks.

Habitat. As the name implies, this species is found along the borders of woodland streams. It occurs in both brushy hardwood and coniferous forests but never far from the banks of a river, lake, stream, or spring. Here it tunnels in the moist alluvial soil under rocks and roots along the eroding banks. It makes nocturnal excursions back some distance into the forest but is never far from the cover of logs, stumps, ferns, and brush piles. It seldom ventures out into open bogs or swales, which are occupied by the meadow jumping mouse.

Reproduction. The breeding season commences as soon as the females emerge from hibernation. In June, woodland jumping mice have been observed indulging in a curious erratic bounding 'dance.' The females appear to dominate the smaller males and to pursue them. Parturition occurs between early June and late August. The females are seasonally polyoestrous, and post-partum oestrus occurs. Probably only two litters are born in a summer, however. The gestation period is twenty-three days, and the average litter size is 4.4 (4–6).

The young 'jumper' is small and is relatively undeveloped at birth, weighing about 1 g. It has a relatively long, pointed tail. The ear pinnae unfold at the age of ten days, and at twelve days the dorsum appears noticeably grey and the tip of the tail is flesh-coloured. By the seventeenth day the back is well furred with a golden coat. The eyes open on about the twenty-sixth day, and the auditory canal opens at about the same time. The youngsters begin to hop about at this stage and assume the many characteristic poses of jumping mice. Weaning takes place at the approximate age of thirty-four days. The juvenile coat is much duller and browner than the adult's at this stage. The moult to adult pelage takes place between sixty-three and eighty days of age.

The juveniles probably do not mature until the following spring.

Economic Status. This interesting forest dweller is not known to have any economic significance, unless one considers its insect diet to be of benefit.

Distribution. The woodland jumping mouse is restricted to eastern North America.

Canadian Distribution. The species occurs throughout the Maritime Provinces (except Newfoundland), southern Labrador, southern Quebec, central Ontario, and west-

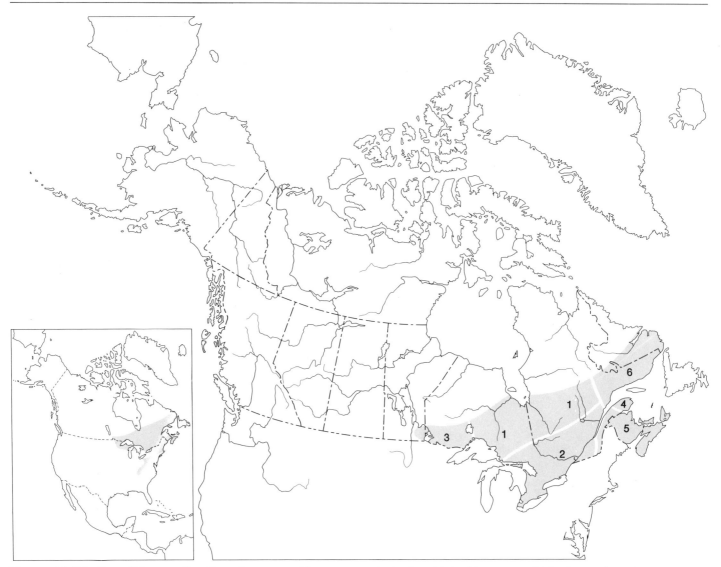

Map 97 Distribution of the woodland jumping mouse, *Napaeozapus insignis*: 1 *N. i. abietorum*, 2 *N. i. algonquinensis*, 3 *N. i. frutectanus*, 4 *N. i. gaspensis*, 5 *N. i. insignis*, 6 *N. i. saguenayensis*

ward to extreme southeastern Manitoba. Six subspecies are currently recognized in Canada (see Map 97).

Napaeozapus insignis abietorum (Preble), 1899, N. American Fauna 15: 36. A large subspecies with heavy dentition, found in central Ontario and Quebec.

Napaeozapus insignis algonquinensis Prince, 1941, Occas. Paper Roy. Ont. Mus. Zool. no. 7, p. 1. The form found in south-central Ontario and western Quebec, north of the St Lawrence River, characterized by bright tawny flanks and a less clearly defined dorsal stripe.

Napaeozapus insignis frutectanus Jackson, 1919, Proc. Biol. Soc. Washington 32: 9. A paler-sided, darker-backed-subspecies, found in the Rainy River district of western Ontario and southeastern Manitoba.

Napaeozapus insignis gaspensis Anderson, 1942, Ann. Rept. Provancher Soc. Nat. Hist. Quebec 1941: 39. Found in the Gaspé Peninsula, Quebec; characterized by pale flanks and a dark dorsal stripe.

Napaeozapus insignis insignis (Miller), 1891, American Nat. 25: 742. The typical form, found in the Maritime Provinces and the Eastern Townships of Quebec.

Napaeozapus insignis saguenayensis Anderson, 1942, Ann. Rept. Provancher Soc. Nat. Hist. Quebec 1941: 40. A large, dark race from southern Labrador and the north shore of the Gulf of St Lawrence.

REFERENCES

Preble, Norman A. 1956. Notes on the life history of *Napaeozapus*. Jour. Mamm. 37(2): 197–200.

Whitaker, J.O. Jr. 1963. Food, habitat and parasites of the woodland jumping mouse in central New York. Jour. Mamm. 44(3): 316–21.

Wrigley, R.E. 1972. Systematics and biology of the woodland jumping mouse, *Napaeozapus insignis*. Illinois Biol. Monogr. 47.

Family **Erethizontidae** / New World Porcupines

The New World porcupines belong to a diverse assemblage of rodents (suborder Caviomorpha), the ancestors of which reached the tropical Americas at an early period and evolved there in relative isolation. They are characterized by a greatly enlarged infraorbital canal, which permits the passage of a large slip of the masseter muscle. This muscle originates on the side of the rostrum. The zygomatic plate, which is nearly horizontal, lies below the infraorbital canal. The lower border of the posterior angle of the mandible is strongly inflected. The tibia and fibula are separate.

The dentition of New World porcupines is heavy. The cheek teeth, which are flat-crowned and rooted, have complex enamel loops. The fourth premolar is molariform. The incisors are very strong.

The body form is large and sturdy. The pelage is characterized by long, sharp spines on the dorsum and tail. The females possess four pectoral teats.

AMERICAN PORCUPINE
Porc-épic d'Amérique. *Erethizon dorsatum* (Linnaeus)

Description. This large, spiny, sluggish rodent is familar to most Canadians, but few know that it is the only member of a typically South American group of rodents that crossed the Isthmus of Panama during the Pleistocene period and invaded North America of its own accord. In this it resembles the opossum, *Didelphis virginiana*, which has a similar history. In contrast, Old World porcupines, *Hystrix* sp., belong to another family and illustrate convergent evolution.

This is Canada's second largest rodent next to the beaver; it measures approximately 3 feet long and weighs up to 25 pounds. It has a robust body; small head, eyes, and ears; a blunt muzzle; a very thick tail; and short, strong legs armed with powerful, long, curved black claws. It has four toes on the forefeet and five on the hind feet. The soles of the feet are fleshy and naked (Plate 23).

The porcupine's skull is heavily constructed; the zygomatic arches are narrow and depressed; the rostrum and interorbital regions are elevated and flattened. The large incisors are orange coloured on the anterior surface. The four cheek teeth are of uniform size (Figure 54).

The pelage of the species is composed of sensory hairs, a dense woolly brown undercoat, long cream-tipped guard hairs, and stiff quills. The hairs are arranged in transverse rows; the quill rows are separated from the rows of coat hairs. The quills are located on head, neck, rump, and tail, and vary greatly in length and diameter. Those on the middle of the back are the longest (about 63 mm), the tail quills are about 30 mm long, and those on the forehead are about 25 mm in length. The quills, which are easily pulled out, are replaced in ten days to six months. They grow about 0.5 mm per day and at the tip have a long hair-like filament, which is soon lost. The brown tip of each quill is covered with backward-projecting scales, which prevent the free withdrawal of the quill and cause the tip to gradually work its way inwards. The quills and hair can be erected in defence, but when not in use they are normally directed posteriorly. It has been estimated that a porcupine has 30,000 quills. The ventral surface and the legs are clothed only with stiff black hairs. The coat hairs are moulted once annually, between spring and midsummer. The moult progresses from the nose and crown posteriorly to the tail. Broken quills are replaced at the same time. Albino porcupines are often seen.

Average measurements of adults: length 772 (648–860), tail 214 (148–300), hind foot 106 (86–124) mm; weight 6.4 (3.3–9.5) kg.

Habits. During most of the year, porcupines are solitary and cantankerous, but they pair up during the mating season. Small family groups occasionally den together. They are vocal during the mating season, and their squeals and grunts may be heard from a considerable distance. Although they have poor eyesight, their hearing and their sense of smell are good.

Porcupines usually shuffle along the ground, leaving pigeon-toed tracks. If alarmed, they break into a slow, lumbering gallop, but they may be easily overtaken. In winter they plow trenches in the soft snow because of

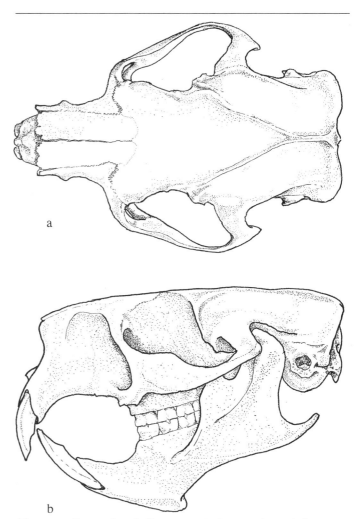

Figure 54 Porcupine skull: (a) dorsal view, (b) lateral view (× 1)

their short legs. They frequently travel below windfalls in the forest and dig long snow tunnels. They are excellent climbers and use the stiff bristles on the under side of their tails as a prop in climbing. Surprisingly, porcupines are also excellent swimmers and take readily to water to cross lakes and rivers or to feed on water-lily leaves. On one occasion when I was attracted to a swimming animal several hundred yards from the shore of a northern lake, I was much surprised when I reached the spot in my canoe to find a high-floating porcupine paddling unhurriedly for the far shore of the lake.

Primarily nocturnal, porcupines spend much of the daylight hours resting, draped over a limb in a favourite tree, which is usually a prominent conifer with a bushy top. They are active all winter.

These sluggish animals are well known for their unique mode of defence. When pressed, they try to find a log or stone to protect their heads, and then they turn their backs on their adversary and elevate their quills. If the enemy gets too close, they lash out with their club-like spiny tail. It is popularly thought that they throw their quills, but this is not true. A lightning-fast blow can be delivered with the tail, and the lateral quills are easily detached and left impaled in the attacker.

When I was a lad I shot my first porcupine, and when it started to fall from branch to branch of a tall tree I stood fascinated below. Suddenly realizing that it was going to fall directly on me, I just managed to crouch before it hit me on the back. I spent a painful ten minutes while my companions gleefully extracted about a dozen quills. The stinging was much too generalized for me to realize that one had been missed, and that evening I was too much embarrassed to report the incident to my parents. About six months later, long after the accident had been forgotten, I discovered a needle-like object rising through the skin of my stomach. Eventually the sharp point reached the surface and stuck in my shirt. The result was a visit to the family doctor, who made a short incision and withdrew the inch-long tip of a slender porcupine quill. The consensus was that it had worked itself around from the back in the superficial muscles until it reached the linea alba, from which it was forced upwards to the surface.

The porcupine makes use of ground shelters, particularly during the winter months. Rocky talus slopes, quarries, caves, and rocky road fill are favourite spots. It also uses road culverts, hollow logs, brush piles, and the roots of windthrown trees. Often a snow tunnel leads to its winter retreat. In summer it may follow regular paths from its dens to favourite feeding areas.

Tagged porcupines ranged over thirty-two to thirty-six acres during a thirty-day period. The average diurnal movement was about eighty-eight yards, and the average nocturnal movement about a hundred and twenty-one. The population density has been estimated at six to eight animals to a square mile in New Brunswick and twenty to twenty-eight to a square mile in Maine.

Porcupines have lived nine years in captivity and probably live almost as long in the wild.

The summer diet of porcupines consists of a wide variety of lush green leaves of forbs, shrubs, and trees. They are particularly fond of the leaves of the yellow pond lily, the aspen, and the white birch. They are also fond of clovers, alfalfa, and young corn. In winter they feed on the cambium layer and inner bark of trees as well as on the new twigs and buds. Among their favourite trees are eastern and western hemlock, balsam fir, tamarack, ponderosa pine, eastern white spruce, and red spruce. Among the broad-leaved trees, they prefer sugar maple, American beech, and basswood. In spring they eat the unfolding poplar and basswood leaves. They cut off quite a few small branches, which fall to the ground and are eaten by rabbits and deer.

Porcupines avidly chew bones and antlers they find on the ground, which have nutritional value because of their high mineral content.

Although the porcupine's defences are formidable, a number of large carnivores know how to kill the porcupine without being converted into pin-cushions themselves. These specialists are the wolverine, the fisher, and the bobcat. All excellent climbers, they may tackle the porcupine while it is treed. Somehow they manage to get a paw under the porcupine and flip it over onto its back, exposing its undefended underparts. Porcupines are attracted to roads on which salt has been sprinkled to melt the snow. During the winter, it is common in Banff National Park, Alberta, to see the tracks of a wolverine leading to each culvert, where it has been systematically hunting porcupines. Wolves, coyotes, and foxes occasionally kill porcupines, but they seem to be less adept than wolverines, fishers, and bobcats, and frequently have their jaws spiked with quills. The fact that porcupine quills have turned up in the pellets and stomach contents of great horned owls and weasels has afforded an opportunity for speculation on how these small predators managed to eat a porcupine.

Habitat. The porcupine is found in both deciduous and coniferous forested regions. Occasionally, however, especially in summer, it is found on the prairies far from trees and in eastern farmland.

Reproduction. It seems appropriate to start a résumé of reproduction in the porcupine with the time-honoured question: 'How do porcupines mate?' The answer is, 'Carefully!' Porcupines mate during the months of November and December. The male follows the female during this period and often climbs the tree the female is occupying. The male serenades her with grunts and low humming; the female may voice her displeasure at these unsolicited attentions by squealing loudly. When she is ready to mate, however, the pair indulge in a comical, roughhouse sort of dance. They rise on their hind feet and advance towards each other, whining and grunting. They may place their paws on each other's shoulders and rub noses; then they cuff each other affectionately on the head and usually bowl one another over with blows and shoves. Usually prolonged association is necessary before a male will mate with a female, but the female appears less choosy and may mate with several males. If the autumn mating is not successful, the female may come into heat again in January or April. The gestation period is relatively long for a rodent, 209 to 217 days. The young porcupines are born between mid-May and the end of July. Usually only one porcupine is born each summer; twins are rare.

Young porcupines are unique among young Canadian rodents because they are born at a relatively advanced stage of development and because they are precocious. Their weight is approximately 530 g at birth, and they are covered with long black hair and quills approximately one inch long. Their quills are flat and limp at birth, but the air soon hardens them. Their eyes are open, and they can walk briskly in a short time. On one occasion a new-born porcupine that had been delivered by caesarean section and carried back to camp in a saddle bag, receiving much jostling along the way, nevertheless took off across the yard at a good clip as soon as it was released. Soon after birth young porcupines display the instinctive behaviour pattern of backing into any proffered hand. They will also follow anyone who moves away from them, and rub against one's face if he whines. In marked contrast to their stolid elders, they are very playful. Since their mothers are nomadic, the young porcupines must follow them soon after birth. They are weaned during their second week, and from that time on they tag along, sampling the green foliage. They reach sexual maturity at approximately two and a half years of age.

Economic Status. Foresters find little attraction in the porcupine and classify it as one of the most important mammalian forestry pests. It damages merchantable timber by girdling and killing it outright, by girdling the tops of trees to produce 'stagheads,' or by clipping the leaders to produce multi-stemmed trees. It usually attacks trees less than six inches in diameter at breast height, the most important of which are the ponderosa pine, the lodgepole pine, and the eastern white and red spruces. In the 1940s porcupine damage was estimated to be 11.5 to 36 cents per acre in Maine, 45 cents to $1.10 per acre in Colorado, and $1.66 per acre of pine plantation in Montana, per porcupine per year.

In a survey of porcupine damage in Fundy National Park, New Brunswick, in 1951, I found the following incidence of recent damage on 125 random trees: balsam fir 72 per cent, spruce 12 per cent, mountain maple 7 per cent, birch 4 per cent, sugar maple 4 per cent, and beech 1 per cent. Not all feeding is detrimental to good forestry practice, of course, because porcupines often thin out dense stands of saplings and kill weed trees such as balsam firs.

These animals also do a great deal of damage to cottages, sheds, and wooden tools. Because of their craving for salt, they will chew up any object on which salt has fallen or any object that has been touched by a perspiring hand or stained with urine. Some of the newer animal repellents offer some protection against porcupine damage. Porcupines are also a menace in agriculture because they trample and destroy corn, alfalfa, and clover. Occasionally they maim cattle that come too close to inspect the curious animals ambling across the meadow. Cattle with quills in their muzzles will not feed.

On the positive side of the ledger, porcupine quills have been used by Indians for many centuries in decorative work. Easily killed with a club, this animal provides nutritious and tasty meat. It is often stated that it provides food for those lost or starving in the forests, and I know of one Royal Canadian Mounted policeman who owes his life to the discovery of a porcupine in the last trees on the edge of the tundra zone of the Northwest Territories.

Porcupines may be controlled by shooting, and the most opportune time and place would be after sunset along roads or on forest borders. The most efficient control method in forests is the distribution of strychnine and salt blocks. The bait is made by thoroughly mixing one ounce of powdered alkaloid strychnine with one pound of finely crystallized table salt, some powdered yellow dextrin, and sufficient water to form a stiff paste. It is then pressed into auger-made holes in soft wood blocks. The blocks should be firmly wedged far back in the rocky dens or nailed, high up, about one and one-half inches above a main branch, to the trunk of a favourite loafing tree.

Small agricultural plots may be protected by the erection of a low metal-screen electric fence.

Distribution. The porcupine inhabits most of North America from northern Mexico to Alaska and from the Atlantic to the Pacific.

Canadian Distribution. This mammal occupies all of continental Canada north to the treeline in northern Quebec, Labrador, Northwest Territories, and Yukon Territory. It does not occur on Newfoundland, Anticosti, Prince Edward, Cape Breton, Grand Manan, or Campobello islands in the east, or on Vancouver Island or the Queen Charlotte Islands in the west. Four geographical subspecies occur in Canada (see Map 98).

Erethizon dorsatum dorsatum (Linnaeus), 1758, Syst. Nat., 10th ed., 1: 57. The typical form, which occupies eastern Canada, most of the Prairie Provinces, and eastern Mackenzie District, Northwest Territories.

Erethizon dorsatum epixanthum Brandt, 1835, Mem. Acad. Imp. Sci. St. Petersburg, ser. 6, Sci. Math. Phys. et Nat. 3: 390. This subspecies occurs in Canada only in the extreme southern short-grass region of Alberta and Saskatchewan. It is characterized by paler greenish-yellow-tipped guard hairs.

Erethizon dorsatum myops Merriam, 1900, Proc. Washington Acad. Sci. 2: 27. A subspecies, characterized by a brownish colour and long rusty-yellow-tipped guard hairs, found in the Yukon, in the western part of the Mackenzie District, extreme northeastern British Columbia, and northwestern Alberta.

Erethizon dorsatum nigrescens J.A. Allen, 1903, Bull. American Mus. Nat. Hist. 9: 558. A blackish-haired porcupine with rusty-yellow tips to the long guard hairs,

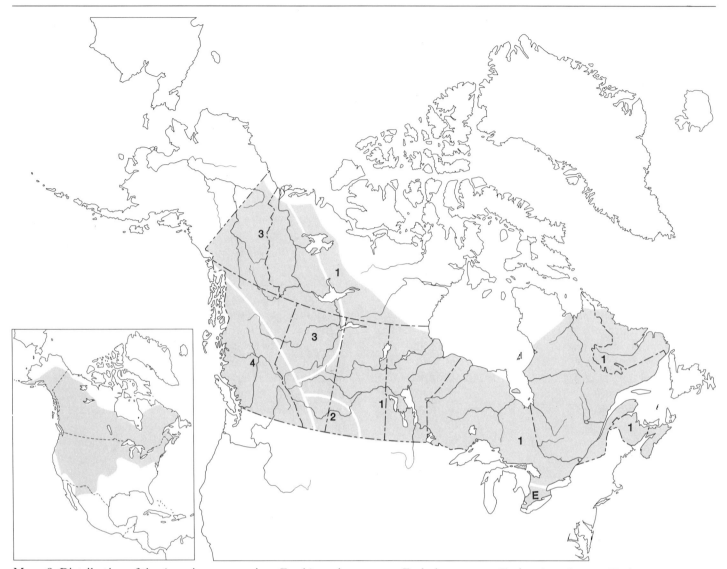

Map 98 Distribution of the American porcupine, *Erethizon dorsatum*: 1 *E. d. dorsatum*, 2 *E. d. epixanthum*, 3 *E. d. myops*, 4 *E. d. nigrescens*, E extinct

found in British Columbia and the Rocky Mountain region of Alberta.

REFERENCE

Taylor, W.P. 1935. Ecology and life history of the porcupine (*Erethizon epixanthum*) as related to the forests of Arizona and the southwestern United States. Univ. Arizona Biol. Sci. Bull. 3.

Family **Capromyidae** / Hutias and Coypus

This family contains an assortment of the little-known hutias from the West Indies and the well-known South American coypu. They have a robust body and variable tails: some long and scantily haired and others much reduced. The pollex is small, and the remaining digits are clawed. These rodents exhibit arboreal or aquatic adaptations. Their skulls are rugged; the molars, which are rooted or rootless, have high crowns with deep enamel folds; the auditory bullae are hollow; the paraoccipital processes are elongate.

COYPU
Nutria. *Myocastor coypus* (Molina)

Description. The coypu is a large aquatic rodent, native to southern South America, which has been introduced to North America as a ranch fur-bearer. It is an otter-sized amphibious mammal weighing up to 23 pounds. It has a flat triangular head, a blunt muzzle, small eyes; small, naked, round ears; and a long, round, scaly tail, which is sparsely haired. Its vibrissae are long and stiff. Its forefeet are small, and its pollex reduced. Its hind feet are larger than its forefeet; the hallux and first three toes are enclosed in a web, but the fifth toe is free and is possibly used as a comb.

The skull of the coypu is heavily ridged for the attachment of muscles, and the mandible is similarly powerful. The nasals are arched; the infraorbital canal is enlarged;

236

the paraoccipital processes are elongate, with prominent lateral processes. The cheek teeth are hypsodont, increasing in size and diverging posteriorly; the incisors are broad and powerful (Figure 55).

The soft, thick pelage is composed of a dense water-proof underfur and long, coarse guard hairs. The muzzle is silvery grey, the upper parts are glossy chestnut brown, the underparts grey brown, and the tail is dark brown. The National Museum of Canada has an albino specimen from Calumet Island, Quebec.

Average measurements of adults: length 701 (596–858), tail 273 (224–343) mm. Weight of mature animals 4.90 (2.72–10.40) kg.

Habits. Coypus are colonial, marsh-dwelling rodents. They excavate short burrows, about eight to nine inches in diameter and four feet in length, in the banks of streams and marshes. There are usually two entrances to their burrows above the water level. Their nests consist of bulky piles of cattails, reeds, and sedges.

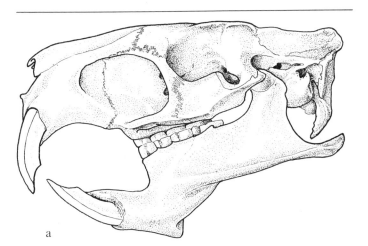

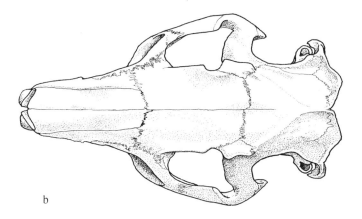

Figure 55 Coypu skull: (a) lateral view, (b) dorsal view (× 1)

The food of this species consists of cattails, burr-reeds, sedges, water weed, water milfoil, and arrowhead. Where their population becomes dense, they may destroy much of the vegetation.

The coypu is a relatively long-lived animal, attaining up to ten years in captivity.

There are few predators powerful enough to kill an adult coypu; probably the otter, the mink, and the coyote are the main possible predators. Weasels, hawks, and owls may take a larger toll of the young than of the adults.

Habitat. Marshes, lakes, and slow-moving rivers where the shores are lined with emergent aquatic vegetation are the coypu's favourite haunts.

Reproduction. The females are polyoestrous and may breed all year in fur farms where the temperature is kept above 60°F. In the wild, however, two litters per year is usual. The gestation period lasts 127 to 132 days, and the average litter size is 9.6. The young are precocious; born with fur and with eyes open, they weigh approximately 200 g. The female's four teats are laterally placed so that the young can nurse while she is feeding. Soon weaned, they eat the same food as the adults. The young mature at about five months of age, and the juvenile females produce their first young at eight to nine months of age.

Economic Status. The coypu is a valuable fur-bearer in South America, and its pelt is marketed as 'nutria.' It has been introduced into Europe, northern Asia, and North America as a ranch animal but has escaped and formed feral populations in many areas. During the fur season of 1965–66 in Canada, 3,417 ranch-raised nutria pelts were sold at an average value of $2 a pelt.

It is feared in some quarters that coypus may supplant the native muskrat in some southern marshes.

Distribution. The coypu's original distribution included southern South America from the Straits of Magellan northward to Bolivia and southern Brazil. Feral populations are now found in southern North America, Europe, and western Asia.

Canadian Distribution. Escaped coypus have established feral populations in the lower Fraser delta of British Columbia, in the Whitefish River drainage of Thunder Bay district, Ontario, and in the Ottawa River drainage of western Quebec and eastern Ontario. It is likely, however, that the climate of most of Canada is too severe for these south temperate zone mammals. The form introduced to North America is reported to be:

Myocastor coypus bonariensis (St Hilaire), 1805, Ann. Mus. Hist. Nat. Paris 6: 82.

REFERENCE

Laurie, E.M.O. 1946. The coypu (*Myocastor coypus*) in Great Britain. Jour. Animal Ecol. 15 (1): 22–34.

Order **Cetacea** / Whales, Dolphins, and Porpoises

Whales, dolphins, and porpoises, which form the order Cetacea, although now completely modified for an aquatic life, still carry evidence that they evolved from terrestrial mammals a long time ago. The external form is streamlined; the skin is smooth; the typical mammalian covering of hair is reduced to a few bristles around the lips of several species; sweat glands are absent. Under the skin is a thick, oily, fibrous layer (blubber), which serves to conserve the body heat in the absence of hair.

The forelimbs in Cetacea are short and paddle-shaped but contain four or five digits embedded in fibrous tissue, which are used as vanes, articulating only at the shoulder. The organs of propulsion are a pair of horizontal tail flukes, which drive the fusiform body ahead at each upstroke. The hind limbs are normally absent (vestigial knobs have been reported occasionally). All that remains to prove that the early ancestors of whales possessed hind legs is a pair of small pelvic bones floating in the body musculature. Occasionally vestigial femurs and tibias may be associated with these bones. Whales have small fixed eyes; the lachrymal glands exude tears of grease rather than water. The ears are very small, the pinnae are absent, and the auditory canal is restricted or absent. The nostrils (either a single or a paired orifice) are on the top of the head and lead to the lungs through a closed canal to keep water from entering from the throat. There is a single pair of teats situated in grooves on each side of the genital opening. The male's genital organs are likewise situated internally.

The skulls of whales are characterized by elongate rostra and much telescoped crania (to accommodate the dorsal nares). Though teeth are present in the suborder Odontoceti, they are found only in the foetuses of the whalebone whales of the suborder Mysticeti. The whales of the latter suborder are characterized by numerous parallel plates of baleen, which hang from the gums of the upper jaw. The baleen plates are very much frayed on the inner side and act as strainers, when the large tongue is elevated, to separate out the small crustacean 'krill,' which is the food of these giants of the deep.

The whale's great body is supported only by the massive but relatively simple vertebral column and by the rib cage. The cervical vertebrae are thin and crowded, often

fused, a characteristic that accounts for the neckless appearance of whales in general. The whale's other vertebrae are relatively unmodified and are thick and cylindrical with prominent vertebral discs. The flukes are not supported by bone.

This order includes the largest animals that have ever lived. Because they reverted to the primordial sea, they resemble other marine types such as sharks, bony fishes, and the ancient reptile ichthyosaur, but their anatomy and their behaviour clearly demonstrate that they are mammals.

Recent research has elucidated several interesting features of the whale such as its use of sonar to find food and evade barriers, and the property of its fusiform body that permits the laminar flow of water past it with a minimum expenditure of energy. The cetacean ear is much modified to receive underwater sound waves. Sound travels in water five times faster than it does on land (or approximately at one mile per second). Sound also has better propagation properties in water than in air. In water, sound waves pass directly through body tissues because they are approximately the same density as the surrounding water, and therefore an external ear orifice is unnecessary. The middle and inner ears are united in a tympanoperiotic bone, which is suspended from the skull by ligaments instead of being embedded in the skull as in most higher mammals. This large conch-like bone, which is one of the densest bones known, is very persistent. The interior is filled with foamy material, which is thought to transmit the sound waves.

The commercial hunting of whales commenced in the Bay of Biscay during the twelfth century. Basque fishermen pursued the slow 'scrag' whale, *Eschrichtius robustus*, and the 'Biscayne' whale, *Balaena glacialis*, in small sailboats and killed them with hand-thrown harpoons. As the whale populations in western European waters declined, the hunt was carried northward in sailing ships to Spitsbergen and North Cape (where *Balaena glacialis* was known as the 'Nordkaper'). The hunt was carried across the Atlantic Ocean to Newfoundland waters by Basque fishermen early in the sixteenth century.

After Hudson's voyage to Hudson Bay in 1611, the

exploitation of the bowhead whale, *Balaena mysticetus*, in Greenland waters commenced.

The whaling industry was in full swing in western Atlantic arctic waters by the start of the nineteenth century. Between 1804 and 1817, 193,522 right whales, *Balaena glacialis*, were killed. The peak of the European whaling industry in Hudson and Baffin bays was between 1818 and 1868. American whalers turned their attention to the stocks of bowhead whales in the Bering and Beaufort seas between 1870 and 1920.

The 'scrag' whale was exterminated in the Atlantic Ocean sometime during the seventeenth century, before zoologists became aware of its existence as a distinct species, and the right and bowhead whales were reduced to near extinction in Atlantic waters by the end of the nineteenth century. As these whales became reduced to the point of diminishing returns the whalers turned their attention to the slow humpbacked whale, *Megaptera novaeangliae*, and the more dangerous sperm whale, *Physeter catodon*, between 1800 and 1850.

By the middle of the nineteenth century the technology of the whaling industry had changed considerably. Steamships took over from sailing ships, and Norwegian whalers introduced the explosive harpoon gun. With the changed technology, the whalers began to hunt the speedy rorquals (family Balaenopteridae) that had formerly been too fast for the sailing ships and hand-rowed dories. During the early part of the twentieth century, 1913–31, blue whales, *Balaenoptera musculus*, were hunted in the northern seas, until their numbers were much reduced. Attention was switched to the Antarctic after 1920.

By 1930 the final refinements in whaling technology were introduced. These included the hollow lance shaft, by which compressed air could be pumped into the whale carcass to keep it from sinking, and factory-ships with their brood of small steam catchers. The Second World War, 1939–45, brought a halt to the whale hunt in Antarctic waters, but many whales were 'sunk' for submarines during the conflict. The southern hunt recommenced in 1945, with the added sophistication of sonar detection. As successive species have become reduced to the point of diminishing returns, attention has been focused on smaller and smaller species: the fin whale, *Balaenoptera physalus*, after 1945, and the sei whale, *Balaenoptera borealis*, after 1962.

Hopes for the conservation and rational management of whales have been placed in the International Whaling Commission, but this international agency has been unable to restrain the exploitation of declining stocks. Canada temporarily closed the three remaining active whaling stations in Newfoundland and Nova Scotia in the autumn of 1972. Canada also supported the proposed general ten-year moratorium on commercial whaling at the meeting of the commission in London in June 1973; however, the proposal was defeated.

ARTIFICIAL KEY TO FAMILIES OF CANADIAN CETACEA

1   Baleen plates in mouth (no adult teeth), paired blow-holes.   2

2   Throat grooves present, baleen plates narrow and short (less than 3 feet), mouth straight.   3

3   Many throat pleats and a small dorsal fin.
               BALAENOPTERIDAE

3′   Two to four short throat grooves, no dorsal fin.
               ESCHRICHTIDAE

2′   No throat grooves, huge arched mouth containing long, wide baleen plates (up to 8 feet).   BALAENIDAE

1′   Teeth in mouth, single blow-hole.   4

4   Only one or two pairs of functional teeth in tip of lower jaw, which is slightly longer than upper jaw and is usually prolonged into a 'beak,' central crescentic nostril, tail flukes not notched.   ZIPHIIDAE

4′   Many teeth in lower jaw.   5

5   Weak lower jaw which fits into groove on ventral surface of bulbous head, s-shaped blow-hole on left side of snout.   6

6   Large, bulbous-headed whale with a row of dorsal bumps in place of a dorsal fin.   PHYSETERIDAE

6′   Small whale (15 feet long) with a blunt head and a dorsal fin.   KOGIIDAE

5′   Lower jaw matches upper in a normal short mouth with a fixed 'smile,' a projecting upper lip of variable width, no throat grooves, and notched flukes.   7

7   Snout blunt with only a narrow upper 'lip,' pectoral flippers blunt, no dorsal fin, cervical vertebrae unfused.
               MONODONTIDAE

7′   Snout generally prolonged, dorsal fin present (except *Lissodelphis*), pectoral flippers falcate, at least two cervical vertebrae fused.   DELPHINIDAE

4″   Long tusk projects from upper jaw, no teeth in lower jaw.
               genus MONODON

Family **Ziphiidae** / Beaked Whales

This family includes a number of small- to medium-sized toothed whales. All have a single, median, crescentic nostril. The forelimbs are short and round and usually enclose five digits. There is a short, falcate dorsal fin, about two-thirds of the distance to the caudal flukes.

The beaked whales' skulls are relatively small, with a slender, dense rostrum. Many species in the family have markedly asymmetrical skulls caused by a prominence in the nasal region. The mandibles have a long, fused symphysis and often many vestigial teeth embedded in the gums. The males have one or two pairs of prominent broad tusks in the mandibles; these tusks are characteristic of the group. The tusks of the females seldom erupt. The stomach of a beaked whale has from nine to fourteen compartments. The tail flukes are usually convex medially, and are not notched. There are two or more throat furrows, which converge anteriorly to form a v. The first three or more cervical vertebrae are usually fused.

GIANT BEAKED WHALE
Grande baleine à bec. *Berardius bairdii* Stejneger

Description. This is the largest of the beaked whales: the males may reach 39 feet (12 metres) in length and the

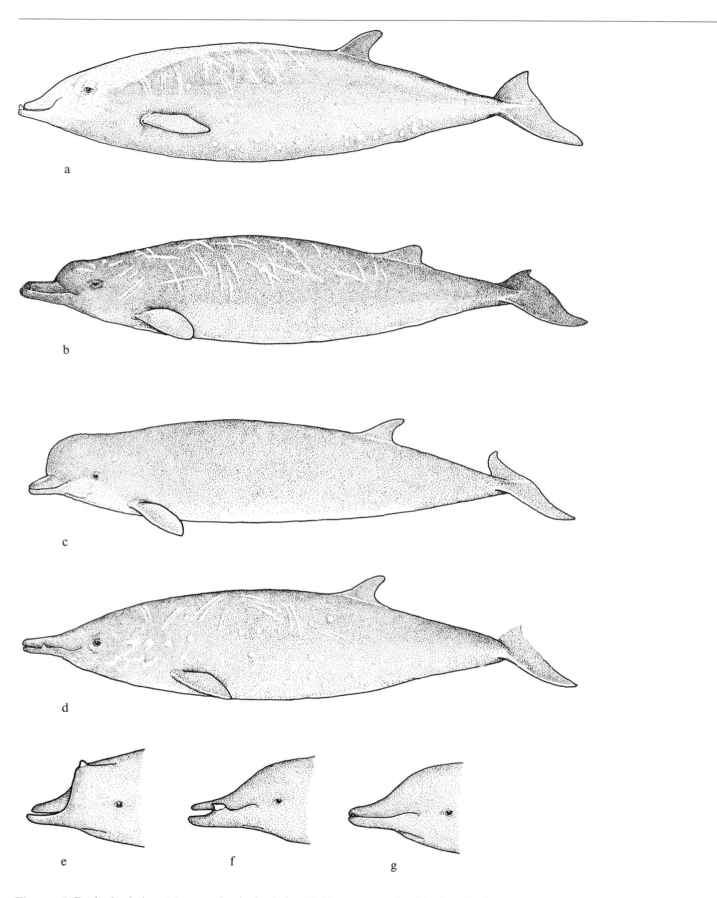

Figure 56 Beaked whales: (a) goose-beaked whale, *Ziphius cavirostris*; (b) giant beaked whale, *Berardius bairdii*; (c) northern bottlenosed whale, *Hyperoodon ampullatus*; (d) Sowerby's beaked whale, *Mesoplodon bidens*; (e) Blainville's beaked whale, *Mesoplodon densirostris*; (f) Stejneger's beaked whale, *Mesoplodon stejnegeri*; (g) True's beaked whale, *Mesoplodon mirus*

Map 99 Distribution of the giant beaked whale, *Berardius bairdii*

females 42 feet (12.8 metres). There is a narrow elongate beak separated from an elevated forehead by a groove in the males. In the tip of the mandible, which projects beyond the tip of the upper jaw, there are two pairs of triangular teeth. A pair of throat grooves converge to meet anteriorly. The flippers are rounded; the small dorsal fin is situated well back from the mid-point of the dorsum. The broad flukes may show a slight median notch. The body is thickest near the flippers and tapers posteriorly.

The dorsal colour of this species is black, and the ventral slightly paler, with some white spots along the mid-ventral line. The dorsum is usually marked with long white scars, perhaps made by the teeth of other whales during fights, or by the 'beaks' of the squid on which they feed (Figure 56b).

Habits. These whales are gregarious, travelling generally well offshore in gams (herds) of ten to twenty individuals, including calves. They blow rapidly about fifteen times in quick succession before diving, and raise their flukes in the air during a dive. A harpooned male will dive deeply, rapidly taking out 500 fathoms of line.

The whale's food consists of squids, octopuses, small rockfish, and herrings. This species is parasitized by stomach round-worms and externally by caprellid amphipods (whale lice) about the jaws.

Reproduction. Nothing is known of the reproduction of this species.

Economic Status. These whales are not hunted regularly in American waters, but a few 'bottlenose' whales are reported to have been taken over the years at Pacific coast whaling stations. About fifty are taken annually in Japanese waters, however, and their oil is usually sold as sperm whale oil.

Distribution. The giant beaked whale is restricted to the northern Pacific Ocean from central California to the Aleutian Islands, Bering Sea, the Commander Islands, the Sea of Okhotsk, and Japanese waters (see Map 99).

Canadian Distribution. This whale was first identified from two specimens taken off the north coast of Vancouver Island. The first was secured about ten miles off Kains Island, Quatsino Sound, on July 5, 1950, and the second, twenty miles east-southeast of Cape St James, Queen Charlotte Islands, on August 9, 1951. From 1950 to 1966, 23 specimens were taken by whalers from Coal Harbour, Vancouver Island. The form is:

Berardius bairdii Stejneger, 1883, Proc. United States Nat. Mus. 6: 75. Coastal British Columbia.

REFERENCE

Pike, G.C., and I.B. MacAskie. 1969. Marine mammals of British Columbia. Fish. Res. Bd. Canada Bull. 171: 5–9.

SOWERBY'S BEAKED WHALE
Baleine à bec de Sowerby. *Mesoplodon bidens* (Sowerby)

Description. The smaller beaked whales belonging to this genus are poorly known because they are not hunted commercially and are known only from occasional strandings. This species reaches a maximum length of 16 feet (4.9 metres). Its body is spindle-shaped; its head tapers to a long, slender beak; in males the lower jaw exceeds the upper; there are two converging grooves under the lower jaw and a crescentic blow-hole on the head. The small flippers are paddle-shaped, and the small dorsal fin, which is placed posteriorly, is concave behind. The dorsal colour is shiny blue-black; the underparts are blue-grey with irregular light spotting. There may be many white scratches on the skin from tooth-marks (Figure 56d).

The skull is slightly asymmetrical as a result of the maxillary prominence; the beak is long and slender. In the adults there is a single pair of mandibular teeth, situated behind the symphysis at a distance of about a third the length of the mandible. The males have a large projecting triangular tooth, but the teeth of juvenile females do not project above the gum line.

Habits. These small whales are not gregarious and are usually observed alone or in groups of two or three. They are not considered migratory. Their food is thought to consist of squids.

One specimen was kept alive out of water for two days, in 1835, in France. It was offered moistened bread but could not be prevailed upon to eat. It was reported to have frequently given vent to loud bellowing, like the lowing of a cow. This species is occasionally preyed upon by killer whales.

Habitat. Sowerby's beaked whale is found in deep offshore boreal waters.

Reproduction. One calf is born at a time.

Economic Status. None.

Distribution. This species occurs in the North Atlantic Ocean from Cape Cod and Newfoundland to France, Great Britain, and Norway. It is more common on the European side, especially in the North Sea (see Map 100).

241

Map 100 Distribution of Sowerby's beaked whale, *Mesoplodon bidens*

Map 101 Distribution of Blainville's beaked whale, *Mesoplodon densirostris*

Canadian Distribution. Specimens have been stranded twice on the shores of Newfoundland, one at Trinity Bay on August 26, 1952, and the second at Notre Dame Bay on September 23, 1953. The species is known as:

Mesoplodon bidens (Sowerby), 1804, The British Miscellany ..., p. 1.

REFERENCE

Sergeant, D.E., and H.D. Fisher. 1957. Sowerby's beaked whale. *In* The smaller cetaceans of eastern Canadian waters. Jour. Fish. Res. Bd. Canada 14(1): 83–115.

BLAINVILLE'S BEAKED WHALE
Baleine à bec de Blainville. *Mesoplodon densirostris* (Blainville)

Description. This is one of the smaller beaked whales, males measuring less than 15 feet (4.6 metres) in length and mature females as little as 12 feet (3.6 metres). The body form is regularly ziphioid. The most striking feature is the great height of the mandibles and the teeth, so that the upper jaw lies in a trough. The forehead rises gradually from the beak and is actually lower than the male's projecting tusks. The colour is black, with some reddish patches on the underparts, between the flippers and the genital opening, and with some irregular light grey spots on the belly. A specimen taken off Nova Scotia weighed 1,783 pounds (810 kg) (Figure 56e).

The skull of this species is characterized by an exceedingly slim, heavy rostrum (beak); deep rostral grooves, anterior to the maxillary foramina; and the great depth of each mandibular ramus in the vicinity of the tooth. The

male's teeth, which may be 6 inches high and a little over 3 inches wide, are embedded in a thick fibrous cushion, and probably erupt only at maturity. Those of the female are smaller and may remain embedded in the fleshy gum.

Habits. Practically nothing is known of the life history of the species.

Habitat. This small beaked whale appears to live a pelagic life in tropical waters. Those that have been stranded in northern waters are thought to be sick individuals.

Reproduction. No details are known.

Economic Status. None.

Distribution. Only sixteen specimens of this species are known from widespread strandings. It occurs in tropical waters of the North Atlantic, the South Pacific, and the Indian oceans. It is not known as yet from the South Atlantic or North Pacific (see Map 101).

Canadian Distribution. Only two specimens of Blainville's beaked whale are known from Canadian waters. The first was an adult male captured at Peggy's Cove, Nova Scotia, in February 1940, and the second was washed ashore at Fourché Bay, Newfoundland, in December 1968, which is the most northern record for the western Atlantic.

The species is known as:

Mesoplodon densirostris (Blainville), 1817, Nouv. Dict. Hist. Nat. ..., 2nd ed., 9: 178.

REFERENCE

Raven, H.C. 1942. On the structure of *Mesoplodon densirostris*, a rare beaked whale. Bull. American Mus. Nat. Hist. 80, Art. 2: 23–50.

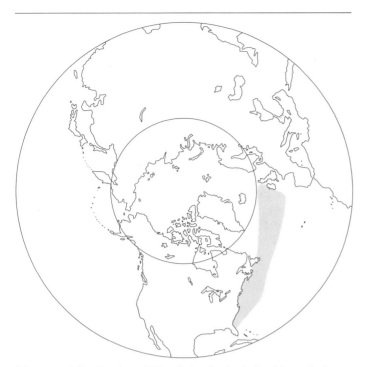

Map 102 Distribution of True's beaked whale, *Mesoplodon mirus*

TRUE'S BEAKED WHALE
Baleine à bec de True. *Mesoplodon mirus* True

Description. This North Atlantic beaked whale measures up to 17 feet (5.3 metres) in length. Its deep body is spindle-shaped but rather laterally compressed. Its head is prolonged into a slender beak, the lower jaw projecting a little beyond the upper. There are two prominent throat grooves, which meet anteriorly to form a v. The forehead of this whale rises gradually to the crescentic blow-hole. Its flippers are rounded, its dorsal fin is small, and its flukes are broad but unnotched. It has a smooth, thin skin. The dorsal colour is glossy slate black, and the venter is somewhat mottled with greys and purples.

The diagnostic feature of this little whale is the presence of a pair of teeth at the tip of the mandible. The teeth of adult males are fairly large and flat and project beyond the gum, but those of females are small and slender and remain embedded in the gum (Figure 56g).

This whale's skull is characterized by a long, slim, straight rostrum which lacks basal grooves. The asymmetrical maxillary prominence protrudes into the lateral outline of the rostrum to form a notch.

Habits. Little is known of the life of this small pelagic whale.

Habitat. This whale inhabits the deep, cold waters of the North Atlantic Ocean.

Reproduction. No details are known.

Economic Status. None.

Distribution. This species is known only from twelve strandings. Eleven of them are thought to indicate the normal distribution, which includes the east coast of North America from Cape Hatteras to Cape Breton Is-land, and the northern British Isles. The twelfth was in Florida (see Map 102).

Canadian Distribution. True's beaked whale has appeared only once in Canadian waters at South Gut, St Anne's Bay, Cape Breton Island, on August 5, 1938. A companion was reported, but it escaped. The species is known as:

Mesoplodon mirus True, 1913, Smiths. Misc. Coll. 60(25): 1.

REFERENCES

Allen, G.M. 1939. True's beaked whale in Nova Scotia. Jour. Mamm. 20: 259–60.
Ulmer, F.A. Jr. 1941. *Mesoplodon mirus* in New Jersey, with additional notes on the New Jersey *M. densiros-tris*, and a list and key to the ziphoid whales of the Atlantic Coast of North America. Proc. Acad. Nat. Sci. Philadelphia 93: 107–22, pl. 20, 21.

STEJNEGER'S BEAKED WHALE
Baleine à bec de Stejneger. *Mesoplodon stejnegeri* True

Description. This species is the least known of our small beaked whales. It has the typical spindle-shaped body form and may attain a length of 17 feet (5.3 metres). The diagnostic feature is the presence of a pair of large blade-like teeth in the mandible, about a third of the way back from the tip and behind the short symphysis. Unlike for *M. densirostris*, the mandible of this species is not greatly enlarged in the alveolar region. The forehead rises gradually from the protruding beak (Figure 56f).

The skull of this beaked whale lacks the grooves at the base of the rostrum typical of *M. densirostris*, and the premaxillary bones form a crest above the nares.

The colour is black except for the jaws, which are white. The back is often scarred by tooth-marks.

Habits. This small beaked whale is reported to occur in small groups of two or three half a mile to a mile offshore on salmon-trolling grounds. It blows once or twice between dives. Its only enemy is the killer whale.

Habitat. The species has a pelagic life in the cold sub-arctic North Pacific Ocean.

Reproduction. No details are known.

Economic Status. None.

Distribution. Stejneger's beaked whale is found in the North Pacific Ocean from the coast of Washington State to Bering Sea, and in Japanese waters (see Map 103).

Canadian Distribution. The species is known from three specimens stranded on Vancouver Island and one at Prince Rupert, British Columbia. The Canadian form is:

Mesoplodon stejnegeri True, 1885, Proc. United States Nat. Mus. 8: 585.

MOORE'S BEAKED WHALE
Baleine à bec de Moore. *Mesoplodon carlhubbsi* Moore

Description. This species was recently described on the basis of skull characteristics, but there is little information

Map 103 Distribution of Stejneger's beaked whale, *Mesoplodon stejnegeri*

on the external appearance of the whale. It would be very difficult for anyone other than a cetaceologist to identify the species in the field. The type specimen is an adult male, 17 feet (5.3 metres) long. A juvenile male measuring 9 feet (2.7 metres) in length was estimated to weigh about 400 pounds (180 kg). The body form is typical of other species of the genus. The colour is greyish, dark slate grey dorsally shading to a dull yellow white ventrally. The pair of teeth in the males are situated about 3 inches from the tip of the lower jaw and stand erect in their sockets, arched slightly inwards. The 'beak' appears slightly arched in dorsal outline.

Habitat. This species is believed to inhabit waters of the north temperate zone.

Reproduction. No information is available.

Economic Status. None.

Distribution. This species is found in the North Pacific Ocean from Japan to the west coast of North America. It does not enter the more northern subarctic waters.

Canadian Distribution. Two specimens of stranded beaked whales, one at Long Beach, Vancouver Island, on July 3, 1963, and a second from Rivers Inlet in 1965, have been identified as belonging to this species. The coast of southern British Columbia is believed to be the northern limit of its distribution.

Mesoplodon carlhubbsi Moore, 1963, American Midl. Nat. 70(2): 422.

REFERENCE

Pike, G.C., and I.B. MacAskie. 1969. Marine mammals of British Columbia. Fish. Res. Bd. Canada Bull. 171: 9–11.

GOOSE-BEAKED WHALE

Baleine à bec de Cuvier. *Ziphius cavirostris* G. Cuvier

Description. The goose-beaked whale is larger than the beaked whales of the genus *Mesoplodon*, adults measuring from about 18 to 26 feet in total length. The female is larger than the male, and its body is also much more rotund. Its 'beak' is very short, and its 'forehead' rises regularly behind it. The lower jaw overlaps the upper, and the corners of the short mouth turn up in a fixed smile. In the male a simple pair of peg-like teeth project from the tip of the lower jaw, but in the female these teeth remain embedded in the gum. This species also possesses a series of smaller teeth embedded in the lower jaw behind the front ones. The eyes are located diagonally behind the corners of the mouth. There are no external ear orifices. The crescentic nostril is placed dorsally a little ahead of the eyes. The usual v-shaped gular groove appears on the throat. The flippers are small and round; the short dorsal fin is concave behind and is located posteriorly on the back. There is a slight caudal peduncle just ahead of the flukes, which are very slightly notched medially (Figure 56a). From the specimens at hand the colour of this whale seems quite variable. Most are very dark grey below and posteriorly, with a creamy white throat, jaws, head, and shoulders. The darker colour includes the flippers and area surrounding the eyes. Young specimens are much paler. Adults are much scarred with long scratches and ovoid white blotches, thought to be caused by the teeth of other whales.

The rostral 'beak' of the skull in this species is shorter and broader than those of species of the genus *Mesoplodon*. The premaxillae are massive, forming with the nasals an asymmetrical cup around the nostril.

Habits. Very little is known of the life story of this species. It is thought to be gregarious. One individual, captured alive in California and held a day in a tank, appeared very docile. It breathed two or three times at ten- to twenty-second intervals and then held its breath for one minute and fifteen seconds. In the sea this species is reported to dive for half an hour at a time. Its food is reported to consist principally of squid, but a few stalked barnacles have occasionally been found on its lips. The species may occasionally be preyed upon by killer whales.

Habitat. The specific marine environment requirements of this species are not known. It appears to be pelagic like most of the family.

Reproduction. The young are born in late summer or early autumn.

Economic Status. A few are taken regularly in Japanese waters.

Distribution. The goose-beaked whale is known from many oceans and seas and may be cosmopolitan in distribution.

Canadian Distribution. Five strandings have occurred on the coast of Vancouver Island, British Columbia (at Cape Scott, Victoria, Estevan Point, Bella Bella, and Jordan River) and two on the Queen Charlotte Islands. On the western side of the Atlantic coast, this whale does not

Map 104 Distribution of the goose-beaked whale, *Ziphius cavirostris*

seem to occur north of Rhode Island, but it reaches the British Isles and Scandinavia in European waters (see Map 104). The form is:

Ziphius cavirostris G. Cuvier, 1823, Recherches sur les ossements fossiles ..., 2nd ed., 5: 352.

REFERENCE

Moore, J.C. 1963. The goose-beaked whale: where in the world? Chicago Nat. Hist. Mus. Bull. 34(2): 2–3, 8.

NORTHERN BOTTLENOSED WHALE
Baleine à bec commune. *Hyperoodon ampullatus* (Forster)

Description. The bottlenosed whale is one of the better-known medium-sized whales of the North Atlantic Ocean. Adults measure between 20 and 30 feet (6.1–9.3 metres) in length, and a 21-foot (6.5 metre) female weighed 2 tons 18 hundredweight (2.6 metric tons).

The 'beak' of this whale is short. The adult males are characterized by a bulbous 'forehead' rising abruptly from the beak, but in females and young males the forehead rises only moderately above it. A pair of spindle-shaped teeth are embedded in the tip of the lower jaw, which projects slightly beyond the upper. These teeth usually erupt only in the adult males. There are as a rule a number of other small conical teeth embedded in the gums of both upper and lower jaws. The usual two ziphioid throat grooves are present. The crescentic nostril is located a little farther back than that of the goose-beaked whale; the pectoral 'fins' are also more pointed than in that species.

The remainder of the body is typical of the family. The dorsal fin is placed about two-thirds of the length of the body from the nose; it is small and concave posteriorly. The caudal flukes are broad but unnotched (Figure 56c).

The colour is quite variable: young whales are blackish, paler beneath, but the older ones are light brown. The very old males are yellowish brown, with whitish beaks and heads.

The skull of the bottlenosed whale is quite remarkable. The lateral edges of the maxillary bones at the base of the rostrum are elevated to form two crests ahead of the nares. These crests continue to grow in the males until they form inflated parallel masses of bone, which surround a solid lump of fat about twice the size of a watermelon. Usually the first six cervical vertebrae are fused in this species.

Habits. Bottlenosed whales are gregarious and are usually met in gams of four to ten individuals, composed of young females and calves. The bulls usually travel alone. They are unsuspicious and sportive about ships. They show strong social ties, and if one is harpooned, others close in around the wounded one, probably attracted by its underwater distress signals. In this way it was often possible for early whalers to capture all the individuals of a single gam. Bottlenosed whales are very active, leaping out of the water, twisting their heads, and crashing into the water again head-first.

They are migratory and spend the winter months in the North Atlantic Ocean from New York across to the Mediterranean Sea. In early spring (March) they migrate northwards to the edge of the arctic ice-floe from Davis Strait and the Greenland and Norwegian seas as far as Novaya Zemlya. During the summer months of June to August they remain within a day's run of the arctic floe-edge, reaching as far as latitude 77° N in the Greenland Sea. In September and October they migrate southwards, passing through the North Sea from Scandinavia and along the west coast of Great Britain.

The bottlenosed whale is one of the deepest divers among the whales. One harpooned male took out 700 fathoms of line in its initial sounding and stayed under for two hours.

The food of the bottlenose consists of arctic squid, *Gonatus fabricii*. Bottlenosed whales are parasitized by whale lice (Cyamidae), which are specialized skeleton shrimps of the crustacean order Amphipoda.

Habitat. This pelagic whale frequents cold subarctic waters.

Reproduction. At birth the single young is about 10 feet long. Young whales often linger farther south than adults.

Economic Status. With the decline of the right whales in arctic waters around 1880, European whalers turned their attention to these smaller whales. One whaler took 203 in May and June 1885, but very few are taken nowadays off our east coast. A full-grown bottlenosed whale yields two tons of oil in addition to two hundredweight of spermaceti (see section on economic status of the sperm whale) from the bulbous head. The oil is very similar to sperm oil.

Distribution. This species is confined to the northern Atlantic Ocean southward to New York and the Mediter-

Map 105 Distribution of the northern bottlenosed whale, *Hyperoodon ampullatus*

ranean. A closely related species, *H. planifrons*, inhabits the antarctic oceans.

Canadian Distribution. This species migrates along our east coast as far as latitude 70° N in Davis Strait. A few are reported to linger near Frobisher Bay, Baffin Island, Resolution Island, and Cape Chidley, Labrador. Immature individuals are seen on the Grand Banks (see Map 105).

The first Canadian record was of a 22-foot 1-inch female, which was stranded near Sainte-Anne de la Pocatière, Gaspé Peninsula, Quebec, on September 4, 1940. A second 22-foot male was taken at Dildo, Trinity Bay, Newfoundland on July 27, 1953. A companion escaped. A third was stranded on Sable Island in 1968. The species was described as:

Hyperoodon ampullatus (Forster), 1770, *in* Kalm, Travels into North America ..., 1: 18.

REFERENCES

Flower, W.H. 1882. On the whales of the genus *Hyperoodon*. Proc. Zool. Soc. London 1882: 722–6.
Gray, David. 1882. Notes on the characters and habits of the bottlenose whale (*Hyperoodon rostratus*). Proc. Zool. Soc. London 1882: 726–31.

Family **Physeteridae** / Sperm Whale

This family contains only the sperm whale, a toothed species with a very large bulbous head and a weak underslung lower jaw containing rows of strong conical teeth. The head contains a reservoir of spermaceti; the single, curious s-shaped nostril is situated asymmetrically on the left side near the tip of the snout. The dorsal fin is replaced by a series of humps.

SPERM WHALE
Cachalot macrocéphale. *Physeter catodon* Linnaeus

Description. This is probably the best-known whale, perhaps partly because of Herman Melville's romantic book *Moby Dick or the Whale*. Moby Dick was supposedly an albino bull sperm whale or cachelot, and it is interesting to note that one or two albino sperm whales have been taken in recent years.

The sperm whale's head is enormous, comprising about a third of the body length. It has a single, dorsal s-shaped nostril on the left side, near the tip of the barrel-shaped snout. The slim underslung mandible fits into a groove on the ventral surface of the snout. The lower jaw contains from sixteen to twenty-six pairs (average twenty-three) of strong conical teeth up to 8 inches in length, firmly anchored in the mandibles. These teeth fit into deep sockets in the upper jaw, alongside one to three pairs of rudimentary maxillary teeth. The eyes are relatively large; there are vestigial auditory canals; the pectoral fins are relatively small and paddle-shaped; there are two or more roughly parallel throat grooves; the usual dorsal fin is replaced by a ridge of humps, diminishing in size posteriorly; there is a ventral caudal peduncle as well. The broad caudal flukes are deeply cleft medially. There are a number of corrugations on the back, flanks, and chest (Figure 57a).

The skull of this species is massive; the rostrum is long and broad; the cranium is markedly telescoped and is asymmetrical in the maxillary region. The right nasal bone is absent, and the parietals are almost eliminated. The skull cradles the reservoir of spermaceti, which fills the inflated snout. Vestigial posterior limb-bones, including ilium and femurs, have been reported in one sperm whale.

Normally the colour is uniformly slate grey dorsally, lighter on the ventral surfaces with white splashes at the navel and on the lower jaw. Old animals often have a pale grey whorl on the snout. The palate and tongue are light grey. The blubber varies from 4 to 12 inches thick on the back.

Mature males measure from 11 to 18.5 metres (36–60 feet) in length, and mature females measure between 8 and 12.3 metres (26–40 feet). A 59-foot male weighed 52 tons. The bulls have larger heads and relatively smaller caudal parts than the cows. In the males the caudal humps are more posteriorly situated, and the snout projects more beyond the lower jaw.

Habits. Sperm whales are gregarious, but the gams or schools are usually composed of certain age and sex classes. There are schools of females with one to three 'schoolmasters' (bulls), gams of bachelor bulls, nursery schools of cows with new-born calves without 'schoolmasters,' and gams of unattended pregnant females. Non-breeding bulls remain solitary.

These whales are relatively slow swimmers, averaging about three to four knots when unhurried or ten to twelve knots when pressed. They are among the deepest divers. Sperm whales have become entangled in transoceanic cables lying on the floor of the oceans at depths between 65 and 620 fathoms. They usually submerge for about seventy minutes and then remain quietly at the surface and 'blow' sixty to seventy times in ten to eleven minutes. The spout is a bushy spray directed diagonally forward.

Sperm whales emit a variety of underwater sounds. There is a muffled smashing sound, a sound reminiscent of a grating rusty hinge, and a series of twenty or so sharp clicks, two to five per second, which are probably used in echo location.

These whales are migratory. They are plentiful at all times in tropical waters, but the bulls are found in the higher latitudes only during the summer months. The sperm whales of the North Atlantic spend the winter in the vicinity of the Cape Verde and Canary islands, and migrate northward towards the Azores Islands in spring in large gams of fifty to a thousand animals. The cows, calves, and 'schoolmasters' remain in the Gulf Stream during the summer, but gams of non-breeding bulls continue northward to arctic waters between April and September. The herds of sperm whales in the Southern Hemisphere migrate to antarctic waters in the southern summer – November to March.

The food of the sperm whale consists primarily of giant squid. In the Azores region eight species are taken. The largest specimen of the genus *Architeuthis* measured 10.5 metres (34 feet 5 inches) long and weighed 184 kg (405 pounds), but the average size is 2 to 8 feet (62–244 cm) in length. A few fish are also taken: basking sharks, barracuda, albacore, and deep-sea angler fish. A rag fish, *Acrotus willoughbyi*, was taken off the Queen Charlotte Islands. In the Bering Sea, 64 per cent of the stomachs examined contained squid, 26 per cent squid and fish, and 9 per cent fish only. The farther the whales travelled beyond the Commander Islands the poorer the food supply became.

Sperm whales are parasitized by whale lice (Cyamidae), copepods (*Penella*), and stalked barnacles. The snout is often pitted with circular scars from the giant squid suckers, and there are often other circular scars on the hide caused by sea lampreys.

Physical maturity is reached at eighteen years, when the males average 52 feet in length and the smaller females average 36 feet in length. There is no date on longevity in this species, and man is its only predator.

Habitat. The sperm whale is pelagic, inhabiting deep tropical waters. It is most common near oceanic islands. Only the mature bulls migrate to subarctic waters.

Reproduction. The whale stocks of the northern and southern hemispheres are six months out of phase, reproductively. In the northern populations the bulls have a protracted sexual season lasting from November to May. Oestrus occurs between January and July in the females, soon after lactation has ceased following the previous pregnancy. The females experience two or more ovulations in each breeding season, if the first one does not result in a pregnancy. The oestrous cycle occurs normally about every three years.

The bulls are polygamous: each gam of cows is attended by one, rarely more, 'schoolmaster.' The peak of mating is about April, during the northward spring migration. The gestation period is sixteen months, and normally one calf (rarely twins) is born between May and November. The peak of births occurs in August near the Azores.

The young sperm whale measures 3.71 to 4.10 metres (12 feet 2 inches to 13 feet 4 inches) in length and is dark grey in colour. The mandibles lack teeth at birth. The calf nurses by inserting its short lower jaw into the mother's

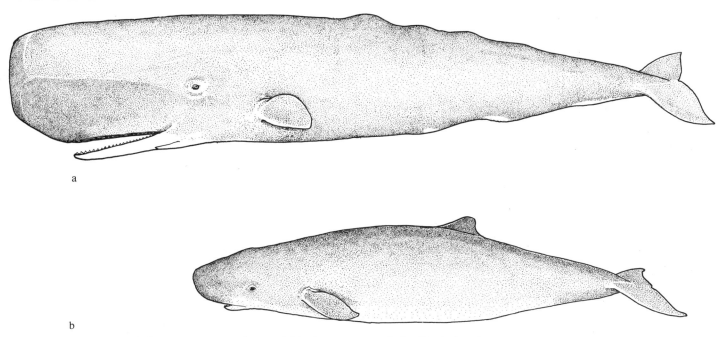

a

b

Figure 57 (a) sperm whale, *Physeter catodon*, and (b) pigmy sperm whale, *Kogia breviceps*

Map 106 Distribution of the sperm whale, *Physeter catodon*

mammary groove, and the mother pumps the milk into its mouth. The calves are weaned when they are a year old and measure 21 feet (6.4 metres) long. The mandibular teeth do not erupt until they are between 8.4 and 9.5 metres (28–31 feet) long. In the meantime they live on smaller squids.

The juvenile bulls mature at an age of four or five years, when they are about 31 feet long. The females mature at four years of age, when they are approximately 31 feet long, and grow very slowly thereafter.

Economic Status. The sperm whale formed the backbone of the whaling industry in the early nineteenth century. It was the source of three valuable products: spermaceti, ambergris, and sperm oil.

Spermaceti is a clear, colourless oil when tapped from the 'case' or reservoir in the head of the whale. It is dipped out in buckets and casked separately, where it turns into a waxy substance on exposure to the air. A large sperm whale yields 15 barrels of the the substance, which is used for candles, for the dressing of fabrics, for medical purposes, and also in the preparation of cosmetics.

Ambergris, which forms in the sperm whale's intestines, is a solid grey or blackish concretion deposited around cuttlefish beaks. It is occasionally found floating in the sea or washed ashore. It is very valuable and is used as a vehicle for retaining the fragrance of expensive perfumes.

Sperm oil, which is rendered by boiling the blubber, was used as illuminating oil. The introduction of petroleum in 1859 caused a decline in the industry, although the oil still has important specialized industrial uses. Now the spermaceti is rendered along with the sperm oil and is not sold separately.

After 1839 the catch of sperm whales declined because of overexploitation during the sailing and hand-harpoon whaling days. Now whaling is done from steamships, and explosive harpoon guns are used. Sperm whales are hunted off the shores of Japan, Natal, Chile, and Azores. During the thirties the annual world catch was about 2,000 to 2,500 sperm whales and in 1957 it rose to over 18,000, but in the 1962–63 season it dropped to 12,588.

Pelagic whaling is now controlled by the International Whaling Commission, which establishes restrictions. At present the minimum legal limit for sperm whales is 38 feet for pelagic whaling and 35 feet for shore-based installations. These legal lengths should provide protection for the bulk of the cows, and since the species is polygamous, the taking of males should not jeopardize the survival of the species.

Distribution. The sperm whale is cosmopolitan in the oceans and seas of the world.

Canadian Distribution. Bull sperm whales migrate past our Atlantic and Pacific coasts during the summer months (see Map 106), travelling as far north as Davis Strait (latitude 66°N). Twenty-eight have been taken commercially off Labrador in three years. Over 5,000 have been taken off the British Columbia coast since whaling operations commenced in 1905, from whaling stations at Rose Harbour and Coal Harbour.

The genus is monotypic:

Physeter catodon Linnaeus, 1758, Syst. Nat., 10th ed., 1: 76.

REFERENCES

Clarke, R. 1956. Sperm whales of the Azores. Discovery Repts. (Cambridge, England) 28: 237–98.
Matthew, L.H. 1938. The sperm whale, *Physeter catodon*. Discovery Repts. (Cambridge, England) 17: 93–168.
Pike, G.C., and I.B. MacAskie. 1969. Marine mammals of British Columbia. Fish. Res. Bd. Canada Bull. 171: 13–15.

Family **Kogiidae** / Pigmy Sperm Whales

The two species of pigmy sperm whales have recently been assigned to a separate family distinct from the related sperm whale. They have less bulbous heads and a distinct dorsal fin.

PIGMY SPERM WHALE
Cachalot pygmée. *Kogia breviceps* (Blainville)

Description. The pigmy sperm whale, which attains a maximum length of only 11 feet, is one of the smallest cetaceans. It has a blunt head and a weak underslung lower jaw that gives the animal a shark-like appearance. The protruding conical teeth (nine to fifteen pairs) in the bowed mandible fit into sockets in the upper jaw, which occasionally carries vestigial teeth, and the single nostril is on

Map 107 Distribution of the pigmy sperm whale, *Kogia breviceps*

Economic Status. None.

Distribution. This is a rare whale, known only from about sixty strandings. It appears to be cosmopolitan in all the oceans.

Canadian Distribution. There are only two records of this whale in Canadian waters. The first was that of an adult female which was found dead under the ice in Halifax Harbour, Nova Scotia, on January 17, 1920, and the second was stranded on Sable Island in January 1969 (see Map 107).

Kogia breviceps (Blainville), 1833, Ann. Anat. Phys. 2: 337 (*Kogia* is a latinized corruption of 'coger').

REFERENCES

Handley, C.O. Jr. 1966. A synopsis of the genus Kogia (pigmy sperm whales). Chap. 4, pp. 62–9, *in* Whales, dolphins, and porpoises, *edited by* Kenneth S. Norris. University of California Press, Berkeley and Los Angeles.

Piers, H. 1923. Accidental occurrence of the pigmy sperm whale (*Kogia breviceps*) on the coast of Nova Scotia: an extension of its known range. Proc. and Trans. Nova Scotia Inst. Sci. 15: 95–114.

the left side of the head. It has a falcate dorsal fin, and the pectoral fins are relatively longer and narrower that those of the larger sperm whale. The caudal flukes are deeply cleft. The colour is black above and pale grey below (Figure 57b). Four bristles appear on the side of the snout of the foetus, but these are apparently shed soon after birth. There are also throat grooves in the foetus, which disappear in adult life. The rostrum is exceedingly short; the zygomatic arches are incomplete; there is a small 'case' of spermaceti in the head. The cervical vertebrae are fused, and pelvic bones are lacking. Unlike for the sperm whale, the sexes are approximately the same size in this species. The average total length of eight males was 2.7 (2.2–3.3) metres and of eight females 2.4 (2.2–3.2) metres; weight 318–408 kg.

Habits. This small whale usually occurs either alone, or as a female with her calf, or in small gams. It is slow-moving and rather lethargic, and is not known to have regular migrations. Its food consists of small squids and crabs.

Habitat. The pigmy sperm whale appears to inhabit warm, shallow coastal waters. The fact that it is more common on the western shores of the great oceans bordering the Orient and eastern North America has led to the conclusion that it favours the warm tropical currents passing along the western shores of the larger oceans.

Reproduction. The scanty evidence available indicates that this species possibly mates in late summer and has a gestation period of nine months and a parturition period in spring. Females which were both pregnant and lactating have been taken. The single calf stays with its mother during its first year of life.

Family **Monodontidae** / White Whale and Narwhal

The two small arctic whales of this family are believed to be primitive dolphins. They are differentiated by a number of anatomical features, including the lack of dorsal fins and the possession of short, rounded pectoral fins and blunt snouts. The cervical vertebrae are free, and there are other primitive features of the skull, including the middle ear sinus system. Both species have teeth in both jaws, but the narwhal's tusk is unique.

WHITE WHALE
Béluga. *Delphinapterus leucas* (Pallas)

Description. This whale is frequently called 'beluga,' the Russian name of the species, which means 'whitish.' It is a small whale, which attains, though rarely, a maximum length of 17 feet (a length found only in old males of the Okhotsk Sea subspecies). It has a fusiform body with a blunt snout. The upper jaw protrudes slightly ahead of the melon, and the regular mouth has a fixed 'pleasant' smile. Adults are creamy white with brown eyes; there are vestigial ear orifices; the back is ridged; the pectoral fins are short and rounded; the caudal flukes are deeply notched. In old males the pectoral fins turn up at the tips (Figure 59a).

Young calves are a dark slate in colour the first year. The juveniles are various shades of grey, and the adult's white colour is not attained until the whales are about 10 to 12 feet long, at four or five years of age. The skin of this species is smooth and thin.

The white whale's skull is flat on top; the rostrum is broad and depressed. The upper jaw contains sixteen to twenty peg-like teeth, and the mandible contains a similar number, which intermesh with the upper teeth. The nares are displaced to the left behind the eyes. The single external nostril is semicircular when open and crescentic when closed (Figure 58).

The size of these whales depends upon the particular stock involved. Populations in the Gulf of St Lawrence and the Beaufort Sea are larger than those in Hudson Bay. Males are larger than females. Average length of males from Churchill was 10.4 (5–14) feet or 3.2 (1.5–4.3) metres and of females 9.6 (5–12.5) feet or 2.9 (1.5–3.8) metres, calves included. Males from the Beaufort Sea averaged 15 feet (4–6 metres) and females 13 feet (4 metres). An old male, 14 feet 2 inches (4.4 metres) long, weighed 2,981 pounds (1,360 kg). The maximum weight reported from the western Pacific is 4,000 pounds (2 metric tons).

Habits. White whales are sociable beasts, and are usually found in small groups or in loose gams of a hundred or more individuals. Groups of two or three are common, and these consist of a female with a young calf or with a calf and an immature animal, probably her previous calf. Small gams of ten to twenty adult bulls are occasionally met as well. This migratory species spends the summer months in shallow arctic waters, retreating to deep, open water when the shallow bays freeze over.

Herds spend the winter in Baffin Bay, Davis Strait, and Ungava Bay, and migrate into the bays and straits of the Arctic Archipelago in summer. Most beluga frequenting Hudson Bay in summer pass in and out of Hudson Strait in spring and autumn. Small groups may remain along the floe-edge in northern Hudson Bay and along the west coast of Greenland. Other populations inhabit Bering Sea and migrate along the northwest coast of America in spring and autumn, but there also appear to be small resident populations along the floe-edge in the Beaufort Sea and Amundsen Gulf. The population in the Gulf of St Lawrence also has an annual migratory pattern.

The white whale is vocal, and in early whaling literature was called the 'sea canary.' It utters a variety of puffs, whistles, and squeals. Bulls have been reported to bugle. Although some of these calls probably have social significance, others are used as sonar in detecting obstacles and in locating food.

These whales seldom dive deeply. Usually they make a series of short dives, breathing intermittently with a rocking motion, with first the head above water, blowing, and then the back appearing. Very little of the body is exposed above the water line. The maximum duration of dives is ten to fifteen minutes. White whales are slow swimmers, and have a normal cruising speed of about six knots although they may reach nine knots when pressed.

White whales feed in shallow estuaries on a variety of food, which includes such fish as capelin, herring, cisco, sculpin, sand lance, Atlantic cod, tomcod and Greenland cod, flounder, and char. They also feed on numerous invertebrates such as octopuses, squids, shrimps, and paddleworms (*Nereis*).

Their chief predators are the killer whale and man.

Habitat. This whale is one of three species that live only in the arctic zone and bear their young only in arctic waters. It frequents uniformly cold, shallow estuarine waters, not less than 4 feet in depth. Usually it enters the river mouths on the rising tide and leaves on the ebb tide, but it also ascends large rivers discharging into arctic seas – one was taken 700 miles up the Yukon River. As many as 162 'spouts' per mile have been seen in the mouth of the Churchill River in summer.

Reproduction. This species is polygamous. Mating occurs in the spring. (Andrew Graham of the Hudson's Bay Company reported that the animals take a vertical position, belly to belly, with the heads protruding out of the water.) The gestation period is thirteen to fourteen months, and the young are born between March (in west Greenland) and August (in Hudson Bay), with a peak in June. Usually one calf is born every two years, and rarely twins are born. The calf at birth is 5 feet long and slate blue in colour. At one month it weighs about 185 pounds (84 kg). During its first summer it grows to about 7 feet (2.1 metres) in length and 450 pounds (203 kg) in weight, and as a yearling, it measures about 9 feet (2.7 metres). The calf nurses for about six months.

The females become sexually mature at three years of age, and the males at four years of age.

Economic Status. The white whale is one of the most important marine resources of the Arctic. The skin (raw or cooked) provides the Eskimo delicacy 'muktuk' and, as 'porpoise' leather, is used in boots and laces. The Eskimo also used to cover their skin whale boats (umiaks) with it. The oil (one white whale yields about thirty [15–185] gallons) is used for lamp oil, in edible products such as margarine, or in industry. The meat is used as food for humans, dogs, or ranch fur-bearers.

White whales are captured by harpoons and nets, or by

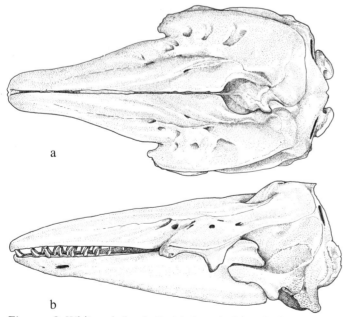

Figure 58 White whale skull: (a) dorsal view, (b) lateral view (× 1/8)

Map 108 Distribution of the white whale, *Delphinapterus leucas*

moves into Lancaster Sound, Fox Basin, and Hudson Bay, but a gap in the distribution occurs between Somerset Island, Prince of Wales Island, and Banks Island and Amundsen Gulf, which are frequented by western stocks from the Pacific Ocean and the Beaufort Sea (see Map 108). The Canadian form is:

Delphinapterus leucas leucas (Pallas), 1776, Reise durch verschiedene Provinzen des Russischen Reichs, 3(1): 85.

REFERENCES

Sergeant, D.E., and P.F. Brodie. 1969. Body size in white whales, *Delphinapterus leucas*. Jour. Fish. Res. Bd. Canada 26: 2561–80.

Vladykov, V.-D. 1944. Etudes sur les mammifères aquatiques, III. Chasse, biologie et valeur économique du marsouin blanc ou béluga (*Delphinapterus leucas*) du fleuve et du golfe Saint-Laurent. Contrib. Inst. Biol., Univ. Montréal 15.

– 1947. Etudes sur les mammifères aquatiques, IV. Nourriture du marsouin blanc ou béluga (*Delphinapterus leucas*) du fleuve Saint-Laurent. Contrib. Inst. Biol., Univ. Montréal 19.

NARWHAL
Narval. *Monodon monoceros* Linnaeus

Description. The narwhal is the basis of the fabulous medieval unicorn. The first tusks of the narwhal to reach Europe were thought (perhaps quite naturally) to belong to a terrestrial animal, which was assumed to have the form of a horse. It was not until 1655 that the Danish scientist Wormius announced that the remarkable tusk belonged to a whale. So bizarre is this creature that its name and form are well known to most readers. It is surprising, however, that, though over three hundred years have passed since Wormius's time, there is little more known about the narwhal.

This whale grows to a maximum length of about 16 feet, exclusive of the tusk. It has a short, blunt head; a regularly shaped mouth; small, rounded pectoral fins; and short, broad caudal flukes that are medially notched. The striking feature of the narwhal is the presence of a long, spirally twisted horn, which projects through the upper lip of the male. This is a maxillary tooth. In both sexes of the adult narwhal only a single pair of teeth are present in the upper jaw. In the female these usually remain embedded in the gum, but the left maxillary tooth in the male grows in a clockwise direction through the gum and may attain a length of 9 feet. The right tooth usually remains suppressed, but sometimes it is the one that grows, or sometimes both become elongate. Occasionally a female may have a short tusk (Figure 59b).

Although many writers have speculated on the use of this short tusk, it still is not known how the narwhal uses it. It appears to be a secondary sexual character, and one might suppose the males use it in some kind of contest. Since, however, these whales are rarely scarred, as are

drives to strand them at low tide. Until 1939 they provided a local industry in the estuary of the St Lawrence River. The best year was 1935, when 558 animals were taken. A commercial plant for processing whales was operated at Churchill, Manitoba, from 1949 to 1960, and took an average of about 450 whales annually. The meat was ground up and sold as food to prairie mink farmers. The Hudson's Bay Company has also maintained a factory at Pangnirtung, Baffin Island, for the export of white whale hides to Europe.

At present the hunting of white whales in the Canadian arctic region is restricted to local residents. The total catch in the eastern Arctic is about one thousand whales a year, and an additional two hundred are taken in the western Arctic in the native fishery. The whales are hunted in shallow estuaries using small boats. They are harpooned first, then shot, and finally dragged ashore and butchered, the blubber being boiled down for oil and the meat preserved for dog food.

Distribution. This whale is holarctic in distribution. It occurs as far north as latitude 81°35′ N in Kennedy Channel; it is also found near Spitzbergen, northern Norway; in the White, Kara, and Chukchi seas; and in the Okhotsk Sea south to Sakhalin Island in the western Pacific. Stragglers have appeared at Cape Cod, U.S.A.; Firth of Clyde, Scotland; and in the Baltic Sea off Sweden.

Canadian Distribution. Relict populations are found in the Bay of Fundy and in the St Lawrence estuary from Quebec City to Natashquan on the north shore and to the Bay of Chaleur on the south. Strays have recently been taken at Halifax and at Kildore River, Nova Scotia. The species is extremely rare off Newfoundland and Labrador but occupies Davis Strait and has reached Kane Basin between Greenland and Ellesmere Island. In summer it

Figure 59 Dolphins and porpoises: (a) white whale, *Delphinapterus leucas*; (b) narwhal, *Monodon monoceros*; (c) blue dolphin, *Stenella caeruleoalba*; (d) Dall's porpoise, *Phocoenoides dalli*; (e) white-beaked dolphin, *Lagenorhynchus albirostris*

Figure 6o More dolphins: (a) bottlenosed dolphin, *Tursiops truncatus*; (b) common dolphin, *Delphinus delphis*; (c) Pacific pilot whale, *Globicephala macrorhyncha*; (d) harbour porpoise, *Phocoena phocoena*; (e) northern right-whale dolphin, *Lissodelphis borealis*

Figure 61 More dolphins: (a) Atlantic white-sided dolphin, *Lagenorhynchus acutus*; (b) Pacific white-sided dolphin, *Lagenorhynchus obliquidens*; (c) killer whale, *Orcinus orca*; (d) grey grampus, *Grampus griseus*; (e) Atlantic pilot whale, *Globicephala melaena*

beaked whales, it does not appear to be used as a weapon, and it cannot be important in feeding because the females, which normally lack a tusk, eat well. The tip is usually worn smooth and is frequently broken off, and this brings up the most curious fact of all: in the hollow tip of a broken narwhal tusk, occasionally one finds the tip of a smaller tusk jammed in and broken off. Since there is no evidence that teeth are replaced in Cetacea, there remains the mystery of how a narwhal 'fills' the cavity in its broken tusk with the tip of a smaller tusk. It has been suggested, though this seems like wild speculation, that it provokes a younger male whale to charge directly – tusk to tusk – and when the younger whale's tusk has penetrated its broken tip, the larger whale breaks it off with a twist of the head.

Adult narwhals are pale grey below, marbled with slate-grey blotches dorsally. The young at birth are slate grey in colour and become lighter with age.

Males, which average 6.1 metres in length, are larger than females, which average 4.2 metres. The females average about 600 kg in weight, and the males may weigh up to a metric ton.

Habits. Narwhals are socially gregarious and usually appear in gams, which may include more than a thousand individuals. Sometimes the gams consist of only one sex. Narwhals are very noisy and utter gargling groans or exhaling whistles that may be heard three miles off. They swim quite quickly but spend much time loafing or even sleeping at the surface with their backs awash.

Narwhals feed on squids, octopuses, shrimps, molluscs, polar cod, flounders, halibut, and skates. They descend to approximately 200 fathoms and then return to the surface to breath for some time before diving again. In breathing they roll, exposing a flipper but never the tusk.

This species is migratory, but insufficient information is available to present a clear analysis of its annual movements. Narwhals probably spend the winter months offshore in Davis Strait, Baffin Bay, and Lancaster Sound, which remain open all winter. In spring they migrate westward through Hudson Strait and Lancaster Sound. They occur in spring only on the south shore of Hudson Strait as far as Cape Weggs. After that point they turn northwestward toward Mills and Southampton islands and Foxe Basin. They enter Cumberland and Eclipse sounds on the east coast of Baffin Island. Large gams of females start to pass through Admiralty Inlet and Eclipse Sound about the first of July. By late August the reverse eastward migration is in full swing near Pond Inlet and Bylot Island.

Narwhals also migrate northward into Smith Sound between Ellesmere Island and Greenland. They appear along the ice edge toward the end of May and enter the bays when the ice breaks up and drifts out. They travel north of Melville Bay in the summer, but many remain in the vicinity of Inglefield Bay all summer. Others press northward to Hall Basin. In gams of several hundred they migrate on the rising tide into the fiords and leave on the ebb. By October they have left the Thule district of Greenland.

Occasionally in early winter, when the sea pack-ice is

carried against the shores and freezes fast before the bay freezes, small gams become trapped in bays along the coasts of Baffin and Southampton islands and Greenland. The narwhals, and sometimes white whales as well, become increasingly restricted to the shrinking open water until they are crowded into small holes. These they manage to keep open by butting the thin, new ice with the sturdy 'melons' on the tops of their heads. They do not use their tusks for this purpose. Old males have, however, been observed sleeping in tidal cracks with their tusk projecting out onto the surface of the ice.

An eyewitness account of a Greenland hunt of trapped narwhals (in *Grønlandsposten*, 1943: 145) provides a vivid picture of the spectacle:

We may have been driving for about one hour when a glimpse in the night showed that we were approaching the front. There were flashes ahead and to both sides. We drove on until a volley of guns just to the left made us stop. We ran to the place and found that three men with raised rifles were staring fixedly at the black glassy surface of an opening in the water as large as the site of Greenlander's house. Everything was calm and motionless. Then the smooth surface was suddenly broken by black shadows and white animals which in elegant curves came up and disappeared – narwhals and white whales by the score. Side by side they emerged so close to each other that some of them would be lifted on the backs of the others and turned a somersault with the handsome tail waving in the air. First rows of narwhals, then white whales and then again narwhals – each species separately. It seethed, blobbed and splashed in the opening. With a hollow whistling sound they inhaled air as if sucking it through long iron tubes. The water was greatly disturbed, shots cracked and the waves washed over the ice. Then all was calm again. The black, smooth surface was there again as suddenly as it had just disappeared. A single dead white whale was floating at the surface. The animal was now harpooned and made fast to the ice edge to be pulled out of the water and flensed on occasion.

The narwhal's enemies, in addition to Eskimo hunters, include the killer whale and the rogue bull walrus. A dead narwhal and a bull walrus, locked in mortal combat, have been found. The walrus had buried its tusks into the belly of the whale, and there was whale meat in its stomach.

Habitat. The narwhal prefers the edge of landfast ice and ice-floes and therefore occurs farther north than the white whale. It also frequents deep waters and shuns shallow bays. It occurs most commonly in deep fiords along the coasts of Baffin, Ellesmere, Devon, and the northeast coast of Southampton islands and of Greenland.

Reproduction. Few details are known, except that it is common to find foetuses of various lengths in pregnant females, a circumstance that indicates a prolonged breeding season. Narwhals are about 1.5 metres long at birth. Usually one calf, rarely two, is born in June or July. Females are said to bear calves every two years.

Economic Status. Arctic whalers hunted the small narwhal for a brief period when the Greenland whale fishery gave out. In one season they took as many as 2,800 narwhal in Eclipse Sound. The narwhal oil was considered superior in quality to other whale oil.

At present the utilization of narwhals is limited to Eskimo hunters, who harpoon them from frail kayaks. The oil is used for lamps, the black skin and flesh are esteemed,

Map 109 Distribution of the narwhal, *Monodon monoceros*

and the tusk is valuable as ivory for carving purposes. The hide is sometimes used for covering uniaks or whale boats and for boot soles.

Distribution. The narwhal is found in the Atlantic sector of the Arctic Ocean (see Map 109).

Canadian Distribution. The narwhal is commonly distributed in Canadian eastern arctic waters, centred on Davis Strait and Baffin Bay. Its occurrence in the Canadian western Arctic rests solely on the observation that in 1826 spearheads and ice-picks of narwhal ivory were used by Eskimos at Toker Point east of Mackenzie Delta. The genus is monotypic.

Monodon monoceros Linnaeus, 1758, Syst. Nat., 10th ed., 1: 75.

REFERENCES

Porsild, M.P. 1922. Scattered observations on narwhals. Jour. Mamm. 3(1): 8–13.

Vibe, Christian. 1950. The narwhal. *In* The marine mammals and the marine fauna in the Thule district (Northwest Greenland) ... Medd. om Grønland (Copenhagen) 150(6): 77–84.

Family **Delphinidae** / Dolphins and Porpoises

This family includes the well-known, speedy, agile dolphins, the porpoise (the smallest cetacean), and the rapacious killer whale. Dolphins (the mammals as opposed to the large game fish known by the same name) are distinguished from porpoises by having a short beak. Porpoises have blunt heads. Dolphins and porpoises are more common in warmer seas than in colder waters.

The members of this family range from the smallest cetaceans to the 30-foot killer whale. Their bodies are usually slim and streamlined. They have distinctive features in common, with few exceptions: most of them have many peg-like teeth in both jaws; most have medially placed dorsal fins and long, pointed pectoral fins; all have medially notched caudal flukes; most possess a few facial bristles, in the embryo stage at least.

Skeletal characters include two or more fused cervical vertebrae, a moderate rostrum in the skull, fused lachrymal and malar bones, no maxillary crest, and a short mandibular symphysis. The single nostril is placed medially on top of the head above the eyes.

BLUE DOLPHIN
Dauphin bleu. *Stenella caeruleoalba* Mayen

Description. This little-known dolphin may reach a length of 9 feet. Its body is streamlined; its snout extends into a slender beak, which is separated from the sloping 'forehead' by a shallow groove. It has pointed pectoral fins, a dorsal fin about halfway down the back, and deeply notched, broad flukes. The upper and lower jaws contain forty-six to fifty pairs of small conical teeth, which increase in size posteriorly (Figure 59c).

The colour of this species is dark brown or bluish black above (including the beak); the flukes and fins are white below. It has a prominent dark flank stripe from the beak to the anal region. From this main stripe a branch leads ventrally to the point of insertion of each pectoral fin and a second one to behind the fin. A pale tan stripe above the dark one extends above each eye.

Males are generally a little longer than females, and adults measure 2.19 to 2.89 metres in standard length.

Habits. These dolphins occur in small gams of up to fifteen individuals. They are believed to feed on fish.

Reproduction. No information is available.

Habitat. These dolphins occur in offshore and coastal waters in both warm and cold seas.

Economic Status. These dolphins are utilized in Japan.

Distribution. Cosmopolitan in the oceans of the world.

Canadian Distribution. This species has been found on both our Atlantic and Pacific coasts. Three specimens have been taken from the coastal waters of Vancouver Island, British Columbia, and four have been found on the beaches of Sable Island, Nova Scotia. The Canadian form is known as:

Stenella caeruleoalba euphrosyne (Gray), 1846, *in* The zoology of the voyage of H.M.S. *Erebus* and *Terror* ..., I (Mamm.): 40.

REFERENCES

Pike, G.C., and I.B. MacAskie. 1969. Marine mammals of British Columbia. Fish. Res. Bd. Canada Bull. 171: 15–17.

Sergeant, D.E., A.W. Mansfield, and B. Beck. 1970. Inshore records of Cetacea for eastern Canada, 1949–68. Jour. Fish. Res. Bd. Canada 27: 1912.

COMMON DOLPHIN

Dauphin commun. *Delphinus delphis* Linnaeus

Description. This is the common dolphin of the Mediterranean Sea that played such an important role in the art, literature, and lore of classical Greek and Roman cultures. A pictographic seal from Crete, representing a dolphin, is estimated to date from 3500 to 2200 B.C., The dolphin's stylized form – a short beak, large eye, arched back, and flukes – is recognizable on coins, vases, statuary, and wall paintings in southern Europe, at least until medieval times. A dolphin appears on the coat of arms of the eldest son of the King of France, who consequently was called 'Le Dauphin.'

Classical literature contains many references to the friendly and co-operative relationship of dolphins to humans as if the dolphin recognized man as a 'kindred spirit' in a different medium. A good example is the story of Arion, as told by Herodotus in the sixth century B.C. Arion, on board a ship sailing from Corinth to Sicily, was threatened by the sailors. Upon throwing himself into the sea, he was rescued by a dolphin, which carried him on its back to shore.

Pliny, in the first century, describes several incidents involving friendship between boys and dolphins, including some of boys riding dolphins across bays. The 'boy on a dolphin' motif has been repeated many times in classical sculpture.

It is easy to shrug off these tales of long ago and relegate them to mythology, but, like the existence of Troy itself, co-operation between dolphins and humans has recently been found to have a factual basis. Incredible as it may seem, a wild dolphin appeared in 1956 off the beach of Opononi, New Zealand, and began to frolic with the children. It learned to toss beach balls with the youngsters and took small children on its back for short rides before dunking them. Unfortunately, however, one day towards the end of that same season, as the tide ran out it became stranded on a rocky ledge and died. There have also been recent accounts of floundering swimmers who have been pushed roughly ashore by dolphins.

And so it seems likely that centuries ago when man was closer to nature he had time to observe and recount these wonderful incidents of friendly contact with another intelligent species in the warm Mediterranean waters.

The common dolphin is a small cetacean, which attains a length of 6 to 8 feet. Its body is streamlined; the narrow, 6-inch beak is separated from the reclining forehead by a deep groove; the medially placed dorsal fin is moderately high; the pectoral flippers are tapered; the flukes are narrow and notched. Each jaw has forty to fifty pairs of small conical teeth. Behind the tooth rows are palatine grooves. At birth there are five to seven short bristles on each side of the snout. The eyes are moderately large, and situated behind and below them are vestigial ear orifices.

The dorsum in this species is dark brown or black, and the venter is white. The black dorsal colour dips downwards below the dorsal fin. The flanks are coloured with overlapping bands of grey, beige, and green. The eye is encircled by a black ring, which is joined by a stripe to the groove at the base of the beak. There is a white stripe above this black one. A greenish band leads from the lower jaw to the base of the pectoral fin (Figure 60b).

The average length attained is about 1.82 (1.62–2.29) metres. A male measuring 1.90 metres weighed 80 kg (175 pounds). The males are a little larger than the females.

Habits. These dolphins are highly social, travelling in gams that may number over a thousand animals. When travelling they group themselves on a broad curved front, several ranks deep. They often leap simultaneously and then swim underwater about 100 yards before they again rise to blow in unison. When their bodies crash into the sea, the sound is like a heavy thunderstorm with lashing rain. They often play about ships, and by tilting their flukes and flippers to the correct angle they may coast 'downhill' on the bow wave of vessels for prolonged 'free rides.' Dolphins are among the swiftest animals in the sea. They normally swim at six to eight knots but may reach top speeds of up to eighteen knots. They communicate by a variety of underwater squeals, and they navigate by sonar 'ticks.'

The dolphin's food consists of a variety of pelagic schooling fishes, such as sardines, anchovies, bonetos, and seuries. One taken off Nova Scotia contained the remains of billfish, *Scomberesox saurus*, and a Newfoundland specimen contained the beaks and pens of small squid, *Illex illecebrosus*.

Habitat. This species normally lives a pelagic existence in the warmer seas and oceans.

Reproduction. The breeding season extends from spring to early summer. The gestation period is eleven months, and the lactation period extends six months into the next pregnancy. With the oestrous cycle of twelve months the female eventually comes into heat after the males have passed their breeding condition, so she misses about one pregnancy in four years.

The single new-born calf is about 1.17 metres (3 feet 10 inches) in length. It is toothless and has a moustache of short bristles. Born in early spring it follows its mother closely for six to nine months.

Sexual maturity is reached at a length of 1.70 metres.

Economic Status. These dolphins were once used for human food in the United States and Great Britain, and are still used as food to some extent in Japan.

Distribution. Cosmopolitan in warm and temperate seas.

Canadian Distribution. The common dolphin is anything but common in Canadian waters. Small gams of eight to ten appear off the edge of the Grand Banks and Flemish Cap in July to September each year. They frequent the warmed 'slope water' between the Labrador and Gulf

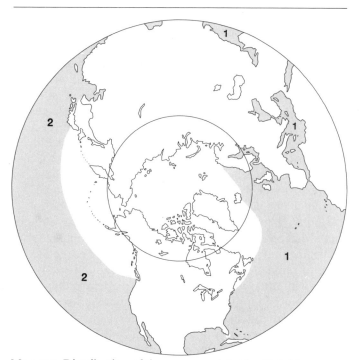

Map 110 Distribution of the common dolphin, *Delphinus delphis*: 1 *D. d. delphis*, 2 *D. d. bairdii*

currents at temperatures between 11° and 17°C. This is the northern limit of their range in the western Atlantic Ocean (see Map 110).

A single atypical specimen was taken in Trinity Bay, Newfoundland, on July 22, 1957. Another specimen was stranded at Victoria, British Columbia, on April 8, 1953. Two subspecies occur in Canadian waters:

Delphinus delphis bairdii Dall, 1873, Proc. California Acad. Sci. 5: 12. Pacific Ocean.
Delphinus delphis delphis Linnaeus, 1758, Syst. Nat., 10th ed., 1: 77. Atlantic and Indian oceans.

REFERENCE

Sergeant, D.E. 1958. Dolphins in Newfoundland waters. Canadian Field-Nat. 72(4): 156–9.

BOTTLENOSED DOLPHIN
Dauphin à gros nez. *Tursiops truncatus* (Montague)

Description. This is the species exhibited in most marine aquaria. It has been studied intensively at several marine studios and is therefore, by far, the best-known cetacean. Undoubtedly many of the details of this dolphin's way of life are applicable to other whales, but it is difficult at present to know how far to extend them.

The bottlenosed dolphin is larger than the common dolphin and may attain a maximum length of 12 feet. The body is typically streamlined. The beak is shorter and broader than in the previous species, and each jaw carries twenty to twenty-five pairs of peg-like teeth. The dorsum, including the beak, flippers, and flukes, is dark grey, which shades to white on the lower jaw and belly. The tip

of the lower jaw projects a little beyond the upper jaw. The dark coloration includes the laterally compressed caudal peduncle behind the anus (Figure 60a).

Average length of adults, 2.58 (1.79–3.65) metres. Two adult females weighed 557 and 690 pounds (255 and 310 kg), but the maximum weight may reach 800 pounds (360 kg).

Habits. Dolphins are probably among the most intelligent animals, but since they live in the water and have no hands it is difficult to appraise their intelligence. The percentage ratio of a dolphin's brain weight to its body weight is 1.17 (man's ratio is 2.1 and the chimpanzee's is 0.7). Dolphins are highly social and are usually met in groups of five to twenty-five individuals. Occasionally, in migration, the groups are much larger. They exhibit many types of social co-operation, such as trying to assist wounded 'fellows.' They will support a new-born calf, a wounded individual, or even a dead one, on the surface to allow it to breathe. A dolphin has been observed supporting a dead calf, or even a dead shark, on its back at the surface. There is also co-operation between females when a calf is born. The calf is bunted to the surface and supported and guided between the dorsal fins of its mother and a 'midwife.'

This species of dolphin may associate with pilot whales and other dolphins.

Dolphins utter a variety of underwater sounds. There are jaw-clapping sounds to indicate irritation or intimidation, courting 'yelps,' and echo-sounding 'clicks,' 'clacks,' and 'whistles.' The sounds are produced in air sacs in the nasal passages. The valves that close the air passage when the dolphin submerges are thought to vibrate. Dolphins navigate and locate their food by means of echo location or 'sonar.' The clicks are of a half-second duration and range between seven and fifteen kilocycles per second in frequency. By means of this frequency-modulated echo location, dolphins are able to locate small fish prey and even to locate the entrances in nets.

It is believed that the dolphin's hearing is receptive to much higher frequencies than man's. Its eyesight is only adequate, and dolphins have only a rudimentary sense of smell.

These dolphins are also very swift. Their normal cruising speed is three to four knots, and the maximum is twelve to eighteen knots. The skin and blubber covering is loose and pliable, and forms corrugations when the animal speeds along. This is thought to be a reaction to the variations in water pressure along the fusiform body and, as such, reduces drag.

Dolphins usually respire one to three times at ten-second intervals and then dive for one to two minutes. They do not normally dive as deep as the larger whales. They spend the days foraging in the bays and retreat to open water at dusk. Bottlenosed dolphins are migratory along the eastern coast of North America, moving northward in spring and southward in autumn. They are resident in the Gulf of Mexico.

The food of dolphins consists primarily of a wide variety of marine fishes. On the Texas coast, mullet composed 83 per cent of the diet. Other fish eaten include croakers, gizzard shad, flounder, queen fish, corbina, barred surf perch, shiner perch, white sea perch, and topsmelt. Usually they live on small fish less than ten inches long, which they swallow whole. Larger ones are first broken up by rubbing them on the bottom, tossing them in the air, and biting off the heads.

The dolphin's only predators are the killer whale, which it evades by swimming into shallow surf, and man. Dolphins are reported to kill or drive off sharks at every opportunity. One dolphin, beached on the English coast, was reported to have choked to death on a four-foot shark. Another was observed in the Gulf of Mexico playing with the carcass of a small shark, while another bit the head off a basking shark.

Habitat. The bottlenosed dolphin frequents shallow, warm and temperate coastal waters, lagoons, and bays, and even enters river mouths. It is seldom observed more than twelve miles from shore.

Reproduction. Mature males fight younger males and drive them away from the gams. In the spring the male goes through an elaborate courtship of the female. This includes constant companionship, posturing, the emitting of yapping cries, nuzzling, patting the female with fins and flukes, and rubbing against her body. The birth of a calf in the gam arouses the male's desire for the gam.

Mating usually takes place in the early spring – February to May – and the calves are born during the same period after a gestation period of twelve months. The female bears a calf every other year.

The dolphin calf is surprisingly large at birth (3 feet 9 inches to 5 feet 1 inch, or 115 to 155 cm), approximately half the length of its mother. It is normally born flukes first and immediately after birth is nudged to the surface to breathe. A second female (the 'midwife') takes up a position beside the mother, and the two guide the faltering calf between their backs. Although at birth the calf's dorsal fin is folded sideways, it soon straightens up. The full-term 'foetus' has a few blond hairs on the snout. The calf is toothless and darker than the adult. The mother rolls on her side to feed the calf, and when it inserts its short beak into the mammary groove, she squirts the rich milk directly into its mouth. During the first few days it remains near the mother's dorsal fin, but when it becomes a stronger swimmer, it takes up a position just below and behind the flukes. It is weaned after about eighteen months, but continues the close association with its mother for about six years.

The juvenile female matures at the age of six years and bears its first calf at the age of seven. By that time it has had considerable experience acting as 'midwife' and 'babysitter' for other calves.

Economic Status. Near the end of the last century there was a small dolphin industry at Cape Hatteras, U.S.A. At present dolphins from American and European waters are not utilized.

Distribution. The bottlenosed dolphin occurs off the coasts of Europe (including the Baltic, Mediterranean, and Black seas), in the western Atlantic from the West Indies to Maine, South America, New Zealand, Bay of

Map 111 Distribution of the bottlenosed dolphin, *Tursiops truncatus*

Bengal, Japan, Hawaii, and the Pacific coasts of North and Middle America. It is resident along the Atlantic coast from New Jersey south (see Map 111).

Canadian Distribution. The bottlenosed dolphin has appeared on our coast only as a single straggler, which was stranded at the head of tidewaters on the Petitcodiac River, New Brunswick, on September 15, 1950. A second probable specimen was observed at Milford, Nova Scotia, on September 3, 1968. The Canadian form is:

Tursiops truncatus truncatus (Montague), 1821, Mem. Wernerian Nat. Hist. Soc. 3: 75. The Pacific subspecies *gillii* has not appeared in Canadian waters.

REFERENCES

Kellogg, W.N. 1961. Porpoises and sonar. University of Chicago Press.

Sergeant, D.E., D.K. Caldwell, and Melba C. Caldwell. 1973. Age, growth and maturity of the bottlenosed dolphin (*Tursiops truncatus*) from northeast Florida. Jour. Fish. Res. Bd. Canada 30: 1009–11.

NORTHERN RIGHT-WHALE DOLPHIN
Dauphin à dos lisse. *Lissodelphis borealis* (Peale)

Description. The right-whale dolphin differs from other dolphins in that it lacks a dorsal fin. It is a small, slim dolphin with a slender beak, a slightly protruding lower jaw, a low slanting forehead, pointed pelvic fins, and an extremely slender, keeled caudal peduncle. It grows to a maximum length of about 8 feet. Its colour is mostly black above, with a large, roughly diamond-shaped white blaze on the chest, extending to a long, narrow white band from

Map 112 Distribution of the northern right-whale dolphin, *Lissodelphis borealis*

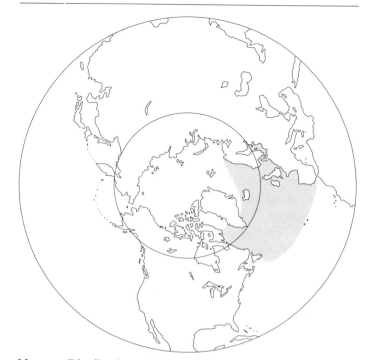

Map 113 Distribution of the white-beaked dolphin, *Lagenorhynchus albirostris*

the umbilicus to the base of the flukes. The ventral surfaces of the tips of the flukes are grey, and the tip of the lower jaw is white. There are forty-three to forty-seven small sharp teeth in each row on the long, slender jaws (Figure 60e).

The average length of three specimens was 2.13 (2.08–2.18) metres. The smallest weighed 56.2 kg (125 pounds).

Habits. Very few details of the life history of this species are known. It is highly social and congregates in large gams, which sometimes include over a thousand individuals. It sometimes associates with other species such as pilot whales. It communicates by sonar. Its food consists mainly of squid.

Habitat. This dolphin is primarily pelagic in cool or cold waters.

Reproduction. No details are known.

Economic Status. None.

Distribution. North Pacific Ocean from California to the Bering Sea (see Map 112).

Canadian Distribution. Although this dolphin is probably a normal visitor off our British Columbia coast, only a pair have been sighted to date. This species is known as:

Lissodelphis borealis (Peale), 1848, Mammalia and ornithology in U.S. Explor. Exp. ..., 1838–1842 ... Philadelphia, 8: 35.

REFERENCE

Norris, K.S., and J.H. Prescott. 1961. Northern right whale dolphin. *In* Observations on Pacific cetaceans of Californian and Mexican waters. Univ. California Pub. Zool. 63(4): 323–6.

WHITE-BEAKED DOLPHIN
Dauphin à nez blanc. *Lagenorhynchus albirostris* Gray

Description. Dolphins of this genus may be characterized by their rather stout streamlined bodies, scarcely discernible beaks, high slender dorsal fins, and keeled caudal peduncles. Internally, they have special skeletal characteristics, such as fewer teeth and a larger number of vertebrae (80–90) than other dolphins.

The white-beaked dolphin attains a maximum length of about 10 feet. Four males found in Canadian waters averaged 2.22 (2.11–2.39) metres, and a single female measured only 1.96 metres. Their colour is mainly blue-black above (including the narrow pointed fins and flukes) and white below. There is a pale band across the short beak, although the lips are outlined in black. There are vague pale areas on the flanks beneath the dorsal fin and an oval greyish area between the eye and the pectoral flipper. There are twenty-two to twenty-five relatively large conical teeth in each row (Figure 59e).

Habits. These dolphins are gregarious in nature and have been reported in groups of up to 1,500 individuals, although gams observed in Canadian waters usually include smaller numbers (six to eight). They are migratory and travel northward along our east coast during the spring months of March to May and again southward during October and November. They appear off the Labrador coast in July and August. They eat such fish as cod, herring, and whiting.

Habitat. Offshore and pelagic in cold arctic waters.

Reproduction. The young, which measure about 4 feet (1.22 metres) long at birth, are born in midsummer.

Economic Status. Occasionally utilized in Newfoundland.

Distribution. North Atlantic Ocean from the Grand Banks and North Sea northward.

Canadian Distribution. The species is a regular inhabitant of our eastern coastal waters (see Map 113). Occasionally small groups of white-beaked dolphins are either trapped by ice and stranded in Newfoundland bays, or driven ashore or harpooned. The species is known as:

Lagenorhynchus albirostris Gray, 1846, Ann. Mag. Nat. Hist. ser. 1, 17: 84.

REFERENCE

Sergeant, D.E., and H.D. Fisher. 1957. White-beaked dolphin. *In* The smaller cetaceans of eastern Canadian waters. Jour. Fish. Res. Bd. Canada 14(1): 93–5.

ATLANTIC WHITE-SIDED DOLPHIN
Dauphin à flancs blancs. *Lagenorhynchus acutus* (Gray)

Description. This is a slightly smaller species, reaching a maximum length of about 9 feet (2.75 metres). It is similar in outline to the previous species, but the keeled caudal peduncle is more pronounced and the teeth are smaller and more numerous (30–34 in each row). It is black above and white below. In this species the white areas are larger and include the base of the pectoral fins. There is a long white band (wholly enclosed by black) on the flank below and behind the dorsal fin, and a black stripe runs from the corner of the mouth to the junction of the pectoral fin (Figure 61a).

Habits. This is a gregarious species, usually met in large gams. It often associates with other species such as pilot whales. It appears to be a little more stolid in behaviour than most other dolphins and does not seem to play on ship's bow waves, or to panic or assist when one of its group is killed.

This species' food includes herring, mackerel, and small squid.

Habitat. Offshore in temperate waters.

Reproduction. Mating occurs in the early autumn, and the young are believed to be born in early summer after a gestation period of about ten months. The calf is about 1 metre long at birth.

Economic Status. The species is occasionally utilized by Newfoundland whalers in Trinity Bay and in Norway.

Distribution. The species occurs in the North Atlantic Ocean from Cape Cod north to Greenland, along the Atlantic coasts of Ireland and Scotland, in the North Sea, and along the Norwegian coast as far north as Trondheim Fiord. It appears to prefer slightly warmer water than the white-beaked dolphin.

Canadian Distribution. This dolphin is fairly common off the coasts of our Maritime Provinces in summer (July to October) (see Map 114). The dolphin is identified as:

Lagenorhynchus acutus (Gray), 1828, Spicilegia zoologica ..., 1: 2.

Map 114 Distribution of the Atlantic white-sided dolphin, *Lagenorhynchus acutus*

REFERENCE

Jonsgard, A., and O. Nordli. 1952. Concerning a catch of white-sided dolphins (*Lagenorhynchus acutus*) on the west coast of Norway, winter, 1952. Norwegian Whaling Gazette 41(5): 229–32.

PACIFIC WHITE-SIDED DOLPHIN
Dauphin à flancs blancs du Pacifique. *Lagenorhynchus obliquidens* Gill

Description. The Pacific white-sided dolphin is the smallest of the three dolphins of this genus that frequent Canadian waters. It attains a maximum length of about 7½ feet. The form is typical: the beak is very small, the dorsal fin is slender and hooked, and the tail stock is slender and keeled. The teeth number twenty-nine to thirty-two in each row (Figure 61b).

The dorsal colour is black, fading to dark grey on the flanks, fins, and flukes. The underparts are white, from the lower jaw to the base of the flukes, prominently bordered by a black line. The tip of the lower jaw is black. There are two pale grey or white stripes on the flanks and a second posterior pair on the tail stock. Partial albinos, which are white except for a grey mid-dorsal line, have been observed.

Average measurements of American specimens: total length 1.89 (1.44–2.29) metres, weight 104 (82–124) kg, or 239 (190–280) pounds.

Habits. The Pacific white-sided dolphins are sociable animals. They often congregate in great gams, numbering a thousand individuals. Often other animals, such as California sea lions, elephant seals, and fur seals, as-

261

Map 115 Distribution of the Pacific white-sided dolphin, *Lagenorhynchus obliquidens*

sociate with them. When they are migrating, they swim swiftly in packed columns, often breeching in unison, but when feeding they segregate into smaller groups of similar age and sex composition and disperse across the ocean surface. They may attain a speed of fifteen knots.

These dolphins are very acrobatic: they leap gracefully out of the water in unison, they lob-tail and fall back into the water sideways with a loud splash, and they even turn complete somersaults in the air.

They are solicitous of their fellows and rush to support and assist their wounded comrades.

This species is migratory to a certain degree. Most observations made off the northern coasts have been restricted to the summer period. These dolphins appear far off California coasts during the summer and autumn, but when the coastal waters cool off in winter and spring they then appear in inshore waters.

The food they eat consists of small squid and many varieties of small fishes such as lantern fish, anchovies, sardines, herrings, sauries, mackerel, and hake.

Habitat. This dolphin seems to prefer cool temperate to subarctic waters.

Reproduction. The young are born during the summer from early June to late September. They are only about 30 inches (76 cm) long at birth and weigh approximately 30 pounds (13.8 kg). During their first few weeks they swim very close to their mothers' flanks and manage to 'steal a ride' on the water currents created by her swimming effort. When they are older they join groups of their fellows and play and jump together.

Distribution. This dolphin is confined to the north Pacific Ocean from Baja California to Alaska and westward to Japanese waters (see Map 115).

Canadian Distribution. The only Canadian specimen was stranded at Estevan Point, Vancouver Island, British Columbia, in June 1943. The observation of a large gam of approximately a thousand individuals, covering half a square mile of sea off the Queen Charlotte Islands on June 16, 1959, indicates, however, that it is probably fairly common off our Pacific coast in summer. Large schools of 200 to 250 are found in inshore waters around Hecate Strait from October to January. The species was described as:

Lagenorhynchus obliquidens Gill, 1865, Proc. Acad. Nat. Sci. Philadelphia 17: 77.

REFERENCES

Pike, G.C., and I.B. MacAskie. 1969. Marine mammals of British Columbia. Fish. Res. Bd. Canada Bull. 171: 17–19.
Scheffer, V.B. 1950. The striped dolphin, *Lagenorhynchus obliquidens* Gill, 1865, on the coast of North America. American Midl. Nat. 44(3): 750–8.

KILLER WHALE
Épaulard. *Orcinus orca* (Linnaeus)

Description. The killer whale is the largest member of the dolphin family: adult males may attain a total length of 31 feet from the snout to the notch between the flukes. The head is large and blunt, with only a hint of an abbreviated beak on the upper jaw, and passes backwards into a powerful streamlined body without indication of a neck. The pectoral flippers are ovate rather than pointed, as is usual in the family. The dorsal fin is situated at the mid-point on the back and is high and triangular. The caudal flukes are broad, powerful, and notched; the tail stock is dorsally keeled (Figure 61c).

In killer whales there is considerable disparity between the sexes. The males are larger and have longer appendages. The dorsal fin on an adult male may be 6 feet high and is shaped like an acute triangle; that of a female is only about 2 feet high and is relatively broader and hooked at the apex. This difference makes sex determination possible in the water. The pectoral fins of the males are also enlarged.

The rostrum of the skull is broad and elongate, and the premaxillae are narrow and flat. The powerful jaws are armed with ten to fourteen pairs of large, conical, recurved interlocking teeth. The first two or three pairs are smaller than the others in the series. The front teeth show more wear, and in old individuals they may even be worn down to the gum line. Of a total of fifty-two vertebrae, the first three cervical vertebrae are fused.

The killer whale is strikingly marked, shiny black above and white below. The white ventral band extends from the lower jaw to the base of the pectoral fins, where it is widest; then it narrows to form a three-pronged trident-shaped mark. The central narrow prong extends down the mid-ventral line to the base of the flukes. The two lateral prongs arch around onto the posterior flanks. There is also a bean-shaped white spot behind the eyes and a grey indistinct saddle across the back behind the dorsal fin. The ventral surface of the flukes is also pale.

Albino killer whales have frequently been reported from the west coast (seventy-four reports between 1923 and 1959). The same albino individual was observed a number of times near Victoria, British Columbia, during 1958.

Average lengths of killer whales from Canadian waters: adult males 6.61 (6.00–7.08) metres, adult females 5.75 (5.15–7.47) metres. These are very close to the measurements given for killer whales from Japanese waters: average length of males 21 feet (6.4 metres), maximum 31 feet (9.4 metres); average length of females 20 feet (6.1 metres), maximum 27 feet (8.2 metres).

Habits. The killer whale is truly the monarch of the deep. Only the giant sperm whale and the bull walrus seem to have no fear of it, all other large marine mammals fleeing whenever it appears. Yet it seems that these whales can be easily tamed in aquaria and make interesting performers. These whales travel and hunt in 'wolf packs,' which may include three to forty individuals. They are bold, cunning, and rapacious. Like the smaller dolphins, they are acrobatic and can leap distances up to forty feet out of the water. One was observed to leap straight up until its flukes were about eight feet above the sea before it fell back on its side with a thunderous splash. This species loafs along at about four knots, but can probably swim up to eighteen knots when playing or hunting.

Killer whales usually take three to five short dives, ten to thirty-five seconds apart, with intervening 'blows.' These 'blows' produce a bushy spray five to fifteen feet high, accompanied by an audible breathy puff. Occasionally killer whales blow near small boats, and the stench of their breath is reported to be overpowering. After a series of short dives the whales sound for a period of one to four minutes.

Killer whales are migratory. Most Californian migratory records are for the autumn, winter, and spring months. They are rarely reported off our east coast in winter but migrate northward along the coast from April to June. They follow the migrating herds of rorqual and beluga far into arctic waters in summer, where they are fairly common along the ice-floe edges. October again finds them migrating southward along our east coast.

The herds are usually formed of distinct age and sex groups; the bulls generally travel alone, except during the mating season, and the calves and juveniles accompany the cows. It has been estimated that the life-span may lie between twenty and thirty years.

The killer whale is the only cetacean that lives primarily upon warm-blooded prey, in contrast to the sperm whale's diet of giant squid and fish. The stomach of one killer whale contained thirteen porpoises and fourteen seals. In hunting a killer whale pack surrounds the gam of dolphins or herd of seals and compresses it; then individuals rush in bunting the prey or knocking one into the air, and finally they strike it a stunning blow with their flukes. A pack of six killer whales was observed off the California coast

herding a group of frantically swimming California sea lions towards the coast. The whales would rush in, playfully tossing the sea lions high in the air. Eventually they surrounded the herd and killed all of them before they could reach the beach. Young walruses are reported to climb on the backs of their mothers to escape from killer whales but they rise from below and knock them off into the water, where they are captured. Narwhals, white whales, and seals seek refuge among the narrow leads in the shore ice from the attacks of killer whales, which seldom venture into such places. Seals climb upon floes, but the killer whales rise under them, breaking them up or tilting the occupants into the sea again. One killer whale momentarily stranded itself while trying to catch a barking dog on a narrow rock-ledge jutting into the sea.

Packs of killer whales even attack the large baleen whales, the giants of the seas, which may be three times their size. Often they worry the females while other members of the pack kill the small calves, but they are reported to kill even the largest whales. It is stated that they grab the flukes, fins, and lips of the large whales and thresh about until the latter are exhausted and 'loll out their tongues.' The killers then grab hold of the tongues and eat them along with parts of the heads, leaving their prey to slowly die. The species preyed upon include the humpback, finback, and bowhead whales; dolphins; beaked whales; white whales; narwhals; sea lions; sea otter; hair seals; fur seals; elephant seals; geese; fishes, including salmon, halibut, electric rays; and squid.

Killer whales are feared by Eskimos, whalers, sealers, and fishermen. Although they could easily upset a frail kayak or skiff, there seems to be no record of them adding man to their diet. In Antarctica there was an incident of a whale bumping the ice-floe on which a man was standing, but the whale's motives did not become clarified.

Habitat. Killer whales are cosmopolitan in the oceans of the world. They are more common in polar and temperate seas and in coastal rather than pelagic waters.

Reproduction. Mating occurs in spring and early summer, from May to July. The whales often leap gracefully out of the water in pairs during their courtship ritual. The gestation period is approximately sixteen months. The single calf (rarely twins) is born in November or December. It measures approximately 9 feet (2.75 metres) at birth, and is coloured similarly to the adults, except that the white areas are yellowish. Sexual maturity is reached in males at three years of age.

Economic Status. Killer whales were not hunted by nineteenth-century whalers. A few have been taken at our coastal whaling stations in recent years. Three were captured in Newfoundland in 1957, and a number have been captured alive in nets in British Columbia waters and transported to aquaria for display purposes. These whales were important figures in the folklore of the Haida Indians of the Queen Charlotte Islands. Stylized killer whales with square toothy jaws and high dorsal fins pierced by a hole are common motifs in wooden totem poles, argillite carvings, and silver jewellery. They are considered important

Map 116 Distribution of the killer whale, *Orcinus orca*

Map 117 Distribution of the grey grampus, *Grampus griseus*

predators of Pacific salmon and sometimes tear up salmon nets. In the Arctic, they drive the narwhals, seals, and white whales close to shore, where they are more easily captured by the Eskimos.

Distribution. In all seas and oceans.

Canadian Distribution. The killer whale is of regular occurrence along our Pacific and Atlantic coasts. It occurs in the Canadian Arctic in Baffin Bay, Lancaster Sound, Davis Strait, the entrance to Hudson Strait, Admiralty Inlet, Eclipse Sound, Cumberland Sound, and Frobisher Bay, but it does not enter Hudson Bay. It is a rare visitor to the Beaufort Sea, but it occurs regularly in the Gulf of St Lawrence (see Map 116).

Because these whales often hunt close to shore, they occasionally become stranded in large numbers at ebb tide. Eighteen killer whales became stranded at Estevan Point, Vancouver Island, on June 13, 1945. On the other hand, nineteen killer whales were forced ashore by heavy ice in Trinity Bay, Newfoundland, on April 27, 1957. The species is known as:

Orcinus orca (Linnaeus), 1758, Syst. Nat., 10th ed. 1: 77.

REFERENCES

Carl, G.C. 1946. A school of killer whales stranded at Estevan Point, Vancouver Island. Provincial Mus. Nat. Hist. Anthrop. Rept. (Victoria, B.C.) 1945: B21–B28.

– 1960. Albinistic killer whales in British Columbia. Provincial Mus. Nat. Hist. Anthrop. Rept. (Victoria, B.C.) 1959: 1–8.

Pike, G.C., and I.B. MacAskie. 1969. Marine mammals of British Columbia. Fish. Res. Bd. Canada Bull. 171: 19–23.

GREY GRAMPUS
Dauphin gris. *Grampus griseus* (G. Cuvier)

Description. This is another of the lesser-known small cetaceans. There is only a suggestion of an upper 'lip'; otherwise the front of the head rises abruptly in a 'melon' of adipose tissue. The short mouth has a fixed smile, caused by an upward curve, which terminates just below the eyes. The ear orifices are vestigial; and the crescentic narial opening is above the eyes. The pectoral flippers are ventrally placed and are long and falcate. The tall dorsal fin, which is centrally located, has a posterior concave surface. The flukes are regularly formed.

The lower jaw of the grampus contains three to seven pairs of conical teeth, placed near the apex. The moderately broad, flat rostrum is slightly shorter than the cranium and tapers to the apex. The dorsal surface of the cranium behind the nares is smooth. The total number of vertebrae is sixty-eight, and seven cervical ones are fused.

The colour is generally grey, but almost black on the dorsal fin, tail stock, and flukes; the flanks are paler; the face and underparts are creamy grey. The skin is usually scarred with long, parallel scratches (Figure 61d).

This dolphin attains a maximum length of 12 to 13 feet (3.65–3.90 metres).

Habits. This species is gregarious and often associates with other species of dolphins. It is migratory, reaching northern seas in early spring. Its food consists of squid.

Habitat. Pelagic.

Reproduction. The calves, which measure about 6 feet (1.85 metres) long at birth, are born about the first of January. They are coloured much like the adults, except for a more pronounced yellow on the face. They have a moustache of six to eight white bristles on each side of the upper jaw.

Economic Status. None.

Distribution. Cosmopolitan.

Canadian Distribution. In recent years four small gams of one to six individuals have been observed off Vancouver Island and one was killed at Big Bay, Stuart Island, British Columbia, in May 1964 (see Map 117).

Grampus griseus (G. Cuvier), 1812, Ann. Mus. Hist. Nat. Paris 19: 14.

REFERENCE

Flower, W.H. 1872. On Risso's dolphin, *Grampus griseus*. Trans. Zool. Soc. 8(1): 1–21.

ATLANTIC PILOT WHALE

Globicéphale noir de l'Atlantique. *Globicephala melaena* (Traill)

Description. This species, known locally as the 'pothead' whale, provides a marine resource of considerable economic importance to Newfoundlanders. It is one of the larger members of the dolphin family: adult males may attain a length of 22 feet. In some ways its body resembles a giant tadpole. The generic name, *Globicephala*, describes the swollen, maxillary melon that bulges over the upper jaw. This melon attains its maximum size in adult males, and is smaller in immature animals, in which a narrow rostral rim or 'upper lip' is still evident. The broad mouth is carried upwards at the corners in a fixed smile. The pectoral fins are rather ventrally and anteriorly placed: they are long and sickle-like (about a fifth the body length). The dorsal fin is placed slightly anterior to the mid-point of the back. It has a long base, but it does not rise very high. The leading margin is straight, the tip points backwards in a hook, and the posterior margin is concave. The body behind the pectoral fins is slender; the tail stock is slender and keeled; the caudal flukes are slender and medially notched. The skull has a short, broad rostrum, which is shorter than the cranium. The large, flat premaxillae do not project over the margins of the maxillae. The jaws contain nine to twelve pairs of conical teeth situated toward the tip of each jaw.

The colour is mostly grey-black when wet, or dark brown when dry. There is an indistinct dark grey saddle behind the dorsal fin and a smaller dark grey spot behind each eye. On the throat is a prominent pearl grey, kedge-shaped patch. The central column runs from the throat to the anus as a narrow mid-ventral ribbon, narrow anteriorly between the pectoral flippers, but broader between the umbilicus and the anus. At the anterior end, two broad lateral branches lead to the bases of the pectoral flippers (Figure 61e).

Males are larger than females. In addition to possessing more bulbous melons, their dorsal fins also have a more rounded, thickened leading edge, and their pectoral flippers are longer, thinner, and similarly shaped. Sexual maturity is reached at 15 feet (3.70 metres), the average is

18.5 feet (5.65 metres), and the maximum length in Newfoundland waters is 20.2 feet (6.17 metres).

Females reach sexual maturity at a standard length of 12 feet (2.79 metres); the average is 14 feet (3.40 metres), and the maximum length attained in Newfoundland waters is 16.8 feet (5.11 metres). The weight of an average-sized whale (13 feet, or 3.96 metres) is approximately 1,800 pounds (800 kg). The weight of the largest male is about 3 tons (2,750 kg).

Habits. Pilot whales are gregarious and occur in gams, which on the average include about twenty individuals and rarely over a hundred at sea. In the Newfoundland 'drives' the average size of the herd is eighty-five, but this is probably made up of several smaller herds. Strandings of herds of up to two hundred individuals have been reported.

The gam is an integrated social unit. The whales communicate by a variety of underwater sounds: whistles, squeals, grating snores, and whines. These sounds are produced by the lips and by the valves of the narial openings, as well as by the deeper air sacs. Pilot whales seem to rely a great deal upon each other's company. They sleep on the surface in compact groups, often with their flippers touching, with the result that, if one is aroused, all are alerted simultaneously. There is often a strong urge to 'follow the leader' and to panic in the face of danger, a characteristic which whalers use to their advantage when herding. They lance one or two whales, the wounded rush ahead of the gam, and the others follow to become stranded on the beach. It has often been noticed that individual whales that have been towed away to safety from a stranded school frequently return to become stranded again. It is thought that the cries of the stranded individuals recall the free-swimming members of the gam to their doom. When stranded, most toothed whales lie on their bellies, but the pilot whale lies on its side with the result that one flipper becomes embedded in the sand. When the tide rises, the blow-hole becomes flooded before the body is refloated, and the pilot whale drowns.

Pilot whales are sociable towards other species, and mixed groups of various species of dolphins often associate with them; they have even been observed with schools of blue fin tuna and seem in general to be inoffensive to other species. They lack the agility of the smaller dolphins in brief encounters.

Pilot whales normally swim at a rate of about four to five knots, but when hard-pressed they may reach a speed of twenty knots. They usually sound for periods of less than four minutes and may dive to depths of 400 to 1,200 feet. The longest dive recorded was of almost five minutes' duration. When migrating they usually roll along briskly in line, abreast. The formation becomes erratic when feeding. At times they seem to be loafing and may 'stand' bolt upright, exposing about five feet of their bodies, scanning the surface for intruders or sounding with a resounding smack of their flukes.

These whales are migratory. They spend the cold months from late September to early July in the Gulf

Stream southeast of the Grand Banks of Newfoundland, and migrate in summer northward and shoreward to the Maritime Provinces, the Gulf of St Lawrence, the Labrador Sea, Greenland, and northern European waters.

Their food consists primarily of a number of species of small squid: *Illex illecebrosus* in the northwest Atlantic, *Ommastrephes sagittatus* in European waters, *Gonatus fabricii* off Greenland, and *Loligo pealei* in the Gulf of St Lawrence. Since these squid come to the surface at night, much of the feeding is probably done at that period. The squid is undoubtedly detected by the whale's sonar system. Hydrographic conditions, such as water temperature, govern the distribution of squid, so that, since the pilot whales follow the immense swarms of squid, in some years the whales may be abundant at certain localities while in other years they may be absent. In summer, the warming up of the surface waters off the east coast of Newfoundland, Labrador, and the Gulf of St Lawrence attracts the pelagic swarms of squid inshore to these regions, and the pilot whale gams follow them into the bays. A pilot whale consumes about sixty pounds (27 kg) of squid a day or about ten tons of squid in a year.

When squid are not available, pilot whales feed on cod, flounders, or amphipods.

It is probable that the killer whale preys upon the pilot whale to some extent, although definite records are lacking. The pilot whale is utilized by man.

It has been estimated that the female may attain an age of fifty years and the male an age of forty.

Habitat. This species inhabits cold temperate waters, both pelagic and offshore.

Reproduction. There are indications of a mating ritual. The partners are reported to face each other and then to crash head-on, bumping their melons together. They are also reported to rear up, with their heads out of the water, facing each other, chest to chest. The mating season occurs during the spring months of April and May, before the animals leave the wintering grounds. The gestation period is about fifteen and a half months, and the calves are born during the summer, with a peak in August.

The young males measure 5 feet 10 inches (1.78 metres) in mean length at birth, and the females 5 feet 8½ inches (1.74 metres). They are paler grey than their mothers and devoid of teeth. Teeth begin to erupt when they are 7 feet (2.13 metres) long, and are fully erupted when they attain 9 feet (2.74 metres). The calves begin to take squid at a mean length of 7½ feet (2.30 metres) at an estimated age of six to nine months. They are fully weaned after twenty-one or twenty-two months.

Females ovulate for the first time at an estimated mean age of six years, at an approximate length of 12 feet (3.56 metres). Males do not mature sexually until they are approximately twelve years old and 16 feet (4.90 metres) long.

Economic Status. These whales have been utilized commercially for about four hundred years in a few localities such as the Faroe, Orkney, and Shetland islands, and Newfoundland. At present the practice has been

Map 118 Distribution of: 1, the Atlantic pilot whale, *Globicephala malaena*, and 2, the Pacific pilot whale, *Globicephala macrorhyncha*

abandoned in the Shetland and Orkney islands. Prior to 1947, pothead whale hunting had been desultory in Newfoundland, but in that year the hunt was commercially organized in Trinity Bay with the aid of small whale catchers, and from then on the gams in the open bay have been rounded up and herded down to the head of one of the smaller bays with a shelving beach. Inside the small bay, a flotilla of small motor boats and dories takes over and drives the whales onto the gravel beach. Unfortunately, because of the absence of squid in the coast waters during the summers of 1948 and 1949, few whales were taken at first, but more successful seasons were to follow, and almost ten thousand whales were taken in the summer of 1956. Then there was a decline in numbers, probably because of the failure of the squid crop, but the total take of whales rose again to 6,262 in 1961. The meat is used by fur ranchers.

Distribution. The Atlantic pilot whale has a bipolar distribution, being found in the North Atlantic and southern subarctic seas but not in tropical waters. It occurs along the eastern coast of North America from New Jersey northward at least as far as Disko Island, west Greenland.

Canadian Distribution. This species is a common summer visitor to our east coast. It appears first on the Grand Banks in late June and remains until early November. The distance these whales travel north along the Labrador coast depends upon the temperature of the water and the squid crop. They have been observed as far north as Ungava Bay. Single strandings have occurred at Digby, Nova Scotia, in 1949, and at Yarmouth, Nova Scotia, in 1954 (see Map 118).

Atlantic pilot whales occur regularly also in the Gulf of St Lawrence during the summer, at least as far upstream as the mouth of the Saguenay River. In 1930 there was an unusual migration of squid, *Loligo*, up the St Lawrence. A herd of twenty-one whales was seen stranded on August 31 of that year at Trois Pistoles, and a single animal at Ste Anne de la Pocatière and another at Boischatel, Ile d'Orleans, just below Quebec City, at the limit of penetration of salt water, in October. In the same year 200 were stranded at the mouth of Enore River, Prince Edward Island, on August 29, and 50 at Borden, Prince Edward Island. Further incursions occurred in 1934 and 1936, but they were not so spectacular.

The Atlantic pilot whale is known as:

Globicephala melaena (Traill), 1809, Jour. Nat. Phil. Chem. Arts 22:81.

REFERENCE

Sergeant, D.E. 1962. The biology of the pilot or pothead whale *Globicephala melaena* (Traill) in Newfoundland. Fish. Res. Bd. Canada Bull. 132.

PACIFIC PILOT WHALE

Globicéphale du Pacifique. *Globicephala macrorhyncha* Gray

Description. At present the Pacific pilot whale is considered to be a distinct species, but in future studies it may prove to be a subspecies of the Atlantic pilot whale. It is very similar to the previous species and may be distinguished only by the following characteristics. The blaze on the throat being darker grey makes the streak connecting the kedge-shaped patch and the inguinal patch inconspicuous; the dorsal saddle-mark is reddish grey and a v-shaped lighter area surrounds the blow-hole. The pectoral flippers are slightly shorter (14.4 per cent of the body length compared to 18.7 per cent for *G. melaena*). The average number of teeth per row is reported to be slightly smaller (8–12), and the premaxillae are expanded to overlap the maxillae (Figure 60c).

The Pacific pilot whale is slightly smaller then the Atlantic form, averaging 11 feet 5 inches (3.48 metres) in length. The range of adult males is 2.75 to 5.56 metres and of adult females 2.08 to 4.73 metres.

Habits. The life history of the Pacific form is similar to that of the Atlantic species.

Distribution. This species is confined to the north Pacific from Guatemala to the Alaskan peninsula and northern Japan (see Map 118).

Canadian Distribution. Only one small specimen has been taken off our British Columbia coast, and other small groups have been seen west of Vancouver Island. The species is known as:

Globicephala macrorhyncha Gray, 1846, *in* The zoology of the voyage of H.M.S. *Erebus* and *Terror* ..., 1 (Mammals): 33.

REFERENCE

Norris, K.S., and J.H. Prescott. 1961. Pacific pilot whale. *In* Observations on Pacific cetaceans of Californian and Mexican waters. Univ. California Pub. Zool. 63(4): 336–48.

HARBOUR PORPOISE

Marsouin commun. *Phocoena phocoena* (Linnaeus)

Description. Porpoises are distinguished from dolphins by their blunt snouts, which lack beaks or 'upper lips,' and by the peculiar flattened, spade-shaped teeth, instead of the conical teeth of the dolphins. The harbour porpoise is the smallest whale and seldom exceeds a length of 6 feet. It is frequently referred to as 'puffing-pig' because of the snuffling sounds it makes when breathing. It has a stout body, a blunt head, a short straight mouth, a triangular dorsal fin that carries six small tubercules on its leading edge, almost oval-shaped flippers, a keeled tail stock, and notched flukes (Figure 60d).

The skull of this porpoise is small: the rostrum is broad and flat; the pterygoids are vestigial and widely separated; the premaxillae form bosses in front of the nares. There are twenty-two to twenty-seven pairs of spatulate teeth in each jaw. The vertebral column is composed of sixty-four or sixty-five vertebrae.

Dorsally the colour of this species is dark slate grey to blackish, with light grey to white underparts. The flanks are greyish, and black stripes run from the flippers to the corners of the mouth and lower lip.

Males and females are approximately the same size: average total length 1.50 (1.15–1.85) metres, average weight 55 (27–88) kg (60–197 pounds).

Habits. Harbour porpoises usually occur in small groups of two to five animals, occasionally up to a dozen. They do not seem to be as gregarious as some of the dolphins. The sexes are segregated much of the time; gams of mature males travel together, while the females, calves, and young males associate in other groups. They seem to be less playful than many other dolphins and usually do not frolic near ships, nor do they often associate with other species of cetaceans.

In calm water they roll leisurely, exhale with a puff, and inhale with a whine. In choppy water they breathe quickly, throwing up a spray as they plunge into the waves. They seldom leap out of the water. They take a series of three or four quick breaths before they sound. They have been known to dive to a depth of forty-four fathoms.

These porpoises are migratory. They winter off the coast of Washington and British Columbia, migrating northward in summer. In European waters most porpoises migrate out of the Baltic Sea in autumn through the Strait of Kattigat.

The food of this species consists of herring, hake, pollock, capelin, whiting and sable fish, squid, and crustacea. One porpoise is reported to have choked to death on a one-pound shad, and another on a small shark.

Map 119 Distribution of the harbour porpoise, *Phocoena phocoena*

Harbour porpoises are preyed upon by killer whales and large sharks, and occasionally by man.

Habitat. Harbour porpoises inhabit inshore waters such as bays, channels, and harbours. They seldom venture more than twenty miles offshore.

Reproduction. Mating takes place in July and August, and the single calf is born some time between the end of May and early July after a gestation period of ten to eleven months. Since adult females breed each year, they are pregnant most of their lives.

At birth the calf measures 80 to 86 cm in total length (more than half the adult length) and weighs 6 to 8 kg. It has one to three bristles on each side of the snout, which are lost soon after birth. It is generally a little darker in colour than the adult.

The mother usually raises the calf in some sheltered bay during the early days of its life. She turns on her flank to suckle it so that its blow-hole remains above water. The youngster grows rapidly. The calf cuts its teeth at about five months of age, at a weight of about 25 kg, and after that it starts to take some solid food. It weighs 30 to 45 kg at six months and is weaned at eight months.

The yearling females become sexually mature at fourteen months, at an approximate length of 1.48 metres and weight of 50 kg. The males probably mature a little later. The porpoises are essentially full-grown at eighteen months, and the young females bear their first calves near their second birthdays.

Economic Status. Harbour porpoises were hunted regularly in Europe until recent times. They were also harpooned by the West Coast Indians. They are frequently caught in salmon traps or gill nets, which they may seriously damage.

Distribution. This species occurs widely in northern seas: the Pacific Ocean from Point Barrow to southern California; the north Atlantic; the North, Baltic and White seas (a relict population occurs in the Black Sea); southward to the New Jersey coast. It also ascends the large rivers – Columbia, Thames, and Rhine – to the head of tide.

Canadian Distribution. Each June large gams enter Passamaquoddy Bay and travel up the St Croix estuary. They depart in late September. In June and July they occur off the Newfoundland coast. Occasionally they are captured in cod traps in Trinity Bay. They reach the west Greenland coast in spring and travel as far as latitude 69°N, but ice along the Canadian coast of Davis Strait discourages them from foraging in Canadian waters. Although infrequent along the Labrador coast, they have been reported from the outer reaches of Cumberland Sound, Baffin Island. They are resident off the coast of British Columbia (see Map 119).

One specimen was secured at Dildo, Newfoundland, on July 9, 1952. There are seven British Columbia records.

The species is known as:

Phocoena phocoena (Linnaeus), 1758, Syst. Nat., 10th ed., 1: 77.

REFERENCE

Mohl-Hansen, U. 1954. Investigations on reproduction and growth of the common porpoise (*Phocoena phocoena* (L)) from the Baltic. Vidensk. Medd. Dansk. Naturhist. Forening, Copenhagen 116: 369–96.

DALL'S PORPOISE
Marsouin de Dall. *Phocoenoides dalli* (True)

Description. The porpoises of this genus are confined to the North Pacific Ocean. This species is characterized by having a stout body, by being beakless, but by having a pointed head and a prominent dorsal keel on the tail stock. Its mouth is short but straight; the auditory canal is sealed over by the skin; the dorsal fin is short and triangular and is slightly hooked; the pectoral flippers are anteriorly placed and pointed.

The rostrum is relatively broad and flat at the base; the intermaxillaries have elevated bosses ahead of the nares; the pterygoids are widely separated; the temporal fossae are small. The minute teeth are loosely embedded in the gums. Instead of individual alveoli, there are long alveolar grooves in the jaws; the anterior teeth are vestigial. There are twenty-two to twenty-seven pairs of teeth in each jaw. The vertebral column has eighty-eight to ninety-seven vertebrae (Figure 59d).

The dominant colour is slate grey to black, with a white blaze on the belly, which extents onto the flanks as an ovoid patch below and behind the dorsal fin. This blaze may have black streaks on it, particularly on the mid-

269

Map 120 Distribution of Dall's porpoise, *Phocoenoides dalli*

larly in broad channels between offshore islands. It is seldom observed far at sea or in shallow bays.

Reproduction. The single calf is born in July or August.

Economic Status. These porpoises are hunted in Japanese waters. The meat is used for human consumption, the blubber for oil, and the skeleton for fertilizer. The market price for a dolphin in 1949 was about $7.50.

Distribution. Dall's porpoise occurs in the North Pacific from Santa Catalina Island, California, north to the Aleutian Islands and westward to the Okhotsk Sea and the Sea of Japan south to about latitude 39° N. It seems to be more common on the American side (see Map 120).

Canadian Distribution. This porpoise occurs off our Pacific coast in summer, being regularly observed among the outer islands. There are about ten specimens from British Columbia waters. The species is known as:

Phocoenoides dalli (True), 1885, Proc. United States Nat. Mus. 8: 95.

REFERENCE

Cowan, I. McT. 1944. The Dall porpoise, *Phocoenoides dalli* (True), of the north Pacific Ocean. Jour. Mamm. 25(3): 295–306.

ventral line. The tip of the dorsal fin and the posterior margin of the tail flukes are also white. The ventral surface of the tail stock and flippers may be pale grey or blotched.

Average length of males 6.2 feet or 1.88 (1.72–2.00) metres; average weight of males 242 pounds or 110 (95–132) kg. Average length of females 5.7 feet or 1.75 (1.63–1.98) metres; average weight of females 209 pounds or 95 (67–150) kg.

Habits. This is another gregarious small porpoise that usually occurs in gams of approximately a dozen individuals but occasionally is met in larger groups of perhaps a hundred individuals. It does not appear to associate with other small cetaceans. It is among the swifter species of the family, attaining speeds of fifteen to twenty knots. It is very fond of leaping about ships, coasting on the bow wave, and cutting across the bows.

This species seems to be nervous and intolerant. When captured it is the exception among the smaller whales in that it struggles and soon exhausts itself.

These porpoises are migratory. They visit southern California waters between mid-October and early May but are residents about the Farallon Islands to the north. They are summer visitors to Canadian waters from the Strait of Juan de Fuca northward. They have been observed migrating in single file, each about one hundred feet from its neighbour.

They have been heard squealing, and they probably produce other inaudible sounds in their nasal sinuses.

Their food consists of hake, horse mackerel, capelin, herring, sauries, and squid. This porpoise is probably preyed upon by the killer whale.

Habitat. Dall's porpoise inhabits the waters of the continental shelf at less than five hundred fathoms, particu-

Family **Eschrichtidae** / Grey Whale

This is the first family of the suborder Mysticeti, or baleen whales, which consists of whales, mostly larger, in which numerous panels of baleen take the place of true teeth, which are absent after birth. The food consists primarily of small crustaceans or 'krill.'

Other diagnostic features are the paired nostrils and the termination of the maxillary bones just in front of the orbits so that they do not take part in the formation of the elongate rostrum. Usually four digits are enclosed in the pectoral flippers.

The present family consists of only one member – the grey whale – whose head is quite different in appearance from that of other baleen whales. The large mouth bisects the head, cutting off a relatively high snout. The baleen plates are short (less than 20 inches). A series of low humps replaces the dorsal fin of other baleens; there are two to four short throat grooves. The skull is characterized by a long, slender, but deep, depressed rostrum and straight mandibles. The cervical vertebrae are distinct.

GREY WHALE
Baleine grise de Californie. *Eschrichtius robustus* (Lilljeborg)

Description. The grey whale is one of the larger whales. It has a relatively small head; a slightly bowed large mouth; a fusiform body; eyes immediately behind and a little above the corners of the mouth; paired nostrils on the top of the head, above the eyes; and vestigial ear openings midway between the eyes and the pectoral flippers. The pectoral flippers are large, broad, and pointed; the caudal flukes are broad, thick, and medially notched. It has no dorsal fin, but there is a row of about eight humps, which begins two-thirds of the distance along the back and continues down the tail stock. The grey whale might be considered one of the hairiest of whales: there are irregular rows of hair on the upper and lower jaws with concentrations on the lips. There are 138 to 174 yellow baleen plates, 14 to 16 inches in length, on each side of the mouth.

The basic colour is greyish, heavily flecked with white scars that are caused by parasites. The body is usually heavily parasitized with whale 'lice' and barnacles embedded in the hide. The concentration of these barnacles often causes roughened knobby areas on the snout (Figure 62b).

These whales average about 40 to 45 feet in length (12–14 metres) but may reach a maximum length of 50 feet (15 metres). As is common among baleen whales, the females usually exceed the males in size. They weigh approximately 36.4 tons (33.6 metric tons).

Habits. Grey whales are generally solitary animals on their summer and winter ranges, but they travel in loose gams of a few to a dozen or more individuals during migration. The calves accompany the females, and the bulls form small gams. Grey whales are usually placid in disposition, but when wounded or harried for prolonged periods they become angry and may attack the offending boat.

These whales have acute hearing and can produce sounds as well. Occasionally they leap high out of the water or merely lift their heads high. It has been suggested that this behaviour is to permit them to see the coastline or objects on the sea.

They normally cruise at a rate of four knots, but when they are pursued they increase this to a maximum of ten knots. When loafing along, they take three to five 'blows' about fifteen seconds apart before sounding for six- to ten-minute intervals. Normally they do not dive much below 75 to 135 feet (15–25 fathoms). In diving, their bodies slide smoothly down with a casual flip of the tail fins.

These whales undertake annual migrations of about 5,000 miles in each direction along the Pacific coast of North America. From their winter range in the sheltered lagoons of Baja California they migrate northward to their summer range in the Bering and Chukchi seas. They pass San Diego, California, in peak numbers during February and March, and Vancouver Island in April and early May, reaching St Lawrence Island towards the end of May or early June. Most of them pass to the west of that island and press north into the Chukchi Sea in July and August, following the break-up of the frozen seas. The northward passage is at a leisurely rate of approximately two nautical miles an hour. They leave the northern areas in September and October and swim southward more rapidly, at a rate of approximately four nautical miles an hour, passing Vancouver Island in December and San Diego in late De-

cember and January. The cows, which are heavy with calf at that period, give the impetus in the drive southward.

During migration the whales travel close to shore, usually within six miles, except when crossing bays or sounds; often they are just offshore. It is thought that they navigate by sight, using mountains or underwater landmarks to guide them. They pass Kodiak Island and enter the Bering Sea between Unimak Island and the Alaskan peninsula. A few continue northward along the Alaskan coast and pass Wainright and Point Barrow in late June and early July. A few even press as far eastward as Flaxsman Island in the narrow coastal lead. On the return migration they pass Point Barrow between mid-August and mid-September.

The most interesting feature of the food habits of this species is that it feeds only during the summer months and fasts for the remainder of the year. Northward-migrating whales may feed casually along the route, but the southward-migrating whales do not. This means that they feed for five to six months and fast for six to seven.

Grey whales are bottom feeders in shallow seas. When surfacing after feeding, they are often covered with mud, and their activity may be traced by muddy slicks on the sea. It has been suggested that they plow through the silty bottom, straining the silt through their baleen plates and trapping their food inside. Their food consists of amphipod crustaceans, gastropods, bivalve molluscs, polychaete worms, ascidians, and small crabs.

Grey whales are preyed upon by killer whales, the calves being the particular target. In defence, the grey whales seek the shallowest bays and sand bars. They are reported to lift their small calves out of the water on their flippers when pressed by killer whales. Grey whales will flop through the shallowest water and may become temporarily stranded, but they do not die as most other whales do, but wait for high tide to refloat. When attacked in the open sea, they often flop over, exposing their bellies and flippers above the water when exhausted.

Habitat. These whales inhabit shallow continental shelves where the water is temperate. Deep oceans and tropical and arctic water masses are barriers to migration. The coastal waters of the American side of the Bering Sea are warmed by a northward current.

Reproduction. The single calves are born in shallow lagoons along the coast of Baja California between latitude 24° and 28° N. The cows enter these lagoons, but most of the bulls cruise about the entrances to the coves. At birth the calf measures 13 to 17 feet (4–5.2 metres) in length and weighs between 1,500 and 3,000 pounds (680–1,360 kg). The cow feeds her calf by pumping milk into its mouth, which is inserted into the mammary groove and sealed by the mammary lips. The calf is weaned at six months of age.

Mating occurs immediately after the birth of the calf, which usually takes place in January. The cows are polyandrous, and two bulls frequently follow each rutting cow. The gestation period is twelve months, and a calf is born each winter.

Economic Status. Because of their regular migratory

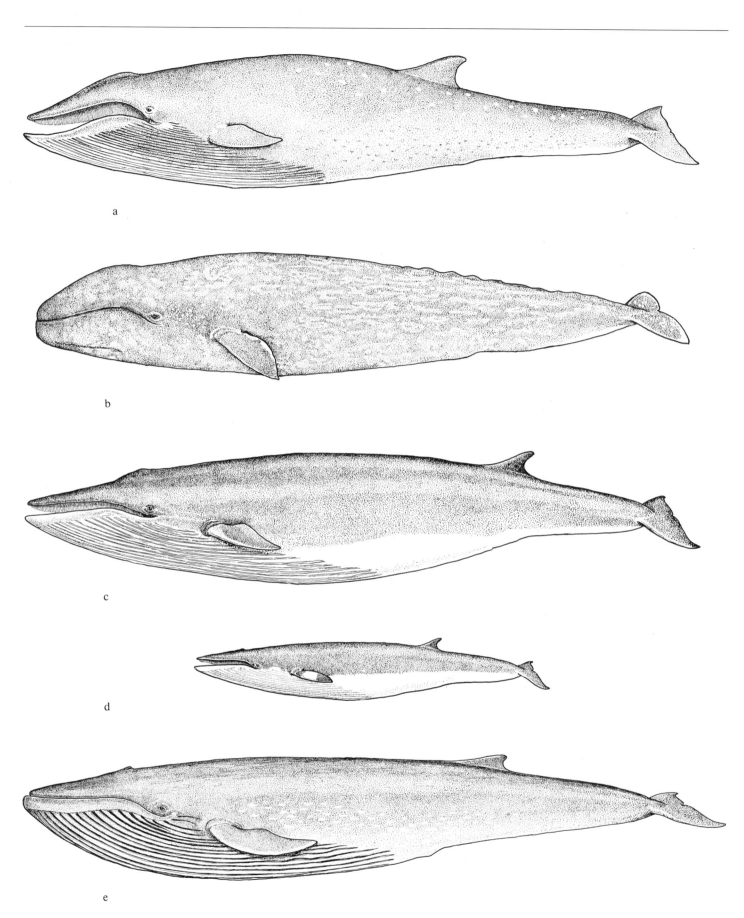

Figure 62 Grey whale and Canadian rorquals: (a) sei whale, *Balaenoptera borealis*; (b) grey whale, *Eschrichtius robustus*; (c) fin whale, *Balaenoptera physalus*; (d) minke whale, *Balaenoptera acutorostrata*; (e) blue whale, *Balaenoptera musculus*

Map 121 Distribution of the grey whale, *Eschrichtius robustus*

whale (*Eschrichtius gibbosus*). Jour. Fish. Res. Bd. Canada 19(5): 815–38.

Rice, D.W., and A.A. Wolman. 1971. The life history and ecology of the gray whale (*Eschrichtius robustus*). American Soc. Mamm. Spec. Pub. 3.

Family **Balaenopteridae** / Rorquals

This family contains the largest animals that have ever lived (even larger than the giant dinosaurs). The rorqual's body is elongate; its head comprises less than a quarter of the body length; a small falcate dorsal fin is situated aft; the pectoral fins are long and pointed; the caudal flukes are relatively small and are deeply indented medially. The rostrum is flat and broad; the eyes are located above the corners of the mouth; the paired nostrils are located on a protuberance slightly in front of the eyes; the lower jaws are bowed. The diagnostic feature of this family is the numerous throat grooves, or pleats, which permit the enlargement of the mouth capacity, somewhat like a pelican's pouch.

The skeleton is characterized by the elongate, flat, pre-maxillary rostrum, the bowed mandibles, the short baleen plates, the distinct cervical vertebrae, and the four digits enclosed in the pectoral flipper. There is a cervical rib fused to the first thoracic rib, making it a double-headed rib.

FIN WHALE
Rorqual commun. *Balaenoptera physalus* (Linnaeus)

Description. The long, sleek finback has been called the greyhound of the deep. When viewed from above, the flat snout is wedge-shaped. There are about sixty throat grooves, which extend from the tip of the lower jaw to the navel. The dorsal fin is about 15 inches (38 cm) high and is strongly hooked behind; the pectoral flippers are about a ninth the total body length; the tail stock is ridged behind the dorsal fin. The snout and lower jaw carry a variable number of bristles. There are up to 370 baleen plates, approximately 95 cm (37 inches) long. Twenty-six to twenty-eight vertebrae make up the vertebral column.

The colour of this species is dark slate blue above and pure white below. The dorsal surfaces of the pectoral fins and caudal flukes are similarly slate grey above and pale grey below. The colour pattern, however, is curiously asymmetrical: the right side of the face is much paler than the left, particularly on the lower jaw. The baleen on the right side is similarly pale grey in front, but it is dull blue grey behind and on the left side (Figure 62c).

There are distinct populations of fin whales in the northern and southern hemispheres, those found in the Northern Hemisphere being smaller. The average length of North Pacific Ocean males is 62 feet (19 metres), and the females attain an average length of 66 feet (20 metres). The maximum length is 70 feet (21.5 metres). The fins of those in the Southern Hemisphere may reach a maximum length

pattern and inshore habitat, these whales were almost exterminated by the Pacific whaling industry in the last half of the nineteenth century. With the decline of 'sail' whaling the population again increased to support a small industry during the 1920s and 1930s, but the population then again declined to the point of extinction. In 1937 the capture of grey whales was prohibited by international agreement, and since that date they have increased dramatically. The American winter population was estimated at 3,000 whales in 1967. Several grey whales have been taken by Alaskan Eskimos in recent years.

Distribution. The grey whale is now confined to the North Pacific Ocean. Besides the population of the west coast of North America, there is a second population on the Asian side, which winters off the Korean coast and spends the summer in the Sea of Okhotsk. The species also inhabited the North Atlantic Ocean during historic times. It was known as the scrag whale by European whalers. Their coastal habitat and slow speed led to their early extinction by Basque whalers. Their bones have been dug up in the reclaimed Zuyder Zee of the Netherlands.

Canadian Distribution. Grey whales are regular spring and autumn migrants along the west coast of Vancouver and the Queen Charlotte Islands, British Columbia, as well as in Hecate Strait (see Map 121). A few stragglers may spend the summer in these waters as well. The species is known as:

Eschrichtius robustus (Lilljeborg), 1861, Forh. Skand.
Naturf. Ottende Møde, Kjøbenhavn for 1860, 8: 602.

REFERENCES

Pike, Gordon C. 1962. Migration and feeding of the grey

of 82 feet (25 metres), but the average length has been decreasing in recent decades from 70 feet (21.5 metres) in 1931–32 to 66.3 feet (20.1 metres) in 1958–59.

Habits. Fin whales are gregarious and usually appear in small groups of about two to seven individuals, but occasionally gams of two to three hundred form during migration. They are swift swimmers for their size and normally cruise at about twelve knots but perhaps reach twenty knots in short bursts. They float very low in the water, exposing the narrow, hooked dorsal fin. The spout is a single, high, vertical, inverted cone of moisture-laden air, repeated at three- to seven-second intervals. They slide under when sounding, with only a slight hump showing and without exposing their flukes. They may remain submerged for twenty minutes, but the average submersion is more like four minutes.

This species is migratory. It spends the summer in polar and subpolar waters and then travels to tropical and subtropical waters in winter. Since the seasons are reversed in the two hemispheres, the northern and southern stocks never meet. Fin whales appear on the summer feeding grounds later than blue and humpback whales. The older animals also migrate before the younger ones do.

The summer food of fin whales consists of krill, which they find by echo location and, to a lesser degree, by sight and touch. An adult fin whale may consume 1.0 to 1.5 metric tons of food in a day. During migrations this species may also eat herrings and capelin, and one was known to feed upon squid. Fin whales are preyed upon by killer whales.

The age of baleen whales may be estimated by counting the laminations in their waxy ear plugs. By this means it has been estimated that fin whales reach physical maturity at twenty-two to twenty-five years of age and attain a maximum life-span of about thirty years.

Habitat. Fin whales are pelagic creatures, inhabiting the deep oceans of the world. They are usually found about twenty-five miles from shore.

Reproduction. Mating and parturition take place in tropical waters during the winter. The old females leave the arctic feeding grounds early and mate before the younger whales arrive on the breeding grounds. This is between November and January for the northern stock. The gestation period is twelve months, and calves are born every two or three years. Usually a single calf is born, but twins are not unusual and as many as six foetuses have been found in a pregnant cow. The calves measure 21 feet (6.5 metres) at birth, which may occur in tropical waters or soon after the northward migration has begun. The calves are weaned when they are about ten and a half months old, by which time they have doubled in size.

Juvenile females reach sexual maturity at four to five years of age, at an average length of 61 (55–68) feet or 18.5 (16.8–20.5) metres, while males mature at five to six years of age at 58 (55–63) feet or 17.5 (16.8–19.3) metres in length.

Economic Status. Because of their speed, their thin blubber layer, and the fact that they sink when killed,

rorquals were not hunted during the early sail-whaling days. The introduction of the harpoon gun, mounted on a powerful catcher boat, by the Norwegians in 1864 opened the way for the exploitation of this whale family. Blue whales dominated the whale catch during the early twentieth century, but since 1945 fin whales have composed about 50 per cent of the world catch. During the 1962–63 whaling season, 20,587 fin whales were taken, mostly in pelagic whaling operations, based on floating factory ships and small catchers in the Antarctic.

Canada had only a small shore-based whaling industry with whaling stations at Hawkes Harbour, Labrador (which burned down in 1959); Williamsport, Port Blandford, and Dildo, Newfoundland; and Coal Harbour, Vancouver Island. Ninety-nine fin whales were taken off Labrador and Newfoundland between 1956 and 1959, and 836 were processed at Coal Harbour from 1962 to 1967, when the station was closed.

The present world stocks of fin whales appear to be declining in spite of the steps that have been taken to conserve them. These included the establishment of a Pacific Antarctic Sanctuary in 1937 (recently opened to hunting again), the restriction of pelagic hunting to the area south of latitude 40°s, a restricted season of sixty-nine days for hunting fin whales, and minimum length restrictions.

The whale products utilized include whale oil rendered from the blubber and whale meat for human and animal consumption.

Distribution. Although fin whales occupy almost all oceans, at least six distinct breeding stocks have been recognized. These are named for their locations: South Atlantic, South Indian, Western Pacific, Eastern Pacific, North Atlantic, and North Pacific. The last two populations are the ones that enter Canadian waters.

The North Atlantic stock winters from the Caribbean Sea and the Azores to the Mediterranean and migrates northward in March past the Gulf of Maine to reach southwest Greenland, Iceland, the Faroes, and Spitsbergen in June and July. In these arctic waters they feed on swarms of krill along the ice-edge. In September they have been observed migrating southwesterly past Ireland, and they have been reported from the Bay of Biscay in October.

The North Pacific stock winters from Baja California and Central American waters to Japan. They migrate northward as early as March and in summer reach the Bering Sea.

Canadian Distribution. Fin whales reach the Gulf of St Lawrence in March, where they feed among the ice-floes. They are common off Newfoundland in June and off the Labrador Coast in July and August. They do not frequent the Baffin Island coast of Davis Strait because of the unfavourable ice conditions there. A group of twelve fin whales was stranded in St George's Bay on the west coast of Newfoundland by incoming ice in March 1959. Another was stranded at Stanhope Beach, Prince Edward Island, during a violent storm on the night of October 25, 1958. A

Map 122 Distribution of the fin whale, *Balaenoptera physalus*

number of mass strandings along the west coast of New-foundland and the north shore of the Gulf of St Lawrence occurred again in 1968.

Fin whales reach the Vancouver Island coast in March and remain fairly common far off the British Columbia coast during most of the summer (see Map 122).

The subspecies that occurs in the Northern Hemisphere is the nominate one:

Balaenoptera physalus physalus (Linnaeus), 1758, Syst. Nat., 10th ed., 1: 75.

REFERENCES

Ohsumi, Seiji, Masaharu Nishiwaki, and Takashi Hibiya. 1958. Growth of fin whale in the north Pacific. Sci. Repts. Whales Res. Inst. Tokyo 13: 97–133.
Sergeant, D.E., A.W. Mansfield, and B. Beck. 1970. In-shore records of Cetacea for eastern Canada, 1949–68. Jour. Fish. Res. Bd. Canada 27: 1905–6.

SEI WHALE
Rorqual boréal. *Balaenoptera borealis* Lesson

Description. The sei whale is a smaller edition of the fin whale. There was much confusion among nineteenth-century whalers concerning the various species of rorquals, and the nomenclature of these whales has been straightened out only during the last thirty years. Although this species bears a strong superficial resemblance to the blue and fin whales, it may be distinguished by the following characteristics. The body form is relatively heavier; the relatively large dorsal fin is situated relatively forward; the posterior edge is only moderately falcate; and the pectoral flippers are relatively short. There are an average of forty-seven (40–62) throat grooves, which terminate in front of the navel; the mouth is relatively smaller (Figure 62a).

The skull of the sei whale is characterized by a pointed, ridged, slightly bowed rostrum. The baleen plates are fine, narrow, and bluish black. The interior edges are shredded into white silky threads. On the average there are 326 (296–342) baleen plates, which measure 35 to 80 cm in length; the vertebral column consists of twenty-two or twenty-three vertebrae.

The dorsal colour is bluish grey (lighter than the fin whale). The flanks have bands of grey that extend from the lower jaw backwards and meet on the abdomen. There are irregular white splotches on the throat and chest. The grooves are pinkish.

The average length of Atlantic Ocean male sei whales is 13 (7.8–17.1) metres, or 42.8 (25.8–8.56) feet, and of females 13.3 (11.0–17.4) metres, or 43.8 (36–57) feet. The antarctic whales are a little larger, males averaging 14.5 metres in length and females 16 metres. The largest female measured attained a length of 18 metres or 59 feet.

Habits. Sei whales are usually met in small gams. Their movements are rather irregular, and occasionally large gams form on the feeding grounds.

The sei whale surfaces obliquely, showing its snout, and slides under without showing its hump or exposing its flukes. It 'blows' with a metallic whistling sound like air rushing through pipes. The spout is a single vertical 'bush' of vapour about eight to twelve feet high (smaller than for the fin whales). The nostrils protrude and open wide on inspiration. Sei whales often swim for long distances just under the surface of the sea and may attain a rate of twenty knots in short bursts.

This species exhibits the same migratory pattern as the other rorquals. It feeds in temperate and subpolar seas in summer and migrates to subtropical seas in winter to breed. The pregnant cows are the first to migrate in the autumn.

The adults reach physical maturity at ten to eleven years. The oldest whale examined so far was fifteen years old.

These whales feed mainly in subpolar seas in summer, but seldom when they are in subtropical waters. They often feed on the surface, twisting and turning to catch schools of small fish or plankton bloom. In polar seas their food is mainly krill and the copepod *Calanus*. They feed upon sardines, anchovies (in Japan), and also on sauries. Their acceptance of fish makes it possible for them to remain in some areas after the krill has gone and other whales, such as the giant blue whale, are forced to leave.

Sei whales are preyed upon by killer whales. They support a few external parasites such as the stalked copepod *Penella* and the barnacle *Coronula*.

Habitat. The sei whale is pelagic, normally occurring far offshore. It does not inhabit cold polar seas but prefers subpolar or temperate seas, such as the northern reaches of the Gulf Stream.

Map 123 Distribution of the sei whale, *Balaenoptera borealis*

Reproduction. The females breed every other year. There is a seven-month anoestrous period after the weaning of the calf. Sometimes irregular oestrus occurs after the loss of a calf. The males exhibit no sexual season; some are fertile all year.

The whales pair off during a protracted breeding season, which stretches from November to February in the Northern Hemisphere and from May to July in the Southern. The gestation period is twelve months. The calves measure about 4.5 metres (14.5 feet) at birth. They grow rapidly and are weaned at five months, by which time they have grown to 8 or 9 metres in length. The juvenile females reach sexual maturity at eighteen months and first breed at the time of their second birthday.

Economic Status. These small, lean whales were scorned by the early whalers because it took approximately six sei whales to produce the same quantity of oil that one blue whale produced. Even in recent years sei whales are hunted only if other species are absent. The world catch of sei whales for the 1962–63 season was 8,043. Eighteen were taken off Labrador between 1956 and 1959, and one at the Dildo, Newfoundland station in 1959. The six catcher ships operating from Coal Harbour, Vancouver Island, captured 2,154 between 1962 and 1967.

Distribution. Sei whales migrate northward in summer in the temperate Gulf Stream to Greenland, Iceland, and Spitsbergen and North Cape in Norway, between May and early September. On rare occasions they continue as far as Novaya Zemlya. They migrate past Ireland from mid-May to mid-June and past the Shetland Islands from mid-June to mid-July. On the west coast of the Atlantic they migrate from Florida to Labrador. In the North Pacific they spend the winter off southern Japan and migrate northward to the Kuriles between April and July.

They leave the northern waters before September. Sei whales are also found in southern seas.

Canadian Distribution. Sei whales do not migrate as far north as blue and fin whales. They were reported as 'swarming' off the south coast of Newfoundland in August and September during the nineteenth century. They regularly appear in the Labrador Sea in July and August. An early record off our Pacific coast was supplied in 1913, when two were reportedly taken. Now it is known that they occur off our British Columbia coast for a protracted period in summer (see Map 123).

The species is known as:

Balaenoptera borealis Lesson, 1828, Histoire naturelle ... des mammifères et des oiseaux découverts depuis 1788, cétacés, p. 342.

REFERENCE

Matthews, L.H. 1938. The sei whale, *Balaenoptera borealis*. Discovery Repts. (Cambridge) 17: 183–290.

MINKE WHALE
Petit rorqual. *Balaenoptera acutorostrata* Lacépède

Description. The minke or little piked whale is a pocket-edition rorqual, seldom exceeding 30 feet in total length. It has a typically streamlined body; a medially ridged and pointed rostrum; a small mouth; and about fifty (40–70) throat pleats, which terminate halfway between the tip of the flippers and the navel. The fins are not particularly remarkable in shape.

The baleen plates number about 304 (270–348), are yellowish white in colour (which is a good distinguishing mark), and are approximately 23 cm long.

The dorsal colour is dark slate grey; the flanks are lead grey, and the underparts from lower lip to flukes are white, including the under surfaces of fins and flukes. A diagnostic feature of this species is the occurrence of a broad white band across the upper surface of the pectoral flippers (Figure 62d).

The average length of males in Norwegian waters is 6.58 (4.88–8.28) metres or 21.5 (16–27) feet, and of females 7.35 (4.80–9.14) metres or 24 (15.8–30) feet. Canadian males average 23.3 feet (7.10 metres) and females 24.9 feet (7.60 metres).

Habits. These whales are usually met singly or in small groups. They may be paired during much of the year. They are swift swimmers and quite playful, at times gambolling about ships and leaping out of the water, often belly uppermost.

Minke whales are migratory, travelling to the polar seas in summer and retreating to temperate or subtropical seas in winter. Usually the adults migrate farthest towards the poles, and the juveniles remain in temperate seas all summer. The sexes are often segregated during migration. This species often penetrates the ice-floes and may become trapped under continuous ice-fields. At such times, to breathe, they thrust their heads perpendicularly out of the restricted cracks between the floes, as reported for the narwhal.

Map 124 Distribution of the minke whale, *Balaenoptera acutorostrata*

Minke whales feed on a wide variety of small fish, krill, copepods, and squids. The most important fish eaten are herring, cod, haddock, capelin, anchovy, sand lance, croaker, salmon, catfish, ling, sprat, pollock, whiting, and coalfish. Among the crustaceans eaten are *Euphausia*, *Calanus*, and *Thysanoessa*. Their wide choice of food permits them to remain in restricted areas after the plankton bloom has passed.

These small rorquals are preyed upon by killer whales.

Habitat. The minke whale inhabits polar and temperate seas but rarely frequents tropical waters. It is also found in the continental shelves but rarely met in the deep seas.

Reproduction. Mating occurs in the spring between January and May, and the single calf is born between November and March after a gestation period of ten months. The females experience two oestrous cycles a year: one from February to March, and the second from August to September. Most females are impregnated during the first cycle and bear a calf each year, but a few may miss the first period and bear a calf after a lapse of eighteen months.

The calf is 2.4 to 2.7 metres (8–9 feet) long at birth, and is weaned at the age of four to five months. It grows to a length of approximately 6 metres (20 feet) during its first year, and males reach about 6.7 metres (22 feet) and females 7.3 metres (24 feet) in length at the age of two years. Sexual maturity is reached at two years of age.

Economic Status. This whale is too small and its oil content too meagre to interest the large pelagic whalers. Shore stations on Newfoundland, however, have taken about ten to sixty minke whales each year since 1947. The meat is processed for ranch fur-bearers.

Distribution. The minke or little piked whale is found in both hemispheres from the polar ice-caps to the borders of subtropical waters. There are two stocks in the North Pacific Ocean: one in the Japan Sea and the other in the open ocean. This species migrates to Japanese (Honshu) waters in spring from Asiatic wintering grounds and leaves in the autumn. On the American coast it winters as far north as Baja California and reaches Alaskan waters in summer.

The North Atlantic stocks migrate northward in spring from the Mediterranean and Florida Keys to southwest Greenland, Spitsbergen, and as far as the Barents Sea. In the autumn they return southward again.

Canadian Distribution. Minke whales make their appearance off our Atlantic coast in spring at the same time as the capelin spawn, from late May to late July. They may travel as far northward as Ungava Bay but seldom enter the ice off the Baffin Island coast. They migrate southward along the Labrador coast in November and December, just before freeze-up. These small rorquals also enter the Gulf of St Lawrence and congregate at the mouth of the Saguenay River in summer. They also occur in Hamilton Inlet and Passamaquoddy Bay, New Brunswick. They occur off our British Columbia coast for a prolonged period during the warmer months (see Map 124).

The North Atlantic and Pacific stocks are considered distinct subspecies:

Balaenoptera acutorostrata acutorostrata Lacépède, 1804, Histoire naturelle des cétacés ..., p. xxxvii. North Atlantic.

Balaenoptera acutorostrata davidsoni Scammon, 1872, Proc. California Acad. Sci. 4: 269. North Pacific.

REFERENCE

Sergeant, D.E. 1963. Minke whales, *Balaenoptera acutorostrata* Lacépède of the western North Atlantic. Jour. Fish. Res. Bd. Canada 20(6): 1489–1504.

BLUE WHALE
Rorqual bleu. *Balaenoptera musculus* (Linnaeus)

Description. Many readers may believe that one of the extinct Mesozoic dinosaurs was the largest animal that ever existed on this planet. The largest sauropod dinosaur attained a total length of about 72 feet and weighed about 36 tons. It is dwarfed, however, by the present-day blue whale, which may attain a maximum length of 100 feet and weigh 145 tons. Even the ancestral whales were smaller than the blue whale, the order having reached its maximum dimensions in recent times.

This giant whale has the regular streamlined torpedo shape of the rorquals. Its low, small dorsal fin is situated well aft; its pectoral flippers are pointed. Its great rostrum is parallel-sided posteriorly and blunt-tipped. Its ventral throat grooves extend from the lower mandible to the navel and include the area behind the eyes. The average number of grooves is 90, but the number may vary between 70 and 118. There are scattered rows of short hairs on the lips, rostrum, and around the nares, and a 'beard' at the tip of the lower jaw. The baleen plates are short (45–98 cm), coarse, and uniformly blue-black, including the shredded internal filaments. The plates number 316 (250–400) on each side. The vertebral column consists of twenty-eight vertebrae.

As the name implies, the ground colour is dark blue-grey, mottled with light blue-grey oval spots on the flanks, back, and belly. The under surfaces of the flukes and flippers are paler, and there may be creamy white blotches on the throat and navel (Figure 62e).

The females are larger than the males, and the antarctic stocks are larger than those of the Northern Hemisphere. Although the largest whale may attain a length of 100 feet (30.5 metres), the largest authentic specimen was a 97-footer (29.5 metres), which entered the Panama Canal. The average length of antarctic females is 88 (73–95) feet or 27 (22.5–29) metres, and the males average 81.5 (67–89) feet or 25 (20.5–27.3) metres. The largest North Atlantic specimen measured 88 feet 7 inches (27 metres). Large whales taken have weighed 119, 120, and 145 tons.

Habits. The blue whale is usually met singly or in small groups of two or three individuals. This giant is remarkably placid and shy. It usually swims at twelve knots on the surface, but may attain eighteen to twenty knots in short bursts of speed. It normally dives to depths of between twenty-five and fifty fathoms, the maximum depth recorded for the species being 194 fathoms. It can remain submerged for fifty minutes, but ten to fifteen minutes is the more normal extent of its submergence. When on the surface it spouts eight to fifteen times, each spout sending a column of vapour perhaps twenty feet in the air. Blue whales sound without showing the flukes.

Blue whales are also migratory, travelling to the edge of the polar ice in the spring and back to temperate waters in the autumn. These migrations are six months out of phase for the stocks in the northern and southern hemispheres. The adults generally travel first, and the juveniles follow.

These giant mammals feed exclusively on planktonic crustacea, or 'krill,' usually composed of species of the genus *Euphausia*. The cold polar seas in summer teem with krill, usually in the first five fathoms of surface water. This species swims into the planktonic 'bloom' and then opens its cavernous mouth by relaxing its throat pleats. When its mouth is full, it contracts its muscular pleats and elevates its tongue, straining the sea water out through the baleen plates and between the massive lips. The crustaceans are trapped on the inner shredded baleen fibres and swallowed down the five-inch-diameter oesophagus. These whales also feed when on their winter ranges in warm water.

Female blue whales reach full maturity at ten years of age, at which time they measure approximately 88 feet (27 metres). The males mature about a year earlier at an average length of 81.5 feet (25 metres). These whales live approximately thirty years.

External parasites are not common in polar seas, but in the tropics blue whales become parasitized by whale lice, copepods, and barnacles. In these waters they also pick up a tropical diatom film, and lampreys may attack them as well.

Habitat. Blue whales are pelagic denizens of polar and temperate seas and are less frequently found in purely tropical waters.

Reproduction. Mating occurs from May to September in the Northern Hemisphere, with a peak of activity in June and July. After a gestation period of ten and a half months the calves are born in April or May, as the whales are migrating northward in temperate waters. Usually a single calf is born, rarely twins. The females bear calves normally every other year. Young blue whales measure 7 metres (23 feet) long at birth and weigh about 2 metric tons. They grow rapidly and are weaned in December at seven months of age, by which time they measure about 16 metres (52 feet). At their first birthday they measure about 18 metres (58 feet), and by their second birthday females have attained an average length of 23.7 metres (77 feet) and males approximately 22.6 metres (74 feet). The juvenile females reach sexual maturity at about five years of age (3–7 years) along with the young males (4–5 years).

Economic Status. The giant blue whales dominated the whaling industry from 1913 to 1931, after the decline of the humpback whale. A single blue whale yields approximately eighty barrels of oil (maximum 305 barrels), and this species composed approximately 90 per cent of the total catch until 1931, when over 30,000 blue whales were taken. Since that date the blue whale population has declined.

The International Whaling Commission established 'Blue Whale Units' (1 blue whale equals 2 fin whales, 2½ humpbacks, or 6 sei whales) as the basis for present management. The current quota for antarctic pelagic whaling is 10,000 B.W.U. per annum. Other conservation measures taken included: the establishment of the South Pacific Sanctuary, restriction of the open season to forty-four days before April 7, and the complete closure of the North Atlantic to whaling operations. During the 1962–63 season, 1,035 blue whales were taken, mostly in Antarctica, but 27 of them were taken off our Pacific coast by whale catchers operating from Coal Harbour. Nine were taken in 1965. The blue whale has been protected in the North Atlantic Ocean since 1955, and hunting of them in the North Pacific has been prohibited since 1965.

In recent years, stocks of this species continue to decline. The mean length of southern 'blues' decreased from 84 feet (25.5 metres) in 1931–32 to 78.3 feet (24 metres) in 1958–59, and the average age at puberty decreased and fecundity increased, an indication of natural compensation to heavy exploitation. By 1971, only 3,000 blue whales were thought to exist in the world's seas.

Distribution. The species is cosmopolitan and migratory in the oceans of the world. Those in the North Pacific migrate in spring to the seas off the Aleutian Islands, seldom entering Bering Sea. The North Atlantic stocks migrate northward to Davis Strait, Spitsbergen, and the Barents Sea. Southern stocks enter the zone of drifting ice that surrounds Antarctica in the southern summer. It is

Map 125 Distribution of the blue whale, *Balaenoptera musculus*

unlikely that there is much equatorial exchange between the northern and southern stocks.

Canadian Distribution. Blue whales reach the Laurentian Channel south of Newfoundland in March. They enter the Gulf of St Lawrence in April and continue to stay in Newfoundland and Labrador waters until July. During July and August most press northward to southwestern Greenland and Iceland. The return migration in autumn is unknown, but it is unlikely that they tarry in Canadian waters during the winter.

I found the base of a cranium of a blue whale, reportedly stranded in 1960, near Percé, Quebec. Blue whales are occasionally met at the entrance to Passamaquoddy Bay, New Brunswick, where they have been mistaken for uncharted reefs (see Map 125).

The species is known as:

Balaenoptera musculus (Linnaeus), 1758, Syst. Nat., 10th ed., 1: 76. Recently an unnamed 'pigmy' race has been discovered in Antarctica.

REFERENCES

Mackintosh, N.A., and J.F.G. Wheeler. 1929. Southern blue and fin whales. Discovery Repts. (Cambridge) 1: 257–540.

Small, George E. 1971. The blue whale. Columbia University Press, Irvington, N.Y.

HUMPBACK WHALE
Rorqual à bosse. *Megaptera novaeangliae* (Borowski)

Description. The humpback whale has a short, stout body, in contrast to the slim, graceful body of the rorquals. The long scimitar-shaped flippers (often a third of the body length) are also unique. These flippers carry a number of knobs and indentations on the forward edge. The typical, low, falcate dorsal fin is situated well aft of the mid-point of the back. The ventral pleats, which extend from the rim of the lower jaw to the navel, are spaced much farther apart than in the rorquals and therefore total only twenty-eight (21–36) in average number. Irregular rows of tubercules line the snout and lower lip, and usually carry a number of short bristles. The terminal edge of the broad caudal flukes is scalloped (Figure 63a).

The rostrum is short, broad, and flat. The baleen plates, which number 320 to 360 per side, are coarse and grey to black in colour, with pale grey shredded fibres. The baleen of mature whales measures about 80 cm in length (maximum 107 cm).

The normal colour of humpback whales is black above and white below; the forward edges and the under surfaces of the flippers and flukes are white as well. There is considerable variation in colouring, however, and some individuals are marbled on the flanks or are entirely black with only a few white splotches on the throat grooves and belly.

The average length of adult males from the Pacific Ocean is 41 (36–47) feet or 12.5 (11.0–14.3) metres and of females 43 (38–48) feet or 13 (11.6–14.6) metres. The average weight is 30 (20–44) tons.

Habits. The humpback is one of the clowns of the 'deep.' It plays by turning gigantic somersaults half under water and then throwing itself out of the water in a belly-up leap and crashing into the sea head-first again. It rolls on the surface, slapping the water with its great flippers, or it leaps out of the water flapping its flippers as if trying to fly. These whales are usually rather docile and are easily approached. During migration they are usually met in gams, from a few individuals to as many as 150. They pair off during most of the winter period.

This species is one of the slower whales; it usually cruises along at about four knots but is capable of short bursts of speed up to ten knots. It derives its common English name from the hump that is seen above the water prior to sounding. Immediately after the hump disappears, the flukes appear and may wave about like a giant bird's wings before disappearing into the sea. Humpbacks can remain submerged for fifteen to twenty minutes, after which time they surface and blow for a number of times between a series of short dives. The spout is relatively low and bushy.

Humpback whales occur in both hemispheres, migrating in summer to the polar seas to feed and retreating in winter to tropical waters to breed. In the North Atlantic they are found from January to April about the Cape Verde Islands, the Azores, Bermuda, the Lesser Antilles, and the Caribbean Sea. In April and May they migrate northwards along the North American and European coasts, and by June and July reach the coasts of Greenland, Iceland, Spitsbergen, and Bear Island. In late summer they reach their northern limits and in late September and October they return southward.

In the North Pacific Ocean, these whales frequent the west coast of Mexico during the winter months. They migrate past the California coast in March and April, and past Vancouver Island in May and June. Some of the groups remain to feed near the Aleutian Islands in July and August, and others pass through Bering Sea and reach Bering Strait. They stay in Bering Sea as late as mid-September. Humpbacks return to the California coast in October and November. Other stocks occur on the Asiatic coast and migrate between Formosa and the Okhotsk Sea and Kamchatka Peninsula.

Humpbacks also feed primarily in polar seas on krill and other planktonic crustacea. They are known to feed also upon herring, capelin, and cod. One whale was found to have six cormorants in its stomach and a seventh in its throat. The birds were undoubtedly feeding on the same school of fish the whale attacked.

This whale reaches physical maturity at an age slightly less than ten years. There are few direct observations of longevity but an embedded hand harpoon was retrieved from a whale eighteen years after it has been thrown at the whale. Humpbacks are preyed upon by killer whales. They are also parasitized by whale 'lice' and acorn barnacles, particularly around the protuberances on the snout and on the flippers.

Habitat. The humpback is a coastal species, frequently

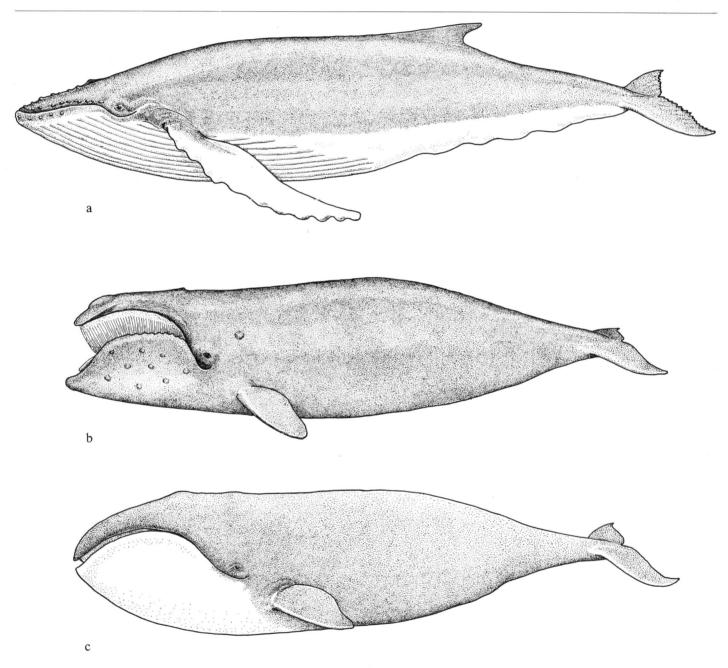

Figure 63 More Canadian whales: (a) humpback whale, *Megaptera novaeangliae*; (b) right whale, *Balaena glacialis*; (c) bowhead whale, *Balaena mysticetus*

entering bays and estuaries. It uses the great ocean currents along continental shores as its highways during migrations.

Reproduction. The mating season for the Northern Hemisphere stocks extends from March to May, while the whales are migrating towards their summer feeding grounds. The period in the Southern Hemisphere extends from August to November. During this period the adults pair off and indulge in gambols and in love pats with their flippers, which may be heard for miles. The females are polyoestrous, and if not impregnated during the primary oestrous period, they may mate again during a second oestrous cycle. The gestation period is eleven months, and most females bear a calf every other year or occasionally twice in three years.

The single calves are born in February or March in the Northern Hemisphere (August in the Southern Hemisphere while the whales are on the winter range in tropical seas). At birth the calves measure 4.5 to 5 metres in length (16–17 feet). They grow even more rapidly than the rorquals and are weaned at five months of age when they measure 7.5 to 8 metres (24.5–26.2 feet) in length. They reach sexual maturity at five years of age, when the males measure 37–39 feet (11.3–11.8 metres) and the females 39–40 feet (11.8–12.2 metres).

Economic Status. The humpback whale was a prime target for whalers during the early days when sailboats and the hand harpoon were in use because it is slow-moving and lacks caution when feeding or during the mating season. Its one important disadvantage was the fact that it sank when killed, so that the whalers had to wait several days for the carcass to decompose sufficiently to refloat. It was, however, a good producer of oil and whalebone. In 1905, humback whales composed 97 per cent of the total catch of whales, and in 1910 in the seas about South Georgia 6,000 were taken. After a brief period of exploitation, the stocks declined markedly after 1916, and the humpback has formed only a small portion of the catch in recent years. During the 1962–63 whaling season, 482 humpback whales were taken. Sixty-eight were taken off Coal Harbour, British Columbia between 1962 and 1965, and four were taken off our east coast in 1958. These whales are also speared occasionally by Eskimos and Aleuts.

Distribution. The humpback whale is cosmopolitan in all the oceans. The northern stocks are found mainly between latitudes 10° and 40°N between October and March. The southern stock occasionally passes north of the equator in August, and so some population exchange may take place.

Canadian Distribution. In recent years these whales have been observed in considerable numbers on the Grand Banks of Newfoundland. The earliest record is that of a cow and calf on March 7, 1961, on the southern edge of the Grand Banks. These may have been early migrants, or their presence may have been an indication of the northern edge of the winter range. The numbers increase in June, and a northward dispersal is evident by late summer. They

Map 126 Distribution of the humpback whale, *Megaptera novaeangliae*

have been seen on the banks of Newfoundland as late as November 30. Occasionally one enters Conception Bay or Hermitage Bay, Newfoundland. A cow and calf were taken in the latter location in June 1903 by whalers.

In summer a few humpbacks occur along the west coast of Vancouver and the Queen Charlotte Islands, British Columbia. They rarely enter the Straits of Georgia (see Map 126).

The species is known as:

Megaptera novaeangliae (Borowski), 1781, Gemeinnüzzige Naturgeschichte des Thierreichs ..., 2(1): 21.

REFERENCE

Matthews, L. Harrison. 1937. The humpback whale, *Megaptera nodosa*. Discovery Repts. (Cambridge) 17: 7–92.

Family **Balaenidae** / Bowhead Whales

In the early days of whaling with sail and hand harpoon, these large, slow whales were the main quarry and hence earned the English name 'right' whales. Members of this family are thickset baleen whales which lack the throat grooves of the rorquals. The two species found in the Northern Hemisphere also lack the dorsal fin. The mouth is very large, and the lower lip extends high above the jawbone. The rostrum is slender and decurved and is surrounded by the arched lower lip. The baleen plates are long (up to 14 feet or 4.25 metres), narrow, and flexible.

RIGHT WHALE
Baleine noire. *Balaena glacialis* Borowski

Description. The right whale is a large, thickset black whale with large, paddle-shaped pectoral flippers and with neither dorsal fin nor throat grooves. The head is large, comprising about a quarter of the body length. The thick lower lip extends upwards in a high medial bow on each side with a crenulated edge, and the slender decurved snout is snugly surrounded by it. At the tip of the snout is a large, oval rugose callosity, approximately one foot square, known as the 'bonnet.' Other smaller warty protuberances occur on the snout and lower lip and above the eyes. These callosities are usually infested with whale lice and acorn barnacles. The eyes are just above the corners of the mouth. Short white hairs are scattered along the snout and edge of the lower lip, particularly on the 'chin.' The blubber layer is unusually thick on these whales, often as much as 25 cm (10 inches) on the belly (Figure 63b).

In this species, the skull is marked by a long, slender, depressed rostrum and by bowed mandibles. The seven cervical vertebrae are fused; the vertebral column consists of fifty-five to fifty-seven units; and the flippers enclose five digits. The baleen plates are black, slender, and long (2.21 metres or 7.5 feet) with black shredded fibres, and number 228 to 259 on each side of the long, slender palate.

Right whales are usually completely black, but irregular white splashes are found on the bellies of about 10 per cent of the population.

The average length of adult males is 13.7 (10.9–14.6) metres or 45 (36–48) feet and of adult females 14.0 (9.5–16.5) metres or 46 (31–54) feet. The females are usually a little larger than the males but seldom exceed 54 feet (16.5 metres) in length. The average weight is 23 metric tons for females and 22 for males.

Habits. Formerly these whales were gregarious in nature and were found in gams of up to a hundred or more individuals. They are usually rather tame and are easily approached. They are quite sportive and often roll in the water, waving a giant flipper, lobtailing, or breeching. They are slow swimmers, averaging about four knots.

When diving, right whales arch their backs and expose their flukes. As a rule they remain submerged ten to twenty minutes; then they surface and blow five or six times. The spout, which is double and slanted forward, sends a v-shaped spray, which may reach fifteen feet in height on a calm day.

Right whales are migratory: they spend the summer months in cool temperate waters and then travel to subtropical waters in the winter months. The migrations of the northern and southern hemispheres are naturally six months out of phase. The stocks of the western Atlantic formerly wintered from November to March in considerable numbers from Cape Cod to the southern tip of Florida, Bermuda, and the Gulf of Mexico. Those of the eastern Atlantic wintered in the Bay of Biscay. On the Pacific coast of America they wintered from Vancouver Island to Oregon and occasionally to California waters.

The spring migration passed the New England States from late March to mid-May, and the whales travelled northward to the Gulf of St Lawrence, Newfoundland, the Labrador coast, and southwest Greenland. The European stocks travelled northward to the Orkney and Shetland islands, Iceland, and the North Cape in Norway during a brief six-week summer period. The northern Pacific stocks frequented the waters about the Aleutian Islands and Kamchatka and of the Bering and Okhotsk seas.

Their food consists of krill and other pelagic crustaceans such as copepods. There is some evidence that herrings are also eaten.

Apart from man, the killer whale is the only predator.

Habitat. Right whales frequent coastal temperate seas.

Reproduction. Mating occurs regularly in December and January (atypically in July). The gestation period is eleven to twelve months in duration. The calves are 5 to 6 metres (16–20 feet) long at birth and are nursed until they are six to seven months old. The young whales reach puberty at a length of 14 to 15 metres (42.5–45.5 feet).

Economic Status. Commercial whaling began with the exploitation of this species. It produced high yields of whalebone and oil and had additional advantages: it was unwary, it was a slow swimmer, and its body floated after death. The European industry, which was well established by the twelfth century, started with Spanish Basque fishermen along the Bay of Biscay. These fishermen harvested 700 to 1,000 whales a year, until the stock of 'Biscayne' whales was depleted towards the end of the fifteenth century. Then, in the sixteenth century, the Basque fishermen pursued their quarry across the seas to Newfoundland waters as well as to Spitsbergen and Iceland. The Norwegians took up the hunt off their coast, where this whale became known as the 'Nordkaper.' Right whales were commonly distributed off the New England coast during the seventeenth century and were cited as one of the main resources of the coast by early New England settlers. They hunted the whales in small boats from the harbours, but by 1670 the coast was deserted by the whales and the whalers were forced to build larger whaling ships to pursue the whales at sea and in the Gulf of St Lawrence.

During the nineteenth century the southern right whales were exploited, and between 1804 and 1817 right whales numbering 193,522 were killed in southern waters. The stock could not stand this pressure, and the catch dropped to 397 off South Georgia between 1909 and 1918. Between 1920 and 1927, only four right whales were captured off the southern coast of Africa. During the height of the southern pelagic whaling industry in the 1933–34 season, almost 40,000 whales were captured, of which two were right whales. In the same year, two were killed off the Alaskan coast.

The end of the right whale commercial hunt in the North Atlantic Ocean was reached off the Orkney and Shetland Islands between 1899 and 1908, when Norwegian whalers took the last sizable catch.

The species has been harried to the point of extinction,

Map 127 Distribution of the right whale, *Balaena glacialis*:
1 *B. g. glacialis*, 2 *B. g. japonica*

The bowhead or Greenland whale is larger than the right whale and may attain a maximum length of 65 feet. It resembles a monstrous tadpole with an enormous head, which is a third the body length, and with a chunky cylindrical body tapering from the flipper region to the tail stock. The great mouth, 15 to 20 feet long, with lips 5 to 6 feet high, forms a trough from the front, cradling the narrow depressed snout inside the arched lower lip. The lips and snout bear irregular rows of short white bristles but lack the bonnet and protuberances of the right whale, as well as the crenulations on the lower lip. The ox-sized eyes are situated about a foot above the corners of the lips. The near-by ear canals are of the diameter of a goose quill. The pectoral flippers are blunt and thickset; the caudal flukes measure 18 to 26 feet from tip to tip (Figure 63c).

The skull has a broad, heavy cranium, bowed mandibles, and a long, slender bowed rostrum. The cervical vertebrae are fused. The baleen plates are exceedingly long and narrow (9 to 10 feet on the average, but up to a maximum of 14 feet or 4.3 metres in length). These blue-black plates carry shredded filaments at the tip and on the external side. There are approximately 360 plates to a side, and the longest ones are in the middle of the mouth. These formed the 'whalebone' of nineteenth-century commerce used in ladies' corsets and hoop skirts, and in sofas and carriage springs.

The colour of this species is mainly blue-black over most of the body, except for irregular creamy blotches on the lower jaw, white flashes on the belly, and a pale grey area on the tail stock. The layer of blubber is very thick, up to 18 inches.

Few measurements of actual specimens are available. The females are known to attain a larger size than the males. Although the largest authentic specimen from Pond Inlet, Baffin Island, measured 65 feet (20 metres) in total length along the belly, from snout to notch in the flukes, a more normal maximum length is 58 feet (17.5 metres).

Habits. These whales are gregarious, feeding in small groups of three or four individuals, but often in their heyday gathering in large gams of several hundred whales during migration. They are usually timid and sluggish in behaviour, but when attacked females defend their calves with determination. Since they often sleep on the surface of the water, they are easily killed when so discovered. Bowhead whales are less active than right whales. They swim slowly at speeds of two to four knots and sound for periods of up to thirty minutes. After surfacing, they 'blow' five or six times, the spout being similar to the right whale's. When sounding they lift their flukes clear out of the water.

This species is migratory, travelling northward in early spring after the retreating ice front and again southward in early winter ahead of freeze-up.

The food consists of crustacean krill. The whale usually feeds near the surface, opening its cavernous mouth by dropping the lower jaw to form a scoop. Then it closes its mouth, raises its great tongue, and strains the water through the baleen plates and lips, trapping the small crustaceans on the shredded internal filaments.

but, fortunately, today, under full protection, a few right whales are reappearing in their old haunts.

Distribution. Formerly cosmopolitan in the cooler seas, but absent in tropical waters between about latitudes 25°N and 30°S. Now very rare.

Canadian Distribution. Formerly common along our Atlantic and Pacific coasts in summer and during migrations. Now only occasional records occur. A 35- to 40-foot right whale was stranded at Pugwash, Nova Scotia, in October 1954 (see Map 127). A 41-foot male was taken off the coast of Vancouver Island in May 1951.

Two subspecies occur off our coasts:

Balaena glacialis glacialis Borowski, 1781, Gemeinnüzzige Naturgeschichte des Thierreichs ..., 2(1): 18.
Balaena glacialis japonica Lacépède, 1818, Mém. Mus. Hist. Nat. Paris 4: 473. A larger race, found in the North Pacific Ocean, which may reach a weight of 100 tons at a length of 17 metres.

REFERENCE

Allen, J.A. 1908. The North Atlantic right whale and its near allies. Bull. American Mus. Nat. Hist. 24, art 18: 277–329.

BOWHEAD WHALE
Baleine boréale. *Balaena mysticetus* Linnaeus

Description. So similar is this species to the right whale that for many years it was uncertain whether one or two species of right whale existed. The bowhead was one of the first resources of our arctic regions to be exploited by Europeans.

Physical maturity is reached for both sexes at an approximate length of 51 feet (15.5 metres).

The bowhead whale also differs from the right whale in the general scarcity of external parasites such as barnacles and whale lice. It is preyed upon by the killer whale, and it will enter narrow leads between ice-floes to evade it.

Habitat. This species, which inhabits the icy Arctic Ocean, is seldom found far from ice-floes. It penetrates farther north than any other whale with the possible exception of the narwhal. When it migrates south to its winter range, it occupies the northern distribution of the right whale and several species of rorquals. On its summer range it frequents bays, straits, and estuaries.

Reproduction. Practically nothing is known of the reproduction of this species. Mating is reported for February to March or June to July. The gestation period may be ten or twelve months in duration. The calves are reported to be born in March and April in the Labrador Sea and during May in Chukchi Sea. Usually a single calf, measuring 13 feet (4 metres), is born, but occasionally twins occur. Because of the long nursing period, which lasts twelve months, the English whalers called the young 'suckers.'

Economic Status. The hunt for bowhead whales began in 1611 in the waters surrounding Spitsbergen, where Basque fishermen searched for right whales, and continued until the whales declined in about 1720. In the meantime Henry Hudson had reported seeing whales in the western Atlantic, and the Dutch began whaling operations in 1719 in Davis Strait, off the southwest coast of Greenland. As a result of reports of the abundance of whales in Baffin Bay between 1818 and 1824, by the British explorers Ross and Parry, a British whaling fleet was outfitted from the British ports of Hull, Dundee, Kirkcaldy, Peterhead, Fraserbugh, and Aberdeen to pursue the whale. By 1868 this fleet included thirty steam and sailing vessels, but by 1904 it had declined to six steam vessels, and the last voyage took place in 1912. American whalers first entered eastern Canadian arctic waters in sailing vessels in 1846, but they transferred to the Pacific after 1870. The first American whaling ships passed through Bering Strait in 1848 to hunt in the Chukchi and Beaufort seas. They ventured farther eastward until in 1888 the first vessel wintered at Herschel Island, off the Yukon coast. Fifteen vessels and eight hundred men spent the winter of 1894–95 at Herschel Island, and other ships wintered as far east as Langdon Bay. The peak year was 1893, when 309 bowhead whales were taken in the Beaufort and Chukchi seas. The average take for a two-year cruise was about sixty-five whales. The hunt in these waters was terminated in 1912, however, because of the collapse of the whalebone market. These northern whalers had confined their harvest to the whalebone and had not bothered about whale oil.

The Scottish whalers in Baffin Bay usually returned to port each winter, but the American whalers wintered-over in the Arctic. In return for the Eskimo collection of whalebone and furs, the whalers supplied the Eskimos with small whale boats and hunting gear. The Eskimos became dependent upon the whalers for supplies of food, utensils, and weapons, and the departure of the whalers in 1912 was a severe economic blow to the coastal Eskimos of the Canadian Arctic. The Eskimos have continued to take a small harvest of whales in the Arctic using umiaks, whale boats, hand harpoons, and rifles. The boiled 'black-skin' is considered a delicacy; the flesh is used for dog food, the oil for fuel, and the bone for implements. Bowhead whales were traditionally hunted by the Eskimos of Tigara and Point Barrow. The annual catch of Alaskan Eskimos is ten to fifteen whales per season, but the Canadian Eskimo catch is much smaller. Pond Inlet and Southampton Island are two areas of native whaling in the Canadian Arctic. The bowhead whales have been protected from modern whaling operations since 1937, and are now slowly recovering from the verge of extinction in arctic regions.

Distribution. Bowheads are confined to arctic and sub-arctic regions from Spitsbergen to Wrangell Island, Siberia. Originally they migrated past Jan Mayen Island between late March and the end of April and reached Spitsbergen between mid-May and the end of June. After tarrying in the bays of Spitsbergen they moved northwestward to the region of permanent ice during the summer. August and early September found them moving southward again, down the east coast of Greenland.

Canadian Distribution. In Canadian eastern arctic waters they entered Hudson Strait in April and travelled westward to northern Hudson Bay. In June and July they congregated along the floe-edge from Marble Island northward to Roes Welcome Sound and Frozen Strait. As the summer progressed, they followed the melting ice northward into Foxe Basin. In late autumn they migrated eastward through Hudson Strait.

Other whales first appeared in Davis Strait off frozen Frobisher Bay in March. Later they crossed over to the southwest Greenland coast and followed the warm northward current to Melville Bay, which was reached in early summer. They then recrossed westward to Smith, Jones, and Lancaster sounds during July and August. Pond Inlet on northern Baffin Island was a favourite late summer haunt. Afterwards they followed the ice-choked southern current down the east coast of Baffin Island to Cumberland Sound in October and remained along the edge of the new-formed ice, off the coast of southeastern Baffin Island, until early December, and then they vanished (see Map 128).

In former years, before the advent of Europeans, bowheads migrated in winter down the coast of Labrador through the Straits of Belle Isle and into the Gulf of St Lawrence. The discovery of a bowhead whale skull buried under six feet of sand at Ste Anne des Monts, Gaspé Peninsula, in May 1949 confirmed its former occurrence in this region. A few also wintered along the southwest coast of Greenland from Disco Bay to Holsteinborg. In the North Pacific region, these whales wintered off the Aleutian and Kurile islands and migrated northward from early April to mid-June. They passed Tigara and Point Barrow

Map 128 Distribution of the bowhead whale, *Balaena mysticetus*

and travelled as far east as Banks Island in midsummer. They migrated southward past Point Barrow again between late August and early November.

The species is known as:

Balaena mysticetus Linnaeus, 1758, Syst. Nat., 10th ed. 1: 75

REFERENCES

Brown, R. 1868. Notes on the history and geographical relations of the Cetacea frequenting Davis Strait and Baffin's Bay. Proc. Zool. Soc. London 1868: 533–56.

Low, A.P. 1906. Whaling. Chap. 10, pp. 248–82, *in* The cruise of the *Neptune*, 1903–1904. Govt. Printing Bureau, Ottawa.

Mansfield, A.W. 1971. Occurrence of the bowhead or Greenland right whale (*Balaena mysticetus*) in Canadian arctic waters. Jour. Fish. Res. Bd. Canada 28: 1873–5.

Order **Carnivora** / Carnivores

The mammals of this order, as their name indicates, are primarily flesh-eaters, although a few, such as the raccoon and the bear, have become, secondarily, omnivores. They vary in size from the mouse-sized weasel (*Mustela nivalis*) to the huge Alaskan brown bear (*Ursus arctos*). The trenchant characters of the group are found in their dentitions, which are indicative of their diet. Their incisors are small; their canines are long, conical, and recurved; their premolars are usually laterally compressed and blade-like; their rear molars are often rotated, 90 degrees or less, or are absent. The diagnostic feature is the enlargement of the fourth upper premolar and the lower first molar to act as a pair of shears in cutting meat and tendons. These are referred to as the carnassial teeth, which are highly developed in most carnivores but reduced in the raccoons and bears. The lower jaw articulates with the skull by means of a transverse condyle which fits snugly into a trough-shaped glenoid cavity, permitting only vertical movement.

The legs of carnivores are moderately long; the radius, ulna, tibia, and fibula are all distinct. The feet have four or five toes, tipped with sharp claws; the animals walk either on their toes (digitigrade) or on their heels (plantigrade).

The skulls are ruggedly constructed; the brains are large and convoluted; the senses are well developed.

ARTIFICIAL KEY TO FAMILIES OF CANADIAN CARNIVORA

I	Feet with five clawed digits.	2
2	Tail rudimentary.	URSIDAE
2'	Tail of average length.	3
3	Tail with alternating black and tan rings.	PROCYONIDAE
3'	Tail not annulated.	MUSTELIDAE
I'	Rudimentary clawed toe on forefoot, four toes on hind foot.	4
4	Sharp claws retractile.	FELIDAE
4'	Blunt claws not retractile.	CANIDAE

Family **Canidae** / Dogs

Wolves, dogs, and foxes form a group of cursorial predators. This means that they chase their prey and kill it by snapping and slashing. For this mode of attack they are admirably equipped: they have long legs, muscular bodies, long fluffy tails that act as balancing organs, long slender snouts, and an almost complete dentition with strong canines and carnassials. They are digitate and have strong non-retractile claws. They have five toes on the forefeet, but the pollex is high on the inside of the leg, and there are only four digits on the hind feet (Figure 64). The humerus lacks an epicondular foramen.

Members of this family are cosmopolitan, although it is thought that the Australian dingo was introduced by man. They all have a highly developed sense of smell and acute hearing. They are intelligent and social. Man has domesticated at least one of the group – the dog.

COYOTE
Coyote. *Canis latrans* Say

Description. The scientific name of the species means 'the barking dog'; this is particularly appropriate on the Canadian prairies where the coyote's nocturnal serenades are a characteristic of the true spirit of the land. The common name is of Spanish derivation from the original Aztec name *coyotl*.

The coyote is a medium-sized dog, very much like a small collie. It has a slender muzzle, a black nose pad less

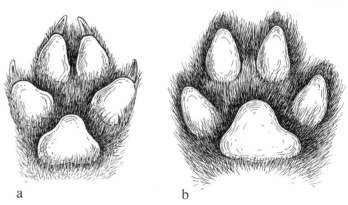

a   b

Figure 64 Comparison of hind feet of (a) a canid (*Canis lupus*) and (b) a felid (*Felis concolor*) (× 1/2)

286

than one inch in diameter, very large pointed ears, long slender legs, relatively small feet, and a tail slightly less than half the body length with a well-developed brush. A scent gland is situated on the back, above the base of the tail (Plate 22).

The coyote's canine teeth are relatively long and slender (about 1.5 inches). When the jaw is closed, the tips extend below the anterior mental foramina of the mandible.

The general colour of this species is a buffy grizzled grey. The muzzle, the outer side of the ears, the forelegs, and the feet are fulvous-coloured. The throat and belly are white. The underfur on the back is fulvous, but the long guard hairs are black-tipped, producing a prominent black dorsal stripe and grizzled flanks. The buffy tail is black-tipped. There is also a dark cross on the shoulders. Albino coyotes are rarely seen. There is one prolonged moult each spring: only slight loss of hair takes place in early March, but shedding is profuse in June and complete by July. The moult starts on the tail and progresses to the lower limbs, upper limbs, flanks, and back. The back and belly are the last areas to shed. The guard hairs drop before the underfur. The new summer coat, which is composed of short, harsh guard hairs, makes the animals appear much slenderer than in winter. The guard hairs and undercoat lengthen during August and September and produce the long, dense winter coat.

Males are larger than females. Adults measure approximately: length 120 (105–132), tail 35.0 (30.0–39.4), hind foot 18.0 (17.7–22.0) cm. The average weight of northern coyotes is about 13.2 kg (29 pounds). The maximum weight reported is 34 kg (75 pounds), but that particular specimen had a stomach full of sheep meat.

Habits. Coyotes are intelligent, but they are timid and suspicious in the presence of man. They are very social. The family pack, consisting of a mated pair and the pups, constitutes the basic social unit. Occasionally larger packs are seen, particularly in winter, but these are thought to include closely related individuals, such as members of previous litters. Both parents are involved in raising the young, and the dog, as well as standing guard, assumes the responsibility of bringing food to the den for the bitch and pups. The growing pups are very playful and romp and scuffle much like domestic pups. Even the adults show affection among themselves and occasionally high spirits, such as when they toss sticks about or carry bones in their mouths over long distances.

Their calls, which are so characteristic of the open prairies, consist of a quick series of yelps, followed by a falsetto howl. These are given usually in the evening, at night, or in the early morning. Often the pack sits in a circle and joins in uttering the shrill yip-yaps prior to a hunting excursion. They also whine and bark, like small dogs. They rely mainly on their acute hearing and sense of smell. Their sense of sight is less developed, and they use it primarily to note movement.

Coyotes trot lightly or run with their tails depressed. They can bound distances of up to fourteen feet. Their maximum speed lies somewhere between thirty-five and forty-three miles an hour. They also swim well. Though primarily nocturnal in activity, they are occasionally about during the mornings and late afternoons in remote regions.

Coyotes living in mountainous country undertake vertical seasonal migrations, travelling to the high country in summer and retreating to the valleys in winter.

Little information is available on home ranges and population densities. The packs maintain a hunting territory around the den, which may be as much as twelve miles in diameter, and usually travel along fixed routes or trails. There are indications that the bitch returns year after year to whelp in the same territory and may maintain it for life. However, others may travel far. Tagged coyotes have been recaptured as much as 400 miles from the original site.

Captives have lived fifteen years, but the normal life-span in the wild is probably much less.

Coyotes feed largely upon small mammals and carrion and to a lesser extent on birds, deer, antelope, insects, and vegetation. Based upon stomach analysis, their diet has been estimated to consist of approximately 33 per cent cottontails and hares, 25 per cent carrion, 18 per cent mice and ground squirrels, 4 per cent deer and antelope, 2 per cent nesting birds, 2 per cent vegetation, 1 per cent insects, and 14 per cent domestic mammals and birds. One cannot generalize about the diet of any particular coyote, however. Many live in areas where antelope and deer are lacking, and others live in areas that are remote from domestic stock and poultry.

It is very interesting to watch a coyote on a 'mousing' expedition. It stalks slowly and carefully through the grass, sniffing each clump and burrow. Eventually it stiffens and then suddenly pounces, its four legs held stiffly together, upon the hapless prey. The capture of an antelope or deer, on the other hand, calls for teamwork. For this the coyotes use every advantage, such as wind, topography, and crusted snow, to trap their quarry. They may take turns pursuing the deer to tire it, or they may drive it towards hidden members of the pack. For the coyote and the deer, however, the relationship between the prey and predator is so finely balanced that frequently a single coyote is chased and tormented by its expected prey. In Banff National Park I watched two doe mule deer try, unsuccessfully, to spear a lone coyote by jumping on it stiff-legged. The coyote managed to dodge between their legs and eventually made its escape. On another occasion I watched a coyote chase a ram mountain sheep across a slope towards a knoll of rocks. As soon as the ram reached the base of the rocks it wheeled around and drove the coyote back across the meadow it had just won.

The coyote also pursues the bobcat and the fox with great glee. The bobcat usually quickly 'trees,' but the fox appears to be more agile, managing usually to elude the coyote and gain its burrow. Occasionally the coyote receives the worst of an encounter with a porcupine and gets its jaws filled with quills.

The coyote, in turn, must be on the alert for a number of larger predators such as the wolf, the cougar, the black

Map 129 Distribution of the coyote, *Canis latrans*: 1 *C. l. incolatus*, 2 *C. l. latrans*, 3 *C. l. lestis*, 4 *C. l. thamnos*

bear, and the grizzly bear. Even the golden eagle has been known to attack a young coyote. A unique relationship exists between the coyote and the American badger, *Taxidea taxus*. One has occasionally been known to follow a hunting badger and station itself at one of the exits to a ground squirrel burrow which the badger is in the process of digging out, and to pounce on any animal (be it a ground squirrel, pocket gopher, kangaroo rat, mouse, or wood rat) that attempts to escape. It is not clear how the badger benefits from this relationship, yet badgers have been observed following coyotes. Perhaps the badger is aggressive enough to drive the coyote off its prey; it could certainly never catch a coyote if it decided to run off with the prey.

Habitat. The coyote is an adaptable animal, which occupies alpine tundra, boreal forests, aspen parklands, and short-grass steppes. It appears to prefer hilly country with poplar 'bluffs' and willow-lined stream banks. It is one of the few native mammals that have been able to adjust to human settlement and to thrive in the vicinity of farms and towns. When I lived in Banff, it was a regular occurrence

to see coyotes tripping down the residential streets on their dawn patrol of the garbage cans.

Reproduction. Unlike the domestic dog, the coyote bitch is monoestrous, coming into heat for a period of four or five days between late January and late March. The dog is similarly sexually active only during a three- or four-month period in early spring. The same couple may remain paired for a number of years, but not necessarily for life, although with man's toll on coyotes this often turns out to be the case. The gestation period is sixty to sixty-three days. The litter is born in late April or early May, the average litter size being 5.7 (1–19). Since the female possesses only eight teats, there is little chance for large numbers of young to survive.

The litter is born in a burrow, which the bitch digs with her forepaws. Usually she enlarges a marmot or badger burrow. The entrance may be concealed by a stump, log, or bush, but the fresh pile of earth and abundant tracks usually are a giveaway to the occupied den. The den may have a second escape entrance, or there may be other burrows close by to provide shelter should the natal den be

288

discovered. The burrows are usually six to nine feet in length, and the den is about three feet underground. Bedding is scarce or lacking. Rarely two litters of different ages have been found in a single den. Their mothers might belong to the same pack, or one litter might be adopted and sheltered after their den has been molested.

The whelps are sleek, blind, pug-nosed, limp-eared, and helpless at birth. Their puppy coats are dark grey-brown and woolly, with a black dorsal stripe. The adult pelage is not assumed until four weeks of age. The eyes open and the ears perk up some time after nine days of age. One pup weighed 1 pound 5 ounces (600 g) at ten days of age. Pups appear at the den entrance when they are about three weeks old and are weaned between five and eight weeks of age. They are then fed regurgitated food by their parents. Soon after they are two months old, they leave the den and travel short distances with their parents.

Juvenile coyotes are fully grown at one year but do not reach sexual maturity until just prior to their second birthday.

Economic Status. Because of their predilection for small game, including lambs, calves, and poultry, coyotes came into direct competition with poultry and stock-raising during the early development of western agriculture. Bounties were placed on their heads in the United States in 1825, only two years after the species had first been described for science. In many areas bounties are still paid (usually $10 per animal), but in other areas a reaction to this persecution has set in, and coyotes are protected because of their toll on hares, ground squirrels, prairie dogs, and mice, which are all agricultural pests. Over the years, man has employed a variety of devices against the coyote, including bounties, strychnine, '1080,' coyote-getters, snares, and steel traps, but the coyote still flourishes and has even expanded its range. Although control programs may be warranted in areas of concentrated stock-raising, it is to be hoped that this species will be permitted to survive in wilderness areas.

Coyote fur is frequently used for trimming parkas, and the price received for a pelt has been as high as $17. In 1922 as many as 12,000 were taken for their fur in Saskatchewan alone, and during the 1971–72 fur season 46,500 pelts were taken across Canada at an average price of $15.64 each, for a total value of $727,258.

These wild dogs also constitute a public health menace of some significance because they are important wildlife reservoirs of rabies. In a serious outbreak of rabies in western Canada in 1951–63, coyotes constituted an important source of infection for domestic animals. They also harbour the adult stage of a tapeworm, *Echinococcus granulosus*, which normally progresses through its larval stage in a big game species such as deer, although humans may become infected with the 'hydatid' larvae through contact with coyote or wolf faeces.

Coyote pups, taken at an early age from the den, make interesting pets. They are, however, always suspicious of strangers and tend to become rather snappy as they grow older. They will mate with domestic dogs and produce fertile hybrids. It was thought at one time that some of the small domesticated dogs of the Plains Indians were derived from wild coyotes, but it seems more likely that the Indians brought their dogs with them when they immigrated to North America.

Distribution. Coyotes were originally found in western North America from central Mexico northward to the central Prairie Provinces. During the sixteenth century, after the Spanish invasion and the introduction of livestock, they expanded their range southward to include most of western Central America.

Canadian Distribution. Between 1829 and 1907 coyotes extended their distribution northward from the fifty-fifth parallel of latitude to embrace southern Alaska, Yukon Territory, and Mackenzie District. After 1907 the northward movement continued until by 1931 they had reached the Mackenzie River delta, northern Yukon Territory, and most of Alaska. About the same time, coyotes started to move eastward across northern Ontario, and between 1918 and 1948 they occupied all of central and southern Ontario and western Quebec. From the St Lawrence valley they spread into New York and the New England States.

Four subspecies are currently recognized in Canada (see Map 129).

Canis latrans incolatus Hall, 1934, Univ. California Publ. Zool. 40: 369. A large cinnamon-coloured race with little black showing, found in Yukon Territory, Mackenzie District, and northern British Columbia and Alberta.

Canis latrans latrans Say, 1823, *in* Long, An account of an expedition to the Rocky Mountains ..., 1: 168. The typical form, found on the prairies and parkland of southern Alberta and Saskatchewan.

Canis latrans lestis Merriam, 1897, Proc. Biol. Soc. Washington 11: 25. A dark grey race, found in southern British Columbia and the southern Rocky Mountain region of Alberta.

Canis latrans thamnos Jackson, 1949, Proc. Biol. Soc. Washington 62: 31. A large grizzled brown race, found from the eastern Saskatchewan border to western Quebec.

REFERENCES

Dobie, J. Frank. 1949. The voice of the coyote. Little Brown, Boston.
Young, S.P., and H.H.T. Jackson. 1951. The clever coyote. Stackpole Company, Harrisburg, Pa., and Wildlife Management Institute, Washington.

WOLF
Loup. *Canis lupus* Linnaeus

Description. For many millennia the wolf as a competitor was intimately associated with the northern races of man. This relationship continued down to recent years on our frontiers. It is still difficult to view the animal objectively, and most of our opinions are unconsciously influenced by superstitions and folklore such as is found in the story of *Little Red Riding Hood*.

Although the wolf is similar in appearance to a large German shepherd or a husky sled dog, it is lankier and has longer legs, larger feet, and a narrower chest. Its face is larger and less pointed than that of a coyote; its black muzzle is more than 1¼ inches in diameter, and its ears are more rounded. Its tail is long, bushy, and black-tipped (Plate 24).

The wolf has a large, heavily constructed skull, large teeth with widely spaced premolars, and relatively shorter and thicker canines than the coyote. When the lower jaw is in place, the tips of the canines do not project below the mental foramina of the mandible (Figure 65).

This species has a dorsal tail gland covered with bristly hair, and the pollex is high on the inside of the foreleg.

The colour of wolves is extremely variable: from snow white to coal black, and all intermediate degrees of cream, grey, brown, and orangy black. Grizzled grey individuals predominate. Differently coloured pups may occur in the same litter, and there is no geographical uniformity of colour, although white wolves predominate in the arctic regions. The coat is composed of long, coarse guard hairs and short, soft underfur. The naked foot pads of northern wolves are protected by stiff tufts of hair, which grow between the pads in winter.

The wolf has one protracted annual moult in late spring. The new, short summer pelage grows into the long, silky winter coat. The underfur grows during the autumn.

Male wolves are noticeably larger than females. Unfortunately a good series of measurements is lacking. The total length may vary from 150 to 205, the tail from 36 to 50, and the hind foot from 22 to 32 cm. A large male wolf may measure slightly over 6 feet in total length and stand almost 3 feet high at the shoulders. Wolf skins may, however, be stretched to a length of 8 feet. Adult wolves weigh between 26 and 79 kg (57–175 pounds) – the specimen of maximum weight unfortunately included a full stomach of sheep meat! The largest wolves are found in northwestern Canada, and the smallest ones in the arctic islands.

Habits. The wolf is often described by using subjective anthropomorphic terms, such as villainous, cowardly, cruel, vicious. In contrast, the domesticated wolf, or dog, is described as 'man's best friend,' loyal, brave, friendly, playful. Actually the wild wolf possesses all the behavioural characteristics of its domestic relative with the possible exception of the trait of fawning for man's favours. The wolf still maintains its independent aloofness towards man. It has extremely complex social instincts. The family pack, composed of parents, whelps, and close relatives, is the social unit. Within the pack there is a social hierarchy. The leader is usually the largest and strongest dog, followed by younger or senile males, then the mate of the dominant dog, other females, and finally the pups in order of strength. The usual pack numbers between four and seven individuals but may include anywhere from two to fourteen. All members of the pack accept considerable responsibility for the education, protection, and feeding of the pups. The father brings food to the nursing female and later to the young. If the mother is killed, the father will look after the young as well as possible, and if they are still nursing, another mother may adopt them. The extra wolves, which may be uncles, aunts, or grandparents, take turns in 'babysitting' for the puppies while the parents are away hunting. The adults show a considerable amount of mutual respect and affection. There is much tail-wagging, caressing, romping, and occasionally tricks, ruses, and friendly brawls; but strangers are usually driven off, except in winter when several packs may unite to hunt.

Wolves possess a very keen sense of smell and acute hearing. Their eyesight is less keen, so that from a distance they can see objects moving but they cannot tell what they are. This fact was well illustrated by a personal incident which occurred on the arctic tundra. From our tent I watched my companion walking along an esker towards our camp. I noticed a single wolf quartering across the esker about a quarter of a mile upwind. The wolf suddenly stopped when it saw my companion on the crest, and then it commenced a deliberate stalk toward him bounding from rock to rock. When it reached a distance of about a hundred yards, it crouched and started to crawl towards him with its belly pressed close to the ground. My companion changed his direction slightly to head straight for the tent. About that time I decided to reach for my rifle and take part in the episode. As I glanced up again, my companion picked up a rock to defend himself. The wolf approached stealthily to within twenty yards, at which point it crossed his trail. It suddenly leaped up, stared at him momentarily, and then bounded off – a clear case of mistaken identity. It had not been able to identify the moving object until it caught the scent. Many of the instances where wolves have stalked man are, I believe, the results of misidentification or curiosity before the scent of the object has been caught.

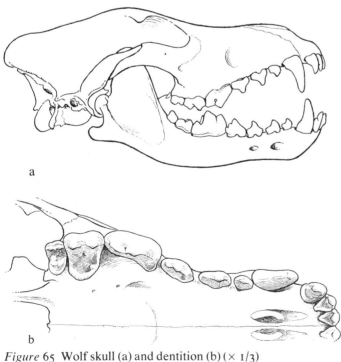

Figure 65 Wolf skull (a) and dentition (b) (× 1/3)

The wolf's howl – a long, gutteral, quavering wail – has been described as the most dismal sound ever heard by human ears. In spite of the veneer of modern civilization, even the most seasoned woodsman may pause when he hears the call and speculate on its proximity and meaning. To voice various emotions wolves also bark, yelp, whine, and snarl.

Wolves trot or run with a lumbering, bounding gait, tail streaming behind or slightly elevated. They may attain a speed of twenty-eight miles per hour over a short distance, or twenty-two to twenty-four over a mile or two. The endurance of the wolf is remarkable. One trapped near Île à la Crosse, Saskatchewan, escaped with the trap and toggle attached to its front foot. It was finally killed a month later near Green Lake, about ninety miles away, with the trap and toggle still attached. During the nineteenth century, Plains Indians used to run down wolves for sport. In 1865, Thomas Kessik ran one down between Fort Pelly and the Touchwood Hills, Saskatchewan (a distance of nearly a hundred miles), finally falling exhausted on the wolf and managing to kill it with his knife.

Wolves use dens during the breeding season in a variety of locations, such as under a shelf of rock or in a cave, a hollow log, an abandoned beaver lodge, or an enlarged badger or fox den. The dens are usually located on a promontory near water. The bank burrow, consisting of an enlarged former badger, fox, or marmot burrow, is most common. A large pile of fresh sand usually discloses the entrance, which is broader than high (about 20 by 26 inches). The tunnel may be between six and thirty feet in length. The natal chamber at the end of the tunnel is dry and hard-packed. Above the den are the beds where the adults may lie and keep watch over the valley below. There are usually other dens or funk holes near by. In early spring wolves may have to dig a snow tunnel to the den entrance.

Wolves often use winter shelters under the roots of fallen trees. I found a most interesting winter den in Banff National Park in a tangle of windthrown trees with a large wapiti hide draped over the roof and entrance.

The wolf pack occupies a fixed home range around the den, which may be, at least during the summer months, anywhere from 100 to 260 square miles in area. Over this area the pack usually travels along fixed runways, which follow game trails, logging roads, rivers, lakes, and portages. Wolves are one of the few species of northern animals that will cross large frozen lakes in winter. Their runways are well marked with urination posts, by which the pack not only lays claim to the route but also keeps track of interlopers. In Prince Albert National Park, Saskatchewan, I found runways varying from twenty-seven to eighty-seven miles in length. The shorter routes were in areas supporting the denser populations of big game. The packs often patrol these routes at regular intervals of about a week. In other studies wolf movements are reported as being more irregular. The pack may split up to hunt but rejoin again at a later date.

Some individuals undertake longer emigrations. A wolf pup ear-tagged in Banff National Park, Alberta, was later taken in Jasper National Park, 162 miles away.

The density of wolves in wilderness areas varies considerably, depending on the density of big game. In Prince Albert National Park it was approximately one wolf to 40 to 80 square miles. On concentrated winter game ranges in Jasper National Park, containing an estimated 300 to 400 head of big game, it was about one wolf to 10 square miles between 1947 and 1951.

Wolves undertake seasonal migrations in certain parts of their distribution. They follow the game down to the valleys in winter from high summer pastures in the Rocky Mountains. In northern Canada bands of 'arctic' wolves follow migrating caribou herds to distances of 500 miles from the tundra in summer to the boreal forest in winter. In the foothills and forests of central Canada they are more static in distribution.

Over much of northern Canada the wolf is the arch-predator as the lion is in Africa. The grizzly, the polar bear, and the mountain lion, though stronger individually, will give way before a pack of wolves. Wolves are primarily hunters of big game. This item formed 80 per cent of the diet in Jasper National Park and 68 per cent in Mount McKinley National Park, Alaska. It includes moose, caribou, wapiti, mule deer, white-tailed deer, mountain sheep, bison, and muskoxen (to a limited extent), depending on the availability of the various species in the wolves' territory. (White-tailed deer formed 90 per cent of the diet in an eastern study.) Small game, such as rabbits, hares, marmots, ground squirrels, beavers, muskrats, and mice, also constitute an important item of diet varying from about 18 per cent in Jasper Park to 32 per cent in Mount McKinley Park. Ground-nesting birds, fish, berries, fruit, insects, and grass form incidental items in the diet. Wolves do not relish carrion as much as coyotes do. They will often return to their own kills and clean up the carcasses, but they seldom touch other carcasses unless driven to eat them by starvation. In agricultural areas they will kill domestic stock, such as cattle, sheep, pigs, poultry, and occasionally horses. In Jasper National Park horses which were allowed to range freely in winter in isolated valleys were seldom molested by local packs of wolves, which were feeding on wapiti and deer, but horses on open ranges, particularly in the Yukon Territory, have been killed by wolves.

Wolves are not particularly fast, and all their regular prey species can outrun them in a straight race. They therefore have to resort to cunning to obtain the advantage over their prey. They may course over their territory with the pack extended in line and outflank their quarry, or they may take turns in chasing their prey in order to tire it, but more often the pack splits up, and part of it circles around the quarry to drive it towards others that lie in wait. At other times environmental conditions such as swamps, glazed ice, or crusted snow give the wolves the advantage over the long-legged ungulates. In mountainous terrain wolves often chase their prey down steep hillsides, causing the quarry to stumble and fall. Even a single adult wolf can pull down the largest bull moose under the ideal conditions of deep, crusted snow.

Occasionally lone game animals are able to stand off a pack of wolves when the advantage is on their side. Ungulates usually head for water when pursued in summer. If they reach it, they are more or less safe because the short-legged wolves are at a disadvantage if the water is over three feet in depth. In winter, however, the water may be a trap for the prey; for if they are winded, they may collapse in the freezing water; or if the lake has been freshly frozen with clear ice, the ungulates may skate about on their hooves, while the wolves obtain better traction from their furry pads. In mountainous areas bighorn sheep, mountain goats, and wapiti find relative sanctuary on steep, rocky walls, and moose occasionally beat off their adversaries when they can protect the flank and rear by means of a rock or an overthrown tree. It has often been stated that wolves always hamstring their prey, but this seems to be uncommon. Usually they grab at the nose, or throat, or slash at the abdomen or tail end.

After the pack has killed a large animal and initially fed upon it, it may cache the remaining meat in the snow or in a hollow log or stump. If there are pups in the den, the wolves will carry food back and cache it near the den. If food is plentiful and is easily obtained, they may eat only the choice parts and leave the carcass to be cleaned up by the lesser predators such as coyotes, wolverines, martens, and weasels. Ravens, eagles, crows, jays, and chickadees also feed on wolf kills. It has been estimated that a single wolf kills between one and one and a half large animals each month.

Some people believe that wolves prey only upon the fattest animals, but quantitative studies indicate that they prey primarily upon calves and aged and sick animals, that is, upon the animals that are most easily caught. This fact has been proved for Dall sheep, bighorn sheep, caribou, moose, and bison, but is less clearly indicated for wapiti and deer. Wolves therefore tend to cull the herds of big game in their territory by removing the aged, sickly, and unwary adults, along with the very young when they are unprotected.

Wolves show a marked hostility towards mountain lions, bears, and coyotes, particularly in the vicinity of their dens. The mountain lions usually quickly 'tree' when rushed by wolves. The bears defend themselves quite effectively and retire from the scene. The wolves show no inclination for close combat with grizzly, black, or polar bears. Wolves also pursue coyotes, which fortunately can dodge quicker and run faster. However, I have observed signs in the snow in Prince Albert Park which indicated where a pack of wolves caught and ate a coyote on a frozen pond. It should also be mentioned that packs also kill and sometimes eat lone wolves entering their territory.

It will be noted that the wolf population is not controlled by natural predation. The population does not, however, increase quickly. Other factors, such as starvation and disease, are important checks, as are rabies, distemper, and sarcoptic mange. In normal wolf populations, the proportion of pups is usually small, but when the population is subjected to intensified control programs, the ratio of pups rises significantly, indicating that a previous factor limiting the population was operative.

The longevity record for a wolf in captivity is eighteen years.

Habitat. Wolves show little preference for special habitats. They are found on the arctic tundra, on mountain-tops, and on plains, as well as in coniferous and eastern deciduous forests.

Reproduction. Female wolves are monoestrous. The oestrous period lasts for about a month in late winter, but the bitches are in heat for only the last five days of the period. The peak of the mating season extends from about late February to mid-March. This is the 'Mad Moon,' a very active period in the wolves' calendar. At this period they are very vociferous and are socially inclined. Wolves are reported to mate for life. The gestation period is between sixty and sixty-three days. The pups are born in early May in Canada, but the reproductive period is earlier farther south (March 10 to April 1 in Arizona). The average litter size is seven (5–14). The female possesses eight teats in two rows. The whelps are sooty blue at birth, sleek, blind, and pug-nosed, and have floppy ears. Between five and nine days of age the eyes open, the ears become erect, and they stagger about the den. The puppy coat is woolly, and the first adult coat appears at an age of about a month. The pups are weaned when they are six to eight weeks old. When they are approximately three to four weeks old, they first appear above ground to gambol and wrestle at the den entrance. As they grow they become rougher in play. When they are about two months old, they are usually moved from the natal den to another summer den for reasons of sanitation or to be closer to better hunting opportunities. If the female is forced to move her pups while they are still young, she carries them individually in her mouth by the loose skin on their backs. After they have been weaned, the adults feed them by disgorging meat from their kills. By late August or early September the pups join the adults in their first hunting lessons. Juvenile females becomes sexually mature at two years of age, but the males do not reach sexual maturity until the third year.

Wolves and dogs frecly interbreed. Eskimos and Indians occasionally stake out their bitches in heat so that they will be bred by wolves and produce larger and stronger sled dogs. These hybrid wolf-dogs tend to be suspicious and unreliable when they mature.

Economic Status. The hand of man has been against the wolf almost since the dawn of history, but this is not the universal picture. In some Indian cultures the wolf was considered as a sort of 'wild brother' and left alone.

The payment of a bounty on the scalp of the wolf is one of the earliest control methods, dating back to early Grecian times, about 600 B.C. Bounties have been paid on wolves for over 300 years in North America without any clear evidence that they have ever led to the elimination of the animal. In more recent years, the government-paid predatory animal hunter has been more effective in removing individual wolves that cause damage in agricultural

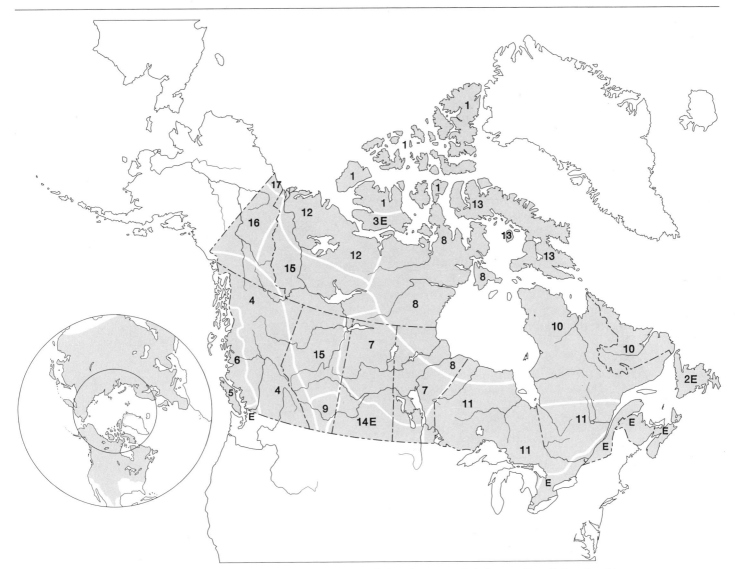

Map 130 Distribution of the wolf, *Canis lupus*: 1 *C. l. arctos*, 2 *C. l. beothucus*, 3 *C. l. bernardi*, 4 *C. l. columbianus*, 5 *C. l. crassodon*, 6 *C. l. fuscus*, 7 *C. l. griseoalbus*, 8 *C. l. hudsonicus*, 9 *C. l. irremotus*, 10 *C. l. labradorius*, 11 *C. l. lycaon*, 12 *C. l. mackenzii*, 13 *C. l. manningi*, 14 *C. l. nubilis*, 15 *C. l. occidentalis*, 16 *C. l. pambasileus*, 17 *C. l. tundrarum*, E extinct

areas where control measures are warranted. Traps and snares as well as cyanide-guns (coyote-getters) and strychnine pellets have been effectively used for the kill.

Before the advent of Europeans, Eskimos and Indians used such devices as deadfalls, pits, and snares to kill wolves. A clever device was invented by the Eskimos for the purpose, which was constructed by twisting a length of whale baleen into a coil and securing it with a piece of sinew. This was then dipped in fat, moulded into a ball, and placed near a wolf kill. After the wolf had eaten and digested it, the baleen coil sprang open and pierced the wolf's gut, causing peritonitis and death.

Wolves have long constituted a reservoir of sylvatic rabies in North America. Indians and early western explorers dreaded rabid wolves, which entered their encampments and bit people and dogs alike, often resulting in the death of the victims. They also constitute a public health menace by harbouring the tapeworm *Echinococcus*

granulosus, which may cause hydatid disease among humans through contact with wolf faeces.

Although wolves are generally thought to attack people, authentic cases in North America are extremely rare (far fewer than attacks by bulls, for instance). Many so-called attacks are merely cases of curiosity or mistaken identity, as explained previously. There is, however, one authentic attack, which took place near Poulin in northern Ontario on December 29, 1942. At about 8:15 in the morning, a railway section man, who was travelling at about ten miles an hour on a speeder to inspect the tracks, was attacked by a wolf, which jumped on him. The force of the impact knocked him and the gasoline speeder off the track. He reached for an axe and defended himself until a freight train came along and the crew jumped off and killed the wolf. Since that was before the outbreak of rabies among wolves in the north in 1947–53, rabies was not suspected and no tests were made.

Wolves are important fur-bearers; during the 1971–72 season 3,804 were taken at an average price of $30.40, for a total value of $115,628.

Distribution. The wolf has a holarctic distribution. Originally it occurred in western Europe from Spain and Ireland through central and northern Asia to Japan, and formerly it occurred throughout North America from the Mexican plateau to northeast Greenland. Only coastal California and parts of the arid southwestern states were devoid of wolves.

Canadian Distribution. Wolves were once spread throughout Canada with the exception of the Queen Charlotte Islands. They have now been exterminated in large blocks of the southern parts of British Columbia, the Prairie Provinces, Ontario, Quebec, the Maritime Provinces, and Newfoundland.

North American wolves have been split into a large number of subspecies based upon slight differences in size, skull, and colour. Seventeen of these are currently recognized as occurring in Canada (see Map 130), but the number may be drastically reduced in future studies.

Canis lupus arctos Pocock, 1935, Proc. Zool. Soc. London, for 1935, part III: 682. A nearly pure white silky wolf, found on the Queen Elizabeth Islands of the Arctic Archipelago.

Canis lupus beothucus G.M. Allen and Barbour, 1937, Jour. Mamm. 18: 230. A large whitish subspecies, which formerly occurred on Newfoundland but was exterminated about 1913.

Canis lupus bernardi Anderson, 1943, Jour. Mamm. 24: 389. A large whitish race, originally found on Banks and Victoria islands, which may have been swamped by immigrants from the Queen Elizabeth Islands in recent years.

Canis lupus columbianus Goldman, 1941, Proc. Biol. Soc. Washington 54: 110. A large dark form, found in the southern Yukon Territory, central British Columbia, and the southern Rockies of Alberta.

Canis lupus crassodon Hall, Univ. California Pub. Zool. 38: 420. A medium-sized dark grey race limited to Vancouver Island.

Canis lupus fuscus Richardson, 1839, *in* The zoology of Captain Beechey's voyage in His Majesty's *Blossom* ..., p. 5. A small, dark cinnamon-coloured race, found in coastal British Columbia.

Canis lupus griseoalbus Baird, 1858, Mammals, *in* Repts. Expl. Surv. ... Rail. to Pacific, 8(1): 104. The form occurring in the north-central part of the Prairie Provinces.

Canis lupus hudsonicus Goldman, 1941, Proc. Biol. Soc. Washington 54: 112. A medium-sized whitish subspecies with certain distinctive cranial differences, found in northern Manitoba in winter and in Keewatin and eastern Mackenzie districts, Northwest Territories, in summer.

Canis lupus irremotus Goldman, 1937, Jour. Mamm. 18: 41. A large pale-coloured race, found on the southern plains of Alberta; now very rare.

COLOUR PLATE

30

Fisher, *Martes pennanti*

31

Black-footed ferret, *Mustela nigripes*

Canis lupus labradorius Goldman, 1937, Jour. Mamm. 18: 38. A large light-coloured subspecies, found in Labrador and northern Quebec.

Canis lupus lycaon Schreber, 1775, Die Säugethiere ..., Theil 2, Heft 13, pl. 89. A small dark subspecies that inhabited all of southeastern Canada. It has been exterminated in southern Quebec south of the St Lawrence River and in New Brunswick since about 1880, and in Nova Scotia prior to 1900. There appears to be no reference to wolves on Prince Edward Island.

Canis lupus mackenzii Anderson, 1943, Jour. Mamm. 24: 388. A small race, found in the northern Mackenzie District, Northwest Territories.

Canis lupus manningi Anderson, 1943, Jour. Mamm. 24: 392. A small race, found on Baffin Island.

Canis lupus nubilis Say, 1823, *in* Long, An account of an expedition ... to the Rocky Mountains ...,1: 169. The 'buffalo' wolf that formerly followed the herds of buffalo across the great plains of southern Manitoba and Saskatchewan; now possibly extinct.

Canis lupus occidentalis Richardson, 1829, Fauna Boreali-Americana 1: 60. A large form in which the black colour phase occurs commonly, found in southern Mackenzie District and northern Alberta.

Canis lupus pambasileus Elliot, 1905, Proc. Biol. Soc. Washington 18: 79. A very large, frequently dark-coloured wolf that occurs in central Alaska and Yukon Territory.

Canis lupus tundrarum Miller, 1912, Smiths. Misc. Coll. 59(15): 1. A whitish race, found on the arctic coast of Alaska and the Yukon Territory.

REFERENCES

Kuyt, E. 1972. Food habits of wolves on barren-ground caribou range in the Northwest Territories. Canadian Wildlife Serv., Rept. Ser. 21.

Mech, L. David. 1966. The wolves of Isle Royale. Nat. Parks Serv., Dept. Interior, Fauna Ser. 7, Washington.

Rutter, Russell J., and Douglas H. Pimlott. 1968. The world of the wolf. J.B. Lippincott, Philadelphia and New York.

Young, S.P., and E.A. Goldman. 1944. The wolves of North America. American Wildlife Institute, Washington.

ARCTIC FOX
Renard arctique. *Alopex lagopus* (Linnaeus)

Description. The arctic fox is about the size of a terrier. It has short legs, a round head, a blunt nose, and short, rounded ears. The soles of its feet are thickly furred. Its tail is approximately half the body length and forms a thick brush. When in its long, silky winter coat, the arctic fox looks much plumper than the red fox, but its long pelage is deceiving. The irises of its eyes are golden yellow (Plate 25).

The skull of the arctic fox is shorter and flatter than that of the genus *Vulpes*. The frontal region is elevated above the short rostrum. Sagittal and occipital crests are only slightly developed. The canines are short and weak, and so is the bite.

There are two winter colour phases: white and blue. The blue winter coat varies from almost blue-black to pearl grey. It fades considerably under the spring sunlight. There is a great variation in the ratio of blue to white foxes in various populations. In the central Canadian Arctic the percentage of blues varies from 0.1 to 0.7. In the eastern Arctic (Baffin Island and coastal Labrador) it varies between 1.1 and 4.4 per cent. In Greenland the ratio is approximately 50:50. In the Aleutian and Pribilof islands blue foxes predominate, and in Iceland only blue foxes occur. Braestrup, the Danish biologist, believes that the colours indicate two races of arctic foxes, the white ones being lemming foxes and the blue ones coastal foxes.

There is only one summer coat, which is much shorter than the winter coat. The back, tail, and outer sides of the legs are brown, and the belly and flanks are yellowish white. There are two annual moults. The brown summer coat first appears among the guard hairs as early as February 28 and as late as March 6. Later the long guard hairs and underfur peel off the head and limbs in long strips. The foxes appear spotted and ragged in June, but they assume the complete summer coat by the beginning of July. This coat is worn for only a short time, however, and by late August the growing winter pelage gives the fox a greyish cast. The new coat appears first on the abdomen, flanks, and back. The head, neck, and tail moult last. The snow-white coat is virtually complete by mid-November, although a few small patches may remain until December.

Males are larger than females. A series of adult males from the Canadian Arctic averaged: length 886 (885–910), tail 317 (280–340), hind foot 151 (130–161), ear 55 mm; weight 3.5 (3.2–4.0) kg. A series of similar females averaged: length 821 (750–850), tail 289 (265–320), hind foot 139 (128–148) mm; weight 2.9 (2.5–3.3) kg.

Habits. Except during the breeding season these foxes are primarily solitary. When a group congregate about a whale carcass or a garbage dump, they scrap among themselves. They are active, nervous, and unsuspecting around human habitation until they have been molested; then they become more wary. They are great camp thieves and will steal anything that is not tied down, edible or not. They are primarily nocturnal in activity, hunting from dusk till dawn. During the arctic summer, however, they are abroad during the period of the midnight sun. They are solicitous of their young, and both sexes attend to their needs and bring them food.

Arctic foxes have an acute olfactory sense. They can detect lemmings in their nests under the snow as they can a carcass at a considerable distance. They have a high-pitched husky bark that sounds like the yapping of a small dog at a distance. Besides barking, they hiss and scream when fighting, but they do not howl.

The arctic fox runs lightly over the tundra with its tail stiffly extended. It also swims readily and floats high in the water.

These foxes dig their dens in light, sandy soils in river banks, eskers, or small hillocks. Most entrances face to-

wards the south, and the tunnels slope down towards the permafrost. There are numerous entrances and side tunnels, especially in old dens. The average number of entrances is twelve, but counting the entrances of connecting tunnels the number can vary from one to sixty. The diameter of the entrance is about eight inches. Not all dens are burrows; occasionally arctic foxes den among rocks in a talus slope or a rock field. The entrances to fox dens are characterized by a growth of lush dark-green vegetation caused by the nitrogen supplied by the faeces. Sometimes the dens are very numerous in suitable habitat, but, on the average, they are 900 (50–3,000) metres (average about 1/2 mile) apart. The same dens are used by generations of arctic foxes, and each year only a portion of the available dens are used for rearing the young, depending upon the fox population. In winter, arctic foxes seek shelter in tunnels in snowbanks. The home range of a pair of foxes may vary between 16 and 25 square kilometres (6.2–9.7 square miles) when the population is high, and there may be six occupied dens for every square kilometre or 0.386 square mile.

The population of arctic foxes fluctuates dramatically. Peaks are reached every three to five years, and then the population crashes to a low point. The crashes usually follow a year after a lemming crash, but it has been reported that blue fox populations do not fluctuate as much as lemming fox populations. The population after a crash has been estimated to be approximately 0.086 fox to a square kilometre.

These foxes also undertake spectacular migrations, especially after a lemming population crash. In March 1832 a wave of arctic foxes swept across Sweden from Lapland to Scania (the southernmost province). They have also penetrated the boreal forests of Siberia as far south as Yeniseisk, a distance of 1,300 km (800 mi). White foxes have migrated across the drifting ice of Baffin Bay from arctic Canada to northwest Greenland, temporarily swamping the normal ratio of blue foxes. These migrations are most obvious soon after freeze-up in November and occur in a series of waves, the first being composed primarily of well-fed males. Many single trails lead along the shores of the Arctic Ocean at that time of year.

Arctic foxes live primarily upon lemmings and other arctic voles. They may be seen carefully following the progress of a lemming under the snow, either by sound or by smell. Suddenly they pounce and dig rapidly with their forefeet down to the lemming in its nest or tunnel. In summer they catch lemmings mainly when they are scurrying over the tundra and seldom have to dig them out of their burrows. During the summer months they feed upon ground squirrels, young hares, and the eggs and fledglings of ground-nesting birds. They also feed upon flightless geese and ducks and clamber about sea-bird colonies on cliffsides, eating eggs and pulling young auklets, murres, and dovekies from their nests. Although it is a period of plenty for foxes they are provident enough to cache piles of lemmings, birds' eggs, and fledglings for future periods of want.

In winter there are lemmings, arctic hares, and ptar-

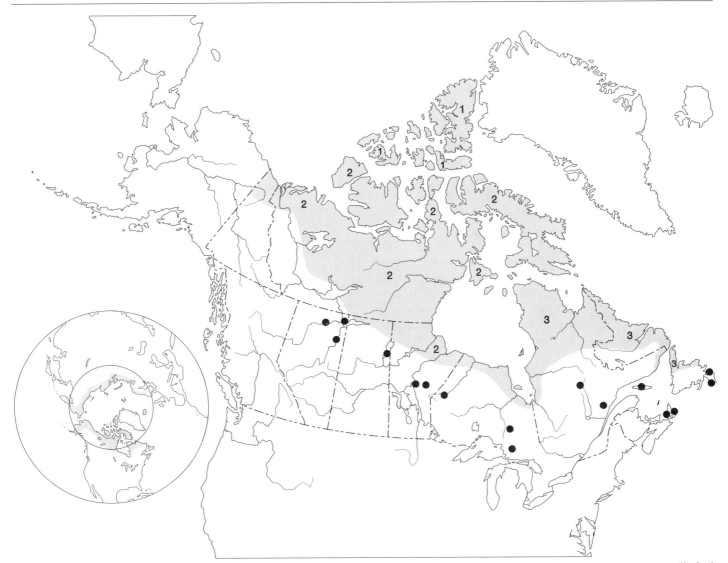

Map 131 Distribution of the arctic fox, *Alopex lagopus*: 1 *A. l. groenlandicus*, 2 *A. l. innuitus*, 3 *A. l. ungava*, ● extra-limital occurrences

migan to hunt, but carrion plays a more important role in the diet during that season. They trail timber wolves in order to clean up what is left of caribou carcasses, and follow polar bears across the frozen seas to feed upon the carcasses of seals left by them. They may also kill new-born ringed seals in their dens. In Iceland, foxes are accused of killing sheep. Under severe stress they may even turn cannibalistic (they are quick to eat their own species when they have been caught in traps). They are fond of fish and become quite adept at catching burbot, arctic cod, salmon, and char in shallow water. They are reported to stir the water with their paws to attract the attention of the fish and then snap at them when they surface. The coastal foxes prowl along the strandline and eat molluscs, crabs, sea urchins, and fish trapped in tidal pools.

On the other hand foxes are alert to keep out of reach of wolves and polar bears. They are also careful not to molest the nests of snowy owls or peregrine falcons. Wolves are their chief predators, and occasionally one finds signs on the snow to indicate that a wolf pack has

caught and eaten an arctic fox. Recently immigrating red foxes to the tundra zone harry arctic foxes. Besides predation, the foxes suffer from a variety of canine maladies such as rabies, encephalitis, and distemper, which decimate their populations, especially during peak years. Arctic foxes live approximately eight to ten years.

Habitat. This species inhabits the arctic and alpine tundra zones and the boreal forest border during the winter months. It also ventures far out on the frozen polar seas to trail polar bears and has reached the remotest arctic islands in this manner.

Reproduction. The vixens are monoestrous, and the oestrous period lasts twelve to fourteen days. One notices the onset of the breeding season by the appearance of paired tracks where previously the foxes had been travelling alone. The breeding season occupies approximately a forty-day period between mid-February and the end of April, depending upon the physical condition of the foxes. If food is plentiful, the breeding season is early; if it is a year of starvation, the season is late or is even missed

297

completely. Tracks indicate that the fox is most active during this period. It is monogamous, and the pairs dig the snow out of the natal dens toward the end of March. The average gestation period is fifty-one (49–57) days, and the young foxes are born between mid-May and mid-June.

Arctic foxes bear surprisingly large litters, which average 6.4 (4–25) whelps, depending on the lemming population. If food is abundant, litters are large; if food is scarce, the litters are small or only a few foxes will breed.

The young foxes are helpless, blind, deaf, and toothless (altricial) at birth, and weigh approximately 57 g each. They have a velvety, close, dark brown undercoat and lack the guard hairs. This coat grows quickly and becomes paler on the flanks and belly as the guard hairs begin to grow through. Growth is rapid; the whelps emerge from the dens at the age of two to four weeks, and they are weaned at approximately the same age. The young foxes are very trusting, and will approach humans and gambol and play in full sight of them. They may be moved by the parents from the natal den to another den in midsummer. However, after a brief period of being brought food by their parents, they are abandoned first by the dog and then by the vixen in mid-August. They are then on their own and soon disperse. Sexual maturity is reached the following spring at the age of nine to ten months.

Economic Status. The arctic fox is one of the most valuable natural resources of the Canadian arctic regions. Its pelt commands a high price, which has fluctuated between $6 and $75 in recent years. In the 1971–72 fur crop season, 33,655 white foxes were sold at an average price of $11.33 and 70 blue foxes at an average price of $12.46, for a total value of $383,902.

Originally Eskimos and Indians caught the arctic fox by using snares, deadfalls, and pits, but now they trap it. The trap is placed in a shallow hole scooped out of the snow and then covered by a thin slice of snow to prevent the wind from filling the mechanism with snow. Bait in the form of frozen meat balls is placed over the trap. Arctic foxes are not suspicious and are easily trapped.

Recently arctic foxes from Banks and Cornwallis islands and Eskimo Point on the west coast of Hudson Bay have been found to harbour the tapeworm *Echinococcus multilocularis*. The larval stage of this parasite may form a dangerous cerebral cyst in infected humans.

Distribution. The species is holarctic in distribution, inhabiting the tundra zone of northern Europe, Asia, North America, Greenland, Iceland, and Spitsbergen. Timberline usually forms the natural southern boundary of its range, but rarely foxes penetrate to southern Sweden, Latvia, and southern Siberia as far as the estuary of the Amur River. There is a relict population on the tops of the Altai Mountains in Central Asia. Fox tracks have also been seen on the polar ice as far north as latitude 85°N.

Canadian Distribution. The white fox is widely distributed in northern Canada, including the northern Yukon Territory, Mackenzie District, east of the Mackenzie River, and all of Keewatin and Franklin districts, the coasts of Hudson Bay in northern Manitoba, Ontario, and northern Quebec, and coastal Labrador. During excep-

tional migrations they have occurred as far south as Fort Chipewyan, Alberta; Reindeer Lake, Saskatchewan; and Norway House, Manitoba. Arctic foxes frequent the southward-drifting ice-floes off the Labrador coast in winter, and have been carried occasionally to Newfoundland and through the Straits of Belle Isle to Anticosti Island and Cape Breton Island (1923, 1935). In the spring of 1922 there was a large-scale immigration to the north shore of the Gulf of St Lawrence, where they did considerable damage to nesting eider duck colonies.

Three subspecies are recognized in Canada (see Map 131).

Alopex lagopus groenlandicus (Bechstein), 1799, Thomas Pennant's allgemeine Uebersicht der vierfüssigen Theire, 1: 270. A large form in which the blue colour phase appears regularly, found on the northern Queen Elizabeth Islands.

Alopex lagopus innuitus (Merriam), 1902, Proc. Biol. Soc. Washington 15: 170. A smaller race, found in the central Canadian Arctic.

Alopex lagopus ungava (Merriam), 1902, Proc. Biol. Soc. Washington 15: 170. Found in northern Quebec and Labrador.

REFERENCES

Braestrup, F.W. 1941. A study on the arctic fox in Greenland. Meddelelser om Grønland (Copenhagen) 131: 1–101.
Macpherson, A.H. 1969. The dynamics of Canadian arctic fox populations. Canadian Wildlife Serv. Rept. Ser. 8.

RED FOX
Renard roux. *Vulpes vulpes* (Linnaeus)

The red fox is another mammal familiar to most people in the Northern Hemisphere. Somehow its image seems to shrink with the advancing years. The fox of the nursery stories was usually depicted as a bold, sly, cunning animal, which usually got the better of its neighbours, but our first glimpse of a fox in life is of a shy, nervous animal trying to remain hidden from sight.

This fox resembles a slender, small dog with sharp pointed face and ears, long silky fur, and a thick brush. Unlike the dog, however, it has furred foot pads. It has a more oval forefoot print, and its toe pads are smaller than those of the grey fox (Figure 66).

The skull of this species is long and slender, particularly in the rostral region, and the cranium rises gradually and only slightly above it. Two parietal ridges run from the supraorbital processes in front and unite behind to form a single sagittal crest. The anterior incisors are lobed; the canines are long and slender; the palate terminates medially in front of the last molar.

In the red fox the underfur is long and thick, grey at the base and buffy towards the tips. The guard hairs are long and are usually banded. The vibrissae are long and black. In wild populations there are three distinct colour phases. The most common is the normal red phase, which occurs in 46 to 77 per cent of the population. In this phase the lips, chest, abdomen, inside of the ears, and tip of the tail are creamy white; the face and flanks are ochraceous; the cheeks, dorsum, rump, and tail are rufous. There is also a scattering of black guard hairs down the mid-dorsal line, and black hairs are prominent in the tail in a subterminal band. The backs of the ears and the anterior portions of the legs are black. The second colour phase is found in what is called the cross fox. This fox is ochraceous or greyish brown, with a strong suffusion of long black guard hairs on the dorsum, which form a cross from shoulder to shoulder. These foxes usually constitute about 20 to 44 per cent of the population. The least common phase is termed the 'silver fox,' which forms 2 to 17 per cent of the population. Silver foxes are totally black except for white tips on the tail and a variable amount of frosting caused by silver tips on the guard hairs. There are two other rare, naturally occurring pelage mutations: Samson foxes lack guard hairs completely, and the underfur appears woolly; and bastard foxes are buffy throughout. Under domestication in fur farms other colour mutations, such as the platinum, have arisen.

The three usual colour phases of the red fox are thought to be caused by the action of a single pair of gene alleles. The homozygous dominants produce red foxes, the homozygous recessives produce silver foxes, and the heterozygous forms produce the cross foxes. The recessive gene for the silver colour phase is thought to have arisen twice independently, once in eastern Canada and again in northwestern Canada. It has not occurred in the Old World. Variations in the population percentages are thought to be due to migration, selective pelting, and variation in the identification of the cross fox.

The red fox is reported to have a single, prolonged annual moult in the Old World.

There are few recorded measurements for the red fox. Males are slightly larger than females. The range of measurements of adults is: length 900–1,117, tail 350–420, hind foot 145–171 mm. The weight is between 3.6 and 6.8 kg.

Figure 66 Red fox, showing cross and silver colour phases

Habits. Red foxes are shy, nervous animals, which are seldom tamed as pets. The family is the basic social unit during half the year – from the mating period until the pups disperse. After that, the animals are solitary during the autumn and winter until the next mating season. During the denning period, the parents are solicitous towards their young, bringing them food in the form of small game, transporting them from den to den, and teaching them to hunt. After the young leave the den, the family stays together, using several rallying points for social intercourse until the family bonds weaken during the autumn. An unusual interspecific tolerance between the red fox and the woodchuck, with both species occupying the same burrow, has been described.

Foxes are most active during the hours of darkness but may be seen about during late afternoon and early morning. They have acute hearing and a keen sense of smell and possess a high-pitched bark. They run with a light, quick, airy gait, and leave tracks almost in line in the snow. When galloping the tracks appear in groups of four.

These foxes usually modify an abandoned woodchuck burrow to serve as a den, although occasionally they excavate their own burrows. The dens are usually located in sandy or gravelly soil, on small knolls in pastures, along the banks of streams, along a fence row, or on the edge of a forest. A den may be anywhere from ten to thirty feet in length, and three to ten feet below the surface. The foxes usually start to clean out an old den for occupancy in January or February. The same dens may be enlarged and used year after year. As a rule they prepare several dens in close proximity for escape purposes, and the dens have two or three entrances.

Foxes may travel up to five miles on a nocturnal forage. The home range of a single fox or family has been estimated to be between 1.4 and 3.14 square miles. Average fox densities in agricultural land have been estimated to be about one fox per 1.6 square miles. During years of abundance as many as five litters have been raised within 200 acres, and twenty-five foxes have been trapped within such an area prior to the autumn dispersal. Red fox populations show regular fluctuations, with peaks between eight and ten years apart. These peaks do not occur simultaneously across the whole country, however, and it usually takes three to four years for peak populations to occur country-wide.

Red foxes are mobile animals. Tagging experiments have shown that young males may disperse as much as 166 miles in the autumn, although the average is about 43 miles; juvenile vixens disperse less widely. During periods of peak abundance, the proportions of the colour phases change, indicating a considerable immigration of foxes into areas of peak populations.

These animals have an omnivorous diet, utilizing whatever is most readily available. There is a considerable annual shift in diet. During the winter months meat is high on the menu, whereas in summer invertebrates and vegetable matter are more important. Small mammals form the principal prey, constituting about 37 per cent of the diet. These include moles and shrews (not favoured), wood-

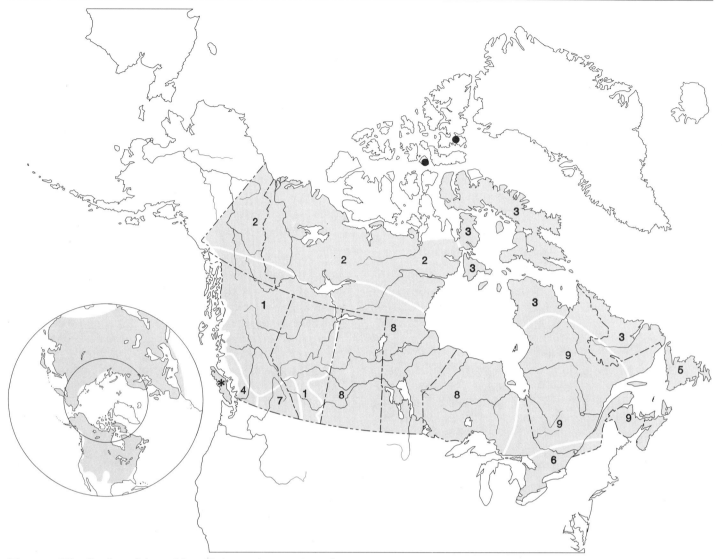

Map 132 Distribution of the red fox, *Vulpes vulpes*: 1 *V. v. abietorum*, 2 *V. v. alascensis*, 3 *V. v. bangsi*, 4 *V. v. cascadensis*, 5 *V. v. deletrix*, 6 *V. v. fulva*, 7 *V. v. macroura*, 8 *V. v. regalis*, 9 *V. v. rubicosa*, * introduced, ● extra-limital record

chucks, squirrels, mice (particularly field voles, *Microtus* sp.), muskrats, cottontails, and snowshoe hares (which form 56 per cent of the diet in Newfoundland). Birds constitute about 20 per cent of the diet, including grouse, quail, pheasants, ducks, small ground-nesting birds, and domestic chickens. Invertebrates such as crayfish, crickets, grasshoppers, beetles, and caterpillars constitute about 26 per cent; plant material such as acorns, grasses, corn, berries, cherries, strawberries, plums, and apples form approximately 16 per cent; and cold-blooded vertebrates, including snakes, fish, and frogs, make up an insignificant 1 per cent.

Mice are stalked and dug out of the snow in winter by the red fox. Cottontails are usually caught after a short race. Red foxes cache a considerable amount of food under sand, leaves, or snow for future requirements. Often other predators discover the caches before the owner returns.

Red foxes are preyed upon by coyotes and bobcats in

particular, but seem to be too agile for the more cumbersome wolves.

Tagging experiments have indicated a longevity of at least three years, but there seems to be a large turnover each year.

Habitat. Red foxes prefer semi-open country such as agricultural areas, lakeshores, river valleys, natural clearings in the forests, and alpine and arctic tundra. They are seldom found in the heart of dense forests.

Reproduction. The vixens possess eight mammae. They are monoestrous and come into heat between December and the end of March. The peak of breeding lies between mid-January and mid-March. The dogs reach breeding condition eight to ten weeks before the vixens. During the mating season the vixen may be courted by several dogs, but monogamy is the usual situation, and the pair bond is fixed. The gestation period is between fifty-one and fifty-three days. The young whelps are born between March and May, depending upon latitude, and the average litter size is 5.1 (1–10). Rarely as many as sixteen whelps have been found in one den, but these probably represent the litters of two vixens.

The whelps weigh approximately 100 g at birth and are altricial in development. Their juvenile pelage is brown and woolly because of the lack of guard hairs, which appear later. Their eyes open during the second week of life. The pups are weaned and appear above ground to romp at the den entrance after they are a month old. The adults then bring them mice, rabbits, and birds to feed on, and may move them to another den at that point. The young disperse when they are fourteen to sixteen weeks old, and sexual maturity is reached at ten months of age.

Economic Status. Red foxes are important fur-bearers and were commonly raised in fur farms a couple of decades ago, until their long fur went out of style. In 1919–20 a silver fox skin brought $246.46 and a cross fox $63.18, and in 1929–30 the average value for a red fox pelt was $29.82. During the 1971–72 trapping season 51,348 red and cross foxes were traded at an average price of $15.97, and 470 silver foxes for $17.94, for a total value of $828,314.

Individual foxes may become serious pests to poultry farmers. In the fifties fox populations rose in agricultural areas of eastern Canada. Unfortunately an epizootic of rabies swept through this high population towards the end of that decade, and foxes became a serious public health menace to rural areas.

Distribution. Red foxes are widely distributed in the Northern Hemisphere – in Europe, North Africa, Asia, and North America.

Canadian Distribution. Red foxes occur right across Canada from Newfoundland to the southwestern coast of British Columbia. They were introduced to Vancouver Island, but they are very rare on the southern plains of Alberta and southwestern Saskatchewan. They also occur sparsely on the southern continental tundra of the Northwest Territories. In 1918 or 1919, red foxes crossed Hudson Strait from the Ungava Peninsula to southern Baffin Island, and by the late forties they had occupied all of Baffin Island. In 1950 they crossed Fury and Hecla Strait to Melville Peninsula and expanded southward to Repulse Bay. In 1962 they crossed Lancaster Sound north of Baffin Island and reached Resolute Bay on Cornwallis Island and Grise Fiord on the southern coast of Ellesmere Island. It appears that the Ungava race has adapted well to the arctic tundra habitat to compete with the arctic fox.

American red foxes are now accepted as belonging to the same species as the Old World foxes. Nine subspecies are currently recognized as occurring in Canada (see Map 132).

Vulpes vulpes abietorum Merriam, 1900, Proc. Washington Acad. Sci. 2: 669. North-central British Columbia and Alberta and southern Yukon and Mackenzie District.

Vulpes vulpes alascensis Merriam, 1900, Proc. Washington Acad. Sci. 2: 668. The largest race, found in northern Yukon and Northwest Territories.

Vulpes vulpes bangsi Merriam, 1900, Proc. Washington Acad. Sci. 2: 667. An ill-defined race, reported from Labrador and northern Quebec.

Vulpes vulpes cascadensis Merriam, 1900, Proc. Washington Acad. Sci. 2: 665. A small, short-tailed, small-toothed race, found in southwestern British Columbia.

Vulpes vulpes deletrix Bangs, 1898, Proc. Biol. Soc. Washington 12: 36. A pale, straw-coloured form, found on the island of Newfoundland.

Vulpes vulpes fulva (Desmarest), 1820, Mammalogie ..., pt. 1, p. 203, *in* Encyclopédie Methodique ... The typical American race, found in southern and central Ontario.

Vulpes vulpes macroura Baird, 1852, *in* Stansbury, Exploration and survey of the Great Salt Lake of Utah ... (Special Session United States Senate, Exec. 3, app. c, p. 309). A large, long-tailed race, found in southeastern British Columbia and southwestern Alberta.

Vulpes vulpes regalis Merriam, 1900, Proc. Washington Acad. Sci. 2: 672. A large, richly coloured race, found from eastern Alberta, Saskatchewan, and Manitoba to northwestern Ontario, and in the southern portions of the Northwest Territories.

Vulpes vulpes rubicosa Bangs, 1898, Science, n.s. 7: 272. A small, slender, dark red fox, found in the Maritime Provinces and southeastern Quebec.

REFERENCES

Butler, L. 1947. The genetics of the colour phases of the red fox in the Mackenzie River locality. Canadian Jour. Res. D, Zoology 25(6): 190–215.

Cross, E.C. 1941. Periodic fluctuations in numbers of the red fox in Ontario. Jour. Mamm. 40(3): 294–306.

Philippe, L. 1950. Le renard roux (*Vulpes fulva fulva* Desmarest) et son influence écologique et économique durant la saison hivernale sur une partie de l'île de Montréal, Le Naturaliste Canadien 77(1–2): 5–43.

Scott, T.G., and W.D. Klimstra. 1955. Red foxes and a declining prey population. South Illinois Univ. Monogr. Ser. 1.

SWIFT FOX
Renard véloce. *Vulpes velox* (Say)

Description. This species is very close to the kit fox (*Vulpes macrotis*) and may be only subspecifically distinct. It is a small slender fox, about the size of a large house cat, with relatively large ears. Its skull is smaller and lighter than a red fox's, but the auditory bullae are relatively larger.

The underfur in this species is thick but harsh, and the guard hairs are thinly scattered. The legs, shoulders, and back of the ears are ochraceous buff; the flanks are yellowish grey; the forehead, back, and tail are grizzled grey. The cylindrical tail is tipped with black. The underparts and the inside of the ears are creamy white. There are two prominent black spots on each side of the snout below the eyes (Figure 67a).

The spring moult takes place between April and July; the summer coat is rather thin; the winter coat, which starts to grow in late summer, is attained by late October.

Average measurements of adults: length 844, tail 280, hind foot 130 mm. Males are a little heavier than females: 2.0 (1.7–2.5) kg against 1.9 (1.6–2.1) kg.

Habits. Swift foxes are solitary except during the breeding season. They are timid creatures, but unfortunately for their survival they are often quite unwary of men. They are primarily nocturnal and spend the daylight hours asleep in their burrows. Their usual calls are shrill yaps, but they also purr, growl, croak, and whine. They appear to be swift runners, as their name implies, and they seem almost to float along close to the ground with their tails extended. However, their speed is deceptive because of their small size and also because of their pale coloration, which blends with the surroundings. They reach a maximum speed of about twenty-five miles an hour in the first burst but soon tire. They evade dogs and coyotes by quick changes of direction in seeking the safety of burrows.

The dens of swift foxes are located in sandy soil on open, bald prairie, along fence rows, or occasionally in ploughed fields. The mounds of fresh earth are a giveaway to the entrances, and there is usually no shade about them. The entrances average about four (1–7) in number and are eight to ten inches in diameter. The burrows, which are either excavated by the foxes themselves or are usurped burrows of badgers or marmots, vary from seven to twelve feet in length. The natal chamber, which is about three feet below the surface, is about twelve inches across and is

Map 133 Distribution of the swift fox, *Vulpes velox*: E extinct

bare of nesting material. This chamber has several side tunnels, in which abundant remains of prey are usually lying about.

A tracked swift fox travelled about six miles during a night's forage. The density of foxes on ideal range is about one fox to two square miles.

The food of the swift fox consists of 64 per cent mammals (jack rabbits, cottontails, ground squirrels, pocket mice, kangaroo mice), 9.6 per cent birds (prairie chickens and small ground-dwelling birds), 8.8 per cent invertebrates (mostly insects), plus a few lizards and fish, and 17.6 per cent vegetable matter (grasses and berries). In winter these foxes commonly cache excess food, such as mice, under the snow.

The chief predators of this species are coyotes, golden eagles, and rarely wolves.

Habitat. Swift foxes are typical of arid short-grass plains and shrubby deserts.

Reproduction. The females are thought to pair for life, but burrows occasionally are reported to contain one dog and two vixens. They are monoestrous, the oestrous period occurring between late December and early February. The gestation period is unknown. The pups are born in March or April, and the litter size is usually four or five, but one double litter of fifteen has been reported.

The young are very small with soft woolly coats during the first month. They weigh 0.5 kg at two weeks of age but grow quickly until they reach adult weight about the first

Figure 67 (a) Swift fox, *Vulpes velox*, and (b) grey fox, *Urocyon cinereoargenteus*

of August. Around the beginning of May the first adult pelage commences on the forehead and back. The pups appear above ground in July and disperse by the beginning of October.

Economic Status. Since this little fox lives mainly in deserts, it seldom has the opportunity to earn the farmer's wrath by raiding chicken coops. Its toll of rodents and rabbits is beneficial to agricultural interests. Its pelt has no commercial value.

Distribution. The swift fox was found in the arid plains of central North America from Texas to southern Canada, but is now much restricted in distribution.

Canadian Distribution. This fox was commonly met on the southern prairies, from the Pembina Hills of Manitoba to the foothills of the Rockies, when the region was first settled. It was easily trapped, however, and soon disappeared as the land came under cultivation. The last specimen was taken at Glovenlock, Saskatchewan, in 1928, and the species is now believed to be extinct in Canada. The form found in Canada was the northern subspecies (see Map 133).

Vulpes velox hebes Merriam, 1902, Proc. Biol. Soc. Washington 15: 73.

REFERENCE

Egoscue, H.J. 1962. Ecology and life history of the kit fox in Toocle County, Utah. Ecology 43(3): 481–97.

GREY FOX
Renard gris. *Urocyon cinereoargenteus* (Schreber)

Description. The shorter legs of the grey fox make it appear smaller than the red fox, but actually both species weigh about the same, 8 pounds. This species has a shorter muzzle, rounder footprints, larger toe pads, and more curved claws. There are trenchant differences in the skull: two distinct parietal ridges run from the supraorbital processes back to the occipital crest without uniting to form a median sagittal crest; the upper incisors are not lobed; and the lower mandible has a unique posterior step.

The grey fox has been confused with the cross phase of the red fox, but the coat is quite distinctive. The pelage is harsh. The upper parts are grizzled grey, caused by the white bands and black tips on the guard hairs. The under-fur is buffy. The legs, cheeks, and chest are ochraceous. There is a prominent black muzzle patch below each eye and on the lower jaw. The upper lip otherwise is whitish, as are the throat and belly. The brush is long and thick. There is a prominent dorsal stripe of stiff black hairs and a black tip to the tail (Figure 67b).

Average measurements of adults: length 988 (800–1,125), tail 372 (275–443), hind foot 142 (100–150), ear 75 mm. The males are heavier than the females: males average 4.1 (3.6–5.9) kg and females 3.9 (3.4–5.4) kg.

Habits. Grey foxes have much the same habits as red foxes except for their unique habit of climbing trees. They can jump easily from branch to branch if these are not angled too steeply, and can even scramble up steep trunks using their sharp, hooked claws. Though the males assist the vixens in raising the whelps, they do not usually remain near the natal den. After the young have dispersed, the males, too, tend to desert their mates. Vixens show amazing spunk in defending their whelps and have been known to stand their ground and growl at intruders. This fox is mostly nocturnal in activity. The vixen usually remains in the den with the pups during the daylight hours.

In the southern portions of their distribution grey foxes make their dens in hollow logs and stumps or in rock piles, but in the north they are more prone to use burrows. In Florida the average home range is about two miles in diameter. These foxes are also great travellers: tagged juveniles have been known to disperse as much as fifty-two miles from their natal den. Population densities may be in the order of 3.4 foxes per square mile of good habitat.

Grey foxes feed primarily upon small mammals. They seem to be particularly fond of cottontails, which constitute about 20.5 per cent of their diet. Rodents such as woodchucks, deer mice, and harvest mice constitute another 20.5 per cent, and shrews 1 per cent. Birds such as chickens, pheasants, ducks, and passerine birds form 26 per cent, insects 2.5 per cent, fish 2.5 per cent, and plant material 28.6 per cent. They consume more plant material, such as corn, apples, nuts, and fruit, than the red fox.

The bobcat is the only known predator.

Habitat. The grey fox prefers forests and marshes and is less at home in farm lands than the red fox.

Reproduction. The vixens normally possess only six functional mammae. They are monoestrous and normally monogamous, though occasionally polygamous. Two vixens occasionally rear their litters in the same den. The foxes pair off and run together during the oestrous period, which may occur between the last week of January and mid-May, with a peak in early March. The exact gestation period is not known. Parturition occurs from March 21 in the south to mid-June in the north. Grey foxes generally breed about a month later than red foxes. The litter averages about 3.7 (1–7) whelps, which weigh about 100 g each. They retain their woolly coats for one month. At twelve weeks of age they are weaned and leave the den to follow their mother on short hunts. They drop their milk teeth in August, at about four months of age, and then start to hunt for themselves. By that time they weigh almost seven pounds (3 kg), but they do not reach adult size until early winter.

Most juvenile females reach sexual maturity before their first birthday, but about 7 per cent do not breed until the second year.

Economic Status. This fox is too rare in Canada to be of any economic significance.

Distribution. This is primarily a southern species found in the southern half of North America and in Central and South America.

Canadian Distribution. From early historical accounts and from archaeological excavations it is known that grey foxes occurred in considerable numbers in southern Ontario as far north as Midland and in southern Maine in the

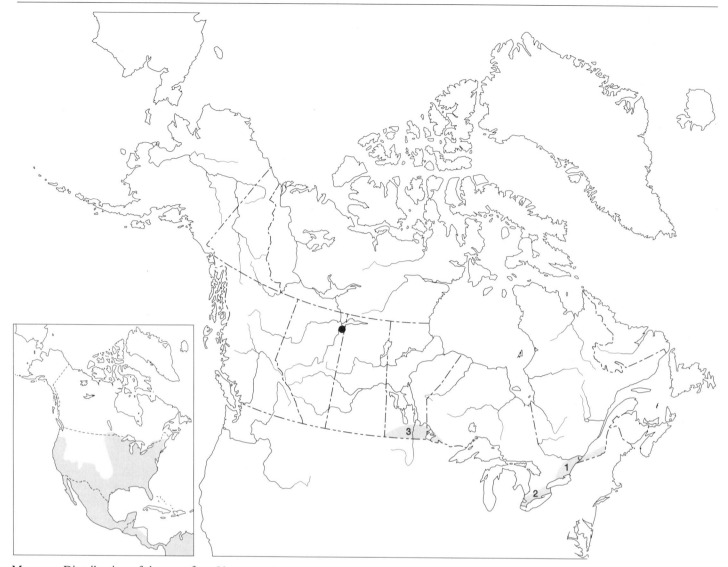

Map 134 Distribution of the grey fox, *Urocyon cinereoargenteus*: 1 *U. c. borealis*, 2 *U. c. cinereoargenteus*, 3 *U. c. ocythous,*
● extra-limital record

middle of the seventeenth century. After that period they vanished for 300 years from the northern fringe of their distribution only to reappear in the middle of the twentieth century. They have entered Canada at three points, and each population represents a distinct subspecies (see Map 134).

Urocyon cinereoargenteus borealis Merriam, 1903, Proc. Biol. Soc. Washington 16: 74. A sight record from the Eastern Townships of Quebec. In 1942 this subspecies first crossed the St Lawrence into the eastern Ontario counties of Leeds, Stormont, Dundas, and Glengarry.

Urocyon cinereoargenteus cinereoargenteus (Schreber), 1775, Die Säugethiere ..., Theil 2, Heft 13, pl. 92. In 1948 this subspecies entered the Ontario counties of Welland and Lincoln, bordering the Niagara River.

Urocyon cinereoargenteus ocythous Bangs, 1899, Proc. New England Zool. Club 1: 43. This subspecies entered the Rainy River district of western Ontario in 1944; it was reported at Sprague, Manitoba, in 1946–47 and at St

Adolphe, Manitoba, in 1957. A wandering grey fox was trapped by an Indian at Old Fort Point, Lake Athabasca, Alberta, on January 12, 1950.

REFERENCES

Lord, R.D. Jr. 1961. A population study of the gray fox. American Midl. Nat. 66(1): 87–109.
Peterson, R.L. et al. 1953. Early records of the red and gray fox in Ontario. Jour. Mamm. 34(1): 126–7.

Family **Ursidae** / Bears

Many of the aquatic toothed whales are larger than bears, but bears are the largest terrestrial carnivorous mammals. Bears also constitute one of the most recently evolved family groups. They are heavy-set, bob-tailed mammals with five clawed toes on each foot. They are plantigrade (walk on their heels). Bears do not restrict themselves to a strictly carnivorous diet, a fact which is reflected in their low-crowned, flattened molars, which they use for crushing and chewing food. The first premolars are peg-like, or often lacking. The tympanic bullae are not inflated. The humerus lacks an epicondylar canal. All Canadian bears hibernate to some extent.

AMERICAN BLACK BEAR
Ours noir. *Ursus americanus* Pallas

Description. The large, heavy, lumbering shape of the black bear is familiar to most readers. Adults stand a little less than 3 feet high at the shoulder and measure 5 to 6 feet in length, including the 4-inch stubby tail. The snout of the bear tapers gradually into the broad head. The bear has small black eyes, prominent rounded ears, a short neck, and a back and shoulders that form almost a straight line (Plate 28). Its legs are thick, and each has five toes, armed with short, curved, non-retractile claws. Its large foot pads are naked (Figure 68).

The bear's skull is massive, with a large cranium, strong sagittal crest and zygomatic arches, and a broad frontal region. The canines are short and strong; the upper incisors are all approximately the same length; the premolars are weak or lacking; the molars are flat-crowned, the last only moderately larger than the premolars (Figure 69).

The pelage of the bear is coarse and long. The commonest colour is black, except for the tan muzzle and white v on the chest. Cinnamon-coloured bears occur commonly in western Canada. There are also honey-coloured bears, and colour phases of white and blue, the latter two being restricted to locations on the Pacific coast. There is one annual moult in late spring after the bear emerges from hibernation.

Males are larger than females. Average measurements of adult males: length 168 (137–188) cm, tail 100 (77–177) mm, hind foot 265 (232–365) mm, ear 120 (110–135) mm, weight 169 (115–270) kg. Average weight of adult females

136 (92–140) kg. Bears become very fat in the autumn but are quite thin in the spring when they emerge from their winter dens.

Habits. During most of the year black bears are solitary beasts, but they pair up briefly during the mating season. The cubs remain with the sow for about a year. When a number of bears congregate at a garbage dump, they try to keep out of each other's way. The bears are rather cantankerous and might attack young cubs if it were not for the sow's savage protection of them. They are bold and truculent and often become roadside beggars in parks. Black bears are semi-arboreal and climb trees to feed on young shoots, buds, and fruit, as well as to protect themselves. They also swim well. They have a keen sense of smell and acute hearing, but their eyesight is poor. They utter a variety of sounds: squeals, growls, and grunts. When very young, a bear cries when afraid and hums when contented. A bear's usual gait is a lumbering walk, but it can move quickly when it has to, and then it looks like a large black ball bouncing through the woods as it gathers its feet under its heavy body for each spring. Bears may be observed at all hours but are most active at night.

The home range of the black bear has been estimated to include about seventy-eight square miles; old bears are thought to range farther, up to fifteen miles from their home base. There is much overlapping in home ranges with little sign of conflict. The bear has the peculiar habit of standing beside a tree, such as a birch or aspen, and clawing the bark as high as it can reach. These marking-posts are supposed to have some significance in expressing territorial claims. The density may be in the order of one bear to every 5.56 square miles.

In the autumn the black bear seeks the shelter of a cave, rock crevice, hollow log, windthrown stump, or merely a mossy hollow under the low, sweeping branches of a

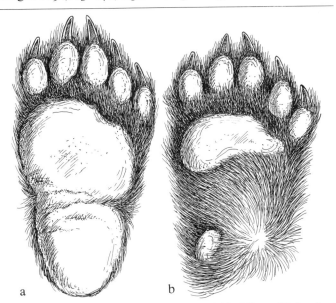

Figure 68 Soles of feet of black bear: (a) hind foot, (b) forefoot (× 1/3)

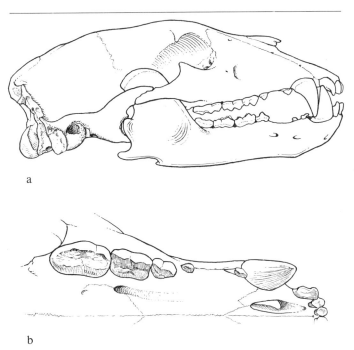

Figure 69 Black bear skull (a) and dentition (b) (× 1/4)

spruce or fir for its winter den. It drags in some spruce boughs, rotten wood, or heather for bedding. The reason for the bear's winter dormancy is not completely understood. In October bears appear satiated and lethargic. The date for entering winter dormancy depends upon latitude and the local weather: in Alaska it may be early October, but on the southern tip of Vancouver Island it may be delayed until late December, and an occasional bear may even be seen about all winter. When bears enter a state of lethargy in winter, their body temperatures drop from about 38°C to 31–34°C, and the rate of breathing declines to two to four respirations per minute. The metabolic rate is depressed, and no growth occurs during the winter months. The bears may be aroused, however, by shouting. They sleepily stare at the intruder and then amble off to seek another shelter. When hibernating, the temperature of the hair tips may be only 5°C, and light snow will gradually melt off, or the bears may shake it off in turning in their sleep. Usually well-protected dens become completely covered by snow, except for a breathing-hole, out of which a small column of vapour rises on crisp days. Bears desert their winter beds in April, when melting snows flood them.

Black bears are omnivorous and not too selective in their feeding habits. Twigs and leaves are consumed along with berries. If they are feeding on garbage, they may consume paper, cardboard, rags, string, and pieces of wood. When they first emerge from hibernation they are still in fair condition but decline rapidly because food is scarce at that time of year. At first they will eat spruce needles; tear logs open for carpenter ants, grubs, and beetles; clean up carrion resulting from winter losses; graze on fresh sprouts of grasses and sedges; and browse on tree buds. As the summer progresses, ripening fruits command their attention, including strawberries, raspberries, blackberries, Juneberries, cherries, cranberries, crowberries, and hazelnuts. They also eat roots, cowparsnips, and locoweed. In autumn they consume grasshoppers, crickets, beechnuts, acorns, wild grapes, and apples. Although these are the staples, bears are opportunists and never pass up the chance of seizing mice, cottontails, woodchucks, fish, or perhaps a calf moose, deer fawn, calf, or piglet. Their love of honey is well known; they are also attracted by sweet, ripe corn in autumn and have been known to create havoc in cornfields at that time. The annual diet consists of approximately 76.7 per cent vegetable matter, 7.4 per cent insects, 15.2 per cent carrion, and 0.7 per cent small mammals.

Black bears have few natural enemies, but the grizzly bear is one. Wherever the distributions of these two species overlap, the black bear is constantly on its guard for fear of meeting a grizzly. One evening about ten years ago I was watching, from the safety of a warden's truck, some black bears feasting on the Jasper Park Lodge garbage dump. They had been there since early evening, and about fifteen had gathered. As dusk approached they became more apprehensive, and several sows led off their cubs. Suddenly two grizzlies appeared in the shadows at the far end of the clearing. Pandemonium broke loose as the bears scrambled down the slope accompanied by the rattling of pails and cans. Heading for a grove of tall lodgepole pines below the dump, they quickly climbed them and hung from the branches like oversized black plums. In the meantime three grizzlies stalked majestically into the clearing with only an occasional glance or sniff towards the trees. We stayed until it was quite dark, but the black bears remained in their trees, and we could hear the occasional whine of a cub coming from the tops of the pines.

Black bears have lived as long as twenty-three years in captivity.

Habitat. Black bears inhabit either coniferous or deciduous forest regions, as well as swamps and berry patches.

Reproduction. The sows have three pairs of mammae: one inguinal and two pectoral. The oestrous period lasts from about June 20 to July 10. Oestrous usually occurs every second year because of lactation anoestrus, but if the cubs are lost early, an oestrous period will occur the following summer. The bears are sexually active between mid-April and late August of each year. Noisy pairing occurs for this very brief period each season; otherwise the bears remain alone.

The gestation period lasts for about 220 days, and the cubs are born between mid-January and early February, while the sow is in dormancy. Bears exhibit a reproductive phenomenon known as delayed implantation. The fertilized eggs lie dormant for several months, so that it is October or November before the blastocyst is implanted in the uterus, and the embryo develops only during the last ten weeks of pregnancy.

The average number of cubs in each litter is 2.4 (1–5). The cubs are remarkably small and underdeveloped at birth, a 300-pound black bear giving birth to cubs about the size of squirrels. At birth the cub measures about 20 cm long and weighs 240 to 330 g; its head and forelimbs are large, but its hindquarters are underdeveloped; it is naked and blind. The black fur appears on the dorsum during the first week, and the eyes open after five or six weeks. The milk teeth are in place when the cub leaves the den in April, and the first permanent teeth appear when it is about three months old. It weighs about five to ten pounds (2.3–4.5 kg) at that time. The cubs are weaned at five months of age and are self-sufficient by the time they are six to eight months old. They den up with the sow the second winter of their lives but disperse the following spring before she mates again. When danger threatens the family, the sow sends the cubs up a tall tree. She may remain on guard below or she may leave the area, but she is always within earshot. The third winter the cubs may den together or seek individual beds.

Juvenile females reach sexual maturity in the wild when they are four to five years old, and the males reach sexual maturity a year later.

Economic Status. Black bears constitute an important big game resource. Their flesh is palatable, and bear hunting is a popular sport. At one time their hides were commonly used as rugs and robes for sleighs, but now about

Map 135 Distribution of the American black bear, *Ursus americanus*: 1 *U. a. altifrontalis*, 2 *U. a. americanus*, 3 *U. a. carlottae*, 4 *U. a. cinnamomum*, 5 *U. a. emmonsii*, 6 *U. a. hamiltoni*, 7 *U. a. hunteri*, 8 *U. a. kermodei*, 9 *U. a. randi*, 10 *U. a. vancouveri*, E extinct

the only use for their pelts is for the fur busbies worn by Guards Regiments. During the 1971–72 fur season 2,522 black bear pelts were sold for an average price of $24.74, for a total value of $62,395.

On the debit side of the ledger, black bears are a considerable nuisance around garbage dumps and as camp robbers. Tourists should be aware of the potential danger involved in photographing or feeding beggar bears. These bears have lost their natural fear of man, and their behaviour is quite unpredictable. A twelve-year-old girl was pulled off a porch in Jasper National Park a few years ago and killed. In another incident, in 1948, an emaciated black bear killed a three-year-old girl at a forest ranger's station near Sault Ste Marie, Michigan.

Distribution. The black bear occupies most of North America from the Mexican plateau north to the treeline in Alaska and Labrador.

Canadian Distribution. The black bear occurs right across forested Canada from Newfoundland to the Queen Charlotte Islands, British Columbia. Ten local subspecies are recognized (see Map 135).

Ursus americanus altifrontalis Elliot, 1903, Field Columbian Mus. Pub. 80, Zool. Ser. 3: 234. The black bear of southwestern British Columbia, characterized by a high forehead.

Ursus americanus americanus Pallas, 1780, Spiciligia zoologica ..., fasc. 14: 5. The typical race of eastern and central Canada, in which the brown colour variety is rare.

Ursus americanus carlottae Osgood, 1901, N. American Fauna 21: 30. A large form with broad, massive skull, found on the Queen Charlotte Islands, British Columbia. No brown phase reported.

Ursus americanus cinnamomum Audubon and Bachman, 1854, The viviparous quadrupeds of North America, 3: 125. The brown phase occurs almost as commonly as the black. A large race.

307

Ursus americanus emmonsii Dall, 1895, Science, n.s. 2: 87. The so-called blue bear, or glacial bear, a rare colour phase from the St Elias Mountains of southwestern Yukon Territory.

Ursus americanus hamiltoni Cameron, 1957, Jour. Mamm. 37: 358. The black bear of Newfoundland, characterized by an inflated cranium.

Ursus americanus hunteri (Anderson), 1945, Ann. Rept. Provancher Soc. Nat. Hist. Quebec 1944: 22. Southeastern Yukon Territory and southwestern Mackenzie District.

Ursus americanus kermodei Hornaday, 1905, 9th Ann. Rept., New York Zool. Soc. 1904: 82. This is the white bear of Gribble Island, British Columbia, named in honour of Francis Kermode, who was director of the Provincial Museum in Victoria for many years. It was later discovered that white bears formed only a small percentage of the population there, but the bears of coastal British Columbia from Burke Inlet north to the Nass River seem to have some physical characteristics in common.

Ursus americanus randi (Anderson), 1945, Ann. Rept. Provancher Soc. Nat. Hist. Quebec 1944: 19. A small race from central Yukon Territory.

Ursus americanus vancouveri Hall, 1928, Univ. California Pub. Zool. 30: 231. A large black bear with massive skull, from Vancouver Island, British Columbia. No brown phase reported.

REFERENCES

Erickson, A.W., John Nellor, and G.A. Petrides. 1964. The black bear in Michigan. Michigan State Univ. Agr. Exp. Station, Res. Bull. 4.

Jonkel, J., and I. McTaggart Cowan. 1971. The black bear in the spruce-fir forest. Wildlife Monogr. 27.

Rausch, R.L. 1961. Notes on the black bear, *Ursus americanus* Pallas, in Alaska, with particular reference to dentition and growth. Zeits. f. Saügetierkunde 26(2): 65–128.

GRIZZLY BEAR
Ours brun. *Ursus arctos* Linnaeus

Description. The grizzly bear has gained the reputation of being the most ferocious and the most dangerous mammal in North America. Captain Meriwether Lewis and Captain William Clark, while on their famed expedition to the Pacific via the Missouri River in 1804–06, were the first Europeans to provide a detailed description of this bear and to collect specimens. Actually, earlier references to the grizzly on the Canadian prairies go back over 100 years before that to the French Jesuit missionary Claude Jean Allouez, who was told of this terrible bear by Indians living near the Assiniboine River, Manitoba, in 1666. Henry Kelsey of the Hudson's Bay Company stood on the edge of the woods in Manitoba on August 20, 1691, and saw grizzlies and bison feeding on the prairie in front of him. In the early days this bear was called either 'grizzly' because of its grizzled grey coat, or 'grisly' because of its

terrifying reputation. Recent studies have shown that the American bear is only subspecifically distinct from the Eurasian brown bear.

The grizzly bear is larger than the black bear. Its snout is relatively longer and rises abruptly into the broad, concave face. Its broad head is capped by two small, rounded, heavily furred ears. It has a prominent hump on the shoulders. The claws of the forefeet are long, slender, and pale yellow or brown in colour. (The claws of bears in the autumn are much worn after a summer of digging.) There is much individual variation among grizzlies: some are rangy and others are more heavily built; some have long, slender heads and others have short, broad heads (Plate 26).

The trenchant differences between black and grizzly bears are found in their dentition. In the grizzly the third pair of upper incisors is longer than the central two pairs, and so when the lower canine locks in place, in front of the upper canine, it appears as though the skull has two pairs of upper canines. The teeth are much heavier, and the last molar is noticeably larger than for the black bear (Figure 70).

The grizzly's pelage is very long, especially the ruff on the shoulders, which flops about as the bear runs; it is variable in colour, from creamy yellow to almost black. On the northern tundra many grizzlies are creamy yellow on the back, with rufous-coloured legs and underparts. In the Rocky Mountains the 'silver tip' colour phase, in which the bears are dark brown, with the long hairs of the shoulders and back frosted with white, is dominant. Usually there are some white-tipped hairs around the face and over the shoulders. In late spring and early summer the thick underfur is rubbed off, and the bears are thinly clad for the duration of the warmer weather. The new growth commences in mid-August, and by October the bears are in their long, glossy winter coats.

There are few accurate measurements of grizzly bears. The type specimen collected by Lewis and Clark in 1805 was reported to measure 8 feet 7 inches (2.6 metres) in

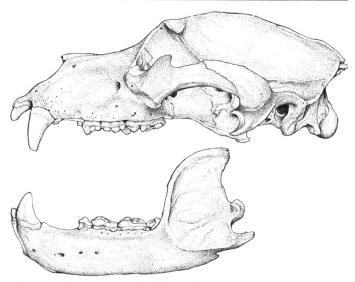

Figure 70 Grizzly bear skull, lateral view (× 1/4)

length and to stand 53 inches (1.3 metres) high at the shoulders. A medium-sized male, killed in Jasper National Park, measured: length 186 cm, tail 75 mm, and hind foot 260 mm. Adults weigh from 136 to 526 kg (300–1,153 pounds), the maximum weight being recorded for an old zoo bear.

Habits. Most of the literature dealing with grizzlies concerns bear hunting and stresses their intelligence, wariness, ferocity, and vitality; very little is known about their everyday lives. The adults are solitary most of the time, except during the short mating season. They are extremely shy and flee from contact with man, but they are courageous and will attack if cornered, wounded, or separated from their cubs. Occasionally grizzlies congregate at favourite feeding spots such as salmon streams or garbage dumps, but they always keep out of one another's way, the smaller bear giving way to the larger one. They also have special clawing posts and claw the bark from trees as far up as they can reach, or bite out chunks of bark. These posts may be territorial signs. They do not climb trees because their long foreclaws are not adapted for climbing.

Grizzlies have poor eyesight but excellent hearing and an acute sense of smell. They growl and roar when fighting. The usual gait is a slow walk with the low-slung head swinging from side to side. They can move very quickly, however, and can easily catch a black bear. Indeed a horse must put forth its best effort to evade the grizzly's rush. I recall surprising a grizzly drinking at a mountain stream in Waterton Lakes National Park, Alberta. The bear took off up the opposite hillside in a rolling gallop and did not pause until it disappeared over the crest of the mountain more than a thousand feet above – an exhibition of tremendous stamina. Grizzlies are also excellent swimmers.

This species is most active during the evening, night, and early morning hours. It sleeps in a bed in alder thickets or on high alpine slopes during the daylight hours. Occasionally it moves about and feeds during the day when food is scarce. Practically nothing is known of its home range or population density. It appears to exhibit territoriality and drive off strangers. Tagged grizzlies have travelled up to fifty miles.

In the late autumn grizzlies seek the shelter of a cave, hollow tree, or windfall for their winter dens. They usually den high in the mountains, and if they cannot find a natural shelter, they will dig a hole under a projecting rock on a steep slope. Grizzlies spend less time dormant than black bears, seldom retiring before mid-November and emerging in April. Occasionally a lone grizzly may wander about until December, even in the Arctic. Then its long coat may be filled with ice from blizzards or fishing forays. When grizzlies emerge in the spring, their dens may be buried beneath snowbanks, necessitating the excavation of a snow tunnel to the surface.

Grizzlies have lived to an age of twenty-nine years in zoological gardens.

The feeding habits of these bears are omnivorous. Upon first emerging from their dens, they usually make their way down to the valleys to graze on new grass or to dig up the roots of licorice root, glacial lillies, spring beauty, angelica, and skunk cabbage. They also clean up any carcasses of winter-killed big game animals which they find. In summer, fruit such as elderberries, highbush cranberries, salmon berries, crowberries, and bearberries attract their attention, though they also continue to graze on grass and horsetails. From late June until early September, the grizzlies along the west coast crowd the river banks to feed upon spawning and spent Pacific salmon. At all times of the year they consume insects, fungi, and roots. They also dig mice, ground squirrels, and marmots out of their burrows. The grizzlies of the Canadian Rockies are quite carnivorous and hunt moose, elk, mountain sheep, goats, and even black bears. Occasionally they come down from the mountain fastness and kill cattle on the ranges in the foothills. If they kill a large mammal, they will first cache the remains in a snowbank or drag some branches over it, and then bed down close by, returning to feed upon it until it is consumed. I once saw a grizzly drag a horse carcass a hundred yards into a grove of trees – an example of their prodigious strength.

In autumn, after the ground squirrels and marmots have gone into hibernation, the grizzly bears tear up great furrows in the tundra to find the lethargic rodents.

Habitat. The grizzlies prefer open areas. At present they inhabit the alpine tundra and subalpine forests of the Rocky Mountains and extensive areas of arctic tundra. Until the advent of Europeans to this continent they also inhabited the Great Plains region.

Reproduction. The sows breed every second year, oestrus being supressed in the intervening years because they are nursing the cubs at heel. Mating occurs from late June to early July. The males are polygamous, and the sows polyandrous. The gestation period is between 229 and 266 days. Delayed implantation occurs, and the cubs are born to the sow in dormancy some time between mid-January and early March. The average litter size is two, but one to four cubs may be born. At birth the cubs are the size of small kittens (17–20 cm) and weigh about 340 to 680 g. They are clothed with fine, dark fur. They grow rapidly and weigh 15 kg at three months and 25 kg at six months.

The cubs stay close to their mother's heels during the first summer, and are weaned at four to five months of age. The mother is courageous in their defence, because she knows that a wandering grizzly boar would make short work of them if he found them. The sow and her cubs den together the second winter, but they disperse before her next mating period. The third winter the two-year-olds may den together. Sexual maturity is attained at an age of six to seven years.

Economic Status. In former times the grizzly was a dangerous opponent to Indians and Eskimos, armed only with bows, arrows, spears, and knives. For that reason considerable lore arose concerning the bear. Bears were used in totems, there were bear dances, and the Mandans of the Missouri valley prized necklaces of grizzly claws. The early muzzle-loaders were still inadequate defence against a grizzly, but today's high-powered rifles have made bears prime sporting quarry in the Rocky Mountains

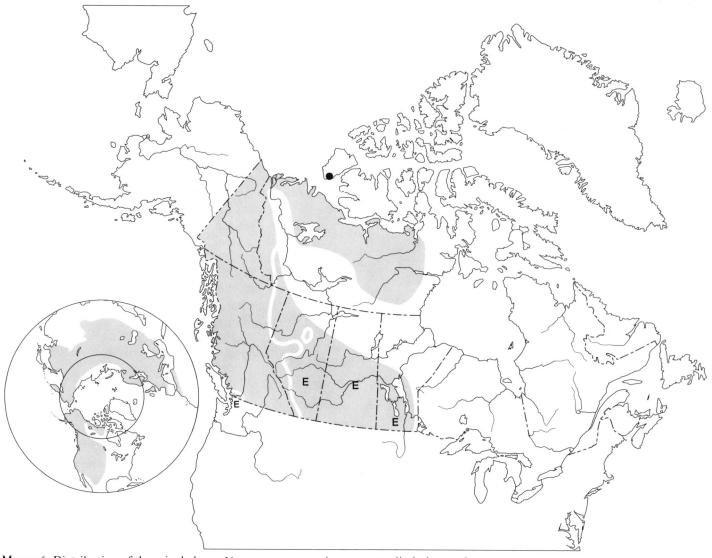

Map 136 Distribution of the grizzly bear, *Ursus arctos*: E extinct, ● extra-limital record

of Alberta, British Columbia, and the Yukon Territory. The hunting incentive is mostly the trophy, and little use is made of the meat or hide. In the 1971–72 fur season, 7 grizzly bear hides were traded at an average price of $130.71, for a total value of $915.

Grizzlies occasionally are a hazard about camps and ranches. Although most of them are extremely shy and try to evade contact with man, there is considerable risk in confronting one at close quarters. Travellers in high country are well advised to give them plenty of room. There are a number of cases of deaths and injuries from bear maulings in western Canada. Occasionally a lone grizzly becomes a cattle killer, and then it is necessary to destroy it.

Distribution. The grizzly once occupied almost all of western North America from the Mexican Highlands to the Arctic Ocean. It is now restricted to the Rocky Mountain region; there are a few in northern Mexico, a few scattered through the western United States, and the remainder are in Canada and Alaska. The closely related European brown bear occurs in Europe, Asia, and Asia Minor.

Canadian Distribution. Grizzlies once occurred on the prairies as far east as the Red River valley, Manitoba (see Map 136), but they were exterminated along with the bison in the early days of exploitation. Now they are restricted to the Rocky Mountains of western Alberta and British Columbia with the exception of the Swan Hills, south of Lesser Slave Lake, Alberta, where an isolated colony, numbering perhaps 400, was discovered in 1953. Farther north they inhabit all of the Yukon Territory and the mountains west of the Mackenzie River. A distinct population known as the barren-ground grizzly occurs on the arctic tundra of northern Yukon Territory and of northern and eastern Mackenzie District and has spread recently into central Keewatin District. One grizzly was even taken on Banks Island in the winter of 1951–52.

Ursus arctos horribilis Ord, 1815, *in* Guthrie, A new geography, history, comm. grammar ..., Philadelphia, American ed. 2: 291, 299.

The American grizzly bear was first described by Ord, based upon the specimens and information collected by

Lewis and Clark in 1804–05. In 1918 C.H. Merriam, in a review of these bears, recognized eighty-seven kinds of grizzlies and brown bears in North America. Recent studies have indicated that all these supposed species refer to individual variations in one species of bear. Because of the extinction of grizzly bears over much of their range, it may never be possible to assign reasonable subspecific names to different populations.

REFERENCES

Holzworth, J.M. 1930. The wild grizzlies of Alaska. G.P. Putnams Sons, New York.
Mundy, K.R.D., and D.R. Flook. 1973. Background for managing grizzly bears in the national parks of Canada. Canadian Wildlife Serv., Rept. Ser. 22.

POLAR BEAR
Ours blanc. *Ursus maritimus* Phipps

Description. Polar bears may surpass in size the grizzlies of the Gulf of Alaska. The shape of the polar bear is quite different, however; its body, especially the neck and the legs, is much longer, and it has a long, narrow head and very small ears. Its foot pads are covered with fur; its rhinarium, claws, and tongue are black; its eyes are brown (Plate 27).

The polar bear's skull is long and massive; the canines are large; the cusps are more elevated on the molariform teeth than those found in other species of bears. These characteristics confirm the fact that polar bears are the most carnivorous of the group.

This species' pelage is coarse, thick, and long. The colour is creamy white; in summer it is thinner and yellowish white. Old males have a mane. The annual moult occurs between the end of May and August.

Males are approximately a fourth to a third larger than females. They measure 2–3 metres (7–11 feet) in length, tail 8–13 cm, hind foot 33 cm, ear 9–11 cm, height at shoulder 120 cm (4 feet). Adult males weigh usually between 420 and 500 kg (900 and 1,100 pounds) with a maximum weight of 700 kg (1,600 pounds).

Habits. Polar bears are solitary, sagacious, stolid creatures. Their usual gait on land is a shuffling walk. They often stand on their hind legs and stretch their necks for a better view of their surroundings. In the water they tread water and stretch their necks up to peer about, or when travelling across ice-floes they climb the ridges for a better view. They seem to have excellent eyesight and an acute sense of smell, but they pay little attention to sounds. When disturbed on land, polar bears make for the sea at a rolling gallop of approximately twenty-five miles per hour. In the water they swim at a speed of four miles per hour and can remain submerged for two minutes. They swim by paddling with their forefeet only, trailing their hind feet. If the water is rough, they swim with muzzle submerged, raising the head regularly to breathe.

Polar bears are carried southward on drifting ice-floes in spring and early summer. When the ice breaks up in August, they come ashore and make their way northward along the coasts. They are occasionally observed as much as seventy-five miles inland at that time. Polar bears will swim great distances across open water to reach the coast.

In late autumn, the pregnant females excavate dens in snowbanks on hillsides or on the sides of pressure ridges of ice, in which they spend the winter and bear their young. Most female polar bears disappear by mid-November and reappear in late March with their cubs. Pregnant females spend 160 to 170 days in dormancy; non-pregnant females spend only 115 to 125 days in hibernation; young males and young females spend about 105 days under cover; and adult males are active most of the winter and take cover for only 50 to 60 days during the darkest days of winter, from about November 23 to January 23. If the seas are frozen and if seals are rare, the old males take to hibernacula, but by early February the tracks of an occasional old male may be seen travelling towards leads in the sea ice.

The polar bear's diet is mostly meat. In early spring it searches for new-born ringed seals in snow caves or 'igloos' on the ice. At other times it preys upon ringed seals, at their breathing-holes. It also hunts harbour and bearded seals and young walrus on ice-floes by skilful stalking or by swimming under water to the edge of the floe. During the summer months it feeds upon shoreline carrion, fish, mussels, crabs, starfish, and the eggs and nestling young of waterfowl and cliff-dwelling sea birds. It has been known to swim under eiders and catch them when they dive in fright. It also grazes on grasses and eats mushrooms, crowberries, and lemmings.

A stranded whale carcass is a real windfall for the polar bear and as many as forty-two of them have been observed congregated at a bowhead whale's carcass. When eating seals, the polar bear consumes the skin and blubber first, the meat last. It has been reported that polar bears throw chunks of ice at walruses to maim them before attacking.

Aside from man, the polar bear has few natural enemies. Occasionally a male walrus or a killer whale may kill one.

Polar bears have lived for as long as thirty-five years in captivity, but their natural longevity is probably less.

Habitat. These bears frequent the southern broken edge of the arctic ice pack. They avoid solidly frozen sea ice and the open seas.

Reproduction. The females experience short oestrous periods every second year. The breeding season occurs from April to May, and the animals pair off during a brief two-week period. The females are polyandrous, and the males fight among themselves for their attention. The gestation period varies from 228 to 254 days after mating. Delayed implantation occurs. Parturition takes place between late November and early January while the females are in their hibernacula. The average litter size is two (1–4). The young cubs are about 30 cm in length, weigh less than 1 kg (2 pounds), and are naked and blind at birth. Their eyes open at about six weeks of age. Their first coat is white and woolly. At three months of age the cub is about 60 cm long, weighs 9 kg, and has a coat of krinkly white fur. Cubs den with their mother the first winter and stay with her until the next summer. By that time they

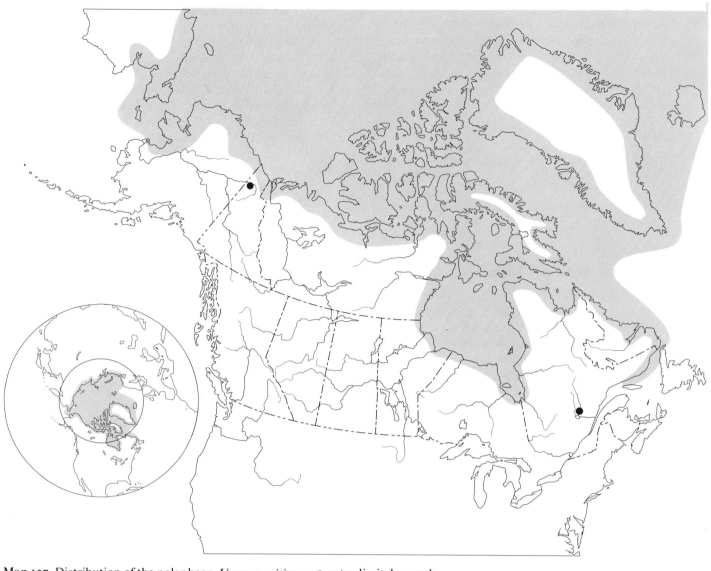

Map 137 Distribution of the polar bear, *Ursus maritimus*: ● extra-limital records

weigh 90 to 180 kg (200–400 pounds) and are half-grown. Their mother drives them off during her next oestrous period. Sexual maturity is reached at an age of five to seven years.

Economic Status. Polar bears are hunted by Eskimos in the Canadian Arctic with the aid of sled dogs. When a bear is met on the trail, the dogs are often cut loose to bring the bear to bay so that the hunter can catch up and shoot it. In winter, dogs are sometimes used to sniff out hibernating bears from their dens. A small hole is dug in the snow so that the bear's head can be located and used as the target. In the 1971–72 fur season, 389 hides were sold at an average price of $329.05, for a total value of $128,000. The Eskimos retain a few more hides for waterproof boots, pants, sleeping-bags, and sled covers. The meat is eaten by men and dogs.

Polar bear livers are poisonous because of the excessive concentration of vitamin A. When eaten, the liver causes nausea, cramps, and temporary blindness. Polar bears also harbour the nematode *Trichinella spiralis*, and the consumption of raw meat may lead to the parasitic disease trichinosis.

Polar bears also have the reputation of being predators of man. They are shy and wary in summer but have been known to attack men during the winter darkness – perhaps because of extreme hunger, or because those particular bears had never before met a man.

Distribution. The polar bear is circumpolar in distribution, inhabiting all arctic seas and coastlines. It is relatively common on the pack-ice off the Alaskan coast north of Bering Strait, off the coasts of Greenland, and along the Eurasian arctic coast from Spitsbergen to Wrangell Island. Only rare stragglers reach Iceland. Individual bears have been seen on the frozen Arctic Ocean as far as latitude 88°N, only two degrees from the North Pole.

Canadian Distribution. This species is found along our arctic coasts from Alaska to Labrador and from the tip of James Bay to northern Ellesmere Island. It is common in the Beaufort Sea and Amundsen Gulf areas, but less common from Coronation Gulf to Boothia Peninsula because of the generally prevailing sluggish currents and solid ice cover. It is again more common east of Boothia Peninsula. Polar bears are most abundant in the north end of Hudson Bay around Southampton Island and in the Arctic Archipelago.

Occasionally stragglers have been met in the interior near Fort MacPherson and Great Bear Lake, Northwest Territories. Bears are regularly carried on the spring pack-ice through the Straits of Belle Isle into the Gulf of St Lawrence, making their way ashore along the north coast of the gulf as far west as Anticosti Island. A most unusual record was that of an old female shot near Peribonca, Lake St John District, Quebec, on or about October 20, 1938 (see Map 137).

No subspecies of polar bears are recognized now.

Ursus maritimus Phipps, 1774, A voyage towards the North Pole ..., p. 185.

REFERENCES

Harington, C. Richard. 1968. Denning habits of the polar bear (*Ursus maritimus* Phipps). Can. Wildlife Serv. Rept. Ser. 5. Ottawa.

Loughrey, A.G. 1956. The polar bear and its protection. Oryx 3(5): 233–9.

Family **Procyonidae** / Raccoons and Their Allies

This family is primarily Tropical New World in distribution, except for the anomalous pandas of eastern Asia. One representative occurs in Canada. They are a diverse group of small to large carnivores in which the specialization of the carnassial teeth is lacking. The molars are low-crowned and usually reduced to two in number in the lower jaw. The plantigrade feet each possess five toes with non-retractile claws. Most species possess moderately long to long tails with prominent coloured annulations.

RACCOON
Raton laveur. *Procyon lotor* (Linnaeus)

Description. The raccoon resembles a fat cat. Its stout body is clothed in a long, thick coat; its short, bushy tail has four to six prominent black rings; its face tapers from the short, rounded ears to a sensitive button-like nose. Its legs are short, and its narrow feet carry five toes each, tipped with strong recurved claws. The soles of its feet are naked, and its stance is plantigrade (Figure 71).

The pelage of the raccoon is long and dense; the undercoat is brown and woolly; the guard hairs are long, and white- or creamy-tipped on the belly and flanks but black-tipped on the back. The tail is alternately ringed with buffy brown and black bands of stiff hairs. The black facial mask, which extends across the cheeks, eyes, and nose, gives the animal a mischievous appearance. The effect of the mask is heightened by pale grey bars above and below and the large, sparkling black eyes. The pointed face is

framed by a ruff of grey hairs behind the cheeks and alert white-tipped ears. Although the general colour effect is usually grizzled grey, there is a wide range of variation from almost black to fulvous, pale grey or even white specimens (Plate 29). A prolonged annual moult occurs during the summer months, at which time the pelage is noticeably shorter than in winter.

The raccoon's skull is rather broad, with a high, rounded cranium. The first premolars are peg-like, the carnassials are rounded, and the molars are flat-crowned, an indication of an omnivorous diet. The auditory bullae are laterally compressed, with a short, central auditory canal (Figure 72).

Males are larger than females. Average measurements of adults: length 846 (730–950), tail 235 (220–250), hind

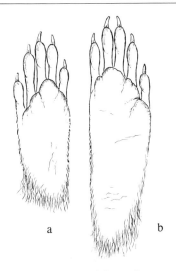

Figure 71 Soles of feet of raccoon: (a) forefoot, (b) hind foot (× 1/2)

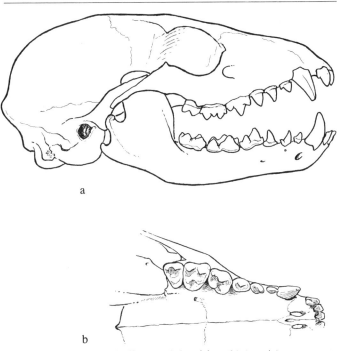

Figure 72 Raccoon skull (a) and dentition (b) (× 2/3)

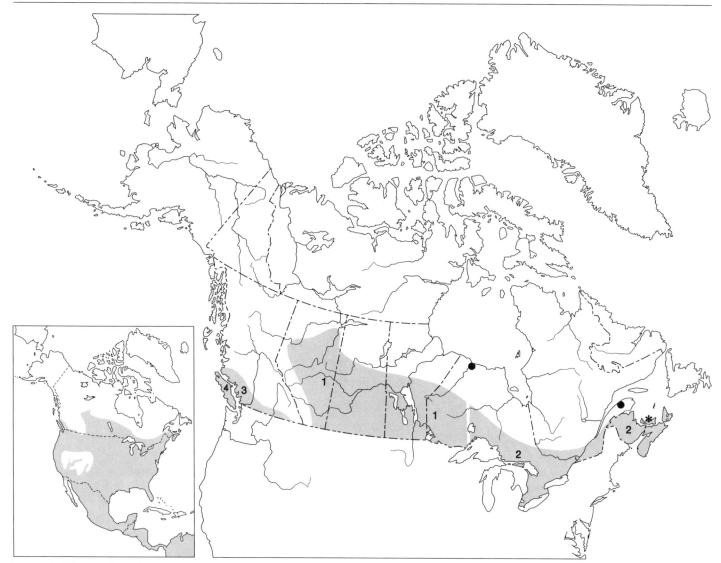

Map 138 Distribution of the raccoon, *Procyon lotor*: 1 *P. l. hirtus*, 2 *P. l. lotor*, 3 *P. l. pacificus*, 4 *P. l. vancouverensis*, *introduced (PEI), ● extra-limital record

foot 112 (105–120) mm. Average weight of adult males 8.6 kg (18.8 pounds) and of adult females 7.5 kg (16.5 pounds). The heaviest raccoon reported weighed 62 pounds 6 ounces (28 kg).

Habits. Raccoons are highly intelligent, moderately sociable animals. The adults usually forage alone, except for the females with half-grown young. However, when raccoons meet there is often a social exchange and sometimes playful tussles. The young are extremely playful. They show a remarkable aptness in finding stored food and overcoming all sorts of protective devices. Although generally mild-mannered and easily tamed, they will fight bravely against great odds when cornered.

Their senses are acute, especially the sense of touch in their fingers and muzzle. Their eyesight is good, particularly at night, when their eyes glow like red coals in the ray of a flashlight. Their hearing is also good, and they seem to be particularly sensitive to ground vibrations.

Raccoons are nocturnal and are seldom active before dark; they spend most of the daylight hours sleeping in a den or in a crotch of a tree. They are excellent climbers and swimmers but run rather slowly with a rolling gallop.

They utilize dens in hollow trees, particularly elms, maples, and basswoods. Their dens are usually situated over ten feet from the ground, and the entrances are 7 to 17 inches (18–43 cm) in diameter. Raccoons also occupy caves, hollow logs, overturned stumps, and burrows excavated by marmots, skunks, or foxes; and around human habitation they often use culverts, drain pipes, and abandoned barrels for temporary shelter. Their dens are lined with leaves or wood chips. In the northern part of their distribution, raccoons become dormant during the severest winter weather, but mild spells in midwinter will usually encourage them to make local forays.

The population density for raccoons has been estimated at two families per square mile of good habitat, or ten individuals to a square mile. They usually range over a mile of territory but may travel as far as five miles.

Raccoons are omnivorous. Sweet corn tops their palatability list in agricultural areas. They are also fond of fruit such as wild cherries, gooseberries, elderberries, and wild grapes. Crayfish are a favourite food item, and these they carefully capture by touch from under the boulders of stream beds. June beetle grubs, grasshoppers, crickets, and molluscs are also avidly eaten. Among the vertebrates eaten are small fish, frogs, and turtles, also meadow voles, deer mice, cottontails, squirrels, and small birds. Although they occasionally kill chickens, most of their food is obtained from river banks, which are their favourite haunt.

Raccoons are a nuisance in suburban areas because of their depredations on garbage tins.

Because of their size and climbing ability raccoons have few natural predators. Bobcats, red foxes, and coyotes manage to catch a few, and great horned owls capture the young animals.

Animals in captivity have lived as long as thirteen years.

Habitat. Raccoons primarily dwell in forested areas near water courses. They occupy river valleys and isolated copses of trees in the grasslands, but are not necessarily confined to the close vicinity of water.

Reproduction. The females are monoestrous, and possess four pairs of mammae. Mating occurs between late January and the beginning of March. After a gestation period of sixty-three days the young coons are born between the middle of April and the middle of May. The average litter size is 3.5 (1–6). The new-born are well furred, except for their slender tails. Their eyes do not open until they are approximately three weeks old. The mother is a solicitous parent and teaches the youngsters to climb and hunt during their first summer. She will even lead the dogs away from her young during the autumn hunting season. The family usually remains together the first winter, but the young females become sexually mature during the next spring, at which time the family breaks up.

Economic Status. 'Coon hunting with hounds is a popular sport in the United States and has some devotees in Canada as well. The flesh is good to eat. However, the main economic importance of raccoons is as fur-bearers. During the 1971–72 fur season, 28,303 raccoon pelts were traded at an average price of $5.44, for a total value of $154,038. The price has been much higher in the past, when 'coonskin coats were in vogue. During their heyday, there were a number of raccoon ranches.

Distribution. The raccoon is native to North and Central America from southern Canada southward. It has been successfully introduced to the Soviet Union as a fur-bearer.

Canadian Distribution. The raccoon occurs in the Maritime Provinces with the exception of Newfoundland (it has been introduced to Prince Edward Island); it occurs in southern Quebec, central Ontario, the aspen parkland of the Prairie Provinces (there is one exceptional record from Wood Buffalo Park, Alberta), and southern British Columbia. There are recent sporadic records for northwestern Ontario (Severn River) and northern Manitoba (Oxford House). Four geographical subspecies are recognized in Canada (see Map 138).

Procyon lotor hirtus Nelson and Goldman, 1930, Jour. Mamm. 11: 455. A large ochraceous subspecies inhabiting the southern and central Prairie Provinces. Increasing and spreading northward.

Procyon lotor lotor (Linnaeus), 1758, Syst. Nat., 10th ed., 1: 48. Eastern Canada.

Procyon lotor pacificus Merriam, 1889, N. American Fauna 16: 107. A dark grey race, found in southwestern British Columbia.

Procyon lotor vancouverensis Nelson and Goldman, 1930, Jour. Mamm. 11: 458. A small blackish race, found on Vancouver and other islands in the Straits of Georgia.

REFERENCE

Whitney, L.F., and A.B. Underwood. 1952. The raccoon. Practical Science Publishing Company, Orange, Conn., U.S.A.

Family **Mustelidae** / Weasels and Their Allies

The members of this family vary from extremely small (weasel) to moderate-sized carnivores (sea otter). They usually have elongate bodies and short legs, each of which carries five digits. The claws are non-retractible. Their stance is digitigrade or semiplantigrade. All members possess a pair of prominent anal scent glands.

The skull of these animals has a shortened rostrum and an elongate, flattened cranium with compressed auditory bullae. The dentition is reduced. The incisors are weak; the canines and carnassials are strongly developed; the molars are reduced to one above and one or two below; the last upper tooth is rotated 90 degrees. The palate extends a considerable distance beyond the molars. The alisphenoid canal is lacking.

AMERICAN MARTEN
Martre d'Amérique. *Martes americana* (Turton)

Description. The marten is a mink-sized arboreal weasel, with a slender body, short limbs, broad feet, and, arming the digits, sharp, flattened recurved claws, admirably suited for climbing (Figure 74). Its bushy tail is about half the length of the body. It has a broad head, tapering to a sharp nose; relatively large ears; and relatively large, bright, beady black eyes (Figure 75). Its stance is digitigrade. Both sexes possess abdominal scent glands, which they rub on logs and rocks during the mating season (Figure 73).

The marten has a relatively long, slender skull, the frontal region of which is broad and flat; it has slender zygomatic arches, a rounded cranium, and relatively inflated auditory bullae. Like all species of the genus *Martes* it possesses four premolars in each row. A slight sagittal crest develops on the older males.

The marten's pelage is long and lustrous; the tan underfur is dense and soft; the guard hairs are long and glossy, particularly in the winter coat. The summer coat is short and rough. There is only one prolonged summer moult. The guard hairs commence shedding in early spring, and the tail appears slenderer in summer. The undercoat is shed in summer. The new coat first appears on the tail and legs in early September, and the complete winter coat is assumed by mid-October.

The colour is extremely variable from dark brown – almost black – to pale buff dorsally, and shows a certain amount of geographical variation: there are foci of dark-

Figure 73 American marten

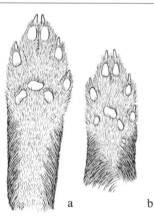

a   b

Figure 74 Soles of feet of marten: (a) hind foot, (b) forefoot (× 1/2)

Figure 75 American marten face (× 1/2)

316

coloured martens (which are the most valuable) in British Columbia and northern Quebec. The dorsum is generally dark brown; the bushy tail and legs are almost black; and the head is light grey. The well-furred ears are pale; the underparts are pale brown, with irregular creamy or orange-coloured breast spots, which may be only on the throat or may extend from the chin to abdomen.

There is a marked difference in the size of the sexes (as for most of the weasel family). The males are about 15 per cent larger than the females. Average measurements of adult males: length 600 (551–645), tail 175 (150–199), hind foot 89 (80–95), ear 42 (35–45) mm; weight 995 (700–1,300) g. Average measurements of adult females: length 538 (490–602), tail 156 (135–182), hind foot 77 (71–98), ear 36 (34–38) mm; weight 661 (600–775) g.

Habits. Martens are primarily solitary animals. The females raise the young, and they form the only groups met. The males are pugnacious and associate with the females only at breeding time. The young martens show the only signs of humour found in the species when they roll and scrap like kittens, but even so they resist being handled after they are three weeks old. Martens have an insatiable curiosity and appetite, which could be mistaken for tameness when they learn to come to feeding stations at isolated cabins in the forest. These same characteristics lead to their easy capture in all sorts of traps.

Although martens are generally considered to be tree-dwellers, they do, in fact, spend considerable time on the ground. When hunting on the ground they bound along, placing the hind feet in the prints of the forefeet and leaving pairs of twin tracks in the snow. They will occasionally swim across rivers and lakes and can dive and swim underwater to escape. They are primarily nocturnal in activity, from dusk to dawn, but may be seen about during late afternoons on cloudy days. They are active all winter. The young are born and raised in leaf-lined nests in hollow trees or in cavities in piles of rocks. They may use overturned stumps or brush piles as temporary shelters.

The males occupy larger home ranges than the females: 0.92 square mile as opposed to 0.27 square mile. During the mating season the males may wander more extensively. Usually they occupy their home ranges permanently, but in mountainous terrain they may undertake seasonal altitudinal migrations because of the changing availability of an adequate food supply in the winter. Transplanted tagged marten have returned twelve miles to their home ranges. Population densities vary from 1.5 to 4.4 animals per square mile of good habitat. It was formerly thought that the marten population exhibited a ten-year cycle of abundance, but there has been little evidence of regular fluctuations since 1922.

Food preferences are broad, and they are not dependent upon a particular prey species. Over a number of years the diet fluctuates widely, depending on the prey species which are available. Mice constitute the main source of food (66 per cent of food items in one study). Although the red-backed vole is the favourite prey, various other voles of the genera *Microtus*, *Synaptomys*, and *Phenacomys* are commonly taken, as well as deer mice and jumping mice.

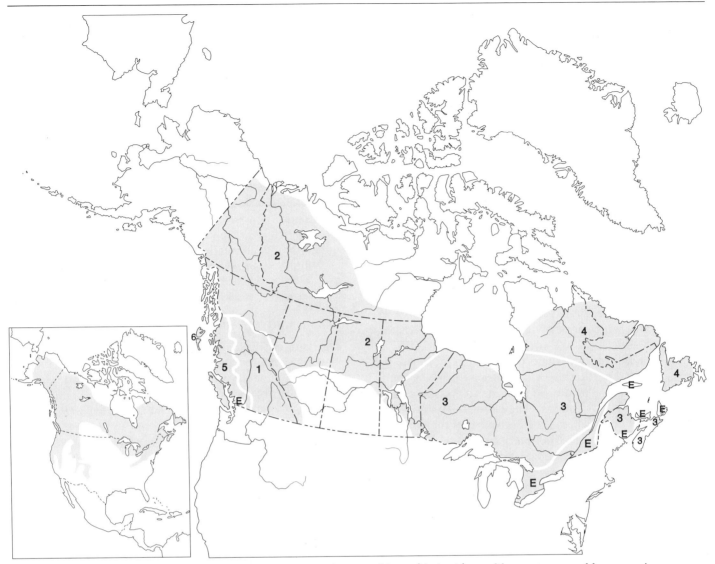

Map 139 Distribution of the American marten, *Martes americana*: 1 *M. a. abietinoides*, 2 *M. a. actuosa*, 3 *M. a. americana*, 4 *M. a. atrata*, 5 *M. a. caurina*, 6 *M. a. nesophila*, E extinct

Red squirrels and flying squirrels are another important source of food (10.2 per cent). Snowshoe hares and pikas are eaten (3 per cent in a study when hares were scarce and 40 per cent in a study when they were abundant). Birds, including grouse and smaller birds, constituted 12.3 per cent of the food in a northern British Columbia study. Fruit such as strawberries, blueberries, and raspberries are eaten during the summer, occasionally forming up to 17 per cent of the diet. Insects, particularly beetles, bugs, and wasps, are also eaten to an extent of about 5 per cent of the normal diet, and carrion in the form of deer and elk carcasses is also eaten.

Aside from man, martens suffer little natural predation. Fishers, lynx, coyotes, great horned owls, and golden eagles are reported to prey on them to a limited extent. Martens have lived up to eleven years in captivity.

Habitat. These animals are typical denizens of the climax coniferous forest. They are found in Douglas fir–cedar–hemlock forests in the west and black spruce–white cedar swamps in the east. They avoid burned-over

or logged areas. Forest fires are a serious menace to marten habitat.

Reproduction. The mating season occurs in July and August each year. The males are polygamous. This species also exhibits delayed implantation in its reproductive cycle. After the eggs are fertilized, further development is arrested in the blastocyst stage for seven to eight months until implantation in the uterus occurs in February or later. The foetuses then develop quickly during the next twenty-eight days to parturition, which occurs in late March or April. The total gestation period is 220 to 275 days. The average litter size is 2.6 (1–4).

The young martens are born helpless, blind, deaf, and practically naked. At birth their weight is about 28 g, and they are covered with a thin coat of yellowish hairs. Their development is altricial. Dark stripes appear dorsally between the eighth and tenth day. The dark greyish juvenile coat is worn until the end of the third week, when they moult into a dark brown subadult coat. Their ears open at twenty-six days of age, and their eyes at thirty-nine days.

317

They begin to crawl at about forty-six days and are weaned at about six weeks of age.

Although the juveniles reach adult size in about three and a half months, they do not mature sexually until they are fifteen to seventeen months old, and even then only about 20 per cent of the most vigorous young females breed. Most do not reach sexual maturity until they are two years old; they bear their first litter near their third birthday.

Economic Status. The marten is one of the more valuable Canadian fur-bearers. The skins are used for collars, capes, and stoles. In the mid-nineteenth century, the Hudson's Bay Company traded as many as 180,000 skins from Canada in a single season, but in recent years the annual harvest has dropped to about 28,000 skins per year. When the market for fine furs was at its peak in the 1940s, marten hides were worth as much as $100 each, and the total harvest was worth approximately two million dollars. However, the marten has fallen from favour in recent years, and in the 1971–72 season 56,231 marten were traded at an average price of only $8.33, for a total value of $468,280.

Distribution. Marten once occurred in a broad belt across forested northern North America from Newfoundland and the Appalachian Mountains to Alaska and the southern Rocky Mountains. They remain today only in pockets, particularly in the northern parts of their distribution, because of the destruction of habitat and excessive trapping. The closely related pine marten, *M. martes*, and the stone marten, *M. foina*, occur in Eurasia.

Canadian Distribution. The validity of several subspecies names is in doubt at present because of recent taxonomic studies. I have tried to include below those geographical subspecies that appear to be acceptable (see Map 139).

Martes americana abietinoides Gray, 1865, Proc. Zool. Soc. London 1: 106. A small dark race, found in the Rocky Mountains of eastern British Columbia and southwestern Alberta.

Martes americana actuosa (Osgood), 1900, N. American Fauna 19: 43. A large greyish form, found in the Yukon and Northwest Territories and possibly in the northern parts of the Prairie Provinces.

Martes americana americana (Turton), 1806, A general system of nature ..., 1: 60. A small reddish form found in Ontario, southern Quebec, and the Maritime Provinces, now extinct on Prince Edward Island and Cape Breton Island.

Martes americana atrata (Bangs), 1897, American Nat. 31: 162. A large dark race, occurring in Newfoundland, Labrador, and northern Quebec. Now extinct on Anticosti Island.

Martres americana caurina (Merriam), 1890, N. American Fauna 4: 27. The last two subspecies are situated on the Pacific coast and are more clearly differentiated from the previous forms by certain skull characteristics: lower, broader skulls; shorter, broader auditory bullae; and larger upper molars. The present race is more cinnamon brown above with a dark orange throat patch. It occurs along the Pacific coast of British Columbia west of the Coast Range, including Vancouver Island.

Martes americana nesophila (Osgood), 1901, N. American Fauna 21: 33. A large pale form with heavy dentition, found on the Queen Charlotte Islands.

REFERENCES

Dodds, D.G., and A.M. Martell. 1971. The recent status of the marten, *Martes americana americana* (Turton), in Nova Scotia. Canadian Field-Nat. 85(1): 61–2.

Hagmeier, E.M. 1961. Variation and relationships in North American marten. Canadian Field-Nat. 75(3): 122–38.

Weckwerth, R.P., and V.D. Hawley. 1962. Marten food habits and population fluctuations in Montana. Jour. Wildlife Mngt. 27(1): 55–74.

FISHER
Pékan. *Martes pennanti* (Erxleben)

Description. The fisher resembles a large black cat, but its body is slenderer, its limbs are much shorter, and its long, bushy tail tapers towards the tip. It has a broad head that tapers to a black button-like nose, short rounded ears, small eyes, and large feet armed with narrow, curved, horn-coloured claws (Plate 30).

The fisher's skull is much larger and heavier than that of the marten. The rostrum is relatively long. The adult male has strong, broad zygomatic arches and pronounced sagittal crests. The female's skull is slenderer than the male's and has a smooth, rounded cranium.

The fisher's thick pelage is coarser than the marten's. The grey, buff-tipped underfur is long, dense, and woolly. The long brown guard hairs have a variable grey subterminal band. This light band, which is broad on the head, shoulders, and upper back, gives the animal a grizzled grey mantle. The rump, tail, feet, and belly are dark chocolate brown, almost black in some specimens. There may be small irregular white spots on the chest and abdomen. Fishers also show much individual variation from pale grizzled grey individuals to almost black ones. An albino fisher has also been reported.

Males are about 20 per cent larger than females. Average measurements of males: length 940 (847–1,073), tail 350 (328–373), hind foot 118 (97–125) mm; weight 3.7 (2.6–5.5) kg. Average measurements of females: length 808 (703–946), tail 306 (253–364), hind foot 100 (87–107) mm; weight 2.1 (1.3–3.1) kg.

Habits. Fishers are usually solitary animals, and only occasionally are two sets of adult tracks noted together outside of the breeding season. However, young fishers travel with their mother most of their first year. They are secretive animals and are seldom observed. They are less arboreal than the marten and do most of their hunting on the ground. They appear to prefer walking on fallen logs. Fishers are also good swimmers. They are about both night and day and remain active throughout the winter months except during the severest weather, when they

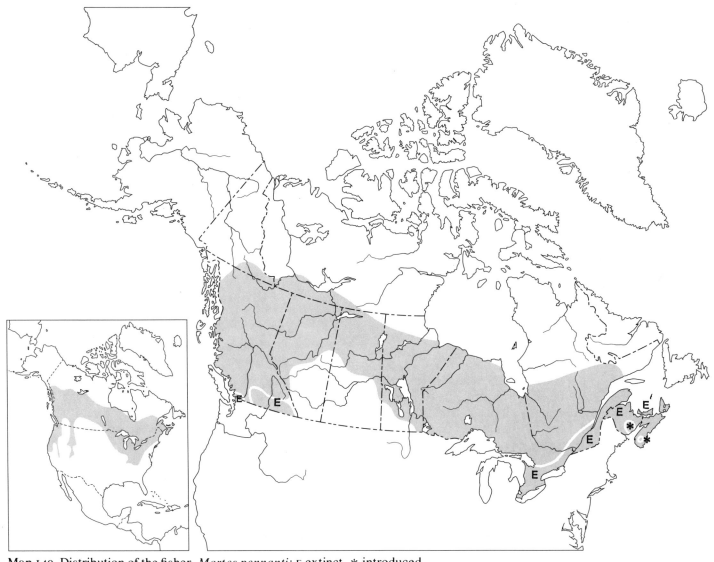

Map 140 Distribution of the fisher, *Martes pennanti*: E extinct, * introduced

take temporary shelter. They construct their dens in hollow trees and logs, in rock crevices and brush piles, and under boulders. They use temporary dens while on the trail, which may be shallow snow dens or even inside the frozen carcass of a large game animal.

Fishers travel along regular hunting circuits much like wolves. These circuits may be as much as sixty miles in length and encircle a home range approximately ten miles in diameter. The population of these carnivores appears to fluctuate with a periodicity of about ten years.

Mammals constitute about 80 per cent of the diet of the fisher. Among the favourite food items are red squirrels (17 per cent), flying squirrels (2 per cent), red-backed voles (17 per cent), snowshoe hares (17 per cent), shrews (13 per cent), porcupines (8 per cent), deer mice (7 per cent), along with traces of mink, muskrat, and other small mammals. Fishers are considered the classical predators of porcupines, which they manage to bite on their unprotected bellies. Carrion also forms an important part of their diet, and the finding of deer, moose, caribou, and beaver in studies of their diet is usually attributed to their

feeding on carcasses of these large animals, although there are records of fishers attacking and killing young fawns.

Other classes of food include birds (11.7 per cent), particularly the blue jay and ruffed grouse, fish (1.7 per cent), insects (3.3 per cent), and fruit (23.4 per cent). During the summer months they eat mountain ash berries, cherries, beechnuts, and probably many other berries as well. Occasionally traces of frogs and toads turn up in their diet.

Man is the only important predator of the fisher.

Habitat. This animal is a denizen of the climax coniferous forest. It prefers the vicinity of water courses. Unlike the marten, it will venture into subclimax deciduous groves and old burns.

Reproduction. The fisher has a remarkably long gestation period for an animal of its size, comparable to the gestation period of some of the largest whales. Postpartum oestrus occurs six to eight days after parturition. The breeding season occurs in March and April, and the young are born the following year between March 23 and April 27. The average gestation period is 352 (338–358) days, but implantation of the blastocysts is delayed until

319

late January or early February. The average litter size is 2.7 (1–4). The young are born blind and helpless. Development is altricial. The eyes open at about seven weeks. Sexual maturity is reached at two years of age, although some young animals in captivity may breed as yearlings.

Economic Status. Fisher skins are used as coat collars, capes, and stoles. The pelage of the large male skins is harsh, and the smaller female skins are more valuable. Small fine skins were valued up to $345 each in 1920. During the 1971–72 fur season, 8,278 fisher skins were traded at an average price of $29.35, for a total value of $242,963.

Distribution. The fisher is unique to North America and is quite distinct from the Eurasian sable, *Martes zibellina*. It is more southern in distribution than the marten and occupies the broad band of boreal forest that traverses north-central North America. It also occurs in the eastern hardwood forest and the southern Cordilleran region of the west coast.

Canadian Distribution. Never so common as the marten, the fisher has been reduced to pockets in the forested regions of Canada from New Brunswick (extinct in Nova Scotia since 1922) to British Columbia. It extends its range northward as far as the southern Mackenzie District and Yukon Territory but is absent from the coastal islands (Newfoundland, Prince Edward Island, Vancouver Island, and the Queen Charlotte Islands; see Map 140). Recent studies have indicated that there is probably only one variable form in North America.

Martes pennanti (Erxleben), 1777, Systema regni animalis …, p. 470.

REFERENCES

DeVos, A. 1952. The ecology and management of fisher and marten in Ontario. Ontario Dept. of Lands and Forests Tech. Bull.

Dodds, D.G., and A.M. Martell. 1971. The recent status of the fisher, *Martes pennanti pennanti* (Erxleben), in Nova Scotia. Canadian Field-Nat. 85(1): 63–5.

Rand, A.L. 1944. The status of the fisher *Martes pennanti* (Erxleben), in Canada. Canadian Field-Nat. 58(3): 77–81.

ERMINE or STOAT
Hermine. *Mustela erminea* Linnaeus

Description. This ferocious little carnivore is familiar to both North Americans and Europeans alike. Its long, slender body, including the tail, scarcely reaches 12 inches. Its small intense face is no broader than its serpentine neck. Its slender furred tail is approximately a third of the total length. It has short oval ears, which are thinly furred. The vibrissae are long, befitting a fossorial mammal. A pair of prominent anal scent glands give the animal a strong musky odour, particularly when it is aroused (Figure 76).

The skull of the ermine is long, narrow, and flattened;

the rostrum is short; the auditory bullae are elongate; the post-orbital processes are blunt. The mouth is small, and the premolars are reduced to three in each row (Figure 77).

The ermine's pelage is short and fine and exhibits a pronounced seasonal variation. In summer the dorsum, the outer sides of the legs, and the flanks are a rich chocolate brown, which is cut off abruptly from the creamy white ventral parts including the lips, and from the undersides of the legs and toes. The terminal third of the tail is tipped with long, stiff black hairs. The brown pattern is provided by the guard hairs, which when parted disclose the greyish underfur.

In winter the pelage is longer and denser than in summer, and the soles of the feet are well furred. The colour then is clear white throughout, except for the black tip of the tail and frequently a yellowish staining around the rump, caused by the discharge of the scent glands. Albino

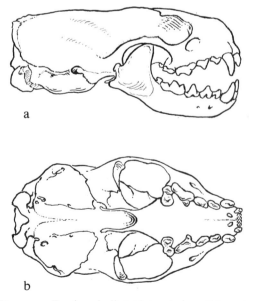

Figure 76 Ermine

Figure 77 Ermine skull: (a) lateral view, (b) ventral view (× 1½)

white ermines have been observed in summer. Not all ermines turn white in winter, however. Those of south-western British Columbia, where winter snow cover is uncommon, remain brown throughout the year.

The drastic change in colour takes place during a period of from three to five weeks, twice a year: in late March and April, and again in late October and November. In spring the brown coat first appears as a mid-dorsal strip and gradually spreads over the flanks and rump to the lateral demarcation line. The belly is the last region to moult, and white hairs remain on the toes. In autumn the process is reversed, the new coat appearing first on the belly and spreading to the dorsum. The duration of daylight is the major initiating factor for the moult, although the temperature is also significant, but to a lesser degree. The changing light stimulus is received by the eyes and transferred to the pituitary gland, which alters the amount of gonadotrophic hormone produced. The actual coat change may be detected by changes in the hair follicles some time before the moult appears. The spring moult is also associated with the breeding season.

Males are approximately twice the size of females in this species. Average measurements of adult males: length 272 (251–315), tail 75 (65–90), hind foot 35 (32–38) mm; weight 80 (67–106) g. Average measurements of adult females: length 236 (215–255), tail 55 (42–70), hind foot 30 (28–33) mm; weight 54 (45–74) g.

Habits. This bold little hunter is muscular, agile, and quick in its actions. It appears and disappears among the logs and foliage of the forest floor with confusing rapidity. The slender, serpentine body permits it to enter small rodent burrows and reminds one of a quick looping caterpillar as it lopes along a log. Its voice is shrill and piping. Its insatiable curiosity and appetite drive it to bold activity when confronted by man. An ermine may clamber up a man's clothing to reach food or attack someone who releases it from a trap. It frequently takes up residence in cabins and lives off the kitchen scrap, boldly taking food from table and pantry alike. The female is courageous in the defence of her young and will carry them away from danger in her mouth, even if the half-grown offspring is almost as large as herself. The family hunts together until the young disperse. The young ermines indulge in rough-and-tumble play.

Although primarily terrestrial, ermine can climb well and often pursue squirrels and chipmunks in trees. They can also swim and often cross small streams. In winter their hunting forays leave a maze of little paired tracks over new snow, exploring every stump, shrub, and hole. They also follow mouse runways beneath the snow or make tunnels themselves. On one occasion in Prince Albert National Park, Saskatchewan, as I paused on my snowshoes to regain my breath, I was startled to see the head and little body of an ermine rise out of the clean trackless snow before me. Although occasionally met during the daylight hours, they are mostly nocturnal in activity.

Ermine commonly take over the burrows of mice, ground squirrels, chipmunks, or pocket gophers and adapt them to their own occupancy. They use the fur and feathers of their prey or dry grasses and shredded leaves to line their nests. Other sections of the burrows are used as toilet and larder. Not all ermine live underground. Some build dens in hollow logs and under roots and buildings and in abandoned farm machinery. I surprised a female who had built a nest of grass in a hollow rafter in a barn. She carefully transferred her half-grown young, one by one, along the rafter to the safety of the hayloft.

Populations exhibit drastic fluctuations, depending upon the population of mice. When mice are abundant, so are ermine, and when mouse populations crash, they disappear also. In years of peak abundance their crushed bodies are commonly observed along highways.

A nematode, *Skrajabingylus nasicola*, parasitizes the frontal sinuses of weasels and causes the holes that are occasionally observed in the frontal bones of their skulls.

Admirably suited for killing small mammals, these carnivores make quick dashes to capture their prey, grab them around the shoulder region, and bite through the neck at the base of the skull. If the prey is small, they stand over it, but if it is large, they may be thrown sideways, where they kick and claw while maintaining a grip with their jaws. Cottontails and small hares are about the largest prey they can manage to kill, but practically no resting animal is safe from their attacks. One ermine was observed harrying a red-tailed hawk from perch to perch. All weasels are accused of a lust for killing far more than their immediate needs, but the fact that they store the extra carcasses in larders does not bear out this statement. As winter approaches these animals begin to amass an underground larder full of mice.

An analysis of the ermine's diet has indicated the following percentages: mice 50.7, shrews 22.5, hares 8.7, porcupine 6.2, birds 5.0, squirrels 2.5, fish 1.2, and unidentified flesh 3.7. Voles of the genera *Microtus* and *Clethrionomys* and mice of the genera *Peromyscus* and *Mus* are most frequently taken. These are consumed in the proportion of their availability. Larger game include rats, ground squirrels, pocket gophers, chipmunks, pikas, and mountain beavers. Occasionally larger males become specialists at killing poultry. Ermine have been reported to feed their young on earthworms. They also eat snakes and frogs.

In turn, these small carnivores are hunted by larger carnivores such as coyotes, badgers, foxes, hawks, owls, martens, wolverines, and fishers.

Habitat. Ermine occupy a wide range of habitats. They seem to be more at home in boreal coniferous or mixed forests, but they also inhabit tundra, boundaries of meadows, shrubby river banks, and lakeshores. They stay close to the cover of rock talus, stone walls, hedgerows, stumps, and logs. They occur from sea level to alpine tundra – up to an elevation of 10,000 feet.

Reproduction. Adult males appear to be in reproductive condition from late February or March to August. Postpartum spontaneous ovulation occurs in the female in the spring, and since further oestrous cycles follow at about monthly intervals, the females may be considered poly-

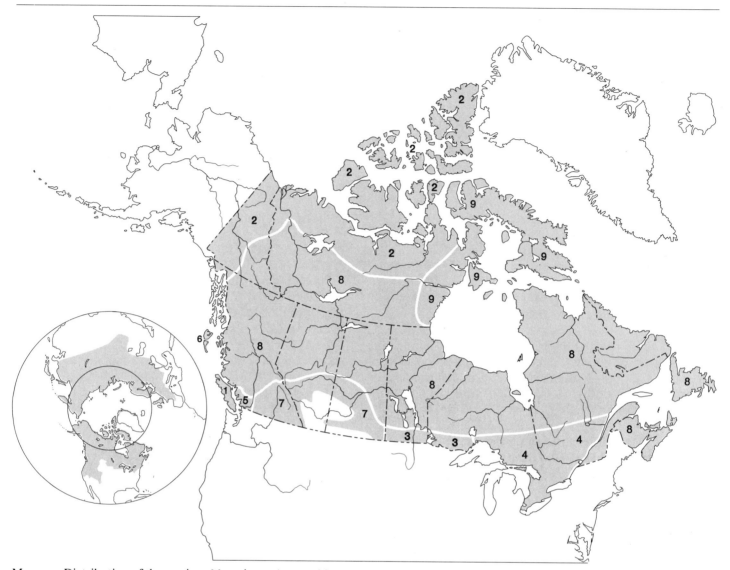

Map 141 Distribution of the ermine, *Mustela erminea*: 1 *M. e. anguinae*, 2 *M. e. arctica*, 3 *M. e. bangsi*, 4 *M. e. cicognanii*, 5 *M. e. fallenda*, 6 *M. e. haidarum*, 7 *M. e. invicta*, 8 *M. e. richardsonii*, 9 *M. e. semplei*

oestrous. Mating may take place in early summer, but the implantation of the blastocyst is delayed until the following March, and parturition occurs about a month later. The apparent gestation period is therefore approximately ten months.

One litter is born each year between mid-April and early May, which averages six (4–9) young. The female possesses ten mammae. The tiny young ermines are covered with fine white hair at birth, and their eyes and ears are sealed. Although altricial in development, growth is rapid. The young have well-developed manes at three weeks (which distinguishes them from young long-tailed weasels), their eyes open at five weeks, and the youngsters are soon travelling short distances with their mother. Young males at seven weeks are as large as their mothers. Since the young juvenile females mature sexually very quickly, at two to three months of age, all female ermines are capable of bearing young each spring. The males mature

the following February or March and take part in reproduction the next summer.

Economic Status. The ermine derives its common name from its white winter coat, which is considered fit to grace the shoulders of royalty. The small skins are used for trimming coats, stoles, and neck-pieces. Unfortunately no distinction is made between the white winter skins of our three species of weasels in the fur trade, and they are all called 'ermine.' This species, however, makes up the bulk of the furs. In the 1971–72 fur season, 38,964 skins were traded at an average price of $0.64, for a total value of $25,047.

Distribution. The ermine, or stoat, has a very wide circumpolar distribution, inhabiting Europe, North Africa, Asia, northern North America, and northeastern Greenland.

Canadian Distribution. The ermine is found in all of Canada with the possible exception of a few offshore islands. Nine subspecies are currently recognized (see Map 141).

Mustela erminea anguinae Hall, 1932, Univ. California Pub. Zool. 38: 417. Found on Vancouver, Saltspring, and North Pender islands, British Columbia. Distinguished by a narrow white ventral band; usually remains brown in winter.

Mustela erminea arctica (Merriam), 1896, N. American Fauna 11: 15. A large subspecies, found on the tundra and taiga of the Yukon and Northwest Territories, including the Arctic Archipelago exclusive of Keewatin District and Baffin and Bylot islands.

Mustela erminea bangsi Hall, 1945, Jour. Mamm. 26: 176. Southern Manitoba and western Ontario.

Mustela erminea cicognanii Bonaparte, 1838, Charlesworth's Mag. Nat. Hist. 2: 37. A small subspecies with broad white ventral band, which occupies southern Ontario and Quebec.

Mustela erminea fallenda Hall, 1945, Jour. Mamm. 26: 79. Distinguished by its darker brown coat, including the upper lip, which it usually carries all year. It is found in southwestern coastal British Columbia.

Mustela erminea haidarum (Preble), 1898, Proc. Biol. Soc. Washington 12: 169. Confined to the Queen Charlotte Islands, British Columbia. The under side of the base of the tail is coloured the same as the belly.

Mustela erminea invicta Hall, 1945, Jour. Mamm. 26: 75. Southeastern British Columbia and southwestern Alberta.

Mustela erminea richardsonii Bonaparte, 1838, Charlesworth's Mag. Nat. Hist. 2: 38. A large form that inhabits boreal Canada from Newfoundland to British Columbia including the southern Yukon and Northwest Territories.

Mustela erminea semplei Sutton and Hamilton, 1932, Ann. Carnegie Mus. 21: 79. A small subspecies, characterized by its short, blunt muzzle and broad forehead, found on Bylot, Baffin, and Southampton islands and eastern Keewatin District, Northwest Territories.

REFERENCES

Criddle, N., and S. Criddle. 1925. The weasels of southern Manitoba. Canadian Field-Nat. 39(6): 142–58.
Hall, E.R. 1951. *Mustela erminea. In* American weasels. Univ. Kansas Pub., Mus. Nat. Hist. 4: 87–167.

LONG-TAILED WEASEL
Belette à longue queue. *Mustela frenata* Lichtenstein

Description. This is the largest of the three species of weasels found in Canada; males attain a total length of about 20 inches. The long, slender tail is approximately half the length of the body (Figure 78c). The legs are sturdy and strong. The skull is similarly more ruggedly constructed than the ermine's; old males possess a sagittal crest. The cranium is relatively shorter, and the postorbital processes are pointed.

The summer coat of the species is cinnamon brown above, including the face, legs, and basal portion of the tail, and ochraceous or buff-coloured on the ventral surface. The winter coat is pure white (including the vibrissae) except for the black terminal quarter of the tail. Long-tailed weasels in the southern part of their distribution in the United States remain brown all winter. Rarely melanistic specimens have been encountered.

The autumn moult occupies approximately thirty days between early October and early December, and the spring moult occupies about twenty-five days between late February and late April. The new white winter coat first appears on the abdomen, feet, and tail and gradually spreads over the flanks, neck, and face. In the meantime the back becomes paler, with the appearance of white guard hairs. The rump and back of the head are the last regions to show the brown coat. The spring moult progresses in the reverse direction: the new brown coat first appears behind the shoulders and ears, then on the dorsum, and spreads over the flanks. The changing length of daylight is again the main causative factor involved in the moult.

Males are approximately 25 per cent larger than the females. Average measurements of eastern adult males: length 406 (374–456), tail 135 (124–153), hind foot 45 (42–51) mm; weight 225 (196–267) g. Eastern adult females: length 325 (306–362), tail 108 (95–117), hind foot 37 (35–41) mm; weight 102 (72–126) g.

Habits. As far as is known, the habits of the long-tailed weasel do not differ markedly from those of the ermine except as a result of its larger size. It appears to occupy a larger home range, which has been variously estimated to include from 10 to 300 acres. Although the home ranges of several weasels may overlap, weasels seldom meet except during the breeding season. Populations fluctuate but not

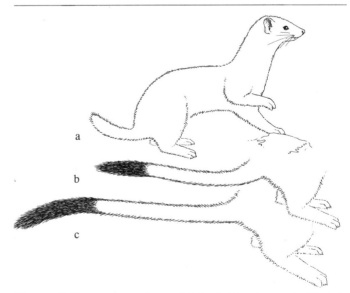

Figure 78 Comparison of weasel tails: (a) least weasel, *Mustela nivalis*; (b) ermine, *Mustela erminea*; (c) long-tailed weasel, *Mustela frenata* (× 1/2)

323

Map 142 Distribution of the long-tailed weasel, *Mustela frenata*: 1 *M. f. altifrontalis*, 2 *M. f. longicauda*, 3 *M. f. nevadensis*, 4 *M. f. noveboracensis*, 5 *M. f. occisor*, 6 *M. f. oribasus*

so rythmically as those of the ermine. Densities have been estimated to vary from one weasel per 6.5 acres to one weasel per 38.2 acres of open forest.

Because of its larger size and greater power this weasel can subdue larger game than the ermine, but the bulk of its diet consists of small mammals. It clings tenaciously to larger animals with its teeth and stubby legs, and wraps its slim muscular body around its prey in much the same manner as a large snake. The weasel, when cornered or when men have come between it and its prey, has been known to attack. In one study the percentage of food items was as follows: meadow voles 52, deer mice 19, chipmunk 18, pocket gophers 3.9, ground squirrels 2.6, pikas 1.3, prairie dogs 2.6. The weasel also eats cottontails, wood-rats, red squirrels, harvest mice, house mice, Norway rats, roof rats, shrews, and least weasels, when those prey species are available. Specimens have been found with porcupine quills embedded in their faces, indicating that they will even tackle these well-defended creatures.

Birds constitute a less important prey group. The re-mains of tree sparrows, field sparrows, horned larks, brown creepers, and teal have been found in weasel stomachs. They undoubtedly take a toll of young ground-nesting birds as well. It is this species that probably accounts for most of the predation in chicken coops. In a study in southern Michigan long-tailed weasels accounted for 59 per cent of the predation on chickens and 1 per cent of the total chicken population. On the other hand, they undoubtedly kill many rats, which also prey upon young chicks.

Weasels also eat small numbers of insects: grasshoppers, vesper wasps, and flies. They occasionally kill snakes and may eat berries during the summer months.

Their predators are foxes, coyotes, wolves, domestic cats, and dogs.

Habitat. This species shows a greater preference for open country grasslands, aspen parklands, and river bottom lands. It prefers the vicinity of water. In the southern Rocky Mountains it occurs in the alpine tundra zone to an elevation of 10,000 feet.

Reproduction. The females possess four pairs of abdominal mammae, and are monoestrous. Oestrus occurs 65 to 104 days after the birth of the young. Implantation of the embryos is delayed from September to March; then the foetuses develop for approximately twenty-seven days prior to birth. Males are sexually active from April to August; their gonads regress in September. Both sexes are sexually inactive during the period when the white winter coat is worn.

Mating occurs in July and August. The young are born between early March and early April, after a gestation period of 279 (220–337) days (including the seven-month period of delayed implantation). The average litter size is six (3–9).

New-born weasels are pink and wrinkled and are sparsely covered with white hairs. The head seems unusually large and the neck unusually long. They weigh approximately 3.1 g when one day old. Development is altricial. They are clothed in a fuzzy white coat by one week, which grows into a sleek coat by two weeks. However, they lack the mane of young ermines. Their eyes open between thirty-six and thirty-seven days of age, and they are weaned at three and a half weeks. The female takes the young on foraging parties.

The juvenile females mature very quickly by the age of three to four months, but the males do not mature sexually until they pass their first birthday.

Economic Status. Unfortunately the two larger weasels are not differentiated in the fur trade, though fewer long-tailed weasels are trapped because of their more limited distribution in Canada. This species is a more important predator on chickens than other species. It is best controlled by setting baited steel traps under the chicken coop.

Distribution. Unlike the other two weasels, this one is strictly New World in distribution and occurs from northern South America to southern Canada.

Canadian Distribution. Six geographical subspecies are currently recognized in Canada (see Map 142). This species is confined to the southern boundary of Canada except in the northwest where it reaches central British Columbia and Alberta.

Mustela frenata altifrontalis Hall, 1936, Carnegie Inst. Washington Pub. 473: 94. A large chocolate brown form with yellow or orange underparts, found only in the Fraser delta region of British Columbia.

Mustela frenata longicauda Bonaparte, 1838, Charlesworth's Mag. Nat. Hist. 2: 38. A large pale race, found in the southern Prairie Provinces.

Mustela frenata nevadensis Hall, 1936, Carnegie Inst. Washington Pub. 473: 91. A small dark race in which the yellow colour of the underparts continues onto the under side of the forefeet and the base of the tail; found in south-central British Columbia.

Mustela frenata noveboracensis (Emmons), 1840, A report on the quadrupeds of Massachussetts, p. 45. A paler brown race with longer black tip to the tail; found in southern Ontario and Quebec.

Mustela frenata occisor (Bangs), 1899, Proc. New England Zool. Club 1: 54. Very long black tip to the tail; found in southern New Brunswick and the easternmost townships in southern Quebec (Kamouraska).

Mustela frenata oribasus (Bangs), 1899, Proc. New England Zool. Club 1: 81. A form characterized by the prolongation of yellow on the ventral surface of the tail and on the dorsal surface of the paws; found in the Rocky Mountains and Caribou plateau of British Columbia and the Peace River district of Alberta.

REFERENCES

Hall, E.R. 1951. *Mustela frenata. In* American weasels. Univ. Kansas Pub., Mus. Nat. Hist. 4: 193–405.
Soper, J.D. 1919. Notes on Canadian weasels. Canadian Field-Nat. 33(1): 43–7.

LEAST WEASEL
Belette pygmée. *Mustela nivalis* Linnaeus

Description. This mammal is the smallest carnivore. It is scarcely larger than the mice on which it preys, and seldom exceeds 8 inches in total length. It has the typical slender, lithe body and short legs of its large relatives, but its short stubby tail lacks the black tip in summer and winter (Figure 78a). Its face is blunt, and its short oval ears scarcely protrude beyond the fur (Figure 79).

The tiny skull is elongate; the rostrum is shortened; the cranium is elongate but more elevated than that of *Mustela erminea*. The post-orbital processes are pointed.

In summer, this weasel's coat is walnut brown above and white below, from upper lips to base of tail. It has whitish feet, and brown spots may occur on the cheeks. The soles of the feet are furred. In winter, throughout most of the range, its coat turns completely white with the possible exception of a few black hairs at the tip of the tail. In southern populations in the eastern United States, the

Figure 79 Least weasel

white belly is more restricted and the brown or mottled brown coat is worn all winter.

The autumnal moult begins on the ventral surface, and the vernal moult begins on the mid-dorsal line and proceeds as outlined for the ermine.

Males are larger than females. Average measurements of adult males: length 196 (183–217), tail 34 (27–42), hind foot 22 (21–23), ear 13 (12–15) mm; weight 43.7 (34.5–63.5) g. Average measurements of adult females: length 176 (170–181), tail 25 (22–29), hind foot 19 (18–21), ear 12 mm; weight 41 (25–58) g.

Habits. The habits of this diminutive predator are similar to those of the larger ermine. It appears to be even more agile in its movements, however, and is seldom observed or captured, except by accident in a small trap. Its voice is reported to be a shrill shriek. It is primarily nocturnal and is active all winter.

These weasels usurp the nests and burrows of their victims, and adapt them for themselves, lining them with fine grass or mouse fur, which they pluck from the carcasses of their prey. In winter the fur lining may be an inch thick and may be matted like felt. In it they keep themselves warm, or thaw out a frozen mouse carcass from their larders. Once established for the winter in a burrow of a vole, a pocket gopher, or a mole, they drag in the carcasses of other mice secured on short hunting forays, and cache them in their larders. Near by is situated the toilet area. Occasionally their nests are discovered in straw or clover stacks. The home range has been estimated at two acres, and the weasel seldom travels more than 100 yards from its home.

Least weasels feed almost exclusively on mice, such as meadow voles, prairie voles, red-backed voles, deer mice, house mice, and harvest mice. They hunt by scent and pounce on the hapless animal, biting through the back of its skull with their minute canines. They may also eat amphibians and insects in summer. They have very high metabolic rates and consume approximately one gram of food per hour, which adds up to more than half the body weight of an adult least weasel per day.

This species is eaten, in turn, by long-tailed weasels, by great horned and barn owls, and frequently by feral house cats.

Habitat. This species, which also accepts a wide choice of habitats, may be found in stubble fields, meadows, river banks, parklands, and mixed forests.

Reproduction. Studies on captives have shown that in spite of its similarity to other weasels the least weasel resembles the ferret in reproductive biology. Females are polyoestrous, and two or possibly more litters are born each year. The period of heat lasts about four days. There is no delayed implantation, and the gestation period is only thirty-five to thirty-seven days. In North America mature males are sexually active from February until mid-November. Nestlings have been discovered in the wild during the months of July, August, December, January, February, and March. The litter size averages five (3–10) young. The young are weaned after twenty-four days, and

34

Some Canadian seals: (a) bearded seal, *Erignathus barbatus*; (b) ringed seal, *Phoca hispida*; (c) northern elephant seal, *Mirounga angustirostris*; (d) hooded seal, *Cystophora cristata*; (e) grey seal, *Halichoerus grypus*

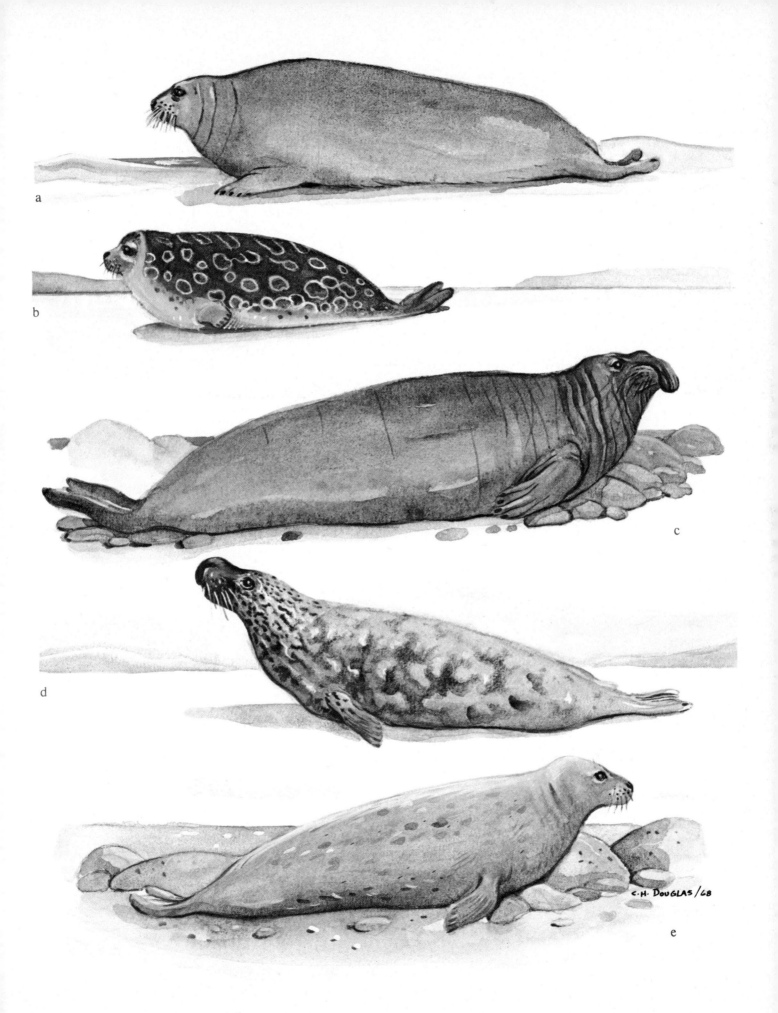

a

b

c

d

e

C.H. Douglas/68

35

their eyes open after thirty days. The juveniles reach sexual maturity at approximately four months.

Economic Status. This weasel is quite rare and therefore of little significance in the fur trade. Among the Indians the trapping of a weasel was considered a good omen. It is a valuable check on mouse populations.

Distribution. This species also occupies a broad circumpolar distribution through western Europe, North Africa, Asia, and northern North America.

Canadian Distribution. The least weasel occupies most of continental Canada with the exception of the Maritimes, southern Ontario and Quebec, coastal British Columbia, and the northeastern tundra of the Northwest Territories. Two subspecies are currently recognized (see Map 143).

Mustela nivalis eskimo (Stone), 1900, Proc. Acad. Nat. Sci. Philadelphia 52: 44. Northern Yukon Territory and northwestern Mackenzie District.

Mustela nivalis rixosa (Bangs), 1896, Proc. Biol. Soc. Washington 10: 21. The remainder of Canada.

REFERENCES

Criddle, Stuart. 1947. A nest of the least weasel. Canadian Field-Nat. 61(2): 69.

Heidt, G.A. 1970. The least weasel *Mustela nivalis* Linnaeus. Developmental biology in comparison with other North American *Mustela*. Michigan State Univ. Pub. of the Museum, Biol. Ser. 4 (7): 229–82.

Polderboer, E.B. 1942. Habits of the least weasel (*Mustela rixosa*) in northeastern Iowa. Jour. Mamm. 23(2): 145–7.

Saunders, W.E. 1932. Least weasel, *Mustela rixusa* (Bangs) in Ontario. Canadian Field-Nat. 46: 146.

BLACK-FOOTED FERRET
Putois d'Amérique. *Mustela nigripes* (Audubon and Bachman)

Description. This large, mink-sized weasel is now perhaps the rarest mammal in North America. Its body is thicker than the smaller weasels'; its legs are stout; its tail is rather short, and well furred but not bushy; its oval ears are more prominent. Large males may reach 23 inches in length.

The skull of this species is massive and broad. The zygomatic arches are widely spread. The rostrum is short and convex. The skull is prominently constricted behind the post-orbital processes. The sagittal and lambdoidal crests are well developed. The broad auditory bullae are obliquely flattened.

The over-all colour is creamy white. The underfur is white, and short brown-tipped guard hairs project through on the dorsum to give a tan-coloured cap and saddle markings. There is a dark chocolate brown mask across the eyes, the cheeks, and the feet; the legs and terminal third of the tail are similarly coloured. The muzzle, forehead, ears, throat, belly, and base of the tail are white. There is a brownish wash on the fur between the legs, and a thin black mid-line on the lower abdomen. The foot pads are furry, with long hairs hiding the claws (Plate 31).

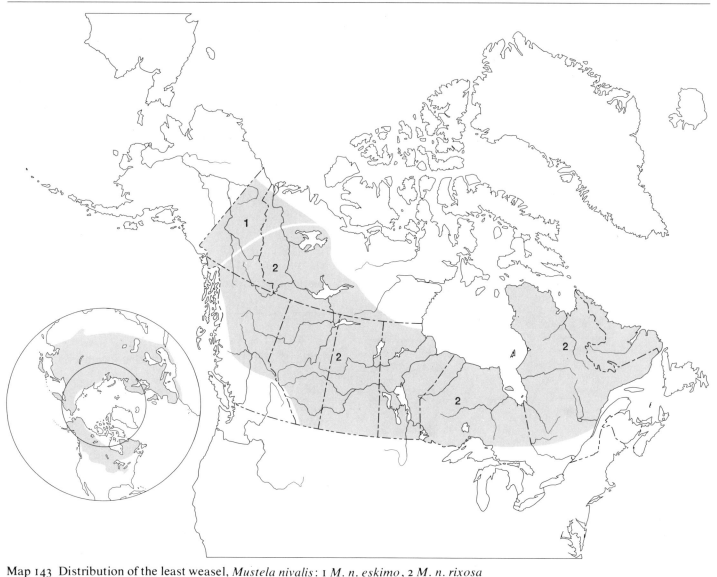

Map 143 Distribution of the least weasel, *Mustela nivalis*: 1 *M. n. eskimo*, 2 *M. n. rixosa*

The ferret's summer coat is thin and more buffy in colour than the winter one. The winter coat, though relatively short, is glossy and silky. Specimens taken in late November and early December were moulting. The vibrissae remain black the year round.

Average measurements of Canadian adult males: length 533 (512–573), tail 127 (114–139), hind foot 59 (51–64), ear 27–30 mm. Weights of three adult males: 535, 588, 633 g. Adult females are about 10 per cent smaller than the males; measurements of one adult female: length 500, tail 128, hind foot 61 mm.

Habits. Very little is known of the habits of this species. The animals are playful when young but have the reputation of being ferocious as adults. They are fastidious and scratch sand over their refuse and toilet heap, which is located near the entrance to their burrows. They often squat on their hind quarters and stretch their slender bodies erect to get a better look at their surroundings. They travel with graceful leaps across the ground. When cornered, they chatter angrily.

Ferrets are most active at dawn and dusk, but they may be observed occasionally at midday. They remain active all year but may spend some days in their burrows during the worst winter storms.

Ferrets usurp rodent burrows for their dens, but usually modify them by enlarging the entrance and constructing various chambers and connecting tunnels. They deposit large mounds of fresh earth near the entrance.

The black-footed ferret is believed to live primarily on prairie dogs. Most ferrets that have been observed were in the 'dog towns' running from one burrow to another. Since prairie dogs are active most of the winter over much of their range, they provide a continuous supply of food. Ferrets are also known to eat several species of ground squirrels, cottontails, jack rabbits, voles and mice, snakes, and many ground-nesting birds including sharp-tailed grouse. There is even one record of a black-footed ferret attacking a new-born pronghorn antelope. Voles increase in importance for them during the winter months, when several of the other species, such as hibernating

328

Map 144 Distribution of the black-footed ferret, *Mustela nigripes*: E extinct

ground squirrels, are not available. Since the prairie dog has such a restricted distribution in Canada, other species must assume larger roles in the ferret's diet.

Habitat. The black-footed ferret is confined to arid short-grass prairies.

Reproduction. Nothing is known of the reproduction of this species in North America. An Asian relative mates in late winter and bears three to six young in early spring. There is no evidence of delayed implantation in ferrets, and the gestation period is thirty-seven days. Nursing females have been taken in late June in North America, and a light tan youngster, with its eyes open, has been observed on July 10.

Economic Status. The pelt is of no commercial value. The ferret is economically beneficial because of its rodent diet.

Status. The last Canadian specimen was secured on December 7, 1937, at Climax, Saskatchewan, and the species is now believed to be extirpated in Canada. Although never common, it has been reduced to the verge of extinction in the United States as a result of the prairie dog eradication program. Scattered observations of ferrets in North and South Dakota have been made as recently as 1963, and the last observation from Montana was in 1957. Elsewhere they are believed to be extirpated.

Distribution. The black-footed ferret originally occupied the central grasslands from Texas to the southern prairies of Canada. The American species is closely related to the common pale steppe ferret *Mustela eversmanni* of eastern Europe and central Asia. That form is increasing and spreading northward.

Canadian Distribution. Originally met on the western prairies south of Calgary, Alberta, and Regina, Saskatchewan. Now extinct (see Map 144). The species was named:

Mustela nigripes (Audubon and Bachman), 1851, The viviparous quadrupeds of North America 2: 297.

REFERENCE

Henderson, F.R., P.F. Springer, and R. Adrian. 1969. The black-footed ferret in South Dakota. Dept. of Game, Fish and Parks, Pierre, South Dakota.

AMERICAN MINK
Vison d'Amérique. *Mustela vison* Schreber

Description. The mink is our most valuable fur-bearer. It has a long lithe body, short sturdy legs, a long serpentine neck, and a flat, pointed face (Figure 81). It has a bushy tail about half the body length, and small ears. It possesses anal glands, which emit a strong musky odour. Large males may reach 2 feet in total length (Figure 80).

Figure 80 American mink

Figure 81 American mink face (× 1/4)

329

The mink's skull is sturdily constructed, with short, flat rostrum, narrow zygomatic arches, an ill-defined postorbital constriction, and a flattened cranium. The auditory bullae are flattened, and the last upper molar is dumbbell-shaped.

The pelage is soft and lustrous, with thick greyish-brown underfur and long, glistening guard hairs. The thick pelage is about the only aquatic adaptation that this amphibious weasel possesses. The soles of the feet are only sparsely haired. The coat colour varies from a rich brown to almost black, but is paler on the ventral surface, which has white splashes on the lower lip, the chest, and sometimes the lower abdomen. There are a number of colour mutations, which are bred on fur farms. Two of these at least – pearl and albino – occasionally occur in wild populations.

Male mink are much larger than their mates. Adult males average: length 535 (491–620), tail 174 (158–210), hind foot 60 (56–68) mm; weight 2.07 (1.68–2.31) kg. Average measurements of adult females: length 509 (420–597), tail 149 (128–180), hind foot 50 (47–54) mm; weight 0.89 (0.79–1.20) kg.

Habits. Although playful as kits, adult mink are considered bold, ferocious, and untamable. They usually live solitary lives, except during the mating season when they run together briefly. There are questionable reports of males assisting the females in feeding the young. They utter a variety of cries from a soft cooing during the mating season to screams and hisses when fighting.

As is well known, mink are excellent swimmers; they also lope along the ground with a typical musteline gait. They are primarily nocturnal in activity and remain active all year, except during the severest weather.

Mink inhabit dens under the roots of trees along stream banks, or occasionally use beaver lodges, muskrat houses, or stumps and hollow logs in the forest. Usually they merely usurp the bank burrows of beavers and muskrats, but occasionally they dig their own dens. Females normally occupy one or two dens, in which they raise their kits; but males range widely and may take shelter in a large number of bank burrows.

The females restrict their travels to an area of from nineteen to fifty acres, but males range over territories of up to three square miles. Prior to the trapping season, mink populations may be of the order of 8.5 to 22 animals per square mile of good habitat. In less favourable agricultural areas, after the trapping season the population may be as low as three or four animals per square mile. In these areas most of their travel is along water courses. There is little information on longevity in the wild, but there is almost a complete replacement of individuals over a three-year period.

The mink's diet has been studied in detail in New York State. Small mammals make up 38.3 per cent of the food items identified in stomachs and intestinal tracts. Leading the list of mammals taken are the meadow vole (12.4 per cent), the muskrat (5.4 per cent), the shrew (4.8 per cent), and the cottontail (2.9 per cent). In other studies muskrats have been more important (as high as 36 per cent of the

diet). At periods of low water level and when the juvenile muskrats are dispersing in the autumn, they are particularly vulnerable to mink predation. Fish forms the next most important group (33.3 per cent). Favourite species are minnows, dace, shiners (14 per cent); followed by trout (2.5 per cent) and sunfish (1.7 per cent). Frogs (18.9 per cent) and salamanders (3.2 per cent) are important items, too, as are crayfish (14.1 per cent). Insects (6.8 per cent), birds (2.7 per cent), and earthworms (2.4 per cent) are less important. An item that does not appear in this study is snakes, although mink are known to kill quite a few.

Male mink feed upon larger game than the smaller females, eating mostly muskrats and cottontails. This diet is a reflection of their wider cruising range. The more sedentary females feed upon smaller game in their restricted territories.

Mink predators are few, but include the great horned owl, the bobcat, the red fox, the coyote, the wolf, and the black bear.

Habitat. Mink inhabit stream banks, lakeshores, forest edges, large swamps, and tidal flats. In late winter the water level usually drops below the ice level in rivers and lakes, leaving a thin layer of air, which permits them to travel widely underneath the ice.

Reproduction. Because of the economic importance of the mink, its reproductive processes have been studied in detail. The females possess three pairs of inguinal mammae, and are polyoestrous to the extent that the follicles ripen in several waves, seven to ten days apart, during the mating season in the absence of fertilization. Ovulation is induced by coitus and occurs thirty-six to thirty-seven hours afterwards. After a short period of development, the embryo enters a short restive period in the blastula stage. This period is variable, depending upon the stage in the breeding season. This season lasts from late February to early April. The later the mating the shorter the delay in implantation so that the period of birth is a restricted one between late April and early May. For the reasons outlined above, the gestation period varies widely from thirty-nine to seventy-six days, with an average of fifty days. The males are in breeding condition in February and March and mate promiscuously.

Only one litter, which contains from two to ten kits (average five), is born each year. The young mink are pink and wrinkled and are covered with fine white hairs; they are blind and deaf. Development is altricial. The eyes open at the age of about five weeks, and the youngsters are weaned soon after. They follow their mother on her hunting excursions during the early summer but fend for themselves after two months and disperse in the autumn. The juvenile females reach adult weight at four months, but the males grow more slowly, reaching adult weight at about nine to eleven months. The females reach sexual maturity at twelve months and the males at eighteen months.

Economic Status. Mink has always been an important fur-bearer, but in recent years, when short-tailed species have been favoured in fur styles, it has come to dominate the fur market. A large number of wild mink are still

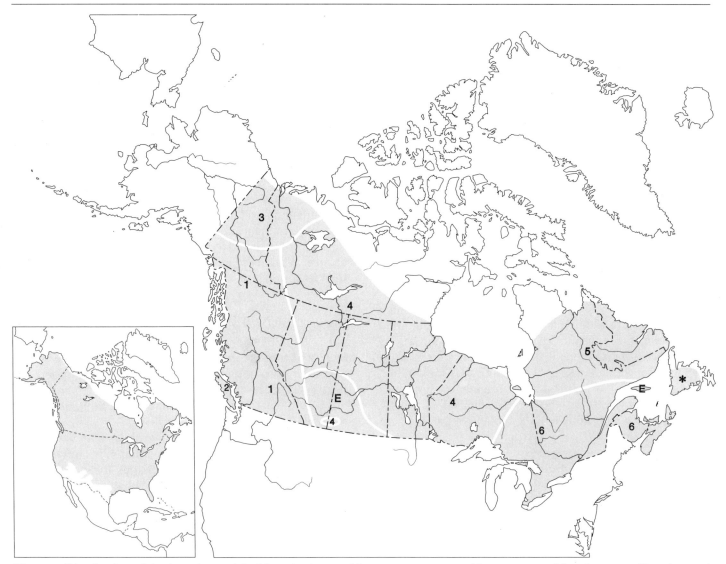

Map 145 Distribution of the American mink, *Mustela vison*: 1 *M. v. energumenos*, 2 *M. v. evagor*, 3 *M. v. ingens*, 4 *M. v. lacustris*, 5 *M. v. lowii*, 6 *M. v. vison*, * introduced, E extinct

trapped (in the 1971–72 fur season, 72,674 mink were trapped at an average value of $11.72 apiece, for a total value of $855,806), but many more mink are raised on mink ranches. During the 1971–72 fur season, 1,155,020 ranch-raised mink were pelted and sold for $14,633,981 at an average price of $12.67. Most of these mink are raised in Ontario, Manitoba, and British Columbia.

Occasionally mink are involved in depredations on hen houses, but they are far more damaging in forages about fish hatcheries.

Distribution. The American mink is distinct from its close relative the Eurasian mink. Our species occurs throughout most of northern North America.

Canadian Distribution. Six subspecies are currently recognized in Canada (see Map 145). The species occupies all of Canada south of the treeline with the exception of Newfoundland, Anticosti Island, and the Queen Charlotte Islands. It has been introduced to Newfoundland.

Mustela vison energumenos (Bangs), 1896, Proc. Boston Soc. Nat. Hist. 27: 5. A small dark race, found in south-

ern Yukon and Mackenzie District, British Columbia, and western Alberta.

Mustela vison evagor Hall, 1932, Univ. California Pub. Zool. 38: 418. A large pale race, found on Vancouver Island, British Columbia.

Mustela vison ingens (Osgood), 1900, N. American Fauna 19: 42. A large brownish race, found in northern Yukon and Mackenzie districts.

Mustela vison lacustris (Preble), 1902, N. American Fauna 22: 66. A small pale race, found in central Canada west and south of Hudson Bay.

Mustela vison lowii Anderson, 1945, Ann. Rept. Provancher Soc. Nat. Hist. Quebec 1944: 57. A small dark race, from northern Quebec and Labrador.

Mustela vison vison Schreber, 1777, Die Säugethiere ..., pl. 127b. Typical form found in eastern Canada as far as James Bay.

REFERENCES

Hamilton, W.J. Jr. 1959. Foods of mink in New York. New York Fish and Game Jour. 6(1): 77–85.

Hansson, A. 1947. The physiology of reproduction in mink (*Mustela vison*) with special reference to delayed implantation. Acta Zoologica 28: 1–136.

Mitchell, J.L. 1961. Mink movements and populations on a Montana river. Jour. Wildlife Mngt. 25(1): 48–54.

Mustela macrodon (Prentiss), 1903, Proc. United States Nat. Mus. 26: 887.

REFERENCE

Wright, B.S. 1962. The sea mink of Fundy. *In* Wildlife sketches – near and far, pp. 143–51. Fredericton, N.B.

SEA MINK
Vison de mer. *Mustela macrodon* (Prentiss)

Description. The sea mink is an outstanding example of man's thoughtless exploitation of wildlife resources; it was exterminated before it was recognized as a distinct species.

The sea mink was described as being fully twice the size of the American mink, the female sea mink being as large as the largest male common mink. It had a much larger skull than *M. vison*, with a wide rostrum, a large opening of the anterior nares, and an antiorbital foramen; it was also characterized by very large teeth. Its fur was much coarser and more reddish than that of the more common mink, and it was reported to have a peculiar odour.

This species was originally described from a portion of a skull found in an Indian shell heap near Brookline, Maine, and since that date other skeletal fragments and skulls have been described from the New England coast.

Habits. Nothing is known of the biology of this species.

Habitat. It occurred along the rocky coasts and offshore islands, a habitat now occupied by American minks.

Reproduction. No details are known for this species.

Economic Status. The remains of this mink found in shell heaps indicate that it was used by the Indians for food. The fur buyers of Maine during the first half of the nineteenth century recognized the 'sea mink' pelts and paid a 'special price' for them because of the size.

Status. It is thought that the sea mink was exterminated in New England about 1860 or 1870. The last specimen secured was taken at Campobello Island, New Brunswick, about 1894, and has been mounted.

Distribution. The exact limits of the distribution are unknown. It occurred from Connecticut northward to the Bay of Fundy.

Canadian Distribution. The only Canadian record is the last specimen ever taken. That it may have had a wider distribution in the Maritimes is suggested by an early reference to an unidentified mammal by Thomas Pennant in *Arctic Zoology* in 1785. He reports 'a strange animal seen by Mr. Phipps and others in Newfoundland, of a shining black: bigger than a fox; shaped like an Italian greyhound; legs long; tail long and tapered. One gentleman saw five sitting on a rock with their young, at the mouth of a river; often leaped in and dived, and brought up trouts, which they gave to their young. When he shewed himself, they all leaped into the water and looked at him. An old furrier said he remembered a skin of one sold for five guineas.' This reference could have applied to an otter equally well, but Pennant was familiar with the otter, which he described elsewhere.

WOLVERINE
Carcajou. *Gulo gulo* (Linnaeus)

Description. Probably no other northern mammal plays such an important role in camp-fire tales and folklore as does the wolverine. It is accredited with prodigious strength and ferocity – enough to drive off a grizzly bear – and superhuman intelligence, which enables it to evade the traps of men and to rob the most elaborately protected caches. Although the wolverine is in real life slightly less than its reputation, it is in many ways a remarkable mammal.

It is one of the larger species in the weasel family: about the size of a fat spaniel or a bear cub. It has a stout, muscular body; a short, bushy tail; relatively long, strong legs; and large, bear-like paws with five, strong, partly retractile horn-coloured claws, suitable for climbing. Its head is broad; its ears are short and rounded; its small eyes are beady black; and its face tapers to a prominent black muzzle (Plate 32).

The wolverine's skull is massive and broad, with strong spreading zygomatic arches; the cranium is crowned by a strong sagittal crest, which overhangs the occiput. The teeth are massive and are admirably suited for crushing bones. The second lower incisors are displaced back into a

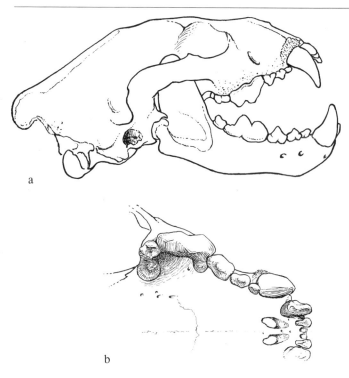

Figure 82 Wolverine skull (a) and dentition (b) (× 1/2)

second row, and the third upper incisor is larger than its mates, reminiscent of the grizzly bear's. There are four premolars rather then three, as found in *Mustela*. The bullae are small, with elongate auditory canals. The lower mandible is firmly hinged to the skull (Figure 82). The stance is semiplantigrade.

In this species the pelage is long and coarse and includes a dense underfur. The general colour is a rich, glossy, dark brown, darkest on the mid-dorsal saddle, the feet, and the tail. The forehead and tips of the ears are grizzled grey. Two pale buff stripes originate on the shoulders and sweep along the flanks, meeting again at the base of the tail. The underparts are dark brown splashed with irregular creamy-white spots on the chest and throat. The soles of the feet are furred. There is a difference of opinion on whether there are one or two annual moults.

Males are larger than females. Average measurements of adult males: length 1,000 (940–1,070), tail 231 (218–260), hind foot 184 (178–190), ear 55 mm; weight 14.8 (11.3–16.2) kg. Average measurements of adult females: length 901 (865–932), tail 223 (210–250), hind feet 160 (155–165), ear 48 (38–56) mm; weight 10.6 (6.6–14.8) kg.

Habits. Like other members of the weasel family the wolverine is pugnacious, curious, bold, and strong, and these characteristics seem to be developed in proportion to its size. It is said that a wolverine will defend its food against the attack of a wolf or even a grizzly bear. It has well-developed scent glands and puts its 'mark' on its food, which further discourages intruders. It is primarily a solitary nomad and will not tolerate the visit, to its territory, of another wolverine of the same sex. The sexes associate only briefly during the mating season, and the only wolverine groups comprise the females and their cubs during the first summer.

The wolverine appears to have poor eyesight and seldom recognizes objects at any great distance. It often sits on its haunches and peers about, and reports have it that it shades its eyes with a raised paw. Its hearing seems to be indifferent, but its sense of smell, by which it tracks its prey, is acute.

The normal gait is a clumsy, though not fast, gallop, which it can maintain tirelessly. Often it walks slowly and deliberately, mile after mile, leaving a line of slightly wavy single footprints in the snow, suggestive of a wolf's track. The wolverine is an excellent climber and sometimes uses low branches to drop onto the back of its prey. It is also an excellent swimmer. It barks, growls, and makes furious hisses when cornered. It is active both day and night and all winter long, seldom seeking shelter even during the most extreme weather.

The wolverine constructs a rough bed of grass and leaves, under a fallen tree trunk, upturned root, rocky crevice, or low, sweeping leafy bough, which serves as a lair. When on the trail during the winter it may dig a snowy den under a snow-burdened evergreen bough for a night's shelter. The home range is extensive; individual animals have been trailed sixty to eighty miles over the snow.

The wolverine is omnivorous; it consumes a wide range of edible roots and berries, small game such as mice and ground squirrels, birds' eggs, fledglings, and fish. Wolverines sometimes are able to catch beavers on their way from feeding grounds to ponds. They also have a particular liking for porcupines, although they do not seem to have mastered the art of killing them with impunity, a few of them having succumbed later because of the piercing of the stomach by the undigested quills. It also manages to kill large game animals with some regularity. Wolverines have been observed killing or worrying moose, caribou, and mountain goats by biting them at the shoulders and the base of the neck.

The wolverine is primarily a scavenger, however, and its dentition shows some parallel developments to the Eurasian hyenas. It follows migrating caribou herds and cleans up the carcasses left by wolves and bears, crushing the bones and cutting the sinews with its powerful carnassials.

One might expect this powerful adversary to have no enemies, but at least one wolverine has fallen victim to a pack of wolves, and, as has been mentioned, others have succumbed to the lowly porcupine.

Habitat. The wolverine formerly inhabited the boreal forests of North America. Although few remain today in the forests, more are found on the tundra between the treeline and the arctic coasts. There are also good populations in the alpine tundra areas of the Rocky Mountains. During the winter months these alpine wolverines descend into the valleys, where game is more plentiful.

Reproduction. The females are monoestrous, with one breeding period a year. The males become sexually active in April, and the breeding season stretches from late April to early September. There is delayed implantation, and the blastocyst does not become implanted until January. The young are born between late March and mid-April after a gestation period of approximately seven to eight months. The litter varies between two and five young.

The first natal coat is fuzzy and creamy white, with darker paws and face mask. The tail is quite stubby. The young are suckled for eight to nine weeks. The female aids their digestion by licking their tummies after each feeding. The mother may attack intruders when the litter is very young and helpless, but when the cubs are older she usually withdraws to safety. During the early summer the cubs remain in the den, and the mother brings food to them. Later they follow her, and she teaches them to hunt. The cubs remain with their mother the first winter of their lives and disperse in spring.

The juveniles mature as yearlings, and the females mate during their second summer.

Economic Status. It is easy to understand how this animal would come into competition with trappers and prospectors in its country. They follow traplines and destroy the trapped fur-bearers. They sometimes learn how to remove the bait from traps without getting caught, and often even hide the traps set to catch them in the snow. They also break into caches of food, furs, and camping gear. The food is often cached elsewhere or 'marked' and

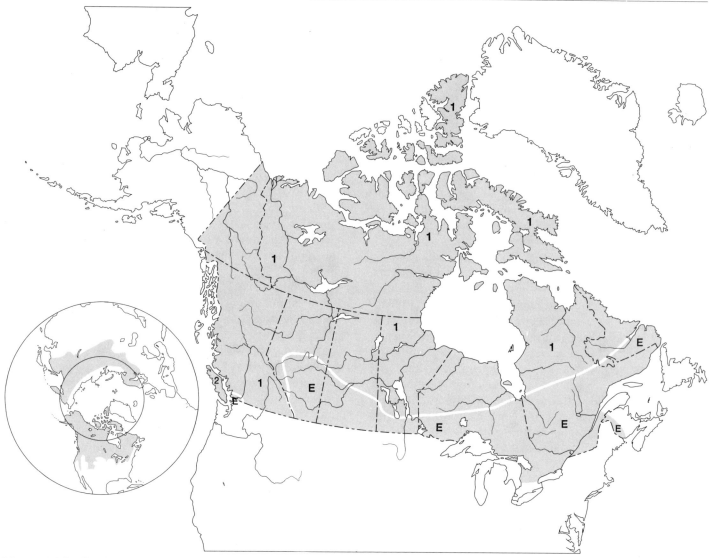

Map 146 Distribution of the wolverine, *Gulo gulo*: 1 *G. g. luscus*, 2 *G. g. vancouverensis*, E extinct

rendered useless for the trappers' use, and the fur and gear are chewed and strewn about. They can roll off the heavy stones a man has lifted onto a food cache. The only safe caches are those constructed as overhanging platforms on tall, peeled poles, ringed by wide metal collars and placed in clearings.

Wolverine fur has little commercial interest, but it is highly regarded by the inhabitants of arctic and subarctic regions because of its quality to resist frosting. It is used by them for parka hoods, collars, and wristlets. The guard hairs are long, sparse, and straight, projecting well above the thick, even underfur, and it is this combination of factors that makes the hairs much less likely to frost than wolf or coyote fur.

During the 1971–72 season, 561 wolverines were sold at an average price of $71.46, for a total value of $40,089. Many more wolverines are trapped annually but are kept by the trappers to trim parkas.

Distribution. This species is another member of the holarctic fauna, occurring in northern Europe, Asia, and North America. In recent years hunters and trappers have greatly reduced its numbers.

Canadian Distribution. Wolverines are still sparsely distributed in the boreal forest from Labrador to Alaska and southward in the Rocky Mountains to the northwestern United States. The present centre of abundance is, however, in the tundra zone of the Yukon and the Northwest Territories. The animal also inhabits the Arctic Archipelago as far north as northern Ellesmere Island. It has not been recorded in Newfoundland, Prince Edward Island, and Nova Scotia; and was exterminated in New Brunswick and southeastern Quebec around 1850 (see Map 146).

Gulo gulo luscus (Linnaeus), 1758, Syst. Nat., 10th ed., 1: 47. Continental North America.

Gulo gulo vancouverensis Goldman, 1935, Proc. Biol. Soc. Washington 48: 177. A smaller race, with chestnut rather than buffy flank stripes, found only on Vancouver Island.

REFERENCES

Krott, Peter. 1958. Tupu-tupu-tupu. Hutchinson, London.

Van Zyll de Jong, C.G. 1975. The distribution and abundance of the wolverine (*Gulo gulo*) in Canada. Canadian Field-Nat. 89: 431–7.

AMERICAN BADGER
Blaireau d'Amérique. *Taxidea taxus* (Schreber)

Description. The badgers are relatively large members of the weasel family. The American badger is a smaller species than the Old World form. Its body is stout, but flattened dorso-ventrally; it has short ears, legs, and tail, and broad semiplantigrade feet. The ivory-coloured claws on the forefeet are extremely long, but those on the hind feet are short (Figure 84). Its small head is broad between the ears and tapers to a pointed snout. There are prominent anal glands, and a belly gland that emits a musky odour when the animal is excited (Figure 83).

The badger's skull is robust and rather triangular in shape, with a broad, flat occipital wall and a tapered, short rostrum; the cranium is flattened. There are four upper teeth behind the canines and five lowers. The mandible is firmly articulated with the skull.

In this species the dorsal pelage is coarse and longer than that on the venter, particularly on the flanks where it forms a fringe, which exaggerates the flattened effect of the body. The base of the dorsal hairs is creamy or buff-coloured; then follows a subterminal black band and a white tip, giving the back a grizzled appearance. The stubby tail is covered with stiff buffy-brown hairs; the underparts are creamy or buffy white; the legs are chocolate brown, and the broad feet are blackish; the foot pads are naked. The badger's head has a very distinctive pattern: the muzzle, crown, and hind neck are dark brown to almost black, and the whole area is divided by a narrow white mid-dorsal line, which runs from the muzzle to the shoulders. This white line is matched on each side of the face by white cheeks and white ears trimmed with black. Behind the eye on each cheek is a black crescentic spot. The fur is much shorter on the head than on the back.

Males are larger than females. Four males from British Columbia averaged: length 801 (775–845), tail 142 (130–157), hind foot 125 (123–130) mm; weight 6.15 (3.6–7.71) kg. Large males may weigh as much as 11.4 kg (25 pounds).

Habits. Very little is known of the American badger's habits. It is primarily a fossorial animal, as indicated by its body form and long digging claws. It is a very powerful digger and a courageous fighter. It seems to be a solitary dweller except during the mating season, which may include much of late summer. Its unique hunting partnership with coyotes has been mentioned in connection with that species.

Either the badger's senses are not particularly keen, or else it chooses often to ignore human observers. If followed too closely, it may hiss and snarl and try to intimidate its pursuer. Badgers are not very agile and run close to the ground with a trotting movement when pursued. Their normal gait is a leisurely waddle.

Badgers are primarily nocturnal in activity, but may be observed regularly sunning near their burrows in the early morning, or hunting during the late afternoon. They are unusual among the weasel family in that they tend to hibernate during the winter months. In Canada this is general from November to April, but farther south they may spend only a few weeks in their dens during the severest weather and remain active during mild spells.

Badgers live in large burrows, which may be as long as thirty feet and as deep as ten feet, situated on the open prairie. The entrances are clearly indicated by great mounds of excavated earth. Bulky nests of grasses are constructed in the enlarged chamber at the end of the burrow. Badgers often take over and enlarge the burrows of prairie dogs or ground squirrels.

The badger's food consists primarily of ground squirrels, pocket gophers, prairie dogs, kangaroo rats, and lesser rodents such as pocket mice, mice, and voles. They also consume ground-nesting birds, snails, and insects.

Figure 83 American badger

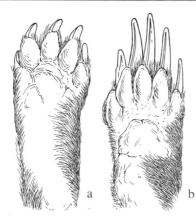

Figure 84 Soles of feet of badger: (a) hind foot, (b) forefoot (× 1/3)

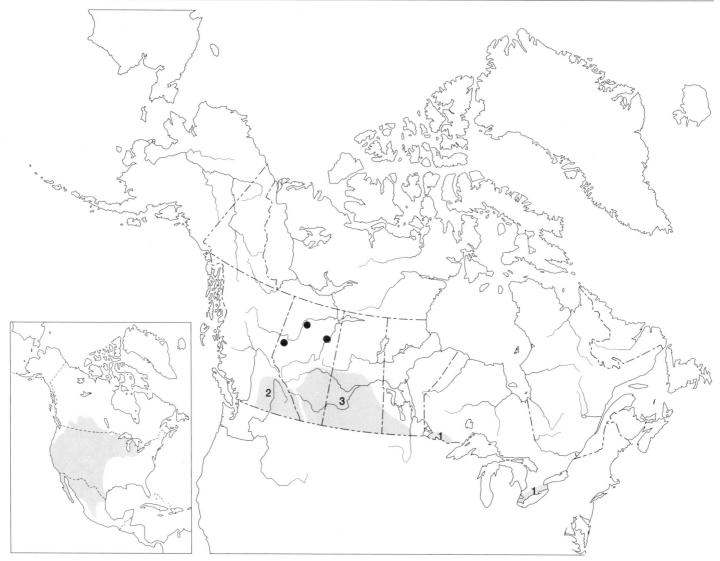

Map 147 Distribution of the American badger, *Taxidea taxus*: 1 *T. t. jacksoni*, 2 *T. t. jeffersonii*, 3 *T. t. taxus*, ● extra-limital records

There is one record of a badger killing a rattlesnake and also a report of their appetite for honey.

Badgers obtain most of their food by excavating the burrows of large fossorial rodents, which they do with such gusto that areas almost an acre in extent may be torn up in their efforts. The badger has developed another unique hunting method: it digs into a back entrance of a ground-squirrel burrow, enlarges it to within about a foot of the front entrance to fit its body, blocks the rear entrance with dirt, and then lies concealed until an unwary animal rushes into the burrow and its waiting jaws.

The badger is too powerful an adversary and too quick a digger to have any other predator but man.

Habitat. Badgers inhabit open prairies, farmlands, and parklands. They do not frequent forests.

Reproduction. Mating occurs in August and September, but implantation of the embryo is delayed until about mid-February. The young, which average four (2–5) in number, are born between late April and mid-May. The young badgers romp playfully around the den mouth in early summer. Although weaned when half-grown, they are brought food by the mother until they are two-thirds grown.

Economic Status. Although badgers perform a useful role in controlling ground squirrels and other rodents, their large excavations are not appreciated by farmers. Badger holes also constitute a serious hazard to horsemen on the open range. Badgers may occasionally raid apiaries, but seldom are a serious risk to chicken houses.

At one time, badger hides were popular as 'throws' over armchairs and chesterfields, and the animals were actively trapped for their pelts, but today their hides have little use in the fur market. During the 1971–72 fur season 2,121 badgers were taken at an average value of $11.02, for a total value of $23,384.

Distribution. The badger occupies a large area of central and southwestern North America.

Canadian Distribution. The badger was once common on the Canadian prairies, but now its numbers are much reduced. It occurs also in the mountain valleys of southeastern British Columbia and in the open, flat farmlands of southwestern Ontario from whence there are a few records (see Map 147).

Taxidea taxus jacksoni Schantz, 1945, Jour. Mamm. 26: 431. A small subspecies with a relatively narrow skull found in southern and western Ontario.

Taxidea taxus jeffersonii (Harlan), 1825, Fauna Americana, p. 309. A large, dark subspecies found in British Columbia.

Taxidea taxus taxus (Schreber), 1778, Die Säugethiere ..., Theil 3: 520. The typical form found in the Prairie Provinces.

REFERENCES

Long, Charles A. 1972. Taxonomic revision of the North American badger, *Taxidea taxus*. Jour. Mamm. 53(4): 725–59.

Seton, E.T. 1909. Common badger of America. *In* Life-histories of northern animals, 2: 995–1009. Scribner's Sons, New York.

WESTERN SPOTTED SKUNK
Mouffette tachetée. *Spilogale gracilis* Merriam

Description. This little skunk is known by a variety of names such as civet cat, polecat, and hydrophobia cat. It is slimmer and more weasel-like than the larger striped skunk; it has a small head, short legs, long foreclaws, naked soles, and a semiplantigrade stance. The skull is small and rounded, with a flattened cranium and swollen auditory bullae.

The pelage is short, silky, and black, with six white stripes extending down the back, flanks, and rump. These stripes are often broken into spots for part of their length. The long black tail is tipped with a white plume, and there are white spots between the eyes and in front of the ears. No two spotted skunks are patterned alike (Figure 85).

Average measurements of adult males of the British Columbia race: length 412 (353–460), tail 126 (101–158), hind foot 48 (41–54) mm; weight 816 (784–847) g. Average measurements of adult females: length 384 (323–439), tail 120 (85–140), hind foot 44 (40–48) mm.

Habits. The spotted skunk is quick, agile, and secretive in its activities, and it resembles the weasels more than the sluggish, confident larger skunks. However, unlike the weasel, it is quite sociable. The families stay together much of the year and often hibernate in community dens. The youngsters romp and play like kittens.

The spotted skunk possesses the same defensive weapon employed by the larger skunks. It discharges a strong musky fluid from a pair of scent glands situated under the base of the tail. This fluid has been described as resembling a highly concentrated onion extract, and experts may detect a difference between it and the musky discharge of the larger striped skunk. The droplets may be projected distances of from six to twelve feet. This species has a unique threatening attitude. Its first warning is to raise its tail and let the white plume cascade over its back. If the intruder pays no heed, the skunk does a handstand on its forefeet, elevates the tail and spreads its hind feet. It may even advance a few feet towards its adversary on its forefeet, or perform a little dance on them. If its tormenter approaches within about six feet, the skunk will spray.

This species has a variety of gaits. It usually trots about its tasks but may bound like a weasel or gallop like a striped skunk. Its maximum speed is about four and a half miles per hour. It is an excellent climber and may climb to the top of a tree to escape. It utters a variety of grunts and screeches. These skunks are primarily nocturnal in activity – with two peaks of activity shortly after sunset and again before dawn – and are seldom seen about during daylight hours. Their spotted pelts make them practically invisible in deep shadows.

Spotted skunks construct their dens in a variety of locations. They may usurp a woodchuck burrow, or use hollow logs, stumps, straw stacks, hollow trees, or dwell under a pile of logs, the floor of a building, or in any place that is dark and dry.

Skunks do not truly hibernate, but several will bed together in a den during severe winter weather. The winter home range consists of about 160 acres and contains several active dens. In spring the males wander over a larger territory of two to four square miles, while the females remain more static. Populations may reach thirteen skunks per square mile of good agricultural land.

The spotted skunk is more carnivorous in diet than the striped skunk, although it still eats a considerable amount of vegetable matter in season. Mammals form the bulk of the winter and spring diet. These include cottontails, field voles, Norway rats, house mice, and native mice. Corn is also an important part of the winter diet in agricultural areas. Insects and plant material form the bulk of the summer and autumn diet. Beetles and larvae are favourite items along with fruit such as grapes, mulberries, and

Figure 85 Western spotted skunk

Map 148 Distribution of the western spotted skunk, *Spilogale gracilis*

ground cherries. Birds and birds' eggs are also eaten during these seasons. Spotted skunks readily accept offal and carcasses at all seasons, and occasionally lizards, snakes, and frogs are eaten.

The spotted skunk's most active predators are men and dogs and cats around farms. Its most dangerous natural predator is the great horned owl, which seems to relish it. Since birds have limited olfactory senses, the skunk's natural defence is not effective against avian predators.

Habitat. The spotted skunk inhabits scrubland, canyons, and farmlands. It avoids heavy forests and wetlands. It often enters buildings.

Reproduction. Much is yet to be learned concerning the reproduction of this species. In the northern part of its distribution, mating apparently takes place in late winter, and the young are born in early summer after a gestation period of at least 121 days. In the southern part of its range, however, a second litter may be born in late summer. It is not yet known whether delayed implantation occurs in this species. The average litter size is four or five.

At birth, young spotted skunks measure about 100 mm in length and weigh about 22.5 g. Their skin is smooth and black with white stripes and is covered with sparse, short, thin hair. Their eyes and ears are closed. They are much more wrinkled by the time they are one week old, but by the time they are three weeks old they have a dense coat in

the adult colour pattern and can crawl about the nest. At thirty-two days of age their eyes open and the youngsters develop the typical defence stance, although the scent glands do not become functional until they are about six weeks old. At the age of three and a half months, they are about adult size and venture out on their own.

Economic Status. In parts of southwestern North America these skunks may be carriers of the rabies virus and hence their name 'hydrophobia cats.' In parts of the southeast they are encouraged to take up residence in barns to control rats. Occasionally individual spotted skunks become chick killers and egg stealers.

Their pelts are in continual demand today for striped short-length ladies jackets. Unfortunately they are too restricted in distribution in Canada to be of any economic significance.

Distribution. The spotted skunk is confined to Central America and southern North America.

Canadian Distribution. Only one subspecies reaches the southwestern coastal area of British Columbia at present, but a central prairie form, *Spilogale spissigrada*, occurs up to the Manitoba–Ontario boundary and may cross the border in the near future (see Map 148).

Spilogale gracilis latifrons Merriam, 1890, N. American Fauna 4: 15. Southwestern British Columbia.

REFERENCE

Crabb, W.G. 1948. The ecology and management of the prairie spotted skunk in Iowa. Ecol. Monogr. 18: 201–33.

STRIPED SKUNK
Mouffette rayée. *Mephitis mephitis* (Schreber)

Description. Skunks are well known to most Canadians, either from first-hand experience or by reputation. The English name is derived from an earlier Indian name. Adults are about the size of a house cat and have a stout, 'hippy' body; small head, eyes, and ears; and a long, bushy tail. This skunk has short legs and plantigrade feet, which have naked soles. The claws of the forefeet are long and make excellent digging tools; those on the hind feet are short (Figure 86).

The skunk's best-known feature consists of a pair of internal perineal musk sacs, which discharge into the anus through a pair of tubes ending in projecting nipples. When a skunk decides to spray, it elevates its tail stiffly over its back, everts the anal orifice exposing the twin jets, and by contracting sphincter muscles ejects twin streams of musky fluid. The streams unite about one foot behind the animal and eventually break up into a fine spray, which may be felt five to six yards away. The skunk possesses uncanny accuracy and can hit an adversary situated a short distance away in any direction – behind, beside, or in front of it – by twisting its rump towards the target. There is a commonly held misconception that skunks cannot eject their musk unless the hind feet are on the ground and that, therefore, they can be lifted by the tail with impunity.

338

Unfortunately this is not true – as many experimenters can testify! The skunk is loath to waste its musk and does not discharge it unless its life is at stake. Seemingly many skunks do not feel their lives are at stake when lifted by the tail, but they will squirt if struck a blow or jerked. It is therefore important to make sure that the offensive battery is directed away from the holder's body when handling them. This is done by grabbing the skunk by the back of the neck and tail.

The skunk's musk is an oily fluid creamy to greenish in colour, which was described by the Canadian naturalist E.T. Seton as 'a mixture of strong ammonia, essence of garlic, burning sulphur, a volume of sewer gas, a vitriol spray, a dash of perfume musk, all mixed together and intensified a thousand times!' The active ingredient is a sulphide called 'mercaptan.' It is highly repellent to all mammals and causes nausea to some individuals, but it is not blinding as many believe. If sprayed on the eyes, it causes intense burning, excessive tear flow, and momentary blindness. The pain is short-lived, however, and normal eyesight returns within a few minutes. Indeed, some say that the vision is improved after a bath of skunk musk.

This species has a sturdy skull, and a prominent sagittal crest on the cranium. The auditory bullae are small. The palate terminates behind the last molar.

The pelage of the skunk is long and lustrous. The basic colour is shiny black, with a narrow frontal white stripe between the eyes and two broad white dorsal stripes, which originate at the nape of the neck and unite again at the base of the tail. There is a great amount of individual variation in pelage, some skunks having only short thin stripes on the shoulders, and others having broad white bands and black-and-white plumed tails. There are two annual moults, in the spring and fall.

The males are approximately 15 per cent larger than the females. Average measurements of adult males: length

Figure 86 Striped skunk

571 (522–610), tail 224 (195–250), hind foot 67 (61–81), ear from crown 15 (13–18) mm; weight 1.66 (1.27–2.44) kg. Adult females: length 551 (512–593), tail 221 (199–246), hind foot 63 (57–67), ear from crown 15 (11–18) mm; weight 1.29 (0.95–2.10) kg.

Habits. The striped skunk is a very placid, sluggish animal, confident in its defensive weapon. It moves with a deliberate walk, a slow trot, or a clumsy gallop. Its top speed has been estimated at nine miles an hour. It swims well enough but climbs very little. Skunks utter a variety of sounds: hisses, growls, squeals, and soft cooings. Although they are primarily nocturnal in activity, they are often observed just at dusk and occasionally one may be seen about in broad daylight.

They build bulky nests of dried grasses and leaves in underground burrows, two to six yards in length. They usually usurp the burrows of woodchucks or cottontail rabbits but occasionally excavate their own. Or they may take up residence under a building, in a wood-pile, or under a stump.

In late October or early November, skunks start gathering material for their winter beds. In our latitudes most skunks begin hibernation during the first cold spell of early December. The adult females and young seldom reappear until late March, but the males may become active during mild spells throughout the winter. Farther south they become dormant only during winter cold spells. Skunks become very fat in the autumn. The females may lose between 10 and 30 per cent of their weight by spring, but the more active males lose only about 10 per cent, since they feed during mild spells. The animals den-up in community dens containing up to a dozen individuals or more, mostly adult females with their young.

The skunk's home range covers about 10.4 acres, and populations average about 13.5 per square mile of agricultural land.

Striped skunks are omnivorous in diet. Their fall and winter diet consists of about 26.7 per cent by bulk of fruit (wild grapes, Virginia creeper, cherries, horse nettle), 19.6 per cent mammals (field voles, deer mice, cottontail rabbits), 6.8 per cent insects (grasshoppers, beetle larvae), 10.8 per cent grasses, leaves, and buds, 13.5 per cent carrion, and 11.3 per cent grains (corn) and nuts. The ratios are different during the spring and summer months, at which time their diet consists of 43 per cent insects (grasshoppers, white grubs), 27.5 per cent fruits, 16.2 per cent mammals (voles, mice, moles, shrews, chipmunks, cottontails), and 8.7 per cent grains. They also occasionally eat birds' eggs and nestlings, crayfish, minnows, molluscs, frogs, lizards, and snakes.

Skunks have few natural enemies, the chief being the great horned owl. Other carnivores such as bobcats, foxes, coyotes, and fishers may take the odd skunk if they are really desperate for food.

Habitat. Striped skunks reach their greatest densities in agricultural lands, but they also occur in forests and along river valleys.

Reproduction. The two sexes consort together only during the brief breeding season. The males are polygamous

Map 149 Distribution of the striped skunk, *Mephitis mephitis*: 1 *M. m. hudsonica*, 2 *M. m. mephitis*, 3 *M. m. nigra*, 4 *M. m. spissigrada*

and are driven off by the females after the termination of their short, three-day oestrous period. The females are monestrous, and the mating period occurs in late February and early March. The young are born in their mother's den around the middle of May after a gestation period of about sixty-two days. The average litter size is five or six (2–10) young.

At birth the little skunks are blind and deaf and are wrinkled and thinly clothed with short, fine fur. The black-and-white colour pattern is already clearly outlined. At three weeks of age they are fully furred, they begin to crawl about, and their eyes start to open. At four weeks they first assume a defensive position with elevated tail. From five to seven weeks they are very playful and at the end of that period they first emit musk. Fully weaned at an age of six to seven weeks, they leave the den and follow their mother on her evening forages in late summer and throughout the autumn. They then hibernate with her when winter approaches.

Economic Status. Striped skunks are reported to be good to eat, although I cannot vouch for this from personal experience. They have long been considered palatable by the Indians, as shown by their remains in kitchen middens. Our chief interest in skunks at present is their over-all effect on agricultural lands, which is largely beneficial because of the vast number of injurious insects and voles they consume. Their nocturnal digging activities for grubs on lawns is, however, an annoyance, and they do occasionally become poultry raiders. They are easily trapped, however, and can be got rid of by live-trapping them and moving them away a couple of miles. It has been shown that they will not return if moved two and a half miles.

Their pelts are not valuable at the present time. During the 1971–72 fur season, 179 skunks were taken in Canada at an average value of 28 cents.

In eastern Canada at present, striped skunks form an important wildlife reservoir of sylvatic rabies.

Everyone is interested in an effective means of removing the musk odour of the skunk's spray from clothing, skin, and pets. It is, of course, nearly impossible to deodorize an object quickly, but gasoline or ammonia removes most of the odour in a first washing. Soaking in tomato juice is also recommended. In the woods, smoking the clothing above a juniper or cedar fire is effective.

Distribution. The striped skunk is found over much of North America.

Canadian Distribution. Four subspecies of striped skunks occur across the country from the Maritime Provinces to the Fraser delta of British Columbia (see Map 149). They are absent from Newfoundland, Cape Breton and Anticosti islands, Labrador, northern Quebec, most of the Northwest Territories, Yukon Territory, and coastal British Columbia. It is believed that they have spread into Nova Scotia since 1850. They were introduced to Prince Edward Island as fur-bearers, but after the market declined they were permitted to escape from fur farms and thereupon became a nuisance. From 1932 to 1956, approximately 4,000 striped skunks were submitted annually for a $1 bounty.

Mephitis mephitis hudsonica Richardson, 1829, Fauna Boreali-Americana 1: 55. A large dark race with bushy black tail, found from western Ontario to the Coast Range of British Columbia and north to the southern Mackenzie valley, Northwest Territories.

Mephitis mephitis mephitis (Schreber), 1776, Die Säugethiere …, Theil 3, Heft 17, pl. 121. The typical form with narrow white stripes and a white plume to the tail, found in eastern Canada from the Maritimes to northeastern Manitoba.

Mephitis mephitis nigra (Peale and Palisot de Beauvois), 1796, A scientific and descriptive catalogue of Peale's museum, Philadelphia, p. 37. White stripes variable, tail usually wholly black except for white tip. Found in southern Ontario and the Eastern Townships of Quebec.

Mephitis mephitis spissigrada Bangs, 1898, Proc. Biol. Soc. Washington 12: 31. A small race, found in the Fraser delta region of southwestern British Columbia.

REFERENCES

Allen, Durward A. 1939. Winter habits of Michigan skunks. Jour. Wildlife Mngt. 3: 212–28.

Verts, B.J. 1967. The biology of the striped skunk. Univ. Illinois Press, Urbana.

RIVER OTTER
Loutre de rivière. *Lontra canadensis* (Schreber)

Description. The otter possesses many adaptations for an amphibious way of life. Its body is long and streamlined from the bulbous nose pad to the long tapered tail. Its head is broad and flattened; its eyes and ears are small (the ears may be closed under water); its muscular neck is scarcely narrower than the head. It has short, powerful legs, fully webbed toes, and furred soles. Its maximum length is about 4½ feet, and maximum weight about 30 pounds (Figure 87).

The otter's skull is sturdy; the rostrum is short, and the cranium is swollen and flattened. The dentition is heavy; the auditory bullae are flattened (Figure 88).

The American otter is very similar to the Eurasian species; however, the nose pad is much larger and there are several features of the skull, such as the strong supraorbital processes, that distinguish it from that species.

As is characteristic of all amphibious mammals, the pelage is thick and lustrous. The underfur is dense, and the guard hairs are a glossy dark brown. The long vibrissae and the throat are silvery grey.

Average measurements of adult males: length 1,126 (1,000–1,313), tail 424 (340–507), hind foot 127 (110–138) mm; weight 7.75 kg. Females: length 1,094 (1,000–1,158), tail 414 (385–447), hind foot 122 (120–123) mm; weight 7.20 kg.

Habits. Although wary of humans in the wild state, otters are sociable, docile, playful animals, exhibiting a

Figure 87 River otter

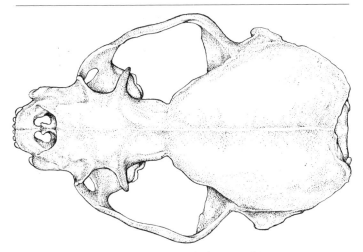

Figure 88 River otter skull, dorsal view (× 3/4)

341

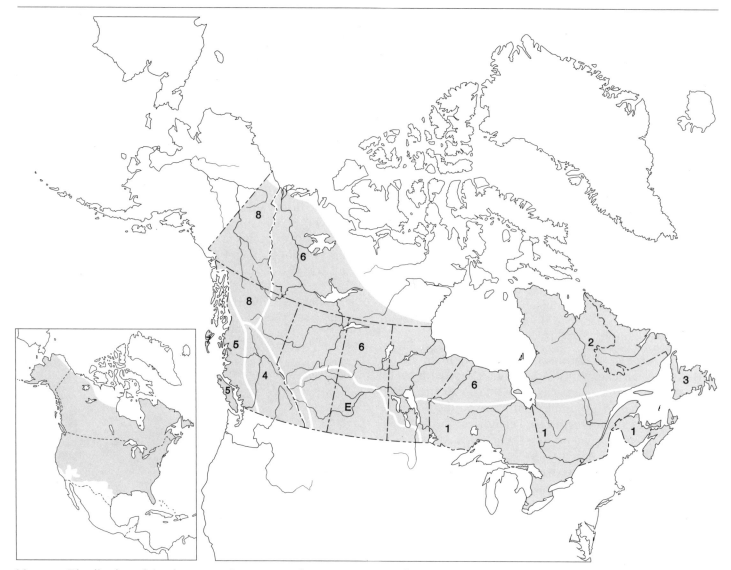

Map 150 Distribution of the river otter, *Lontra canadensis*: 1 *L. c. canadensis*, 2 *L. c. chimo*, 3 *L. c. degener*, 4 *L. c. evexa*, 5 *L. c. pacifica*, 6 *L. c. preblei*, 7 *L. c. periclyzomae*, 8 *L. c. yukonensis*, E extinct

strong family loyalty. The males are pugnacious only during the breeding season, and the females drive them off when the young are small. After the young otters have grown somewhat, the father rejoins the family and assists in raising the youngsters. Otters are extremely intelligent and are unusual among the weasel family in their capacity for domestication.

The otter's senses are keen. The most commonly heard sound is a shrill whistle, but it also chuckles and grunts in alarm. Otters swim with a swift, undulating, serpentine motion both on the surface and under water. They may tread water and extend the necks high above the water and peer about. These characteristic motions have caused some observers to report 'sea monsters' in Loch Ness, Scotland, and perhaps elsewhere. Otters are also at home on land and run with the typical musteline looping gait. On snow-covered surfaces they progress by a series of three jumps and a slide that may carry them six to eight yards.

On a frozen lake they can reach eighteen miles an hour in this manner. They are very fond of 'tobogganing' down snowy slopes on their bellies, with their forelegs extended and their hind legs trailing. Such otter 'slides' are often seen on river banks along well-used otter trails. In summer they resort to grassy or muddy slopes for 'tobogganing.'

Otters are primarily nocturnal in activity but may be about in early morning and late afternoon in remote areas. They are active all winter except during the most severe periods, when they may take shelter for a couple of days.

They construct beds of dry wood chips, bark, and leaves in hollow logs, stumps, roots, and beaver lodges, or they usurp a bank burrow of a beaver or muskrat. They do not excavate their own burrows. Occasionally they occupy large, bulky, open nests of grasses in a marsh- or river-bank thicket. They forage widely and may travel fifty to sixty miles of stream bank during a year, although usually three to ten miles of stream suffices for a single family. The males may travel far overland during the breeding season. An exceptional record of homing was provided by a pair of tame otters from Victoria, British Columbia, which were taken to Stanley Park Zoo in Vancouver. They escaped, recrossed the Straits of Georgia – seventy miles – and returned to their haunts at Victoria within three weeks.

The river otter has been known to live at least sixteen years in captivity.

Otters obtain most of their food by capturing it under water. They also obtain some food by grubbing along the bottom, their long vibrissae being extremely useful tools in this type of foraging. Most of the studies of otter food have been conducted in fresh water, but otters are also commonly distributed along sea-coasts, where they live largely on crabs and other marine invertebrates.

In a Montana study, fishes occurred in 93 per cent of otter faeces. These included minnows, sunfish, trout, catfish, sculpins, and perch. Invertebrates (dragonfly and stonefly nymphs, water beetles, bugs, and crayfish) occurred in 41 per cent; amphibians (frogs, tadpoles, and newts) in 18 per cent; and mammals such as muskrats, meadow voles, shrews, and beavers in 6.1 per cent.

Otters are often reported to be predators of beaver, but the actual situation is not clear. It is doubtful whether an otter could kill an adult beaver, and the evidence suggests that fish are their preferred diet. They might well kill young beaver found alone in a lodge.

Occasionally coyotes and wolves manage to kill an otter caught migrating overland. Otherwise they are fairly secure in their aquatic environment.

Habitat. The otter is amphibious and prefers to spend its life on the shores of deep, clear water in lakes, rivers, large marshes, and ocean bays. It may even occur in lakes and rivers in the tundra north of the treeline.

Reproduction. The American otter is monoestrous, with a long (42–46 day) oestrous period, during which successive periods of heat occur about six days apart if fertilization does not take place. Delayed implantation also occurs in this species, which is different from the situation reported for the Old World otter. The mating season is from late winter to early spring, immediately after the birth of the young (post-partum oestrus). The apparent gestation period varies between nine and a half and twelve and a half months, including the delayed implantation period, and the average litter size is 2.5 (1–4).

A new-born otter measures about 275 mm long and weighs about 132 g. It is fully furred, and has a large head and a stubby tapered tail. Its growth is atricial. The eyes open after thirty-five days, and the young otters begin to play at five to six weeks of age. They venture out of their nest at ten to twelve weeks, and their mother then begins to teach them to swim and hunt. The father usually joins the family group after they are six months old. Otters mature sexually at two years of age, but the males are not successful breeders until they are six to seven years old.

Economic Status. Otters are easily tamed, and the Old World species was used to catch fish for the table in ancient times. In America the species is sought for its valuable fur, which was once popular for men's fur coats but is now used chiefly for fur collars, stoles, and coats for women. Otters are extremely wary and are difficult to trap: precautions must be taken to remove all human scent from the traps. In the 1971–72 fur year, 15,261 otters were trapped across Canada at an average value of $33.54, for a total value of $511,877.

Otters are also considered to be a serious menace to fish hatcheries. If one manages to get into the holding tanks, it can do a great deal of damage among the small trout in one night.

Distribution. This species is limited to North America.

Canadian Distribution. Eight subspecies of otter are currently recognized as occurring in Canada from Newfoundland to Vancouver Island and north to Yukon Territory (see Map 150). More critical studies will, however, probably show that many of these races do not merit recognition.

Lontra canadensis canadensis (Schreber), 1776, Die Säugethiere ..., Theil 3, Heft 18, pl. 126B. The typical form found in the Maritimes, southern Quebec, Ontario, and Manitoba.

Lontra canadensis chimo (Anderson), 1945, Ann. Rept. Provancher Soc. Nat. Hist. Quebec 1944: 59. Characterized by the possession of a longer, heavier skull; found in northern Quebec and Labrador.

Lontra canadensis degener (Bangs), 1898, Proc. Biol. Soc. Washington 12: 35. A small, dark (almost black) race, found in Newfoundland.

Lontra canadensis evexa (Goldman), 1935, Proc. Biol. Soc. Washington 48: 182. A small, pale race, occupying the western slope of the Rocky Mountains in British Columbia.

Lontra canadensis pacifica (Rhoads), 1898, Trans. American Phil. Soc., n.s., 19: 429. A large, dark race from the west coast of British Columbia, including Vancouver Island.

Lontra canadensis periclyzomae (Elliot), 1905, Proc. Biol. Soc. Washington 18: 80. A very large form, found in the Queen Charlotte Islands, British Columbia.

Lontra canadensis preblei (Goldman), 1935, Proc. Biol. Soc. Washington 48: 178. Characterized by the large, heavy skull and dentition; from the Mackenzie valley, Northwest Territories, and northern parts of the Prairie Provinces.

Lontra canadensis yukonensis (Goldman), 1935, Proc. Biol. Soc. Washington 48: 180. From the Yukon Territory, with a small skull.

REFERENCES

Greer, K.R. 1955. Yearly food habits of the river otter in the Thompson Lakes region, northwestern Montana, as indicated by scat analysis. American Midl. Nat. 54(2): 299–313.

Hamilton, W.J. Jr., and W.R. Eadie. 1964. Reproduction in the otter *Lutra canadensis*. Jour. Mamm. 45: 242–52.

Liers, E.E. 1951. Notes on the river otter (*Lutra canadensis*). Jour. Mamm. 32(1): 1–9.

SEA OTTER
Loutre de mer. *Enhydra lutris* (Linnaeus)

Description. The sea otter's adaptations to the aquatic environment far exceed those of other amphibious members of this family. Indeed it bears a strong resemblance to the seals of the next order, Pinnipedia. It is the largest of the mustelids, reaching a length of over 5 feet and a weight of 82 pounds. It has a broad, flat head; a short, thick neck; a body that has been likened to a long rubber bag half-full of water, which sloshes about on land; and a short, stout tail. Its forelimbs are short and weak; its foot is rather mitt-like, with a roughened pad, barely distinguishable toes, and five minute claws. The hind limbs are short and powerful; the long toes are webbed to form long flippers furred on both sides; the claws are flattened. The nose pad is blunt; the eyes are black and beady; the short, fleshy, naked ear pinnae also serve as valves under water. The vibrissae are stiff and long, resembling the walrus's moustache. The skin seems much too large for its body and forms loose folds on the neck and chest (Figure 89).

The sea otter's skull is short and heavy, with an inflated cranium having a prominent sagittal crest. The rostrum is extremely short, the orbits are large, and the auditory bullae small. The teeth are large and broad – useful for crushing marine invertebrate shells (Figure 90).

The sea otter's crowning glory is its lustrous pelt. The underfur is very soft and dense, forming a plush coat about an inch thick. The longer guard hairs are scattered and are especially prominent on the head and shoulders. Other marine mammals such as seals and whales have thick layers of fat to insulate them against the cold water, but the sea otter lacks this protection and relies solely on its coat. The pelt varies among individuals from rusty red through dark brown to almost black. Usually it is paler on the throat, chest, and head. The pale guard hairs on the head and neck give a grizzled appearance. The coat undergoes a continual, gradual moult throughout the year.

Average measurements of adult males: length 1,430 (1,270–1,634), tail 360, hind foot 220 mm; weight 34.4 kg (50–82 pounds). Average measurements of adult females: length 1,207 (1,095–1,289), tail 273 (259–280), hind foot 197 (150–222) mm; average weight 19.7 kg (38–50 pounds).

Habits. These animals appear placid and sociable. They usually congregate in 'pods' of various age and sex groups, although the females and young form separate nursery groups in summer. They are sedentary and seldom travel far from favourite feeding, resting, and sleeping quarters and spend much of their leisure time preening their fur, scratching, and playing with other members of the pod. They are usually unwary and tolerate man's activities, but they do not form the same attachment to men as do river otters. They have a keen sense of smell but poor eyesight. They are vocal and squeal, hiss, snarl, and grunt.

This species is primarily aquatic in activity and swims gracefully with an undulating motion of the whole body,

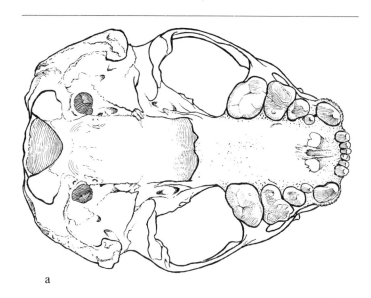

a

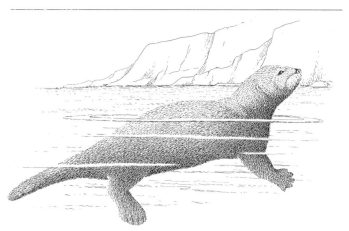

Figure 89 Sea otter

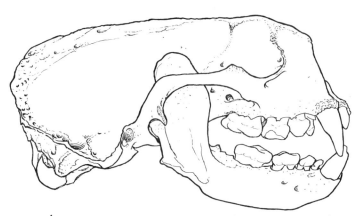

Figure 90 Sea otter skull: (a) ventral view, (b) lateral view (× 1/2)

propelled by alternate strokes of the broad flippers. The forepaws are not used in swimming but are pressed against the chest. Sea otters spend much of the time swimming on their backs with their heads elevated. They also tread water and peer about with necks outstretched, and leap out of the water and roll in it. They remain under water on the average of fifty-five seconds (15–150) while foraging for food. On land, sea otters are clumsy and drag and twist their heavy bodies over the boulders. Their flippers are awkwardly pointed forward in walking on land, much like the fur seal's.

They are diurnal with two peaks of feeding activity: in the early morning and late afternoon. During their rest periods they sleep on their backs in patches of kelp, often wrapping themselves in it. When asleep they often cover their eyes with their paws. As night approaches, they either crawl ashore on some rocky reef to sleep or retire to favourite kelp beds off shore.

Sea otters are active all winter but seek the shelter of grassy beds among the boulders along rocky shores during severe storms.

There is no indication of territoriality in this species. Longevity is approximately eight years. Studies in Alaska have indicated that the diet of the sea otter consists of 75 per cent sea urchins, 9 per cent mussels, 4 per cent crabs, 4 per cent limpets, 1 per cent snails, and 1 per cent fish. In addition, traces of starfish, octopus, and seaweed are found in their stomachs. In California, abalones are an important item in the diet. The otters dive for their food in coastal waters between ten and twenty-five fathoms deep, carry the food to the surface in their paws, roll over onto their backs, and using their chests as dining tables lift the food to their mouths with their forepaws. The hard tests of the sea urchins are crushed with their teeth.

This species shares with man and the chimpanzee the unique ability to use tools. When it brings hard-shelled molluscs to the surface, it often also brings a flat stone from the bottom, which it places on its chest and uses as an anvil for pounding the mussel shell until it breaks and the soft parts can be extracted. The same stone may be used to crush several mussels.

Sea urchins appear to contain little nourishment, and otters must consume thirty-five to forty per day to survive. On the other hand, approximately 20 pounds of fish per day supplies an adequate diet. In zoos, sea otters eat each day between 20 and 35 per cent of their body weight.

Aside from the depredations of man, the killer whale is the sea otter's only predator.

Habitat. The sea otter lives almost entirely in the sea, off rocky reefs, islets, and rocky coasts. It seeks the shelter of kelp beds to rest and sleep.

Reproduction. Very few details of reproduction are known for this species. Breeding is polygamous. Mating occurs in the water in spring or summer, and the single young is usually born in spring. Delayed implantation is suspected. Only one set of twin embryos has been reported.

The young sea otters are born on shore and immediately

Map 151 Distribution of the sea otter, *Enhydra lutris*

carried to the sea. The youngsters are large and well developed. They measure between 500 and 635 mm in length and weigh between 1.5 and 2.0 kg. Their eyes are open, and their milk teeth are already cut. Their coat is reddish brown and woolly. The new-born young float high in the water but cannot swim. The female otters are very solicitous of their young and carry them about on their chests. When the mother dives for food, she leaves her youngster floating in the kelp bed. If danger threatens, she will seize the youngster in her teeth and dive. While the mother floats leisurely on her back, the young otter nurses from the two inguinal teats. The otter is weaned at about two months, but the mother continues to feed it tidbits which she places on her chest. Otters are not deserted by their mothers until they have learned to swim and dive for food, which occurs after seven or eight months. By their first birthday they have moulted into the dark brown adult coat, but they do not reach sexual maturity until they are three years old.

Economic Status. The Chinese mandarins were the first to admire the dark, lustrous plush pelts of the sea otter. It was not until the early voyages of Bering to the northwest coast of America in 1741 and of Cook in 1779 that Europeans learned of the tremendous wealth to be obtained by trading sea otter pelts to the Chinese. For the next 150 years European captains pursued a ruthless exploitation of the sea otter along those coasts. In the middle of the nineteenth century as many as 120,000 pelts were secured in a single year from Russian territories, and the price for a single pelt was as high as $2,500. It is no wonder that sea otters reached the verge of extinction by 1910. An international treaty of 1911 granted them full protection, and by

1913 the Aleutian populations started to make a comeback on the establishment of a sanctuary by the United States.

Distribution. Sea otters formerly inhabited a ribbon of coastal waters in a long arc from northern Japan, Sakhalin Island, Kamchatka Peninsula, and Commander, Kurile, and Aleutian islands to the Pacific coast of North America as far south as Baja California.

Present Status. The present world population of sea otters is believed to be between 25,000 and 40,000 animals. The Alaskan population totals approximately 20,000 animals, mostly in the Aleutian Islands, and there is an isolated population of southern sea otters off the Monterey coast of California.

Canadian Distribution. Sea otters were formerly distributed along the whole British Columbia coast (see Map 151). The original population was extirpated about the beginning of the century (last records: Nootka Island in 1909, Queen Charlotte Islands prior to 1919, and Kyukuot in 1929). Stock from Amchitka Island, Alaska, was reintroduced in 1971. The Canadian subspecies is:

Enhydra lutris lutris (Linnaeus), 1758, Syst. Nat., 10th ed., 1: 45. From Vancouver Island to Japan.

REFERENCES

Barabash-Nikoforov, I.I, et al. 1962. The sea otter (Kalan). Israel Program for Scientific Translations, United States Dept. Commerce, OT.S. 61-31057, Washington.

Kenyon, K.W. 1963. Recovery of a fur bearer. Nat. Hist. 72(9): 12–20.

Murie, O.J. 1940. Notes on the sea otter. Jour. Mamm. 21: 119–31.

Family **Felidae** / Cats

The cats are the most specialized of the carnivores in structure and habits. They vary in size from the domestic cat to the lion and the tiger. Their heads are short and broad; their lower jaws have a distinct chin; their muzzles are short; and their orbits are directed forward. Their teeth show a high degree of specialization for biting and bolting food: the incisors are in a straight line, the large canines are compressed and placed well forward, the carnassials are highly developed as shears, and the other premolars and molars are reduced. Their bodies are sinuous and powerful; their stance is digitigrade on naked pads. There are five toes on the forefoot (the pollex is high on the wrist), and the hind foot carries only four toes. Each toe is armed with a compressed, curved, retractible claw, which is withdrawn in walking but extended in climbing and slashing prey.

Cats are generally solitary, stealthy, nocturnal hunters. They possess keen eyesight and generally abhor water.

They are almost cosmopolitan in distribution, except for Australia and Madagascar.

MOUNTAIN LION
Couguar. *Felis concolor* Linnaeus

Description. The mountain lion or cougar is among our largest and most powerful predatory animals, exceeded in size only by the bears. Large males have measured up to 8 feet in total length and have weighed up to 272 pounds. In spite of its size, very few people have observed a cougar in its natural haunts because of its extreme wariness.

The cougar's body is long and lithe; its head is quite small; its ears are small and rounded; since its forelegs are shorter than its hind legs, the hindquarters are higher than the shoulders; the cylindrical tail is about 30 inches long. The paws are relatively large (Plate 33).

The massive skull has a short rostrum, widely arched orbits, and well-developed sagittal and lambdoidal crests overhanging the foramen magnum. The mandible is short and deep, the nasals are expanded, and the powerful canines are compressed but only slightly grooved (Figure 91).

The pelage is short and coarse. The over-all adult colour varies from tawny brown to greyish brown, darker on the mid-dorsal line and pale buff on the belly. The chest and throat are white, and the backs of the ears, tip of the tail,

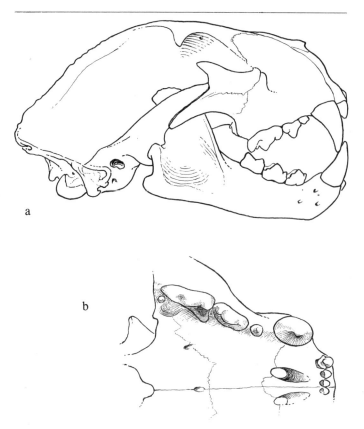

a

b

Figure 91 Mountain lion skull (a) and dentition (b) (× 1/3)

and stripes on the muzzle are black. The vibrissae are long and pale. There are no definite periods of moult, only a gradual replacement of fur throughout the year. The summer coat tends to be brighter and the winter coat darker and longer.

Males are much larger than females. Measurements of adult males: length 171–274, tail 66–90, hind foot 24–29 cm; weight 67–103 kg. Adult females measure: length 150–233, tail 53–82, hind foot 22–27 cm; weight 36–60 kg.

Habits. Cougars are solitary animals except during the mating season or on those occasions when the female is accompanied by kittens. All their senses are keen. Primarily nocturnal in activity, they prowl noiselessly among the shadows seeking their prey. They are excellent climbers and can swim, although they take to water reluctantly and only when pursued or when seeking new hunting grounds. They have a varied repertoire of growls, hisses, cries, and a loud purr of contentment.

The cougar lair is usually a cave or a crevice among rocks, but it may be merely a shelter under an overhanging bank or tree, or in a hollow stump or thicket. Each cougar patrols his own home range over set trails which may be twelve to eighteen miles in extent. The males mark their territories with scratched scent posts. I have observed where one had stretched up a balsam poplar and sharpened its claws like a giant tabby cat, tearing long strips of bark off the tree trunk, which had littered the snow beneath. Population densities have been estimated as one cougar per township (thirty-six square miles).

These animals have lived up to eighteen years in captivity.

The cougar feeds primarily upon larger mammals. It hunts by stalking like a domestic cat. When close enough, it springs from its hiding place onto the back of its prey. Occasionally, if cover is scarce, it may have to make a short dash before it leaps. Deer are its favourite food, and the cougar likes to land on the prey's shoulder, bite deep into the back of its neck, and rake the head and flanks with its claws. Usually the deer is knocked down by the impact and killed almost instantly. During the western outbreak of hoof and mouth disease in 1951, I was called upon to inspect a mule deer buck in Banff National Park, which was drooling and limping. It was decided to shoot the animal as a precautionary measure. Upon closer inspection, it was found that the animal had a broken jaw and bore long, deep gashes from shoulder to elbow. It had undoubtedly just survived the attack of a cougar.

After the kill the cougar usually lifts or drags the carcass to a safe eating place. If game is scarce, the big cat will rake leaves and branches over the carcass to hide it for a later feeding, but if game is plentiful, it may feed only once on the carcass. These cats prefer fresh meat and normally do not scavenge from old kills unless they are very hungry.

Besides mule and white-tailed deer cougars hunt wapiti and moose, bighorn sheep, mountain goats, porcupines, beaver, snowshoe hares, mountain beaver, mice, and birds; and rarely coyotes, foxes, lynx, bobcats, and skunks. They also occasionally prey upon domestic stock such as calves, pigs, dogs, and colts. They are reported to be particularly fond of horse flesh.

Detailed studies of stomach contents and scats have revealed the following diet: deer 77 per cent, porcupine 8.8 per cent, domestic animals 4 per cent, beaver 3.4 per cent, hares 2.1 per cent, and traces of other items such as grasses.

Habitat. Although the cougar is now associated generally with mountainous terrain, canyons, and rimrock, it also occupies a wide variety of habitats from swamps and wooded river valleys to dense coniferous forests. Altitudinally, it occurs from sea level to at least 10,000 feet in the mountains of California.

Reproduction. This species does not have a restricted breeding season. The kittens may be born in any month of the year, although there appear to be two peaks of births: in late winter and in midsummer. The females are seasonally polyoestrous, although there are few data on the frequency of oestrous periods. There is good evidence of an occasional post-partum oestrous period, although development may be prevented by lactation. Ovulation is assumed to be induced by copulation, as in most cats investigated. When in heat, the female attracts the attention of a male by entering his domain. There may be vicious fights between two males courting the same female. For the purpose of raising her kittens alone, the female separates from her mate before the birth of the young. Males have been known to kill young kittens found undefended in the lair.

The gestation period is between ninety and ninety-six days, and the average litter size is two to four (1–6). The female possesses three pairs of abdominal teats. The kittens stay with their mother for about a year, and the litters are born, on the average, every other year.

Young cougar kittens are about 300 mm long at birth and weigh 400 g. Their eyes are closed, and they are covered with a woolly, spotted coat, striped on the stubby tail. Their development is altricial. Their eyes open after ten days, and from a wobbly start they develop into rather rough but playful kittens. They begin to eat meat brought by their mother at an age of six weeks, and by three months they are fully weaned. As soon as they are able to travel, the mother leads them to her kills, and the family finds temporary shelter near by. They lose their spots at about six months of age and assume a juvenile brown coat. Until they are one year old, they remain with their mother, learning to hunt. The juvenile females reach sexual maturity at two and a half years, and the males at three years of age.

Economic Status. The cougar is one of the top predators in the ecological pyramid of numbers. In wilderness areas it serves the useful role of assisting to keep the large herbivores within the carrying capacity of their food supply. In areas hunted by man, the cougar is a competitor, and its activity is often noted with some alarm. In agricultural areas, the depredations of certain individuals on livestock require control operations.

Cougars are most easily hunted with hounds. They

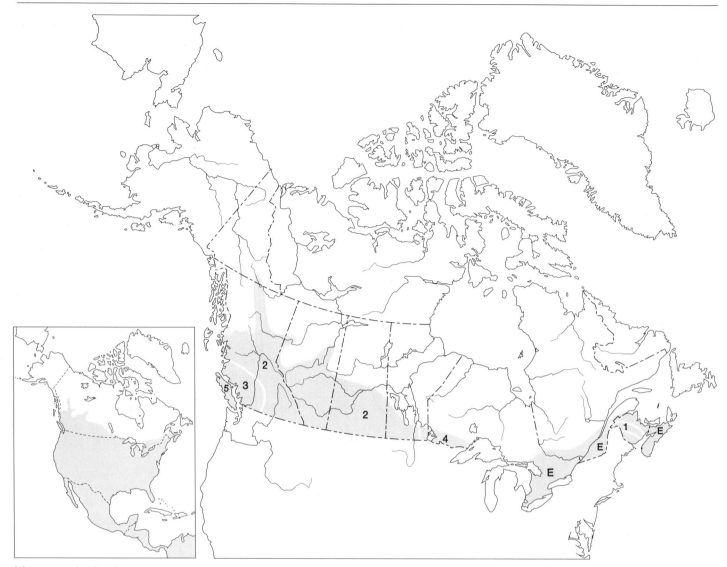

Map 152 Distribution of the mountain lion, *Felis concolor*: 1 *F. c. couguar*, 2 *F. c. missoulensis*, 3 *F. c. oregonensis*, 4 *F. c. schorgeri*, 5 *F. c. vancouverensis*, E extinct

'tree' readily upon their approach, and it is then easy to shoot them. They may also be trapped at carcasses and baited with catnip.

There are a small number of records of cougar attacks upon man, especially children. On Vancouver Island, between 1949 and 1952, there were several cases, including maulings and fatalities. The animals involved were usually small, starving individuals. There was an apparent shortage of food at that time. Another fatality, in California, was caused by the bite of a rabid cougar. It would appear wise to keep such a risk in mind where children walk alone in deep woods frequented by these animals.

Distribution. This species had one of the most extensive distributions of any mammal in the Western Hemisphere. It was originally found from the Atlantic to the Pacific and from Patagonia to northern British Columbia.

Canadian Distribution. The species has been greatly reduced or extirpated over much of its former range in central and eastern Canada but still occurs regularly in British Columbia and in the Rocky Mountains of Alberta (see Map 152). Five races are reported within our boundaries.

Felis concolor couguar Kerr, 1792, The animal kingdom ..., p. 151. Formerly found in New Brunswick, peninsular Nova Scotia, southern Quebec, and Ontario. Recently thought to be extinct, but a few individuals are now known to occur in New Brunswick. A small reddish race with dark dorsal stripe.

Felis concolor missoulensis Goldman, 1943, Jour. Mamm. 24: 229. A very large, pale subspecies, originally occupying the Rocky Mountain and Cascade ranges of British Columbia, western Alberta, and the southern Prairie Provinces. Now the race is found in fair numbers only in the Rocky Mountains, where it has pushed northward during the past thirty-five years; it has been reduced to stragglers in the river valleys and wooded hills of the Prairie Provinces, north to Prince Albert National Park and to the Pasquia Hills of Saskatchewan and east to near Winnipeg, Manitoba.

Felis concolor oregonensis Rafinesque, 1832, Atlantic Jour. 1: 62. A large, dark subspecies, found in the Coast Ranges of British Columbia north to the Bella Coola valley.

Felis concolor schorgeri Jackson, 1955, Proc. Biol. Soc. Washington 68: 149. Reported rarely from northwestern Ontario.

Felis concolor vancouverensis Nelson and Goldman, 1932, Proc. Biol. Soc. Washington 45: 105. A small, dark reddish race, found on Vancouver Island and occasionally on near-by Saltspring and Quadra islands.

REFERENCE

Seidensticker, J.C. IV, M.G. Hornocker, W.V. Wiles, and J.P. Messick. 1973. Mountain lion social organization in the Idaho Primitive Area. Wildlife Monogr. 35.

LYNX
Loup-cervier. *Lynx lynx* (Linnaeus)

Description. The lynx is a medium-sized cat with a short body, long legs, very large padded feet, and a stubby tail. A prominent ruff surrounds its face. Its ears are pointed and are tipped with long pencils of black hairs (Figure 92).

The skull of the lynx is sturdy, with a very short rostrum, widely spread zygomatic arches, and a rounded cranium, surmounted by a weak sagittal crest. There are only three cheek teeth behind the canines in both upper and lower jaws (Figure 93). The trenchant difference between the skull of this and other species of *Lynx* is the separation of the anterior condyloid foramen and the foramen lacerum posterius on the basicranium (Figure 96b).

The pelage of the lynx is long, lax, and thick. The underfur is buffy brown. A broad grey subterminal band and the black tips on the guard hairs give the coat a grey-frosted appearance on the back. The underparts are more buffy. The dorsal surfaces of the ears are grey with black margins and terminal tufts. The tip of the tail is black. There are also black stripes on the forehead and around the facial ruff, and other indistinct dark spots on the belly and insides of the forelegs.

The long guard hairs are moulted twice a year: in October and November, and again in April and May. The summer coat is shorter and browner, and the spotting is more distinct. The kittens moult into the adult coat at the age of eight to ten months.

The males are larger than the females. Average measurements of adult Newfoundland males: length 890 (740–1,065), tail 104 (51–138), hind foot 233 (204–325) mm; weight 10.6 (6.7–17.2) kg. Average measurements of adult Newfoundland females: length 845 (765–965), tail 97 (76–122), hind foot 225 (180–250) mm; weight 8.6 (5.1–11.6) kg.

Habits. Lynx are solitary, silent hunters of the deep forests. They travel in pairs only briefly: during the mating season and during the first winter of the kittens' lives when they accompany their mothers. They are nocturnal, appearing first about two hours before dark and remaining active until about one hour after sunrise. They prowl about silently on their large furry pads through the dark forests in search of food. They generally hunt by sight or hearing and do not seem to have a keen sense of smell. Although generally silent, I have heard shrieks and caterwauling at night in the northern forests that could only be ascribed to these animals. They frequently pause in their forages to sit on their haunches to survey the forest, or they lie silently on their paws hidden under an alder bush, awaiting some movement. They leave many urination

Figure 92 Lynx

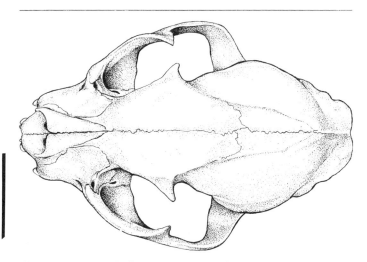

Figure 93 Lynx skull, dorsal view (× 3/4)

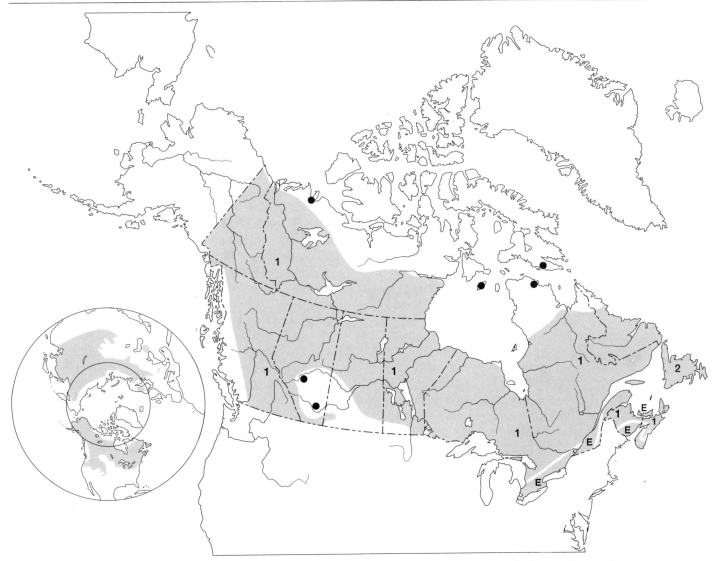

Map 153 Distribution of the lynx, *Lynx lynx*: 1 *L. l. canadensis*, 2 *L. l. subsolanus*, ● extra-limital records, E extinct

posts along their trails as a means of communication. In rest periods they preen and lick their coats. Lynx spend most of their time on the ground but are excellent climbers and occasionally swim across rivers. They often make long leaps over logs or brush, or to low branches, but in the open they gallop rather clumsily.

Lynx construct only rough beds under a rocky ledge, windfall, or low branch; occasionally they enter caves. They remain active all winter except during the severest weather when they simply bed-down in the snow under an evergreen branch or log. They occupy a home range of six to eight square miles and have an average daily cruising range of 2.6 miles. A tagged lynx has been known to travel sixty-four miles. Although usually sedentary, lynx will migrate great distances when food is scarce.

Populations of lynx show dramatic fluctuations, with peak intervals approximately ten years apart. Peak populations of lynx occur just after peak populations of snowshoe hares, their main food supply; and lynx populations 'crash' after the hares disappear.

An investigation of the stomachs and scats of lynx in Newfoundland indicates that the diet consists of: snowshoe hares 73 per cent; birds such as ducks, ptarmigan, sparrows, flickers, and chickens 21 per cent; meadow voles 14 per cent; and moose and caribou carrion 20 per cent. On the mainland, lynx have been reported to eat ground and tree squirrels, foxes, and skunks. They occasionally kill deer, caribou fawns, and mountain sheep lambs. One lynx might consume 170 to 200 hares per year and additional mice and birds.

Besides man, lynx have few predators except cougars and wolves. Lynx can always escape from a pack of wolves in the forest by climbing, but they are no match for them in the open.

Habitat. The dense climax boreal forest with its dense undercover of thickets and windfalls is the favourite haunt of the lynx. It also roams for short distances on the tundra beyond the treeline, and in starvation years it ventures far out onto the tundra in search of arctic hares, lemmings, and ptarmigan.

350

Reproduction. Few details are known for this species because they are difficult to study in the wild or to breed in captivity. The females possess four teats, and seem to be monoestrous. Oestrus occurs in Newfoundland between March 11 and April 6, when they mate. The gestation period is approximately nine weeks, and the kittens are born some time between the middle of May and the middle of June. The average litter size is between two and three (1–5). There is only one litter a year.

The kittens are furry little grey balls with vague longitudinal stripes on the back and flanks and barred limbs. At birth their eyes are closed and their ears are folded. They measure between 163 and 185 mm in total length and weigh between 197 and 211 g. Their development is altricial. Their eyes open after twelve days, and they lose their fluffy natal coat at the age of two months. They are as playful as any other young kittens.

Economic Status. The long, soft, grey, lustrous coat of the lynx has made it popular for fur collars, coat trimming, jackets, hats, and muffs. After a long period of unpopularity, the lynx pelt is again returning to its former position of high style. In the 1971–72 fur season, 53,589 lynx pelts were traded at an average price of $38.07, for a total value of $2,040,085.

Individual lynx may attack domestic animals on remote farms, particularly chickens. However, they are usually fairly easily trapped or hunted with hounds.

Distribution. This is another widely distributed holarctic species found in the forested regions of Spain, Portugal, Poland, the Balkan Peninsula, Scandinavia, the Soviet Union, Asia Minor, Kashmir, and China, as well as in the northern forests of North America.

Canadian Distribution. The lynx inhabits the broad boreal forest belt across Canada from Newfoundland to Yukon Territory. The southern boundary has receded northward in recent years in the Maritimes, southern Quebec, Ontario, and the Prairie Provinces. It is unknown from coastal British Columbia. There are isolated records from Franklin Bay (1917), Lake Harbour, southern Baffin Island (1918), and Coates Island, Northwest Territories (about the same time). The distribution of the two recognized Canadian subspecies is outlined in Map 153.

Lynx lynx canadensis Kerr, 1792, The animal kingdom ..., 1: 157. Now found only on Cape Breton Island, Nova Scotia, having been exterminated in peninsular Nova Scotia about 1930 and in New Brunswick in 1943. Occurs in the Gaspé Peninsula of Quebec, central and northern Ontario (two killed in Ottawa in 1963 and 1964), westward to British Columbia and the Yukon.
Lynx lynx subsolanus Bangs, 1897, Proc. Biol. Soc. Washington 11: 49. A small, brownish race, restricted to the Island of Newfoundland.

REFERENCES

Saunders, J.K. Jr. 1963. Food habits of the lynx in Newfoundland. Jour. Wildlife Mngt. 27(3): 384–90.

– 1963. Movements and activities of the lynx in Newfoundland. Jour. Wildlife Mngt. 27(3): 390–400.
– 1964. Physical characteristics of the Newfoundland lynx. Jour Mamm. 45(1): 36–47.

BOBCAT
Lynx roux. *Lynx rufus* (Schreber)

Description. The bobcat is very similar to the lynx in appearance and requires fairly close scrutiny to distinguish it from its northern relative. Generally the bobcat is smaller, although some individuals have weighed up to 69 pounds. Its legs are shorter, and its feet lack the large furry pads of the lynx. Its tail is a little longer and is characterized by a white tip, a broad black dorsal distal band, and several dark proximal bands (Figure 94). It has rounded ears and much shorter ear tufts. Its coat is more heavily spotted (Figure 95).

The trenchant character of the bobcat's skull is the confluent foramina lacerum posterius and anterior con-

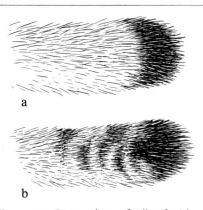

Figure 94 Comparison of tails of (a) lynx and (b) bobcat (× 1/3)

Figure 95 Bobcat

351

dyloid on the basicranium below the foramen magnum (Figure 96a).

The general coat colour in this species is tawny brown above, with numerous black spots and black-tipped guard hairs. The underparts are whitish with black spots; the limbs are tawny with black horizontal bars. The face has a black nose pad, white vibrissae, and a black striped ruff and forehead. The dorsal surface of the ear is black with a central white spot, as opposed to the lynx's grey ears with black margins. Albino and melanistic bobcats have been recorded as well.

There are two moults: in spring and in autumn. The summer coat is shorter and more rufous; the winter coat is longer and greyer.

Males exceed the females in size. Average measurements of adult males: length 827 (800–876), tail 157 (130–170), hind foot 170 (165–185), ear 77 (65–85) mm; weight 9.6 (6.4–18.3) kg. Adult females: length 768 (710–804), tail 143 (127–165), hind foot 156 (146–170), ear 70 (60–76) mm; weight 6.8 (4.1–15.3) kg.

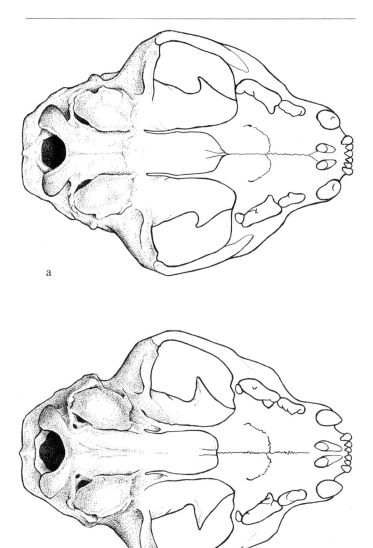

a

b

Figure 96 Comparison of skulls of (a) bobcat and (b) lynx (× 2/3)

Habits. Bobcats are solitary, bold, silent stalkers of small game. Although they have a reputation for fierceness ('he could lick his weight in wildcats'), this was based upon their actions when held in traps or brought to bay by hounds. People have found them to be interesting and reliable pets when raised from kittens, although they are rather rough in play and hard on the furniture. They share many of the same behaviour patterns as the cougar and lynx. They have well-travelled paths, use urine posts ('scrapes') to communicate, and sharpen their claws on tree trunks. Their eyesight and hearing are good, and their sense of smell is of secondary importance. They have the same variety of calls as the cougar and the lynx, from purring to caterwauling. They climb well and often leap over logs or onto low boughs. They run with an ungainly bounding gait and swim reluctantly if pressed by hounds. Bobcats are generally nocturnal but are probably more frequently observed during the daylight hours than the lynx.

The bobcat constructs its lair of dry moss or leaves in a hollow log, rock crevice, or thicket, or under a stump.

Bobcats usually occupy established home ranges. In a Montana study the mean distances between tagging points and recapture points for females were 3.2 miles and 5.3 miles. The longest distance travelled by a tagged bobcat was twenty-three miles in eighteen months. They have lived fifteen years in captivity.

Although primarily small game predators, bobcats occasionally kill deer. They are a little too small to handle these animals effectively, however, and may be carried about clinging to the shoulders of their intended prey. On rare occasions they may be injured or killed by the trampling of the deer. Long-term studies in the United States have indicated the following bobcat diet based on stomach analysis: lagomorphs (principally snowshoe hares and cottontail rabbits) 45 per cent, mice and rats 28 per cent, squirrels 10 per cent, kangaroo rats and pocket mice 5 per cent, pocket gophers 2 per cent, porcupines 1 per cent, deer 2–4 per cent, shrews 2 per cent, birds 3 per cent, livestock 2 per cent (mostly lambs and kids), and traces of poultry, snakes, lizards, insects, and vegetation. Bobcats have been known to kill many other creatures such as muskrats, mountain beavers, red and grey foxes, mink, bats, house cats, weasels, herons, and turtles. In some areas porcupines form a more important role in the diet than indicated above.

In turn, bobcats are preyed upon by cougars, coyotes, and wolves. Great horned owls and foxes are important predators upon the kittens.

Habitat. The bobcat is less restricted in habitat choice than the lynx. It inhabits swamps, woodlots, second-growth forests, deserts, and rocky hillsides. It is this adaptability to changing environment that has led to its occupancy of agricultural lands and the outskirts of cities. The bobcat has thrived in spite of human changes in the environment, while its close relative the lynx has declined.

Reproduction. Our knowledge of reproduction in this species is scanty. The females are thought to be seasonally

Map 154 Distribution of the bobcat, *Lynx rufus*: 1 *L. r. fasciatus*, 2 *L. r. gigas*, 3 *L. r. pallescens*, 4 *L. r. rufus*, 5 *L. r. superiorensis*, E extinct, ● extra-limital record

polyoestrous. There appears to be a prolonged breeding season. Most of the litters are born between late April and mid-May, but there is evidence of a second group of births between late August and early October. It would appear that there is a second oestrous period if the female is not impregnated during the first oestrous cycle, from late February to early March, when the bobcats normally pair off. The gestation period is thought to be between fifty and sixty days. The average litter size is 2.69, but the number of young may vary from one to seven. There may be a regular second autumn litter in the southern portion of the bobcat's range. The mature males are probably fecund all year.

The young at birth are fully clothed with a soft woolly coat, dull tawny olive in colour with obscure black patches, and weigh approximately 283 to 368 g. The mother drives off her mate when the kittens are born, but later when they are weaned she permits him to assist in bringing food for them. The development of the kittens is altricial. Their eyes open after nine days, and they are

weaned by the age of two months. They remain with their mother until January, after which they strike off on their own. They weigh between a pound and a pound and a half by late autumn.

The juvenile female kittens mature as yearlings.

Economic Status. The bobcat's fur is soft and not very durable. It finds a small market for sports jackets and coat trim. During the 1971–72 fur season 3,842 pelts were traded at an average value of $21.31, for a total value of $81,862.

Bobcats occasionally make depredations upon poultry, turkey, and sheep ranches. They are hunted with hounds, a sport quite popular in the United States. Readily 'treed' when pursued by hounds, they are then shot.

Unfortunately bobcats are susceptible to rabies, and a rabid bobcat may attack dogs, horses, or even men. There are several records of spontaneous maulings by bobcats but no fatalities.

Distribution. This species is confined to southern North America.

353

Canadian Distribution. The bobcat is found only along our southern boundary, where the evidence suggests a recent invasion since the beginning of this century. Five subspecies are currently recognized across the continent (see Map 154).

Lynx rufus fasciatus Rafinesque, 1817, American Monthly Mag. 2(1): 46. A rufous form, found in southwestern British Columbia.

Lynx rufus gigas Bangs, 1897, Proc. Biol. Soc. Washington 11: 50. A large, dark reddish subspecies, found in peninsular Nova Scotia, New Brunswick, and probably southern Quebec. Formerly in southeastern Ontario (prior to 1906).

Lynx rufus pallescens Merriam, 1899, N. American Fauna 16: 104. A large, pale race, found in central and eastern British Columbia and in the southern portions of the Prairie Provinces.

Lynx rufus rufus (Schreber), 1777, Die Säugethiere ..., Theil 3, Heft 95, pl. 109B. The typical race of the eastern United States, which has recently invaded southern Ontario and Manitoba.

Lynx rufus superiorensis Peterson and Downing, 1952, Contrib. Royal Ontario Mus. Zool. and Palaeontol. 33: 1. The form found in northwestern Ontario, characterized by certain differences in skull measurements.

REFERENCE

Young, Stanley P. 1958. The bobcat of North America. Stackpole Company, Harrisburg, Pa.

Order **Pinnipedia** / Seals, Sea Lions, and the Walrus

Seals are profoundly modified for an aquatic life. Most are marine, but a few live in fresh water. Unlike whales, they are not wholly committed to the water but must return to the land (or ice-floes) to bear their young. Some are pelagic during migrations, but many spend the greater part of their lives near rock islets or within sight of land.

The pinniped body is streamlined: the face is short; the nostrils are valvular and slit-like; the large eyes are close together; the vibrissae are long and coarse; the external ears are reduced; the neck is long and powerful, yet supple. The limbs are short and paddle-like, the proximal portions being enclosed within the general body outline. The tail is reduced. The skin is thick and is covered with hair and underlaid by a thick layer of blubber.

The skull of this order is usually flattened; the teeth are peg-like and far apart. There are five nailed digits enclosed in a web on each foot. The liver is large and multilobed. The kidneys are also lobulated. Most seals are highly gregarious, with complex social groupings.

ARTIFICIAL KEY TO FAMILIES OF
CANADIAN PINNIPEDIA

1	Hind flippers long and capable of rotation forward under the body.	2
2	Body well furred.	OTARIIDAE
2′	Body practically naked.	ODOBENIDAE
1′	Hind flippers short and permanently pointing backwards.	PHOCIDAE

Family **Otariidae** / Eared Seals

These seals are less specialized for an aquatic environment than the other families of pinnipeds. They have short, stiff, pointed ears; a thick coat of fur; and hind limbs that are turned forward to support the body on land so that they can shuffle along fairly easily. The soles of the flippers are naked. The nostrils are at the end of the snout; the teeth resemble those of the carnivores more closely. The skull has well-developed supraorbital processes and an alisphenoid canal.

These seals occupy the North Pacific Ocean and antarctic seas. They are gregarious and breed in large rookeries on offshore islands.

NORTHERN SEA LION
Otarie de Steller. *Eumetopias jubata* (Schreber)

Description. The pinnipeds are on the average much larger than the terrestrial carnivores, and several are larger than the largest bears. This species, the largest of the eared seals, is much larger than any bear. George Wilhelm Steller, the German naturalist who accompanied the Bering expedition to the northeast Pacific, provided the first description of this sea lion, which he observed on Bering Island on June 20, 1742. Its body is cylindrical and streamlined. The cow is slim, but the bull has massive forequarters and a swollen neck. The sea lion's head is bearlike: the muzzle is straight; the eyes are large; the ears are small, stiff, and pointed; the pale mystacial vibrissae are long (50 cm) and stiff. The flippers are large; the first digit is the largest; and the hind flippers face forward. Richly supplied with sweat glands, sea lions fan themselves with their flippers when under heat stress (Plate 35).

The skull is massive, with quadrate supraorbital processes. The teeth are large. The third upper incisor is caniniform, and the lower jaw has only two pairs of incisors. There are five cheek teeth in each ramus of the jaw, with a decided gap between the fourth and fifth.

In this species the pelage is short and coarse and lacks an undercoat. The bulls are buffy above and reddish brown on the belly, and have dark brown flippers. There is a slight mane on the hind neck. The cows are a uniform brown in colour, and the young are sleek and dark brown.

The mature bulls are approximately double the size of the cows. Adult males average 2.95 (2.70–3.20) metres (approximately 12 feet) in length and weigh up to 1 ton. The cows average 1.85 to 2.15 metres in length and weigh 275 to 365 kg (600–800 pounds).

Habits. Sea lions are highly gregarious; they occupy dense rookeries during the breeding season, swim in herds, and haul out onto rocky islets together during the remainder of the season. The bulls are bellicose. There is a definite social hierarchy on the breeding grounds, with barren cows, bachelor bulls, and yearlings hauling out together at some distance from the breeding colonies. In the water sea lions may be playful, playing tag in the waves, or the younger animals may play 'king of the

Map 155 Distribution of the northern sea lion, *Eumetopias jubata* : ● extra-limital record

'castle' on a rock or toss pebbles at one another. On land there is much bickering between neighbours, much movement of their sinuous necks, and a constant bedlam of roaring bulls, barking cows, and whining pups. Viewed from a distance, sea lions, when disturbed by an approaching plane or boat, look like a brown carpet slipping off the rocky islets as they plunge into the sea. Usually they haul out during the afternoons, especially during bright, calm weather, but they prefer to stay in the sea during stormy weather.

The annual movements of these sea lions is not well known at present. There appears to be some northward dispersal during the autumn as well as an offshore movement in winter. The only sign of territorial behaviour is the harem master's vigorous defence of his encompassed breeding area in the breeding rookery.

Sea lions are continuous feeders, except during the breeding season when the harem bulls starve themselves for two or three months. Their intestinal tracts are 80.5 metres (275 feet) long, or thirty-eight times their body length. Their food consists of a wide variety of inverte-

brate marine life and fishes: coelenterates, sand dollars, worms, molluscs, crabs, squid and octopus, lamprey, pollack, flounders, sculpins, cod, herring, skate and dogfish, sea perch, halibut, salmon, sable fish, eulachon, rockfish, hake, greenling, and lumpfish. A study of 382 stomachs indicated the following diet: squid and octopus 36 per cent, sand lance 25 per cent, rockfish 11 per cent, clams 29 per cent, crabs 9 per cent, flounder 4 per cent, halibut 2 per cent, greenling 4 per cent, lumpfish 2 per cent, and unidentified fish remains 18 per cent.

The northern sea lion has only a few predators besides man; these are the killer whale and one or two species of large sharks. They have been known to live seventeen years in the wild.

Habitat. This species spends most of its life in a narrow belt of coastal water, hauling out on rocky offshore islets. One was captured 150 km (93 miles) inland on a river bank in Oregon. It is not known how far to sea they wander during migrations.

Reproduction. The bulls are polygamous. Only the larger ones serve as harem masters, the younger bachelor

356

bulls remaining outside the breeding colonies awaiting their turn to serve. The old bulls stay on their territories from about mid-May to early August and fast throughout the period. As an adaptation to the marine environment, their sexual organs are folded into the body cavity.

The females also show several adaptations. The mammary glands are sheet-like on the flanks and belly, and the abdominal teats may be retracted when the pups are not feeding. The uterus is bicornuate. Each ovary sheds a single egg in alternate years, and the embryo develops in each branch of the uterus in alternate years. The cows are monoestrous, and post-partum oestrus follows a few days after the birth of the pup. There appears to be delayed implantation as the gestation period is almost exactly a year in duration.

The cows reach the breeding colony ahead of the bulls, in early May. The harems consist of ten to thirty cows to each harem master. There is, however, much interchange of females, which are much quicker and can easily out-manoeuvre the cumbersome bulls. The pups are born between late May and late June. The females are solicitous and defend their offspring and teach them to swim.

The new-born pups have a sleek, dark brown pelage, are 89 to 102 cm long, and weigh between 18 and 22 kg (40–45 pounds). Their development is precocious. Their milk teeth disappear before or soon after birth. They grow rapidly, attaining 32 to 36 kg after two months and about 68 to 91 kg (150–200 pounds) at the age of one year. They nurse most of the first year of their lives.

The females mature at three years, and the bulls reach sexual maturity at six or seven years of age, though they are unable to compete for harems until they are nine or ten years old.

Economic Status. Fishermen distrust the northern sea lion. They accuse it of eating commercial fish, and it certainly does destroy fish in nets and traps and damages fishing gear as well. Sometimes it may be unjustly condemned as were the two sea lions killed at the mouth of the Klamath River, California, during a salmon run. Stomach analysis showed that these two had been feeding exclusively on lampreys. There has, however, been a continuing control program on the British Columbia coast for many years. As early as 1917, 8,000 sea lions were destroyed by professional hunters. The population of sea lions in British Columbia waters was estimated at 11,000 to 12,000 from an aerial census in 1956–57. The authorities undertook a heavy reduction program in 1959 and 1960, and the population was reduced to about 4,000 animals in 1969.

Status. The total world population of sea lions is thought to be approximately a quarter of a million, of which 180,000 occupy Alaskan waters.

Distribution. North Pacific Ocean from Japan, Kamchatka, and the Commander, Pribilof, and Aleutian islands south along the west coast of North America to southern California (see Map 155).

Canadian Distribution. Coastal waters of British Columbia. One record from Herschel Island, Yukon Territory. The main Canadian rookeries are off the Scott Is-

lands and Cape St James, Queen Charlotte Islands. In winter they occur off Vancouver Island. The genus is monotypic:

Eumetopias jubata (Schreber), 1776, Die Säugethiere ..., Theil 3, Heft 17, pl. 83B, p. 300.

REFERENCES

Pike, Gordon D. 1961. The northern sea lion in British Columbia. Canadian Audubon 23(1): 1–5.
Spalding, D.J. 1964. Comparative feeding habits of the fur seal, sea lion and harbour seal on the coast of British Columbia. Bull. Fish. Res. Bd. Canada 146.
Thorsteinson, F.V., and C.J. Lensink. 1962. Biological observations of Steller sea lions taken during an experimental harvest. Jour. Wildlife Mngt. 26(4): 353–65.

CALIFORNIA SEA LION
Otarie de Californie. *Zalophus californianus* (Lesson)

Description. This is the performing 'seal' of circuses and zoological parks. It has a fusiform body; the hind flippers trail when swimming but rotate forward when resting on land. The ear pinnae are stiff and inconspicuous, and the mystacial vibrissae are long and stiff. The California sea lion is slenderer than the northern sea lion, and the bulls lack the grossly thickened neck of that species. However, the bulls possess a prominent bony crest on the crown of the head, which serves as a good distinguishing mark.

The skull of this species is more slender and elongate than the northern sea lion's. Cows and younger bulls have markedly slender nasal bones. There are usually six upper cheek teeth behind the canines, with a long gap between the fifth and sixth.

The stiff pelage lacks an undercoat. When wet, the animal appears almost black, but when dry the coat varies from buff to sepia brown.

Average measurements of adult males: length 2.42 metres, tail 115 mm, hind foot 470 mm, weight 227–271 kg (500–600 pounds). Average measurements of females: length 1.83 metres, tail 75 mm, hind foot 395 mm, weight 45.4–90.8 kg (100–200 pounds).

Habits. These animals, though gregarious, are not very sociable. They are usually shy and wary of intruders. When young they are very playful, gracefully leaping out of the water, riding the surf, or diving off rocky prominences. They are graceful swimmers, swimming on their sides and rolling like corkscrews. They propel themselves with their front flippers. On the breeding rookery there is much bickering among neighbours. They possess a behaviour pattern that has been highly developed among performing circus animals. If a stone is thrown at a sea lion on the shore, it will attempt to catch it in its teeth and toss it away. It will even attempt to catch a large rock that would break its teeth.

The cries of this species are quite different from those of the larger northern sea lion. The bulls utter a honking bark, the cows occasionally utter a quavering howl, and the pups bleat, but this species never roars. Its senses are not particularly keen, but it has been shown that, much like the whale, it uses a type of sonar echo-sounding to locate fish and underwater obstacles.

California sea lions are mostly nocturnal in feeding activity and spend much of the morning and the mid-day period sleeping on beaches. There seems to be a general northward migration after the breeding season.

The California sea lions' food consists of squid, octopus, abalones, and a variety of fishes such as herring, sardines, rockfish, hake, and ratfish. They bring the prey to the surface, bite through the neck, snap off the head with a powerful shake, and then bolt the body 'head first.'

Aside from man, killer whales and large sharks prey upon these sea lions. They have been known to live eighteen to twenty years in captivity.

Habitat. This species chooses a different habitat for its breeding rookeries and hauling-out spots than the other sea lion. It prefers sandy or boulder beaches, backed by precipitous cliffs, and sometimes sea caverns. It seldom frequents the rock islets used by the northern sea lion.

Reproduction. About the beginning of June the bulls first go ashore on the rookeries to establish their stations and territories. They will not feed for the next two months. The females go ashore later to breed, but they are free to move about between the bulls' territories and to return to the sea. The single pups are born between June 1 and 20, after a gestation period of 342 to 365 days. Shortly after giving birth the cow seeks the attention of a harem master and then concerns herself for the remainder of the summer in raising the pup. Both post-partum oestrus and delayed implantation are therefore indicated.

The pups, which bear initially a dark pelage, weigh about 16.5 kg (36 pounds) at birth. The mothers are very solicitous of their own offspring but toss about and crush the other pups in the colony. In learning to swim, the pups often seek asylum on their mothers' backs. They nurse for almost a full year but also eat fish on the side.

Economic Status. In the latter part of the last century (1860–80) many sea lions as well as whales were taken along the Pacific coast for their oil content. Later a trade developed in sea lion hides for the manufacture of glue, and these sold for five cents a pound. The dried 'trimmings' found a ready market in China for medicinal purposes. This trade was terminated in 1909 when the animals received legal protection. In the 1920s a small but profitable trade developed in capturing young sea lions in seine nets for zoos and circuses.

California sea lions are reported to eat commercial fish in nets and on lines and to damage fishing gear.

Status. In 1947 two to three thousand California sea lions were reported along the California coast.

Distribution. This species inhabits the coastal waters of the North Pacific from the Tres Marias Islands, Mexico, to Vancouver Island, British Columbia. There are also three small isolated populations in the Sea of Japan.

Canadian Distribution. This sea lion is known only from specimens taken at Ucluelet and Effingham Inlet, Vancouver Island, but it is reported as a regular visitor to

36

Mule deer, *Odocoileus hemionus*

37

White-tailed deer, *Odocoileus virginianus*

38

39

Allan Brooks

COLOUR PLATE

38

Moose, *Alces alces*

39

Wapiti, *Cervus elaphus*

Map 156 Distribution of the California sea lion, *Zalophus californianus*

Barkley Sound and Race Rocks near Victoria. The Canadian race is:

Zalophus californianus californianus (Lesson), 1828, Dict. Class. Hist. Nat. 13: 420. Vancouver Island (see Map 156).

REFERENCE

Peterson, R.S., and A. Bartholomew. 1967. The natural history and behaviour of the California sea lion. American Soc. Mamm. Spec. Pub. 1.

NORTHERN FUR SEAL
Otarie à fourrure. *Callorhinus ursinus* (Linnaeus)

Description. This is one of the most important fur-bearers, for from its pelt is fashioned the luxurious Alaskan seal coat. The northern fur seal is smaller than the related sea lions. It has a small head, with large eyes, short pointed snout, high forehead, and moderately long, stiff, slender ears. The bull's body is massive, with a swollen neck, but the cows are more gracefully proportioned. The limbs are short; the flippers are very long, and are capable of forward rotation on land; the toes are of equal length, and only the central three digits support flattened nails. The tail is insignificant (Figure 97).

The fur seal's skull is moderate in size; the rostrum is short and depressed; the frontal bones rise abruptly; the intraorbital region is long. The dentition is weak: there are six upper and four lower cheek teeth.

The pelage is composed of long, scattered (20–30 mm) guard hairs and a dense, velvety underfur about 14 mm in length. The hair grows in bundles, each containing one

359

guard hair and thirty-five to forty undercoat hairs. The bulls are almost black dorsally, brownish ventrally, with a grizzled grey mantle on the neck and shoulders. The flippers are naked, exposing the black skin. The limbs are reddish brown. The cows appear dark in the water, but the coat is pearly grey when they first emerge and start to dry out. After some time ashore at the rookery, they turn rather brownish. Both sexes as juveniles have long brown whiskers, which turn white in adulthood. The pups are born in a first black coat, which they moult at thirteen weeks of age to assume a silvery coat.

The adults moult annually, commencing in late September or October and continuing for four or five months. The moult is gradual, each fur bundle being shed individually so that no drastic moult line develops. The yearlings moult earlier, in August.

The difference in size between the sexes is extreme in this species, the adult bulls weighing about four times as much as the adult females. Average measurements of adult bulls: length 1.95 (1.89–2.15) metres, tail 50 mm, ear 50 mm, weight 192 (150–272) kg (average 427 pounds). Average measurements of adult cows: length 1.30 (1.10–1.42) metres, tail 50 mm, ear 45 mm, weight 42.5 (38–54) kg (average 94 pounds).

Habits. While at sea, fur seals are either solitary or slightly gregarious. The females abandon the pups on the rookery, and the youngsters are on their own their first winter. However, during the mating season, when the adult seals mass on the rookery in dense numbers, a complex social grouping is formed (see section on Reproduction for the explanation). The yearlings and younger animals do not take part in this society during the height of the breeding season but remain on the fringes of the colony.

The seals do most of their feeding at night when the fish are near the surface, and spend most of the daylight hours resting and preening. They often swim lazily with one flipper waving in the air. On land they wave a hind flipper to perspire. They can fall into a profound sleep, either on

Figure 97 Northern fur seal

land or at sea. They have been known to dive to depths of forty fathoms. In the wild, bulls have been known (by tagging experiments) to live fourteen years, and cows as long as twenty-one years.

Northern fur seals are strongly migratory. In October each year the cows and younger animals pour through the eastern channels between the Aleutian Islands. About ninety-five per cent of the Pribilof Islands herd spreads out over the northeastern Pacific Ocean as far south as the Mexican border, and up to five per cent head westward towards Japan. They reach the southern limits of their winter range off the California coast in December and then begin the northward spring migration in March, streaming by Vancouver Island, about thirty miles offshore, in late March, April, and May. The pups leave the rookery by themselves, a little later than the cows. Many spend the winter months in the protected northern fiords along the Alaska and British Columbia coasts, particularly in Hecate Strait. They seldom enter the Straits of Georgia. There is considerable mortality during winter storms, and the carcasses of emaciated pups are often washed ashore along Pacific coast beaches. The yearlings do not all return to the natal rookery, and those that do return in September and early October, later than the breeding adults. As they mature, more of an age class return at earlier dates to the rookery. The adult bulls do not undertake such long annual migrations. They remain in the vicinity of the Pribilof Islands until late autumn and then move offshore to wintering areas in Bering Sea and the Gulf of Alaska. They are therefore able to return to the rookery in spring earlier than the cows.

The food of the northern fur seal consists primarily of fish and squid, but birds are taken occasionally. Their diet varies considerably with the geographical location. Off the British Columbia coast the following percentages of food items have been noted: herring 78.6 per cent, eulachon 2.3 per cent, salmon 4.6 per cent, pilchard 1.4 per cent, sand lance 1.4 per cent, rockfish 0.8 per cent, other fish 4.1 per cent, squid 1.1 per cent, and a trace of marbled murrelet. In the Bering Sea, whiting, tomcod, and squid form the staple food supply. Of 2,129 stomachs examined from North American waters, only 3.2 per cent contained salmon. Off the Asiatic coasts lantern fish are commonly eaten. The stomachs also frequently contain an array of rocks.

Large sharks and killer whales are the chief predators, along with man.

Habitat. Fur seals are mostly pelagic in distribution during the autumn, winter, and spring but come ashore to breed during the summer. Young animals more commonly are found in coastal waters during the winter. The rookeries are formed on rocky beaches.

Reproduction. The breeding habits of this species are known in considerable detail because of its economic importance. It is also a species of unusual interest because of the extreme development of polygamy. The mature adult bulls climb ashore on the Pribilof Islands in late May or early June. These are the 'harem masters,' which are probably about ten years of age or older. They go without

Map 157 Distribution of the northern fur seal, *Callorhinus ursinus*: ● extra-limital record

food or water for over two months until the close of their breeding season. During the first weeks there is savage fighting between them to establish stations and territories, which are governed by the strength of the bull and the topography of the beach. Eventually the bulls will collect harems of ten to one hundred cows. These harems are not fixed, however, but fluctuate widely because of the movements of the cows and the pirating actions of neighbouring harem masters. The bulls will try to compel pre-oestrous cows to remain until mated but will permit them to travel on their feeding forays afterwards.

The adult cows arrive at the rookery from mid-June until mid-July. They climb ashore and seek the company of other cows, which means that the larger harems close to the shore grow more quickly than the inner ones. A neighbouring bull must kidnap four or five cows in order to establish a harem; otherwise the cows will disperse back to the larger groups. Eventually the shore harems are so crowded that the late arrivals must shuffle farther up the beach to find room. The pups are born two to three days after the cow's arrival. The peak of the pupping period is

July 15, and it usually terminates about August 1. Mating occurs four to seven days after the pup is born, which gives a gestation period of about 360 days. Normally a single birth occurs, but there is one record of twins.

The female fur seal is monoestrous. The ovaries function in alternate years, ripening a single ovum. Oestrus is post-partum, and the ovum is released spontaneously. Delayed implantation occurs the following December. The sexually mature juvenile cows come ashore after the end of the main breeding season in August and early September. By that time the harem masters are exhausted and have returned to the sea, so the young females are served by the bachelor males – that is, the young males which, though sexually mature, were not strong enough to win a territory in the rookery and were forced to hang around its borders.

At birth the pups weigh about 5 kg (11 pounds) and have their eyes open. The cow remains close to her pup for the first week, nursing it (the female has four abdominal mammae). Then the day after she has mated, she leaves the harem for a hunting foray at sea, which may last six to eight days. After that she returns for a day to nurse her pup before departing again. The pup must therefore go about six days between feedings; yet it grows quickly, and by the time it is weaned at four months, in November, it weighs about 13 to 14 kg (30 pounds). By that time, having been deserted by its mother, it must fend for itself.

Juvenile females reach sexual maturity at three to four years of age. Approximately eleven per cent of the four-year-olds and fifty per cent of the five-year-olds are pregnant. The males mature about the same time, but it may be some years before they take part in breeding activities.

Economic Status. Since the discovery of the Pribilof Islands rookeries in 1786–87 by the Russian navigator and fur-trader Gerassim Pribilof, seals have been continuously harvested for the fur trade, first under Russian management and later under American jurisdiction. The fine plush-like fur was first prized by Chinese mandarins, and later by Russian princes and European nobles. By the turn of the present century, the northern fur seal herds had been greatly reduced. The Convention for the Conservation of North Pacific Fur Seals, signed by the North Pacific powers in 1911 and extended in 1957, prohibited pelagic sealing and permitted the United States to manage the Pribilof Islands herd and the Soviet Union to manage the Commander Island herd. Both Canada and Japan receive 20 per cent of the profits of the program. Approximately 65,000 seals are taken annually from the Pribilof Islands herd, and the profit is approximately $50 per pelt, so that Canada's share is approximately $650,000 annually. (In the 1971–72 fur season, Canada received $310,728 from 9,138 seal skins.) In addition, between 1912 and 1940, nearly 50,000 fur seals were taken in British Columbia waters by native Indians using canoe and spear.

The pelts are taken before the moult starts in September. For many years only three- to five-year-old bachelor bulls were taken, but in view of the favourable size of the herd in 1956 a number of females were also pelted. In 1957 the number of skins taken on the Pribilof Islands was 78,919. The transformation of the raw pelts into finished furs requires 125 individual operations, including dehairing, leathering, dyeing, and processing, all of which takes more than three months for an individual hide. The final processing is done in St Louis, Missouri.

Status. The world population in 1957 was estimated to be 1,978,000 animals, of which 1,800,000 bred on the Pribilof Islands, 60,000 on the Commander Islands, and 60,000 on Robben Island, off Sakhalin Island in the western Pacific Ocean.

Distribution. The species occurs in the North Pacific Ocean from Point Barrow and Bering Sea south to California on the eastern coasts, and the Commander Islands and Bering, Copper, and Robbin islands in the western Pacific south to the Sea of Japan (see Map 157).

Canadian Distribution. Fur seals frequent the coastal waters of British Columbia in winter and during the spring and autumn migrations. There is one extra-limital record from the arctic coast of the Yukon Territory, about the first of October 1951. The animal was an emaciated

juvenile that had travelled over 1,000 miles from its normal distribution. The species is monotypic:

Callorhinus ursinus (Linnaeus), 1758, Syst. Nat., 10th ed., p. 37.

REFERENCES

Clements, W.A., J.L. Hart, and G.V. Wilby. 1936. Analyses of stomach contents of fur seals taken off the west coast of Vancouver Island in April and May, 1935. Canada, Dept. Fisheries, Ottawa.

Craig, A.M. 1964. Histology of reproduction and the oestrus cycle in the female fur seal, *Callorhinus ursinus.* Jour. Fish. Res. Bd. Canada 21(4): 773–811.

Kenyon, K.B., and V.B. Scheffer. 1954. A population study of the Alaskan fur-seal herd. Special Science Rept., Wildlife No. 12, United States Dept. Interior, Washington.

Scheffer, V.B. 1961. Pelage and surface topography of the northern fur seal. N. American Fauna No. 64. Washington.

Family **Odobenidae** / Walrus

The fossil record for the walrus indicates that it evolved from an ancestral member of the Otariidae in early Pliocene times (about seven million years ago). It seems distinct enough from the eared seals today to merit separate family status. Its specialized bottom-feeding habits and its unique form are quite distinct from the remainder of the group. Its body is thick and heavy; its head is short and broad; the external ears are reduced to mere skin folds; the hind limbs are capable of forward rotation; the hair covering is much reduced, and older animals are practically naked. The characteristic feature is the prolongation of the two upper canines into downward-projecting tusks. Walrus possess fifteen thoracic and five lumbar ribs instead of fourteen and six, as found in other seals.

WALRUS
Morse. *Odobenus rosmarus* (Linnaeus)

Description. On land the walrus apppears as an awkward, ugly creature. Its head seems too small for its swollen, creased neck. The thick, wrinkled, beige-brown skin is sparsely covered with short, wiry, reddish-brown hairs above, and the skin changes to reddish-brown on the belly and at the base of the flippers. The walrus's face is a sight not soon forgotten – the broad muzzle with its ridiculous moustache of about four hundred bristles up to a foot in length, and the small widely spaced eyes and long ivory tusks protruding between fleshy lips. The limbs are short and stout, and the short tail is enclosed in a fold of skin. The flippers carry five small, distinct claws. The bulls are much larger than the cows and may weigh up to $1\frac{1}{2}$ tons. Their swollen necks are covered with coarse tubercules and scars (Figure 98).

The skull of the walrus is heavily constructed and is almost rectangular in shape (Figure 99). The cranium is flattened; the small orbits lack supraorbital processes; the halves of the mandible are firmly fused in adults. The dentition is reduced and specialized and is often irregular. The milk teeth develop in the foetus. The average permanent dentition includes eighteen teeth. The tusks first erupt with enamel tips, which are soon worn off, and the adults' tusks are composed of pure dentine. A series of annual annular ridges develops on the roots, by which the

Figure 98 Walrus

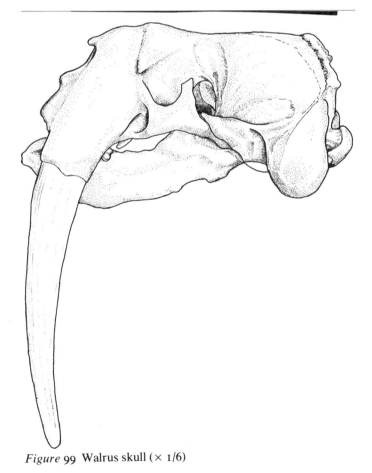

Figure 99 Walrus skull (× 1/6)

age of the animal may be determined. The tusks continue to grow during early adult life and reach an average length of 14 inches in the Atlantic race and 24 inches in the Pacific race. The tusks cease to grow in old age and may wear down to stubs. The permanent cheek teeth are columnar and are surrounded by layers of cementum. The tip of the tongue is rounded rather than notched as in the fur seals.

The fresh pelage consists of short, sparse silver-grey hairs, which turn reddish brown by the time the old coat is moulted in the summer.

Eastern arctic adult bulls average 3.05 (2.54–3.56) metres in length (120 inches) and the cows average 2.56 (2.29–2.92) metres (102 inches). The average weight for these adult males is 760 kg (1,650 pounds) and for the cows 570 kg (1,250 pounds). The Pacific Ocean race is significantly larger, and bulls have weighed up to 1,268 kg (2,795 pounds) and their cows 850 kg (1,874 pounds).

Habits. Walruses are gregarious, foraging and migrating in herds and hauling out on rocky promontories in densely packed groups during spells of fine weather. Away from land, they spend much of their time huddled on ice-floes. There is much petty squabbling among the group; neighbours are used as pillows to rest upon, often receiving jabs from the tusks. When sleeping on promontories or ice-floes, one member of the group will rear up from time to time, peer about, and then flop down reassured; however, their senses do not seem very acute. Originally confiding animals, they have become very wary in recent times and have deserted many of their historic hauling-out spots (*ooglit* in Eskimo) on open beaches. There is a pronounced segregation of the sexes during most of the year.

On land, walruses laboriously hunch their heavy bodies forward, rather caterpillar-like. When alarmed they plunge into the sea. Then their bulk is supported and hidden by the water, and they swim with slow, majestic grace, blowing in unison before rolling under the waves. It seems difficult to believe that these ponderous creatures have been observed to travel fifteen to twenty miles across land on the snow. They utter a variety of bellows and grunts. The bellows of the bulls may be heard for a mile or more when the herd is still out of sight. Bulls, especially when wounded, have been reported to attack boats in the water. On land they are less aggressive, only occasionally standing their ground in the face of approaching men and dogs.

Walrus usually feed in the early morning, and then haul out and rest for the remainder of the day. Occasionally they may fast for a whole week during pleasant, clear weather. They appear to feed heavily in autumn in shallow water until the bays freeze over. At this time they try to keep breathing-holes open by bunting the new soft ice with their heads. Eventually they retreat to the shore lead, which develops about a mile offshore during the winter. If the water is too deep at the edge of the pack-ice, they migrate to shallower water.

The Pacific walruses show a definite migration pattern. They spend the winter months in the shallow Bering Sea and then migrate in summer northward to the edge of the

Map 158 Distribution of the walrus, *Odobenus rosmarus*: 1 *O. r. divergens*, 2 *O. r. rosmarus*, ● extra-limital records

arctic pack-ice along the northern coasts of Siberia and Alaska. The Atlantic walruses are more sedentary, carrying out only local migrations when solid ice forms over the narrow coastal shelves.

By counting the cementum rings on their teeth, it has been estimated that walruses reach an age of thirty-five years.

This species lives primarily on molluscs, which it digs from the shallow sea bottom. There is still speculation concerning its feeding methods, but it seems probable that it 'stands on its head' in the water and rakes the sandy or muddy bottom with its tusks by turning its head from side to side. Walruses' stomachs may contain up to eighty-five pounds of the feet and siphons of burrowing bivalve molluscs, the shells being rarely found. Either they nip off the projecting mussels' feet and siphons, or they crush the shells with their molars and spit them out. Their bristle-like vibrissae must perform an important tactile function in finding food, because the bristles are worn short in old animals. Bottom sea life such as an-

nelids, crustacea, tunicates, and holothurians are also eaten.

Walruses seem to fast during the spring mating season, and the bulls appear to feed very little during the summer.

Occasionally a mature bull becomes a rogue and turns to eating seals or even young narwhals and belugas. These rogue bulls may be identified by their yellowish (fat-stained) scratched tusks.

Bull walruses fear few predators aside from man, but polar bears and killer whales frequently attack younger animals.

Habitat. This species is confined to the shallow northern seas of the continental shelves with depths between fifteen and eighteen metres (50–60 feet). The animals spend much of their time in the vicinity of the edge of the polar pack-ice. Formerly they spent much of the summer on land but they are now wary of man's interference.

Reproduction. Active spermatogenesis commences in the males in late autumn and continues until early June. The females possess four mammae: an inguinal pair and an abdominal pair. Mating probably occurs promiscuously on the ice-floes in April and May. The females mate every second year. Post-partum oestrus occurs too late for the first breeding season, but autumn ovulations may account for the rare off-season births. There is no delayed implantation, and the calves are born in May and June, the peak period being between May 14 and 26. There is a rare case of a birth on January 31. The gestation period lasts for 366 to 376 days. Usually only single births occur, but rarely twins are born.

The new-born calf, which weighs 46 to 68 kg (100–150 pounds), is covered with a short silvery-grey coat, which is moulted at the age of two months, when a thinner adult coat is assumed. The calves are born on the ice-floes, but they can swim soon after birth, and their development is precocious. The permanent tusks with their enamel caps erupt at three months of age. The calves remain with their mothers a full two years and nurse for most of that period. The females are solicitous mothers, and orphaned calves are adopted by other females.

Sexual maturity for juvenile females is reached at an age of four to five years, and the males reach sexual maturity about a year later.

Economic Status. The walrus is an important game resource to the Eskimo sea-hunting culture. The flesh, fat, skin, and viscera are used for either human consumption or dog food. The hides are used for covering boats and for thongs and dog traces. The intestines are used for raincoats and containers, and the bones are used for tools such as harpoon heads. Nowadays walrus ivory carving is a lucrative business, worth about $150,000 annually in Alaska. The Eskimo formerly hunted the walrus by spearing them from kayaks or by fishing for them, using blubber baits on hooks. Now most of the hunting is by rifle, with auxiliary use of harpoons to bring the animal in and secure it to floats before it can sink after death.

During the period 1860–80, approximately 10,000 walrus were taken annually by European whalers in Bering Sea for their ivory and oil, and similar numbers were probably taken by whalers in the eastern Canadian Arctic. At present 900 to 1,000 are taken annually in Alaska and approximately 1,700 in the eastern Arctic.

Status. The Pacific walrus population was estimated to be approximately 45,000 animals in 1957. Unfortunately, similar figures are not available for the eastern Arctic, but the population does not appear to be declining significantly.

Distribution. The walrus inhabits the edge of the polar ice-sheet in the Arctic Ocean southward to Bering Sea, James Bay, and the Labrador coast. The range is interrupted in the Canadian Arctic Archipelago and in the Severnaya Zemlya Archipelago, U.S.S.R. There are four distinct populations in the Atlantic, the Pacific, the Kara Sea, and the Laptev Sea.

Canadian Distribution. Formerly the range extended much farther south to Kamchatka, the southern Alaskan coast, the Mackenzie delta, and Franklin Bay in the east, and to the Gulf of St Lawrence, the Bay of Fundy, and the Massachusetts coast. Jacques Cartier discovered large colonies of walrus on Sable Island, Cape Breton Island, and the Magdalen Islands in 1534. These colonies were exploited by early explorers and fishermen in the sixteenth and seventeenth centuries, and as a result the walrus population has retreated northward. It is possible that a simultaneous warming trend in the climate also had a bearing on this shift. Recent extra-limital records came from the Bay of Fundy and Prince Patrick Island in the western Arctic in 1963. The distribution of the two sub-species is shown in Map 158.

Odobenus rosmarus divergens (Illiger), 1811, Abh. Preuss. Akad. Wiss. Berlin, p. 68. The Pacific walrus is larger than the Atlantic form and has longer, slenderer, more divergent tusks. It occurs only occasionally along the coast of the Beaufort Sea east to Banks Island.

Odobenus rosmarus rosmarus (Linnaeus), 1758, Syst. Nat., 10th ed., 1: 38. The Atlantic walrus is now found in the eastern Arctic from the Labrador coast and Hudson Bay to Kane Basin, and westward to Barrow Strait.

REFERENCES

Brooks, J.W. 1954. A contribution to the life history of the Pacific walrus. Alaska Cooperative Wildlife Research Unit, Rept. 1.

Loughrey, A.G. 1959. Preliminary investigation of the Atlantic walrus *Odobenus rosmarus rosmarus* (Linnaeus). Wildlife Mngt. Bull. 14, Canadian Wildlife Service, Ottawa.

Family **Phocidae** / True Seals

These seals constitute the most highly specialized, most numerous, and most widespread family of the pinnipeds. They have a streamlined body and short limbs. Their hind limbs alone are used for propulsion; turned posteriorly, they cannot be rotated forward. The forelimbs are smaller and are used only for steering and braking. They have broad heads, large luminous eyes, and ear orifices that lack external pinnae. Their pelage is composed of a coat of stiff over-hairs and a shorter, thin undercoat; both surfaces of the flippers are furred. The skulls are broad and flat, with inflated auditory bullae, but lack alisphenoid canals and post-orbital processes.

BEARDED SEAL
Phoque barbu. *Erignathus barbatus* (Erxleben)

Description. This species is often referred to as the 'square flipper' because of the unusual shape of the foreflippers, which is created by the almost equal length of the digits (the third digit being only slightly longer than the others). It is a very large, robust seal with large eyes and a conspicuous moustache composed of long, regular vibrissae that tend to curl at the tips when dry, prominent ear orifices, and a thickened neck (Plate 34a).

The skull of this seal has a relatively vaulted cranium, which lacks a sagittal crest, and a short, high rostrum. The jugal bone is short and broad. The dentition is very weak, and the small, widely separated teeth are usually much worn (Figure 100).

The pelage is composed of a coat of stiff hairs, which is smoky grey with a darker brown cap and dorsum. The annual moult occurs between March and June.

Both sexes are similar in size, averaging 235 (210–285) cm in length (approximately 8–9 feet) and possibly reaching a maximum weight of 397 kg (875 pounds).

Habits. Very few details of the social life of these seals are known. They are not gregarious and are seldom found in large numbers. It is reported that they are curious and easily attracted, but, when suddenly confronted by a hunter, they may 'freeze.' They are also reported to whistle to their pups while under water but are relatively quiet on land or ice. Although they do not undertake regular long migrations, they may be carried about erratically on drifting ice.

Their teeth are less useful as a means of age determination than in the other species, but their strong foreclaws

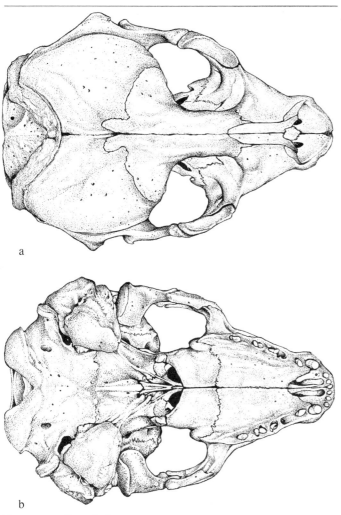

Figure 100 Bearded seal skull: (a) dorsal view, (b) ventral view (× 1/3)

show annual rings. A light band forms during the breeding season and a ridge during the subsequent moult. Ages up to sixteen years have been assigned by this method.

Their food consists of bottom-living animals such as whelks, clams, holothurians, crabs, octopuses, and bottom-dwelling fish such as polar cod, flounders, and sculpins. It is thought that their strong claws and long moustaches are in some way associated with their feeding habits. Bearded seals resemble the walrus in these details.

The natural enemies of the bearded seals are killer whales and polar bears.

Habitat. Bearded seals inhabit arctic and subarctic shallow seas over continental shelves, which are choked with pack-ice in winter but are largely open water in summer.

Reproduction. Female bearded seals are unique among northern seals in possessing two pairs of abdominal teats. They are probably monoestrous. Though mating occurs in mid-May in the Canadian Arctic, implantation is delayed about two and a half months until August. The apparent gestation period is about eleven and a half months. The pups are born in April and May, with a peak of births about the first of May. There is no post-partum oestrus, and the females do not ovulate again until early June, when the males are out of breeding condition. Therefore they must wait a year to be mated again, and the pups are born only every second year – a unique condition among the seal family.

The pups measure about 120 cm (47 inches) at birth and weigh about 36.3 kg (80 pounds). They are born with a woolly, mouse-brown natal coat. They do not seem to develop as quickly as most other seals and reportedly follow their mothers for a considerable length of time. It is not known how long they are nursed.

Sexual maturity for both sexes is reached after the sixth year.

Economic Status. These seals are of little commercial interest but are of great economic importance to the Eskimos because of their large size. Their thick hides are used for the covering of tents, kayaks, and whale boats (umiaks) as well as for strong lines and dog traces. The meat is used for human and dog food.

Unfortunately, these seals constitute a public health menace because they harbour the nematode *Trichinella*, and if the seal meat is eaten raw or frozen (as is popular among the Eskimos), trichinosis may follow. The liver may contain a sufficiently high concentration of vitamin A to be poisonous under certain conditions.

Status. These seals are less common than the ringed and harp seals. A recent estimate of the total population has been made at 75,000 to 150,000 animals.

Distribution. This species is holarctic in distribution about the northern coasts of the continents. It does not inhabit the solid polar ice-sheet, however.

Canadian Distribution. Two weakly defined subspecies are reported to inhabit northern Canadian coastal waters from the Yukon border, the Arctic Archipelago, Hudson Bay, and the Labrador coast to the Gulf of St Lawrence (see Map 159).

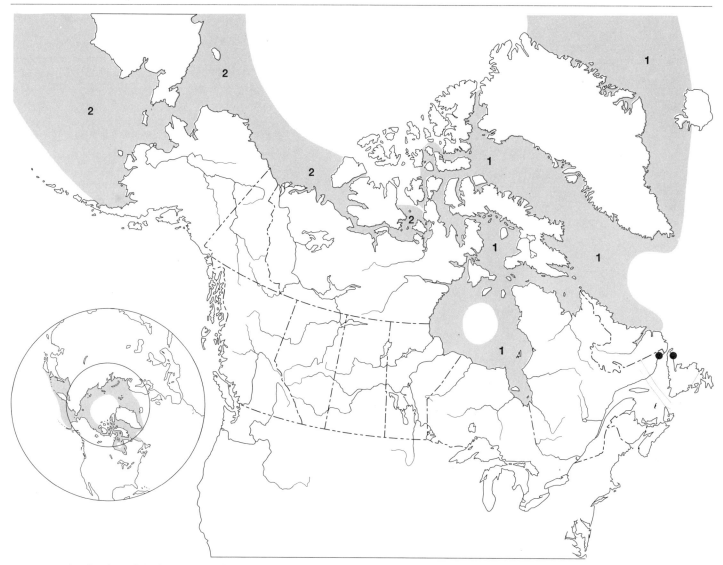

Map 159 Distribution of the bearded seal, *Erignathus barbatus*: 1 *E. b. barbatus*, 2 *E. b. nauticus*, ● extra-limital records

Erignathus barbatus barbatus (Erxleben), 1777, Syst. regni animalis ..., 1: 590. Canadian eastern Arctic, and the North Atlantic to Laptev Sea.

Erignathus barbatus nauticus (Pallas), 1811, Zoographia Russo-Asiatica 1: 108. Canadian western Arctic to Laptev Sea; reported to have a shorter, broader rostrum.

REFERENCE

McLaren, I.A. 1958. Some aspects of growth and reproduction of the bearded seal, *Erignathus barbatus* (Erxleben). Jour. Fish. Res. Bd. Canada 15(2): 219–27.

GREY SEAL
Phoque gris. *Halichoerus grypus* (Fabricius)

Description. This is a large seal with a relatively long, broad, straight snout, which has led to the local name 'horse face.' The flexible forelimbs and the long, slender claws make it more adept on land than most other seals. Some individuals also have slightly larger ear pinnae than

is normal for the family. The adult bulls are more massive than the cows and have swollen, wrinkled necks and broad, slightly 'roman' snouts (Plate 34e).

The skull of the grey seal is arched dorsally, with a high, broad rostrum. The dentition is strong: the cheek teeth are mostly simple cones; the first tooth behind the canines is pushed medially out of line, and there is a gap between the fourth and fifth upper cheek teeth. Old males have prominent sagittal crests.

The adult coat is variable in colour: silvery to dusky grey with obscure black blotches on the flanks and back. The underparts and head are lighter than the back. The bulls are darker brown. The pups are born in a long, crinkly, white coat, which they moult when they are three to four weeks old to assume a dark grey, spotted juvenile coat.

The cows moult annually between late January and April, and the bulls moult a little later, between late February and May.

Adult males may reach a total length of 300 cm (9 feet 10

367

Map 160 Distribution of the grey seal, *Halichoerus grypus*

inches) and weigh 290 kg (640 pounds). Females are smaller, up to 230 cm (7 feet 7 inches), and weigh 249 kg (550 pounds).

Habits. These are gregarious seals, which forage in groups and haul out to breed and moult in dense colonies. Aside from these periods on shore, they spend much of the year feeding in coastal waters. They dominate the smaller harbour seals and usurp favourite skerries at low tide to haul out upon. They have a variety of calls: from hisses and snarls for driving off intruders to short barks and mournful hoots. They crawl quite far inland on deserted islands during the breeding season. When diving they can remain under water for periods of up to twenty minutes. They have been taken on fish hooks set at depths down to seventy to eighty fathoms.

Generally, grey seals are relatively sedentary about the vicinity of the breeding colonies, but the young disperse widely during the first two years of their lives. They exhibit territoriality during the breeding season, the bulls defending a breeding territory and the cows defending an area about their calves. The colonies may vary in size from 100 to 9,000 individuals.

Estimated by dental rings, captive grey seals have reached an age of forty-one to forty-two years, and wild seals have reached an age of up to thirty-five years.

This species feeds primarily on bottom fish such as rockfish, saithe, pollack, cod, flounder, whiting, coal fish, and ling. They also feed to a lesser degree on squid, pelagic crustacea, and schooling fish such as herring and salmon. Aside from man, the killer whale is its chief predator.

Habitat. These seals inhabit exposed rocky coasts, skerries exposed at low tide, and remote islands in temperate seas. They forage for bottom fish on continental shelves.

Reproduction. Grey seals are particularly interesting because their breeding season differs widely with the geographical location of the colony. The older bulls establish territories on rocky or shingle beaches, or in channels at the water's edge, or on ice shelves. They collect small harems of eight to ten dispersed cows with their calves. They do not feed for four to six weeks during this period. The younger bulls lie in the shallow water and accost passing cows. The bulls challenge intruders with lowered heads, open mouths, and hisses. If the challenger does not withdraw from the territorial bull's shuffling charge, a fierce fight will ensue, in which the contestants grapple with each other's wrinkled necks. Usually the invader retreats, and the territorial bull gives a victory 'roll.'

To bear her young the cow climbs ashore or onto the ice. At first she discourages the bull's attention with a raised flipper and a hoot, but about two weeks after the birth of the young she yields to the near-by bull.

On Canadian shores, parturition and mating occur on the ice or on rocky islets in January and February, as they do also in the Baltic Sea, but on the shores of Britain they occur on rocky points and islands in the autumn, from September to December.

The cows have two abdominal teats, which are normally everted but expand during nursing. There is post-partum oestrus and delayed implantation so that the apparent gestation period is eleven and a half months. Single births are the rule. The pup is about 76 cm (30 inches) long at birth and weighs about 14 kg (31 pounds). It is thin but fills out rapidly, gaining about three pounds a day, so that it weighs 90 to 100 pounds (41–45 kg) by the time it is weaned at sixteen to eighteen days. It begins to moult after the third week, at which time it is deserted by its mother. The pups yap shrilly when their mothers return to the water to feed. When the moult is complete, they make their way to the sea, learn to swim and eat, and then disperse. When caught as yearlings they have changed little in weight (40 kg) but measure 115 to 127 cm in length. Sexual maturity is reached between six and seven years of age.

Economic Status. Grey seals arouse the ire of fishermen because they may feed upon commercial fish such as salmon, and sometimes they damage fish traps and nets. Their destruction is advocated by other people because they act as the terminal host for the codworm, the intermediate stage of which encysts in the flesh of the cod.

Status. This is one of the less common seals, whose world population is estimated at about 40,000, of which about 5,000 inhabit Canadian waters.

Distribution. The grey seal inhabits the temperate waters of the North Atlantic. It is most common about the British Isles, Norway, the White and Baltic seas, and Iceland. An isolated population occurs in the Gulf of St Lawrence in the western Atlantic.

Canadian Distribution. This species is found along the coasts of the Maritime Provinces from the north shore of the St Lawrence to Newfoundland, Prince Edward Island, Nova Scotia, Sable Island, and Grand Manan Island in the Bay of Fundy. It ascends the St Lawrence River as far as Rimouski (see Map 160). The species is monotypic.

Halichoerus grypus (Fabricius), 1791, Skrivter af. Naturh. Selskabet, København, 1(2): 167, pl. 13, fig. 4.

REFERENCES
Cameron, A.W. 1967. Breeding behavior in a colony of western Atlantic grey seals. Canadian Jour. Zool. 45(2): 161–73.
Coulson, J.C., and Grace Hicking. 1964. The breeding biology of the grey seal, *Halichoerus grypus* (Fab.), on the Farne Islands, Northumberland. Jour. Animal Ecol. 33(3): 485–512.

HARBOUR SEAL
Phoque commun. *Phoca vitulina* Linnaeus

Description. The harbour seal is probably the most widespread and best known of the true seals. Its body is short and heavy, averaging about 5 feet in length. It has a round, smooth head and dorsally placed valvular nostrils. Its large convex eyes, also dorsally placed, provide good underwater vision; the mystacial vibrissae, which number about forty-two on each side of the muzzle and measure about 125 mm long, are flattened and beaded. The digits are about equal in length and terminate in flattened claws; the tail is short; the tongue has a terminal notch (Figure 101).

In this species the skull is rounded, with a slight sagittal crest (Figure 102). The broad nasal bones taper gradually; the posterior margin of the palate is v-shaped; a bony nasal septum extends behind the palate. The five cheek teeth are large and are set obliquely in the upper jaw; the third upper tooth is the largest; there are three upper and two lower incisors; the mandible is heavy and deep.

The overcoat is composed of stiff hairs about 11 mm in length, and the undercoat of sparse curly hairs about 5 mm in length. The colour is extremely variable. The background varies from creamy white to dark brown. The usual colour is buff-brown above with irregular dark brown spots, streaks, or blotches. The under side is usually creamy white with scattered dark brown spots. The

Figure 101 Harbour seal

annual moult occurs in late summer and early fall, between August and early November; it proceeds from the posterior to the anterior parts.

Average measurements of adult males: length 150 (122–170) cm, tail 107 (87–115) mm, hind foot 295 (255–338) mm; average weight 72.5 kg, maximum 148 kg (300 pounds). Average measurements of adult females: length 148 (140–160) cm, tail 98 (96–100) mm, hind foot 275 (245–290) mm; average weight 58 kg, maximum 111 kg (243 pounds).

Habits. Harbour seals are gregarious on land but disperse to forage alone in the water. They haul out on sand banks and rocky shoals and lie side by side in loosely organized bands of up to 500 individuals. They are very wary and quick to flop into the water at the appearance of a boat or the report of a rifle. In general they are inoffensive creatures and romp and play in the surf. They have the curious habit of clapping their foreflippers on their chests with a loud splash.

All the senses of harbour seals seem to be acute. They utter a variety of grunts and growls and a high-pitched yapping bark. In the water they snort and snuffle. On land they hitch themselves awkwardly forward by means of their foreflippers (the claws are used to grip the sand and shingles). In the water they scull gracefully with their hind flippers and with undulations of their hind quarters, rolling from their sides onto their backs. They slip under water and rise cautiously; they do not 'porpoise' or splash like sea lions. They have been known to dive as deep as 300 feet for short periods and can remain under water for as much as twenty-three minutes.

Their activity pattern is governed by the tides and the weather. They usually haul out at low tide to rest and sleep, and then resume feeding on the incoming tide. They often ride the high tides far up the coastal rivers, feeding as they go. In stormy weather they shun rocky coasts.

Harbour seals are quite sedentary in habits, remaining in coastal areas all winter, although they come ashore less frequently at that time. In the spring, they often migrate far up large rivers, however, following the eulachon and salmon runs, returning to the coast in the autumn.

This species has lived up to seventeen years in captivity.

The diet of harbour seals consists of 94 per cent fishes and 6 per cent molluscs. Fishes eaten include rockfish, herring, lamprey, flounder, tomcod, hake, salmon, sculpins, pollack, cod, ling, blennies, mackerel, ratfish, silver perch, and sand lance. The molluscs include squid, octopus, and clams of the genus *Yoldia*. They also occasionally eat crayfish, crab, and shrimp. In captivity they eat about four kilograms (8.5 pounds) of fish per day.

Predators include the polar bear, the walrus, the killer whale, and the shark. Golden eagles have been known to prey upon new-born pups resting on sand-bars.

Habitat. This species inhabits coastal waters about ten miles off land. It is found in bays, harbours, and coastal rivers. Its activities are not confined to salt water, and it is found permanently in inland waters such as in Harrison Lake, British Columbia.

Reproduction. The reproductive cycle in this species is highly adapted to its aquatic environment. In the males spermatogenesis commences in July. There is no harem formation, and mating occurs promiscuously in shallow water or upon the sand-bars and skerries where the seals haul out from late July to early September. The females have two abdominal mammae. They are monoestrous, oestrus following the termination of lactation. The implantation of the embryo is delayed two to three months. After an apparent gestation period of about ten months, the pups are born between the middle of May and the middle of June. The peak of the pupping season is the first half of June, but it varies with locality. Usually only a single birth occurs, rarely twins. The pups are born on reefs and skerries, and at the edge of sand-bars. Under the stress of human interference or of stormy weather they may even be born in the water.

At birth, harbour seal pups measure 660–910 mm (26–36 inches) in length and weigh 9–13 kg (20–29 pounds). The first coat (lanugo), composed of long, soft, silvery unspotted fur, is shed just before birth or rubbed off soon afterwards, revealing the second shorter, darker, spotted coat. At birth the eyes are open, and there are small but unmistakable ear folds.

For the first couple of days the pups are too weak to

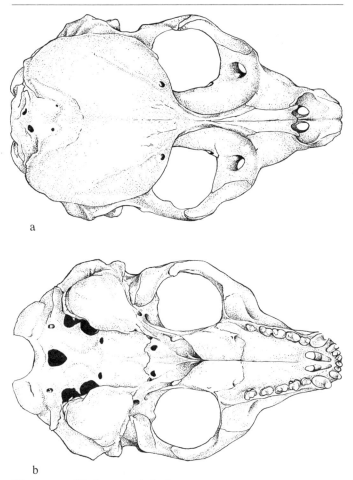

a

b

Figure 102 Harbour seal skull: (a) dorsal view, (b) ventral view (× 1/2)

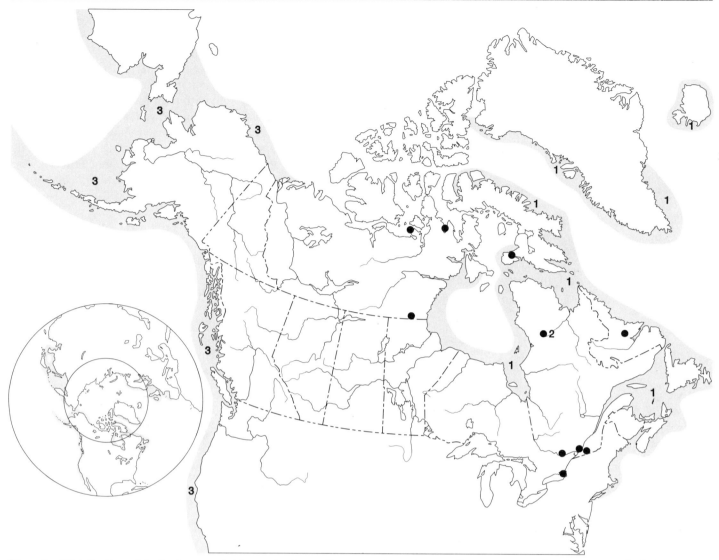

Map 161 Distribution of the harbour seal, *Phoca vitulina*: 1 *P. v. concolor*, 2 *P. v. mellonae*, 3 *P. v. richardii*, ●extra-limital records

climb ashore or dive, and just float around the surface of the shallow water. Their development is precocious, however, and after the first week they can dive in shallow water for short periods and drag themselves ashore. Their milk teeth are replaced by the permanent teeth *in utero*. At first the mother floats on her back on the surface to suckle her pup, but as its strength increases the pup will dive and suckle under water while she floats vertically, or it will nurse while she is resting on shore.

The mothers are very solicitous of their young. When the pups are still helpless, they ride 'pick-a-back' on their mothers' shoulders as they swim. If danger threatens, the females will grasp the pups in their teeth and dive. Later on, they guide their pups in diving and swimming underwater with a front flipper. The pups are weaned after about a month. They grow rapidly and double their weight by the first winter and triple it by their first birthday.

It is thought that sexual maturity is not reached until the seals reach an age of five to six years.

Economic Status. Harbour seals are held in disrepute by fishermen because of their depredations on commercial fishes and damage to fishing gear. They feed on salmon during the period salmon 'run' upriver to spawn. The seals also feed on commercial fish caught in gill nets and occasionally damage the nets themselves. Occasionally, wily seals enter fish traps, eat the fish, and escape.

The actual damage varies a great deal from locality to locality and from season to season, however. Investigations have indicated seal damage to commercial catches of from 1 to 23.8 per cent. Since seals feed on the most available food, they often consume other species that prey upon young salmon.

For many years bounties have been paid on seals on both our coasts. On the British Columbia coast an average of 2,600 seals were taken annually up to 1947, when the bounty was $5 per 'nose.' There was a commercial market for harbour seal pelts from 1963 to 1968, when fur buyers offered up to $65 for prime skins.

Distribution. The harbour seal occurs along the northern coasts of Europe, Asia, and North America.

Canadian Distribution. This species is found on both our Atlantic and Pacific coasts and in the eastern Arctic as far

371

north as Hudson Bay, Foxe Basin, Baffin Bay, and Alexandra Fiord, Ellesmere Island. Stragglers have entered the St Lawrence River and proceeded as far as Lake Ontario and Ottawa. Three subspecies are described on our coasts and inland waters (see Map 161).

Phoca vitulina concolor DeKay, 1842, Mammalia, *in* Zoology of New York, part 1: 53. The race is found along our Atlantic coast.

Phoca vitulina mellonae Doutt, 1942, Ann. Carnegie Mus. 29: 111. A land-locked population, found in the Upper and Lower Seal lakes, Ungava Peninsula, Quebec, about ninety miles east of Richmond Gulf, Hudson Bay. It is estimated that the colony was established during a period of marine submergence, between 8,000 and 3,000 years ago. It is a small, dark subspecies.

Phoca vitulina richardii Gray, 1864, Proc. Zool. Soc. London, p. 28. The British Columbia coast. Distinguished by the premaxillae extending posteriorly along the nasals for 8 to 10 mm in a significantly large proportion of the skulls.

REFERENCES

Fisher, H.D. 1952. The status of the harbour seal in British Columbia, with particular reference to the Skeena River. Fish. Res. Bd. Canada Bull. 93.

Mansfield, A.W. 1967. Distribution of the harbor seal, *Phoca vitulina* Linnaeus, in Canadian Arctic waters. Jour. Mamm. 48(2): 249–57.

RINGED SEAL
Phoque annelé. *Phoca hispida* Schreber

Description. The ringed seal is the smallest of the pinnipeds, averaging only 4 1/2 feet in length. Its body is similar to that of the harbour seal, from which it can be distinguished only by careful examination. The head is rounder, the snout is more pointed, and the large, solemn brown eyes give it a feline rather than canine cast. The claws are triangular in cross-section and have a dorsal ridge. The thick layer of blubber varies from a maximum of 40 per cent of the body weight in late autumn to 23 per cent during the spring fast (Plate 34b).

Compared to the harbour seal's skull, the ringed seal's is more delicately constructed, with a weaker dentition, befitting the primary diet of planktonic crustacea. The cranium is globular and lacks a sagittal crest; the mandibular teeth are aligned with the slender jawbone and are uncrowded; the bony nasal septum does not extend beyond the posterior v-shaped margin of the palate (Figure 103).

The adult coat is harsh to the touch; the stiff guard hairs point backwards. The colour is variable. Dorsally it may vary from brown to bluish black in background colour with irregular creamy rings with dark centres, from which it gets its common name. The ventral surface may be silvery white to creamy yellow with scattered black spots There is often a rusty tint about the mouth and the base o the flippers. The pups are covered with a soft, crinkly,

white coat about an inch in length at birth, which earns them the name of 'whitecoats.' The annual moult occurs between mid-May and mid-July, with a peak in June, but a few moulting individuals have been noted as late as September 1. During the moulting period, the adults spend most of the time fasting and basking on the ice-floes. They scratch off the old pelt with their hind flippers, and pieces of the epidermis slough off as well. At the height of the moult, large areas of their bodies are naked.

The average length of adult males is 135 cm, and the maximum 162 cm. The females average a little shorter, with a maximum of 153 cm. The average weight of adults is 91 kg. The maximum weight recorded for eastern arctic males is 101 kg (225 pounds).

Habits. Ringed seals are primarily solitary, but occasionally appear in loosely dispersed groups. Although they take warning from the actions of their fellows, they act individually. Their sense of sight appears to be poorly developed, and they respond mainly to the movement of close objects. The senses of hearing and smell seem to be keenly developed. They whine and moan on the ice, or growl if trapped at close quarters. They climb clumsily onto the ice but swim with grace and ease. When feeding in shallow water, they usually submerge for periods of three

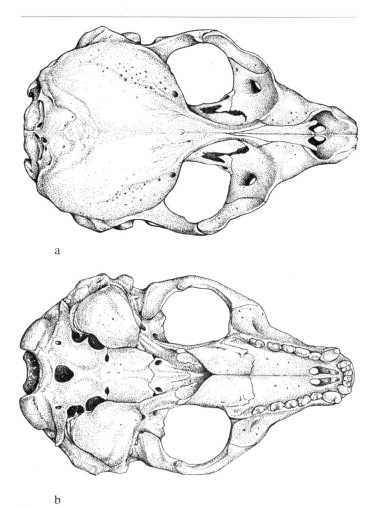

a

b

Figure 103 Ringed seal skull: (a) dorsal view, (b) ventral view (× 1/2)

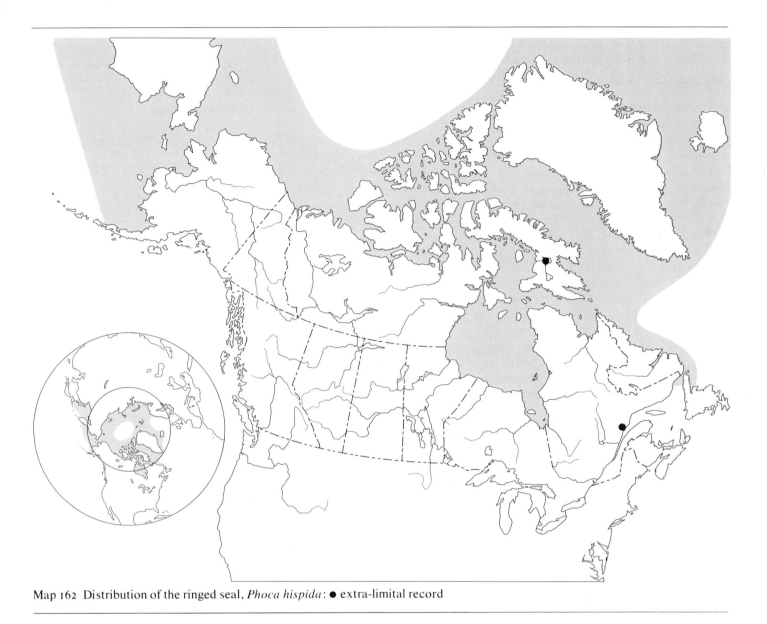

Map 162 Distribution of the ringed seal, *Phoca hispida*: ● extra-limital record

minutes with alternating periods of one and a half minutes on the surface. Their maximum diving potential appears to be to a depth of 300 feet and for as long as twenty minutes.

Little is known of the activity and movements of ringed seals. In the vicinity of land-fast ice the adults are mostly sedentary. In water the young and juveniles are most commonly found at the edge of the shore ice and among drifting offshore floes.

Their populations have been estimated to vary between ten and thirty-five animals per square mile of land-fast ice within a mile of shore, and five seals per square mile beyond that distance.

Their age may be determined by annual annuli on the dentine layers of their teeth. A thin layer is deposited in spring during the fasting period. By this means an old male was estimated to be forty-three years old at death.

Ringed seals feed primarily upon crustacean macro-plankton and to a lesser extent upon small fish. In shallow water they eat crabs, prawns, and fish such as polar cod, herring, whiting, eulachon, and smelts. In deeper water they feed upon pelagic crustacean 'krill.' The choice of

species depends upon availability. The seals fast from April to late June or July during the reproductive and moulting seasons.

Predators of adults include sharks, killer whales, and polar bears. Polar bears and arctic foxes prey upon the new-born 'whitecoats' in their natal dens, and even the larger and more powerful gulls attack exposed young pups.

Habitat. This seal shows an attachment to land-fast ice, or to the more or less solid ice cover of the Arctic Ocean, where it occurs in the shifting leads and pressure ridges as far as the North Pole. It is only infrequently found in the shifting ice-floes of the open seas. There is also a land-locked population in Nettilling Lake, Baffin Island.

Reproduction. The males are sexually active between mid-March and mid-May. At that time they have a very strong, offensive, musky odour. There is no information on mating habits, whether they pair or mate promiscu-ously, but they certainly do not collect harems. The females are monoestrous, and the oestrous period is post-partum while the females are still lactating. The period between the birth of the young and oestrus is not known, but it is believed to be short. Implantation of the embryos is delayed three and a half months until August. The single pup is born sometime between mid-March and mid-April, and mating is thought to occur about the latter date so that the apparent gestation period is about eleven and a half months.

The pups are born in snow dens on land-fast ice. These may be excavated by the female in the snow that covers the ice, or they may be natural snow caves caused by the uptilting of blocks of ice at pressure ridges. Dens are approximately ten feet long and two feet high, and the walls become iced from the body heat of the seals. The only entrance to the den is from a breathing-hole in the ice at one end of the cave. At birth the pups are about 65 cm in length and weigh 4 to 5 kg (10–12 pounds). They are covered with the fluffy white lanugo coat, which they retain for about a month.

The pups are helpless at first and remain in the snow dens, where the females nurse them for a full two months. Longer nursing in sheltered northern bays, where the snow and ice remain longer, produces larger pups. Eventually the young take to the water to learn to swim and hunt for themselves with the breaking up of the ice in summer. Juvenile females reach sexual maturity at the age of six years and the males a year later.

Economic Status. The ringed seal (or *netsik*) is the cornerstone in the native economy of the coastal Eskimos. Its flesh is used as food for man and dog. The liver with its high vitamin A content is particularly prized. The intestines are used for containers and, occasionally, igloo windows. The skins are used for mukluks, parkas, tents, mats, light lines, receptacles, floats, dog harnesses, and *tupik* (tent) covering. The fat is burned for light and heat in the igloos in winter. The bones were once manufactured into various tools.

The seals are carefully stalked upwind by the hunter behind a shield of white canvas or, previously, polar bear skin, stretched on a wooden cross, while they are basking on the ice beside their breathing-holes. For the last few yards the hunter crawls on his belly. After the seal has been shot, there is a wild dash to ensure that it does not slip back into the hole. Previously Eskimo hunters waited patiently at the seal holes for the seals to return to breathe. An ingenious float warned the hunter of the approaching seal, which caused the water to well up in the hole, and the hunter would thrust down with his spear at the unseen animal.

Distribution. The ringed seal is holarctic in distribution, occurring in arctic and subarctic waters south to the Gulf of St Lawrence, the Baltic Sea, and Hokkaido Island in the western Pacific. There are closely related species: the Baikal seal, *Phoca sibirica* Gmelin, and the Caspian seal, *Phoca caspica* Gmelin, which are believed to be relict species landlocked in Lake Baikal and the Caspian Sea of Asia as an aftermath of the last glacial period.

Canadian Distribution. Ringed seals have been known to bear pups on the shore ice as far south as North Cape, Newfoundland, and a few occur along the Labrador coast, but the centre of distribution is around Baffin Island,

40

Caribou, *Rangifer tarandus*

41

42

where the population has been estimated at one million. In the Far North the ice may be so thick as to discourage den construction. At present only one subspecies is recognized for all Canadian arctic coastal waters (see Map 162). Formerly separate subspecies were described for the Beaufort Sea and Nettilling Lake populations.

Phoca hispida hispida Schreber, 1775, Die Säugethiere ..., Theil 3, Heft 13, pl. 86. The typical form of the Arctic Ocean.

REFERENCE

Smith, T.G. 1973. Population dynamics of the ringed seal in the Canadian eastern Arctic. Fish. Res. Bd. Canada Bull. 181.

HARP SEAL
Phoque du Groenland. *Phoca groenlandica* Erxleben

Description. The harp seal is probably the most important of the seals from a commercial point of view. It is one of the smaller species, slightly larger than the ringed and the harbour seal, but smaller than the others. Adults average about 6 feet in length. The form is typically phocid: the face is short, and the large, liquid brown eyes are situated high on the flat forehead (Figure 104).

The skull of the harp seal is a little larger than the skulls of the harbour and ringed seals. The interorbital bridge is extremely narrow; the nasals are long and tapering from front to back; the posterior margin of the palate is arched (not v-shaped), and the median bony nasal septum extends beyond the edge of the palate. The small, widely spaced cheek teeth have accessory cusps; the third tooth is the largest.

The adult pelage is stiff, and the individual guard hairs are about 20 mm long. The coat colour is remarkably variable, depending upon sex and a sequence of immature coats from birth to adulthood. The species derives its common name from the coat of the adult male. The back-

Figure 104 Harp seal

ground colour is steel blue when wet, drying to pale grey, with a dark brown or black head and tail patches, and a large, irregular horseshoe-shaped band straddling the back and uniting across the shoulders. The flippers and belly are whitish with small, irregular black spots. The females may be similarly patterned, except that the 'harp,' the head, and the tail spots are usually greyish brown rather than black, or the back may have blotches with irregular dark grey spots and no clearly defined 'harp.'

The pups at birth are covered with a long, fluffy white coat from which they derive their common name of 'whitecoats.' This first 'lanugo' coat is composed of a layer of long (4–5 cm) guard hairs and a soft undercoat of curly, woolly fur. After about a week, the coat begins to loosen about the face and flippers, and the pups are then called 'ragged jackets.' This coat is completely shed after two weeks, when the pups assume a short, creamy grey one, flecked with black spots about the size of a 'quarter' along the flanks and sparsely on the back. Most pups have a dark grey median band, but occasionally one may be dark all over. The succeeding juvenile coats are more creamy brown with large dark blotches on the flanks, which often merge into the dark median band. These juveniles are called 'bedlamers' by the sealers.

The annual moult has been termed 'catastrophic' in this species; not only does the coat shed, but large patches of the epidermis peel off as well. Most of the seals spend the moulting period basking and dozing on the drifting ice-floes, and they seem reluctant to enter the water at this time. The Gulf of St Lawrence herd is, however, handicapped by the earlier break-up of the spring ice-floes and must terminate the moult in the water. The moult lasts about a month, beginning in early April with the arrival of the adult males and bedlamers. The adult females start to moult about the end of April.

Occasionally very dark 'smutty' seals are observed; these are thought to be melanistic colour forms.

The males are only slightly larger than the females. The average length of adult males is 172 (138–200) cm, and of adult females 168 (142–182) cm. The maximum weight is up to 180 kg (400 pounds).

Habits. Harp seals are highly gregarious. They haul out onto the ice in dense herds to bear their young, to mate, and to moult. They also migrate and feed in loose herds in the sea, although there is some segregation of the sexes out of the breeding season. They are reported to dive to extreme depths of 100 to 150 fathoms and to remain under water for periods of fifteen minutes. They usually frequent the leads between ice-floes but will punch breathing-holes through newly forming ice by bunting it with their heads and then will maintain these holes by frequent visits while the depth of ice is increasing. Eventually a small raised rim is formed about the hole. They are very vocal: the pups whimper and cry, and the adults' loud barks carry great distances across the ice in the crisp winter air.

Very little is written of the diurnal activity of these seals, but their annual pattern of activity is well known because of their spectacular pelagic migrations. They spend most of the year on the edge of the arctic pack-ice.

After the moult ends in late May off the Labrador and Newfoundland coasts, the harp seals of the western Atlantic follow the disintegrating ice northward through Davis Strait and into Baffin Bay. They appear off west Greenland in late May, migrate as far north as Thule and westward through Lancaster Sound into the Canadian Arctic Archipelago in late June, to spend the summer months dispersed in these arctic waters. About September 20, with the freeze-up of the arctic bays, the seals begin their southward migration along the east coast of Baffin Island and eastward through Hudson Strait from Hudson Bay and Foxe Basin. The first migrants reach Cape Chidley at the north tip of Labrador after the middle of October, and the herds stream down the Labrador coast in November and December, aided by the southward-flowing Labrador Current, finally reaching the Straits of Belle Isle about New Year's Day. Here the migrating stream divides, part being swept through the Straits of Belle Isle into the Gulf of St Lawrence and the remainder continuing down the east coast of Newfoundland. For the next month and a half the seals disperse widely in the waters of the southern part of the gulf and off the northern Grand Banks until those waters freeze up in late February. Then the adults approach the edge of the pack-ice to whelp, mate, and eventually to moult both in the gulf and off the southern Labrador coast.

The juvenile 'bedlamers' follow the adults southward during the autumn migration. The young pups move first away from the ice pack where they were born, then drift passively southward in the current until they are eight to ten weeks old, after which they actively migrate northward behind the herds of adults and juveniles in late May.

The females show a sense of territoriality in the breeding colonies on the ice-floes, where they drive off the other females from the vicinity of their pups.

Harp seals feed primarily upon small marine fishes and secondarily upon crustacean macroplankton. When the pups first start eating, they feed on euphausid shrimps and amphipods, the same sort of 'krill' that the ringed seals and baleen whales feed upon. As yearlings and adults, they add prawns to the diet. The juvenile and adult harp seals favour small schooling fish such as capelin and herring. In Greenland waters they feed on various cod, redfish, and cottids. By the beginning of the breeding season in late February, they are very fat, but they then enter a prolonged fast during the breeding and moulting seasons, which leaves them lean by the time they commence the northward migration in May.

This annual fast causes regular growth rings to form in the dentine of the canines, by which the age of the seals may be determined. From these rings it appears that harp seals may live over thirty years.

Aside from sealers, the natural predators of harp seals include Greenland sharks, killer whales, and polar bears.

Habitat. The harp seal is a pelagic species inhabiting the edge of the arctic pack-ice and the subarctic waters of the North Atlantic. It occasionally enters brooks on Cape Breton Island in winter and may ascend them as much as eight miles.

Reproduction. Mating appears to be promiscuous in this species; there is seldom any harem formation, but there are considerable signs of courtship. As the mating season approaches, the males gather in the leads between the ice-floes and 'porpoise,' or swim furiously in circles, or 'rocket' straight onto the ice-floes to attract the females' attention. The females respond by arching their backs, lifting their hind flippers, and bending their heads backwards. Mating occurs either in the water or on the floes, and two males may fight over the attention of a single female. The males are at the peak of their rutting period in early March, at which time they take on a strong musky odour; the reproductive glands regress rapidly in April.

The females are monoestrous, oestrus occurring about two weeks after parturition when the lactation period is drawing to a close. The apparent gestation period is about eleven and a half months, but there is a period of delayed implantation of about two and a half months. Usually only a single pup is born each year, but twin embryos have been found.

The pregnant females whelp on the newly formed winter pack-ice, which consists of large, flat floes varying in thickness from a few inches to about two feet, surrounded by pressure ridges and leads, which are alternately open or frozen over. They haul out some time after mid-February, and the pups are born between the end of February and the middle of March. Usually whelping occurs a few days earlier in the Gulf of St Lawrence than on the 'Front' off the Labrador coast.

In each area the herds are usually concentrated into two 'patches' on the ice, which may vary from 5 to 100 square miles in extent and contain up to 6,000 seals per square mile.

The pups at birth are about 80 cm in length and weigh about 5.5 kg (12 pounds). They are clothed in the long, woolly, white 'lanugo' coat, which keeps them warm and snug on the winter ice. At birth their large eyes are smoky blue but they soon turn to dark brown. Most pups are born near the centre of the ice-floes. The females may have a near-by breathing-hole, which they have kept open since the ice formed, or they may crawl in from the leads. If the leads close, the mother must either stay with the pups or force her way down through the brash ice in the leads.

Young harp seals must rank with the most precocious of young mammals, because they are nursed for only about two weeks and are then abandoned by their mothers. But during that two-week period they grow enormously on their mothers' milk, which is very rich in butter fat. When they are weaned they weigh between 90 and 100 pounds (40–45 kg); half of this weight is composed of fat. What is more surprising is that they are even able to survive at an earlier date if their mothers are accidently killed or if they are lost through storms and break-up of the floes, although they may be stunted in size.

During the first week of their lives the pups are quite passive; they nurse almost continuously and wail if their mothers leave them even temporarily. Among the many 'whitecoats' on the ice-floe the mothers are able to find their own pups by odour, and they harshly reject the entreaties of other pups. Occasionally high storms at this period force the floes to grind, split, and tilt upwards in the formation of pressure ridges, resulting in high pup mortality.

After the pups are abandoned by their mothers, they begin to starve; at the same time they start to moult into their sleek, first juvenile coat. They become restless and make their way to the edge of the floes and eventually topple into the water and learn to swim. Their first efforts are so clumsy that they are called 'beaters' by Newfoundland sealers, though the term also refers to the first spotted coat. Eventually they begin to swim among the ice-floes, and finally, driven by hunger, they learn to feed upon the crustacean 'krill' swarming in the frigid waters. By this time they are about a month old, and their weight has dropped to about 50 pounds (20–22 kg).

The young harp seals as 'bedlamers' migrate rather erratically until maturity is reached, between the ages of five and nine years.

Economic Status. The harp seal is the basis of the traditional sealing industry of Newfoundland, which dates back to 1750, and is now worth about two million dollars annually. The seals are harvested for fur, leather, and oil, rendered from the fat. Originally the 'whitecoats' were the most valuable group. Up until 1951, oil was probably the most important item, but since 1952 there has been an increased demand for the adult pelts, which are called 'sculps' by sealers. This has caused a change in the percentage of adults harvested: until 1946, 'whitecoats' accounted for about 90 per cent of the harvest, but now adult harps account for 40 per cent.

The greatest kills took place between 1820 and 1860, when about 500,000 seals were taken annually. In 1831, 687,000 seals were taken by some 300 ships, manned by 10,000 sealers, principally from Newfoundland, Nova Scotia, Scotland, and Norway.

Recently the hunt was being vigorously pressed by fleets of large, modern, ice-breaker-type vessels, equipped with refrigerated holds and often with helicopters for spotting the seals. These ships came from the Maritime Provinces as well as other countries, such as Norway, France, the United States, Greenland, and the Soviet Union. Added to this marine fleet was a land-based industry in the Gulf of St Lawrence, which used helicopters to transport the sealers. As a result of these modern methods the kill increased from about 230,000 annually in 1949–54 to 310,000 in 1961, of which about 85,000 were juveniles and adults. This harvest apparently exceeded the natural increase, and the western Atlantic population has declined dramatically in the past ten years from an estimated three million to one and a quarter million seals. During the 1971–72 fur season 166,629 'hair seals' were sold at an average value of $8.84, for a total value of $1,473,280.

Conservationists in both western Europe and North America have expressed concern over the excessive harvest of these seals. The Department of the Environment, as a result, has limited the harvest of seals in the Gulf of St Lawrence to 150,000 and prohibited the use of large sealing ships and helicopters in hunting there. Norway, in a

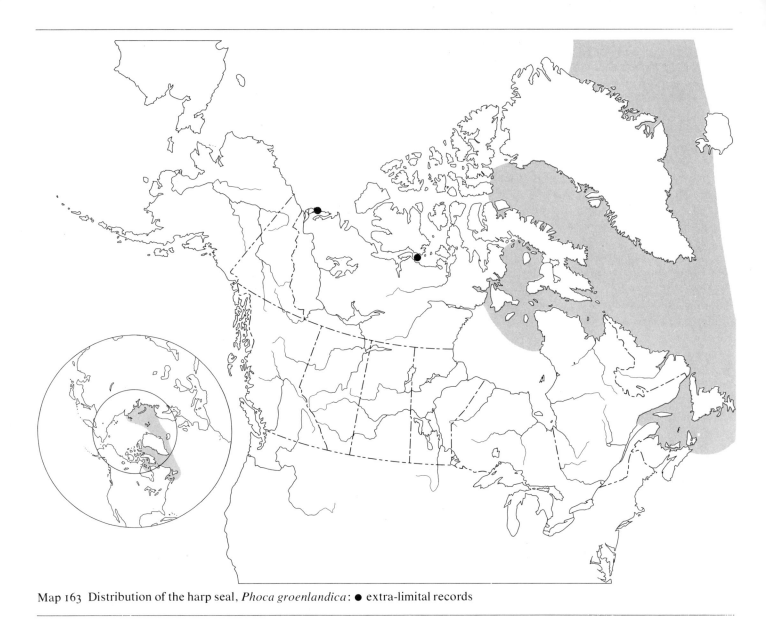

Map 163 Distribution of the harp seal, *Phoca groenlandica*: ● extra-limital records

treaty negotiated with Canada, has agreed to keep its ships out of the Gulf in exchange for a share of the quota.

Status. The population of harp seals whelping in the Gulf of St Lawrence has been estimated at 450,000 animals in 1973.

Distribution. There are three distinct stocks of harp seals in the North Atlantic: those of the western Atlantic, which have been discussed in detail; the West Ice herd, which whelps off Jan Mayen Island north of Iceland; and the herd that whelps in the White Sea off northern Europe. Tagging experiments have indicated little exchange between the herds, although a pup tagged near Prince Edward Island on March 21, 1969, was caught on a salmon longline hook off northern Norway on May 20, 1970. The West Ice herd whelps a month later than the other two groups.

Canadian Distribution. The harp seal is most commonly found in eastern arctic waters in summer, although there is a report of a single straggler from the Mackenzie Delta in 1924. It also occurs southward in winter and early spring to include our coasts off the Gulf of St Lawrence and Nova Scotia (see Map 163).

378

Phoca groenlandica Erxleben, 1777, Systema regni animalis ..., 1: 588. North Atlantic.

REFERENCES

Sergeant, D.E. 1965. Migrations of harp seals *Pagophilus groenlandicus* (Erxleben) in the northwest Atlantic. Jour. Fish. Res. Bd. Canada 22(2): 433–64.
– 1973. Feeding, growth and productivity of northwest Atlantic harp seals (*Pagophilus groenlandicus*). Jour. Fish. Res. Bd. Canada 30: 17–29.
Sivertsen, E. 1941. On the biology of the harp seal *Phoca groenlandica* Erxl. Investigations carried out in the White Sea, 1925–1937. Hvalrådets Skrifter, Nr. 26. Det Norske Videnskaps. Academi, Oslo.

HOODED SEAL

Phoque à capuchon. *Cystophora cristata* (Erxleben)

Description. The hooded seal and the elephant seal belong to a separate subfamily, characterized by the possession of large inflatable probosces in the adult males, by a reduction in the number of incisors, and by the greater length of the first and fifth digits of the hind limbs in comparison with the central digits. The hooded seal is a large species: the males occasionally exceed 10 feet in length and 900 pounds in weight. Its most remarkable feature is the presence of a large elastic nasal cavity, which can be inflated to form a rounded crest or 'hood,' which looks like a black rubbery football and extends from the nostrils to the forehead. When this is relaxed, the snout appears wrinkled. The females and immature males lack this hood. The males can also extrude the nasal sac through a nostril to form a bubble-gum-like balloon when the hood deflates. The claws are straw coloured and particularly strong (Plate 34d).

The skull of the hooded seal has a rounded, flat cranium; the premaxillae are short and do not reach the nasals; there are only two pairs of upper incisors and one pair of lower incisors; the cheek teeth are peg-like.

The adult coat is composed of stiff hairs; the general background colour is steel grey with irregular dark brown spots and blotches, which are more concentrated on the dorsum. The young are born in a distinctive second natal coat – slate blue dorsally, blackish on the head, and cut off sharply from the silvery white underparts – which accounts for their common name 'bluebacks' in contrast to the harp seal 'whitecoats.' The hooded seal pups have an earlier white coat, which is shed *in utero* much like the harbour seal's. The adults moult annually between mid-June and mid-July.

The mature males are larger than the females and vary in total length from about 200 to 250 cm (6½–8 feet) and weigh 300 to 400 kg (700–900 pounds). The mature females measure from 177 to 212 cm (6–7 feet).

Habits. Hooded seals are gregarious, at least during the breeding, moulting, and migration periods. They are noted for their aggressive behaviour, which is uncommon among seals. They are frequently observed during the breeding season in small family groups consisting of the mother with her pup, accompanied by the mother's suitor. The adults will often attempt to defend the pup, rather than desert it as the harp seal does.

These seals also undertake long pelagic migrations. After the completion of whelping on the winter pack-ice off southern Labrador in March, the adults migrate northward in April and cut across Davis Strait towards the southern tip of Greenland. A few continue up its western coast, but most migrate around Cape Farewell in early May and continue up the east coast of Greenland to Denmark Strait in June, where they haul out on the arctic pack-ice to moult. Here they are joined by herds of westward-migrating hooded seals, which have come down from the eastern Atlantic whelping patches north of Jan Mayen Island, northeast of Iceland. After the moult in midsummer, the seals leave the pack-ice to feed, and their exact movements are unknown. The pups follow the adult migration routes about a month later. By August and early September the seals are again migrating around Cape Farewell, this time westward. They cross Davis Strait towards Cape Chidley, Labrador, and migrate down the

coast in October, usually well out to sea. Winter feeding grounds are found on the Grand Banks of Newfoundland until the beginning of the whelping period in late February, when the animals again haul out on the arctic pack-ice to breed.

The seals fast during the breeding and moulting periods when they haul out on the pack-ice. Since these are the times when most specimens are taken, there is little information available on feeding habits. They are reported to feed on mussels, starfish, squid, octopus, and shrimp, as well as herring, capelin, and cod.

This species is reported to live as long as thirty-two years. Aside from man's hunting activities, its chief predator is the killer whale.

Habitat. Hooded seals are a pelagic species, inhabiting the edge of the arctic pack-ice.

Reproduction. The females are monoestrous and exhibit post-partum oestrus and delayed implantation. Breeding appears to be monogamous. Since the single pups are born on thicker pack-ice than is used by the harp seals, the breeding patches are farther offshore. The adults must use the open leads to gain access to the floes, rather than punch holes through thin ice. There are two main breeding areas: one off the south coast of Labrador and northern Newfoundland, and the second north off Jan Mayen Island. Pupping in Newfoundland waters occurs between mid-March and the first week of April. A few pups are born in the Gulf of St Lawrence.

The pups average 100 (87–115 cm) in length and weigh approximately 23 kg (50 pounds) at birth. They are nursed for a very short period, approximately two weeks, and are then deserted by their mothers. They then moult their 'blueback' natal coats and enter the sea about ten days later. It may be noted they are well adapted to the transitory nature of their natal environment, being able to leave the shifting ice-floes on their own about three weeks after birth. The adults mate after the end of the lactation period of the females. Sexual maturity is reached between four and six years of age.

Economic Status. Hooded seals are hunted along with harp seals. The pelts of the 'bluebacks' are particularly sought during the breeding season, and the adults are hunted in Denmark Strait when they haul out to moult. Between 1949 and 1958, approximately 75,000 seals were taken annually, 55 per cent of which were 'bluebacks.' Currently there is no quota on the number of hooded seals that may be taken.

Status. The total population of hooded seals is estimated to be between 500,000 and 750,000, most of which are in the northeast Atlantic. The western Atlantic population is estimated at only 50,000 to 75,000. This population was on the decline between 1920 and 1960, but the Jan Mayen population grew during the same period. It is thought that the warming trend in the north Atlantic region during the period caused the western seals to migrate northward to join the Jan Mayen group.

Distribution. This species occurs regularly in the North Atlantic Ocean from the Gulf of St Lawrence to Spitsbergen and Novaya Zemlya.

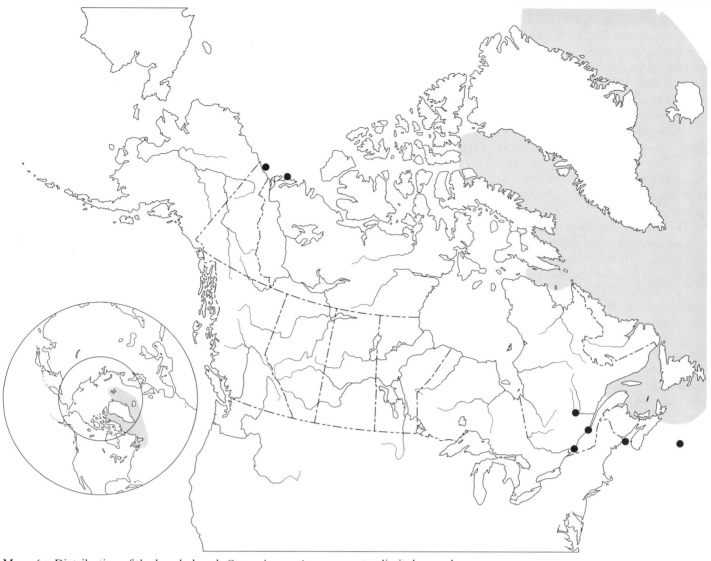

Map 164 Distribution of the hooded seal, *Cystophora cristata*: ● extra-limital records

Canadian Distribution. Hooded seals occur off our Maritime coasts from Nova Scotia, Newfoundland, and the Gulf of St Lawrence northward as far as Cape Sabine, Ellesmere Island, Northwest Territories. Stragglers have also turned up in the western Arctic: one at Herschel Island, Yukon Territory, in 1939, and another at Tuktoyaktuk, east of the Mackenzie Delta, Northwest Territories, in 1942–43 (see Map 164). The species is monotypic.

Cystophora cristata (Erxleben), 1777, Systema regni animalis 1: 590.

REFERENCES

Rasmussen, Birger. 1960. (On the stock of hood seals in the Northern Atlantic.) Fish. Res. Bd. Translation Ser. No. 387. Arctic Unit, Ste-Anne de Bellevue, Quebec.
Sergeant, D.E. 1965. Exploitation and conservation of harp and hood seals. The Polar Record 12(80): 541–51.

NORTHERN ELEPHANT SEAL
Éléphant de mer. *Mirounga angustirostris* (Gill)

Description. This grotesque 'sea monster' is a rare visitor to our Pacific coastal waters. Along with its antarctic relative, the southern elephant seal (*Mirounga leonina*), it is the largest pinniped of all and indeed ranks among the largest living mammals. Adult bulls may reach a length of 20 feet and weigh 4 tons.

This species is obese, with a large head, a long broad snout, large dark eyes, small ear orifices, a thick creased neck, short thickened foreflippers, and bilobed hind flippers. The bilobed appearance is due to the greater length and to the flattening of the first and fifth digits in comparison with the short middle digits. The claws on the hind digits are rudimentary. The adult bulls possess a remarkable foot-long proboscis, which when flaccid hangs over the mouth, but when inflated curves downward into the mouth. It is an extension of the nasal cavity (as in the hooded seal) and is divided by the nasal septum. When inflated, a deep transverse crease develops across the top of the snout. The 'trunk' is not capable of any lateral movement and can only be extended or deflated and held clear of the mouth. The nostrils are located on the broad naked tip of the proboscis. The tough skin of the bull's neck and chest is heavily corrugated with creases. Females and young males lack the proboscis (Plate 34c).

The skull of this species is massive and bear-like, with enlarged canine teeth. The remainder of the cheek teeth are peg-like. The anterior margins of the auditory bullae are concave, and the palatine bones are butterfly-shaped in outline.

The pelage is short, dense, and dull yellowish-grey in colour, darker on the dorsum and paler on the venter. The annual moult occurs in May, June, and July, when the animals return to the land to fast. When the old coat is shed, large patches of skin peel off with the old hair attached.

The adult bulls are about two and a half times larger than the females and may measure between 330 and 650 cm in total length, tail 27.5 cm, and hind flipper 75 cm. The maximum weight recorded is 3,629 kg (8,000 pounds). The adult females vary between 300 and 350 cm in length and weigh up to 907 kg (2,000 pounds).

Habits. These seals are ponderous, lethargic, sedentary animals. On land they are highly gregarious and like to pack together in massed herds; in the sea they forage alone. When young they are quite playful in the surf, but as adults they are short-tempered and spend much time squabbling with their closely packed neighbours. During these tiffs, the opponents rear up, face each other chest to chest, and then lunge at each other. The goal appears to be to fall upon the opponent and crush it with the weight of the foreparts. The northern elephant seal is remarkable for its indifference to the presence of man. Bulls when awake can be approached to within a metre or two, and sleeping seals may be sat on or reclined upon without disturbing them. The cows or younger bulls usually withdraw slowly from approaching men; some take to the water, but others remain on the beach.

These seals are apparently diurnal in activity, although they spend much of the time asleep on beaches. They are particularly sedentary at night. They are extremely clumsy on land and hunch along like monstrous 'inch worms' at a top speed of about four miles an hour. They are much more graceful in the water and plough along just under the surface, raising a considerable bow wave, at an estimated ten to twelve miles an hour. Only the hind flippers are used, alternately, to propel the body with graceful undulations of the hind quarters. The foreflippers are used for braking, steering, and crawling on land. Elephant seals dive to at least 100 fathoms.

These animals have a variety of sounds: snorts, coughs, barks, and snores, but the bellows of the bulls are really unique. When the proboscis is inflated, the tip enters the mouth and the nostrils point to the pharynx, which acts as a resonator. The resulting rhythmic metallic snorts may carry a mile or may completely overpower a lesser adversary at close range.

There is no general migration pattern, but the bulls vanish out to sea from the breeding colonies in spring and disperse widely.

Elephant seals forage in deep water, 50 to 100 fathoms in depth, and feed upon squid, ratfish, hagfish, and small sharks. Young seals, in turn, are preyed upon by large sharks, and the adults are preyed upon by killer whales.

Habitat. These seals are pelagic denizens of warm temperate seas. They breed upon deserted beaches of subtropical continental and oceanic islands.

Reproduction. This species shows a primitive stage in the development of polygamous breeding habits, characteristic of the sea lions and fur seals. The elephant seal bulls vie for a spot among the gregarious females but do not actively collect and defend harems. The mature harem masters lie scattered about in a solid mass of females, while the subordinate bulls are forced to take up positions around the perimeter of the colony. The larger bulls intimidate the subordinates with their resonant bellows and seldom have to fight, but the younger bulls, which have undeveloped probosces, fight viciously among themselves for position.

The cows are monoestrous, oestrus occurring post-partum during the lactation period. Mating occurs in January, February, and early March. The gestation period is approximately eleven months. The period of delayed implantation is not known. The single pup is born between mid-December and the end of January; it is thin at birth and approximately 110 cm long. The natal coat is composed of slightly curly, greyish black hair.

The pups nurse for two to three months on land and rapidly fill out. Although the bulls fast during the breeding period, the cows regularly return to the sea to feed, leaving the pups in the colony for protracted periods. The other cows, however, refuse to nurse temporarily orphaned pups. The gravest risk to the pups is being crushed by the massive bulls, which churn about, oblivious of them. The age at which the juveniles become sexually mature is not known.

Economic Status. These monstrous sedentary animals on their remote breeding islands were exploited for oil as early as 1818. By 1860 their numbers had been so reduced that it was uneconomical to hunt them further, and by 1890 only a single herd of about fifty animals survived on Guadalupe Island. Given complete protection by the Mexican government in 1922, they have increased in numbers from that date.

Status. The current population is estimated at 15,000 animals.

Distribution. Northern elephant seals breed on the islands off the coast of southern California and Baja California. They wander out to sea after the breeding season, and males have been taken as far north as Oregon, British Columbia, and Prince of Wales Island, Alaska.

Canadian Distribution. This species has been reported several times by fishermen off the west coast of Vancouver Island, but the first incontrovertible proof of its

Map 165 Distribution of the northern elephant seal, *Mirounga angustirostris*

occurrence in Canadian waters was the capture of a large male off the north coast of Pine Island, Queen Charlotte Strait, on September 22, 1944 (see Map 165). A second male was driven ashore by killer whales and subsequently shot by a fisherman near Ucluelet on April 10, 1952. The species is monotypic.

Mirounga angustirostris (Gill), 1866, Proc. Chicago Acad. Sci. 1: 33. Pacific coast of North America.

REFERENCE

Bartholomew, G.A. 1952. Reproductive and social behavior of the northern elephant seal. Univ. California Pub. Zool. 47(15): 369–472.

Order **Artiodactyla** / Cloven-hoofed Mammals

The commonly recognized members of this order are characterized mainly by the structure of the foot bones. The main axis of support for the weight of the body runs down the leg between the third and fourth digits. The bones of these digits are equally well developed. Although the terminal phalanges, which bear the hooves, are asymmetrical, they form a symmetrical unit when posed together. (The situation is different in the horse, which belongs to the order Perissodactyla, in which the axis runs through the centre of the dominant third digit.) The second and fifth digits assume secondary support roles, and the first digit is lacking in modern representatives of this order. The astragalus, in the heel, has rounded articular surfaces at both ends, which permit these animals to rise quickly, hind quarters first. The stomach is divided into compartments. The dentition is characterized by a reduction in the number of upper incisors; the premolars are distinct in appearance from the molars; the last molar in the mandible is triple-lobed. The skull lacks an alisphenoid canal.

Domestic swine, sheep, goats, and cattle belong to this order.

ARTIFICIAL KEY TO FAMILIES OF CANADIAN ARTIODACTYLA

1	Feet each with two digits.	ANTILOCAPRIDAE
1′	Feet each with four digits.	2
2	Both sexes carry permanent keratinous horns.	BOVIDAE
2′	Males (occasionally females) carry deciduous bony antlers.	CERVIDAE

Family **Cervidae** / Deer

Deer are easily recognized by the possession of antlers (on the males at least). Antlers, which are replaced each year, are true bony outgrowths of the frontal bones and are covered by furry vascular skin (velvet). During the period of growth the antlers are nourished from the heavily vascularized velvet. Upon maturity of the antler, the blood supply is cut off at the base of the antler (the burr); the skin dries and peels off, or is rubbed off, revealing the polished, bony antler. Eventually a ring of cells breaks down beneath the burr, and the antler breaks off or drops off. A scab grows over the stump, and the cycle begins again the following year.

Deer have other skeletal characteristics: the skull is long and lacks upper incisors. The lower canines are incisiform and lie in the frontal row, which is followed by a considerable gap before the premolars and molars. There is a large vacuity between the frontal and lachrymal bones. The metapodial bones of the third and fourth digits are fused to form canon bones with double distal condyles. The metapodials of digits two and five are much reduced to mere slivers. The stomach has four compartments, and the gall bladder is missing.

CARIBOU or REINDEER
Caribou. *Rangifer tarandus* (Linnaeus)

Description. The reindeer of northern Europe and Asia and the caribou of northern North America are now considered to belong to a single widespread species, although there are some well-marked geographical subspecies. This species possesses a number of features that lead to the conclusion that it is one of the more primitive members of the deer family. These features include: the presence of antlers, generally in both sexes; the relative prominence of the second and fourth lateral digits (the 'dew claws'), and their low placement on the foot so that they bear some of the body weight; the relatively long metapodial bones (splints) associated with these digits; the possession of well-marked tarsal and interdigital glands; and the relatively simple crests on the cheek teeth.

This species also possesses a number of special adaptations to the arctic and subarctic environment: the muzzle is large, blunt, well furred, and rather bovine in appearance; the rhinarium is restricted to a small oval area on the upper lip; the nostrils are valvular; the short, broad ears are heavily furred and rather crowded behind the antlers; the short tail is well furred; the compact body is covered by a long, thick pelage; the feet are unusually large, and the large crescentic hooves facilitate travel over snow-covered or boggy ground. The hooves show an unusual annual development. In summer the foot pads are enlarged and soft; the edges of the hooves are worn quite flat so that the pad rests on the ground. In winter the hooves grow to a remarkable length; the pads shrink and become horny, and the hair between the toes forms tufts that cover the pads, so that the animal then walks on the horny rim of its hooves, thus protecting the fleshy pads from contact with the frozen ground (Plate 40).

Caribou antlers are extremely variable; indeed on any animal one antler is seldom the mirror image of the other. Although the antlers of mature bucks are much larger than those of does, it is difficult to distinguish between the antlers of some young bucks and does. Not all does carry antlers, and in some populations, such as the Newfoundland caribou, as many as 30 per cent of the does are antlerless.

From the burr the main antler beam sweeps dorsally and slightly laterally over the shoulder and then bows gracefully so that the tip points forward. Usually two main tines branch off close to the burr. The first one, called the brow tine, points forward and downward over the forehead and acts as an eye shield. It has a basal stalk and usually expands into a compressed palm with terminal buttons. Generally one brow tine is dominant, and its partner develops as a simple prong, but occasionally two large palms lie side by side over the forehead. The second tine, or bez tine, which arises a short distance behind the brow tine, swings laterally and forward in a graceful arc. Beyond the brow and bez tines, the beams curve gracefully, give off a short posterior tine, and then divide into a group of terminal tines, which may be digitate or palmate.

The annual growth of antlers is approximately six months out of phase between the sexes. Velvet knobs appear on the adult bucks in March, and their antlers grow rapidly from May through July, so that by August they carry large, cumbersome velvet antlers approximately three to four feet in length. The bony cores are remarkably flexible, the great velvet racks springing in and out as the bucks trot. Cores also appear to be sensitive at this period; bucks frequently turn their heads to the side and carefully scratch their antlers with a rear hoof when they itch, or even shake their heads when flies alight on the racks. The antlers have hardened by mid-September, when the bucks rub off the velvet against small saplings. Later in the month most bucks have long strips of velvet hanging from blood-streaked antlers. By October the antlers are polished clean, but these polished antlers are not carried long, for by early November the older bucks begin to drop them, and by February most of the younger animals have dropped theirs as well.

The does' antlers develop during the summer months from June to September. The velvet remains until late October, but does then carry their antlers until April or May. The dropping of the does' antlers is associated with the birth of the fawns.

The skull is characterized by a long rostrum, delicate premaxillae that do not reach the nasals, a moderately expanded cranium, an extreme post-orbital position of the antler pedicels, prominent nasals expanded proximally, a moderate-sized preorbital pit and lachrymal vacuity, and a

post-narial opening divided by a vertical vomerine plate. The dentition is rather weak; the incisors are small and flexible, seated in their alveoli; the inner incisors become notched with age, as a result of feeding habits. Upper canines are generally present in both sexes, but are vestigial and do not pierce the gum (Figure 105).

The long, dense pelage is composed of long, brittle guard hairs and a close, fine crinkly underfur. There is a long ventral mane on the throat; although both adults and young are unspotted, a faint dappling may be noted occasionally on the fawns.

The colour pattern varies widely with different subspecies and according to season. The basic dorsal colour in fresh autumn pelage is clove brown, darker on the face, and on the chest and the dorsal surface of the short tail. The neck and mane are creamy white, and this colour extends above a darker bar in a band across the lower shoulder and flank. The belly, rump, and under surface of the tail are white. The legs are brown, except for narrow white 'socks' just above the hooves. The arctic subspecies are largely white with only a bluish grey saddle on the back, and the forest subspecies are dark sepia brown with the white underparts restricted to the belly and a narrow patch on the rump. The summer coat is generally short and dark, but the winter coat is long, silky, and greyish. By late spring the coat becomes a dirty greyish white because of the bleaching and breakage of the darker tips of the guard hairs.

There are two annual moults. The main moult occurs between July and early September. The yearlings moult first, and the old bucks and the does with fawns moult last. During this period, the long, worn coat of both guard hairs and undercoat is shed in great patches and replaced by a short, sleek coat of dark guard hairs. So much hair is shed that it may form a windrow along river and lake shores

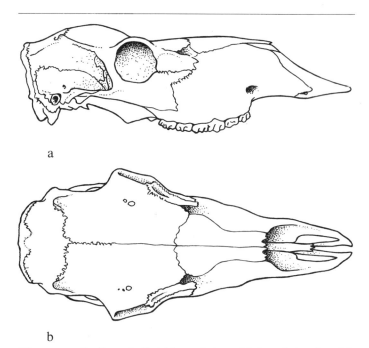

a

b

Figure 105 Caribou skull: (a) lateral view, (b) dorsal view (× 1/4)

after a caribou herd has crossed. In late September the undercoat commences its growth, and a second growth of long guard hairs appears. These are white on the neck, and they soon cover the shorter, dark summer guard hairs to produce the long mane. By October the caribou are covered with a long, thick coat of buoyant hair.

The sexes differ significantly in size, the males being about 25 per cent heavier than the females. There is also a considerable range in size between subspecies. The arctic islands subspecies are small, and the woodland caribou are much larger, weighing up to 600 pounds. The following measurements refer to the American barren-ground caribou, which are about average in size. Average measurements of adult bucks: length 180 (160–210), shoulder height 110 (87–120), hind foot 52 (43–57), length of antlers 96 (52–130) cm; weight 110 (81–153) kg (average 232 pounds). Average measurements of adult does: length 166 (137–186), shoulder height 104 (96–112), hind foot 50 (43–56), length of antlers 39 (23–50) cm; weight 80.7 (63–94) kg (177 pounds).

Habits. Reindeer are gregarious and are usually observed in bands of ten to fifty individuals or in loose herds of approximately a thousand animals, which are social groups consisting of different sex- and age-groups at different seasons. There appears to be an attraction, similar to a magnetic force, that keeps the individuals together. Seen from the air, a migratory herd reminds one of parallel strings of iron filings in a magnetic field: similarly, parallel strings of reindeer flow over the well-beaten trails and funnel through natural defiles. Dispersed individuals, if alarmed while feeding, quickly run together to form a compact band. Caribou in large groups also develop herd behaviour patterns: for example, they become much more indifferent to humans and predators, although individual animals are usually difficult to approach. They may also form a compact, milling circle when troubled by insects.

There are three annual periods of concentration: in late winter prior to the spring migration, immediately after the fawning period, and again before the autumn migration and rutting period. At those times the caribou may occur in massed herds totalling 50,000 to 100,000 animals. In between these periods of concentration there are periods of dispersal, when the caribou are thinly dispersed over wide areas.

Throughout most of the year, bands of caribou are usually formed of like individuals such as adult bucks, adult does with their fawns at heel, barren does, or yearlings. Barren does will regularly associate with the bucks and young bucks with the does, but only during the mating season do all the age- and sex-groups unite.

There does not appear to be a definite pattern in group leadership, although it appears that the social order is most often a matriarchy with an experienced doe leading the group. The leadership often changes, however: it may be a group of bucks in the van of a large herd, or even a young yearling, that moves off first, the rest following. The closest social tie is between the doe and her fawn throughout the first year. Occasionally a yearling follows at a distance. There is some friction between yearlings and fawns and similarly between does and strange fawns. There is only a loose attraction between animals in a similar age or physiological group. When the paths of two grazing bands cross, the bands may be composed of different individuals when they separate.

Reindeer are usually quiet animals, but this does not mean they are voiceless. When surprised or annoyed by insects, they give a loud snort. The usual call is a belch-like grunt, and a band of noisy reindeer reminds one of a herd of swine. The fawns bawl a good deal. The rutting bucks pant frequently and utter prolonged belching bellows.

The reindeer relies almost completely on its sense of smell to detect danger, and it is necessary for the hunter to stalk it upwind. Though its hearing is adequate, it pays scant attention to crackling twigs or soft voices. Either its eyesight is remarkably poor, or it is unusually unresponsive to visual stimuli, for the hunter can often closely approach it by crawling upwind when its head is turned away. A friend of mine managed to crawl up to a lone feeding buck and give it a slap on the rump before it took flight. The stalker should, however, freeze when the reindeer turns its head in his direction, for it is quick to note movement, especially against a background of snow in winter.

Mention must be made of the caribou's so-called curiosity. After taking alarm, it seldom runs far before stopping to look back over its shoulders. Usually the reindeer band gallops off in a wide circle and passes close by, downwind of the intruder, as if to confirm his identity by scent.

This species seems to be primarily diurnal in activity, feeding mostly in the early morning and late evening, and resting during the mid-day and midnight periods.

Reindeer are restless animals. While feeding slowly along a ridge, they may suddenly break into a trot and travel to a new feeding area a short distance away. They have a variety of gaits, from the characteristic loose trot with head and tail held high, to a fast springy pace, in which the legs are thrown stiffly forward. When hard pressed, they break into a laboured rolling gallop, which is seldom maintained for long. The top speed appears to be about thirty-seven to forty-nine miles an hour. A unique characteristic of the reindeer is the clicking sound produced by the slipping of tendons over sesamoid bones in their feet. They are excellent swimmers, and when in their long, thick, buoyant winter coat they float unusually high in the water with much of their backs exposed. The maximum swimming speed is about six miles an hour.

The reindeer's gregariousness is also associated with nomadism: the herds are almost constantly on the move, migrating from one seasonal pasture to another. These migrations may be very extensive. For the tundra subspecies, the tundra summer ranges and forested winter ranges may be 800 miles apart. Other populations inhabiting mountainous regions undertake vertical seasonal migrations from summer alpine tundra zones to lower forested zones in winter. The woodland caribou movements are less widespread but still involve travel from low fens to drier open ridges. The factors involved in these migrations are complex, and include a change in diet as a result of seasonal growth of vegetation, rutting and fawning requirements, snow conditions (caribou abandon areas of crusted, hard-packed snow for areas with lighter snow), destruction of pastures by forest fires, weather, wind direction, and the prevalence of biting flies and mosquitoes. The bucks usually lead the autumn migration to the winter pastures and may penetrate the woods farther than the females, but the bands of pregnant does and their yearlings, driven by the urge to reach safe fawning grounds, lead the herds to the summer pastures.

Reindeer and caribou exhibit no individual spatial home range. The band may have an annual home range, but it would be very large if all the seasonal wanderings were included. For the tundra races, there is some evidence that single herds, deserting familiar pastures for several years, may wander far across the north country. One square mile of excellent spruce–lichen forest could support as many as seventy-five reindeer for one winter, but average forested areas, including some lakes and burns, can support only six to fifteen reindeer per square mile during the winter months.

The average longevity for barren-ground caribou is approximately four and a half years, and the maximum longevity in the wild is about thirteen years.

If horses are called 'hay-burners,' reindeer should be called 'lichen-burners,' because these lowly plants are the mainstay of their diet, especially in winter. Other winter foods include dried horsetails and sedges, and the twigs of willows and birch. The summer diet is more varied and includes mushrooms, lichens, grasses, sedges, forbs such as licorice root and vetch, twigs and leaves of willows and birch, and fruit such as bake-apple. Reindeer also avidly chew discarded antlers for their mineral supplement. It is reported that they eat lemmings as well, when the opportunity presents itself. Woodland caribou appear to rely more on arboreal lichens than the tundra subspecies do. Reindeer eat about ten pounds of lichens in a day.

Undoubtedly man should be listed as the chief predator of these animals. Palaeolithic drawings on cave walls in southern France and Spain clearly show that man has preyed upon the reindeer for at least the last 25,000 years. Reindeer and man may have developed some sort of balanced relationship under primitive conditions. Aside from man, the wolf is their most serious predator. The relationship between the wolf and the caribou is complex, the balance being so delicate that the wolf cannot easily kill its prey unless the conditions have been tipped slightly in its favour. A healthy caribou a few days after birth can outrun a wolf in a direct race, and caribou seem to recognize when they are in immediate danger of attack and when they are relatively safe. The herds may appear little disturbed when a pack of wolves passes leisurely through their midst, but they will be instantly on the alert when a hunting pack appears. Occasionally a stampeding band of reindeer has been observed passing quite close to a wolf, and yet the wolf has been unable to catch one. On other occasions a wolf seems to single out its prey and pursue it through band after band, ultimately catching it.

Aside from the wolf, the grizzly, the wolverine, and the lynx secure a few caribou, particularly the young. Golden eagles are also important predators of new-born fawns.

Habitat. Reindeer inhabit the arctic tundra, subarctic taiga, and boreal coniferous forests. Their distribution extends farther south in mountainous regions, where they inhabit the alpine tundra and subalpine forest zone. In forested regions they utilize the climax forest areas and the edges of open fens and heaths because of the rich lichen growth. In winter they sun themselves on frozen lakes in the afternoons, and in summer they lie on sheltered snowbanks on the north sides of tundra hills to escape the heat and the hordes of mosquitoes.

Reproduction. The bucks are polygamous during the rutting season. They feed only sparingly and spend much of the time rushing about, threshing bushes with their antlers, sparring with other bucks, panting and bellowing. Actual rutting behaviour varies considerably with different populations. The woodland caribou bucks collect and defend harems of twelve to fifteen does; but in the large herds of tundra reindeer rutting occurs promiscuously, the adult bucks dashing through the herds or marshalling long columns of migrating animals. The does are seasonally polyoestrous. The mating period occurs between early October and early November, when the tundra reindeer return to the vicinity of the treeline, prior to the autumn migration. In the Shickshock Mountains of the Gaspé Peninsula, Quebec, the rut occurs on the tundra mountaintops.

The gestation period for the reindeer is approximately seven and a half to eight months in duration, and the fawns are dropped between mid-May and the beginning of July. The northern races are the last to drop their fawns. Most tundra reindeer are born in a two- to three-week period about mid-June. The pregnant does migrate towards rocky, hilly terrain, where the fawns are born. As the doe's time arrives, she drops behind the herd and lies down to bear her young. Single births are usual, but rarely twins are born. At birth the fawn measures about 600 mm in length (24 inches), has a shoulder height of about 510 mm (20 inches), and weighs about 5 kg (11 pounds). The natal coat is rather crinkly; it is fawn-coloured above, with a prominent black muzzle and eye-ring and creamy underparts.

The fawns are remarkably precocious. After the mother licks the fawn, she usually remains lying with it for the first four hours if possible. The youngster usually struggles to stand up on wobbly legs after about thirty minutes and nurses for the first time about two to four hours after birth. If disturbed, however, it can walk with a hopping gait thirty minutes after birth and run several miles after ninety minutes. It can outrun a man when it is a day old and swim 150 yards within a few days. Normally the doe urges the new-born fawn to follow the slowly drifting herd of does and fawns after it is four hours old, and within a day or two it can keep up with the running herd. The young caribou begin to graze on a few choice items after two weeks but depend upon milk for the first month at least. Weaning is often delayed, and in winter a few fawns still supplement

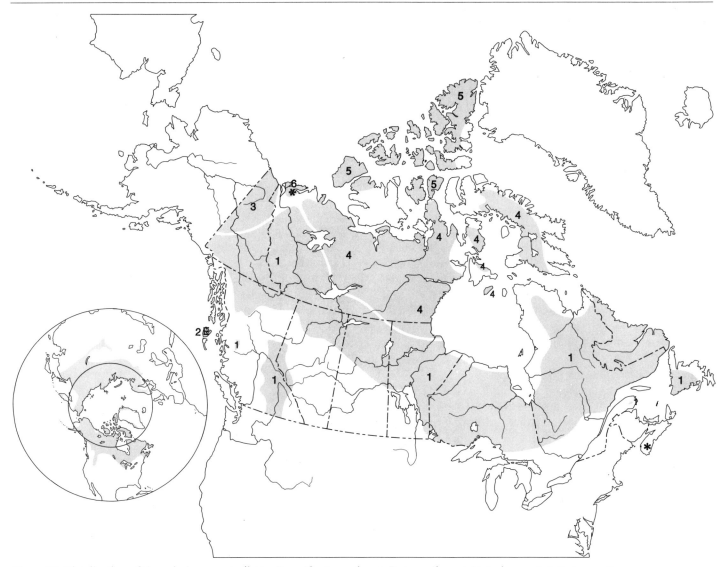

Map 166 Distribution of the reindeer, or caribou, *Rangifer tarandus*: 1 *R. t. caribou*, 2 *R. t. dawsoni*, 3 *R. t. granti*, 4 *R. t. groenlandicus*, 5 *R. t. pearyi*, 6 *R. t. tarandus*, E extinct, * introduced

their diet by sucking occasionally. Reindeer fawns grow antlers in their first autumn. In the juvenile females sexual maturity occurs normally at sixteen months, but it is later in the males.

Economic Status. Before the arrival of Europeans, caribou constituted an important economic resource for northern Eskimos and Indians. Only in the last few decades has it been supplanted, for many residents in remote areas of Canada, by other sources of foods and by manufactured articles. The caribou provided a source of nutritious meat for human consumption and for dog food. Light, warm arctic clothing and bedding, and formerly tepees, were made from the pelts. The sinews were used as thread, the bones as utensils, and the fat for light and heat. Originally the natives had a number of ingenious methods of capturing the caribou, including the use of drift fences and pounds, snares, and pitfalls in snowbanks. More directly they hunted caribou with bows and arrows and speared them in the water at crossing points. In recent decades, firearms have replaced most of these methods.

In 1948 I estimated that the annual kill of barren-ground caribou ran as high as 100,000 animals. By 1957 this had dropped to about 15,000 animals, and more recently to about 10,000. This decrease reflects not only the lessened importance of caribou in the northern economy but also the decline in availability of the animal.

A most unfortunate side effect of the recent testing of atomic weapons has been a disturbing rise in the toxic radioactive by-products, such as cesium-137, in the bodies of Eskimos and Lapps. This effect has been traced to the natural food chain: lichens–reindeer–Eskimos and Lapps. Lichens are unlike arctic perennial plants, which grow only for short periods of the year, receive nourishment through their roots, and drop their leaves annually; and are unlike annuals, which freeze in winter. Lichens grow continually at many points, have no leaves to drop, receive much of their nourishment from the air (especially arboreal lichens), and are extremely long-lived as individuals. Therefore they store considerable amounts of radioactive fallout. While feeding upon lichens, reindeer pick up the radioactive by-products, which in turn contaminate the meat eaten by the northern residents. Caribou-eating Eskimos of Alaska carry a burden of cesium-137 two hundred to three hundred times larger than Washington residents.

Status. The population of Canadian barren-ground caribou was probably about two and a half million animals at the turn of the century. The total had declined to about 670,000 in 1949, 279,000 in 1955, and 200,000 in 1964. A welcome increase to 357,000 was estimated during 1967 surveys. In 1961, I estimated the population of woodland caribou at about 43,000 animals, and of the Peary caribou at about 13,000. A survey of the Porcupine herd of the northern Yukon in 1972 indicated a herd of about 110,000 animals that migrate annually to northeastern Alaska.

Distribution. Wild reindeer formerly occurred in a broad belt across Eurasia from Norway to Siberia and across northern North America. Wild reindeer in Europe are now confined to the mountains of southern Norway and Karelia. In the rest of Europe their place has been taken by herds of domestic animals. Wild reindeer still occur in considerable numbers in the Union of Soviet Socialist Republics.

Canadian Distribution. Five subspecies of reindeer or caribou are currently recognized in Canada (see Map 166). They inhabit most of northern Canada, and their distribution swings southward in the Rocky Mountain region to the United States border. The Queen Charlotte Island race is extinct. In the east, caribou are found in Newfoundland and south of the St Lawrence River only in the Schickshock Mountains of the Gaspé Peninsula of Quebec. They have been extinct in Prince Edward Island since before 1874, in Nova Scotia since 1925, and in New Brunswick since 1927. The currently recognized subspecies are:

Rangifer tarandus caribou (Gmelin), 1788, Linn. Syst. Nat., 12th ed., 1: 177. The woodland caribou of the boreal forest region from Newfoundland and Labrador to British Columbia and the southern Yukon Territory; a large, dark subspecies.

Rangifer tarandus dawsoni Seton, 1900, Ottawa Naturalist 13(11): 257–61. A small, mouse-coloured race, formerly found on Graham Island of the Queen Charlotte Islands, British Columbia. Extinct since 1910.

Rangifer tarandus granti J.A. Allen, 1902, Bull. American Mus. Nat. Hist. 16: 122. Northern Yukon Territory.

Rangifer tarandus groenlandicus Linnaeus, 1767, Syst. Nat., 12th ed., 1: 98. The barren-ground caribou inhabiting southwestern Greenland, Baffin and Bylot islands, and the continental tundra zone across the Mackenzie Delta where intergradation with the Alaskan race *R. t. granti* Allen 1902 occurs in the northern Yukon Territory. Southward in winter to the northern Prairie Provinces. The form as described in the text.

Rangifer tarandus pearyi J.A. Allen, 1902, Bull. American Mus. Nat. Hist. 16: 409. A small, pale subspecies with narrow upright antlers, found on northwest Greenland and the Queen Elizabeth Islands. Intergrading with

the continental form on Banks and Victoria islands.

Rangifer tarandus tarandus (Linnaeus), 1758, Syst. Nat., 10th ed., 1: 67. The European reindeer. A Royal Commission was appointed in 1919 to study the possibilities for reindeer and muskox industries in northern Canada. As a result, A.E. and R.T. Porsild were appointed to investigate suitable ranges for a reindeer industry. They travelled to Alaska in 1926 and then surveyed the region between the Mackenzie Delta and the Coppermine River for suitable range. In 1929, Dr A.E. Porsild supervised the purchase of a reindeer herd of 2,890 animals near Kotzebue Sound. Andrew Bahr, a veteran Lapp herder, took over the reindeer drive, which left Alaska towards the end of December 1929 and reached the Mackenzie Delta five years later, on March 6, 1935, after an epic trek unique in Canadian history. The government reindeer herd at the reindeer station has been maintained subsequently to provide meat and hides for northern residents. The herd totalled about 6,000 animals in 1973.

REFERENCES

Kelsall, John P. 1968. The migratory barren-ground caribou of Canada. Dept. Indian Affairs and North. Develop., Canadian Wildlife Serv.

Parker, G.R. 1972. Biology of the Kaminuriak population of the barren-ground caribou. Canadian Wildlife Serv., Rept. Ser. 20, Part 1.

MULE DEER
Cerf mulet. *Odocoileus hemionus* (Rafinesque)

Description. This is the characteristic deer of the mountains and foothills of western North America. It is larger and stockier than the eastern white-tailed deer. The trenchant characters include larger ears; a shorter (eight-inch) cylindrical tail, which is white or brown and black tipped; and a large metatarsal gland (50–150 mm), which is surrounded by stiff brown hairs and dichotomously branched antlers. The dew claws are situated high on the slender foot (Plate 36).

The skull is typically cervine with long, slender premaxillae and a long diastema between the lower incisors and the cheek teeth (which are larger than those of the white-tailed deer), and lacks upper incisors and canines. The post-nares are divided by a vertical vomerine plate. The lachrymal fossa for the preorbital gland is larger than found in the white-tail.

The mule deer's antlers are quite distinct from those of the white-tail. The beams arise from the rugged burr on the frontal bones above the orbit. A short distance above the burr the basal snag (eye guard) branches off medially. The beams then swing laterally and branch equally to produce a fork. In mature bucks, each fork divides a second time to produce four equal tines on each side, each pointing upwards. Only the bucks normally carry antlers, which grow in the velvet in the summer, rub off completely in August and September, and shed each spring between mid-January and mid-April.

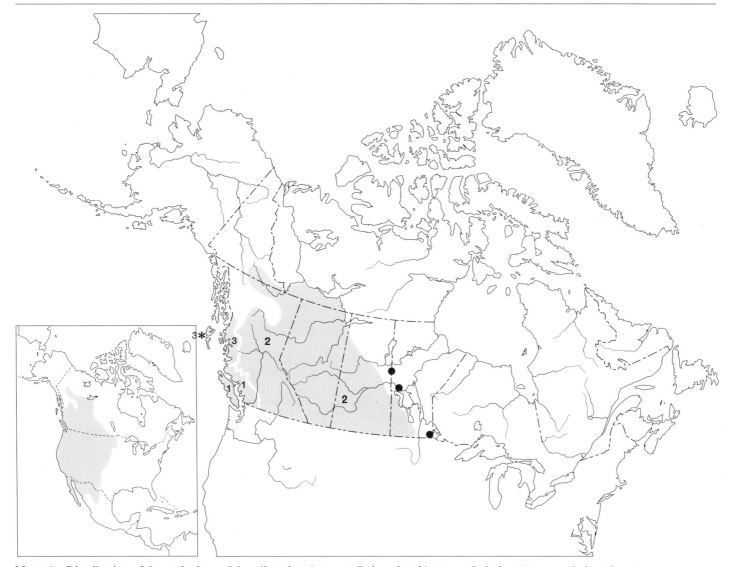

Map 167 Distribution of the mule deer, *Odocoileus hemionus*: 1 *O. h. columbianus*, 2 *O. h. hemionus*, 3 *O. h. sitkensis*, * introduced, ● extra-limital record

The pelage is rather coarse. The summer coat is thin, reddish brown or tawny brown above; the forehead is dark brown; the face is white with a black, moist muzzle and a brown patch on the side of the nose; the ears are black-rimmed; the chest is dark brown or blackish; and the inside of the ears, thighs, belly, throat, and rump patch are white. The winter coat is longer and thicker then the summer one and has an underfur. The dorsal colour is dark brown or grizzled brown. The moults take place in June and September.

The size varies considerably between different subspecies. Adult males measure: length 142–188, tail 15–20, hind foot 41–59, ear 12–25 cm; weight 50–215 kg (110–475 pounds). Measurements of adult females: length 132–152, tail 11–20, hind foot 41–51, ear 12–24 cm; weight 31.5–72 kg (70–160 pounds).

Habits. The mule deer appears to be more gregarious than the white-tailed deer. Small groups of does and bucks band together independently in summer. In winter they form larger mixed bands of all ages and sex groups and even associate with herds of wapiti and pronghorns on winter pastures. The social order of these winter bands is a matriarchy, with an experienced doe as leader. The bucks have lost their antlers and are docile at this period. In spring the does withdraw to bear their fawns. The bucks exercise their dominance only during the autumn rutting season.

Mule deer have a variety of gaits from a sedate walk to a gallop; however, it is their special stiff-legged bounding gait that has led to their common name, jumping deer. They are excellent swimmers and cross straits up to fourteen miles wide between coastal islands.

This species undertakes seasonal altitudinal migrations in the mountains. The bucks are found high up in alpine meadows during the summer, but some does may remain at lower elevations. All migrate down to lower ground in the winter, and seek regions of lower snowfall.

Mule deer have been known to live as long as twenty years.

The mule deer's winter diet is composed of twigs of

389

evergreens, deciduous saplings, and shrubs. Among its favourite winter foods are the Douglas fir, western cedar, Oregon yew, trailing blackberry and huckleberry, salal, aspen, willow, red-osier dogwood, serviceberry, bitter-brush, mountain juniper, and sagebrush. In spring grasses predominate in the diet; in summer, forbs and grasses; and in the autumn, foliage. In the summer mule deer appear to graze more than the white-tails.

Predators of this species include the mountain lion, wolf, coyote, lynx, and bobcat. Bears and golden eagles capture a few fawns, and feral dogs are a menace in settled areas. There is a delicate balance of power between deer and coyotes. I have seen two or three does drive off single coyotes on several occasions. The deer tried to stab the coyote with their forefeet, and the coyotes had to dodge and roll to keep away from their sharp hooves.

Habitat. This is a deer of open coniferous forests, sub-climax brush, aspen parklands, steep broken terrain, and river valleys. It shuns the open prairie and the deep, climax, coniferous forests.

Reproduction. The bucks are polygamous but follow one doe for several days before they switch their attentions to another. Their necks begin to swell in early to mid-October, and they thresh their polished antlers on small saplings as a form of erotic stimulation. The bucks are truculent and dangerous during the rutting period. When following the does, they exhibit the typical ungulate male rutting stance with neck lowered, head held forward, upper lip curled up, and back hunched.

The does are seasonally polyoestrous. The rut occurs between late October and early December, with a peak between October 24 and November 14. It is later in the south. The gestation period is approximately 210 days, and in Canada the fawns are generally born during early June, although they may be dropped any time between March and November. Normally twins are born, but the number of offspring may vary from one to three.

The fawns at birth are chestnut coloured with rows of white spots on the flanks and back. They weigh approximately 3.75 kg (8^1/$_4$–8^1/$_2$ pounds). The does cache their fawns for the first month, usually seeking isolated safe spots for the purpose, such as on islands in lakes and rivers. The fawns moult into the first winter 'blue' coat after the end of August and are weaned after four to five months.

Juvenile mule deer reach sexual maturity somewhat later than white-tailed deer, at the age of eighteen months.

Economic Status. This is an important big-game species in western North America.

The Alberta population is estimated at 175,000 animals. Estimates for other provinces are lacking. Though it seems to be declining in the settled areas of the southern Prairie Provinces, it is increasing in the northern parts.

Distribution. This deer is found in western North America from northern Mexico to southern Yukon Territory and Mackenzie District, Northwest Territories.

Canadian Distribution. Three well-marked subspecies occur in Canada, which have been given well-known vernacular names (see Map 167).

43

American bison, *Bison bison*

44

Muskox, *Ovibos moschatus*

45

46

Odocoileus hemionus columbianus (Richardson), 1829, Fauna Boreali-Americana 1: 257. The black-tailed deer, found on the coast of British Columbia north to Rivers Inlet and on Vancouver Island. A small, dark race, characterized by having the proximal portion of the tail brown and the distal half black. The white rump patch is much reduced.

Odocoileus hemionus hemionus (Rafinesque), 1817, American Monthly Mag. 1: 436. The mule deer, the largest race, found from southeastern Manitoba to the interior of British Columbia, east of the Coast Range and north to the southern Yukon Territory, Fort Simpson, and Great Slave Lake in the Mackenzie District. It is characterized by having a white tail with a black tip and a very large white rump patch. It was seen on the Peace River in northern Alberta by Alexander Mackenzie as early as 1792.

Odocoileus hemionus sitkensis Merriam, 1898, Proc. Biol. Soc. Washington 12: 100. The Sitka deer, the smallest and darkest race with the proximal two-thirds of the tail brownish and the distal third black. The antlers are smaller then those of the other races. This species occurs on the northern coast of British Columbia, on the Alaska panhandle, and on the coastal islands. Between 1900 and 1916 it was introduced to the Queen Charlotte Islands, where it now thrives.

REFERENCE

Taylor, Walter P. (ed.). 1956. The deer of North America: the white-tailed, mule and black-tailed deer, genus *Odocoileus*: their history and management, pp. 332–617. Stackpole Co., Harrisburg, Pa., and Wildlife Management Institute, Washington.

WHITE-TAILED DEER
Cerf de Virginie. *Odocoileus virginianus* (Zimmermann)

Description. The white-tailed deer is probably the most widespread and best known big-game species in North America. Its body is slender and graceful; its legs are slim, with the small dew-claws high on the side of each foot, and the hooves are narrow and pointed. Its crowning glory, however, is its tail, which is almost a foot long, with a broad base, brown above, and a wide white fringe. It is a signal of the animal's spirits, as it flicks from side to side, or waves high over the back, exposing the snowy white under surface. The white-tailed deer may be distinguished from its close relative the mule deer by its tail, its smaller ears, its simple beamed antlers with dorsal tines, and its short metatarsal glands (30 mm) on the side of the hind legs, usually surrounded by some white hairs (Plate 37).

This deer has glands that perform useful functions in communicating. There are the typical cervid preorbital glands and the pear-shaped tarsal glands on the inside of the hocks, surrounded by stiff white hairs, which may be elevated when the animal is excited. These glands emit a musky fluid, which is augmented by the deposition of urine by the does during the rutting season. Interdigital glands between the central toes of each foot emit a strong-smelling waxy substance that leaves a scented trail in the grass.

Normally only the bucks carry antlers, although antlered does are occasionally found. The beams bend gracefully forward from the burrs on the frontal bones above the orbits, and close above the burr the basal snag emerges. A number of tines branch off on the dorsal surface and point forward; the longest ones are at the back, and the shorter ones forward. It is not true that a buck's age can be determined by the number of points on its antlers. One study showed that 15 per cent of yearling 'spike horns' carried three to five points, and 4 per cent carried six to eight points! Tooth eruption and wear are more reliable in determining age.

The antlers of this species develop over a period of twenty weeks from May to August, and the bucks rub the velvet off against saplings in September. The older bucks drop their antlers in early December after the rut, but the younger bucks keep theirs until early February. The development of the antlers depends on hormones secreted by the pituitary gland and the testes, and the shedding of the velvet is associated with an increase in the content of the male sex hormone testosterone in the blood in the autumn.

The skull is typically cervine, with a moderately sized lachrymal vacuity, a high cranium, and a median vomerine plate separating the posterior nares. The upper canines are lacking (Figure 106).

There are two moults each year. The summer coat is short and thin and lacks the underfur. The dorsal colour is reddish fawn, with white on the belly, throat, and eye-ring; inside the ears and legs; on the chin; and on the under

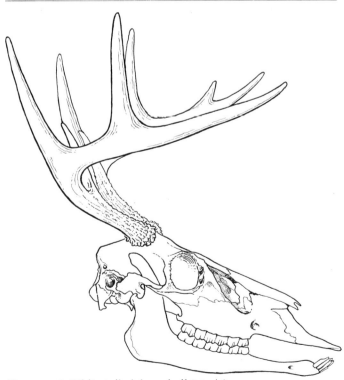

Figure 106 White-tailed deer skull (× 1/4)

side of the tail. The face has a dusky wash and a black bar on the lower jaw. The winter coat is longer and stiffer, with a sparse undercoat. It is grizzled greyish in colour. This coat, which is often referred to as the 'blue' coat, is assumed in late August and September and worn until the spring moult in May and early June. The summer coat is called the 'red' coat. Albino white-tails are occasionally seen.

Average measurements of adult bucks: length 183–198, tail 15–28, hind foot 50, ear 14–24, shoulder height 92 cm; weight 85.5–95.9 kg (189–211 pounds). Weight of adult does 57.0–62.5 kg (126–137 pounds).

Habits. This species may be considered to be generally solitary, particularly in summer. The basic social unit is the doe and her fawns. The bucks are solitary in summer or associate in small groups of two to four, but these groups disband prior to the mating season. In the winter, particularly if the snow is deep, bands of white-tails are formed on favourite feeding grounds, but the association is casual. These bands are usually led by an old doe.

Although white-tails have good eyesight and acute hearing, they seem to depend mainly on their sense of smell. They are quick to note movement but slow to recognize a stationary object such as a standing man. To identify the object the white-tail may approach cautiously, stamping its feet, snorting and flicking its tail, as if trying to frighten the object to see if it moves.

White-tails walk with a springy, cautious gait, tail switching. Alarmed, they flee with three or four graceful bounds, then a high leap, the tail wigwagging from side to side. At maximum effort, they gallop with long, low strides and attain a speed of forty miles an hour. They are excellent swimmers and have been known to swim as far as six miles. They take freely to water to escape from predators or insects. In winter on clear ice they are at a disadvantage compared to more sure-footed dogs, coyotes, and wolves. When a deer is surprised, the most familiar sound is the snort or grunt, but the bucks occasionally bellow during the breeding period, and does murmur to their fawns when they bleat for attention.

Deer are 'twilight' creatures with two peaks of activity, at dawn and again at dusk. In late winter they often sun themselves on open hillsides during the afternoons, but during the summer they bed down in the forest shade to chew the cud during the day. They bed down for the night usually between 11 P.M. and midnight. As most seasoned hunters know, the best days for hunting deer are drizzly, grey days when they are bedded down in sheltered spots in wet woods. They are more restless on windy days.

During winters of deep snow, white-tails 'yard-up' in cedar swamps, forming well-marked trails, and often remain there even though food may be more plentiful in the open clearings. In mountainous areas they undertake altitudinal migrations from alpine meadows in summer to the valleys in winter.

The white-tail is an amazingly static animal and may occupy a home range as small as forty acres of excellent habitat or over three hundred acres of poorer habitat. Within its home range the deer is familiar with every tree, hollow, brook, and trail. It is reluctant to leave its home range, even when hunted by dogs, and usually runs in circles through its familiar territory. In tagging studies it has been found that bucks are recovered an average of 6.7 miles from the initial tagging spot, and does an average of 3.7 miles, although one buck travelled 165 miles after being tagged. As a rule they 'home' to their original territories after being moved up to twenty miles, but beyond that distance they usually scatter. Deer populations have been calculated as being up to thirty-four animals to a square mile.

White-tails have lived as long as twenty years in captivity but seldom surpass ten years in the wild.

Primarily these deer are browsers, living on the buds and twigs of shrubs and saplings in winter. They supplement their diet with tender young grass in summer and with fruit in the autumn. They nibble daintily when on the move and seldom remain in one spot for long. They consume about five pounds of natural browse per hundred-weight each day.

In eastern Canada the basic winter diet of the white-tail is white cedar. Other foods high on the preferred list are mountain, striped, or red maples, red-osier dogwood, mountain ash, sumac, cherry, aspen poplar, ground hemlock, hemlock, balsam, fir, and basswood trees. It is particularly fond of apples in the autumn. Its summer diet includes such forbs as lamb's quarters, jewelweed, asters, and golden-rod. Mushrooms are a favourite delicacy in late summer.

Originally the cougar and the wolf were the chief predators of deer, but these predators are now greatly reduced over much of the deer's range. The lynx and the bobcat regularly kill deer, usually by dropping out of a tree onto their back. The coyote is a serious predator in western Canada, and feral dogs now take a high toll of deer in the countryside. Black bears may manage to capture a few fawns.

Habitat. Contrary to common belief, extensive climax forests of mature hardwoods or conifers are not good deer habitat. The food has all grown out of reach, and the dense shade discourages new growth on the forest floor. Deer prefer an interspersion of cover types, edges of hardwood forests, glades, swamp edges, banks of streams, and cedar swamps. On the prairies they take shelter in wooded coulees during the day and forage on the open prairie during the twilight hours.

Reproduction. The sexual rhythm of deer, like that of many other animals, is influenced by the annual change in hours of daylight. In the Northern Hemisphere, the rutting period occurs in the autumn when the days are growing shorter, but red deer shipped to New Zealand shifted their rutting season to April after only three years in the Southern Hemisphere.

The bucks' necks begin to swell in September, apparently as a result of exercise of the neck muscles in carrying and polishing the heavy antlers and in sparring with their adversaries. During this period the bucks are so much occupied with other matters that they neglect to eat, and they lose about 10 per cent of their weight. The rut commences in mid-October and continues until late December. The bucks paw up muddy hollows in the trails, thresh shrubs with their antlers, and joust with other bucks. Usually these battles are formalized, and the weaker ones withdraw uninjured, but occasionally one of the adversaries is killed or, rarely, the antlers interlock and both bucks die. At this period, tame deer become belligerent and have been known to gore and kill their owners.

The bucks are polygamous, although they may form an attachment and stay with a single doe for several days or even weeks until she reaches oestrus. If she rejects his attentions, he will wander off in search of another doe. Occasionally, does in oestrus may be followed by several bucks, the strongest in the lead and the youngest in the rear.

The does are seasonally polyoestrous and usually come into heat in November for a short twenty-four hour period. If a doe is not mated, a second oestrus occurs about twenty-eight days later. The gestation period is approximately 205 to 210 days.

The doe usually picks a sheltered spot such as a bracken-covered glade to drop her fawns. The fawns may be born any time between April and September, but the peak of the fawning period in Canada lies between late May and mid-June. Twins are the mode, but anything from a single fawn to quadruplets may be born. Usually a young doe bears a single fawn the first time.

The new-born fawns have bright reddish silky coats, dappled with rows of quarter-sized white spots on flanks and back. At birth they weigh approximately six to seven pounds (about 3 kg). They can stand within a few hours and take a few wobbly steps on their long spindly legs. However, the white-tail doe caches her fawns for the first month. If there is more than one fawn, she caches them separately during the day, returning to nurse them at two- to three-hour intervals. The young fawn lies perfectly still with legs folded under its body and neck extended. When picked up, it utters a startlingly loud bleat. For the first week or so, the fawns are odourless, and dogs or coyotes may quarter across the fawning area without finding them. After about three weeks the fawns can run agilely after their mothers. Although they begin to graze at this time, they are not weaned until they are four months old. They moult out of their spotted coats into their greyish winter coats in September. Small buttons of antlers can be palpated under the skin of bucks' foreheads after six months, but their first spikes are not produced until their second winter. Winter fawns weigh about 78 to 80 pounds (about 35 kg).

Most juvenile does mate as yearlings, but a few female fawns reach sexual maturity between late November and early January during their first winter. The males mature as yearlings but probably do not get a chance to mate until they are much older and stronger.

Economic Status. In colonial days the white-tailed deer was an important source of meat and hides for the Indians and the early settlers in the forested regions of eastern North America. Although many believe that the wildlife

393

Map 168 Distribution of the white-tailed deer, *Odocoileus virginianus*: 1 *O. v. borealis*, 2 *O. v. dacotensis*, 3 *O. v. ochrourus*, * introduced

resources were unlimited in the 'good old days,' deer populations were undoubtedly much lower in the eastern climax forests than they are today in the more diversified habitats. The deer populations were decimated during the early period by excessive hunting so that the species was rare or absent over much of its former range during the nineteenth century.

Today the white-tail is the most important big-game species in North America. It is hunted by millions of hunters each autumn, and millions of deer are taken. Yet the white-tail continues to flourish, and since in many areas the populations are excessive, many die of starvation each winter.

These deer cause serious damage to regenerating forests; they also frequently cause extensive damage in orchards and vegetable gardens.

Status. The population of white-tailed deer in Canada is estimated to be approximately two and a half million.

Distribution. This species occupies most of North and Central America, and its range extends into South America.

Canadian Distribution. At present the white-tailed deer is found across southern Canada from Cape Breton Island to southeastern British Columbia and northward to Moosonee, The Pas, and the Peace River district of Alberta. At the turn of the century the distribution was restricted to more southerly areas, but there has been a rapid expansion of this species northward during the past thirty years.

The white-tail was reintroduced to Nova Scotia in 1894. It reappeared by natural immigration into New Brunswick about 1918. It was introduced to Prince Edward Island in 1949, and a small band is now established in the western end of the island. It was also introduced in 1896 to Anticosti Island, where a large population now occurs. Three subspecies occur in Canada (see Map 168).

Odocoileus virginianus borealis Miller, 1900, Bull. New York State Mus. Nat. Hist. 8: 83. The form inhabiting eastern Canada from Lake of the Woods eastward.

Odocoileus virginianus dacotensis Goldman and Kellogg, 1940, Proc. Biol. Soc. Washington 53: 82. A large, pale race with heavy antlers, found in the Prairie Provinces.

Odocoileus virginianus ochrourus V. Bailey, 1932, Proc. Biol. Soc. Washington 45: 43. A small race, found in southeastern British Columbia and through the Rocky Mountain passes into Jasper, Banff, and Waterton Lakes national parks.

REFERENCE

Taylor, Walter P. (ed.). 1956. The deer of North America: the white-tail, mule and black-tailed deer, genus *Odocoileus*: their history and management. Stackpole Co., Harrisburg, Pa., and Wildlife Management Institute, Washington.

MOOSE
Orignal. *Alces alces* (Linnaeus)

Description. The moose, which is about the size of a horse, is the largest living member of the deer family. It has long legs; high, humped shoulders; a homely, long head with a pendulous snout; large ears; a dewlap or 'bell' hanging from its throat; and a stubby tail. Its large, broad muzzle is almost completely covered with short brown hairs, except for a small, triangular-shaped rhinarium on the upper lip. The tarsal glands are small, and the metatarsal glands are lacking. The dew claws are relatively low on the feet. The hooves are long and pointed (Plate 38).

The common American name, moose, is derived from the Algonkian name, which means 'eater of twigs.' The same species is called 'elk' in Europe. Unfortunately, the application of the name 'elk' to the red deer or wapiti in North America by the early English immigrants has led to much confusion.

The skull of the moose is characterized by elongated, narrow premaxillae and very short nasal bones. The lachrymal vacuity is widely open, and the lachrymal pit is large. The upper canines are lacking. The post-narial aperture is undivided. The bulls carry very large shovel-shaped antlers, which arise from the frontal bones behind the orbits. The beams sweep laterally from the rugose burrs for approximately a foot before one or two anterior brow tines branch forward. The beams then flatten and sweep backwards as broad palms with a number of long terminal tines.

The antler growth in this species commences in April, and the bulls carry large velvety antlers until late August or early September, when they begin to rub them clean on shrubs. The older males drop their antlers in December or early January, but the younger ones carry them until late February.

Bull calves develop flat velvety knobs during the first autumn. As yearlings they develop simple spikes or, rarely, forks. When they are two and a half years old, they grow long forked spikes or small palms. The typical large shovels develop after the bull is four or five years old.

The pelage is composed of stiff, coarse black-tipped guard hairs, which are about 3 inches long on the body but may reach 6 inches in length on the shoulders and neck. The moose has a fine, kinky, bluish undercoat in winter. The fresh summer coat is a rich cocoa brown on the back, and old bulls may be almost black. The shoulders are grizzled, the lower legs are grey, and the underparts are brown. This coat fades to a reddish brown in late winter. In late May the spring moult starts on the shoulders and back. The undercoat grows in September, at which time additional brownish guard hairs are added. Albinos are occasionally observed.

The bulls are considerably larger than the cows. Average measurements of adult bulls of the race *andersoni* length 257 (224–279), tail 17, hind foot 80 (76–83), shoulder height 181 (169–192) cm; weight 453 (385–535) kg or 1,000 (847–1,177) pounds. Average measurements of females: length 232 (206–260), tail 17, hind foot 78 (75–81), shoulder height 179 (174–183) cm; weight 350 kg (768 pounds).

Habits. Moose appear to be the least sociable of our ungulates; they are basically solitary animals. The calves remain with their mothers for the first year of their lives, but the cows drive them off as the time approaches for the birth of the new calves. For the next few months, before they become wise in the ways of the woods, the yearlings blunder about the forests quite disconsolately and unwarily. Occasionally moose may feed in the same meadow, but they seem to ignore each other. Even in winter, when yarded in a favourite swamp, the association appears to be one of necessity. Usually when several moose visit a mineral lick together, they exhibit a social peck-order, the older and stronger ones driving off the weaker ones with slashing jabs of their forefeet.

As a rule moose are timid and quick to flee from man's presence. However, the cow will defend her young calf and, with ears laid back, charge intruders. Bulls in the rutting season are truculent and dangerous. Their hearing and sense of smell are both acute. Moose become alert at the crack of a twig, and a hunter can only approach them upwind. They react to movement but do not respond to a stationary object upwind.

Moose are usually silent, except during the mating period. The cows are more vocal than the bulls. Their calls resemble a bovine bellow with a coughing end *mooo agh*. The calves and the yearlings bawl.

Moose can walk carefully and quietly through the underbrush. They can reach thirty-five miles an hour in a rocking running gait but seldom gallop. They are the most amphibious of our deer and spend much of the summer wading in quiet bays. They are strong swimmers and even dive to reach succulent submerged roots. They have been observed diving to a depth of eighteen feet and remaining submerged for thirty seconds.

Moose show some activity throughout the day, especially in winter, but there are definite peaks at dawn and dusk. Much of the summer day is spent bedded down in the forest shade, chewing the cud. They move about less on windy days and are more active on calm days after stormy weather.

Like most other large ungulates, moose also migrate seasonally up and down the mountain slopes, wintering in the valleys. Occasionally lone bulls winter high up on old avalanche slides where there has been thick regeneration of willows. If the snow is over three feet in depth, they restrict their movements to well-worn trails along river banks and to shrubby open woodland. Several moose may use the same restricted favourite area, or 'moose yard.' They often bed down in the same spot for several days if undisturbed. Summer movements may be similarly restricted to the proximity of a favourite water-lily-covered bay. Concentrations of up to ten moose to a square mile of winter range have been observed, but based upon aerial surveys of big game in Canada's national parks I would estimate an average population of two to a square mile of forest.

Moose have been known to live twenty years.

These animals are primarily browsers, as their Algonkian name suggests. In summer they strip the leaves off twigs with a sideways sweep of the head. In winter they break the twigs off with an upward shrug. They also straddle shrubs and ride down the taller stems to reach the tops. Occasionally in early spring they may be observed grazing awkwardly on tender new grasses by bending their wrists on the ground. Their favourite summer feeding habits are pulling up the leaves and tubers of the water lily.

The winter diet of the moose is composed mainly of willows, balsam fir, red-osier dogwood, mountain ash, aspen, birch, beaked hazel, balsam, poplar, pin cherry, maple, and viburnum. The summer diet includes many aquatics, forbs, grasses, and the foliage of many of the trees eaten in winter. The food requirements are approximately five pounds of browse per hundredweight of moose per day. On restricted winter ranges there is often severe competition between deer and moose.

The adult bull moose is a dangerous adversary and is often able to repel the attacks of a small pack of wolves. Wolves do, however, take their toll of the aged, weak, and younger animals. Grizzly bears in the mountains of western Canada also prey upon moose, particularly cows and calves in spring. Black bears often manage to capture a few calves before they are strong enough to escape.

Habitat. Although the moose is considered a forest dweller, it generally shuns monotonous climax coniferous forests for the subclimax stages of shrubby growth and later aspen–birch parkland. It also favours lakeshores and alder swamps and ranges far out onto arctic tundra in summer, moving to drier hardwood slopes in winter.

Reproduction. The bulls are truculent and restless during the rutting season and spend much of their time trotting through the forests searching for cows and challenging other bulls. The bull is polygamous, but remains with one cow until she reaches her oestrous period before abandoning her to find another pre-oestrous cow. Bulls thrash shrubs with their antlers, urinate in muddy depressions,

and then roll in these wallows. Most encounters between bulls are formalized, and the weaker one withdraws as soon as possible, but occasionally fierce battles develop in which the adversaries may be injured by each other's antlers. It happens but rarely that the antlers of the two bulls lock and, when they do, both die of exhaustion and starvation.

The cows are seasonally polyoestrous, usually experiencing four oestrous periods if not impregnated. This season lasts from mid-September to late November. As the cow's period approaches, she utters a pleading bawl, which attracts the bulls. Hunters mimic her call on a birchbark horn to attract bulls. The gestation period is between 240 and 246 days, and the calves are born in late May or early June. The cow usually seeks secluded shrubby lake borders or islands to serve as a nursery. Here she guards the new-born calf for several weeks.

The moose calf wears a light, reddish brown, unspotted coat at birth. Its body is relatively short, and its long legs appear stilt-like. It measures about 3 feet in length and stands 28 to 32 inches high at the shoulders; it weighs about 14 (10–16) kg (30 pounds). Usually twins are born on adequate range, but births vary from singles to triplets. The calves are extremely wobbly and awkward during the first couple of weeks but soon gain strength and follow their mothers even when they swim across a lake. Moose cows are careless about the safety of calves in water and occasionally force one to swim beyond its strength so that it drowns. The calves double their weight in three weeks, and they are weaned and moult in September.

A few female yearlings may mature sexually at the age of sixteen months, but most mature at two and a half years of age. The males may mature at the same time, but they seldom have the opportunity to breed until they are five or six years old.

Economic Status. The moose is a highly prized big-game trophy and provides excellent hunting over much of its Canadian distribution (almost 5,000 being taken annually in Newfoundland alone). It is also a mainstay in the larder of trappers and Indians in remote areas of northern Canada. Its tough hide produces excellent outer clothing, gloves, leggings, and moccasins. Occasionally calves have been domesticated and taught to draw sleighs and wagons. They become intractable as adults, however, and are dangerous to handle during the rutting and calving periods. High populations of moose cause serious damage to forest plantations and pollarding of balsam fir, some pines, cedars, and birches by browsing the leaders.

Moose are susceptible to infections of a small nematode worm, *Pneumostrongylus tenuis*, which moves through the blood vessels to the brain, causing a loss of coordination. The infected animal tends to travel in circles, its head hanging to one side, and one or both ears drooping. The animal may often stagger and show no fear of man. The symptoms have frequently been referred to as 'moose sickness.'

Status. The American moose population is thought to be 200,000 to 300,000 animals.

Distribution. Moose, or 'elk,' are found across northern

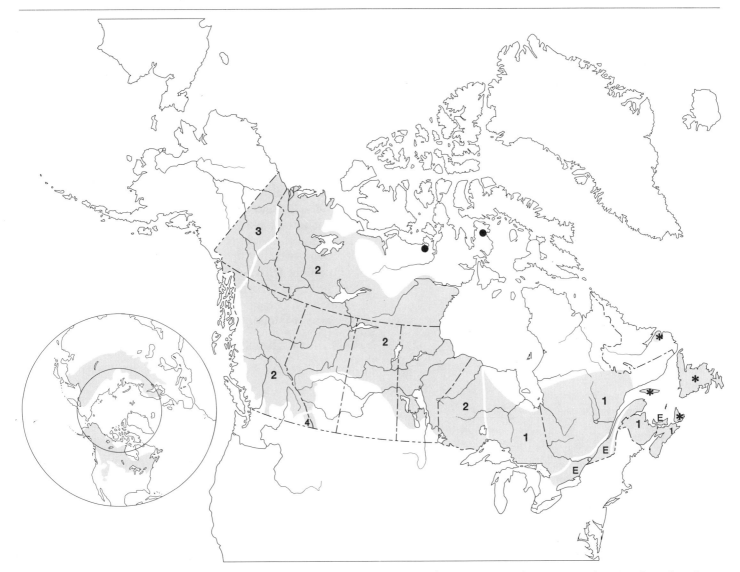

Map 169 Distribution of the moose, *Alces alces*: 1 *A. a. americana*, 2 *A. a. andersoni*, 3 *A. a. gigas*, 4 *A. a. shirasi*, ✱ introduced, E extinct, ● extra-limital records

Europe and Asia from Scandinavia to the Pacific coast and across northern North America from Alaska to Newfoundland and Maine.

Canadian Distribution. The distribution in Canada has changed dramatically during the present century. There is reason to believe that when the European explorers arrived moose were relatively common in the Maritime Provinces, southern Quebec, and Ontario. The distribution extended westward through the boreal forest to the Mackenzie Delta, the Peace River District, and the Rocky Mountains, but it seems that moose were absent from southern British Columbia. As a result of excessive hunting by the colonists and Indians, they were much reduced over their eastern range by the beginning of the nineteenth century. Since 1930 there has been a remarkable resurgence in the moose population, assisted by introductions and natural immigration.

A pair of moose was introduced to Newfoundland in 1878 with doubtful results, but the species was firmly established on that island by the introduction of four animals from Nova Scotia in 1904. Eighteen were reintroduced to Cape Breton Island in 1947 and 1948 to reestablish the species there after its extermination in about 1924. Although moose were greatly reduced in Nova Scotia and New Brunswick during the nineteenth and early twentieth centuries, they have increased during the past twenty-five years. The finding of an occasional antler gives mute evidence of the former occurrence of the moose on Prince Edward Island. Various introductions were made to Anticosti Island between 1895 and 1913 and to southern Labrador in 1953. In the meantime, the distribution expanded naturally into northern Quebec and Ontario, and even into the tundra regions of the Northwest Territories. Since 1920 the species has extended westward to the Coast Range and southward in British Columbia to the international boundary.

Four subspecies are currently recognized in Canada (see Map 169).

397

Alces alces americana (Clinton), 1822, Letters on Nat. Hist. and Int. Res. of New York, p. 193. A medium-sized, relatively dark race, found in eastern Canada as far west as central northern Ontario.

Alces alces andersoni Peterson, 1950, Roy. Ontario Mus. Zool. Occas. Pap. 9: 1. The race of western Canada, based on minor cranial characters.

Alces alces gigas Miller, 1899, Proc. Biol. Soc. Washington 13: 57. The largest of the living races (the bulls are reported to reach 1,800 pounds), with a very dark coat and massive white antlers. This race is found in Alaska, western Yukon, and northwestern British Columbia.

Alces alces shirasi Nelson, 1914, Proc. Biol. Soc. Washington 27: 72. A small, pale race, found in the southern Rocky Mountain region, which has moved into southwestern Alberta and southeastern British Columbia during the last thirty-five years.

REFERENCES

Peterson, Randolph L. 1955. North American moose. Univ. Toronto Press.

Pimlott, D.H. 1959. Reproduction and productivity of Newfoundland moose. Jour. Wildlife Mngt. 23(4): 381–401.

FALLOW DEER
Daim. *Cervus dama* Linnaeus

Description. The fallow deer is an average-sized species about 5 feet in length and about 3 feet high at the shoulders. Since the forelimbs of this deer are somewhat shorter than the hind limbs, the rump is higher than the withers. It has a short neck, a short head that is broad across the antlers and tapers to a pointed nose, short ears, and a relatively long tail. Its hooves are elongate and pointed; the dew claws are vestigial and are situated high on the feet. The lateral metapodial bones are represented by short sections, joined to the proximal end of the canon bones. The preorbital glands are small, and there are interdigital glands on the feet and tarsal glands on the hock.

The bucks have unusual antlers, which are characterized by terminal flattened spades, carried above the head rather than laterally, as in moose antlers. The antlers are shed in March and April.

The skull is short, broad, and flat, with long nasal bones, a small nasal aperture, and an undivided post-narial opening. The upper canine tooth is lacking.

The summer coat is fawn-coloured above, dappled with white spots. It is darker on the rump and tail and creamy white on the underparts. The muzzle is black, with a whitish ring above it on the snout. The winter coat is greyish brown and without the spotting.

Habits. This species is highly gregarious and forms small separate herds of does with their fawns and groups of bucks. The bucks join the does during the mating season in autumn but leave them again in the winter. Their summer diet consists mainly of grasses and forbs. In winter they browse on twigs and on evergreen leaves and needles.

Habitat. Fallow deer prefer brushy, hilly areas with grassy meadows nearby.

Reproduction. The bucks are polygamous and spar considerably among themselves during the rutting season, which occurs during the month of October. The gestation period lasts eight months, and the fawns are born in June. Usually a single spotted fawn is born, but occasionally twins are dropped in the isolated spot to which the doe withdraws. The fawn is weaned after about three months, and the doe with her fawn rejoins the herd in August.

Economic Status. None in North America.

Distribution. Native to the Mediterranean region and Asia Minor, but introduced to many regions, where it flourishes in a semi-wild condition.

Canadian Distribution. Introduced to James Island in the Straits of Georgia, where it is flourishing; individuals occasionally swim across to the Saanish Peninsula of Vancouver Island.

Cervus dama Linnaeus, 1758, Syst. Nat., 10th ed., 1: 67.

WAPITI or AMERICAN ELK
Wapiti. *Cervus elaphus* Linnaeus

Description. There is much confusion over the common name of this species. Early English settlers applied the name 'elk' to this animal in America, although in Europe the same name was applied to *Alces alces*, the animal we know as the moose. Somewhat later, English explorers to western Canada referred to it as the 'red deer,' which is more appropriate since it is the American representative of that Old World species. I prefer the name 'wapiti,' which comes from its Shawnee Indian name meaning 'white rump.'

Call it what you wish, this majestic animal is second in size only to the moose in the deer family. Its head and neck are long; its muzzle is naked and moist; its body is sturdy; its legs are moderately long; its hooves are broadly rounded behind and bluntly pointed in front; and its tail is short and wedge-shaped. It has prominent preorbital glands; oval-shaped metatarsal glands, surrounded by rosettes of stiff golden hairs on the outside of the hocks; and a pair of glands at the base of the tail; but it lacks interdigital glands. The lateral metapodials are represented by slips, joined to the proximal end of the canon bones (Plate 39).

The long, sturdy skull of the wapiti has long nasal bones, a large lachrymal vacuity and pit, an arched cranium, and undivided posterior nares. The dentition is heavy; the central incisors are prominently larger than the outer ones, and both sexes possess large, rounded upper canines ('elk tusks').

The crowning glory of the stag is its majestic antlers, which arise from large burrs, placed high on the cranium behind the orbits. The long, bowed cylindrical beams sweep upwards and back over the shoulders. From the anterior surface, five cylindrical pointed tines arc forward and upward. The first, or brow tine, branches off the beam just above the burr and extends over the face. Shortly beyond it, the bez tine extends laterally above the ear. The trez branches off about a third of the way along the beam, and the fourth, or royal, the longest and stoutest tine, points upwards about three-quarters of the way along the beam. Beyond the royal, the beam angles backwards and appears to fork, forming the last tine, the sur-royal, and the final point, which is the tip of the main beam. The polished antlers in autumn take on a rich brown patina with ivory-coloured points. They are usually round but occasionally are flattened. In some races there may be a terminal cup formed at the base of the royal and the sur-royal tines at the tip of the beam. Occasionally deformed antlers are observed, and rarely a hind carries one or both antlers.

The antlers commence their annual growth in April, the velvet is rubbed off in late August and early September, and the antlers are shed in February, March, and early April. The older stags drop their antlers first. The antlers are heavy, and the animals are at first unaccustomed to the unexpected loss in weight. If only one antler is dropped, the animal goes about with its head on a tilt.

The first set of antlers, which consists of simple long spikes on tall pedicels, grows on the yearling stags. The second set is a miniature rack with three or four points on each side. The third set is heavier with four or five points. Succeeding years usually produce the normal six points on each side. In each successive year, the pedicel below the burr becomes shorter and greater in diameter, as a result of the erosion of a layer of bone under the burr when the antler drops off in successive falls. Yearling spikes are 20 to 50 cm in length, and adult antlers vary from about 110 to 160 cm (4–5 feet) in length along the beam and about the same in spread.

The summer coat is sleek and tawny brown, darker on face, belly, neck, and legs, with a large, buffy rump patch surrounding the tail and including the buttocks. This coat is short and lacks the underfur. The winter coat is composed of long guard hairs and crinkly underfur. It is greyish brown on the back and flanks, and seal brown on the face, neck, belly, and legs. The hair on the neck is longer and forms a ventral mane. The chin and the interior of the pointed ears are buffy. The buffy rump is outlined by a brown line. The stags' flanks are much paler than the hinds' and yearlings', reaching straw colour in winter. The coats lose their gloss and become faded in late winter. The spring moult occurs in May and June, when the animals appear extremely ragged, but the autumn moult in September is barely noticeable.

The stags are larger than the hinds. Average measurements of adult males: length 231 (225–241), tail 14 (10–18), hind foot 64 (60–66), shoulder height 140 cm; weight 315 (265–500) kg or 700 (590–1120) pounds. Average measurements of adult females: length 205 (180–230), tail 14 (12–18), hind foot 63 (60–65), shoulder height 130 cm; weight 225 (188–270) kg or 495 (419–600) pounds.

Habits. Wapiti are gregarious. Bands of hinds and their calves, numbering about twenty-five, forage together during the summer months, while the stags form bachelor bands. In autumn they are divided into harems consisting of hinds with their calves and supervised by a mature stag. After the rutting season, the bands join to form large herds of a hundred or more animals, composed of all ages and sex-groups. In these herds the social order is a matriarchy. The winter herds break up in spring as the hinds separate to bear their calves and the stags move off to form their bachelor bands.

This species is the most vocal deer in Canada. The calves bleat; the hinds squeal or utter a sharp loud bark as an alarm note; and the stags bugle during the mating season. Bugling is a challenge, which starts as a low chesty roar, glides into a high, clear bugling sound, and then subsides to a series of coughing grunts. The high bugle sound carries about a mile on the clear autumn air, but the low coughing grunts are lost at a distance. The stags bugle between late August and November. Wapiti are alert animals and appear to use all their senses to warn of danger.

When feeding, wapiti walk slowly with neck extended forward and head pointed downward, but if alerted they walk with neck and head held high. They trot stiffly with the muzzle pointed a little higher than horizontal, the neck gracefully absorbing the movements. They attain a speed of about twenty-nine miles an hour in a swift gallop. Wapiti swim well and often frolic in shallow water. All age groups are playful at times.

The normal daily pattern is to feed during the early morning and evening periods in summer, then to lie down at mid-day and again after midnight, to chew the cud. The feeding periods are more prolonged in winter, but the bands often bed down in the bright afternoon sunlight in the meadows. Wapiti are migratory; in mountainous regions the stags in particular spend the summer high up in alpine meadows, retreating down to the valleys upon the arrival of heavy snows in October and November. Even on more level terrain they seek wooded hillsides and lake shores in summer and open grasslands in winter. They search out areas of lighter snowfall in winter such as windblown slopes. In spring they follow the melting snowline and freshly sprouting grass up the mountainsides, but some hinds remain behind to bear their calves in the valleys, often on islands in lakes and rivers.

Wapiti do not have a local home range as more static species do. Twelve acres of good pasture is the maximum range requirement of a single animal in a year. They survive a maximum of fifteen to twenty years in captivity.

This is primarily a grazing species, which paws through a light snow cover to reach the grasses in winter. Its favourite summer diet includes blue grass, brome, wheat grass, June grass, and sedge. It also eats a wide variety of forbs such as aster, baneberry, bead lily, columbine, dandelion, fireweed, fleabane, golden-rod, hawkweed, knotweed, marsh marigold, paintbrush, ragweed, strawberry, vetch, licorice root, violet, and clover. It is fond of mushrooms and horsetails.

The winter diet includes a great deal of browse: the twigs of willows, aspen, balsam, poplar, red-osier dogwood, silverberry, chokecherry, mountain maple,

Map 170 Distribution of the wapiti, *Cervus elaphus*: 1 *C. e. canadensis*, 2 *C. e. manitobensis*, 3 *C. e. nelsoni*, 4 *C. e. roosevelti*,
* introduced, E extinct, o location of park herds

shrubby cinquefoil, wild rose, and gooseberry. It is difficult to generalize on the winter diet, however, some herds utilizing browse even when grass forage is available while others merely supplement their grazing with a little browse.

On overstocked ranges, with a scarcity of available grasses and shoots, the wapiti turns to bark and strips trembling aspen and balsam poplar trees as high as it can reach. This results in ugly black scarring or the death of the tree if it is completely girdled. The wapiti will also eat the needles of balsam fir, Douglas fir, and pines if starving, but it cannot eat spruce needles.

The chief natural predators, aside from man, are the mountain lion, the wolf, the grizzly bear, and occasionally the lynx and the coyote. A healthy adult wapiti can defend itself against the attacks of the coyote, and even the hinds can effectively drive coyotes away from their young calves, but senile, sick, or weak individuals occasionally succumb to packs of these animals or feral dogs. The golden eagle, bobcat, black bear, and wolverine some-

times kill unprotected young calves.

Habitat. The wapiti is quite flexible in its choice of habitat. It prefers open areas such as alpine pastures, marshy meadows, river flats, open prairies, and aspen parkland, but occasionally it is found in coniferous forests. Its altitudinal range extends from sea level to 7,500 feet.

Reproduction. The stags are truculent and polygamous during the mating season. It is not clear whether they collect their harems or whether the hinds gather around the stag, but in either case in September and October each mature stag is surrounded by a harem of up to thirty hinds with their calves. The stags' mating behaviour includes threshing bushes with their antlers, which seem to act as erotic organs, rolling in urine-soaked wallows, following the hinds in the typical ungulate mating posture (neck extended, muzzle raised, and upper lip curled), and bugling and driving off intruding stags. The combats between stags include rising on their hind legs and stabbing with their forefeet. They also lower their heads and indulge in shoving contests with their antlers. Usually there is no injury, but occasionally one may receive a puncture on the flank from another's antlers. The antlers seldom lock as do the antlers of moose, caribou, and deer. Although stags drink a great deal during this period, they seldom feed, so that they lose much weight. The hinds are seasonally polyoestrous, and if they are not fertilized the first time they undergo a series of oestrous periods from late September to early November. The rut extends from mid-September to the end of October. The calves are born from late May to early June after a gestation period of 249 to 262 days.

Usually the births are single, but if the range is good twins occur with a frequency of about 25 per cent. The calf is fawn-coloured, with longitudinal rows of creamy spots on back and flanks, and weighs about 37 pounds (17 kg) at birth. For the first few days, the calves are extremely wobbly on their long, stilt-like legs and drop and 'freeze,' neck extended, on the ground at the slightest warning of danger. They are more precocious than deer fawns and follow their mothers about after the first few days. They soon start to nibble on grass but continue to nurse steadily until September, at which time they moult into their uniform, dark brown juvenile coat. Occasionally calves are seen nursing in the winter, but by spring the maternal ties slacken and the calves learn to shift for themselves. As yearlings they may continue to follow their mothers, but the hind's attention is directed toward her new calf.

The juvenile wapiti may mature sexually at the age of sixteen months on good range, but generally the hinds do not bear their first young until they are three years old. It is doubtful if many young stags find the opportunity to mate until they are four or five years old and can challenge another stag.

Economic Status. During the nineteenth and early twentieth centuries the canine teeth of wapiti were prized tokens of a fraternal order and brought as much as $75 a pair. This led to much wasteful killing for the teeth alone. The tines were also harvested for cutlery handles and sold for approximately fifty cents a tine.

At present, wapiti are prized as trophies of the hunt in western Canada. In certain areas, herds cause considerable damage to ranchers' haystacks and to standing crops of green feed during the winter months. The herds cause severe management problems by their excessive utilization of restricted ranges within parks or by their migration to near-by agricultural lands.

Distribution. This species was formerly distributed across most of the northern world from Great Britain, Europe, central Asia, and central North America as far as southeastern Quebec and the Allegheny Mountains in the eastern United States. It has now been restricted to isolated pockets of unexploited habitat.

Canadian Distribution. Formerly the wapiti was found in the Eastern Townships of Quebec, the lower Ottawa valley, and southern Ontario south of Georgian Bay, but it disappeared from this eastern part of its range before 1830. It has been reintroduced to Algonquin Park and near Sudbury. There is an exceptional record from an area two

hundred miles north of Lake Nipigon. On the prairies it ranged from southeastern Manitoba to the Peace River District and eastern British Columbia. A third section of its natural distribution included the lower Fraser valley and Vancouver Island. Wapiti antlers that date back to prehistoric times are also found in Alaska and Yukon Territory. Five subspecies have occurred in Canada (see Map 170).

Cervus elaphus canadensis Erxleben, 1777, Systema regni animalis ..., p. 305. The eastern subspecies, now extinct.

Cervus elaphus elaphus Linnaeus, 1758, Syst. Nat., 10th ed., 1: 66. The European red deer is smaller and darker than the American forms, with a smaller rump patch and a more pointed muzzle, and with antlers that have a tendency to form a terminal cup. Red deer were introduced to Graham Island of the Queen Charlottes but were exterminated between 1942 and 1946.

Cervus elaphus manitobensis Millais, 1915, *in* The gun at home and abroad: Big game of Asia and North America, 4: 281. The prairie form characterized by darker pelage and smaller antlers. It is now restricted to Riding Mountain and Duck Mountain parks and the Interlaken district of Manitoba, to the northern aspen parklands of Saskatchewan from Prince Albert National Park eastwards, and to Elk Island National Park, Alberta. A band of twenty-five was returned to southern Wood Buffalo Park in 1949.

Cervus elaphus nelsoni V. Bailey, 1935, Proc. Biol. Soc. Washington 48: 188. A large, pale form, found in the Rocky Mountain region of southwestern Alberta and eastern British Columbia. Small pockets of native animals also occur in the Selkirk Mountains and northward as far as the Muskwa River, a tributary of the Liard River, in northeastern British Columbia. They have been introduced to other areas such as Princeton, Adams Lake, and Graham Island of the Queen Charlottes. The native stock in the southern Rockies was augmented by introductions from Yellowstone Park to Banff National Park in 1917 to 1920.

Cervus elaphus roosevelti Merriam, 1897, Proc. Biol. Soc. Washington 11: 272. A large, dark race with a marked tendency to produce antlers with terminal cups like the red deer, now restricted to Vancouver Island and the Olympic Peninsula of Washington.

REFERENCE

Murie, O.J. 1951. The elk of North America. Stackpole Co., Harrisburg, Pa., and Wildlife Management Institute, Washington.

Family **Antilocapridae** / Pronghorns

The American pronghorn antelope is the only surviving member of a family of ungulates that contained a host of species in the Pliocene and Pleistocene periods. Some of these had long, bizarre, forked horns; others had spiralled horns; and still others had four horns. The whole assemblage is confined to North America, and the pronghorn is not closely related to the antelopes of Africa and Asia.

The family stands between the Cervidae, with their deciduous antlers, and the Bovidae, with their permanent horns. The pronghorn possesses keratinized branched horn sheaths, over permanent unbranched bony cores, situated on the frontal bones above the orbits. Unlike the bovids, however, the pronghorn sheds the sheath each autumn and replaces it by a new one. The feet lack the lateral digits completely, and glands on the rump and lower jaw replace the interdigital and lachrymal glands. The cheek teeth are high-crowned (hyposodont).

PRONGHORN
Antilope d'Amérique. *Antilocapra americana* (Ord)

Description. The pronghorn is a small, trim ungulate, standing about 3 feet high at the shoulder, with slim clean limbs, short neck and tail, and long pointed ears. The head is rather large, with remarkably large eyes (as large as a horse's). Both sexes carry black horns with an anterior 'prong' or branch and curved tips. The horns of the bucks may reach 20 inches (51 cm) in length, but the does' are much smaller, or occasionally lacking. The hooves are small and pointed. The rump glands exude a musky fluid, and the glands on the bucks' jaws enlarge during the rutting period. The naked, moist rhinarium is restricted to a small black patch between the nostrils (Plate 41).

The skull has a long, broad rostrum without a lachrymal pit. The permanent horn cores are narrow upright blades, situated above the protruding orbits. The cheek teeth are hypsodont, and the upper canines are invariably missing

(Figure 107). The horn cores are covered by a layer of skin with specialized hairs. Between mid-October and mid-November each year the old horn sheath becomes detached from the skin. It is then shed, revealing the newly developing horn sheath, which is at that time composed of a whorl of specialized hairs around the base and a mesh of fine white hairs covering the tip of the core. The new horn is only 3 to 7 cm long in early December, but the keratinized sheath continues to grow until by early July it is about 25 cm long in bucks and 13 cm long in does. The prong develops from a bud on the anterior side of the developing horn. Both sexes rub their horns on bushes until the tips are black and shiny.

The pelage is composed of long, brittle guard hairs, up to 7.5 cm in length on the rump, and a sparse undercoat. The dorsal colour is tan, with a creamy white rosette on the rump. Both the rosette and the black-tipped hairs on the short mane are erectile. The black colouring on the face, which in the buck extends as far as the base of the horns, is restricted to the muzzle in the doe, and the remainder of the doe's rostrum is brown, fading to pale grey about the horns. The lower jaw, the side of the head, the flanks, the belly, and the two bars on the throat are white. The stubby tail is brown. There is an additional black spot beneath the adult buck's ear. Two annual moults occur: the new, thin greyish spring coat develops during a five-week period in May and June; the fresh autumn coat is more reddish.

Males are larger than the females. Average measurements of adult males: length 125–145, tail 6–17, hind foot 39–43, ear 15 cm; average weight of Oregon males 50.5 (45.4–62.8) kg (av. 113 pounds). Measurements of adult females: length 135, tail 6, hind foot 39, ear 14 cm; average weight of Oregon females 41.5 (32.2–47.5) kg (av. 92 pounds).

Habits. Pronghorns appear to possess boundless nervous energy and insatiable curiosity. They are highly gregarious and are found in small herds most of the year, although the does seek privacy when they are about to give birth, and the adult bucks segregate from the does and younger animals in spring and rejoin the does in autumn. Strange objects or the antics of humans arouse their curiosity, and they approach quietly to investigate, only to snort and dash away at high speed when frightened. They signal each other by raising the long hairs of their rump rosettes, which flash in the sunlight for long distances on the prairies. The does and the young kids seem to be high-spirited and indulge in playful chases. When they stop, they shake their coats as dogs do after leaving the water. Observations seem to indicate that there is a recognition of certain social responsibilities: does decoy dogs and coyotes away from cached kids, bucks decoy dogs away from does with young kids, and lone does 'baby-sit' a number of kids while their mothers are feeding or visiting remote springs to drink. Pronghorns mix amicably with bands of cattle, sheep, and mule deer.

Pronghorns have excellent vision, which is exceptional among ruminants. They can see an object three or four miles away, but ignore stationary objects unless they

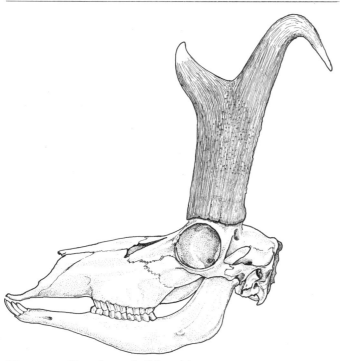

Figure 107 Pronghorn skull (× 1/4)

arouse their curiosity. Their hearing and sense of smell are also fairly keen.

The pronghorn is the fleetest North American mammal. It appears to enjoy racing vehicles and often runs alongside them for a while and then cuts across in front of them. It has been estimated that it may reach fifty to sixty miles an hour in short bursts, but normally it can run at thirty-five to forty miles an hour for distances up to four miles before becoming exhausted. It walks stiff-legged; it can jump considerable distances but not over an object; and it can swim well. Its voice is a soft blow, *cha-oo*. It is most active in early morning and late afternoon, but may feed and move about at any time during the day and night resting intermittently.

In winter, as the hills become snow-covered, pronghorns band together and drift to the valleys. Later they return to steep windblown hillsides, where they paw through the snow to feed. Formerly, pronghorns undertook extensive migrations in Canada to seek areas of lesser snowfall, but the construction of fences, roads, and railways across the prairies has hindered these movements. They refuse to jump even low fences and crawl either under a fence or between the strands. Woven wire fences constitute a complete barrier to their movements, and bands of migrating pronghorns are sometimes trapped by them. Although they occupy an extensive area during a year, the usual limit of their daily movements is about a square mile.

The average life-span of the pronghorn is about four and a half years, and the maximum recorded longevity is twelve years.

Forbs constitute about two-thirds of this species' diet and woody browse forms somewhat less than 30 per cent. Grasses, which are particularly favoured in spring, make up the remaining 3 to 5 per cent. Some of the favourite forbs are clovers, sourdock, wild onion, locoweed, lupin, wild pea vine, larkspur, buttercup, and alfalfa. Browse plants include sagebrush, saltbrush, rabbit brush, and winter fat. Grasses include cheatgrass, wheatgrass, redtop, foxtail, timothy, bluegrass, needlegrass, and sedge. Pronghorns also require water to drink.

Their chief predator is the coyote, especially when the snow is deep. In summer the coyotes concentrate on the young kids, but does will drive off a marauding coyote by trying to spear it with their sharp hooves, sometimes even killing it in this way. Bobcats and grizzly bears are occasional predators, and the chief avian raptores are golden eagles and ravens, which hunt the new-born kids.

Habitat. Pronghorns inhabit plains, steppes, deserts, and foothills. They seek protection in coulees and river valleys.

Reproduction. The bucks commence their curious rutting behaviour about mid-August. This consists of posturing, hanging the head, and waving it from side to side with eyes protruding, and quickly jumping to one side or the other. At the same time they erect their long rosette hairs and mane, often causing waves to pass through the rump fur. The bucks are polygamous and gather harems of does, averaging seven (two to fifteen) in number, during the

mating season. At that time most of the kids play together in groups and ignore their elders. The bucks shed their horns after the completion of the rut.

The does are probably seasonally polyoestrous. Occasionally post-partum mating is reported in the spring. In Oregon the normal rutting period occurs between August 20 and September 20, but in Wyoming it extends until the first of October. The gestation period is between 230 and 240 days. The season of birth is rather prolonged over the range of the species from early March in Texas to mid-June in Wyoming. The average litter size is 1.75 (1–3), twins being the mode.

As a site for the birth of the kids the doe usually picks a small, well-vegetated valley or an island in a lake. After the birth takes place, she retreats about a quarter of a mile away, from which distance she can watch the site where her kids are cached. Normally twins are cached some distance apart from each other. The pronghorn kid weighs about 1.8 to 2.4 kg (4–5 pounds) at birth. Its wavy natal coat is dappled grey with a creamy rump. Its enormous luminous eyes dominate its face. Kids are precocious and rise on wobbly legs to nurse within the first hour. They can run awkwardly on bent legs the second day and are difficult to catch the third day. They appear to be odourless for the first few days of life, and thus dogs and coyotes find them difficult to locate. They remain cached for the first three weeks. By the end of the first week, however, they are most agile and frisky, racing about in playful groups until danger threatens. They follow the does at four to six weeks of age, begin grazing at six weeks, and are weaned by the time they are four months old. They reach independence at that time but continue to follow their mothers during the first winter.

The juvenile does reach sexual maturity at the age of fifteen to sixteen months.

Economic Status. In the past, the pronghorn was probably not an important economic resource for the Plains Indians because it was difficult to stalk and the thin hide and loose hair made it hardly worth the trouble. Today, however, it is a highly prized trophy of the chase.

Stockmen often view bands of pronghorns among their range stock with some concern because of possible competition for food. However, the pronghorn's preference for forbs and shrubby browse does not make it a serious competitor for range grasses.

Status. Originally pronghorns roamed the prairies and steppes of western North America in numbers comparable to the bison, but hunting and the encroachment of civilization in the form of fences reduced the population to an estimated low point of approximately 20,000 in 1908, after disastrous winter losses in 1906–07. Better law enforcement, milder winters, and the establishment of sanctuaries increased the population to approximately 27,000 in the United States and 1,400 in Canada in 1922–24, and 68,000 in the United States and 2,400 in Canada in 1932. In 1945 the number of pronghorns in Canada was estimated at 31,000. Satisfactory population levels have been reached in southeastern Alberta and southwestern Saskatchewan in recent years, and limited hunting has been permitted.

Map 171 Distribution of the pronghorn, *Antilocapra americana*: E extinct

In 1922 Nemiskam National Park was established in southeastern Alberta to preserve a small herd of 42 pronghorns on a 5,000-acre fenced range. The number increased to 235 in 1935. In 1947 the park was closed because the pronghorn population had reached satisfactory levels outside the park.

The gravest risk to the survival of pronghorns in Canada is the occurrence of severe winters, since they are prevented from migrating southward by woven wire fences across their routes.

Distribution. This species is found only in western North America from the southern Prairie Provinces to northern Mexico.

Canadian Distribution. This species, which formerly ranged over most of the treeless prairie region (see Map 171), is now restricted to the adjacent, southern corners of Alberta and Saskatchewan. The Canadian form is typical:

Antilocapra americana americana (Ord), 1815, *in* Guthrie, A new geogr., hist. and comm. grammar ..., Philadelphia, ed. 2, 2: 292, 308.

REFERENCES

Buechner, H.K. 1950. Life history, ecology, and range use of the pronghorn antelope in Trans-Pecos Texas. American Midl. Nat. 43(2): 257–354.

Kitchen, D.W. 1974. Social behaviour and ecology of the pronghorn. Wildlife Monogr. 38.

Rand, A.L. 1947. The 1945 status of the pronghorn antelope, *Antilocapra americana* (Ord), in Canada. Nat. Mus. Canada Bull. 106.

Family **Bovidae** / Antelopes, Cattle, Sheep, and Goats

This familar family of cloven-hoofed mammals has the following characteristics: permanent paired horny sheath covering bony cores on the frontal bones, the lack of upper incisors and canines, and a placenta with numerous cotyledons. As a rule they also have hypsodont cheek teeth, lateral hooves with the distal ends of the metapodial bones lacking, and a gall bladder. From this family, man has domesticated cattle, sheep, and goats, which have been modified through selective breeding to provide meat, dairy products, and wool for man's service.

AMERICAN BISON or BUFFALO
Bison. *Bison bison* (Linnaeus)

Description. The bison is our largest terrestrial mammal. Its massive head and forequarters appear out of proportion to its slim hind quarters. Its head is low-slung, and its shoulders have a massive hump supported by tall dorsal spines on the thoracic vertebrae. Its tail is of moderate length, with a terminal tassel of long hair. Its short black horns rise laterally on the side of the head and have inward-curving tips (the female's horns are slenderer, and the tips point upward); the large nostrils are surrounded by a moistened, black naked rhinarium; and the tongue is slate blue. It has rather short legs with large, rounded hooves; the small lateral hooves are situated high on the hock. A large bull may stand 6 feet high at the shoulder and weigh up to 1 ton (Plate 43). The heavy skull is triangular and flattened, with lateral projecting horns; there is no lachrymal vacuity (Figure 108).

The name buffalo for this species is a misnomer and should be reserved for the Asian and African buffaloes, which are distinct genera.

The pelage is composed of long, coarse guard hairs and a matted, woolly undercoat. The head, shoulders, and forelegs are covered by a shaggy, woolly, dark chocolate-brown mane; the coat on the hind quarters is short, straight, and coppery brown in colour. The head and beard are almost black. There are two annual moults, in spring and in autumn. Albino, pied, and 'blue' individuals

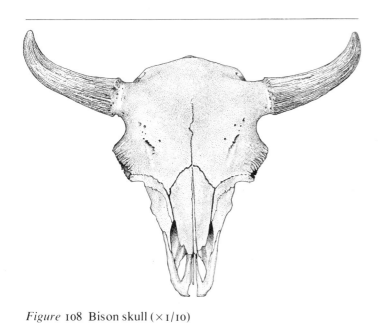

Figure 108 Bison skull (×1/10)

are occasionally observed. White bisons were held in great reverence by the Plains Indians.

The bulls attain adult size at six years of age but continue to grow slowly throughout life; the cows reach maximum size at about four years of age. Measurements of adult males: length 304–380, shoulder height 167–182, tail 43–48, hind foot 58–68 cm; average weight 570 (460–720) kg (1,273 pounds at 6 years). Average measurements of adult cows: length 213, shoulder height 152, tail 45, hind foot 53 cm; weight 420 (360–460) kg (930 pounds).

Habits. Bison are gregarious beasts and travel together in cohesive herds, which may number between four and twenty individuals and which some believe are family bands. These bands may join to form large herds numbering in the thousands. Bison are curious, though wary, and are easily frightened. They mill about under attack and stampede under the influence of contagious excitement. Stampeding bison have little control over their movements, and those behind may trample the leaders if they attempt to change direction abruptly. The assumption of leadership seems to be quite haphazard. The adult bulls are quite stolid and occasionally treacherous. They may charge intruders with little warning and give ground only reluctantly. The tail is elevated during periods of excitement, anger, and rutting. The calves and cows are more playful than the bulls and run and buck in a high-spirited fashion. Much of the time is spent in grooming, which consists of rolling in mud or dust wallows, horning small shrubs and trees, and rubbing against tree trunks.

The sense of smell is keen, and the eyesight is excellent. Odours may be recognized up to a mile away, and moving objects may be observed half a mile away. The calves bawl, the cows snort and cough, and the bulls' bellows during the rut may be heard up to a distance of three miles.

The usual gait is a slow, plodding walk as the herd moves in single file along well-worn paths across the prairie or as it ploughs through deep snow over some frozen northern marsh. If hurried, bison will trot; if frightened, they will break into a curious rocking gallop, which may attain a top speed of thirty-two miles an hour, though they seldom maintain this gait for very long. They are perfectly at ease in water and swim with head and much of the shoulders exposed.

They are mostly diurnal; feeding begins at dawn and continues intermittently throughout the day until nightfall. There are protracted rest periods after noon, when they lie in the shade and chew the cud. On moonlit nights, especially in winter, there is also some movement and feeding activity.

Bison are generally thought of as migratory animals, and their mass movements across the prairies during the spring and autumn months have frequently been described by writers of the past century. It should not necessarily be concluded, however, that the herds found in Saskatchewan in the summer migrated as far as Texas for the winter. It is now thought that all the herds moved southward a couple of hundred miles to more favourable winter pastures. Some writers postulated a circular migration route. The bison herds that spent the summer at higher elevations in the mountains moved down to the river valleys in winter, although lone bulls regularly wintered high in mountain passes. In November and May the bison in Wood Buffalo Park still undertake considerable migrations from the wooded hills to the Peace River valley, a distance of as much as 150 miles. An estimate of the average daily movement of a single animal is 2 miles, and a small herd may stay within a range of 12 square miles in summer and 36 square miles in winter.

Bison are remarkably long-lived and have been known to survive up to forty years.

Bison are primarily grazing animals, living mainly on grasses, forbs, and sedges. Among their staple food items are wheat grass, brome grass, wild rye, wild oats, June grass, blue grass, vanilla grass, reed grass, salt grass, foxtail grass, and spear grass. They also eat horsetail, rushes, sedge, lichens, vetches, pea vine, blueberries, and bearberries.

Only the grizzly bear, the mountain lion, and the wolf are strong enough to kill a bison. Before the advent of Europeans to this continent, the grizzly and the wolf were abundant on the prairies, but it is doubtful that the mountain lion was an important predator. Even a pack of wolves cannot easily overcome a lone bison; they are forced to prey upon lone senile bulls, orphaned or strayed calves, and crippled, wounded, or diseased animals.

Habitat. The bison is found in a wide range of habitats from arid plains to aspen parklands, meadows, river valleys, and even coniferous forests.

Reproduction. The sexes are mainly separated during most of the year, but during the summer the cows are joined by the bulls. The bulls' mating behaviour may be described as temporarily monogamous. Bulls 'tend' cows in oestrus; this consists in constantly following the cow for several days with neck frequently extended, head held horizontally, and upper lip curled. At this time they threaten other bulls that may approach and indulge in shoving contests, which results in the weaker bulls being replaced by stronger ones. Occasionally violent fights occur between evenly matched contestants. The old, outcast bulls do not associate with the rutting herd.

The cows are seasonally polyoestrous. Lactating cows with calves at heel conceive later than dry cows, and bear their calves late the following season. This precludes their breeding during the second normal rutting season, so that they are 'dry' at the beginning of the third season and breed at the onset of the rut. Thus cows normally bear two calves in three years. In Wood Buffalo Park the rutting period normally lasts from early July to late September, with a peak in mid-August. Occasionally, however, there are unseasonal matings. The gestation period is between 270 and 300 days. Parturition occurs between mid-April and the beginning of June, with a peak in the first half of May. Sometimes calves are born in the summer and autumn months. Twins are born only rarely.

The calves, which appear long-legged and short-necked at birth, are covered with an orangy brown crinkled coat. They are precocious and attempt to stand to nurse on wobbly, spidery legs within half an hour after birth. After three hours of life they can run around and buck, and they follow their mother when she moves off. The cow will charge an intruder in defence of her young calf.

The calves follow their mothers closely for the first two to three weeks; the mother recognizes her own calf by scent and rejects strange calves. Later the calves move more freely among the herd in playful groups. Although they start to graze experimentally on tender grass at the age of a week, they are not weaned until they are about seven months old. They moult into their first brown juvenile coat between nine and ten weeks of age.

In captivity young bulls reach sexual maturity as early as fourteen months of age, but an age of two to three years is more general in the wild state. Some precocious heifers conceive as yearlings, but a more normal age is two years, and some 'late bloomers' wait until they are three or four years old.

Economic Status. The bison was the cornerstone in the economy of the Plains Indians, and it figured prominently in the history of western North America. Books have been devoted to the historical and economic aspects of the American bison, and these can only be summarized here. The Spaniard Cortez was the first European to see an American bison – in Moctezuma's zoo in Mexico City in 1521. A countryman of Cortez, Francisco Vázquez de Coronado, saw many in the wild state during his search for the Kingdom of Cibola across the arid plains of southwestern United States in 1540–52. The young Hudson's Bay Company clerk Henry Kelsey was the first European to see bison in Canada, when he stood on the edge of the prairie in Manitoba on August 20, 1691, and overlooked herds of peacefully grazing 'buffles.' Samuel Hearne saw the wood bison in its natural haunts on Great Slave Lake on January 9, 1772, the first European to do so.

The population of wild bison before the advent of Europeans has been estimated at between forty and sixty million, but the quickening pace of European settlement hurried the slaughter of the herds across the land. By 1800 the eastern populations were exterminated, and by 1875 the western herds on the prairies had been reduced to isolated pockets. By 1893 there were only about twenty wild bison in Yellowstone National Park and about three hundred in the Wood Buffalo Park area of the Mackenzie District.

History of Canadian Herds. Walking Coyote, a Pend d'Oreille Indian, captured four calves from a herd of wild bison during a hunt along the Milk River in northeastern Montana in 1873 or 1874. The next spring he drove them to St Ignatius Mission on the Flathead Reservation of western Montana. By 1884, the herd consisted of thirteen head, of which he sold ten to C.A. Allard and Michel Pablo, local ranchers, at $250 a head. In 1893 Allard and Pablo bought the remainder of Buffalo Jones' herd at Omaha (twenty-six pure bison and eighteen hybrid *cattelo*). The amalgamated herd was grazed on Allard's ranch near Ravalli. In 1906 the Canadian government bought Pablo's share of the 709 pure-bred bison for $200,000 in an outstanding conservation move. It took three years to ship these bison by railway from Ravalli to Elk Island National Park, Alberta, a distance of 1,200 miles. Later they were transferred to

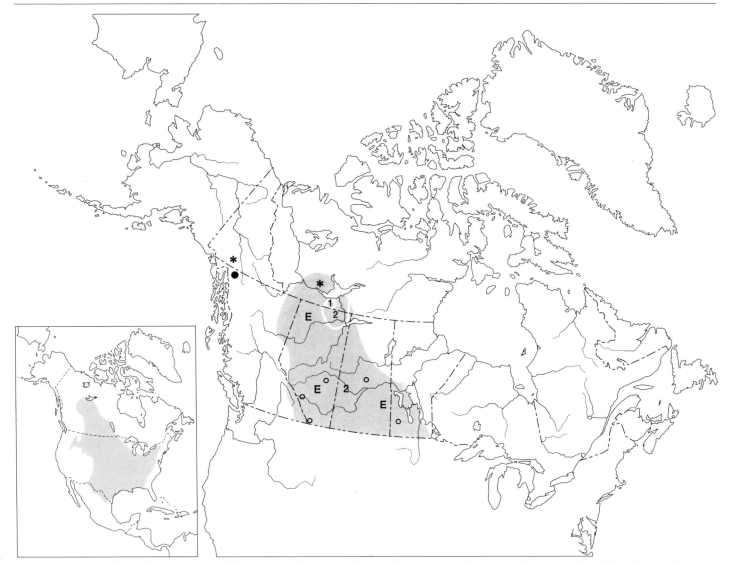

Map 172 Distribution of the American bison, *Bison bison*: 1 *B. b. athabascae*, 2 *B. b. bison*, ○ location of park herds, E extinct, ● extra-limital record, * introduced

Buffalo Park, near Wainwright, Alberta. This herd constituted the basis of the present herd at Elk Island National Park and of other smaller herds at western national parks, in total about a thousand animals.

In 1893 the government of Canada enacted legislation to provide complete protection for the remnant herd of wood bison in the southern Mackenzie District. At first they were given protection by the Royal Canadian Mounted Police. Later, in 1911, the first game wardens were appointed, and by 1914 the population was thought to have increased to about five hundred animals.

Wood Buffalo Park, encompassing an area of approximately 10,500 square miles, was established in 1922 to preserve the native herd of wood bison, then estimated at between 1,500 and 2,000 animals.

Between 1925 and 1928, 6,673 plains bison from the overcrowded Buffalo Park at Wainwright, Alberta, were transported by train and barge to release points along the Slave River. As early as 1925, 400 of the new arrivals had migrated to the meadows of the Peace River delta, which

then was added to the park area, enlarging it to 17,300 square miles. The present size of this mixed herd has been estimated at between 10,000 and 12,500 animals. Unfortunately, bovine tuberculosis, Bang's disease, and, later, anthrax were introduced to this herd.

In 1957 an isolated herd of about two hundred wild bison was discovered in the Nyarling River–Big Buffalo Lake area of the park, separated from the mixed herds by one hundred to two hundred miles of muskeg. The collection of specimens revealed that these were remnants of the native northern race. Steps were taken to preserve this herd in a more suitable area, and a number were transported to an area near Fort Providence, Northwest Territories.

Distribution. The original distribution of bison included most of central North America, from northern Mexico to Great Slave Lake and from Washington to the Rocky Mountain States.

Canadian Distribution. No remains have been found to indicate that bison ever inhabited eastern Canada, but they occurred from eastern Manitoba to eastern British Columbia and northward to the Peace River district and Great Slave Lake region of the Northwest Territories. Two subspecies are recognized (see Map 172).

Bison bison athabascae Rhoads, 1898, Proc. Acad. Nat. Sci. Philadelphia 49: 498. The larger, darker, woolier northern subspecies, formerly found in the Rocky Mountains of western Alberta and eastern British Columbia; known as the wood buffalo. Now reduced to one small wild herd in northern Wood Buffalo Park.

Bison bison bison (Linnaeus), 1758, Syst. Nat., 10th ed., 1: 72. The typical plains form, which also occurred in the hardwood forests of eastern United States. Now found only in semidomesticated herds in many national parks and reserves.

REFERENCES

Fuller, W.A. 1962. The biology and management of the bison of Wood Buffalo National Park. Wildlife Management Bull., ser. 1, no. 16. Canadian Wildlife Service, Ottawa.

Roe, F.G. 1951. The North American buffalo: a critical study of the species in its wild state. Univ. Toronto Press.

Soper, J.D. 1941. History, range and home life of the northern bison. Ecol. Monogr. 11: 347–412.

MOUNTAIN GOAT

Chèvre de montagne. *Oreamnos americanus* (de Blainville)

Description. Although its scientific name (*Oreamnos* from the Greek 'mountain lamb') and its common name suggest that this animal is closely related to sheep and goats, it belongs, in fact, to a small group of mountain antelopes. Its closest relatives are the serow, *Capricornis*, and goral, *Naemorhedus*, of Asia, and a more distant relative is the chamois, *Rupicapra*, of the European Alps. It has a stocky body, with high, ridged shoulders, a short neck, a long, narrow low-slung head, short legs, and a stubby tail. Its hooves are short and oval with thick, spongy pads. The small lateral hooves are situated high on the hock. Its ears are long and pointed; its muzzle is fully furred except for the black-rimmed nostrils and lips. The iris of the eye is yellow, and the oval pupil is dark brown. The short, black, recurved, dagger-like horns with basal annulations and smooth shiny tips are characteristic. The billies' horns curve gradually near the tips, but the nannies' horns are straighter and curve abruptly at the tips. A pair of leathery black glands half-encircle the base of the horns from behind (Plate 42). The skull is long and narrow with pointed premaxillae, and it lacks a lachrymal vacuity or pit. The average length of male horns is 230 (200–300) mm, with an average basal circumference of 140 mm. The horns of the females average 215 (190–260) mm in length, with an average basal circumference of 115 mm. The canon bones of the feet are much shorter than those of sheep or deer (Figure 109).

The mountain goat's coat is creamy white, occasionally with a brownish dorsal line or yellowish wash. Only the black lips, nostrils, horns, hooves, and brown pupils relieve the whiteness. The winter coat is long and silky, and the summer coat is shorter. It has a goat-like double beard. The guard hairs may be up to 175 mm in length on the back, chest, and flanks. The woolly undercoat is finer than cashmere. Between the latter part of May and mid-July, the long fleece is shed in patches, first from the head, shoulders, and legs, and finally from the rump, leaving the animal extremely scraggly in appearance until it assumes the short, trim summer coat. The long guard hairs and the undercoat, which develop in October, give the animal a shaggy appearance that hides its muscular body. At that time the characteristic 'beard' and 'knickers' are prominent.

The billies are decidedly larger than the nannies. Average measurements of adult males: length 179 (156–205), tail 11.5 (9.5–14), hind foot 36.5 (33.5–39.5), ear 13 (11–14), shoulder height 106 (98–114) cm; weight 85.3 (64.9–113) kg or 188 (143–250) pounds. Average measurements of adult females: length 147 (132–159), tail 11 (9–12), hind foot 32 (28–33), ear 11.5 (11.5–12.5), shoulder height 95 cm; weight 61.5 (45.5–96.0) kg or 135 (100–212) pounds.

Because of the remoteness of the mountain goat's domain, information about this 'mysterious' mammal from the accounts of American explorers accumulated very

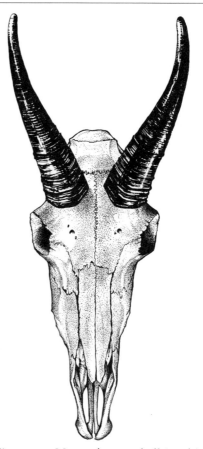

Figure 109 Mountain goat skull (× 1/4)

slowly. Captain James Cook probably saw mountain goat hides and fleece during his visit to Kodiak Island in 1778, when he examined native blankets, but he attributed the hides and fleece to polar bears. Peter Simon Pallas sent a clump of fleece from Kodiak Island to Thomas Pennant in London, some time before 1784, which Pennant identified as Argali sheep wool. Captain George Vancouver is reported to have brought back a skin from his survey of the British Columbia coast in 1792–94. The first clear descriptions of the animal date from the Lewis and Clark expedition of 1806 and from David Thompson's diary of 1807. It was in that year that David Thompson shipped a hundred goat skins back to London from the vicinity of Windermere, British Columbia. From that time on, there has been continual confusion between this species and the native mountain sheep, genus *Ovis*, particularly the northern white sheep *Ovis dalli*. Either species is frequently called mountain 'goat' or 'sheep,' and this has led to much confusion concerning their respective distributions.

Habits. Mountain goats give the appearance of being dispassionate and indifferent animals. In the remote wilderness and in game sanctuaries they seem curious or unwary, but in hunting territory they are usually extremely wary and difficult to approach. They are moderately gregarious; groups of nannies and their offspring are formed during the summer, while the billies remain alone or in loose association with other billies during most of the season, joining the nanny groups only in the autumn. The social order is a matriarchy, with the nannies dominating the more peaceful billies with their sharp horns, except during the mating season. The kids are playful and romp together, but the adults are very deliberate in their movements. They spend much of their time bedded down in slight depressions on mountain slopes, or on ledges from which they can command a broad view of their surroundings, and here they doze and chew the cud. In winter they often resort to caves for protection from the weather. They have curious behavioural patterns of stamping their forefeet and flicking out their tongues when disturbed. The kids bleat, and the adults grunt or occasionally bleat.

This species' eyesight is remarkably well developed for an ungulate, for they notice moving objects at least a mile away. Their sense of smell is probably keen enough, but is often handicapped by shifting breezes in their mountainous domain.

Mountain goats excel in climbing rocky cliffs and following narrow trails along ledges. Their movements are deliberate, muscular, and stiff-legged. They can with ease jump as much as ten feet from one ledge to another. On level ground they run with a slow, rocking gallop. They are mostly diurnal in activity and bed down at dusk.

Mountain goats generally occupy the same ranges in summer and winter and have no marked seasonal migrations. They do, however, abandon some of the highest slopes, where the snow lies deepest, in the depth of winter for lower, more windblown slopes. In spring the nannies seek special natal areas, which are usually grassy ledges on rocky cliffs near some mountain torrent. Spring and early summer are also periods when goats trek to natural salt-licks in the valleys, where the alkaline soil contains minerals such as calcium, manganese, phosphorus, and sodium salts. They frequently cross valleys to distant mountains at this time as well.

Goats have been known to survive at least twelve years in the wild state.

These animals feed throughout the day, with peaks at dawn and dusk. They are snip feeders rather than steady grazers. Their summer diet consists mainly of grasses, sedges, and rushes (71.7 per cent of the stomach contents by volume); forbs, such as lupin, mountain bluebells, *Polemonium*, sweet vetch, bistort, cinquefoil, and penstemon, form 17.2 per cent of the stomach contents; shrubs, such as dwarf huckleberry, swamp current, willow, shrubby cinquefoil, and bearberry, form 3.3 per cent; and conifers, such as pine and juniper, 4 per cent. In the autumn, forbs increase to 20 per cent, and in the winter conifers such as Douglas and alpine fir increase to 24.6 per cent of the diet by volume, and grasses and forbs decrease. In spring the grass consumption begins to rise to the summer peak.

The mountain goats' main predators are mountain lions and eagles, and grizzlies, wolverines, wolves, and coyotes are secondary predators. The mountain goat may fall victim to a bear, a wolf, or a wolverine while feeding on alpine meadows or crossing wooded valleys, but it is safe from these attackers if it can reach a cliff. On the other hand, it often falls prey to a mountain lion in such rocky areas, particularly if it seeks shelter in caves. Eagles, particularly the golden eagle, prey upon young kids and may carry them off if they stray too far from their mothers. For that reason young kids stay close to their mothers, pressing themselves under her flanks if an eagle flies overhead.

Habitat. Mountain goats inhabit the most rugged mountainous terrain imaginable. They prefer steep, grassy talus slopes at the base of cliffs but may also frequent small grassy ledges on the face of steep cliffs and rocky ridges, alpine meadows, and timberline. They occur from approximately sea level on the British Columbia coast to the limit of vegetation at an elevation of about 8,000 feet. Their habitat is characterized by deeper snow than mountain-sheep habitat. Their favourite ledges are often so steep and so exposed that the wind blows the snow off the vegetation, exposing the winter food supply. Their reported animosity to mountain sheep, *Ovis canadensis*, is overrated. The difference in habitat choice is the basis for the observation: 'Sheep on one mountain, goats on another.' Both species are frequently observed on the same slope without signs of animosity other than an apparent ignoring of each other's presence.

Reproduction. The billies have a number of curious behavioural patterns which become evident during the rut. They sit on their haunches like dogs and paw the ground in front of them, covering their flanks and bellies with dirt, which discolours their fur. They mark the vegetation with the fluid from the glands behind their horns, and they posture before nannies. They may diligently tend one nanny in heat and drive off other billies, or they may serve two or three nannies. When courting, they approach

Map 173 Distribution of the mountain goat, *Oreamnos americanus*

the nannies from the rear in a crouch and administer a quick kick to the flank as an opening gesture! Fights are rare between billies but may be vicious when they occur, with the opponents trying to gore each other's flanks with their sharp horns.

The rutting period occurs in November. The nannies are probably seasonally polyoestrous. After a gestation period of about 178 days, the kids are born between the latter part of May and mid-June. Single births are the mode, twins occur in about a quarter of the cases, and triplets are rare.

At birth the kids weigh 2.9 to 3.8 kg (average 7 pounds), measure 62 cm long, and stand 36 cm high at the shoulder. Their large, luminous dark eyes, set in a short face with perky pointed ears, accentuate their whiteness. They have two leathery black spots on the crown where the horns will grow. Slight bony protuberances become apparent to the touch at three days of age, and by autumn the horns are 15 to 25 mm long. The kids follow their mothers very closely and nurse frequently for very brief periods. As their legs grow, they have to kneel to nurse, and the

way in which they wiggle their tails when nursing is reminiscent of domestic lambs. The kids start to nibble on grasses at about one week of age, but are not weaned until they are about six weeks old. They weigh about 10 kg (22 pounds) the first winter, which they spend close to their mothers. In spring, however, they are repelled by their mother before the birth of the new kid and are resigned to follow her at a greater distance during the second summer. The young nannies mature sexually at twenty-seven months and the billies at thirty-nine months.

Economic Status. The meat of a mountain goat is considered unpalatable by our standards, and the animals are hunted solely as trophies. The fine fleece of this species was used by Indians of the northwest coast of North America to weave the famous Chilkat blankets.

Distribution. Rocky Mountain goats are confined to the Cordilleran region of northwest America, from southeastern Alaska to Oregon and northern Idaho. Their distribution is actually spotty over this vast range as they are restricted to suitable habitat.

Canadian Distribution. Mountain goats occupy the Cor-

410

dilleran region of Canada from the international boundary to the southern Yukon Territory. No subspecies are recognized.

Oreamnos americanus (de Blainville), 1816, Bull. Soc. Philom., Paris, p. 80.

REFERENCES

Casebeer, R.L., M.J. Rognrud, and S. Brandborg. 1950. Rocky Mountain goats in Montana. Montana Fish and Game Commission Bull. 5.
Geist, V. 1964. On the rutting behavior of the mountain goat. Jour. Mamm. 45(4): 551–68.
Holroyd, J.C. 1967. Observations of Rocky Mountain goats on Mount Wardle, Kootenay National Park, British Columbia. Canadian Field-Nat. 81(1): 1–22.
Saunders, J.K. 1955. Food habits and range use of the Rocky Mountain goat in the Crazy Mountains, Montana. Jour. Wildlife Mngt. 19(4): 429–37.

MUSKOX
Boeuf musqué. *Ovibos moschatus* (Zimmermann)

Description. The muskox is a relic of the last ice age; its ancestors roamed the European plains and Asiatic steppes along with the hairy mammoth, mastodon, woolly rhinoceros, and reindeer. It is not certain whether the prefix 'musk' was applied by early explorers because of the odour of the bulls during the rut, or whether it was a ruse to link the species with the valuable musk deer of Asia. It was first mentioned by the French author N. Jérémie in 1720 in describing the Hudson Bay region.

This animal bears a superficial resemblance to the bison, but anatomical features such as the lobulated kidneys indicate a closer relationship to sheep and goats. It has a stocky body; short limbs; a stubby tail, completely covered by the body hair; ears that scarcely project beyond the coat; rounded hooves with sharp rims that provide traction on ice and rocks; and a broad, soft heel pad, covered by a tuft of hair projecting between the hooves (Plate 44).

The skull of the muskox is massive; the orbits protrude, and the flattened bosses of the horn cores cover the occipital region. In the males only a narrow groove separates the horn cores. The keratinous horns are ribbed and cracked at the base with worn, polished tips. The horns sweep downwards, close to the skull, and then the tips turn upwards and outwards. The horn colour depends to a great extent upon age – pale in the young, and turning to dark brown in adults. The full development of the bulls' horns takes about six years, and they are much more massive at the base than the cows', allowing only a tuft of hair to grow between the bosses (Figure 110).

In this species the pelage is composed of a soft fleece as fine as cashmere and an overcoat of long, coarse guard hairs, which hangs about the body and blows in the wind like a Scot's kilt and sporran. The guard hairs may be 62 cm long on a bull's neck. The body colour is dark brown to blackish, with creamy to yellowish brown saddle and

'stockings.' The cows and juveniles have lighter hair on the forehead. The fur is short and greyish on the muzzle and legs. The moult begins in late April or early May, and the old coat is shed in patches. At this season, the animals have a tattered appearance with long streamers blowing in the wind, and patches of fleece cling to rocks and bushes on the tundra. By mid-July the new dark undercoat appears. The replacement of the long guard hairs is uncertain – perhaps it continues throughout the year.

The bulls are larger than the cows. Average measurements of adult bulls: length 228 (201–246), hind foot 49 (48–50), tail 14 (11–17), shoulder height 135 (132–138) cm; weight 340 (263–650) kg or 750 (579–1,450) pounds in captivity. Average measurements of adult cows: length 199 (194–201), tail 10 (6–15), hind foot 43.5 (42.5–45.5), shoulder height 123 cm; weight 280–295 kg in captivity (620–650 pounds).

Habits. The muskox is a gregarious animal, usually found in herds numbering between three and a hundred individuals, with an average of fifteen. Outside the breeding season these herds are composed mostly of cows, calves, yearlings, and younger bulls. The bulls usually wander about alone or in small groups during most of the year, but join the herds of cows during the rutting season and possibly remain with them for some time afterwards. Lone animals observed during the late summer are either old and senile bulls, or younger bulls driven away from the herd by the harem master. The cow, her calf, and her two-year-old heifer have strong social ties, which are enlarged to include the herd as a social unit. The muskox's habit of forming a defensive ring or line, with the adults on the outside facing the predators and the calves inside, is an illustration of the herd unity. The muskox also has a peculiar habit of rubbing its preorbital gland on the side of its foreleg when excited. Although generally mild-

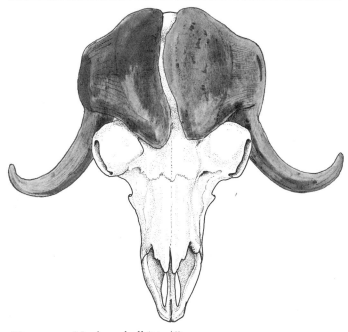

Figure 110 Muskox skull (× 1/6)

Map 174 Distribution of the muskox, *Ovibos moschatus*: E extinct, ● extra-limital record

tempered, muskoxen will charge tormentors briefly when cornered or wounded.

Muskoxen seem to have excellent eyesight and acute hearing. They are usually slow and stolid in their movements, but can run surprisingly fast when pressed. When alarmed, the herd usually runs closely packed. They climb rocky promontories with ease. Their only sound is a deep throaty rumble.

Muskoxen carry on a regular daily pattern of activity even during the prolonged darkness of the high arctic winter. They do not participate in long seasonal migrations and only move short distances, up to fifty miles, from summer to winter feeding ranges. On the banks of the Thelon River in the central tundra, these ranges may only be a few miles apart. There seems to be no territorial competition between herds.

Muskoxen have survived up to twenty-three years in captivity.

These animals are both browsers and grazers and are mobile intermittent feeders, not static intensive grazers

like sheep. Their winter food consists primarily of browse, such as Labrador tea, crowberry, cowberry, bilberry, ground birch, and willow. Their summer diet includes willow, sedge, rushes, blue grass, fescue and other grasses, horsetail, and such forbs as willowherb, bladder campion, knotweed, and fleabane.

The wolf is the main natural predator of the muskox; however, the muskoxen's defensive circle is usually effective, and only occasionally do wolves manage to drag one from it. Wolves also prey upon lone animals, especially the senile bulls. Grizzlies may occasionally attack muskoxen. The defensive circle habit unfortunately leaves it extremely vulnerable to slaughter by hunters with firearms.

Habitat. Muskoxen occur on the arctic tundra. In summer they occupy river valleys, lakeshores, and seepage meadows rich in the growth of willows, heaths, and grasses. In winter they shift to hilltops, slopes, and plateaus, where prevailing winds blow the vegetation free of snow.

Reproduction. The bulls are polygamous and join the harems of cows and their offspring in July. They drive off other intruding bulls and often indulge in serious fights at the height of the rut during the first three weeks in August. The bulls charge each other head-on, then back off slowly, swinging their heads from side to side. Occasionally one is gored in the chest or flank by the sharp horns of its antagonist. The cows have small, densely haired udders with four short teats. After a gestation period of eight months the calves are born in late April or early May. Usually a cow bears a calf every second year, although occasionally a calf is produced in succeeding years; twins are rare.

The muskoxen's natal coat is short, curly, and dark brown in colour. The first moult takes place between mid-July and September when the juvenile winter coat is assumed. This coat is longer and thicker than the natal coat but lacks the long adult guard hairs that develop later, during the third winter. There are no indications of horns at birth, but small bumps appear on the frontal bones after six months. At one year of age the horns are 5 to 7 cm long, and by two years of age they reach a length of 15 to 18 cm, flattened at the base and deflected laterally. The young calf huddles close to the cow's flank, half-hidden by the long guard hairs. They are very precocious and nurse within a few minutes of birth. About a week after birth, they nibble tender grass shoots, but they may continue to augment their natural diet by nursing for twelve to eighteen months. The young heifers reach sexual maturity at three and a half years of age in the wild, but in captivity may mature as early as eighteen months of age. Similarly, the young bulls mature at five years of age in the wild, but in captivity they mature as early as two years of age in more southerly locations.

Economic Status. The original sparse arctic population of muskoxen in Canada was heavily exploited during the nineteenth century for meat and hides. Their long, glossy brown coats were used for sleigh rugs, and between 1864 and 1916 over 15,000 muskox hides were shipped from northern Canada. Many animals were also killed to provide meat for arctic exploration parties. The narratives of certain explorers indicate that 1,000 were killed on Ellesmere Island and 500 on Melville Island to support their travels. The capture of calves for zoological gardens involved the killing of all the adults in the defensive ring. Absolute protection for the species was not provided until 1917, and by that time the population was extremely low. By 1930 it was estimated that only 500 remained on the mainland. Occasionally, under the strain of extreme hardship in remote areas, Eskimos kill a few muskoxen. The Eskimos use the horns of the muskox to fashion bows, which are truly remarkable to see.

Status. The present population in Canada is estimated at 10,000, of which 1,500 are found on the mainland (about a third of these in the Thelon Game Sanctuary, established in 1927), and the remaining 8,500 are distributed on Canada's arctic islands.

Distribution. The muskox is native to northern Canada, northwest Greenland, and formerly the north coast of Alaska. It has been introduced to Iceland, Spitsbergen, and Nunivak Island, Alaska, and to the Kargulen Islands of Antarctica. Introductions to Sweden were not successful.

Canadian Distribution. No subspecies are currently recognized. The distribution (see Map 174) includes the northern continental tundra zone from Chesterfield Inlet to Paulatuk and the following arctic islands: Banks, Victoria, Prince of Wales, Somerset, Devon, Cornwallis, Bathurst, Melville, Ellef-Ringnes, Axel Heiberg, and Ellesmere. Muskoxen are not known ever to have occurred on Baffin and Southampton islands; the population mysteriously disappeared from Prince Patrick Island after 1950, and a population appeared on Banks Island about the same time.

Ovibos moschatus (Zimmermann), 1780, Geographische Geschichte ... 2: 86.

REFERENCES

Hoare, W.H.B. 1930. Conserving Canada muskoxen: being an account of an investigation of Thelon Game Sanctuary, 1928–29. Department of the Interior, Ottawa.

Tener, J.S. 1965. Muskoxen in Canada: a biological and taxonomic review. Department of Northern Affairs and Natural Resources, Ottawa.

BIGHORN SHEEP
Mouflon d'Amérique. *Ovis canadensis* Shaw

Description. This is a large, heavy-bodied sheep with relatively long, slender legs and a straight back. It has a rather long narrow muzzle, short pointed ears, a beardless chin, and a bobbed tail. Its eyes are large; the iris is yellowish or amber-coloured. The preorbital gland is present as well as pedal glands between the hooves. The hooves are concave, and the foot pads are roughened to provide good traction on rocky terrain. The small lateral hooves are situated just below the heel (Plate 45).

The ram's crowning glory is the massive, brown spiralled horns, which curl back and down close to its head with tips projecting forward and outward just below the eyes. These horns are bluntly triangular in cross-section, with the flat base on top and the acute edge on the inside of the spiral. The horns have many annulations, and the more prominent grooves indicate annual growth rings. The ewes' horns are shorter than the rams' more slender ones, which simply curve back laterally from the crown. The skull has a broad cranium supporting conical bony horn cores and a pointed rostrum (Figure 111).

In this species the pelage is smooth and close to the body's contours. It is composed of an outer coat of brittle guard hairs about 60 mm in length, bone white at the base and brown tipped. Underneath is a short (25 mm), thick, grey, crimped fleece, which is analogous to the domestic sheep's wool. The dorsal colour is wood brown, with darker chocolate brown on the chest, face, and legs. The lower belly, the backs of the legs, the muzzle, and the large rump patch are ivory white. The rump patch, which extends from the thighs to the lower back, is centred by the short dark brown tail. The summer coat is a rich glossy brown, but it becomes quite faded by late winter. During early summer (June and July) the old coat becomes matted and is shed in patches, first from the head, shoulders, back, and legs, and finally from the rump; the animals then assume the slick summer coat. Towards late September the guard hairs lengthen, and the fleecy undercoat develops to form the thick winter coat.

Average measurements of adult males from Canada: length 172 (160–185), tail 11.6 (10.0–15.0), hind foot 44.2 (40.5–45.0), shoulder length 97 (82–112) cm, weight 130–156 kg (287–343 pounds). Females are decidedly smaller and measure about 142 cm in length, tail 10, hind foot 37, and shoulder height 80 cm. One weighed 63 kg (139 pounds).

Bighorns were first observed by the Spanish explorer Francisco Vázquez de Coronado in southwestern North America between 1540 and 1552. The species was well illustrated in 1691 by the Spanish missionary Father Piccolo in his account of southern California. It was not until 1804, however, that, based on Duncan McGillivray's account of his first encounter with mountain sheep on the Bow River near the town of Exshaw, Alberta, on November 30, 1800, the species was officially given a scientific name by Shaw. At the time, McGillivray was accompanying the Canadian fur trader and explorer David Thompson on surveys in the Canadian Rockies.

Habits. Bighorns are intensely gregarious. Led by an old ewe, the ewes, lambs, yearlings, and two-year-old rams form bands, which stay together all year. These bands usually number about ten animals but may include as many as a hundred, especially during the winter months when joined by the mature rams. The rams over three years of age form their own bands in spring, and led by an old, experienced ram they migrate to separate summer ranges. They rejoin the ewes again in the autumn in time for the rut, but do not challenge the leadership of the old ewe.

Bighorns give the impression of being confident in their own prowess, not easily excited, sometimes curious, but always alert. They become very 'tame,' and it is easy to approach them when they are given protection in game preserves and parks. The lambs frolic and gambol together, and occasionally the adults indulge in 'high jinks' when they are well fed and comfortable. On the winter ranges this species often fraternizes with deer, domestic sheep, mountain goats, and occasionally wapiti. All age- and sex-groups may indulge in butting jousts at any time of year, but these jousts become more serious among the rams as the rutting season approaches.

Although the senses seem to be acute, these animals appear to pay scant attention to sounds. The sense of sight is remarkable. They often intently watch other animals moving at distances of up to a mile. When bedded down chewing the cud, they maintain watch over the mountain slopes below. Hunters must take the precaution of climbing above their quarry and remaining hidden from view, but mountain breezes are unpredictable and may carry the hunters' scent to the sheep.

Native sheep are far less vociferous than domestic sheep. The lambs bleat, and the ewes respond in summer with a gutteral *ba*. At other times of the year adults utter throaty rumbles, or 'blow' in fright. During the rut the rams frequently snort loudly.

As would be expected bighorns are excellent climbers. Their trails usually follow the contours of steep slopes or zigzag along narrow ledges on the faces of cliffs. They have been 'clocked' at thirty miles an hour on the level and fifteen miles an hour scrambling up mountain slopes, but they are not such fearless climbers as the mountain goats on inaccessible cliffs. Mountain sheep will freely swim across rivers.

These animals are diurnal, with three peaks of feeding activity: in early morning, at noon, and in late afternoon. They usually feed and rest alternately in a one- to three-hour cycle, with lengthened feeding periods in winter. In the evening they bed down for the night in shallow depressions pawed out of the gravel or shale, high on a mountain with a commanding view of the slopes below. During stormy winter weather they seek the shelter of rocks, overhanging cliffs, and shallow caves.

Most sheep bands undertake seasonal migrations, in spring and autumn, between alpine summer ranges and valley winter ranges. These ranges may be anywhere from a few miles to forty miles apart. The rams usually depart first, in May, while the ewes lead the rams to lower elevations in October, when the snow flies. Some sheep bands find suitable range, year round, in close proximity. Most bands will occasionally visit favourite valley salt-licks during the summer, even if it requires a long trek from the summer range. There is no expression of territoriality among mountain sheep, although the bands are very conservative in the use of traditional feeding and bedding areas. In winter, the population density may be as high as

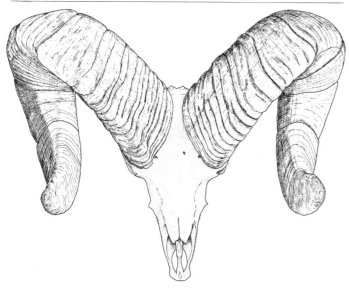

Figure 111 Bighorn sheep skull (× 1/5)

fifty to sixty sheep to a square mile of good range, but while they are dispersed on the summer ranges densities may be as low as one animal to four square miles.

Bighorns may live as long as fourteen years in the wild.

They are primarily grazers, and a heavy use of woody browse plants usually indicates a scarcity of preferred grasses and forbs. Native sheep graze on the move and do not clip the vegetative mat as closely as do domestic sheep. Grasses and sedges compose about 60 per cent of their annual diet, the percentage being higher in the summer and lower in the winter. Forbs, which are eaten most frequently during the summer months, form about 15 per cent of the annual diet. Browse plants such as pasture sage, bearberry, Douglas fir, junipers, willows, and roses constitute about 20 per cent of the annual diet, and are utilized to a greater extent during the winter. Mosses, lichens, and horsetails contribute about 5 per cent of the diet.

The availability of escape terrain in the form of rocky cliffs is important to the survival of this species. If a sheep can reach a rocky outcrop or cliff, it is usually safe from the attack of wolves, coyotes, bears, bobcats, and lynx. I have seen a coyote chasing a band of rams to the foot of a small rocky knoll, and the largest ram of the group turn about and threaten the coyote, which immediately turned away. Only the mountain lion and golden eagle threaten the sheep on rocky slopes. Golden eagles patrol the rugged mountain slopes at lambing time searching for unguarded lambs.

It is when the bighorn bands cross the valleys between mountain ranges that they are most vulnerable to attack from predators. Woodsmen frequently find the evidence of a mountain lion's having dropped out of a tree onto the back of an unsuspecting sheep crossing a gully.

Habitat. Bighorns inhabit alpine meadows, grassy mountain slopes, and foothill country in proximity to rugged rocky cliffs and bluffs. The grassy slopes may be only temporary – the result of forest fires. The winter range usually lies between 2,500 and 5,000 feet in elevation, and the summer range between 6,000 and 8,500 feet. Historically, bighorn also inhabited the badlands and breaks of the Missouri River valley in Montana, but they were never denizens of the plains.

These animals also require drier slopes where the annual snowfall is less than about sixty inches a year, since they cannot paw through deep snow to feed. They therefore are not found on the western slope of the Rocky Mountains north of the Kicking Horse valley. The ewes seek ledges on the steep rocky cliffs near mountain streams on which to bear their young.

Reproduction. As the rutting season approaches, the butting jousts of the rams become more frequent and violent. The contest usually begins with pushing and shoving at close quarters, often accompanied by slashing jabs of a foreleg. Then, according to an established ritual, the antagonists part and walk away about ten yards, turn, rear up on their hind legs, twist their heads to one side as if 'sighting down their noses,' and advance slowly towards each other, still erect. As they approach, their pace quick-

ens, and they lunge forward onto their forelegs, crashing head-on, horn to horn, with a crack that can be heard a mile away. So great is the impact that a shock wave ripples back the length of their bodies. Other near-by rams, attracted to the jousting field, may join the fray.

During the rutting period, the ram's neck becomes swollen; he walks stiff-legged, grunting regularly, and assumes a truculent air, occasionally even towards humans. Mating is completely promiscuous. With nose elevated, head cocked to one side, and upper lip curled, the ram follows any ewe in oestrus. Often several rams may be observed courting a single ewe, quartering back and forth across the mountain slopes, occasionally stopping to bunt and shove one another.

The ewes are probably seasonally polyoestrous. When in oestrus they accept several rams, often frequently, and participate in the mating chases or pose before the rams. The mating season varies greatly throughout the distribution of the species from August to early January. In Canada the peak is in early December, and after a gestation period of 180 days the lambs are born in late May and early June. A single lamb is usual, but twins are born occasionally.

At birth the lambs wear a soft, woolly, creamy-fawn-coloured coat. They have short attractive faces and luminous large eyes. Small horn buttons can be palpated under an unruly patch of matted wool on the crown. They stand about 16 inches high on long wobbly legs. The ewes cache them during the first week, but they soon learn to follow their mothers at a good pace, nursing, or nibbling tender grass along the way. Their development is precocious, and they soon can climb expertly. They are weaned at five to six months of age. The ewes reach sexual maturity at two to three years, and the young rams after three years.

Economic Status. The meat of the bighorn, which was prized by the Indians and early settlers, is generally considered to be the most palatable of all American big-game species. Now bighorns are considered prized trophies by the hunting fraternity. The Indians use the horns to fashion large ceremonial spoons and handles for utensils.

The introduction of domestic sheep to the ranges of the native bighorn has had a disastrous effect upon the native sheep populations because of the introduction of exotic diseases and parasites, such as the lung worm, *Protostrongylus*.

Status. The United States population of bighorn sheep was estimated at 15,000 to 18,000 in 1960, and there were about 5,500 in Canada in 1959.

Distribution. This species is found in the Cordilleran region of western North America from Wapiti Pass, 120 miles south of the Peace River in Alberta, to Baja California and eastward, formerly to the badlands along the Missouri River in western North Dakota and to the Black Hills of South Dakota.

Canadian Distribution. Two subspecies are recognized in western Alberta and eastern and southern British Columbia (see Map 175). The Rocky Mountain bighorn of eastern British Columbia has been introduced to several

Map 175 Distribution of the bighorn sheep, *Ovis canadensis*: 1 *O. c. californiana*, 2 *O. c. canadensis*, ∗ introduced

points in the Selkirk Mountains. The California bighorn is found in the dry interior region of British Columbia in the Ashnola Mountains, Marble Mountains, Chilcotin River canyon, and near Penticton and Lillooet.

Ovis canadensis californiana Douglas, 1829, Zool. Jour. 4: 332. A darker race with more openly curled horns, from the interior of British Columbia.

Ovis canadensis canadensis Shaw, 1804, Naturalists Miscellany, 51. A larger, paler race with more tightly curled horns, found in the Rocky Mountains of Alberta and British Columbia.

REFERENCES

Blood, D.A. 1963. Some aspects of behaviour of a bighorn herd. Canadian Field-Nat. 77(2): 77–94.

Buechner, H.K. 1960. The bighorn sheep in the United States, its past, present, and future. Wildlife Monogr. no. 4, The Wildlife Society, Lawrence, Kansas.

Cowan, I.Mc T. 1940. Distribution and variation in the native sheep of North America. American Midl. Nat. 24(3): 505–80.

Geist, Valerius. 1971. Mountain sheep: a study in behavior and evolution. Univ. Chicago Press, Chicago.

Welles, R.E., and F.B. Welles. 1961. The bighorn of Death Valley. Fauna of the National Parks of the United States no. 6. Washington.

DALL'S SHEEP
Mouflon de Dall. *Ovis dalli* Nelson

Description. The striking colour, graceful form, and aristocratic bearing of the Dall's sheep, combined with the splendour of its lofty alpine domain, make it the favourite big-game species of many sportsmen and naturalists. It is smaller and slenderer in build than the bighorn, with a shorter, more pointed face. Its eye has the same golden bronze iris and horizontal oval pupil of the sheep tribe. The horns and hooves are light amber in colour. The horns are slenderer than those of other species of sheep, and the rams' spirals are more flaring with the tips pointed away from the face. There is a more corrugated keel on the outer curl of the horns than occurs on those of the bighorn sheep. The older rams' tips are usually 'broomed' (the tips worn off). Occasionally rams with more tightly curled horns are observed. The ewes' horns are typically short and are curved backwards (Figure 112).

The Dall's sheep is closely related to the snow sheep, *Ovis nivicola*, of Kamchatka and eastern Siberia. It probably immigrated to northwestern America across the Bering landbridge in the late Pleistocene period after the bighorn had been pushed southward by the continental ice-sheets. Sufficiently detailed studies have not yet been conducted to establish the relationship between this species and its Siberian cousin, and I prefer to retain the American specific name for the present time.

This sheep has two distinctly marked geographical sub-species and an area of intergradation between them. The northern race, which carries the species name, is creamy white over the whole body, occasionally with a few dark hairs along the spine and tail. Only the black rhinarium, which is restricted to the nostrils and upper lip, relieves the whiteness of the coat (Plate 46). The southern race, which is known as Stone's sheep, is slaty brown except for a restricted white rump patch and muzzle and variable amounts of white on the insides of the hindlegs and forehead. Between the ranges of these two typical races are found populations with intergrading colours culminating in the 'saddle-backed' sheep of eastern Yukon territory, where the slaty back is restricted by increasing white on the rump and forequarters.

The short summer coat of the Dall's sheep is attained in June, and by August it is often stained on the chest and

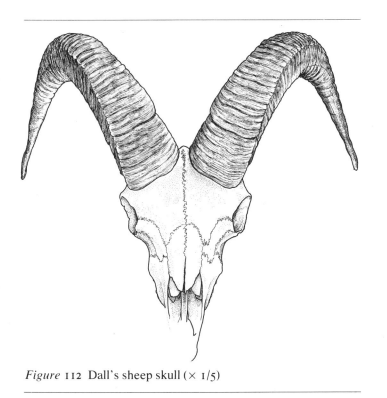

Figure 112 Dall's sheep skull (× 1/5)

underparts by contact with the soil. The winter coat is very long and gives the animal a 'plump' appearance. It reaches its full length by December, and the rams especially possess manes about two inches long.

The southern race, *stonei*, is larger than the more northern populations. Adult males average. length 160 (130–178), tail 10.2 (7.5–10.9), hind foot 43.6 (41.2–45.0), ear 7.5 (6.2–8.5), shoulder height 94 (91–102) cm; weight 91 kg (200 pounds). An adult female measured: length 132, tail 7.7, hind foot 38.2, shoulder height 81.4 cm. The more northern *dalli* measure: adult males, length 142 (134–153), tail 10.2 (8.9–11.5), hind foot 40.8 (39.5–42.1), ear 7.4 (7.0–7.6), shoulder height 94 (92–100) cm; weight 75–90 kg (165–200 pounds). An adult female measured: length 137, tail 9.9, hind foot 38.3 cm; weight about 57 kg (125 pounds).

Habits. This species differs little in social habits from the bighorn sheep. Led by an experienced ewe, the females form spring lambing crèches, and the rams withdraw for the summer. In the autumn the rams indulge in bunting jousts. I have found this species more wary and agile than the heavier bighorns. Even after a decade of protection in the Kluane Game Sanctuary of southwestern Yukon, it was difficult to approach bands without 'spooking' them. Their eyesight is keen, and they easily catch the human scent. The only sounds heard were the bleats of lambs and the soft snorts of the adults.

The rams migrate to higher alpine pastures in summer, and the ewes and lambs often form large herds during those months. All groups descend to the foothills in September and early October. This species has been known to reach fourteen years of age according to the annulations on the horns.

Grasses and sedges predominate in the diet of the Dall's sheep. During the summer months they relish several kinds of herbs, among which are saxifrages, locoweed, licorice root, and horsetails, and through the winter they paw the snows to eat the tender tips of a number of woody plants, such as willow, pasture sage, cranberry, crowberry, and mountain avens.

Their predators include the lynx, wolverine, coyote, grizzly bear, and wolf. Predation by wolves is most critical during the migration periods when the bands may have to cross flat stretches of level tundra to reach their winter ranges. Some winter ranges are on low rolling hills, which lack good escape terrain in the form of rocky outcrops.

Golden eagles also prey upon young lambs. In 1951 I watched an eagle harry a ewe and lamb above Tepee Lake in the Kluane Game Sanctuary, Yukon Territory. The eagle made repeated dives at the pair as they crossed an alpine slope. The ewe made a series of short runs towards a cliff, and each time the lamb pressed itself against her flank. Eventually they reached a narrow ledge and huddled together for some time after the eagle departed. Lambs caught napping at some distance from their mothers are not so fortunate.

Habitat. In summer this sheep inhabits alpine tundra slopes on northern mountains up to an elevation of about

Map 176 Distribution of Dall's sheep, *Ovis dalli*: 1 *O. d. dalli*, 2 *O. d. stonei*

6,000 feet. They descend to lower, drier, southern-facing slopes in winter. Their populations suffer losses during severe winters with heavier than average snowfalls.

Reproduction. The breeding habits of this sheep are similar to those of the bighorn. Mating is completely promiscuous, with several rams serving a band of ewes. The breeding season extends from about mid-November to mid-December. The gestation period seems to be slightly less than six months, and the lambs are born between May 8 and 25, usually a little earlier than the more southern bighorns. Single births are the mode, but occasionally twins are born.

The new-born lambs are not cached but usually lie close to the feeding ewe. Their development is precocious. Lambs a few days old scramble about the cliffs that the ewes chose as lambing quarters. They show great endurance and within two weeks can keep up with their mothers. They begin to nibble grass at ten days of age but continue to nurse for about nine months. By the time they are a month old, the lambs form groups and gambol and frolic together, often several hundred yards away from the feeding ewes. Their bleats carry far from their high cliff retreat when the air is still.

Economic Status. The Dall's sheep is an important food resource for the northern Indians and Eskimos within its range. It is also a popular hunting trophy.

Status. The Alaskan population was estimated to be about 30,000 in 1946. There were approximately 600 in Mount McKinley National Park in 1947, but in 1928 the park population was estimated to have been as high as 5,000 to 10,000 animals. Sizable populations occur in the Canadian part of its distribution as well.

Distribution. This species occupies the mountain ranges of northwestern North America, from northern British Columbia to the Arctic Ocean.

Canadian Distribution. The Canadian range includes northern British Columbia north of the Peace River (see Map 176), the Yukon Territory, and the Richardson Mountains of Mackenzie District, west of the Mackenzie River. Two subspecies are recognized.

418

Ovis dalli dalli Nelson, 1884, Proc. United States Nat. Mus. 7: 13. The typically white sheep of Alaska and the western Yukon District and Mackenzie District.

Ovis dalli stonei J.A. Allen, 1897, Bull. American Mus. Nat. Hist. 9: 111. The black Stone's sheep of northern British Columbia. Intergrades in the Pelly Mountains of southeastern Yukon were formerly called 'Fannin's' sheep or 'saddle-backed' sheep.

REFERENCE

Murie, Adolph. 1944. Chapter 3. Dall sheep. *In* The wolves of Mount McKinley, pp. 62–113. Fauna of the National Parks of the United States, Washington, D.C.

Appendices

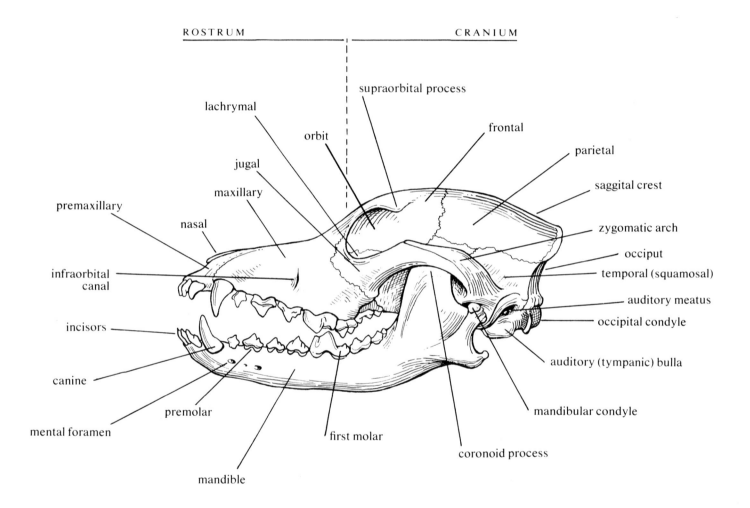

ROSTRUM   CRANIUM

supraorbital process

lachrymal

orbit   frontal

jugal   parietal

maxillary   saggital crest

premaxillary   zygomatic arch

nasal   occiput

infraorbital   temporal (squamosal)
canal   auditory meatus

incisors   occipital condyle

canine   auditory (tympanic) bulla

premolar

mental foramen   mandibular condyle

first molar

coronoid process

mandible

Figure 113 Diagram of a mammal skull showing the various cranial bones

I / Dental formulae, number of digits, and number of mammae for Canadian mammals

I	incisors (see Figure 113)
C	canines (see Figure 113)
P	premolars (see Figure 113)
M	molars (see Figure 113)
Total	total number of teeth
5/4	number of teeth in upper tooth row on one side of mouth/number in lower tooth row on one side of mouth
FL	foreleg
HL	hind leg
ME	total number of mammae
*	pollex vestigial
( )	digits concealed in flippers

Species	Dentition					Digits		
	I	C	P	M	Total	FL	HL	ME
ORDER MARSUPIALIA								
Family Didelphidae								
Didelphis virginiana	5/4	1/1	3/3	4/4	50	5	5	13
ORDER INSECTIVORA								
Family Soricidae								
Sorex cinereus	3/1	1/1	3/1	3/3	32	5	5	6
Sorex vagrans	3/1	1/1	3/1	3/3	32	5	5	6
Sorex obscurus	3/1	1/1	3/1	3/3	32	5	5	6
Sorex palustris	3/1	1/1	3/1	3/3	32	5	5	6
Sorex bendirii	3/1	1/1	3/1	3/3	32	5	5	6
Sorex fumeus	3/1	1/1	3/1	3/3	32	5	5	6
Sorex arcticus	3/1	1/1	3/1	3/3	32	5	5	6
Sorex gaspensis	3/1	1/1	3/1	3/3	32	5	5	6
Sorex trowbridgii	3/1	1/1	3/1	3/3	32	5	5	6
Microsorex hoyi	3/1	1/1	3/1	3/3	32	5	5	6
Microsorex thompsoni	3/1	1/1	3/1	3/3	32	5	5	6
Blarina brevicauda	3/1	1/1	3/1	3/3	32	5	5	6
Cryptotis parva	3/1	1/1	2/1	3/3	30	5	5	6
Family Talpidae								
Neürotrichus gibbsii	3/3	1/1	2/2	3/3	36	5	5	8
Scapanus townsendii	3/3	1/1	4/4	3/3	44	5	5	8
Scapanus orarius	3/3	1/1	4/4	3/3	44	5	5	8
Parascalops breweri	3/3	1/1	4/4	3/3	44	5	5	8
Scalopus aquaticus	3/2	1/0	3/3	3/3	36	5	5	6
Condylura cristata	3/3	1/1	4/4	3/3	44	5	5	8
ORDER CHIROPTERA								
Family Vespertilionidae								
Myotis lucifugus	2/3	1/1	3/3	3/3	38	5	5	2
Myotis yumanensis	2/3	1/1	3/3	3/3	38	5	5	2

Species	Dentition					Digits		
	I	C	P	M	Total	FL	HL	ME
Myotis keenii	2/3	1/1	3/3	3/3	38	5	5	2
Myotis evotis	2/3	1/1	3/3	3/3	38	5	5	2
Myotis thysanodes	2/3	1/1	3/3	3/3	38	5	5	2
Myotis volans	2/3	1/1	3/3	3/3	38	5	5	2
Myotis californicus	2/3	1/1	3/3	3/3	38	5	5	2
Myotis leibii	2/3	1/1	3/3	3/3	38	5	5	2
Lasionycteris noctivagans	2/3	1/1	2/3	3/3	36	5	5	2
Plecotus townsendii	2/3	1/1	2/3	3/3	36	5	5	2
Pipistrellus subflavus	2/3	1/1	2/2	3/3	34	5	5	2
Eptesicus fuscus	2/3	1/1	1/2	3/3	32	5	5	2
Nycticeius humeralis	1/3	1/1	1/2	3/3	30	5	5	2
Lasiurus borealis	1/3	1/1	2/2	3/3	32	5	5	4
Lasiurus cinereus	1/3	1/1	2/2	3/3	32	5	5	4
Antrozous pallidus	1/2	1/1	1/2	3/3	28	5	5	2
Family Molossidae								
Tadarida macrotis	1/2	1/1	2/2	3/3	30	5	5	2
ORDER PRIMATES								
Family Hominidae								
Homo sapiens	2/2	1/1	2/2	3/3	32	5	5	2
ORDER LAGOMORPHA								
Family Ochotonidae								
Ochotona princeps	2/1	0/0	3/2	2/3	26	5	4	
Family Leporidae								
Sylvilagus floridanus	2/1	0/0	3/2	3/3	28	5	4	8
Sylvilagus nuttallii	2/1	0/0	3/2	3/3	28	5	4	8
Lepus americanus	2/1	0/0	3/2	3/3	28	5	4	8
Lepus arcticus	2/1	0/0	3/2	3/3	28	5	4	8
Lepus townsendii	2/1	0/0	3/2	3/3	28	5	4	8
Lepus europaeus								
ORDER RODENTIA								
Family Aplodontidae								
Aplodontia rufa	1/1	0/0	2/1	3/3	22	4*	5	6
Family Sciuridae								
Tamias striatus	1/1	0/0	1/1	3/3	20	4*	5	8
Eutamias minimus	1/1	0/0	2/1	3/3	22	4*	5	8
Eutamias amoenus	1/1	0/0	2/1	3/3	22	4*	5	8
Eutamias townsendii	1/1	0/0	2/1	3/3	22	4*	5	8
Eutamias ruficaudus	1/1	0/0	2/1	3/3	22	4*	5	8
Marmota monax	1/1	0/0	2/1	3/3	22	4*	5	8
Marmota flaviventris	1/1	0/0	2/1	3/3	22	4*	5	10
Marmota caligata	1/1	0/0	2/1	3/3	22	4*	5	10
Marmota vancouverensis	1/1	0/0	2/1	3/3	22	4*	5	10
Spermophilus richardsonii	1/1	0/0	2/1	3/3	22	4*	5	10
Spermophilus columbianus	1/1	0/0	2/1	3/3	22	4*	5	10
Spermophilus parryii	1/1	0/0	2/1	3/3	22	4*	5	10
Spermophilus tridecemlineatus	1/1	0/0	2/1	3/3	22	4*	5	10
Spermophilus franklinii	1/1	0/0	2/1	3/3	22	4*	5	10
Spermophilus lateralis	1/1	0/0	2/1	3/3	22	4*	5	8–10
Cynomys ludovicianus	1/1	0/0	2/1	3/3	22	5	5	8
Sciurus carolinensis	1/1	0/0	2/1	3/3	22	4*	5	8
Sciurus niger	1/1	0/0	1/1	3/3	20	4*	5	8
Tamiasciurus hudsonicus	1/1	0/0	1–2 / 1	3/3	20–22	4*	5	8
Tamiasciurus douglasii	1/1	0/0	2/1	3/3	22	4*	5	8
Glaucomys volans	1/1	0/0	2/1	3/3	22	4	5	8
Glaucomys sabrinus	1/1	0/0	2/1	3/3	22	4	5	8
Family Geomyidae								
Thomomys talpoides	1/1	0/0	1/1	3/3	20	4*	5	8
Geomys bursarius	1/1	0/0	1/1	3/3	20	4*	5	8

Species	Dentition					Digits		
	I	C	P	M	Total	FL	HL	ME
Family Heteromyidae								
Perognathus fasciatus	1/1	0/0	1/1	3/3	20	5	5	6
Perognathus parvus	1/1	0/0	1/1	3/3	20	5	5	6
Dipodomys ordii	1/1	0/0	1/1	3/3	20	5	5	6
Family Castoridae								
Castor canadensis	1/1	0/0	1/1	3/3	20	5	5	4
Family Muridae								
Reithrodontomys megalotis	1/1	0/0	0/0	3/3	16	4*	5	6
Peromyscus maniculatus	1/1	0/0	0/0	3/3	16	4*	5	6
Peromyscus oreas	1/1	0/0	0/0	3/3	16	4*	5	6
Peromyscus sitkensis	1/1	0/0	0/0	3/3	16	4*	5	6
Peromyscus leucopus	1/1	0/0	0/0	3/3	16	4*	5	6
Onychomys leucogaster	1/1	0/0	0/0	3/3	16	4*	5	6
Neotoma cinerea	1/1	0/0	0/0	3/3	16	4*	5	4
Clethrionomys rutilus	1/1	0/0	0/0	3/3	16	4*	5	8
Clethrionomys gapperi	1/1	0/0	0/0	3/3	16	4*	5	8
Clethrionomys occidentalis	1/1	0/0	0/0	3/3	16	4*	5	8
Lemmus sibiricus	1/1	0/0	0/0	3/3	16	5	5	8
Synaptomys cooperi	1/1	0/0	0/0	3/3	16	4*	5	8
Synaptomys borealis	1/1	0/0	0/0	3/3	16	4*	5	8
Phenacomys intermedius	1/1	0/0	0/0	3/3	16	4	5	8
Dicrostonyx torquatus	1/1	0/0	0/0	3/3	16	4*	5	8
Dicrostonyx hudsonius	1/1	0/0	0/0	3/3	16	4*	5	8
Ondatra zibethicus	1/1	0/0	0/0	3/3	16	5	5	6
Lagurus curtatus	1/1	0/0	0/0	3/3	16	4*	5	8
Arvicola richardsoni	1/1	0/0	0/0	3/3	16	4*	5	8
Microtus pinetorum	1/1	0/0	0/0	3/3	16	4*	5	4
Microtus ochrogaster	1/1	0/0	0/0	3/3	16	4*	5	6
Microtus miurus	1/1	0/0	0/0	3/3	16	4*	5	8
Microtus pennsylvanicus	1/1	0/0	0/0	3/3	16	4*	5	8–10
Microtus montanus	1/1	0/0	0/0	3/3	16	4*	5	8
Microtus townsendii	1/1	0/0	0/0	3/3	16	4*	5	8
Microtus oeconomus	1/1	0/0	0/0	3/3	16	4*	5	8
Microtus longicaudus	1/1	0/0	0/0	3/3	10	4*	5	8
Microtus chrotorrhinus	1/1	0/0	0/0	3/3	16	4*	5	8
Microtus xanthognathus	1/1	0/0	0/0	3/3	16	4*	5	8
Microtus oregoni	1/1	0/0	0/0	3/3	16	4*	5	8
Rattus rattus	1/1	0/0	0/0	3/3	16	4*	5	10
Rattus norvegicus	1/1	0/0	0/0	3/3	16	4*	5	12
Mus musculus	1/1	0/0	0/0	3/3	16	4*	5	10
Family Dipodidae								
Zapus trinotatus	1/1	0/0	1/0	3/3	18	4*	5	8
Zapus princeps	1/1	0/0	1/0	3/3	18	4*	5	8
Zapus hudsonius	1/1	0/0	1/0	3/3	18	4*	5	8
Napaeozapus insignis	1/1	0/0	0/0	3/3	16	4*	5	8
Family Erethizontidae								
Erethizon dorsatum	1/1	0/0	1/1	3/3	20	4*	5	4
Family Capromyidae								
Myocastor coypus	1/1	0/0	1/1	3/3	20	4*	5	4
ORDER CETACEA								
Family Ziphiidae								
Berardius bairdii	–	–	–	–	4	(5)	0	2
Mesoplodon bidens	–	–	–	–	2	(5)	0	2
Mesoplodon densirostris	–	–	–	–	2	(5)	0	2
Mesoplodon mirus	–	–	–	–	2	(5)	0	2
Mesoplodon stejnegeri	–	–	–	–	2	(5)	0	2
Mesoplodon carlhubbsi	–	–	–	–	2	(5)	0	2
Ziphius cavirostris	–	–	–	–	2	(5)	0	2
Hyperoodon ampullatus	–	–	–	–	2+	(5)	0	2

Species	Dentition					Digits		
	I	C	P	M	Total	FL	HL	ME
Family Physeteridae								
Physeter catodon	–	–	–	–	34–58	(5)	0	2
Family Kogiidae								
Kogia breviceps	–	–	–	–	18–30	(5)	0	2
Family Monodontidae								
Delphinapterus leucas	–	–	–	–	32–40	(5)	0	2
Monodon monoceros	–	–	–	–	1–2	(5)	0	2
Family Delphinidae								
Stenella caeruleoalba	–	–	–	–	184–200	(5)	0	2
Delphinus delphis	–	–	–	–	160–200	(5)	0	2
Tursiops truncatus	–	–	–	–	80–100	(5)	0	2
Lissodelphis borealis	–	–	–	–	172–188	(5)	0	2
Lagenorhynchus albirostris	–	–	–	–	88–100	(5)	0	2
Lagenorhynchus acutus	–	–	–	–	120–132	(5)	0	2
Lagenorhynchus obliquidens	–	–	–	–	116–128	(5)	0	2
Orcinus orca	–	–	–	–	40–56	(5)	0	2
Grampus griseus	–	–	–	–	6–14	(5)	0	2
Globicephala melaena	–	–	–	–	36–48	(5)	0	2
Globicephala macrorhyncha	–	–	–	–	36–48	(5)	0	2
Phocoena phocoena	–	–	–	–	44–52	(5)	0	2
Phocoenoides dalli	–	–	–	–	44–52	(5)	0	2
Family Eschrichtidae								
Eschrichtius robustus	–	–	–	–	0	(4)	0	2
Family Balaenopteridae								
Balaenoptera physalus	–	–	–	–	0	(4)	0	2
Balaenoptera borealis	–	–	–	–	0	(4)	0	2
Balaenoptera acutorostrata	–	–	–	–	0	(4)	0	2
Balaenoptera musculus	–	–	–	–	0	(4)	0	2
Megaptera novaeangliae	–	–	–	–	0	(4)	0	2
Family Balaenidae								
Balaena glacialis	–	–	–	–	0	(5)	0	2
Balaena mysticetus	–	–	–	–	0	(4)	0	2
ORDER CARNIVORA								
Family Canidae								
Canis latrans	3/3	1/1	4/4	2/3	42	5	4	8
Canis lupus	3/3	1/1	4/4	2/3	42	5	4	8
Alopex lagopus	3/3	1/1	4/4	2/3	42	5	4	8
Vulpes vulpes	3/3	1/1	4/4	2/3	42	5	4	8
Vulpes velox	3/3	1/1	4/4	2/3	42	5	4	8
Urocyon cinereoargenteus	3/3	1/1	4/4	2/3	42	5	4	6
Family Ursidae								
Ursus americanus	3/3	1/1	2–4 / 2–4	2/3	34–42	5	5	6
Ursus arctos	3/3	1/1	2–4 / 2–4	2/3	34–42	5	5	6
Ursus maritimus	3/3	1/1	2–4 / 2–4	2/3	34–42	5	5	6
Family Procyonidae								
Procyon lotor	3/3	1/1	4/4	2/2	40	5	5	8
Family Mustelidae								
Martes americana	3/3	1/1	4/4	1/2	38	5	5	4
Martes pennanti	3/3	1/1	4/4	1/2	38	5	5	4
Mustela erminea	3/3	1/1	3/3	1/2	34	5	5	10
Mustela frenata	3/3	1/1	3/3	1/2	34	5	5	8
Mustela nivalis	3/3	1/1	3/3	1/2	34	5	5	8
Mustela nigripes	3/3	1/1	3/3	1/2	34	5	5	8
Mustela vison	3/3	1/1	3/3	1/2	34	5	5	6
Mustela macrodon	3/3	1/1	3/3	1/2	34	5	5	?
Gulo gulo	3/3	1/1	4/4	1/2	38	5	5	6
Taxidea taxus	3/3	1/1	3/3	1/2	34	5	5	8
Spilogale gracilis	3/3	1/1	3/3	1/2	34	5	5	10

Species	Dentition					Digits		
	I	C	P	M	Total	FL	HL	ME
Mephitis mephitis	3/3	1/1	3/3	1/2	34	5	5	10
Lontra canadensis	3/3	1/1	4/3	1/2	36	5	5	4
Enhydra lutris	3/2	1/1	3/3	1/2	32	5	5	2
Family Felidae								
Felis concolor	3/3	1/1	3/2	1/1	30	5	4	6
Lynx lynx	3/3	1/1	2/2	1/1	28	5	4	4
Lynx rufus	3/3	1/1	2/2	1/1	28	5	4	4
ORDER PINNIPEDIA								
Family Otariidae								
Eumetopias jubata	3/2	1/1	4/4	1/1	34	5	5	2
Zalophus californianus	3/2	1/1	4/4	2/1	36	5	5	2
Callorhinus ursinus	3/2	1/1	4/4	2/1	36	5	5	4
Family Odobenidae								
Odobenus rosmarus	1/0	1/1	3/3	0/0	18	5	5	4
Family Phocidae								
Erignathus barbatus	3/2	1/1	4/4	1/1	34	5	5	4
Halichoerus grypus	3/2	1/1	4/4	1/1	34	5	5	2
Phoca vitulina	3/2	1/1	4/4	1/1	34	5	5	2
Phoca hispida	3/2	1/1	4/4	1/1	34	5	5	2
Phoca groenlandica	3/2	1/1	4/4	1/1	34	5	5	2
Cystophora cristata	2/1	1/1	4/4	1/1	30	5	5	2
Mirounga angustirostris	2/1	1/1	4/4	1/1	30	5	5	2
ORDER ARTIODACTYLA								
Family Cervidae								
Rangifer tarandus	0/3	1/1	3/3	3/3	34	4	4	4
Odocoileus hemionus	0/3	0/1	3/3	3/3	32	4	4	4
Odocoileus virginianus	0/3	0/1	3/3	3/3	32	4	4	4
Alces alces	0/3	0/1	3/3	3/3	32	4	4	4
Cervus dama	0/3	0/1	3/3	3/3	32	4	4	4
Cervus elaphus	0/3	1/1	3/3	3/3	34	4	4	4
Family Antilocapridae								
Antilocapra americana	0/3	0/1	3/3	3/3	32	2	2	4
Family Bovidae								
Bison bison	0/3	0/1	3/3	3/3	32	4	4	4
Oreamnos americanus	0/3	0/1	3/3	3/3	32	4	4	4
Ovibos moschatus	0/3	0/1	3/3	3/3	32	4	4	4
Ovis canadensis	0/3	0/1	3/3	3/3	32	4	4	4
Ovis dalli	0/3	0/1	3/3	3/3	32	4	4	4

	ENGLISH		METRIC	
LENGTH	1	inch	25.4	millimetres
	0.039	inch	1	millimetre
	1	foot	30.48	centimetres
	0.033	foot	1	centimetre
	1	yard	0.914	metre
	1.094	yards	1	metre
	1	mile	1.609	kilometres
	0.621	mile	1	kilometre
	1	fathom (6 feet)	1.828	metres
AREA	1	square yard	0.836	square metre
	1.196	square yards	1	square metre
	1	acre	0.405	hectare
	2.471	acres	1	hectare
	1	square mile (640 acres)	2.590	square kilometres
	0.386	square mile	1	square kilometre
WEIGHT	1	ounce	28.35	grams
	0.353	ounce	1	gram
	1	pound	0.454	kilogram
	2.205	pounds	1	kilogram
	1	short ton	0.907	metric ton
	1.101	short tons	1	metric ton
VOLUME	1	gallon	4.546	litres
	0.22	gallon	1	litre

Glossary

aestivation Dormancy during the summer.

albino An animal with a congenital deficiency in the pigment which results in white skin and hair and pink eyes.

alisphenoid canal Orifice in the wing of the sphenoid bone at the base of the cranium.

altricial Requiring long parental care after birth.

alveolus Tooth socket.

ambient temperature Temperature of the surrounding air.

anchylosed Fused (of bones, joints).

anoestrus Non-breeding period.

arboreal Living in trees.

astragalus Large pivot bone in the ankle.

baculum Penis bone.

baleen Horny plates attached to the upper jaw of whales which act as sieves to strain food from sea water.

basioccipital bone Bone on ventral surface of cranium.

blastocyst Early development stage in embryo.

bluff (poplar) A restricted woods of poplar trees on the prairies.

boreal forest zone Belt of northern, mainly coniferous forest which stretches from the Maritimes to Alaska.

buccal Side of teeth next to the cheek.

burr The permanent base from which deer antlers grow annually.

caecum A blind pouch of the alimentary canal.

calcaneum Heel bone.

calcar A cartilaginous bone extending posteriorly from the heel of certain bats which supports the interfemoral flight membrane.

carnassials A pair of teeth (the upper fourth premolar and the lower first molar) that are blade-like and act as shears to cut meat and tendons (see Figure 113). A diagnostic feature of the carnivores.

caudal vertebrae Bones of the tail.

cervical vertebrae Neck bones.

clavicle Collar bone.

climax vegetation The mature or stabilized type of vegetation which will grow on a certain site.

cline Gradient in a measurement.

cloaca The common chamber into which the intestinal tract, reproductive system, and urinary ducts open in certain animals.

commensalism A relationship between two species living together where one benefits by the other's presence and the other is not particularly harmed by the relationship.

condyle The ball part of a ball and socket articulation between two bones.

Cordilleran region The Rocky Mountain geographical region of western North America.

cotyledons (placental) Buttons of attachment of a large placenta to the uterus as found in certain ruminant mammals.

crepuscular Active during the periods of half-light at dawn and dusk.

cubby A small enclosure of sticks placed around a trap set to capture marten.

cursorial Running.

delayed implantation The condition when the fertilized egg floats freely in the uterus for some months, undergoing only slow, elementary development, before attaching to the uterus and continuing to develop to birth.

diastema A gap (in the teeth).

digitate Finger-like.

digitigrade Walking on the toes (digits).

dimorphism The condition of occurring in two different phases.

diurnal Active during the daylight hours.

dormancy The state of inactivity when in prolonged sleep.

dray A squirrel's nest of leaves.

duff Partially decomposed leaf litter.

epicondylar foramen The canal in the distal end of the humerus of certain mammals.

epizootic An epidemic among wild animals.

erythristic Pertaining to a condition characterized by excessive amount of red pigment.

falcate Sickle-shaped.

fecund The condition of bearing offspring.

femur The thigh bone.

fibula The outer or more slender shinbone.

fluke Half of a whale's tail, or a parasite of the class Trematoda.

follicle The capsule enclosing the mammalian egg cell.

forb Soft-stemmed annual plant.

form A depression used as a nest by a rabbit.

fossorial Adapted for living totally or partially underground.

free water Standing water (not the water content of green vegetation, or water produced by metabolic activity).

fulvous Tawny.

funk hole A hole in which an animal hides when frightened.

fuscous Dingy brown.

gam A herd of whales.

gene allele One of a pair or a group of mutually exclusive hereditary unit characters which occupy a particular locus on a chromosome.

glenoid cavity The socket on the scapula that accepts the condyle of the humerus, or the socket on the squamosal bone that accepts the condyle of the mandible.

gonadotrophic hormone A hormone which influences reproductive activity.

gonads The organs that produce sexual cells.

guard hairs The long hair component as opposed to the shorter undercoat that normally forms the fur coat of mammals.

gular groove Throat groove characteristic of beaked whales (Ziphiidae).

hallux The big toe.

hibernacula Nest or quarters where an animal spends the winter.

hibernation A state of lethargy or dormancy assumed by certain animals during periods of unfavourable climatic conditions. The condition is manifested by lowered metabolic rates, including a body temperature lowered to near the environmental temperature. These animals are able to regain their normal homeothermic temperature only slowly.

holarctic Pertaining to a distribution pattern encircling the North Pole in both the New and Old Worlds.

holocrine gland A gland in which the secretory glands disintegrate and form part of the secretion.

homeothermic Having a constant (warm) body temperature.

humerus The upper arm bone.

hypsodont A high crowned tooth with a hard-wearing ridged surface, well fitted for a vegetarian diet.

incisiform Incisor-like.

incisive foramen A pair of long slits in the palatine bones of the roof of the mouth behind the incisor teeth.

inguinal Pertaining to the groin region.

innominate bones Fusion of ilium, ischium, and pubis bones in pelvis.

in utero 'In the uterus.'

jugal bones (*malar*) A pair of bones that form part of the zygomatic arch (cheek bones; see Figure 113).

keratinous Horny.

kit A young beaver.

krill Small, swarming, planktonic crustacea such as species of *Euphausia* which constitute the food of the baleen whales.

lachrymal vacuity A space on the margin of the lachrymal bone (see Figure 113).

lactating In the process of secreting milk.

lagomorph A member of the order of rabbits, hares, and pikas.

lanugo The first white coat of a young seal.

leporid One of the hares of the genus *Lepus*.

leveret A young hare.

linea alba The tendinous ventral medial line separating the abdominal muscles.

lingual Side of teeth next to the tongue.

loph A highly specialized crest on the crown of a tooth.

marsupium The pouch of marsupial mammals.

masseter muscle A large cheek muscle which raises the jaw.

mast The harvest of forest nuts – acorns, hazelnuts, etc.

maxillary prominences Bumps on the maxillary bones of the upper jaw (see Figure 113).

meatus An orifice (usually the ear orifice; see Figure 113).

melanistic Pertaining to a congenital condition causing an excessive production of black pigment in hair, skin, etc. (i.e. black-furred).

metapodials Foot bones.

metatarsals Foot bones of the hind foot.

midden Storage pile or refuse pile of fodder or conifer cones collected by rodents for winter use.

monoestrous Having a single breeding period each year.

monotypic Pertaining to a genus which has only one species, or an invariable species without discernible subspecies.

murine Mouse-like.

myotid One of many similar small brown bats belonging to the genus *Myotis*.

mystacial vibrissae The 'whiskers' on the snout of a mammal.

nocturnal Active only during the period of darkness.

non-parous The condition of a female that has not yet borne young.

notochord Primitive cellular rod, forerunner of vertebral column.

occipital condyle One of the characteristic two bony knobs (ball joints) at the base of the skull that articulate with the atlas (the first cervical vertebra; see Figure 113). Mammals have a pair, and reptiles a single occipital condyle.

occiput The basal region of the skull.

occlusal Pertaining to grinding surface of the teeth.

oestrous cycle The complete reproductive cycle of a female mammal including the breeding and non-breeding periods.

oestrus The breeding season when the ripe egg is ready for fertilization and the females accept the males.

omnivorous Having an unrestricted diet.

ovulation The expulsion of the egg from the ovary.

palatine bone One of a pair of bones that form the palate.

palmate Palm-like.

paraoccipital processes Processes on the paraoccipital bones at the base of the skull.

parietal ridge A ridge on the side of the cranium (parietal bone; see Figure 113).

parous The condition of a female that has borne young during her lifetime.

parturition Birth.

peck order of dominance A social order where each individual recognizes its superiors and inferiors and either is aggressive towards another or gives way on meeting (based on the example of a hen roost).

peduncle A bony knob.

pelage The coat of fur that clothes a mammal.

pelagic Living on the high seas out of sight of land.

phalange One of the small bones in a digit (finger or toe).

phocid Pertaining to the seals of the genus *Phoca*.

pinna The fleshy external portion of the ear.

placenta Spongy connection composed of maternal and foetal tissues in the uterus by which nutritive and respiratory exchange takes place between maternal and foetal blood systems.

plantar pads Fleshy pads on the soles of mammals' feet.

plantigrade Walking on the heel of the foot.

pollard To prune a tree by cutting the leaders each year.

pollex Thumb.

polyandrous Having several male mates.

polyoestrous Having several breeding periods each year.

polygamous Having several mates.

post-narial opening The posterior opening of the nasal passage in the throat.

post-partum After birth.

precocious Development of the young so that they can quickly look after themselves (i.e. requiring short period of parental care).

pre-oestrous Coming into breeding condition, receptive to the attention of males.

pterygoid bones A pair of bones on the sides of the occiput, usually with prominent processes.

race Subspecies.

radius The outer of two bones of the forearm.

ramus A part of a bone, or a single bone of a natural pair of bones.

refection The reingestion of special incompletely digested faecal pellets, rechewing, and ultimate digestion, as practised by the hares and rabbits.

rhinarium The naked, moist, crinkled (usually black) nose pad of many mammals.

riparian Pertaining to a river bank.

rostrum The portion of the skull anterior to the eyes.

sagittal Pertaining to a vertical section through the mid-dorsal to mid-ventral line.

sagittal crest A crest of bone on the mid-dorsal line of the cranium (see Figure 113).

saltatorial gait Movement by jumping.

samara The winged seed of the maples.

sebaceous gland A gland which secretes fatty matter.

semiplantigrade Walking on the heel partly, or sometimes.

sesamoid bones Small, insignificant foot bones formed in tendons.

spermaceti A clear, colourless oil that is found in the head of sperm whales and bottlenosed whales.

spermatogenesis The formation of sperms.

sphenoid bones A pair of bones forming part of the ventral wall of the cranium.

sphincter A circular muscle which closes an orifice.

squamosal bones A pair of bones on the sides of the skull that are involved in the zygomatic arches (see Figure 113).

sternum Breastbone.

subclimax vegetation A progressive stage in a natural sequence of vegetation, short of the climax stand (e.g. poplars and birch stands in a coniferous forest belt).

submaxillary gland A gland beneath the lower jaw.

sub-oestrus Before oestrus (the rut).

supraoccipital ridge The ridge at the back of the skull above the occiput.

swale Damp meadow (water standing in coarse grass and sedge vegetative cover).

symphysis The line of junction between two bones that have grown together.

taiga A type of arctic vegetation characterized by an open forest of stunted spruce trees among an understory of heaths and lichens.

territoriality Demonstrating the defence of a home range, or feeding and nesting area, against intruders of the same species.

test The sea urchin's shell.

tibia The large shinbone.

toggle A weight, or drag, tied to the end of a trap chain.

torpor A state of sluggishness, inactivity.

tragus An additional lobe at the base of the pinna which is typical of bats.

tuberculate With small lumps.

tundra Arctic or alpine vegetation composed of low shrubs, herbs, grasses, lichens, etc., but devoid of trees.

tympanic bone A bone of the ear (see Figure 113).

ulna The inner bone of the forearm.

ungulates Mammals which walk on their toenails.

unicuspid tooth A tooth with only one cone.

venter The abdominal surface.

vestigial Small and imperfectly formed, disappearing.

vibrissae Long tactile hairs on the face, elbows, or wrists of mammals.

vomerine Pertaining to the vomer bones on the ventral surface of the skull.

whelp A young member of the dog or fox tribe.

zygomatic arches (*zygoma*) Bony arches on the sides of the skull under the eyes (in man the cheek bones; see Figure 113).

Index of Common and Scientific Names

The italic page references refer to the colour plates

435

FRENCH COMMON NAMES

437